CATHAY
AND THE WAY THITHER

CATHAY

AND THE WAY THITHER

BEING A COLLECTION OF MEDIEVAL NOTICES OF CHINA

TRANSLATED AND EDITED

BY

COLONEL SIR HENRY YULE, R.E., C.B., K.C.S.I.

CORR. INST. FRANCE

WITH A PRELIMINARY ESSAY

ON THE INTERCOURSE BETWEEN CHINA AND THE WESTERN NATIONS PREVIOUS TO THE DISCOVERY OF THE CAPE ROUTE

NEW EDITION, REVISED THROUGHOUT IN THE LIGHT OF RECENT DISCOVERIES

BY

HENRI CORDIER, D. LITT., HON. M.R.A.S., HON. COR. M.R.G.S., HON. F.R.S.L.

MEMBER OF THE INSTITUT DE FRANCE PROFESSOR AT THE ECOLE DES LANGUES ORIENTALES VIVANTES, PARIS

VOL. IV

IBN BATUTA—BENEDICT GOES—INDEX

GYAN

Published by

Gyan Publishing House
5, Ansari Road
Daryaganj, New Delhi-110002
Phone: 011-47034999, 9811692060
E-mail: books@gyanbooks.com

Distribution Network
gyanbooks.com
India, USA, Canada, UK, Australia, France

ISBN : 978-81-212-3198-5 (Set)
ISBN : 978-81-212-4820-4 (HB)
First Published, 1916

2nd Impression 2020

Printed at: Gyan Press, Delhi.

Cathay and the Way Thither Vol. IV
Author: Colonel Sir Henry Yule

WORKS ISSUED BY

The Hakluyt Society

CATHAY AND THE WAY THITHER

VOL. IV

SECOND SERIES

No. XLI

ISSUED FOR 1916

COUNCIL

OF

THE HAKLUYT SOCIETY.

CATHAY
AND THE WAY THITHER

BEING A COLLECTION OF
MEDIEVAL NOTICES OF CHINA

TRANSLATED AND EDITED

BY

COLONEL SIR HENRY YULE, R.E., C.B., K.C.S.I.
CORR. INST. FRANCE

WITH A
PRELIMINARY ESSAY
ON THE INTERCOURSE BETWEEN CHINA AND THE WESTERN NATIONS PREVIOUS TO THE DISCOVERY OF THE CAPE ROUTE

NEW EDITION, REVISED THROUGHOUT IN THE LIGHT OF RECENT DISCOVERIES

BY

HENRI CORDIER, D.LITT., HON. M.R.A.S.,
HON. COR. M.R.G.S., HON. F.R.S.L.
MEMBER OF THE INSTITUT DE FRANCE
PROFESSOR AT THE ÉCOLE DES LANGUES ORIENTALES VIVANTES, PARIS

VOL. IV

IBN BATUTA—BENEDICT GOËS—INDEX

LONDON:
PRINTED FOR THE HAKLUYT SOCIETY
MDCCCCXVI

TABLE OF CONTENTS

CATHAY AND THE WAY THITHER

VI. IBN BATUTA'S TRAVELS IN BENGAL AND CHINA (*circa* 1347)

Introductory Notice.

His birth, 1; facilities and stimulus to Mahomedan travelling in those days; its vast field; commencement of his travels, 2; Alexandria; Upper Egypt; Syria; the pilgrimage; Basra, Persia, Baghdad, 3; second pilgrimage; Yemen; Aden, its flourishing state; the African coast, 3; Oman, 4; Hormuz, 5; Central Arabia; third pilgrimage; crosses the Red Sea and travels to Cairo; Syria (second time) and Asia Minor; crosses the Black Sea, 6; Caffa; Majar; Uzbek Khan; visits the city of Bolghar, 7; the *Land of Darkness*; Astrakhan; journey with a Greek Princess to Constantinople; Ukak; Soldaia, 7; Constantinople; the name *Istambul*; Andronicus Senior, 8; returns to Uzbek; visits Khwarizm and Bokhara; Tarmashírín, Khan of Chagatai; Khorasan; passes the Hindu Kush; Pashai, the *Pascia* of Polo; Sind; Sehwán; Larri Bandar, 10; travels towards Delhi; Multan; Mahomed Tughlak, the then Sultan of Delhi, and his character; journey from Multan to Delhi, 10.

Reception at Delhi, and appointment as judge; eight years' residence in India; his extravagance, 13; he falls into disfavour, 15; becomes an ascetic for the nonce, 16; the king sends for him and nominates him ambassador to China; the Chinese embassy which had visited Mahomed; the return presents, 17; his colleagues, 19; they start from Delhi; mishaps near Koel; Kanauj; Gwalior, 20; feats of the Jogis; Daulatābād; Cambay (*note on route from Delhi to Cambay*), 21; Kawe, 22; Gandar; isle of Perim, 23; Gogo; Sindábúr (apparently *Goa*), 23; Hunawar, and its Mahomedan Prince, 24; female education; Malabar; Calicut; Chinese shipping described; ports frequented by the Chinese junks, 25; mishaps attending the start of the embassy, and the traveller left behind, 28; proceeds to Kaulam, 29; goes back to the Mahomedan Prince of Hunawúr,

30; expedition against Sindábúr; Ibn Batuta returns to Calicut; hears of the final wreck and dispersion of his slaves, etc., who had sailed from Calicut; returns a third time to Hunawúr, and to Sindábúr; finding his friends in difficulties, escapes, and returns to Calicut, 31; visits the Maldives, 31; is made Kazi, and marries four wives; his pious reforms; quarrels and leaves for Ceylon; the Pagan chief Arya Chakravarti at Patlam; he travels to Adam's Peak, 32; Kurunaigalla; the Peak; Dondera; Galle; Columbo, 33; sails for Maabar, and again comes to grief, 34; is received by the Sultan of Maabar, whose sister-in-law Ibn Batuta had married at Delhi; that good lady's commemoration by her husband; the Sultan's cruelties; his death, 34; Madura; the traveller's departure again for Kaulam, 35; sets off again for Hunawúr; is robbed, and returns to Calicut, 35; re-visits the Maldives; sails thence to Bengal, 36.

His voyage to China (*see* text following), 36; his return to Arabia, and journey thence by Persia, Irák, Syria (the Black Death), Egypt, Tunis, Sardinia, Algeria, to his native country; his professed joy in returning; his laudations of the West, 37.

Resumes his travels; Tangier, Gibraltar, and Andalusia, 38; sets out for Central Africa, 39; Segelmessa; Taghaza; Malli; Timbuktu, 39; Kaukau; Takadda; the Niger; is ordered home, and returns to Fez, 40.

The Sultan orders his travels to be written, 40; the scribe, Ibn Juzai, 40; how the latter characterises the traveller. Death of the latter, 41.

First knowledge in Europe of Ibn Batuta's book; Seetzen; Kosegarten; Apetz; Lee, 41. Complete MSS. procured by the French in Algeria; Moura's Portuguese translation; partial translations; complete French translation of Defrémery and Sanguinetti, whence the ensuing extracts are translated, 42–3.

Interest of the book and character of Ibn Batuta as a traveller; different views; confused geographical ideas, 43–4; and other instances of loose observation, 44; exaggerations, 46; instances apparently of positive fiction, 48; mistakes in language, 49; chronological difficulties, 50; summing up in favour of general veracity and genuine character, 50; personal character, 51.

Bibliography, 52.

Note A. *On the Value of the Indian coins mentioned by Ibn Batuta*, 54.

Note B. *On the Places visited by Ibn Batuta between Cambay and Malabar*, 63.

Note C. *Remarks on sundry Passages in the Fourth Volume of Lassen's* Indische Alterthumskunde, 66.

Note D. *The Medieval Ports of Malabar*, 72.

THE TRAVELS OF IBN BATUTA IN CHINA, ETC.

Sails from the Maldives to Bengal, 80; that country characterised; its great cheapness, 81; Sadkáwán, 82; the King Fakhruddín, 84; his revolt and wars with the governor of Lakhnaoti (*Gaur*), 84; the traveller visits the country of Kamrú (*Silhet*, vide note E), 86; the Shaikh Jalaluddín; his ascetic life and longevity; his previsions, 87; his treatment of Ibn Batuta; story of the shaikh's goat's hair mantle and his predictions, 88–9; the city of Habank, 90; SunurKáwán (*Sunárganw*), 91; sails for Java (*Sumatra*), 92; BarahNagar (supposed coast near *Negrais*); dog-mouthed people; Java (*Sumatra*), 94; city of Sumatra, 95; the King al Zhahir; departure for China; Mul-Java (*Continent on Gulf of Siam*); Kakula, 96; Kamara (*confusions connected with this name*), 96; elephants; aloes-wood; self-immolation, 97; traveller's account of spices; incense, 97; camphor, 98; Indian aloes-wood, 99; the clove (*his mis-statements*), 101. The Calm Sea, 103; the kingdom of Tawálisi; description of it; the Princess Urdujá governing at Kailúkari, 104; her hospitality; her conversation with the traveller, 106; her present, 107; her warlike character; arrival in China, 108.

The Great River of China, 108; rich products of the country, 109; porcelain, and process of making, 109; Chinese poultry, 110; various characteristics of the people, 110; silk, 111; customs of the merchants, 111; paper money (*note on the word* balisht), 112; fossil coal, 113; Chinese skill in drawing and portraiture, 114; regulations in the ports, 115; forfeitures, 116; regulations respecting foreign traders, 116; travelling accommodations, 116.

City of Zaitún (*Chincheu*), 117; damasks and satins, 118; great amount of shipping; meets the envoys who had been in India, 119; is lodged by the government, and visited by the Mahomedans, 119; sets out on a visit to Sin Kalán (*Canton*), 120; description of that city, 121; immense hospitality of the Mahomedan settlers, 122; the Rampart of Gog and Magog, 123; aged and singular recluse near Canton, 123; his reception of Ibn Batuta; mysterious disappearance, 124; strange stories related of this personage and his mesmeric influence, 125; his peculiar habits. Return to Zaitún, 126; sets out for the capital; Kanjanfú, 126; his grand reception, 127; singular encounter with a countryman from Ceuta, 128; continues his journey, 129; Baiwam Kutlú; Khansá (*Hang chau*), 129; the greatest city on earth; reception; description of the city, 130; the Amír Kurtai, the Viceroy, 131; he gives an entertainment, 133; festival on the water, and songs that were sung; strange exhibition of juggling; further particulars of the city, 133–5; lacker dishes, 135; sets out from Khansa and enters CATHAY, 137. Its great culture and population; arrives at Khánbáliq, 137; the Shaikh Burhán-uddín, 138; the Kán; palace described (*from imagination it would seem*), 139; revolution in progress in Cathay, 140; the Kán slain (*a fiction*), 142; great preparations for his funeral, 142; extraordinary ceremonial, 143. Similar rites in Negroland, 144.

The traveller advised to depart, 145; returns to Zaitún; sails for Sumatra; great storm and darkness, 145; appearance of the rukh, 146; reaches Sumatra, 147; marriage ceremonies of the king's son, 147; departs loaded with presents, 148; arrives at Kaulam; customs during the Ramazan there, 148; Calicut; embarks for Arabia and reaches Zhafár, 149. (*Note on the chronological difficulties of this expedition to China*, 149.)

Note E. *On the* Kamru *of Ibn Batuta* (*the residence of the Shaikh Jalál-uddín*), *the* Blue River, *and the city of* Habank, 151.

Note F. *On the* Mul-Java *of Ibn Batuta*, 155.

Note G. *On the* Tawálisi *of Ibn Batuta*, 157.

Note H. *Regarding the History of the Khans of Chagatai*, 160.

VII. THE JOURNEY OF BENEDICT GOËS FROM AGRA TO CATHAY (1602–1607)

Introductory Notice.

Changes since the time of Ibn Batuta, 169; identity of Cathay with China recognised by the Jesuits in the latter country, not by those in India, 170; expedition to rediscover Cathay projected and Goës chosen for it, 170.

Early history of Goës, 171; a lay-brother of the Jesuits; he is sent to the court of Akbar, 172; circumstance which put it in the head of Jerome Xavier, the head of the mission, to explore Cathay, 174; sanction is received from Europe, and Goës prepares for the journey, 177; his death after accomplishing it at Suchau, 178. Mode in which the narrative was compiled; miserably meagre in consequence; perplexities about the chronology, 179; what may have led to some of the errors, 181.

Chief difficulties in tracing the traveller's route about the Hindu Kush and Badakhshan, 181; passage of the former, 181; Badakhshan, its history and decay from former prosperity, 185; the pass over the Bolor Tagh and Pamir, 186; Chinese Turkestan, its characteristics, 187; history of that region in brief outline, 188. Bibliography of Goës's journey, 194–7.

THE JOURNEY

From the Work of Trigault "De Christianâ Expeditione apud Sinas." Book v, ch. xi, xii, xiii.

Chap. XI. *How the Portuguese, Benedict Goës, a member of our Society, is sent to find out about Cathay.*—Preliminary explanations as to the origin and object of the expedition, 198; Benedict's preparations in character of a merchant, 201; travels to Lahore; his companions, 202; caravan to go to Kashgar, 203; reach Attok, 203; Peshāwar, 203; account of Kafiristan, 204; trouble from robbers in the passes, 205; Kabul, 207; assistance rendered by Goës to the mother of the King of Khotan, 207; two of Goës's companions abandon him, 208; sets out from Kabul; Chārīkār, 208; Parwān, 209; passes the Hindu Kush; Aingharàn, 209; Calcià, 210; Talhan (*Talikhan*); Chemàn (?), 211; trouble with insurgents, 212; the straits of Badakhshan, 214; Serpanil (*Pamir* ?), 214; terrible mountain passes, 214; reaches Yarkand, 215.

Chap. XII. *The remainder of the Journey to Cathay, and how it is ascertained to be all the same as the Chinese Empire.*—Yarkand, 218; delay here, 218; nature of the trade with Cathay under pretext of embassies; pieces of jade the chief import; account of this substance, 219. The King of Yarkand, 220; he is supported by the Prince of Khotan; re-appearance of Demetrius, one of his original companions, and the trouble he caused, 221; Goës makes a journey to Khotan; annoyance from the Mullahs, 222; safe return of Benedict; controversies, 224; the new Caravan chief invites Goës to accompany him to Cathay, 225; Demetrius draws back again, 226; Goës prepares for the journey, and sets out, 227; journey to Aqsù; visit to the young chief there, 229; Caracathai; Kucha, 230; Cialis (*Karashahr*), 232; alarm, which proves unfounded; respect which Goës earned, 233; delays; meets merchants returning from Cathay, who tell him of the Jesuits at Peking, by which he learns that Cathay is China, 235; Goës's bold and dignified conduct, 237; sets out without waiting for the caravan, 237; Pijan; Turfàn, 237; Kamul, 239; enters the wall of China, 239; Suchau; the Tartars on the Chinese frontier and their forays; accident to Benedict on this last part of the journey, 240.

Chap. XIII. *How our Brother Benedict died in the Chinese territory, after the arrival of one of our members who had been sent from Peking to his assistance.*—The garrison towns of Kan chau and Suchau, 241; the Mahomedans at Suchau, and restrictions upon them, 242; the resort of the caravans of merchants professing to be ambassadors; particulars about this system, 243.

Date of Goës's arrival at Suchau, and prosperous state of his affairs, 244; hears further accounts of the Jesuits at Peking from Saracen traders, 244; writes to Matthew Ricci, but his letter miscarries; writes again a letter, which is received after many months, 245; the Jesuits sent a Chinese Christian pupil, John Ferdinand, to his aid, 245; annoyance experienced by Goës during detention at Suchau, 246; arrival of the caravan, 247; John Ferdinand at last arrives, but finds Benedict on his death-bed, 247; his death eleven days later, 248; annoyance to his servant Isaac and John Ferdinand from the Mahomedans, who destroy Goës's journal, 248.

Some remarks on the character of Goës, 249; anecdote of his death-bed, 250.

Trouble of the two survivors, 251; but they outwit the Mahomedans, and get to Peking, 252; relics of Benedict; further history of the faithful Isaac, 253.

Note I.—*The Passes of the Hindu Kush*, 255.

Note II.—*Titles of some Books quoted in this Work by Abbreviated References*, 260.

Note III.—*Corrections and Additional Illustrations*, 266.

INDEX to the whole Work, 272.

ILLUSTRATIONS

Dog-mouthed Islanders (*Sketched from life by the Editor*) *Page* 94

Map of the Passes of the Hindu Kush and Country adjoining, to illustrate the Journey of Goës. *In pocket at end of volume.*

VI

IBN BATUTA'S TRAVELS IN BENGAL AND CHINA

VI

IBN BATUTA'S TRAVELS IN BENGAL AND CHINA

INTRODUCTORY NOTICE

ABU-ABDULLAH MAHOMED, called Ibn Batuta[1], The Traveller (*par excellence*) of the Arab nation, as he was hailed by a saint of his religion whom he visited in India, was born at Tangier on the 24th February, 1304.

The duty of performing the Mecca pilgrimage must have developed the travelling propensity in many a Mahomedan, whilst in those days the power and extension of the vast freemasonry to which he belonged would give facilities for the indulgence of this propensity such as have never been known under other circumstances by any class of people[2]. Ibn Batuta himself tells us how in the heart of China he fell in with a certain Al Bushri[3], a countryman of his own from Ceuta, who had risen to great wealth and prosperity in that far country, and how at a later date (when after a short visit to his

[1] During his travels in the East he bore the name of Shams-uddín (i, 8).

[2] Ricold de Monte Croce is greatly struck with the brotherly feeling among Mahomedans of his day, however strange to one another in blood: "Nam etiam loquendo ad invicem, maxime ad extraneos dicit unus alteri: 'O fili matris meæ!' Ipsi etiam nec occidunt se ad invicem nec expoliant, sed homo Sarracenus securissime transit inter quoscumque extraneos et barbaros Sarracenos" (*Pereg. Quatuor.*, p. 134).

[3] iv, 282. Similar references indicate the French edition and version by Defrémery and Sanguinetti, from which I have translated.

native land the restless man had started to explore Central Africa), in passing through Segelmessa, on the border of the Sahra, he was the guest of the same Al Bushri's brother[1]. "What an enormous distance lay between those two!" the traveller himself exclaims. On another occasion he mentions meeting at Brussa a certain Shaik Abd-Allah of Misr who bore the surname of *The Traveller*. This worthy had indeed made the tour of the world, as some would have it, but he had never been in China nor in the Island of Serendib, neither in Spain nor in Negroland. "I have beaten him," says Ibn Batuta, "for all these have I visited[2]."

He entered on his wanderings at the age of twenty-one (14th June, 1325), and did not close them till he was hard on fifty-one (in January, 1355): his career thus coinciding in time pretty exactly with that of Sir John Mandeville (1322–56), a traveller the compass of whose journeys would be deemed to equal or surpass the Moor's, if we could but believe them to be as genuine[3].

Ibn Batuta commenced his travels by traversing the whole longitude of Africa (finding time to marry twice upon the road) to Alexandria, the haven of which he extols as surpassing all that he saw in the course of his peregrinations, except those of Kaulam and Calicut in India, that held by the Christians at Sudâk or Soldaia in the Crimea, and the great port of Zaytún in China. After some stay at Cairo, which was then perhaps the greatest city in the world out of China[4], he ascended

[1] iv, 377. [2] ii, 321.

[3] [See *Marco Polo*, ii, App. L, 13.—Sir John Mandeville, pp. 598–605.]

[4] The traveller reports that the Plague or Black Death of 1348 carried off 24,000 souls in one day (!) in the united cities of Cairo and Misr or Fostat (i, 229); whilst in 1381 the pestilence was said to have carried off 30,000 a day. George Guccio, who heard this at Cairo in 1384, relates also of the visitation of 1348

the valley of the Nile to Syene, and passed the Desert to Aidhab on the Red Sea, with the view of crossing the latter to Mecca. But wars raging on that sea prevented this, so he retraced his steps and proceeded to visit Palestine and the rest of Syria, including Aleppo and Damascus. He then performed the pilgrimage to the holy cities of his religion[1], and afterwards visited the shrine of Ali at Meshed. From this he went to Basra, and then through Khuzistan and Luristan to Ispahan, thence to Shiraz and back to Kufa and Baghdad. After an excursion to Mosul and Diarbakr, he made the pilgrimage for a second time, and on this occasion continued to dwell at Mecca for three years. When that time had elapsed he made a voyage down the Red Sea to Yemen, through which he travelled to Aden, the singular position of which city he describes correctly, noticing its dependence for water-supply upon cisterns preserving the scanty rainfall[2]. Aden was then a place of great trade, and the residence of wealthy merchants; ships of large burden from Cambay, Tana, and all the ports of Malabar, were in its harbour[3]. From Aden, Ibn Batuta continued

that "according to what the then Soldan wrote to King Hugo of Cyprus, there were some days when more than 100,000 souls died in Cairo!" (*Viaggi in Terra Santa*, p. 291).

[1] Between Medina and Mecca he mentions an additional instance of the phenomenon spoken of at II, p. 262 *supra*. Near Bedr, he says, "in front of you is the Mount of the Drums (*Jibal-ul-Thabúl*); it is like a huge sand-hill, and the natives assert that in that place every Thursday night they hear as it were the sound of drums" (i, 296). [See *Marco Polo*, i, p. 202 *n.*, 207 *n.*]

[2] These cisterns, works of a colossal magnitude, had in the decay of Aden been buried in debris. During the last few years some of them have been cleared out and repaired, and they now form one of the most interesting sights of Aden. [They are said to have been formerly 50 in number, with a capacity of 30 million gallons. Cf. *Marco Polo*, ii, p. 440 *n.*]

[3] Aden, one of those places which nature has marked for perpetual revival, is mentioned, both by Marco Polo and by Marino Sanudo his contemporary, as the great entrepôt of that

his voyage down the African coast, visiting Zaila, Makdashau (Magadoxo of the Portuguese), Mombasa, and Quiloa in nearly nine degrees of south latitude. From this he sailed to the coast of Oman, where, like Marco Polo, he remarks the surprising custom of feeding cattle

part of the Indian commerce which came westward by Egypt, but neither apparently had accurate acquaintance with the route. The former says that "Aden is the port to which the Indian ships bring all their merchandize. It is then placed on board other small vessels *which ascend a river about seven days*, at the end of which it is disembarked, laden on camels, and conveyed thirty days further. It then comes to the river of Alexandria, and is conveyed down to that city." Marino, after speaking of the route by the Persian Gulf, and the three ports of Hormuz, Kis, and Basra, goes on: "The fourth haven is called Ahaden, and stands on a certain little island, joining as it were to the main, in the land of the Saracens; the spices and other goods from India are landed there, loaded on camels, and so carried by a journey of nine days to a place on the river Nile called Chus, where they are put into boats and conveyed in fifteen days to Babylon (Cairo). But in the month of October and thereabouts the river rises to such an extent that the spices, etc., continue to descend the stream from Babylon, and enter a certain long canal, and so are conveyed over the two hundred miles between Babylon and Alexandria." (*Polo*, ii, c: 36; Mar. San. *Liber Fidelium Crucis*, pt. 1, c. 1.)

Here we see that Marco apparently took the Red Sea for a river, misled perhaps by the ambiguity of the Persian *Darya*. In the MS. followed by Pauthier, Marco makes no such mistake as is here referred to. See Pauthier's edition, p. 703. And Marino supposes, as his map also shows, Aden to be on the *west* side of the Red Sea, confounding it probably with *Suákin*, which was also a port of embarcation for India *via* Egypt, as I gather from a MS. of the fourteenth century at Florence on the pilgrimage to the tomb of St. Thomas. The *Chus* of Marino is *Kús*, the ancient *Cos* or *Apollinopolis Parva*, between Keneh and Luxor, described by Ibn Batuta (i, 106) as in his day a large and flourishing town, with fine bazaars, mosques, and colleges, the residence of the viceroys of the Thebaid. That traveller embarked at Kus to descend the Nile, after his first visit to Upper Egypt. It is nearly in the latitude of Kosseir. The *Carta Catalana* calls Kosseir *Chos*, and notes it as the place where the Indian spicery was landed. [At the time of Chau Ju-kua, Aden was perhaps the most important port of Arabia for the African and Arabian trade with India and the countries beyond. It seems highly probable that the Ma-li-pa of the Chinese must be understood as including Aden—of which they make no mention whatsoever, but which was one of "the great commercial centres of the Arabs." Hirth and Rockhill, p. 25 *n.*] [See Ma Huan's *Account of Aden* in *J. R. As. Soc.*, 1896, p. 348; the Chinese Traveller does not mention the cisterns.]

of all sorts upon small fish. After visiting the chief cities of Oman he proceeded to Hormuz, or New Hormuz as he calls the city on the celebrated Island. The rock-salt found here, he observes, was used in forming ornamental vases and pedestals for lamps, but the most remarkable thing that he saw at Hormuz appears to have been a fish's head so large that men entered by one eye and went out by the other[1].

After visiting Kais or Kísh he crossed the Gulf to Bahrain, Al-Kathif, and Hajr or Al-Hasa (or *Al-Ahsa*, v. *supra*, III, p. 65), where dates were so abundant that there was a proverb about carrying dates to Hajr, like ours of coals to Newcastle. Thence he crossed Central Arabia through what is now the Wahabi country, but without giving a single particular respecting it, and made the Mecca pilgrimage again. He then embarked at Jiddah, landed on the opposite coast, and made a journey of great hardship to Syene, whence he continued along the banks of the Nile to Cairo.

After this he revisited Syria, and made an extensive journey through the petty Turkish sultanates into which Asia Minor was then divided[2]. During this tour he tells

[1] Whales (I believe of the Spermaceti genus) are still not uncommon in the Arabian Sea. Abu Zaid mentions that in his time about Siraf their vertebræ were used as chairs, and that houses were to be seen on the same coast, the rafters of which were formed of whale's ribs. (Reinaud, *Relations*, p. 146.) I remember when in parts of Scotland it was not unusual to see the gate-posts of a farm-yard formed of the same.

[2] There were at least eleven of these principalities in Asia Minor, after the fall of the [Seldjukid] kingdom of Iconium in 1308 (Deguignes, iii, pt. ii, p. 76). [Konieh, Iconium, ancient Lycaonia, dynasty of Benu Karaman, 1223–1472; Kastamuni, Paphlagonia, dynasty of Kizil Ahmedlis, 1289–1459; Menteshé, Caria, dynasty of Benu Menteshé, 1300–1426; Aidin, Lydia, dynasty of Benu Sarukhan, 1313–1426; Tekkeh, Lycia, 1300–1427; Hamid, Pisidia, 1300–81; Kermian, Phrygia, 1300–1429; Karasi, Mysia, 1300–36; Abulustein, dynasty of Benu Dhu'lkadr, 1336–1521; Adanah, dynasty of Benu Ramadhan, 1378–1562, and Kingdom of Osmanlis or Othman in Phrygia.]

us how he and his comrade engaged a certain Hajji who could speak Arabic as servant and interpreter. They found that he cheated them frightfully, and one day, provoked beyond measure, they called out to him, "Come now, Hajji, how much hast thou stolen to-day?" The Hajji simply replied, "So much," naming the amount of his plunder. "We could but laugh and rest content," says our traveller.

He then crossed the Black Sea to CAFFA, chiefly occupied, as he tells us, by the Genoese (*Janwiya*), and apparently the first Christian city in which he had found himself, for he was in great dismay at the bell-ringing. He went on by KRIM (or Solghat) and AZOV to MAJAR, a fine city on a great river (the Kuma), where he was greatly struck by the consideration with which women were treated by the Tartars; as if, in fact, creatures of a higher rank than men. From this he proceeded to the camp of Sultan Mahomed Uzbek, Khan of Kipchak [1312–40], then pitched at BISHDAGH, a thermal spring, apparently at the foot of Caucasus[1]. He was well received by the Khan, and obtained from him a guide to conduct him to the city of BOLGHAR, which he was anxious to visit in order to witness with his own eyes the shortness of the northern summer night[2]. He

[1] This place, according to Defrémery (*Journ. As.*, July–Sept. 1850, p. 159), still exists as Besh Tau, and was visited by Klaproth.

Bolghar, sometimes called Bolar, is in 54° 54′, nearly the latitude of Carlisle. It stood near the left bank of the Atil or Volga, about fifty miles above the modern Simbirsk and ninety miles south-west of Kazan. It was sometimes the residence of the khans of Kipchak. There was still a village called Bolgari on the site when Pallas wrote; and there are a considerable number of architectural remains. On these Hammer Purgstall refers to Schmidt's '*Architektonische Umrisse der Ruinen Bolgars*, 1832' (Pallas, Fr. Trans., year II, i, 217; *Gesch. der Gold. Horde*, p. 8; Reinaud's *Abulfeda*, ii, p. 81; [*Marco Polo*, i, p. 7 *n.*; ii, p. 486 *n.*; Bretschneider, *Mediaeval Researches*, ii, p. 82]).

was desirous also to go north from Bolghar to the *Land of Darkness*, of which he had heard still more wonderful things; but this he gave up on account of the many difficulties, and returned to the sultan's camp, which he then followed to HAJ-TARKHAN (Astrakhan).

One of the wives of Mahomed Uzbek was a Greek princess of Constantinople, whom the traveller calls the *Khátún* or Lady Beyálún (*Philumena*? or *Iolanthe*? At iii, 10, it is written *Beilún*), and she was now about to pay a visit to her own people[1]. Ibn Batuta was allowed to join the cortège. Their route seems to have been singularly devious, leading them by UKAK[2] ten days above Sarai, near the "Hills of the Russians," described as a fair-haired, blue-eyed, but ugly and crafty race of Christians, thence to the port of SOLDAIA (perhaps with the intention of going by sea) and then by land the whole way to Constantinople, where they were received in

[1] These marriages appear to have been tolerably frequent as the Greek emperors went down in the world, though the one in question does not seem to be mentioned elsewhere. Thus Húlakú having demanded in marriage a daughter of Michael Palæologus, a natural daughter of the emperor, Mary by name, was sent in compliance with this demand: Húlakú was dead when she arrived in Persia, but she was married to his successor, Abaka Khan. The Mongols called her *Despina Khatun* (Δέσποινα). An illegitimate sister of the same emperor, called Euphrosyne, was bestowed on Nagaia Khan, founder of a small Tartar dynasty on the Greek frontier; and another daughter of the same name in 1265 on Tulabuka, who twenty years later became Khan of Kipchak. Andronicus the Elder is said to have given a young lady who passed for his natural daughter to Gházán Khan of Persia, and a few years later his sister Mary to Gházán's successor, Oljaïtu, as well as another natural daughter Mary to Tuktuka Khan of Kipchak. Also in the genealogy of the Comneni of Trebizond we find two daughters of the Emperor Basil married to Turkish or Tartar chiefs, and daughters of Alexis III, Alexis IV, and John IV making similar marriages. (D'Ohsson, iii, 417, and iv, 315, 318; Deguignes, i, 289; Hammer, *Gesch. der Ilchane*; Preface to *Ibn Batuta*, tom. ii, p. x; Art. *Comneni* in Smith's *Dict. of Gr. and Rom. Biog.*)

[2] Ukaka or Ukek and Majár have already been mentioned at III, p. 84, *supra*. The ruins of Majár exist and have been described by Klaproth (Defrémery in *J. As.*, 1850, p. 154).

great state, the emperor (Andronicus the Younger) and empress coming out to meet their daughter, and the whole population crowding to see the show, while the bells rang till the heavens shook with the clangour. He tells us how, as he passed the city gate in the lady's train, he heard the guards muttering to one another *Sarakínú ! Sarakínú !* a name, says he, by which they called Mussulmans.

It is curious to find the name Istambul in use a century and more before the Turkish conquest[1]. Thus he tells us the part of the city CONSTANTINIA, on the eastern side of the river (the Golden Horn), where the emperor and his courtiers reside, is called *Istambul,* whilst the other side is called Galata, and is specially assigned to the dwellings of the Frank Christians, such as Genoese, Venetians (*Banádikah*), people of Rome (*Ahil-Rúmah*), and of France (*Ahil-Afránsah*).

After a short stay at the Greek city, during which he had an interview with the Emperor Andronicus the Elder, whom he calls King George (*Jirjís*), and after

[1] But even in the ninth century Mas'ūdī says that the Greeks never called their city Constantinia but *Bolin* (πόλιν = *Town* of the Londoner), and, when they wished to speak of it as the capital of the empire, *Stanbolin* (εἰς τὴν πόλιν); and he speaks of these as very old appellations. Indeed the name applied by the Chinese to the Roman Empire in the time of Heraclius (*Folin*) argues that the former term was then in familiar use. In the century following Ibn Batuta, Ruy Gonzalez de Clavijo says that the Greeks called their city, not Constantinople, but *Escomboli* (probably misread for *Estomboli*); and his contemporary Schiltberger tells us the Greeks called it *Istimboli,* but the Turks *Stambol.*

The Orientals found other etymologies for the name. Thus Sadik Isfahani declares that Istanbul signifies in the Turkish language, "You will find there what you will!" And after the capture of the city, some of the sultans tried to change the name to *Islâmbul.*

There are several other names in modern use which have been formed in the same way; e.g. *Isnicmid* from εἰς Νικομήδειαν, *Setines* from εἰς 'Αθήνας. (Jacquet in *Jour. As.*, ix, 459, etc.; Markham's *Clavijo,* p. 47; Schiltberger, p. 136; *Geog. Works of Sadik Isfahani* by J. C., 1832, pp. 7, 8, and *note.*)

receiving a handsome present from the princess[1], he went back to Uzbek at Sarai, and thence took his way across the desert to Khwarizm and Bokhara, whence he went to visit the Khan 'Aláuddín Tarmashírín of the Chagatai dynasty. His travels then extended through Khorasan and Kabul, including a passage of the Hindu Kush. This appears to have been by ANDERAB (which he calls *Andar*), and so by PANCHSHIR (see *supra*, II, p. 263) to PARWĀN and CHAREKAR (*Charkh*). It is remarkable that between Anderab and Parwān Ibn Batuta speaks of passing the Mountain of PASHAI, probably the Pascia of Marco Polo, which Pauthier seems thus justified in identifying with a part of the Kafir country of the Hindu Kush (*Livre de M. Pol,* p. 123)[2]. He then proceeded to Sind, reaching the Indus, probably somewhere below Larkhana, according to his own statement, on the 12th September, 1333. Here he terminates the First Part of his narrative.

Proceeding to SIWASTÁN (Sehwán) he there met with a brother theologian, 'Alá-ul-Mulk, who had been appointed governor of the district at the mouth of the Indus, and after having travelled with him to LAHARI, a fine place on the shore of the ocean, he then turned

[1] Part of this consisted of three hundred pieces of gold called *Albarbarah* (Hyperperæ), the gold of which was bad, he observes. It was indeed very bad, for Pegolotti, if I understand him aright, says these "*perperi*" contained only 11 carats of gold to 6 of silver and 7 of copper (p. 23).

[2] [*Marco Polo*, i, pp. 164–6 *n*.] The name appears still more exactly in another passage of Marco Polo, where he describes the invasion of India by the Mongol prince whom he calls Nogodar. ["He left his uncle who was then in Greater Armenia, and fled with a great body of horsemen, cruel unscrupulous fellows, first through Badashan, and then through another province called Pashai-Dir, and then through another called Ariora-Keshemur. There he lost a great number of his people and of his horses, for the roads were very narrow and perilous." *Marco Polo,* i, p. 98.]. Remarks on the Passes of Hindu Kush will be found in the introduction to Goës, *infra*.

northward to BAKAR, UJAH[1], and MULTAN, where he found assembled a large party of foreigners all bent on seeking their fortunes in India, and waiting at the frontier city for invitations from the liberal sovereign of Hindustan.

This was Mahomet Tughlak, originally called Júna Khan, whose contradictory qualities are painted by Ibn Batuta quite in accordance with the account of Firishta. The latter describes him[2] as the most eloquent and accomplished prince of his time; gallant in the field and inured to war; admired for his compositions in prose and verse; well versed in history, logic, mathematics, medicine, and metaphysics; the founder of hospitals for the sick and of refuges for widows and orphans; profuse in his liberality, especially to men of learning. But with all this he was wholly devoid of mercy and of consideration for his people; the murderer of his father[3]

[1] *Lahari* is still known as Lāhori or "Larry Bunder," though it has disappeared from our recent maps. It stands on the western or Pitti branch of the Indus delta. *Bakár* is Bakhar or Bukkur, the fort in the Indus between Sakkar and Rohri, where the Indus was bridged for Lord Keane's army by Major George Thomson in 1838. *Ujah* is Uchh [High Place] on [the south bank of the Sutlej opposite its confluence with] the Chenāb, below Bahāwalpúr.

[2] Briggs' *Firishta*, i, 411–12; see also Elphinstone, ii, 60.

[3] As the story is told by Ibn Batuta after the relation of an eyewitness, Mahomed had prepared, for the reception of his father on his return from a campaign, a pavilion on the banks of a stream near Delhi. This pavilion was artfully constructed with the assistance of Ahmed son of Ayas the Inspector of Buildings, so that when approached on a certain side by the weighty bodies of elephants the whole would fall. After the king had alighted and was resting in the pavilion with his favourite son Mahmud, Mahomed proposed that the whole of the elephants should pass in review before the building. When they came over the fatal spot the structure came down on the heads of Tughlak Sháh and his young son. After intentional delay the ruins were removed, and the king's body was found bending over that of his boy as if to shield him [1324]. It was carried to Tughlakábad, and laid in the tomb which he had built for himself. This still stands, one of the simplest and grandest monuments of Mahomedan antiquity, rising from the middle of what is now a swamp, but was then a lake. It is said that the parricide Mahomed is also buried therein. This strange

and of his brother, he was as madly capricious, as cruel, bloodthirsty, and unjust as Nero or Caligula. Incensed at anonymous pasquinades against his oppressions, he on one occasion ordered the removal of the seat of government, and of all the inhabitants of Delhi, to Daulatābād in the Dekkan[1], forty days' journey distant; and after the old city had been gradually reoccupied, and he had himself re-established his court there for some years, he repeated the same mad caprice a second time[2]. "So little did he hesitate to spill the blood of God's creatures, that when anything occurred which excited him to proceed to that horrid extremity, one might have supposed his object was to exterminate the species altogether. No single week passed without his having put to death one or more of the learned and holy men who surrounded him, or some of the secretaries who attended him." Or as Ibn Batuta pithily sums up a part of the contradictions of his character, there was no day that the gate of his palace failed to witness the elevation of some abject to affluence, the torture and murder of some living soul[3]. Mahomed formed great schemes of conquest, and carried out some of them. His mad projects for the invasion of Khorasan and of China came to nothing, or to miserable disaster, but

story of the murder of Tughlak Sháh is said to have been re-enacted in our own day (1841 or 1842), when Nao Nihal Singh, the successor of Ranjít, was killed by the fall of a gateway as he entered Lahore.

Ahmed Bin Ayas, the engineer of the older murder, became the Wazir of Mahomed, under the titles of Malik-Záda and Khwája Jahán. (*Ibn Bat.*, iii, 213–14.)

[1] A description of the prodigious scale on which the new city, which was to be called the *Capital of Islam*, was projected and commenced, is given by an eyewitness in the *Masālak-al-Absār*, translated in *Not. et Extraits*, xiii, 172.

[2] Briggs, pp. 420–2; *Ibn Bat.*, iii, 314. Elphinstone says the move was made three times (ii, 67). If so, I have overlooked it in Briggs.

[3] Briggs, pp. 411–12; *Ibn Bat.*, iii, 216.

within the bounds of India he was more successful, and had at one time subjected nearly the whole of the Peninsula. In the end, however, nearly all his conquests were wrested from him, either by the native king or by the revolt of his own servants. Respecting this king and the history of his reign, Ibn Batuta's narrative gives many curious and probably truthful details, such subjects being more congenial to his turn of mind than the correct observation of facts in geography or natural history, though even as regards the former his statements are sufficiently complicated by his contempt for chronological arrangement.

After a detention of two months at Multān, Ibn Batuta was allowed to proceed, in company with the distinguished foreigners, for whom invitations to the court arrived. The route lay by ABOHAR in the desert, where the Indian, as distinguished from the Sindian provinces commenced, the castle of ABŪ BAKHR, AJUDAHAN, SARSATI, HANSI, MASUDABAD, and PALAM, to DELHI[1]. The city, or group of cities, which then bore

[1] I cannot trace Abū Bakhr. *Ajudin* [Ajodhan] or *Pāk Pattan* (The Pure or Holy Ferry) is a town on the right bank of the Sutlej valley, about half-way between Bahāwalpúr and Firuzpúr, the site of a very sacred Mahomedan shrine [the saint Shaik-ul-Islām, Farīd-ul-Hakkwa-ud-Dīn, Shakar Ganj (1173–1265)], for the sake of which Timur on his devastating march spared the few persons found in the town [1398]. *Abohar* is a town in the desert of Bhattiāna, some sixty miles east of Ajudin. [Uboh-har or "the pool of Uboh" after the wife of Jaura, the founder of the town.] The narrative brings Ibn Batuta to Abohar *first*, and then to Abū Bakhr and Ajodin, and I have not ventured to change the order; but this seems to involve a direct retrogression. *Sarsati* [or Sarsūti] is the town now called Sirsa on the verge of the Desert [on the north side of a dry bed of the Ghaggar]. *Hansi* retains its name as the chief town of an English Zillah. Sixty years ago [in 1798] it was the capital of that singular adventurer George Thomas, who raised himself from being a sailor before the mast to be the ruler of a small Indian principality. *Masudabad* I do not know; it must have been in the direction of the modern Bahádargarh. *Palam* still exists, a few miles west of the Delhi of those days, to one of the gates of which it gave its name.

the latter name did not occupy the site of the modern capital built by Sháh Jahán in the seventeenth century, but stood some ten miles further south, in a position of which the celebrated Kutb Minar may be taken as the chief surviving landmark.

The king was then absent at Kanauj, but on hearing of the arrival of Ibn Batuta with the rest, he ordered an assignment in his behalf of three villages, producing a total rent of 5000 silver dinars, and on his return to the capital received the traveller kindly, and gave him a further present of 12,000 dinars, with the appointment of Kazi of Delhi, to which a salary of the same amount was attached[1].

Ibn Batuta continued for about eight years in the service of Mahomed Sháh, though it seems doubtful how far he was occupied in his judicial duties. Indeed, he describes Delhi, though one of the grandest cities in the Mahomedan world, as nearly deserted during his residence there. The traveller's good fortune seems only to have fostered his natural extravagance; for at an early period of his stay at the capital he had incurred debts to the amount of 55,000 dinars of silver, which, after long importunity, he got the Sultan to pay. Indeed, by his own account, he seems to have hung like a perfect horse-leech on the king's bounty.

When Mahomed Tughlak was about to proceed to Maabar to put down an insurrection[2], Ibn Batuta expected

[1] Respecting the value of these dinars, see Note A at the end of this Introduction. The three villages assigned to the traveller lay at sixteen koss from Delhi, he says, and were called *Badlí*, *Basahí*, and *Balarah*. They lay in the *Sadi* or Hundred of *Hindú-but* (or the Hindu Idol; so Defrémery reads it, but the original as he gives it seems rather to read *Hindabat*, and may represent *Indrapat*, the name of one of the old cities of Delhi still existing. Probably the villages could be identified on the Indian Atlas). Two were added later, *Jauzah* and *Malikpúr*.

[2] This must have been on the occasion of the revolt of the Sharíf Jalal-uddín Ahsan in Maabar. The French editors, in

to accompany him, and prepared an outfit for the march on his usual free scale of expenditure[1]. At the last moment, however, he was ordered, nothing loth, to remain behind and take charge of the tomb of Sultan Kutb-uddín, whose servant the Sultan had been, and for whose memory he professed the greatest veneration[2]. He renewed his personal extravagances, spending large sums which his friends had left in deposit with him, and reviling those who were mean enough to expect at least a portion to be repaid! One who scattered his own money and that of his friends so freely was not likely to be backward

the careful chronological table of the events of Mahomed's reign which is embraced in their Preface to the third volume, place this expedition in 1341–2. The sultan fell ill at Warangol [Warangal, 86 miles north-east of Hyderābād City], and returned speedily to Daulatābād [district of Aurangābād, Hyderābād State, or Deogiri, Mohammed Tughlak had the idea of making it his capital] and Delhi.

1 His account of the outfit required by a gentleman travelling in India shows how little such things have changed there in five hundred years, say from 1340 to 1840. (Now they are changing!) He mentions the set of tents and *saiwáns* (or canvas enclosure walls) to be purchased; men to carry the tents on their shoulders (this is never the practice now); the grass cutters to supply the horses and cattle with grass; the bearers (*kaháron*) to carry the kitchen utensils on their shoulders, and also to carry the traveller's palankin; the *farâshes* to pitch his tents and load his camels; the runners to carry torches before him in the dark. Moreover he tells us he had paid all these people nine months' wages beforehand, which shows that the "system of advances" was in still greater vigour than even now.

The French translators do not recognize the word *kaháron*, putting "*gohars?*" as a parenthetic query. But it is still the ordinary name of the caste of people (*Kahārs*) who bear palankins or carry burdens on a yoke over one shoulder, and the name is one of the few real Indian words that Ibn Batuta shows any knowledge of. I think the only others are *tatú* [*ṭaṭṭu*] for a pony; *Jauthri* (for *Chaodri*), "the Shaikh of the Hindus," as he explains it; *Sáha*, as the appellation of a certain class of merchants at Daulatābād, a name (*Sahá*) still borne extensively by a mercantile caste; *Katri* (*Kshatri*) as the name of a noble class of Hindus; *Jogi*; *morah* [*moṛhā*], a stool; *kishri* [*khichṛī*] (for *kichari*, vulgo *kedgeree*, well known at Indian breakfasts); and some names of fruits and pulses (iii, 415, 427; 207; 388; iv, 49, 51; ii, 75; iii, 127–31).

2 This was Kutb-uddín Mubārak Sháh, son of 'Aláuddin, murdered by his minister Khosrū in 1320.

when his hand had found its way into the public purse. The account he gives of the establishment he provided for the tomb placed under his charge is characteristic of his magnificent ideas. "I established in connexion with it one hundred and fifty readers of the Koran, eighty students, and eight repeaters, a professor, eighty *sufis*, or monks, an imam, muezzins, reciters selected for their fine intonation, panegyrists, scribes to take note of those who were absent, and ushers. All these people are recognized in that country as *alarbáb*, or gentlemen. I also made arrangements for the subordinate class of attendants called *alhâshiyah*, or menials[1], such as footmen, cooks, runners, water-carriers, sherbet-men, betel-men, sword-bearers, javelin-men, umbrella-men, hand-washers, beadles, and officers. The whole number of people whom I appointed to these employments amounted to four hundred and sixty persons. The Sultan had ordered me to expend daily in food at the tomb twelve measures of meal and an equal weight of meat. That appeared to me too scanty an allowance; whilst, on the other hand, the total revenue in grain allowed by the king was considerable. So I expended daily thirty-five measures of meal, an equal weight of butcher-meat, and quantities in proportion of sugar, sugar-candy, butter, and pawn. In this way I used to feed not only the people of the establishment, but all comers. There was great famine at the time, and this distribution of food was a great alleviation of the sufferings of the people, so that the fame of it spread far and wide."

Towards the end of his residence in India he fell for a time into great disfavour, the cause of which he relates in this way:

[1] *Rabb*, Dominus, Possessor, pl. *arbáb*; *Hhâshíyah*, ora vestis vel alius rei, *inde* domestici, asseclæ (Freytag in vv).

There was at Delhi a certain learned and pious shaikh called Shihab-uddín the son of Aljām the Khorasani, whom Sultan Mahomed was desirous of employing in his service, but who positively refused to enter it. On this the king ordered another doctor of theology, who was standing by, to pull out the shaikh's beard, and on his declining the office, the ruffian caused the beards of both to be plucked out! Shaikh Shihab-uddín retired from the city and established himself in a country place some miles from Delhi, where he amused himself by forming a large cave, which he fitted up with a bath, supplied by water from the Jumna, and with other conveniences. The Sultan several times sent to summon him, but he always refused to come, and at length said in plain words that he would never serve a tyrant. He was then arrested and brought before the tyrant himself, brutally maltreated, and finally put to death.

Ibn Batuta's curiosity had induced him to visit the shaikh in his cavern before this happened, and he thus incurred the displeasure and suspicion of the Sultan. Four slaves were ordered to keep him under constant surveillance, a step which was generally followed before long by the death of the suspected individual. Ibn Batuta, in his fear, betook himself to intense devotion and multiplied observances, among others to the repetition of a certain verse of the Koran 33,000 times in the day! The surveillance being apparently relaxed, he withdrew altogether from the public eye, gave all that he possessed to darveshes and the poor (he says nothing about his creditors), and devoted himself to an ascetic life under the tutelage of a certain holy shaikh in the neighbourhood of Delhi, called Kamal-uddín Abdallah of the Cave, with whom he abode for five months. The king, who was then in Sind[1], hearing of Ibn Batuta's reform, sent for him to camp. He appeared before the Lord of the World (as Mahomed was called) in his hermit's dress, and was well received. Nevertheless, he evidently did not yet consider his head at all safe, for he redoubled his ascetic observances. After forty days, however, the king summoned him again, and announced his intention of sending him on an embassy to China. According to Ibn Batuta's dates this appears to have been in the spring of 1342.

The object of the proposed embassy was to reciprocate one which had arrived at court from the Emperor of China. The envoys had been the bearers of a present to Sultan Mahomed, which consisted of 100 slaves of both sexes, 500 pieces of *cammucca*[2], of which 100 were of the fabric of Zaitún and 100 of that of King-sze, five maunds of musk, five robes broidered with pearls, five quivers of cloth of gold, and five swords[3]. And the professed object of the mission was to get leave to rebuild an idol temple (Buddhist, doubtless) on the borders of the mountain of KARACHIL, at a place called SAMHAL, whither the Chinese used to go on pilgrimage, and which had been destroyed by the Sultan's troops[4].

[1] This must have been on the occasion of the revolt of Shahú the Afghan at Multān, who murdered the viceroy of the province and tried to set himself up as king. Though Defrémery's chronological table does not mention that Sultan Mahomed himself marched to the scene of action, and Ibn Batuta only says that "the Sultan made preparations for an expedition against him," as the revolt is placed in this very year 1342, it is probable that he had advanced towards Multān (iii, pp. xxi and 362), which according to the view of Ibn Batuta was a city of Sind.

[2] See note, III, p. 155, *supra*.

[3] ["A hundred Mamlūks, fifty slave girls, five hundred dresses of El Kamanjah, five hundred maunds of musk, five dresses wrought with jewels, five quivers wrought with gold, and five swords with jewels." (Lee, *Ibn Batuta*, p. 153.)]

[4] It is interesting to find this indication that perhaps the pilgrimages of the Chinese Buddhists to the ancient Indian holy places were still kept up, but it may have been only the Tibetan subjects of the Great Khan who maintained the practice.

Mahomed's reply was that it was not admissible by the principles of his religion to grant such a demand, unless in favour of persons paying the poll-tax as subjects of his Government. If the Emperor would go through the form of paying this he would be allowed to rebuild the temple[1].

The embassy, headed by Ibn Batuta, was to convey this reply, and a return present of much greater value than that received. This was composed of 100 high-bred horses caparisoned, 100 male slaves, 100 Hindu girls accomplished in song and dance, 100 pieces of the stuff called *bairami* (these were of cotton, but matchless

In our own day I have seen such at Hardwār, who had crossed the Himalaya, from *Mahachin* as they said, to visit the holy flame of Jawálamukhi in the Punjab. *Karachil* is doubtless a corruption of the Sanskrit *Kuverachal*, a name of Mount Kailás, where lies the city of Kuvera the Indian Plutus, and is here used for the Himalaya. In another passage the author describes it as a range of vast mountains, three month's journey in extent, and distant ten days from Delhi, which was invaded by M. Tughlak's army in a most disastrous expedition (apparently the same which Firishta describes as a project for the invasion of China, though Ibn Batuta does not mention that object). He also speaks of it as the source of the river which flowed near Amroha (in the modern district of Morādābād, probably the Ramgunga; iii, 326; ii, 6; iii, 437). The same name is found in the form *Kalárchal*, applied to a part of the Himalaya by Rashíd, or rather perhaps by Al-Birúni, whom he appears to be copying. This author distinguishes it from *Harmakût* (*Hema-Kuta*, the Snow Peaks, one form of the name Himalaya), in which the Ganges rises, and says that the eternal snows of Kalarchal are visible from *Tákas* (Taxila?) and Lahore (Elliot's *Mah. Historians*, p. 30). *Samhal* is probably *Sambhal*, an ancient Hindu city of Rohilkhand (perhaps the *Sapolus* of Ptolemy?), also in Zillah Morādābād. From other passages I gather that the *province* was called Sambhal at that time, and indeed so it was up to the time of Sultan Baber, when it formed the government of his son Humāyūn. I do not find that Sambhal itself has been recognized as the site of Buddhist remains, but very important remains of that character have been examined by Major-Gen. Cunningham, following the traces of Hiuen Tsang, at various places immediately to the north of Sambhal, and one of these may have been the site of the temple in question.

[1] The *Jezía* or "poll-tax...was imposed, during the early conquests, on all infidels who submitted to the Mahomed rule, and was the test by which they were distinguished from those who remained in a state of hostility" (Elphinstone, ii, 457). Its abolition was one of the beneficent acts of Akbar, but Aurangzib imposed it again.

in quality)[1], 100 pieces of silk stuff called *juz*, 100 pieces of stuff called *salatuyah*, 100 pieces of *shirinbaf*, 100 of *shanbaf*, 500 of woollen stuff (probably shawls), of which 100 were black, 100 white, 100 red, 100 green, 100 blue; 100 pieces of Greek linen, 100 cloth dresses, a great state tent and six pavilions, four golden candlesticks and six of silver, ornamented with blue enamel; six silver basins, ten dresses of honour in brocade[2], ten caps, of which one was broidered with pearls; ten quivers of brocade, one with pearls; ten swords, one with a scabbard wrought in pearls; gloves broidered with pearls; and fifteen eunuchs.

His colleagues in this embassy were the Amir Zahír-uddín the Zinjani, a man of eminent learning, and the Eunuch Kāfūr (Camphor) the Cup-bearer, who had charge of the presents. The Amír Mahomed of Herat was to escort them to the place of embarcation with 1000 horse, and the Chinese ambassadors, fifteen in number, the chief of whom was called Tursi[3], joined the party with about 100 servants.

[1] Probably Dacca muslins. *Beirami* is a term for certain white Indian cloths we find used by Varthema, Barbosa, and others, and in Milburn's *Oriental Commerce* we have the same article under the name *Byrampaut* (i, 268). The *Shanbaf* is no doubt the Sinabaffi of Varthema, but more I cannot say. ["1609. A sort of cloth called *Byramy* resembling Holland cloths." (F. C. Danvers and W. Foster, *Letters received by the E. I. Co.*, i, 29.)

Shirinbaf, Pers. *Shīrīnbaf*, "sweet wool," a fine light stuff or cotton whereof the Moors make their cabayes or clothing. (Danvers, *l. c.*, i, 29.)

Shanbaf, *Sinabaffs* [Varthema] is identified by Badger, quoted by Sir G. Birdwood, *Report on the Old Records of the India Office*, p. 153, with *sina-bafta*, "China-woven" cloths.]

[2] Mahomed Tughlak maintained an enormous royal establishment (analogous to the Gobelins) of weavers in silk and gold brocade, to provide stuffs for his presents, and for the ladies of the palace (*Not. et Extraits*, xiii, 183).

[3] ["With whom there was a great Emir," Lee, p. 155.] A statesman called *Turshi* was chief minister in China with great power, a few years after this, in 1347–8 (De Mailla, ix, 584). It is, however, perhaps not probable that this was the same

The king had apparently returned to Delhi before the despatch of the party, for the latter set out from that city on the 22nd July, 1342. Their route lay at first down the Doab as far as Kanauj, but misfortunes began before they had got far beyond the evening shadow of the Kutb Minar. For whilst they were at KOL (Koel or Alīgarh, eighty miles from Delhi), having complied with an invitation to take part in relieving the neighbouring town of JALĀLÍ from the attack of a body of Hindus[1], they lost in the fight twenty-five horsemen and fifty-five foot-men, including Kāfūr the Eunuch. During a halt which ensued, Ibn Batuta, separating from his companions, got taken prisoner, and though he escaped from the hands of his captors, did not get back to his friends for eight days, during which he went through some curious adventures. The party were so disheartened by these inauspicious beginnings that they wished to abandon the journey; but, in the meantime, the Sultan had despatched his Master of the Robes, the Eunuch Sanbul (*Spikenard*), to take the place of Kāfūr defunct, and with orders for them to proceed.

From KANAUJ they turned southwards to the fortress of GWALIOR, which Ibn Batuta had visited previously, and had then taken occasion to describe with fair accuracy. At PARWĀN, a place which they passed through on leaving Gwalior, and which was much harassed by lions (probably tigers rather), the traveller heard that certain malignant Jogis were in the habit of assuming the form

person, as the Indo-Chinese nations do not usually employ statesmen of a high rank on foreign embassies.

[1] That work of this kind should be going on so near the capital shows perhaps that when Firishta says Mahomed's conquest of the distant provinces of Dwara-Samudra, Maabar, and Bengal, etc., had incorporated them with the empire "as completely as the villages in the vicinity of Delhi," this may not have amounted to very much after all (Briggs, i, 413).

of those animals by night. This gives him an opportunity of speaking of others of the Jogi class who used to allow themselves to be buried for months, or even for a twelvemonth together, and afterwards revived. At Mangalore he afterwards made acquaintance with a Mussulman who had acquired this art from the Jogis[1]. The route continued through Bundelkhand and Mālwā to the city of DAULATĀBĀD, with its celebrated fortress of DWAIGIR (Deogiri), and thence down the Valley of the Tapti to KINBAIAT (Cambay)[2].

[1] This art, or the profession of it, is not yet extinct in India. A very curious account of one of its professors will be found in a '*Personal Narrative of a Tour through the States of Rajwāra*' (Calcutta, 1837, pp. 41–4), by my lamented friend Major-General A. H. E. Boileau, and also in the *Court and Camp of Ranjīt Singh*, by Captain Osborne, an officer on Lord Auckland's staff, to which I can only refer from memory. [See *Marco Polo*, ii, 365, 369 *n*.]

[2] I will here give the places passed through by Ibn Batuta on his route from Delhi to Cambay, with their identifications as far as practicable.

DELHI.	
Tilbat, 2½ parasangs from the city . . .	This is perhaps *Tilputa*, a village in the Dadri Parganah, though this is some 17 miles from old Delhi. [Mžik, p. 249, criticizes Yule but does not himself throw any new light on the subject.]
Aú	Possibly *Aduh*, a Pargana town 8 miles west of Bulandshahr. [Mžik, p. 249, says it should be *Adha* or *Edha*.]
Hilú ?	
Beiána, "a great place," with fine markets, and of which one of the chief officers of state had been lately governor	I believe no such name is now traceable. Biana, west of Agra, was a very important city and fortress in the middle ages, but is quite out of place here. [Mžik, p. 249, has Bayāna, 24 English miles west of Koil.]
KÓL, a fine city in a plain surrounded by mango orchards.	*Koel* [or *Koil*], commonly now known as Alīgarh, from the great fort in the vicinity taken by Lord Lake [1803]. *Jalālī* still exists, 10 m. E. of Koel.
(Jalālī, the town relieved)	
Burjbúrah . . .	There is a village *Birjpúr* N.E. of Mainpúri, on the line between Koel and Kanauj.

From Cambay they went to KAWE, a place on a tidal gulf belonging to the Pagan Raja Jalansi, and thence to KANDAHAR, a considerable city on another estuary, and belonging to the same prince, who professed loyalty

Ab-i-Siyah . . .	A Persian rendering of the name of *Kali-Nadi* (Black River), which enters the Ganges near Kanauj. Shari-uddín gives the same name in a Turkish version, *Kara Su* (*H. de Timur Bec*, iii, 121).
KANAUJ	Well known.
Hanaul, Wazirpúr . .	Not traced. The last a very common name.
Bajálisah . . .	Must have been a place of some note as it gave a name to one of the gates of Delhi (iii, 149, and note, p. 461). I should suppose it must have been near the Jumna, *Etāwa* perhaps, or at *Bateswar* Ferry.
City of Maori, Marh .	If the last was Etāwa, Maori may be *Umri* near Bhind.
Alāpúr, ruled by an Abyssinian or Negro giant who could eat a whole sheep at once. A day's journey from this dwelt Katam the Pagan King of Jambil . . .	There is a place, *Jaurasa Alapur*, to the W.N.W. of Gwalior, where Sir Robert Napier gained a brilliant victory over the Gwalior insurgents in 1858, but it seems too much out of the line. The Pagan king is perhaps the Rajah of Dholpúr on the *Chambal*.
GALIÚR	*Gwalior*.
Parwān, Amwari . .	The first may be *Panwári* in the Hamirpúr Zillah, which would be in the line taken, if the next identification be correct.
Kajarrá. Here there was a lake about a mile long surrounded by idol temples, and with buildings in the water occupied by long-haired Jogis .	Appears to be mentioned as *Kajráha* by Rashid, quoted by Elliot (p. 37), who identifies both names with *Kajrái*, on the banks of the Ken river in Bundelkhand, between Chattarpúr and Panna, which has ruins of great antiquity and interest. If so, the route followed must have been very devious, owing perhaps to the interposition of insurgent districts.
Chanderī, a great place with splendid bazaars .	A well known ancient city and fortress on the borders of Bundelkhand and Mālwā, captured by Sir Hugh Rosė in 1858. According to the *Ayin Akbari* (quoted by Rennell) it contained 14,000 stone houses.

to Delhi, and treated them hospitably. Here they took ship, three vessels being provided for them. After two days they stopped to water at the Isle of BAIRAM, four miles from the main. This island had been formerly peopled, but it remained abandoned by the natives since its capture by the Mahomedans, though one of the king's officers had made an attempt to re-settle it, putting in a small garrison and mounting mangonels for its defence. Next day they were at KUKAH, a great city with extensive bazaars, anchoring four miles from the shore on account of the vast recession of the tide. This city belonged to another pagan king, Dunkul, not too loyal to the Sultan. Three days' sail from this brought the party abreast of the Island of SINDÁBÚR, but they passed on and anchored under a smaller island near the mainland, in which there was a temple, a grove, and a piece of water. Landing here, the traveller had a curious adventure with a Jogi, whom he found by the

ZIHAR, the capital of Mālwā. There were inscribed milestones all the way from Delhi to this.	*Dhār*, say the French Editor. But apparently the next station should have come first in that case.
UJJAIN	Well known ancient city, N.E. of Dhār.
(Amjari, where he tells us (iii, 137) he witnessed a Suttee.)	*Amjhera*, a few miles S.W. by W. of Dhār?
DAULATĀBĀD . . .	Retains its name. It appears in Fra Mauro's map as *Deuletabet*, and in the *C. Catalana* as *Diogil* (Deogiri).
Nadharbár. The people here and of the Daulatābād territory *Marhatahs* (iv, 48, 51).	*Naderbar* of Rennell, or *Nandarbár*, on the south bank of the Tāpti.
Sāghar, a great town on a considerable river.	*Saunghar* on the Tāpti.
KINBAIAT, a very handsome city full of foreign merchants, on an estuary of the sea in which the tide rose and fell in a remarkable manner.	*Cambay* [Khambāyat]. We find the *t* expressed by several of the old authors, by Marino Sanudo (*Cambeth*), by Fra Mauro (*Combait*); and much later the Jesuits of Akbar's time have *Cambaietta*.

wall of the temple[1]. Next day they came to HUNAWÚR (or Onore), a city governed by a Mahomedan prince with great power at sea; apparently a pirate, like his successors in later times, but an enlightened ruler, for Ibn Batuta found in his city twenty-three schools for boys and thirteen for girls, the latter a thing which he had seen nowhere else in his travels[2].

After visiting several of the northern ports of Malabar, then very numerous and flourishing, they arrived at CALICUT, which the traveller describes as one of the finest ports in the world, frequented for trade by the people of China, the Archipelago, Ceylon, the Maldives, Yemen, and the Persian Gulf[3]. Here they were honourably received by the king, who bore the title of *Samari*[4] (the Zamorin of the Portuguese), and made their landing in great state. But all this was to be followed by speedy grief, as the traveller himself observes.

[1] For the identification of the places from Cambay to Hunawúr I must refer to Note B at the end of this Introduction. Assuming, as there argued, that Sindábúr was Goa [see *Hobson-Jobson*, s.v.], the small island was probably *Anchediva*, a favourite anchorage of the early Portuguese. "In the middle of it is a large lake of fresh water, but the island is deserted; it may be two miles from the mainland; it was in former times inhabited by the Gentoos, but the Moors of Mecca used to take this route to Calicut, and used to stop here to take in wood and water, and on that account it has ever since been deserted." (*Voyage of Pedro Alvares Cabral*, Lisbon, 1812, p. 118.)

[2] He says the Sultan of Hunawúr was subject to a Pagan monarch called *Hariab*, of whom he promises to speak again, but does not do so, unless, as is probable, he was the same as Bilal Deo (the Raja of Karnata), of whom he speaks at iv, p. 195.

[3] [Ma Huan describes Calicut (*Ku-li*) as "a great emporium of trade frequented by merchants from all quarters. It is three days' sail from Cochin, by which it is bordered on the south; on the north it adjoins Cannanore (K'ân-nu-urh); it has the sea on the west; and on the east, through the mountains, at a distance of 500 *li* (167 miles), is the kingdom or city of K'an-pa-mei." (*J. R. A. S.*, 1896, p. 345.)]

[4] [The word is Malayāl. *Sāmūtiri*, *Sāmūri*, *Tāmātiri*, *Tāmūri*, a *tadbhava* (or vernacular modification) of Skt. *Sāmundri*, "the Sea-King." *Hobson-Jobson.*]

At Calicut they abode for three months, awaiting the season for the voyage to China, viz., the spring. All the communication with that country, according to Ibn Batuta (the fact itself is perhaps questionable), was conducted in Chinese vessels, of which there were three classes: the biggest called *Junk*, the middle-sized *Zao*, and the third *Kakam*[1]. The greater ships had from three to twelve sails, made of strips of bamboo woven like mats. Each of them had a crew of 1000 men, viz., 600 sailors and 400 soldiers, and had three tenders attached, which were called respectively the *Half*, the *Third*, and the *Quarter*, names apparently indicating their proportionate size. The vessels for this trade were built nowhere except at ZAITÚN and SÍNKALÁN, the city also called SÍN-UL-SÍN[2], and were all made with triple sides, fastened with enormous spikes, three cubits

[1] The French editors derive these three words from Chinese terms, said to be respectively, *Ch'wen*, *Sao* or *Seu*, and *Hoa-hang* (M. Pauthier corrects these two last to *Tsao* or *Chéu*, and *Hoa-ch'wen*, "merchant-vessel," *M. Polo*, p. 656). I may venture at least to suggest a doubt of this derivation. *Junk* is certainly the Malay and Javanese *Jong* or *Ajong*, "a great ship" (v. Crawfurd's *Malay Dict.* in *vocib.* and *Hobson-Jobson*); whilst *Zao* may just as probably be the *Dhao* or *Dao*, which is to this day the common term on all the shores of the Indian Ocean, I believe from Malabar westward, for the queer old-fashioned high-sterned craft of those coasts, the *Tava* of Athanasius Nikitin's voyage from Hormuz to Cambay. "*Dow*," says Burton, "is used on the Zanzibar coast for craft generally." (*J. R. G. S.*, xxix, 239.) [It is quite possible that this word *Kakam* is only a corruption of the old Italian *Cocca*, a kind of ship. There has always been great interchange of words connected with navigation. Cf. *Marco Polo*, ii, 252 *n.*]

[2] We have already seen that *Sínkalán* [Ferrand, *l.c.* i, p. xi, remarks that the Persian صين كلان *Čin kelān*=Skr. *Mahācīna*, Great China] is Canton (*supra*, II, p. 179 and III, p. 126), and Ibn Batuta here also teaches us to identify it with the *Sínia-ul-Sín* of Edrisi, which that geographer describes as lying at one extremity of the Chinese empire, unequalled for its size, edifices and commerce, and crowded with merchants from all the parts of India towards China. It was the residence, he says, of a Chinese Prince of the Blood, who governed it as a vassal of the *Faghfur* (the *Facfur* of Polo, *i.e.*, the *Sung* Emperor of Southern China; see Jaubert's *Edrisi*, i, 193, and *Marco Polo*, ii, 148 *n.*).

in length. Each ship had four decks, and numerous private and public cabins for the merchant passengers, with closets and all sorts of conveniences[1]. The sailors frequently had pot-herbs, ginger, etc., growing on board in wooden tubs. The commander of the ship was a very great personage[2], and, when he landed, the soldiers belonging to his ship marched before him with sword and spear and martial music.

The oars or sweeps used on these great junks were more like masts than oars, and each was pulled by from ten to thirty men. They stood to their work in two ranks, facing each other, pulling by means of a strong cable fastened to the oar (which itself was, I suppose, too great for their grasp), and singing out to the stroke, *La, La! La, La!*

The only ports of Malabar frequented for trade by the China vessels were KAULAM, Calicut, and Hili[3];

[1] This account of the great Junks may be compared with those given by M. Polo (ii, p. 249), and F. Jordanus (p. 54).

[2] Because Ibn Batuta says the skipper "was like a great *Amír*," Lassen assumes that he was an *Arab*. For this there seems no ground. Further on Ibn Batuta calls Kurtai the Viceroy of King-sze, who is expressly said to be a Pagan, "a great Amír." All that he means to say of the captain might be most accurately expressed in the vulgar term "a very great swell."

Whilst referring to Lassen's remarks upon Ibn Batuta towards the end of the fourth volume of his *Indian Antiquities*, I am constrained to say that the carelessness exhibited in this part of that great work makes one stand aghast, coming from a man of such learning and reputation. Such a statement needs support, and I refer for it to Note C at the end of this Introduction.

[3] Scarcely any change in India, since the days of our travellers, is more remarkable than the decay of the numerous ports, flourishing with foreign as well as domestic trade, which then lined the shores of the country; and the same remark applies in degree also to the other countries of Southern Asia, both eastward and westward of India. The commencement of this decay appears to date nearly from the arrival of the Portuguese, for at that time most of the ports were found still in an active and prosperous state. Somewhat similar circumstances have had course in our own country. The decay of the Cinque Ports can plead natural deterioration, but a more striking parallel

but those which intended to pass the Monsoon in India, used to go into the harbour of FANDARAINA for that purpose[1]. Thirteen of these ships, of different sizes, were lying at Calicut when Ibn Batuta's party were there.

The Zamorin prepared accommodation on board one of the junks for the party from Delhi; but Ibn Batuta, having ladies with him, went to the agent for the vessel, a Mahomedan called Suleiman ul-Safadi-ul-Shámi, to obtain a private cabin for them, having, it would seem, in his usual happy-go-lucky way, deferred this to the last moment. The agent told him that the cabins were all taken up by the Chinese merchants, who had

occurs on the shores of the Firth of Forth, once lined with sea-ports which each sent out its little squadron of merchant-vessels, the property of local owners, to the Continental trade; ports which now, probably, can boast only a few fishing-boats, and "merchants" only in the French and old Scotch sense of the term.

The decay of the Malabar ports may have begun in forcible monopoly and in devastating wars, from which the country had previously long enjoyed a comparative exemption, but it has been kept up no doubt by that concentration of capital in the hands of large houses, which more and more characterizes modern commerce, and is in our days advancing with more rapid strides than ever, whilst this cause is being reinforced by that concentration of the streams of produce which is induced by the construction of Trunk Railways. Whatever be the causes, it seems to me impossible to read these old travellers without at least an impression that wealth, prosperity, and probably happiness, were then far more generally diffused on the shores of India than they are now. Is there any ground for hope that the present state of things may be one of transition, and that at a future day the *multiplication* of railways will diminish this intense concentration, and again sow the coasts of India with seats of healthy trade and prosperity? If so, it will not be done by railways of wide gauge and heavy cost like those now made in India.

In a note (D) at the end of this Introduction, I propose to append a review of the Ports of Malabar as they were known from the thirteenth to the sixteenth century.

[1] [In the *Yuen Shi*, ch. 94, fol. 11 r° the "three barbarian kingdoms of *Ma-pa-eul* (Ma'abar), *Pei-nan* (corr. *Kiu-nam*, *Coilam*) and *Fan-ta-la-yi-na*" are mentioned. No doubt the last kingdom refers to the *Fandaraina* of Ibn Batuta, and Prof. Pelliot who gives me this information believes it is also, in the middle of the fourteenth century, *Pan-ta-li* of the *Tao yi chi lio*.]

(apparently) "return tickets." There was one, indeed, belonging to his own son-in-law, which Ibn Batuta could have, but it was not fitted up; however if he took that now, probably he would be able to make some better arrangement on the voyage; (it would seem from this that shipping agency in those days was a good deal like what it sometimes is now). So one Thursday afternoon our traveller's baggage and slaves, male and female, were put on board, whilst he stayed ashore to attend the Friday service before embarking. His colleagues, with the presents for China, were already on board. But the next morning early, the Eunuch Hilal, Ibn Batuta's servant, came to complain that the cabin assigned to them was a wretched little hole, and would never do. Appeal was made to the captain, but he said it could not be helped; if, however, they liked to go in a *kakam* which was there, they might pick and choose. Our traveller consented, and had his goods and his women-kind transferred to the kakam before public prayer time. In the afternoon the sea rose (it always did in the afternoon, he observes), and it was impossible to embark. By this time the China ships were all gone except that with the presents, another junk which was going to stop over the monsoon at Fandaraina, and the kakam, on which all the Moor's property was embarked. When he got up on Saturday morning the junk with his colleagues, and the kakam, had weighed, and got outside the harbour. The junk bound for Fandaraina was wrecked inside. There was a young girl on board, much beloved by her master, a certain merchant. He offered ten pieces of gold to any one who would save her. One of the sailors from Hormuz did save her, at the imminent risk of his life, and then refused the reward. "I did it for the love of God," said this good man. The junk with the presents also was wrecked on the reefs outside, and all on board perished. Many bodies were cast up by the waves; among others those of the Envoy Zahir-uddín, with the skull fractured, and of Malik Sunbul the eunuch, with a nail through his temples. Among the rest of the people who flocked to the shore to see what was going on, there came down the Zamorin himself, with nothing on but a scrap of a turban and a white cotton *dhoti*, attended by a boy with an umbrella. And, to crown all, when the kakam's people saw what had befallen their consort, they made all sail to seaward, carrying off with them our traveller's slaves, his girls and gear, and leaving him there on the beach of Calicut gazing after them, with nought remaining to him but his prayer-carpet, ten pieces of gold, and an emancipated slave, which last absconded forthwith!

He was told that the kakam *must* touch at Kaulam, so he determined to go thither. It was a ten days' journey, whether by land or water, so he set off by the lagoons with a Mussulman whom he had hired to attend on him, but who got continually drunk, and only added to the depression of the traveller's spirits. On the tenth day he reached Kaulam, the Columbum of our friars, which he describes as one of the finest cities of Malabar, with splendid bazaars, and wealthy merchants, there termed *Suli*[1], some of whom were Mahomedans.

[1] *Chūliā* is a name applied to the Mahomedans in Malabar. The origin of it seems to be unknown to Wilson (*Glossary*, in v.). The name is also applied to a particular class of the "Moors" or Mahomedans in Ceylon (*J. R. A. S.*, iii, 338). It seems probable that this was the word intended by the author. ["The word is by some derived from Skt. *chūḍā*, the top-knot which every Hindu must wear, and which is cut off on conversion to Islam.... According to Sonnerat the Chulias are of Arab descent and of Shia profession. The *Madras Gloss*. takes the word to be from the kingdom of *Chola* and to mean a person in S. India." *Hobson-Jobson*.]

There was also a Mahomedan Kazi and Shabandar (Master Attendant), etc. Kaulam was the first port at which the China ships touched on reaching India, and most of the Chinese merchants frequented it. The king was an Infidel, called *Tírawari*[1], a man of awful justice, of which a startling instance is cited by Ibn Batuta. One day when the king was riding with his son-in-law, the latter picked up a mango, which had fallen over a garden wall. The king's eye was upon him; he was immediately ordered to be ripped open and divided asunder, the parts being exposed on each side of the way, and a half of the fatal mango beside each!

The unfortunate ambassador could hear nothing of his kakam, but he fell in with the Chinese envoys who had been wrecked in another junk. They were refitted by their countrymen at Kaulam, and got off to China, where Ibn Batuta afterwards encountered them.

He had sore misgivings about returning to tell his tale at Dehli, feeling strong suspicion that Sultan Mahomed would be only too glad to have such a crow to pluck with him. So he decided on going to his friend the Sultan Jamal-uddín at Hunawúr, and to stop with him till he could hear some news of the missing kakam. The prince received him, but evidently with no hearty welcome. For the traveller tells us that he had no servant allowed him, and spent nearly all his time in the mosque—always a sign that things were going badly with Ibn Batuta—where he read the whole Koran through daily, and

[1] This title *Tírawari* may perhaps be *Tirubadi*, which Fra Paolino mentions among the sounding titles assumed by the princes of Malabar, "which were often mistaken for the proper names of families or individuals." He translates it *sua Maestà*, but literally it is probably *Tiru* (Tamul) "Holy," and *Pati* (Sansc.) "Lord." (See *V. alle Indie Orientali*, Roma, 1796, p. 103.)

by and bye twice a day. So he passed his time for three months.

The King of Hunawúr was projecting an expedition against the Island of Sindábúr. Ibn Batuta thought of joining it, and on taking the *Sortes Koranicæ* he turned up xxii, 41, "Surely God will succour those who succour Him"; which so pleased the king that he determined to accompany the expedition also. Some three months after the capture of Sindábúr the restless man started again on his travels, going down the coast to Calicut. Here he fell in with two of his missing slaves, who told him that his favourite girl was dead; that the King of Java (probably Sumatra) had appropriated the other women, and that the rest of the party were dispersed, some in Java, some in China, some in Bengal. So there was an end of the kakam.

He went back to Hunawúr and Sindábúr, where the Mussulman forces were speedily beleaguered by the Hindu prince whom they had expelled. Things beginning to look bad, Ibn Batuta, after some two months' stay, made his escape and got back to Calicut. Here he took it into his head to visit the DHĪBAT-UL-MAHAL or Maldive [*Male dīva*] Islands, of which he had heard wonderful stories.

One of the marvels of these islands was that they were under a female sovereign[1], Kadija, daughter of the late Sultan Jalál-uddín Omar, who had been set up as queen on the deposition of her brother for misconduct. Her husband, the preacher Jamal-uddín, actually governed, but all orders were issued in the name of the princess, and she was prayed for by name in the Friday Service.

[1] As to the occasional prevalence of female rule in the Maldive Islands see introduction to Marignolli, III, p. 192.

Ibn Batuta was welcomed to the islands, and was appointed Kazi, marrying the daughter of one of the Wazirs and three wives besides. The lax devotion of the people and the primitive costume of the women affected his pious heart; he tried hard but in vain to reform the latter, and to introduce the system that he had witnessed at Urghanj, of driving folk to mosque on Friday with the constable's staff.

Before long he was deep in discontent, quarrels and intrigues, and in August 1344 he left the Maldives for Ceylon.

As he approached the island he speaks of seeing the Mountain of Serendib (compare Marignolli's *Mons Seyllani*) rising high in air "like a column of smoke." He landed at Batthálah (PATLAM), where he found a Pagan chief reigning, a piratical potentate called Airi Shakarwati, who treated him civilly and facilitated his making the journey to Adam's Peak, whilst his skipper obligingly promised to wait for him[1].

In his journey he passes MANAR MANDALI[2], and the

[1] *Arya Chakravarti* is found in Ceylonese history as the name of a great warrior who commanded an army sent by Kulasaikera, who is called King of the Pandyans or people of the Madura country, which invaded Ceylon in 1314. The same name reappears as if belonging to the same individual in or about 1371, when he is stated to have erected forts at Colombo, Negombo and Chilaw, and after reducing the northern division of Ceylon, to have fixed the seat of government at Jaffnapatam. It is probable of course that these were two different persons, and indeed one authority speaks of the first Arya as being captured and put to death in the reign of Prakrama Bahu III (1314–19). The second must have commenced his career long before the date in the Ceylonese annals, as Ibn Batuta shows him established with royal authority at Patlam in 1344 (Turnour's *Epitome of the History of Ceylon*, Cotta Ch. M. Press, 1836, p. 47; Pridham, pp. 77–8; Upham's *Rajavali*, 264–9). Tennent supposes the Pandyan invaders to have come from Jaffnapatam, where they were already established, and not from the continent. Indeed we see from Ibn Batuta that the original Pandyan territory was now in Mussulman hands.

[2] *Minneri Mandel* of Tennent's Map, on the coast immediately abreast of Patlam.

port of SALAWAT[1], and then crosses extensive plains abounding in elephants. These however did no harm to pilgrims and foreigners[2], owing to the benignant influence exercised over them by the Shaikh Abu Abdallah, who first opened the road to the Holy Footmark. He then reached KUNAKÂR[3] as he calls it, the residence of the lawful King of Ceylon, who was entitled Kunár, and possessed a white elephant. Close to this city was the pool called the Pool of Precious Stones, out of which some of the most valuable gems were extracted. His description of the ascent to the summit is vivid and minute, and probably most of the sites which he speaks of could be identified by the aid of those who act as guides to Mahomedan pilgrims, if such there still be. He descends on the opposite side (towards Ratnapura), and proceeds to visit DINWAR, a large place on the sea, inhabited by merchants (Devi-neuera or Dondera), where a vast idol temple then existed, GALLE (which he calls *Káli*), and COLUMBO (*Kalanbu*), so returning by the coast to Patlam. Columbo is described as even then one of the finest cities of the island. It was the abode of the "Wazir and Admiral Jalasti," who kept about him a body of 500 Abyssinians. This personage is not

[1] *Chilaw* of our maps.

[2] See *Odoric*, II, p. 172.

[3] Sir J. Emerson Tennent considers this to be *Gampola*, called classically *Ganga-sri-pura*, the name which he supposes to be aimed at in Ibn Batuta's *Kunakâr*. With all respect for such an authority I think that it more probably represents *Kurunaigalla* or Kornegalle, which was the capital of the lawful sovereigns of Ceylon from about 1319 till some year after 1347. During this period the dynasty was in extreme depression, and little is recorded except the names of the kings, Bhuwaneka Bahu II, Pandita Prakrama Bahu IV, Wanny Bhuwaneka Bahu III, Wijayabahu V. It must have been in the reign of one or other of the two last that Ibn Batuta visited the capital. The name *Kunár* applied to him by the traveller is perhaps the Sanskrit *Kunwar*, "The Prince." (See Turnour's *Epitome*, quoted above.)

impossibly the same with the Khwaja Jahan, who so politely robbed John Marignolli (*ante*, III, p. 231). It is not said whose Wazir and Admiral he was.

At Patlam he took ship again for Maabar, but as he approached his destination he again came to grief, the ship grounding some six or eight miles from the shore. The crew abandoned the wreck, but our hero stuck by it, and was saved by some pagan natives.

On reaching the land, he reported his arrival to the *de facto* ruler of the country. This was the Sultan Ghaiás-uddín of Damghân, recently invested with the government of Maabar, a principality originally set up by his father-in-law, the Sherif Jalál-uddín. The latter had been appointed by Mahomed Tughlak to the military command of the province, but about 1338–9 had declared himself independent, striking coin in his own name, and proclaiming himself under the title of Ahhsan Sháh Sultan. Ibn Batuta, during his stay at Delhi, had married one of the Sherif's daughters, named Hhurnasab. "She was a pious woman," says her husband, "who used to spend the night in watching and prayer. She could read, but had not learned to write. She bore me a daughter, but what is become of either the one or the other is more than I can tell!" Thus Ibn Batuta was brother-in-law to the reigning Sultan, who, on receiving the traveller's message, sent for him to his camp, two days' journey distant. This brother-in-law was a ruffian, whose cruel massacres of women and children excited the traveller's disgust and tacit remonstrance. However, he busied himself in engaging the Sultan in a scheme for the invasion of the Maldives, but before it came to anything the chief died of a pestilence. His nephew and successor, Sultan Nasir-uddín, was ready to take up the project, but Ibn Batuta got a fever at the capital,

MUTTRA (Madura), and hurried off to FATTAN[1], a large and fine city on the sea, with an admirable harbour, where he found ships sailing for Yemen, and took his passage in one of them as far as Kaulam.

Here he stayed for three months, and then went off for the fourth time to visit his friend the Sultan of Hunawúr. On his way, however, off a small island between Fakanúr and Hunawúr (probably the Pigeon Island of modern maps), the vessel was attacked by pirates of the wrong kind, and the unlucky adventurer was deposited on the beach stript of everything but his drawers! On this occasion, as he mentions elsewhere incidentally, he lost a number of transcripts of epitaphs of celebrated

[1] This *Fattan* of Maabar is also mentioned by Rashíd, in conjunction with *Malifattan* and *Káïl,* in a passage quoted at III, p. 68 *supra* (see also p. 70). I am not able to identify it. It *may* have been *Negapatam,* but from the way in which our traveller speaks of it, it would seem to have been the port of the city of Madura, and therefore I should rather look for it in the vicinity of Ramnad, as at Devi-patam or Killikarai, which have both been ports of some consideration. A place also called *Periapatan,* near Ramanancor, is mentioned by the historians of the Jesuit missions as much frequented for commerce, and as the chief town of the Paravas of the Fishery coast, but I do not find it on any map (Du Jarric, i, 628). Pattan or Fattan was probably the *Mabar* city of John Montecorvino and Marco Polo (see III, p. 65), and may be that which Abulfeda (probably by some gross mistranscription) calls *Biyardáwal,* "residence of the Prince of Mabar, whither horses are imported from foreign countries." There is indeed a place called *Ninarkovil,* near Ramnad, celebrated for a great temple (*J. R. A. S.*, iii, 165), which may be worth mentioning, because the difference between these two rather peculiar names (Bíyardáwal and Nínarqáwal) would be almost entirely a matter of diacritical points; Kail and Malifattan (or Molephatam) are both to be sought in the vicinity of Tuticorin (see *Fr. Jordanus*, p. 40). [The Rev. Dr Caldwell, quoted by Sir Henry Yule, *Marco Polo*, ii, p. 372 *n.*, writes: "The Cail of Marco Polo, commonly called in the neighbourhood *Old Káyal*, and erroneously named *Koil* in the Ordnance Map of India, is situated on the Tâmraparnî River, about a mile and a half from its mouth...Káyal stood originally on or near the sea-beach, but it is now about a mile and a half inland, the sand carried down by the river having silted up the ancient harbour, and formed a waste sandy tract between the sea and the town...."] Malifattan is no doubt the *Manifattan* of Abulfeda, "a city of Maabar on the sea shore" (see Gildemeister, p. 185).

persons which he had made at Bokhara, along with other matters, not improbably including the notes of his earlier travels[1]. Returning to Calicut he was clothed by the charity of the Faithful. Here also he heard news of the Maldives; the Preacher Jamal-uddín was dead, and the Queen had married another of the Wazirs; moreover one of the wives whom he had abandoned had borne him a son[2]. He had some hesitation about returning to the Islands, as he well might, considering what he had been plotting against them, but encouraged by a new cast of the Sortes he went and was civilly received. His expectations however, or his caprices, were disappointed, for he seems to have stayed but five days and then went on to Bengal.

Ibn Batuta's account of what he saw in Bengal, and on his subsequent voyage through the Archipelago, will be given in extracts or in more detailed abstract, in connexion with the full text of his travels in China. We now therefore take up this short account of his adventures from the time of his return from the latter country.

After coming back from China he proceeded direct from Malabar to the coast of Arabia, visiting again Dhafar, Maskat, Hormuz, Shiraz, Ispahan, Tuster, Basrah, Meshid Ali and Baghdad, and thence went to Tadmor and Damascus, where he had left a wife and

[1] See iii, 28.

[2] He says this boy was now two years old. As the child was not born when Ibn Batuta left the Maldives in August 1344, his second visit must have been (according to this datum) at least as late as August 1346, and perhaps some months later. He goes to China (at the earliest) during the succeeding spring, and yet his book tells us that he is back from his China expedition and in Arabia by May 1347. There is here involved an error one way or the other of at least one year, and of two years if we depend on Ibn Batuta's own details of the time occupied by his expedition to China. See a note on this towards the end of his narrative (*infra*).

child twenty years before, but both apparently were now dead. Here also he got his first news from home, and heard of his father's death fifteen years previously. He then went on to Hamath and Aleppo, and on his return to Damascus found the Black Death raging to such an extent that two thousand four hundred died in one day. Proceeding by Jerusalem to Egypt he repeated the Mecca pilgrimage for the last time, and finally turned his face away from the East. Travelling by land to Tunis he embarked in a ship of Catalonia. They touched at Sardinia (*Jazírah Sardániah*), where they were threatened with capture, and thence proceeded to Tenes on the Algerine coast, whence he reached Fez, the capital of his native country, on the 8th November 1349, after an absence of twenty-four years.

Here he professes to have rejoiced in the presence of his own Sultan, whom he declares to surpass all the mighty monarchs of the East; in dignity him of Irák, in person him of India, in manner him of Yemen, in courage the king of the Turks, in long-suffering the Emperor of Constantinople, in devotion him of Turkestan, and in knowledge him of Java![1], a list of comparisons

[1] In another passage he names as the seven greatest and most powerful sovereigns in the world: (1) His own master, the Commander of the Faithful, viz., the King of Fez; (2) The Sultan of Egypt and Syria; (3) The Sultan of the two Iraks; (4) The Sultan Mahomed Uzbek of Kipchak; (5) The Sultan of Turkestan and Mā-warā-n-Nahr (Chagatai); (6) The Sultan of India; (7) The Sultan of China (ii, 382). Von Hammer quotes from Ibn Batuta also (though I cannot find the passage) the following as the characteristic titles of the seven great kings of the earth. The list differs from the preceding. (1) The *Takfúr* of Constantinople; (2) The *Sultán* of Egypt; (3) The *King* (Malik?) of the Iraks; (4) The *Khákán* of Turkestan; (5) The *Maharaja* of India; (6) The *Faghfúr* of China; (7) The *Khan* of Kipchak (*Gesch. der Gold. Horde*, p. 300).

The King of Fez in question, Ibn Batuta's lord, was Faris Abu Imán, of the house of Beni Merin of Fez, who usurped the throne during his father's lifetime in 1348, and died miserably, smothered in bed by some of his courtiers, November 1358. In a rescript of his granting certain commercial privileges to the

so oddly selected as to suggest the possibility of irony. After all that he had seen, he comes, like Friar Jordanus, to the conclusion that there is no place like his own WEST[1]. "'Tis the best of all countries. You have fruit in plenty; good meat and water are easily come at, and in fact its blessings are so many that the poet has hit the mark when he sings:

> Of all the Four Quarters of Heaven the best
> (I'll prove it past question) is surely the West!
> 'Tis the West is the goal of the Sun's daily race!
> 'Tis the West that first shows you the Moon's silver face!

"The dirhems of the West are but little ones 'tis true, but then you get more for them!"—just as in the good old days of another dear Land of the West, where, if the pound was but twenty pence, the pint at least was two quarts!

After a time he went to visit his native city of Tangier, thence to Ceuta, and then crossed over into Spain (*al Andalús*), going to see Gibraltar, which had just then been besieged "by the Latin tyrant, Adfunus" (Alphonso XI)[2]. From the Rock he proceeded to Ronda

Pisans, 9th April, 1358, he is styled King of Fez, Mequinez, Sallee, Morocco, Sus, Segelmessa, Teza, Telemsen, Algiers, Bugia, Costantina, Bona, Biskra, Zab, Media, Gafsa, Baladt-ul-Jaríd, Tripoli, Tangier, Ceuta, Gibraltar and Ronda, *i.e.*, of the whole of Barbary from Tripoli to the Atlantic coast facing the Canary Islands. But his claim to the eastern part of this territory must have been titular only, as his father had just lost it when Abu Imán seized the government. (Amari, *Diplomi Arabi del R. Arch. Fiorentino*, pp. 309, 476.)

[1] *Fr. Jord.*, p. 55.

[2] *Thághiah-ul-Rúm*. Amari remarks (*op. cit.*, pp. ix–x): "The early Mahomedans used to call all the Christians of Europe *Rúm*, *i.e.*, Romans, but at a later date chose to distinguish between the Greek and German races, the subjects of the two empires, by applying the term *Farang*, *i.e.*, Franks, to the Western Christians, and *Rúm* to the Byzantines; whilst not well knowing what to make of the Latin race, *headless* as it was, they called the Italians and Spanish Christians sometimes *Rúm* and sometimes *Farang*." The same author says elsewhere that *Thágiah* was applied to Christian princes almost in the Greek sense of *Tyrannus*, *i.e.*, as impugning the legality rather than the abuse of their power.

and Malaga, Velez, Alhama and Granada, and thence returned, by Gibraltar, Ceuta, and Morocco, to Fez. But his travels were not yet over. In the beginning of 1352 he set out for Central Africa, his first halt being at SEGELMESSA, where the dates in their abundance and excellence recalled but surpassed those of Basra[1]. Here it was that he lodged with the brother of that Al Bushri who had treated him so handsomely in the heart of China.

On his way south he passed TAGHAZA, a place where the houses and mosques were built of rock-salt, and roofed with camel-hides[2], and at length reached MALLI, the capital of Sudan[3]. Here he abode eight months, after which he went to TIMBUKTU, and sailed down the Niger

[1] Segelmessa was already ruined and deserted in the time of Leo Africanus. ["The citie of Segelmesse was destroied, and till this day remaineth desolate." Dr. R. Brown, in Hak. Soc. ed., iii, p. 780.] ["Sejelmasah is a town of middling size, belonging to the territories of Tahouth. One cannot enter Sejelmasah but by the way of the desert, which the sand renders difficult. This town is situated near the gold mines, between them and the land of the Blacks, and the land of Zouilah. These mines are said to be of the most pure and excellent gold; but it is difficult to work them, and the way to them is dangerous and troublesome. They say that the district of Tahouth is reckoned as belonging to Africa." (Sir W. Ouseley, *Oriental Geography of Ebn Haukal*, Lond., 1800, p. 21.)] According to Reinaud it was in the same valley with the modern *Tafilelt*, if not identical with it. I think dates from the latter place (Tafilat) are exhibited in the windows of London fruiterers. [Sijilmásiyah, Medina ul Amira, the capital of Tafilet; it had been subjugated by the Omeyyads of Spain in 976. Cf. Brown's ed. of *Leo Africanus*, iii, p. 806: "The ruins are in the district of Wad Ifli; and bear evidence to the city having been a large one."]

[2] *Taghazai* is an oasis in the heart of the Sahra, on the caravan route from Tafilelt to Timbuktu, near the Tropic. On the salt-built houses of the Sahra Oases see Herodotus, iv, 185, and notes in Rawlinson's edition. [Ibn Batuta's Tegaza (Tekkada) lies to the S.W. of Agadez. Cf. Brown's ed. of *Leo Africanus*, p. 1101. Teghâzza is the name of a salt mine situated at two days north of Taodeni. Cf. *Tarikh es-Soudan*, p. 22 *n*.]

[3] In passing the great Desert beyond Taghaza he gives us another instance of the legends alluded to at II, p. 262, *supra*. "This vast plain is haunted by a multitude of demons; if the messenger is alone they sport with him and fascinate him, so that he strays from his course and perishes" (iv, 382).

to KAUKAU, whence he travelled to TAKADDA. The Niger he calls the Nile, believing it to flow towards Dongola, and so into Egypt, an opinion which was maintained in our own day shortly before Lander's discovery, if I remember rightly, by the *Quarterly Review*. The traveller mentions the hippopotamus in the river.

He now received a command from his own sovereign for his return to Fez, and left Takadda for TAWAT, by the country of ḤAKKAR[1], on the 12th September, 1353, reaching Fez, and the termination of those at least of his wanderings which are recorded, in the beginning of 1354, after they had lasted for eight and twenty years, and had extended over a length of at least 75,000 English miles[2].

Soon after this the history of his travels was committed to writing under orders from the Sultan, but not by the traveller's own hand. It would appear, indeed, that he had at times kept notes of what he saw, for in one passage he speaks of having been robbed of them. But a certain Mahomed Ibn Juzai, the Sultan's Secretary, was employed

[1] *Melle*, south of *Timbuktu*, *Gogo* or *Gago*, on the Niger, south-east of the same, *Takadda*, *Hogar*, and *Tawat*, are all I think to be found in Dr. Barth's Map in the *J. R. G. S.* for 1860. [Gaó, Gógó or Kâgho, on the Niger, is marked in Barth's Map but the other places are not to be found in it.—Gógó was the capital of the Songhai Empire. See Brown's ed. of *Leo Africanus*, p. 845; *Tarikh es-Soudan*, p. 6. Ibn Batuta sailed from Kabara, the port of Timbuktu to Gógó. The Kingdom of Melli is also mentioned in *Leo Africanus*: "This region extending it selfe almost three hundred miles along the side of a river which falleth into Niger" (*l. c.*, p. 823). Mansa Sleiman was Sultan at the time of Ibn Batuta's visit, and in 1336 he occupied Timbuktu; in A.D. 1433 the Meli empire began to decline (*l. c.*, p. 841). Sultan Kankan Musa was the first king of Melli who made the conquest of Songhai. Cf. *Tarikh es-Soudan*, transl. by O. Houdas, pp. 12–13, 18–21.] It is remarkable that the Catalan Map of 1375 contains most of these Central African names, viz., Tagaza, Melli, *Tenbuch*, *Geugeu*. The first three are also mentioned by Cadamosto.

[2] This is the result of a rough compass measurement, without any allowance for deviations or for the extensive journeys he probably made during his eight years' stay in India, etc.

to reduce the story to writing as Ibn Batuta told it (not however without occasionally embellishing it by quotations and pointless anecdotes of his own), and this work was brought to a conclusion on the 13th December, 1355, just about the time that John Marignolli was putting his reminiscences of Asia into a Bohemian Chronicle. The editor, Ibn Juzai, concludes thus:

"Here ends what I have put into shape from the memoranda of the Shaikh Abu Abdallah Mahomed Ibn Batuta, whom may God honour! No person of intelligence can fail to see that this Shaikh is the Traveller of Our Age; and he who should call him the Traveller of the whole Body of Islam would not go beyond the truth."

Ibn Batuta long survived his amanuensis, and died in 1377–8, at the age of seventy-three.

The first detailed information communicated to Europe regarding his travels was published in a German periodical, about 1808, by Seetzen[1], who had obtained an abridgment of the work in the East, with other MSS. collected for the Gotha library. In 1818 Kosegarten published at Jena the text and translation of three fragments of the same abridgment. A Mr. Apetz edited a fourth, the description of Malabar, in 1819. In the same year Burckhardt's Nubian Travels were published in London, the appendix to which contained a note on Ibn Batuta, of whose work the Swiss traveller had procured a much fuller abridgment than that at Gotha. Three MSS. of this abridgment were obtained by Cambridge University, after Burckhardt's death, and from these Dr. Lee made his well-known version for the Oriental Translation Fund (London, 1829).

[1] The proper title of the book is, "*A Gift for the Observing, wherein are set forth the Curiosities of Cities and the Wonders o Travel.*"

It was not, however, until the French conquest of Algiers, and capture of Constantina, that manuscripts of the unabridged work became accessible. Of these there are now five in the Imperial Library of Paris, two only being complete. One of these two, however, has been proved to be the autograph of Ibn Juzai, the original editor.

P. José de St. Antonio Moura published at Lisbon, in 1840, the first volume of a Portuguese translation of the whole work, from a manuscript which he had obtained at Fez in the end of the last century. I believe the second volume also has been issued within the last few years[1].

The part of the Travels which relates to Sudan was translated, with notes, by Baron McGuckin de Slane, in the *Journal Asiatique* for March, 1843; that relating to the Indian Archipelago, by M. Ed. Dulaurier, in 1847; that relating to the Crimea and Kipchak, by M. Defrémery, in 1850; and the chapter on the Mongol Sultans of the Iraks and Khorāsān, also by Defrémery, in 1851, all in the same journal. M. Defrémery also published the Travels in Persia and Central Asia in the *Nouvelles Annales des Voyages* for 1848, and the Travels in Asia Minor in the same periodical for 1850–1. In it also M. Cherbonneau, Professor of Arabic at Constantina, put forth, in 1852, a slightly abridged translation of the commencement of the work, as far as the traveller's departure for Syria, omitting the preface[2].

Finally, the whole work was most carefully edited in the original, with a translation into French by M. Defrémery and Dr. Sanguinetti, at the expense of the Asiatic Society of Paris, in four volumes, with an

[1] [I have never seen it.—H. C.]

[2] All these bibliographical particulars are derived from the preface of the French translators.

admirable index of names and peculiar expressions attached (1858–9). From their French the present version of Ibn Batuta's voyage to China has been made. The plan of the Asiatic Society appears to have precluded a commentary; but a few explanatory notes have been inserted by the editors among the various readings at the end of each volume, and valuable introductions have been prefixed to the first three. In the fourth volume, which contains the whole of the traveller's history from the time of his leaving Delhi on the ill-fated embassy to China, this valuable aid is no longer given; for what reason I know not.

There can be no question, I think, as to the interest of this remarkable book. As to the character of the traveller, and the reliance to be placed on him, opinions have been somewhat various. In his own day and country he was looked upon, it would seem, as a bit of a Münchausen[1], but so have others who little deserved it.

His French editors, Defrémery and Sanguinetti, are disposed to maintain his truthfulness, and quote with approbation M. Dozy of Leyden, who calls him "this honest traveller." Dulaurier also looks on him very favourably. Reinaud again, and Baron McGuckin de Slane, accuse him either of natural credulity, or of an

[1] See in the App. to vol. iii, at p. 466, an extract from the *Prolegomena of Ibn Khaldún*. It mentions how our traveller, having returned from his long wanderings, was admitted to the court of his native sovereign. The wonderful stories which he related of the wealth and boundless liberality of Mahomed Tughlak excited incredulity. "Those who heard him relate these stories and others of the same kind at the court, whispered to one another that they were a parcel of lies and that the narrator was an impostor." Ibn Khaldún having expressed this view to the Wazír, received a caution against over-incredulity, backed by an apophthegm, which seems to have led him on reflection to think that he had been wrong in disbelieving the traveller. [There does not seem any doubt that Ibn Batuta has borrowed some of his descriptions from the writings of his predecessors; for instance, part of what he says about Mecca is taken from Ibn Jubair.]

inclination to deal in marvellous stories, especially in some of his chapters on the far East; whilst Klaproth quite reviles him for the stupidity which induces him to cram his readers with rigmaroles about Mahomedan saints and spiritualists, when details of the places he had seen would have been of extreme interest and value.

Though Klaproth was probably acquainted only with the abridgment translated by Lee, and thus had not the means of doing justice to the narrative, I must say there is some foundation for his reproaches, for, especially when dealing with the Saracenic countries, in which Islam had been long established, his details of the religious establishments and theologians occupy a space which renders this part of the narrative very dull to the uninitiated. It seems to me that the Mahomedan man of the world, soldier, jurist, and theologian, is, at least in regard to a large class of subjects, not always either so trustworthy, or so perspicacious as the narrow-minded Christian friars who were his contemporaries, whilst he cannot be compared with the Venetian merchant, who shines among all the travellers of the middle age like the moon among the lesser lights of heaven. There seems to be something in the Mahomedan mind that indisposes it for appreciating and relating accurately what is witnessed in nature and geography.

Of the confused state of his geographical ideas, no instance can be stronger than that afforded by his travels in China, where he jumbles into one great river, rising near Peking, and entering the sea at Canton, after passing King-sze and Zaitún, the whole system of Chinese hydrography, partly bound together by the Great Canal and its branches[1]. These do indeed extend from north to south, but in travelling on their waters he must,

[1] See i, 79, and hereafter in his travels through China.

once at least, and probably twice, have been interrupted by portages over mountain ranges of great height. So, also, at an earlier period in his wanderings, he asserts that the river at Aleppo (the Koïk, a tributary of Euphrates) is the same as that called Al' Asi, or Orontes, which passes by Hamath[1]. In another passage he confounds the celebrated trading-places of Siraf and Kais, or Kísh[2]: and in his description of the Pyramids, he distinctly ascribes to them a conical form, *i.e.*, with a circular base[3]. Various other instances of the looseness of his observation, or statements, will occur in that part of his travels which we are about to set forth in full. Sometimes, again, he seems to have forgotten the real name of a place, and to have substituted another, as it would seem, at random, or perhaps one having some resemblance in sound. Thus, in describing the disastrous campaign of the Sultan's troops in the Himalaya, he speaks of them as, in the commencement, capturing *Warangal*, a city high up in the range. Now, Warangal was in the Dekkan, the capital of Telingana, and it seems highly improbable that there could have been a city of

[1] See i, 152, and French editors' note, p. 432. It is a remarkable feature in the Nile, according to Ibn Batuta, that it flows from south to north, *contrary to all other rivers*. This fact seems to have impressed the imagination of the ancients also, as one of the Nile's mysteries, and Cosmas says it flows slowly, because, as it were, *up hill*, the earth according to his notion rising towards the north.

[2] See ii, 244, and French editors' note, p. 456. [*Supra*, I, p. 144 *n.*; II, p. 107 *n.*]

[3] See i, p. 81. He gives a curious story about the opening of the great pyramid by the Khalif Mámún, and how he pierced its solid base with Hannibal's chemistry, first lighting a great fire in contact with it, then *sluicing it with vinegar*, and battering it with shot from a mangonel. Another parallel is found in the Singhalese tradition of the destruction of the great Dam at Padivil by fire and *sour milk* (see Tennent's *Ceylon*, ii, 504). Though Ibn Batuta passes the site of Thebes three times, and indeed names Luxor as one of his halting places, "where is to be seen the tomb of the pious hermit Abu'l Hajáj Alaksori," he takes no notice of the vast remains there or elsewhere on the Nile.

the name in the Himalaya. (See iii, 326.) One suspects something of the same kind when he identifies *Kataka* (Cuttack?) with the Mahratta country (*ib.*, p. 182), but in this I may easily be wrong; even if I be right, however, the cases of this kind are few.

Of his exaggeration we have a measurable sample in his account of the great Kutb Minár at Delhi, which we have still before our eyes, to compare with his description: "The site of this mosque [the Jama Masjid, or Cathedral Mosque of old Delhi] was formerly a *Budkhánah*, or idol-temple, but after the conquest of the city it was converted into a mosque. In the northern court of the mosque stands the minaret, which is without parallel in all the countries of Islam. It is built of red stone, in this differing from the material of the rest of the mosque, which is white; moreover, the stone of the minaret is wrought in sculpture. It is of surpassing height; the pinnacle is of milk-white marble, and the globes which decorate it of pure gold. *The aperture of the staircase is so wide that elephants can ascend, and a person on whom I could rely, told me that when the minaret was a-building, he saw an elephant ascend to the very top with a load of stones.*" Also, in speaking of the incomplete minaret, which was commenced by one of the Sultans (I forget which) in rivalry of the Kutb Minár, he tells us that its staircase was so great that *three elephants* could mount abreast, and though only one-third of the altitude was completed, that fraction was already as high as the adjoining minaret (the Kutb)! These are gross exaggerations, though I am not provided with the actual dimensions of either staircase to compare with them[1]. This test I can offer, however, in reference

[1] The total diameter of the Kutb Minár at the base is 47 feet 3 inches, and at the top about 9 feet. The doorway is a small

to a third remarkable object in the court of the same mosque, the celebrated Iron *Láth,* or column: "In the centre of the mosque there is to be seen an enormous pillar, made of some unknown metal. One of the learned Hindus told me that it was entitled *haft-júsh,* or 'the seven metals,' from being composed of an amalgam of so many. A portion of the shaft has been polished, about a finger's length, and the sheen of it is quite dazzling. Iron tools can make no impression on this pillar. *It is thirty cubits in length, and when I twisted my turban-cloth round the shaft, it took a length of eight cubits to compass it."* The real height of the pillar above ground is twenty-two feet, and its greatest diameter a little more than sixteen inches[1].

one, not larger at most I think than an ordinary London street-door, though I cannot give its dimensions. The uncompleted minaret is certainly not half the height of the Kutb; [it is 82 feet in diameter. It was begun by 'Alá-uddín, the penultimate predecessor of Mubárik Sháh. For this note, as for much other assistance, I have to thank my friend Col. R. Maclagan, R.E.—H. Y.] Ibn Batuta was no doubt trying to communicate from memory the impression of vastness which these buildings had made upon his mind, and if he had not been so specific there would have been little fault to find.

In justice to him we may quote a much more exaggerated contemporary notice of the Kutb in the interesting book called *Masālak-al-Absār*. The author mentions on the authority of Shaik Burhan-uddín Bursi that the minaret of Delhi was 600 cubits high! (*Notices et Extraits*, xiii, p. 180.)

On the other hand, the account given by Abulfeda is apparently quite accurate. "Attached to the mosque (of Delhi) is a tower which has no equal in the whole world. It is built of red stone with about 360 steps. It is not square but has a great number of angles, is very massive at the base, and very lofty, equalling in height the Pharos of Alexandria" (Gildemeister, p. 190). I may add that Ibn Batuta was certainly misinformed as to the date and builder of the Kutb. He ascribes it to Sultan Muizz-uddín (otherwise called Kaikobād), grandson of Balban (A.D. 1286–90). But the real date is nearly a century older. It was begun by Kutb-uddín Eibék when governing for Shahab-uddín of Ghazni (otherwise Mahomed Bin Sam, A.D. 1193–1206), and completed by Altamsh (1211–36). Ibn Batuta ascribes the rival structure to Kutb-uddín Khilji (Mubárik Sháh, 1316–20), and in this also I think he is wrong, though I cannot correct him.

[1] The pillar looks like iron, but I do not know if its real composition has been determined. It was considered by James

As positive fiction we must set down the traveller's account of the historical events which he asserts to have taken place in China during his visit to that country, as will be more precisely pointed out in the notes which accompany his narrative. I shall there indicate reasons for doubting whether he ever reached Peking at all[1]. And his account of the country of Tawalisi, which he visited on his way to China, with all allowance for our ignorance of its exact position, seems open to the charge of considerable misrepresentation, to say the least of it. He never seems to have acquired more than a very imperfect knowledge even of Persian, which was then, still more than now, the *lingua franca* of Asiatic travel, much less of any more local vernacular; nor does he seem to have been aware that the Persian phrases which he quotes did *not* belong to the vernacular of the countries which he is describing, a mistake of which we have seen analogous instances already in Marignolli's account of Ceylon. Thus, in relating the circumstances of a suttee which he witnessed on his way from Delhi to the

Prinsep to date from the third or fourth century. I should observe that the shaft has been recently ascertained to descend *at least* twenty-six feet into the earth, and probably several feet more, as with that depth excavated the pillar did not become loose. But there is no reason to believe that it stood higher above ground in Ibn Batuta's time than now, and I gather from the statement that the diameter below ground does not increase. I am indebted for these last facts, and for the dimensions given above, to my friend Major-General Cunningham's unpublished archæological reports, and I trust he will excuse this slight use of them, as no other measurements were accessible to me that could be depended upon.

[1] When the traveller (iv, 244) tells us that the people of Cathay or Northern China used elephants as common beasts of burden in exactly the same way that they were used by the people of Mul-Jawa on the shores of the Gulf of Siam [see note, II, pp. 163, 164] he somewhat strengthens the suspicion that he never was in Northern China, where I believe the elephant has never been other than a foreign importation for use in war or court pomps. [M. Ferrand, *Textes*, ii, p. 433, has come to the conclusion that Ibn Batuta never went to Indo-China and China and that the narrative of his travels in these countries is a mere invention.]

coast, after eight years' residence in Hindustan, he makes the victim address her conductors in *Persian*, quoting the words in that language as actually used by her, these being no doubt the *interpretation* which was given him by a bystander[1]. There are many like instances in the course of the work, as, when he tells us that an ingot of gold was called, in China, *barkálah*; that watchmen were there called *baswánán*, and so forth, all the terms used being Persian. Generally, perhaps, his explanations of foreign terms are inaccurate; he has got hold of *some* idea connected with the word, but not the real one. Thus, in explaining the name of *Háj-Tarkhán* (Astrakhan) he tells us that the word *Tarkhán*, among the Turks, signified a *place* exempt from all taxes, whereas it was the title of certain privileged *persons*, who, among other peculiar rights, enjoyed exemption from taxes[2]. Again, he tells us that the palace of the Khans at Sarai was called *Altún-Thásh*, or "Golden Head"; but it is *Básh*, not *Thásh*, that signifies *head* in Turkish, and the meaning of the name he gives is *Golden Stone*[3].

[1] The story is related on his first entrance into Hindustan *àpropos* of another suttee which then occurred. But he states the circumstance to have happened at a later date when he was at the town of *Amjeri*, and I suppose this to have been the town of *Amjhera* near Dhar, which he probably passed through on his way from Dhar to Daulatābād in 1342 (iii, 137).

[2] *Tarkhan* is supposed to be the title intended by the *Turxanthus* of the Byzantine Embassy of Valentine (see note near end of Ibn Batuta's narrative, *infra*).

[3] See remark by Tr., ii, 448. Ibn Batuta tells us that it was the custom in India for a creditor of a courtier who would not pay his debts to watch at the palace gate for his debtor, and there assail him with cries of "*Daruhai Us-Sultán!* O enemy of the Sultan! thou shalt not enter till thou hast paid." But it is probable that the exclamation really was that still so well known in India made by any individual who considers himself injured, "*Duhai* Maharáj! *Duhai* Company Bahádur!" Justice! Justice!

There are some remarkable chronological difficulties in his narrative, but for most of these I must refer to the French editors, to whom I am so largely indebted. Others, more particularly relating to the Chinese expedition, will be noticed in detail further on.

After all that has been said, however, there can be no doubt of the genuine nature and general veracity of Ibn Batuta's travels, as the many instances in which his notices throw light upon passages in other documents of this collection, and on Marco Polo's travels (see particularly M. Pauthier's [and Yule's] notes), might suffice to show. Indeed, apart from cursory inaccuracies and occasional loose statements, the two passages already alluded to are the only two with regard to which I should be disposed positively to impugn his veracity. The very passages which have been cited with regard to the great edifices at Delhi are only exaggerated when he rashly ventures on positive statements of dimension; in other respects they are the brief and happy sketches of an eye-witness. His accounts of the Maldive islands, and of the Negro countries of Sudan (of which latter his detail is one of the earliest that has come down to us) are full of interesting particulars, and appear to be accurate and unstrained. The majority of the names even, which he attaches to the dozen great clusters of the Maldives, can still be identified[1], and much, I believe,

[1] The names attributed by Ibn Batuta to twelve of the Maldive clusters are (1) Pálipúr, (2) Kannalús, (3) Mahal, the Royal Residence, (4) Taládíb, (5) Karáidu, (6) Taim, (7) Taladumati, (8) Haladumati, (9) Baraidu, (10) Kandakal, (11) Mulúk, (12) Suwaid, which last he correctly describes as being the most remote. The names corresponding to these as given in a map accompanying an article in the *J. R. Geog. Soc.* are, (1) Padypolo, (2) Colomandus? (3) Malé, the Sultan's Residence, (4) Tillada, (5) Cardiva, (6) ——? (7) Tilladumatis, (8) Milladumadue, (9) Palisdus, (10) ——? (11) Molucque, (12) Suadiva. M. Defrémery had already made the comparison with those given in Pyrard's voyage of 1619.

of his Central African narrative is an anticipation of knowledge but recently regained. The passage in which he describes at length his adventures near Koel in India, when accidentally separated for many days from his company, is an excellent example of fresh and lively narrative. His full and curious statements and anecdotes regarding the showy virtues and very solid vices of Sultan Mahomed Tughlak are in entire agreement with what is told by the historians of India, and add many new details. The French editors have shown, in a learned and elaborate tabular statement, how well our traveller's account of the chief events of that monarch's reign (though told with no attention to chronological succession) agrees with those of Khondemir and Firishta. The whole of the second part of his narrative indeed seems to me superior in vivacity and interest to the first; which, I suppose, may be attributed partly to more vivid recollection, and partly perhaps to the preservation of his later notes.

Ibn Batuta has drawn his own character in an accumulation of slight touches through the long history of his wanderings, but to do justice to the result in a few lines would require the hand of Chaucer, and something perhaps of his freedom of speech. Not wanting in acuteness nor in humane feeling, full of vital energy and enjoyment of life; infinite in curiosity; daring, restless, impulsive, sensual, inconsiderate, and extravagant; superstitious in his regard for the saints of his religion, and plying devout observances, especially when in difficulties; doubtless an agreeable companion, for we always find him welcomed at first, but clinging, like one of the Ceylon leeches which he describes, when he found a full-blooded subject, and hence too apt to disgust his patrons and to turn to intrigues against them. Such are the impressions which one reader, at least, has gathered from the surface of his narrative, as rendered by MM. Defrémery and Sanguinetti[1].

BIBLIOGRAPHY.

—See Henri Cordier, *Bibliotheca Sinica*, col. 2045–2047.

—De Mohammede Ebn Batuta Arabe Tingitano eiusque itineribus. Commentatio academica,...A. D. VII. Martii CIↃIↃCCCXVIII. Avctor Joannes Gothofredvs Lvdovicvs Kosegarten; Ienae [1818], 4to, pp. 51.

Text and Translation of an abridgment of Ibn Batuta of which Seetzen had already given an analysis.

—Descriptio Terrae Malabar. Ex arabico Ebn Batutae Itinerario edita, interpretatione et annotationibus instructa, per Henricum Apetz. Jenae, in officina Groeckeriana, M.DCCCXIX, 4to, pp. 24.

Other fragment of the same abridgment.

—The Travels of Ibn Batūta; translated from the abridged Arabic manuscript copies, preserved in the Public Library of Cambridge. With Notes, illustrative of the History, Geography, Botany, Antiquities, etc., occurring throughout the work. By the Rev. Samuel Lee, B.D....London: Printed for the Oriental Translation Committee...1829, 4to, pp. xix–243.

Dedication to Lieut.-Col. Fitzclarence, pp. v–viii.—Preface, pp. ix–xviii.—Additions and Corrections, p. xix.—The Travels of Ibn Batūta, pp. 1–243.

This translation is made from three Arabic MSS. bequeathed by Burckhardt to the Library of the Cambridge University.

—Viagens extensas e dilatadas do Celebre Arabe Abu-Abdallah, mais conhecido pelo nome de Ben-Batuta. Traduzidas por José de Santo Antonio Moura, Ex-Geral da extincta Congregação da Terceira Ordem de S. Francisco, Lente Jubilado,

[1] In preparing this paper I have to regret not being able to look over Lee's abridgement, though I have had before me a few notes of a former reading of it. [Seen in the present edition.] If I can trust my recollection, there are some circumstances in Lee which do not appear at all in the French translation of the complete work. This is curious. I may add that in the part translated by M. Dulaurier I have on one or two occasions ventured to follow his version where it seemed to give a better sense, though disclaiming any idea of judging between the two as to accuracy. [Yule added this note since: "I now have a copy of Lee's Ibn Batuta, and I find that the circumstances here alluded to as resting in my memory of that version arose only out of a difference of translation and reading. Compare the story of the man taught by the Jogis in Lee, p. 159, with the same in Defrémery, iv, p. 35."]

e Interprete Regio da Lingua Arabica, Official da Secretaria de Estado dos Negocios Estrangeiros, e Socio da Academia Real das Sciencias de Lisboa. Tomo I. Lisboa. Na Typografia da Academia. 1840, small 4to, pp. vii–533 without the errata, 2 ff. n. numbered.

Translated from a MS. purchased at Fez in 1797–8, by Father Moura.

—Description de l'Archipel d'Asie, par Ibn-Bathoutha, traduite de l'arabe par M. Éd. Dulaurier. (*Journal Asiatique*, Février, 1847, pp. 93–134; Mars, 1847, pp. 218–59.)

—Voyages d'Ibn Batoutah, texte arabe, accompagné d'une traduction par C. Defrémery et le Dr. B. R. Sanguinetti. Paris. Imprimé par autorisation de l'Empereur à l'Imprimerie Impériale, MDCCCLIII–LVIII. 4 vol. 8vo, pp. xlvi–443, xiv–465, xxvi–476, 479; and index alphabétique, 8vo, MDCCCLIX, pp. 91 on 2 col.

—Die Reise des Arabers Ibn Baṭūta durch Indien und China. (14. Jahrhundert.) Von Dr. Hans von Mžik. Mit 2 Karten. Hamburg, Gutenberg-Verlag, 1911, 8vo, pp. 490. (*Bibliothek denkwürdiger Reisen*, t. v.)

NOTE A. (See Page 13.)

ON THE VALUE OF THE INDIAN COINS MENTIONED BY IBN BATUTA.

Though I have not been able to obtain complete light on this perplexed question, I will venture a few remarks which may facilitate its solution by those who have more knowledge and better aids available, and I am the more encouraged to do so because the venerable and sagacious Elphinstone, in his remarks on the subject, has certainly been led astray by a passage in the abridgment of our traveller translated by Lee. He observes (*H. of India*, ii, 208): "In Ibn Batuta's time a western dínár was to an eastern as four to one, and an eastern dínár seems to have been one-tenth of a tankha, which, even supposing the tankha of that day to be equal to a rupee of Akber, would be only 2¼*d.* (*Ibn Batuta*, p. 149)."

But the fact deducible from what Ibn Batuta really says is, that what he calls the silver dínár of India *is* the tangah of other authors, corresponding more or less to the coin which has been called rupee (*Rúpiya*) since the days of Sher Sháh (1540–5), and that this *silver* coin was equal to one-fourth of the *gold* dínár of the West (*Maghrib, i.e.* Western Barbary); whilst it was one-tenth of the gold coin of India, to which alone *he* gives the name of Tangah. Thus he says: "The *lak* is a sum of 100,000 [Indian silver] dínárs, an amount equal to 10,000 Indian gold dínárs" (iii, 106), with which we may compare the statement in the contemporary *Masālak-al-Absār* that the *Red* Lak was equal to 100,000 gold Tangah, and the *White* Lak equal to 100,000 silver Tangah (*Not. et Ext.*, xiii, 211–12). We may also refer to his anecdote about Sultan Mahomed's sending 40,000 *dínárs* to Shaikh Burhán-uddín of Ságharj at Samarkand, which appears also in the *Masālak-al-Absār* as a present of 40,000 *Tangahs.* But the identity of Ibn Batuta's Indian silver dínár and the silver Tangah will be seen to be beyond question when this note has been read through.

The late Mr. Erskine, in his *H. of India under Baber and Humayún* (i, 544), says that the Tangah under the Khiljis (the immediate predecessors of the Tughlaks on the throne of Delhi) was a *tola* in weight (*i.e.* the weight of the present rupee), and probably equal in value to Akbar's rupee, or about two shillings. And this we should naturally suppose to be about the value of the Tangah or silver dínár of Mahomed Tughlak, but there are statements which curiously diverge from this in contrary directions.

On the one hand, Firishta has the following passage: "Nizamood-deen Ahmed Bukhshy, surprised at the vast sums stated by historians as having been lavished by this prince (M. Tughlak), took the trouble to ascertain from authentic records that these Tankas were of the silver currency of the day, in which was amalgamated a great deal of alloy, so that each Tanka only exchanged for sixteen copper pice," making, says Briggs, the tanka worth only about fourpence instead of two shillings (Briggs' *Firishta*, i, 410).

I doubt however if this statement, or at least the accuracy of the Bakshi's researches, can be relied on, for the distinct and concurring testimonies of Ibn Batuta and the *Masālak-al-Absār* not only lend no countenance to this depreciation, but seem on the other hand greatly to enhance the value of the Tangah beyond what we may call its normal value of two shillings.

Thus Ibn Batuta tells us repeatedly that the *gold* Tangah (of 10 silver dínárs or Tangahs) was equal to 2½ gold dínárs of Maghrib (see i, 293; ii, 65, 66; iii, 107, 426; iv, 212). The *Masālak-al-Absār* says it was equal to three *mithcals* (ordinary dínárs?). The former says again that the silver dínár of India was equivalent to eight dirhems, and that "this dirhem was absolutely equivalent to the dirhem of silver" (iv, 210).

The *Masālak-al-Absār* also tells us, on the authority of a certain Shaikh Mubarak who had been in India at the court of M. Tughlak, that the silver Tangah was equal to eight dirhems called *hashtkání*, and that these were of the same weight as the dirhem of Egypt and Syria (*o. c.* xiii, 211); though in another passage the same work gives the value as six dirhems only (p. 194). [Ma Huan in his account of Bengal has: "The currency of the country is a silver coin called Tang-ka, which is two Chinese mace in weight, is one inch and two-tenths in diameter, and is engraved on either side; all large business transactions are carried on with this coin, but for small purchases they use a sea-shell called by foreigners *kao-li*" [cowry].—*J. R. A. S.*, 1895, p. 530. Mr. John Beames, *l.c.*, p. 899, remarks that "the Tang-ka is the ordinary silver coin now more generally known as the rupee. The Bengalis, however, still use the term *ṭaṅká* or *ṭáká* for rupee."]

The only estimate I can find of a Barbary dínár is Amari's report from actual weight and assay of the value of the dínár called *Múmini* of the African dynasty Almohadi, current at the end of the twelfth century. This amounts to *fr.* 16·36 or 12*s.* 11·42*d.* (*Diplomi Arabi del R. Archiv. Fiorent.* p. 398). We have seen that ten silver dínárs of India were equal to two and a half gold dínárs of Barbary, or, in other words, that four of the former were equal to one of the latter. Taking the valuation just given we should have the Indian silver dínár or Tangah worth 3*s.* 2·855*d.*...(A).

Then as regards the dirhem. The dínár of the Arabs was a perpetuation of the golden solidus of Constantine, which appears to have borne the name of denarius in the eastern provinces, and it preserved for many hundred years the weight and intrinsic value of the Roman coin, though in the fourteenth century the dínár of Egypt and Syria had certainly fallen below this. The dirhem more vaguely represented the drachma, or rather the Roman (silver) denarius, to which the former name was applied in the Greek provinces (see Castiglione, *Monete Cufiche*, lxi *seqq.*).

The dínár was divided originally into 20 dirhems, though at certain times and places it came to be divided into only 12, 13, or 10. In Egypt, in Ibn Batuta's time, according to his own statement, it was divided into 25 dirhems. His contemporary, Pegolotti, also says that 23 to 25 *diremi* went to the *Bizant* or dínár. In Syria in the following century we find Uzzano to state that the dínár was worth thirty dirhems; and perhaps this may have been the case in Egypt at an earlier date. For Frescobaldi (1384) tells us that the *daremo* was of the value of a Venice grosso (of which there went twenty-four to the sequin), and also that the bizant was worth a *ducato di zeccha* (or sequin) and a quarter; hence there should have been thirty grossi or dirhems to the bizant (Amari in *Journ. Asiat.*, Jan. 1846, p. 241, and in *Diplomi Arabi* u.s.; *Ibn Bat.*, i, 50; *Della Decima*. iii, 58, iv, 113; *Viag. in Terra Santa di L. Frescobaldi e d' altri*, Firenze, 1862, p. 43). The estimates of the dínár also are various. Quatremère assumes the dínár in Irak at the beginning of the fourteenth century to be 15 francs, or 11*s.* 10½*d.*; Defrémery makes 100,000 dirhems of Egypt equal to 75,000 francs, which, at Ibn Batuta's rate of 25 to the dínár, would make the latter equal to 14*s.* 10*d.*, or at 20 dirhems (which is probably the number assumed) 11*s.* 10½*d.* Pegolotti says the bizant of Egypt (or dínár) was worth 1⅛ florin, but makes other statements from which we must deduce that it was 1⅕[1], valuations which would respectively make the dínár equal to 10*s.* 11·66*d.*, and 11*s.* 3·82*d.* Frescobaldi and his companion Sigoli both say that it was worth a sequin (or a florin) and a quarter, *i.e.*, 11*s.* 8·35*d.*, or 11*s.* 9·06*d.* Uzzano says its value varied (in exchange apparently) from 1 florin

[1] For he tells us (p. 77) that 1 oz. Florence weight was equal to 6 bizants and 16¾ carats, the bizant being divided into 24 carats; and in another place (p. 202) that 96 gold florins of Florence were equal to one Florence pound. The resulting equation will give the bizant almost exactly equal to 1⅕ florin.

to $1\frac{1}{5}$, or even $1\frac{1}{3}$; giving respectively values of 9s. 4·85d., 10s. 6·9d., and 12s. 6d. But he also tells us that its excess in weight over the florin was only $1\frac{1}{4}$ carat (or $\frac{5}{91}$), which would make its intrinsic value only 9s. 11d. MacGuckin de Slane says in a note on Ibn Batuta that the dínár of his time might be valued at 12 or 13 francs, *i.e.*, from 9s. 6d. to 10s. $3\frac{1}{2}$d.; and Amari that the dínár of Egypt at the beginning of the fourteenth century was equal to the latter sum (Quat., *Rashideddin*, p. xix; *Ibn Bat.*, i, 95; *Della Decima*, iii, 58, 77; iv, 110 *seq.*; *Viaggi in Terra Santa*, pp. 43, 177; *Journ. Asiat.*, March, 1843, p. 188; *Diplomi Arabi*, p. lxiv). On the whole I do not well see how the dínár of Egypt and Syria in our author's time can be assumed at a lower value than 10s. 6d.

Taking the dínár of Egypt and Syria at 10s. 6d., and 25 dirhems to the dínár (according to our author's own computation) we have the dirhem worth 5·04d., and the Indian dínár or Tangah, being worth eight dirhems, will be 3s. 4·32d....(B).

Or, if neglecting the whole question as to the value of the dínár and number of dirhems therein, we take Frescobaldi's assertion that the dirhem was worth a Venetian groat as an accurate statement of its value, we shall have the dirhem equal to $\frac{1}{24}$ of a sequin or 0s. 4·68d., and the Tanga worth 3s. 1·44d. ...(C).

But even this last and lowest of these results is perplexingly high, unless we consider how very different the relation between silver and gold in India in the first half of the fourteenth century is likely to have been from what it is now in Europe; observing also that all the values we have been assigning have been deduced from the value of gold coins estimated at the modern English mint price, which is to the value of silver as fifteen and a fraction to one.

The prevalent relation between gold and silver in Europe, for several centuries before the discovery of America took effect on the matter, seems to have been about twelve to one; and it is almost certain that in India at this time the ratio must have been considerably lower. Till recently I believe silver has always borne a higher relative value in India than in Europe, but besides this the vast quantities of gold that had been brought into circulation in the Delhi Empire since the beginning of the century, by the successive invasions of the Deccan and plunder of the accumulated treasures of its temples and cities, must have tended still more to depreciate gold, and it is very conceivable that the relative value at Delhi in 1320–50 should have been ten to one, or even less[1].

[1] For some account of the enormous plunder in gold, etc., brought from the south by Malik Kafur in 1310–11 see Briggs' *Firishta*, i, pp. 373–4. See also *supra*, III, p. 68, for a sample of the spoil in gold

On the hypothesis of its being ten to one we should have to reduce the estimates of the dínár (A), (B), (C), by one third in order to get the real results in modern value. They would then become respectively 2*s.* 1·9*d.*, 2*s.* 2·9*d.*, and 2*s.* 0·96*d.*, and the Tangah or silver dínár thus becomes substantially identified with the modern rupee.

The fact that the gold Tangah was coined to be worth ten silver ones may slightly favour the reality of the supposed ratio between gold and silver, as there seems to have been often a propensity to make the chief gold and chief silver coin of the same weight. I think that the modern gold mohur struck at the Company's Indian Mints is or was of the same weight as the rupee. See also (*supra*, II, p. 197) the statement in Wassaf that the *balish* of gold was just ten times the *balish* of silver.

I do not know whether the existence of coins of Mahomed Tughlak in our Museums gives the means of confirming or upsetting the preceding calculations.

In making them the twenty-franc piece has been taken at the value of 15*s.* 10·5*d.* English, and therefore the franc in gold at 0*s.* 9·69*d.* (*Encycl. Brit.*, article *Money*). The Florentine gold florin has been taken at *fr.* 11·8792, or 9*s.* 4·8516*d.* English, and the Venetian sequin at *fr.* 11·82, or 9*s.* 4·284*d.* (Cibrario, *Pol. Economia del Medio Evo*, iii, 228, 248).

***

Shortly after this note had been printed I saw from the *Athenæum* (February 3rd, 1866) that Mr. Edward Thomas, the eminent Indian numismatologist, had been treating of the Bengal coinage of this period before the Royal Asiatic Society, and on my application to him for certain information, he was kind enough to send me a copy of a pamphlet containing his paper ("*The Initial Coinage of Bengal*") as well as of some

appropriated by one of the minor Mahomedan buccaneering chiefs in the Peninsula. The treasures accumulated by Kalesa-Dewar, the Rajah of Maabar, in the end of the thirteenth century, are stated in the Persian History of Wassaf at 12,000 crores of gold, a crore being = 10,000,000! (see Von Hammer's work quoted *supra*, III, pp. 68–9). Note also that there was according to Firishta at this time none but gold coinage in the Carnatic, and this indeed continued to be the prevalent currency there till the present century (Elphinstone, ii, 48). We may observe too that even when the emperor assigns to Ibn Batuta a large present estimated in silver dínárs, it is paid in gold Tangahs (iii, 426). I may add a reference to what Polo tells us of the frontier provinces between Burma and China, that in one the value of gold was only eight times that of silver, in another only six times, and in a third (that of the Zardandan or Gold-Teeth—*supra*, III, p. 131) only five times that of silver; "by this exchange," quoth he, "merchants make great profit" (pt. i, ch. 46, 47, 48). Difficult of access as those provinces were, such an exchange must in some degree have affected neighbouring countries.

former papers of his on the coinage of the Patan Sovereigns of Hindustan.

It appears to me that these papers fairly confirm from numismatic history the conclusions arrived at in Note A from the passages in Ibn Batuta and the *Masālak-al-Absār.*

The chief points, as far as that note is concerned, to be gathered from Mr. Thomas's researches are these:

(1) That the capital coins of Delhi, from the time of Altamsh (A.D. 1211–36) to the accession of Mahomed Tughlak (A.D. 1325), were a gold and silver piece of equal weight, approximating tc a standard of 175 grains Troy[1] (properly 100 *Ratis*).

(2) That Mahomed Tughlak in the first year of his reign remodelled the currency, issuing gold pieces under the official name of *dínár*, weighing two hundred grains, and silver pieces under the name of *'adalí*, weighing one hundred and forty grains.

(3) That the coinage of silver at least was gradually and increasingly debased till A.D. 1330, when Mahomed developed his notable scheme of a forced currency consisting entirely of copper tokens (alluded to at III, p. 150, *supra*). This threw everything into confusion, and it was not till six years later that any sustained issues of ordinary coin recommenced[2].

(4) From this time the old standard (175 grains) of Mahomed's predecessors was readopted for gold, and was preserved to the

[1] These coins appear to have been officially termed respectively *Sikkah* and *Fizzat*; but both seem eventually to have had the popular name of *Tankah.*

The word *Sikkah* just mentioned involves a curious history.

Originally it appears to mean a *die*; then it applies to the coin struck, as here. In this application (in the form of Sicca Rupees) it still has a ghostly existence at the India Office. Going off in another direction at an early date, the word gave a name to the *Zecca*, or *Cecca*, or Mint, of the Italian Republics; thence to the *Zecchino* or *Cecchino* which issued therefrom. And in this shape the word travelled back to the East, where the term *Chickeen* or *Chick* survived to our own day as a comprehensive Anglo-Indian expression for the sum of Four Rupees.

We see how much the commerce and marine of Italy must have owed to Saracen example in the fact that so many of the cardinal institutions of these departments of affairs drew names from Arabic originals; *e.g.*—The Mint (*Zecca*, as above), the Arsenal (*Darsena*), the Custom-House (*Dovana, Dogana*), the Factory (*Fondaco*, see III, p. 229, *supra*), the Warehouse (*Magazzino* from *Makhzan*), the Admiral (from *Amír*), the Broker (*Sensale* from *Simsár*), the Caulker (*Calafato* from *Kiláfat*), to say nothing of the *Cantaro* and the *Rotolo*. It has been doubted whether *Darseṇa* is of Arabic origin. I see, however, that Mas'ūdī uses *Dár Siná'at* (House of Craftsman's work) in speaking of the Greek Arsenal at Rhodes (*Prairies d'Or*, ii, 423; iii, 67). And at III, p. 144, *supra*, a note speaks hesitatingly about the derivation of dogana from *Diwán.* But in Amari's *Diplomi Arabi* the word *Diwán* frequently occurs as the equivalent of Dogana (*op. cit.*, pp. 76, 88, 90, 91).

[2] It is said (July 1866) that the Italian Government is about to issue copper tokens to represent the different silver coins current in the kingdom (*Absit omen !*).

time of Sher Sháh. It does not appear that the old standard was resumed for silver. For though Mr. Thomas alludes to one example of a coin of A.H. 734 (A.D. 1334, and therefore previous to the resumption of a systematic coinage) as containing 168 grains of pure silver, his examples show in the reign of Mahomed's successor Firuz Sháh the gold coin of 175 grain standard running parallel with continued issues of the silver (or professedly silver) coin of 140 grains.

(5) During this time in Bengal the local coinage of silver retained an approximation at least to the old standard of 175 grains, though from about 1336 this seems to descend to a standard of 166. But one gold coin of Bengal *of this period* is quoted in the papers. It is a piece of inferior execution weighing 158 grs.

(6) The old standard silver tankah of 175 grains represented 64 of a coin or value called *kani*, or *gani*.

In applying these facts to the interpretation of Ibn Batuta I conceive that the coin which he calls *Tangah* was the 175 grain gold piece, and not the new dínár of 200 grains; and that what he calls *dínár* was the old 175 grain silver piece, and not the new *'adali* of 140 grains, *i.e.* it was the coin of which the modern rupee is the legitimate representative and nearly the exact equivalent[1].

[1] I considered that the passages referred to in Note A showed sufficiently the sense in which Ibn Batuta uses the terms *tangah* and *dínár*, and also that the tangah was equal to ten dínárs. But as there seems some doubt about this I will here quote all the passages in which the terms are used so as to be of any value.

(I) Tangah *always means with Ibn Batuta a gold coin. Sometimes he calls it a gold dínár.*

1. Locality, *Delhi*. "The weight of the tangah in dínárs of Maghrib is two dínárs and a half" (i, 293).

2. Locality, *Sind*. "The lak is 100,000 dínárs, and this is equal to 10,000 dínárs in gold of India, and the dínár of India is equal to 2½ dínárs of gold of Maghrib" (iii, 106).

3. Locality, *Delhi*. "1000 tangahs = 2500 dínárs of Maghrib" (iii, 187).

4. Locality, *Delhi*. "2000 tangahs of gold" (iii, 264).

5. Locality, *Delhi*. Ibn Batuta receives 6233 *tangahs* as the equivalent of 67,000 – 6700 *dínárs* (iii, 426).

6. Locality, *Delhi*. The tangah = 2½ dínárs of Maghrib (*Ibid.*).

7. Locality, *Bengal*. The dínár of gold = 2½ dínárs of Maghrib (iv, 212).

(II) Dínár, *though sometimes applied by Ibn Batuta to an Indian gold coin, as we have just seen, is the only name he uses for the standard Indian silver coin.* Sometimes the term used is *Dinár Diráham*, which Defrémery in some instances renders "Dínárs of Silver," and in others "Dínárs in Dirhems." Sometimes the term used is *Dinánir fizzat* (see ii, 373).

8. Locality, *Shiraz*. 10,000 dínárs of silver changed into gold of Maghrib would be 2500 dínárs of gold (ii, 65).

9. Locality, *Delhi*. 100 dínárs of silver = 25 dínárs of gold, presumably of Maghrib (ii, 76).

This, as regards the silver coin, seems tolerably clear from a comparison of Ibn Batuta's statement (as rendered by Defrémery) that "a silver dínár (in Bengal) was worth eight dirhems, and their dirhem was exactly equivalent to *the* dirhem of silver," with the statement of the *Masālak-al-Absār* that "the silver tangah of India was equivalent to eight of the dirhems called *Hashtkání* (*eight-káni*), these hashtkani dirhems being of the same weight with the dirhems of Egypt and Syria[1]." For it was the 175 grain piece that represented 64 kánis (and was therefore equivalent to 8 *hashtkanis*) and not the 140 grain piece[2].

Mr. Thomas has also considered the question, to which I was necessarily led, as to the relative values of gold and silver at that day in India. His conclusions are in the same direction to which my remarks (at p. 62) point in the words, "it is very conceivable that the relative value at Delhi should have been ten to one, or even less," but they go much further, for he estimates it at eight to one.

It seems probable that ten to one or thereabouts was the normal relation in the civilised kingdoms of Asia during the thirteenth century, but it is reasonable to suppose that the

10. Locality, *Upper India*. 100 dínárs = 25 dínárs in gold of Maghrib (ii, 374).

11. Locality, *Upper India*. "1000 dínárs, the change of which in gold of Maghrib is equal to 250 dínárs" (ii, 401).

12. Locality, *Sind*. Passage about the lak, quoted under No. 2.

13. From *Delhi*. Mah. Tughlak sends Burhán-uddín of Ságharj a present of 40,000 *dínárs* (iii, 255). *Masālak-al-Absār* says 40,000 *tangahs*.

14. Loc., *Delhi*. Mahom. Tughlak sends the Khalif's son on arrival 400,000 *dínárs* (iii, 262); and assigns Ibn Batuta a salary of 12,000 *dínárs* (iii, 398). These are evidently silver coins.

15. Locality, *Bengal*. Passage about the dínár being worth 8 dirhems, quoted in text (iv, 210).

No. 2 asserts in reference to Sind that the gold dínár was equal to 10 silver dínárs.

Nos. 9, 10, 11, show that the silver dínár of Delhi was worth one-fourth of the gold dínár of Maghrib.

Nos. 1, 2, 3, 6, 7, show that the tangah of India was a gold coin equal to 2½ gold dinars of Maghrib, and that Ibn Batuta asserts this equally in reference to Sind, Delhi, and Bengal. And, from the combination of these last two deductions, again the gold tangah = ten silver dínárs.

[1] Mr. Thomas warns me that the passage from Ibn Batuta about the dirhem of silver is very obscure; and indeed he has interpreted it in his pamphlet on the Bengal coinage in quite a different sense. But the passage from the *Masālak-al-Absār* appears to be free from obscurity, and to have substantially the same meaning as the version of Defrémery; which is surely an argument of some weight in favour of the latter.

[2] Yet the existence of the latter piece perhaps explains the alternative statement (alluded to at p. 55) that the silver dínár of India was equivalent to 6 dirhems only. The 140 grain piece would in fact be equivalent to 6·4.

enormous plunder of gold in the Dekkan during the reign of Mahomed Tughlak himself and his immediate predecessors must for a time at least have diminished the relative value of gold considerably[1].

[1] Some illustration of the popular view of this influx of gold is given at p. 57. Another anecdote bearing on the subject is quoted at II, p. 144 (*supra*). And the *Masālak-al-Absār* says that Mahomed Bin Yusuf Thakafi found in the province of Sind 40 *bahar* of gold, each *bahar* equal to 333 *mann*, *i.e.*, in all some 333,000 pounds of gold.

Mr. Thomas seems to be of opinion that 8 to 1 was about the *normal* relation of gold to silver in Asia during the time of Mahomed Tughlak and the preceding age, and he quotes in support of this the statement of Marco Polo, which I have referred to in a different view at p. 57, that gold in Caraian (part of Yun-nan) bore that relation to silver. But this was a remote province immediately adjoining still more secluded regions producing gold in which the exchange went down to 6 and 5 to 1. I understand Polo as mentioning the exchange of even 8 to 1 as something remarkable.

The relation between the two metals has followed no constant progression. American silver raised the value of gold in the sixteenth and succeeding centuries, whilst recent gold discoveries are now lowering it again. Minor influences of like kind no doubt acted before. Such authorities as I have been able to refer to say that in the time of the early Roman Empire the relation was 12½ to 1; under the Lower Empire, about the time of Justinian, a little more than 14 to 1; in the early Mahomedan times it varied from 13⅓ to 15 to 1. In the "dark ages" of Europe it sunk in some countries as low as 10 to 1; in the time of Charles the Bald in France (843–77) it was 12 to 1. In Florence in 1356 it was 12 to 1; in England about the same time 12 to 1; and this seems to have been the prevailing relation till the American discoveries took effect. But it seems improbable that 8 to 1 could have been maintained *for many years* as the relation in India and other kingdoms of Asia whilst the relation in Europe was so different. The former relation was maintained I believe in Japan to our own day, but then there was a wall of iron round the kingdom.

Supposing, as I do, that Ibn Batuta's tangah and dínár were the old standard gold and silver coins of 175 grs. each, then the fact that the tangah was worth 10 dinars is in my view an indication of what *had been* at least the relative value of the two metals. And the statement of the *Tárikh-i-Wassaf* (see pp. 116, 442) that the gold *balish* was worth ten times the silver *balish* comes in to confirm this.

It has occurred to me as just possible that the changes made by Mahomed Tughlak in the coinage may have had reference to the depreciation of gold owing to the "Great Dekkan Prize-money" of that age. Thus, previous to his time, we have the gold and silver coins of equal weight and bearing (according to the view which has been explained) a nominal ratio of 10 to 1. Mahomed on coming to the throne finds that in consequence of the great influx of gold the relative value of that metal has fallen greatly, say to something like 7 to 1, which as a local result where great treasure in gold had suddenly poured in, is, I suppose, conceivable. He issues a coinage which shall apply to this new ratio, and yet preserve the relation of the pieces as 10 to 1. This accounts for his 200 gr. gold and 140 gr. silver pieces. Some years later, after the disastrous result of his copper tokens, the value of gold has risen, and he reverts to the old gold standard of 175 grs., leaving (as far as I can gather) the silver piece at its reduced weight. At the exchange of ten silver pieces for one of

NOTE B. (SEE PAGE 24.)

ON THE PLACES VISITED BY IBN BATUTA BETWEEN CAMBAY AND MALABAR.

I dissent entirely from Dr. Lee and others as to the identification of the places named by our traveller between Cambay and Hunáwúr.

Kawé or *Kāwa* is by Lee taken for Gógó. But I have no doubt it is the place still bearing the same name, CAUVEY in Arrowsmith's great map, Gongway or Conwa of Ritter (vi, 645–6), on the left bank of the Mahi's estuary over against Cambay. It is, or was in Forbes' time (*Oriental Memoirs*, quoted by Ritter), the seat of a great company of naked Sanyasis.

Kandahār is evidently the corruption of some Indian name into a form familiar to Mahomedan ears. It occurs also as the name of a maritime city near the Gulf of Cambay in the early wars of the Mahomedans of Sind, and in the *Ayin Akbari* (Reinaud in *J. As.*, s. iv, tom. v, 186). Starting from the point just identified, we should look for it on the *east* side of the Gulf of Cambay, and there accordingly, in Arrowsmith's map, on a secondary estuary, that of the Dhandar or river of Baroda between the Mahi and the Nerbudda, we find GUNDAR. We shall also find it in old Linschoten's map (*Gandar*), and the place is described by Edward Barbosa under the name of *Guindarim* or *Guandari*, as a good enough city and sea-port, carrying on a brisk trade with Malabar, etc. De Barros also mentions it as *Gendar*, a port between Cambay and Baroch (see *Barbosa and De Barros* in Ramusio, i; and also the Lisbon Barbosa, p. 277). The title, *Jálansi*, given by Ibn Batuta to the King of Gandar, probably represents the surname of the Rájpút tribe of *Jhálás*, which acquired large fragments of the great Hindu kingdom of Anhilwara on its fall in the beginning of the century, and whose name is still preserved in that of the district of Gujarat called

gold this now represents a relative value of 8 to 1. Bengal, meanwhile, has not shared in the plunder of the south, and there the old relations remain, nominally at least, unaffected. This is a mere speculation, and probably an airy one. Indeed, I find that Mr. Thomas is disposed to think that the object of Mahomed Tughlak's innovations was to ensure a double system of exchange rates, reviving the ancient local weight of 80 Ratis (140 grs.), and respecting the Hindu ideal of division by 4, with which was to be associated the Mahomedan preference for decimals.

Thus the 64 gani silver piece of 175 gr. was reduced to a 50 gani piece of 140 gr., 10 of which went to the current 175 gr. gold Tangah, while the new 200 gr. gold Dínár was intended to exchange against sixteen 50 gani pieces.

Jháláwár (see Forbes' *Rás-Málá*, i, 285–6, and 292 *seq.*). The form heard by Ibn Batuta may have been *Jhálábansí* or *-vansi*. The tribe of *Khwaja Bohrah* who paid their respects to the envoys here must have been the race or sect calling themselves *Ismailiah*, but well known as traders and pedlars, under the name of *Bohrahs*, all over the Bombay presidency. The headquarters of the sect is at Burhánpúr in the east of Khandesh, but they are chiefly found in Surat and the towns of Gujarat (see Ritter, vi, 567).

Bairam I take to be the small island of Perim [Peram], near the mouth of the Gulf of Cambay. It is, perhaps, the Βαιώνης of the Periplus. This island was the site of a fortress belonging to Mukheraji Gohil, Raja of Gógó and Perim, which was destroyed by the Mahomedans apparently in this very reign of M. Tughlak, and never afterwards restored (Forbes, *op. cit.*). This quite agrees with the statements of Ibn Batuta[1].

Kukah is then the still tolerably flourishing port of Gógó on the western side of the gulf, which has already been indicated as the *Caga* of Friar Jordanus (*supra*, III, p. 78). Lee identified Kukah with *Goa*, whilst Gildemeister, more strangely though not without misgiving, and even Defrémery, identify the *Kawe* of our author with that city. The traveller's repeated allusions to the tides point distinctly to the Gulf of Cambay as the position of all the places hitherto named; the remarkable rise and fall of the tide there have been celebrated since the date of the *Periplus*.

The Pagan king Dunkúl or Dungól, of Kukah, was doubtless one of the "*Gohils*, Lords of Gogo and Perum, and of the sea-washed province which derived from them its name of *Gohilwár*" (Forbes, p. 158), and possibly the last syllable represents this very name *Gohil*, though I cannot explain the prefix.

Sindábúr or Sandábúr is a greater difficulty, though named by a variety of geographers, Europeans as well as Arabs. Some needless difficulty has been created by Abulfeda's confounding it more or less with *Sindán*, which was quite a different place. For the latter lay certainly to the north of Bombay, somewhere near the Gulf of Cambay. Indeed, Rawlinson (quoted in *Madras Journal*, xiv, 198) says it has been corrupted into the *St. John* of modern maps, on the coast of Gujarat. I presume this must be the *St. John's Point* of Rennell between Daman and Mahim, which would suit the conditions of Sindán well.

The data which Abulfeda himself quotes from travellers show that Sandábúr was three days south of Tana, and reached (as Ibn Batuta also tells us) immediately before Hunáwúr.

[1] I find that memory misled me here as to Lee's interpretations. He appears (by writing *Goa* for *Kawé* or *Káwa*) to identify the latter name with the modern *Goa*, not with Gógó, and he attempts no identification of Kuka.

Sandábúr is mentioned by Mas'ūdī, thus: "Crocodiles abound in the *ajwán* or bays formed by the Indian Sea, such as the Bay of SANDABURA in the Indian kingdom of *Bághrah*." I cannot discover what *Bághrah* represents. (*Prairies d'Or*, i, 207.) Rashid also names it as the first city reached on the Malabar Coast. The *Chintabor* of the Catalan map, and the *Cintabor* of the Portulano Mediceo agree with this fairly.

I do not know any European book since the Portuguese discoveries which speaks of Sandábúr, but the name appears in Linschoten's map in the end of the sixteenth century as *Cintapor* on the coast of the Konkan below Dabul. Possibly this was introduced from an older map without personal knowledge. It disagrees with nearly all the other data.

Ibn Batuta himself speaks of it as the *Island* of Sandábúr, containing thirty-six villages, as being one of the ports from which ships traded to Aden, and as being about one day's voyage from Hunáwúr. The last particular shows that it could not be far from GOA, as Gildemeister has recognized, and I am satisfied that it was substantially *identical* with the port of Goa. This notion is supported (1) by its being called by Ibn Batuta, not merely an island, but an island surrounded by an estuary in which the water was salt at the flood tide but fresh at the ebb, a description applying only to a Delta island like Goa; (2) by his mention of its thirty-six villages, for De Barros says that the island of Goa was called by a native name [*Tīsvādī*] signifying "Thirty Villages"; and (3) by the way in which Sandábúr is named in the Turkish book of navigation called the *Mohith*, translated by V. Hammer in the *Bengal Journal*. Here there is a section headed "24th Voyage; from *Kuwai Sindabur* to Aden." But the original characters given in a note read *Koah* (*i.e.* Goa) *Sindabur*, which seems to indicate that Sindabur is to be looked for either in Goa Island, or on one of the other Delta islands of its estuary. The sailing directions commence: "If you start from Goa Sindabur at the end of the season take care not to fall on Cape Fal," etc. If we could identify this *Rás-ul-Fál* we might make sure of Sandábúr. [Yule gives other proofs of the identity of Sindábúr with Goa in *Hobson-Jobson*.]

The *name*, whether properly Sundapúr or Chándapúr (which last the Catalan and Medicean maps suggest), I cannot trace. D'Anville identifies Sandábúr with Sunda, which is the name of a district immediately south of Goa territory. But Sunda city lies inland, and he probably meant as the port *Sedasheogarh*, where we are now trying to reestablish a harbour. (D'Anville, *Antiq. de l'Inde*, pp. 109–111; Elliot, *Ind. to Hist. of Mah. India*, p. 43; Jaubert's *Edrisi*, i, 179; Gildemeister (who also refers to the following), pp. 46, 184, 188; *Journ. As. Soc. Bengal*, v. p. 464.)

The only objection to these identifications appears to be the statement of our author that he was only three days in sailing from Kukah to Sándabúr, which seems rather short allowance to give the vessels of those days to pass through the six degrees of latitude between Gógó and Goa. After all however it is only an average of five knots.

NOTE C. (See Page 26.)

REMARKS ON SUNDRY PASSAGES IN THE FOURTH VOLUME OF LASSEN'S *INDISCHE ALTERTHUMSKUNDE*.

The errors noticed here are those that I find obvious in those pages of the volume that I have had occasion to consult. None of them are noticed in the copious Errata at pp. 982 and (App.) 85.

a. P. 888. "*Ma'âber*, which name (with Marco Polo) indicates the southernmost part of the Malabar coast." The same is said before at p. 156.

REMARKS.

a. The most cursory reading of Marco Polo shows that, whatever Maabar *properly* means, it *cannot* mean this with that author, including as it does with him the tomb of St. Thomas near Madras. But see *supra*, II, p. 141 and III, p. 68. If Maabar ever was understood to *include* a small part of the S.W. coast, as perhaps the expressions of Rashid and Jordanus (p. 41) imply, this would seem to be merely because the name expressed a *country*, i.e., a superficies, and not a *coast*, i.e., a line. The name of Portugal would be most erroneously defined as "indicating the south coast of the Spanish peninsula," though Portugal does *include* a part of that coast.

I find that the Arabs gave a name analogous to that of *Ma'bar* (or the Passage) to the Barbary coast from Tunis westward, which was called *Bar-ul-Adwah*, Terra Transitûs, because thence they used to pass into

REMARKS

Spain (Amari in *Journ. Asiat.*, Jan. 1846, p. 228). And it is some corroboration of the idea that the name *Ma'bar* was given to the coast near Ramnad as the place of passage to Ceylon, that a town just opposite on the Ceylonese coast was called *Mantotte*, because it was the *Mahatotta*, the "Great Ferry" or point of arrival or departure of the Malabars resorting to the island (Tennent, i, 564).

b. P. 889. "From *Kâlikodu* or Kalikut, the capital of the Zamorin, he (Ibn Batuta) visited the Maldives.... On this voyage he met the ships on their voyage from *Zaitún*.... On their decks were wooden huts for the crew, which consisted of *five and twenty men*."

b. Nothing is said by Ibn Batuta of meeting these ships on his voyage to the Maldives. He describes them at Calicut, where they were in port. He speaks of the crew as consisting of *one thousand* men.

c. "The captains were *Amirs*, i.e., Arabs."

c. See *supra*, p. 26.

d. "This kind of ship was only built in *Zaitún*."

d. These ships are distinctly stated to have been built in Zaitún, *and in Sín-kalán*.

e. "From the Malabar coast Ibn Batuta sailed to Ceylon."

e. On the contrary, he sailed *from the Maldives*.

f. "The next land that he mentions is Bengal. Our traveller visited this country (about 1346) and found that between it and the southernmost part of the Dekkan *a most active traffic had sprung up, and also with China*."

f. I can find no ground for this statement in the narrative, except that Ibn Batuta got a passage somehow from the Maldives to Bengal, and afterwards in a junk which was going from Bengal to *Java* (Sumatra). At the latter place the sultan provided a vessel to carry him on to China.

g. Pp. 889–890. "From this (Bengal) he directed his travels to Java, as the name of that island is here given according to the more modern pronunciation; the island of

g. From this we should gather (1) that Ibn Batuta calls Java by *that name*, and (2) calls Sumatra *Jaonah*, whilst (3) Lee introduces a name, *Mul-Java*, unknown to the correct narra-

Sumatra he calls *Jáonah*, which, we should rather have expected to be *Jávonah*, as it is known to be called by Marco Polo *Java Minor*." (*In a note*): "The port where Ibn Batuta landed is called in the correct reading *Sumathrah*... in Lee's translation the name is given incorrectly as *Mul-Jâva*."

REMARKS

tive, as that of the port of Sumatra.

The fact is that Defrémery (whom Lassen cites) and Lee are in perfect accordance here. Sumatra Island is called *Java*; some other country, which both those translators take for Java Proper, is called *Mul-Java*, and *Jaonah* is found *absolutely nowhere* except in Lassen's page.

h. P. 890. "Passing hence (from Sumatra) our traveller *visited some of the Moluccas*; this is rendered certain by the fact that the author of these travels gives a pretty accurate description of the spice plants."

h. There is *not one word* in the narrative about any such visit, or anything that can be so interpreted. As for the accuracy of his description of the spice plants, look at it!

i. *Ib*. "On his further travels Ibn Batuta after *seven days* arrived at the kingdom of *Tualiçeh*....

i. The time in the narrative amounts to *seventy-one days* from Mul-Java, the last point of departure, to Tawalisi. There is nothing about seven days, any more than there is about the visit to the Spice Islands.

j. *Ib*...."By which name only *Tonkin* can be meant. The inhabitants of this kingdom, on account of their vicinity, had many relations, both hostile and peaceful, with the Chinese."

j. It is easy to settle difficult questions with a "can only," but there is nothing to make it clear that Tonkin is meant, and strong reasons arise against that view. And absolutely *nothing* is said in the narrative about vicinity to the Chinese. It is only said that the king had frequent *naval* wars with the Chinese, a fact which rather argues an insular position.

k. *Ib*. "In the Middle Kingdom, next to Zaitún the most important place of trade was the Port of *Sin-ossin* or *Sin-kalan*; this name must indicate Canton, which city stands on the river *Tshing-Kuang*, the form of which is

k. Sinkilan is indeed Canton, but it is by sounder reasons than this that it is proved to be so. One does not see why foreigners should call Canton by the name of its river, if Tshing-Kuang *be* the name [the name is Chu Kiang, the "Pearl River"],

REMARKS

tolerably echoed in the second reading of the name."

neither is there any great resemblance in the words. But we have seen that *Sín-kalán* is merely the Persian translation of *Mahá-chín*, and has nothing to do with Chinese words.

Moreover Sín-kalán is not an alternative reading (*Lesart*) of Sin-ossin (*Sin-ul-Sin*), but an alternative *name*.

It may be said that these errors are of trifling moment, and belong to a mere appendage of the subject of the book. But *noblesse oblige*; a work of such reputation as the *Indian Archaeologia* is referred to with almost as much confidence as the original authorities, and instances of negligence so thickly sown are a sort of breach of trust. Those already quoted are, all but one, within two pages. Going further we find others as remarkable:

l. P. 896. The name of one of the pepper ports on the coast of Malabar is quoted from Cosmas Indico-pleustes (with a reference to Montfaucon, p. 337) as *Pandapattana*, a form which is made the basis of an etymology (as from the *Pandiya* kings).

l. The real name in Cosmas (as found in Montfaucon) is however not *Pandapattana* but *Pudopatana* (Πουδοπάτανα), which is much more likely to be "*New-city*," from the Tamul *Pudu*, "New," as in *Pudu-cheri*, commonly called Pondicherry. The port existed by the same name for a thousand years after Cosmas; see List of Malabar Ports, *infra*.

m. P. 911. Lassen quotes the name applied to the Chinese by Theophylactus Simocatta (see the Essay in volume 1) as *Tengast*, citing the Bonn edition, p. 288.

m. The name at p. 283 of the Bonn edition is not *Tengast*, but *Taugast* (Ταυγαστ). I have no longer access to the book, and I cannot say whether it is so differently written at p. 288. This change again (if it is such) favours an identification. The identification may probably be right, but would stand better on a sound bottom.

In the *Corpus Byzant. Histor.* the word is written Ταυγάς, though the Latin version of the same has *Taugast*.

n. In the appended tract on the Chinese and Arab know-

n. (1) Sultan Mahomed's name was not *Togrul* but *Tughlak*.

ledge of India, we have at p. 31 a statement that Ibn Batuta acquired the high favour of the then reigning Emperor of India, Muhammed *Toghrul*, of the *Afghan* dynasty of *Lodi*.

REMARKS

Neither (2) was he in any sense of *Afghan* lineage; nor (3) did he belong to the *dynasty of Lodi*, which came a century after his time, with the Deluge between in the shape of Timur's invasion.

o. P. 84. "I will not omit to remark that *Wilhelm von Rubruck*, *Jean du Plan Carpin*, and *Benedictus Polonus* establish the fact that also, during the wide sway of the Mongol Emperor Jingis Khan and his successors, a commercial interchange existed between several of their provinces and India. The first of these pious envoys of the Roman court visited the Emperor Mangu Khan, who in 1248 was recognized as Supreme Khan of the whole empire; the second visited Kúblái Khan, who from 1259 to 1296 wielded with vigorous hand the sceptre of his forefathers; the third belonged to that branch of the (Franciscan) order which is termed *Fratres Minores* or *Mindern Brüder*; he was the comrade of the second, and joined him in Poland on a journey to Rome undertaken in 1245. He reached in his company the court of the founder of the Mongul empire at *Karakorum*."

o. There are six errors in these few lines. (1) The mission of Rubruquis *followed* and did not *precede*, as is distinctly implied here, that of John of Plano Carpini. The former took place in 1253. (2) Rubruquis was not sent by the *Roman Court*, but by St. Lewis. (3) Plano Carpini and Bennet the Pole did not visit *Kúblái Khan*, but *Kuyuk Khan*, and their travels took place in 1245–7, not after 1259 as is here implied. (4) All the three monks (and all other Franciscans) were *Fratres Minores*, and not Bennet only as is here implied. (5) Bennet did not join Plano Carpini *on a journey to Rome*, but was picked up at Breslau as an interpreter by the latter when on his way from the Pope at Lyons to the Khan at Karakorum. (6) In whatever manner the three travellers may "establish the fact" in question, it is not by saying anything on the subject in their narratives. As far as I can discover not one of the three contains a single word directly or indirectly as to commercial intercourse between the Mongol provinces and India.

p. Turning back; at p. 402. In speaking of the practice of writing on the palm-leaves with a style, Lassen notes: "The leaves of the *Zwergpalme*

p. *Phœnix Fructifera* is, I presume, the same as *Phœnix Dactylifera*, the date tree. If it *be* called dwarf-palm in Germany (which I doubt) it is very

REMARKS

(i.e. dwarf-palm) or *Phœnix Fructifera* are especially used for that purpose."

badly named; but in any case it would puzzle any Dwarf out of Lilliput to write upon its leaves. The leaf most commonly used for the purpose is that of the Palmyra (*Borassus Flabelliformis*), and, in Ceylon and the peninsula adjoining, that of the Talipat (*Corypha Umbraculifera*), a gigantic palm.

q. P. 511. In his description of the *Chandi Sewu* or "Thousand Temples" at Brambanan in Java, he adopts without question Mr. Crawfurd's view (formed fifty years ago when little was known about Buddhism), that these essentially Buddhist edifices have been each crowned with a lingam. Even if the temples were not Buddhist, who ever saw a lingam on the top of a temple? But in fact the objects in question are no more lingams than the cupolas over St. Paul's facade are *dagobas*. Indeed in the latter case the resemblance is much more striking.

r. P. 546. Here, in dealing with the Malay history as derived partly from the native chronicles cited by Marsden, and partly from the early Portuguese writers, Lassen meets with the name of a chief given by the latter as *Xaquem Darxa*. This hero he supposes to be the son of a certain Iskandar or Sikandar Sháh mentioned in the Malay legends, and devises for his odd name a Sanscrit original "Çākanadhara, d. h. Besitzer Kräftiger Besitzungen"; accordingly he enters this possessor of strong possessions as an ascertained sovereign in the dynastic list under the name of Çākanadhara. Yet this *Xaquem Darxa* (*Xaquemdar Xa*) is only a corrupt Portuguese transcript of the name of *Sikandar Shah* himself (see Crawfurd's *Dict. Ind. Islands*, p. 242). King Çākanadhara is therefore as purely imaginary as the Pandyan city ascribed to Cosmas or the Island of Jaonah for which Ibn Batuta is wrongly made responsible.

NOTE D. (See Page 27.)

THE MEDIEVAL PORTS OF MALABAR.

It seems worth while to introduce here a review of the Ports of Malabar as they are described to have existed from the thirteenth to the sixteenth century. Many of these have now altogether disappeared, not only from commercial lists but from our maps, so that their very sites are sometimes difficult to identify. Nor are the books (such as F. Buchanan's *Journey*[1] and others) which might serve to elucidate many points, accessible where this is written. But still this attempt to illustrate a prominent subject in the Indian geography of those centuries will I trust have some interest.

We shall take the Goa River as our starting point, though Malabar strictly speaking was held to commence at Cape Delly. Had we taken the whole western coast from Gujarat downwards, the list would have been enlarged by at least a half.

The authorities recurring most frequently will be indicated thus: B stands for Barbosa (beginning of the sixteenth century) in Ramusio; BL for the Lisbon edition of Barbosa; DEB for De Barros (to whom I have access only in an Italian version of the two first Decades, Venice, 1561, and in Ramusio's extracts); IB for Ibn Batuta; S for the anonymous *Sommario dei Regni* in Ramusio.

Sandábúr, Chintabor, etc., see Note B, *supra*.

Bathecala, a flourishing city on a river, a mile from the sea (Varthema); BEITKUL, in the now again well-known bay of Sedasheogarh [Sedásiva-ghur, Buchanan, iii, p. 178]. I do not find it mentioned by any other of the early travellers, but in the seventeenth century it was the seat of a British factory under the name of Kārwār, the name (Kārwār Head) still applied to the southern point of the bay. [Kārwār, in North Kanara District.]

Anjediva (Varth.); ANCHEDIVA, an island 5 miles south-west of Kārwār Head, which was a favourite anchorage of the early Portuguese, the island affording shelter and good water. [It forms part of the Portuguese Possessions in Western India; see Buchanan, iii, p. 178.]

Cintacola (B), Cintacora (BL), Centacola (Varthema), Ancola? (DEB); ANKOLAH? a fortress on a rock over the river Aliga, belonging to the *Sabaio* of Goa (B), the residence of many Moorish

[1] [The title of the work is: *A Journey from Madras through the countries of Mysore, Canara, and Malabar*....by Francis Buchanan, M.D., ...London, 1807, 3 vol. 4to. I have made use of it. H. C.]

merchants (Varth.). ["Ancola is a ruinous fort, with a small market near it." Buchanan, iii, p. 176.]

Mergeo River (B), Mergeu (BL and DEB), Mirgeo (S). A great export of rice; the river north of KUMTA, on the estuary of which is still a place called MIRJĀN, the Meerjee or Meerzah of Rennell. Of late years I believe the trade has revived at Kumta, chiefly in the export of Dhārwār cotton. ["This traffic has been much affected by the railway through Portuguese territory." *Gaz. India.*]

Honor (B), Onor (DEB and Cesar Federici), Hináwar (IB), Hannaur (Abulfeda), Manor and Hunāwūr of Abdurrazzak, probably Nandor of the Catalan Map, HUNĀWŪR or ONORE (properly *Hunúr*?). A fine place with pleasant gardens and a Mahomedan population (Abul. and IB); a great export of rice and much frequented by shipping (B), but long a nest of pirates. ["Honawera, or Onore, as we call it, was totally demolished by Tippoo after he had recovered it by the treaty of Mangalore. It was formerly a place of great commerce." Buchanan, iii, p. 137.]

Battecala (B), Baticala (BL and DEB), Batigala of Fr. Jordanus, BATKUL. A great place with many merchants, where ships of Hormuz and Aden came to load sugar and rice, but destroyed by the rise of Goa. (An English Factory in the seventeenth century). [Bhatkal; North Kanara District—"Batuculla means the *round town*; stands on the north bank of a small river, the *Sancada-holay*." Buchanan, iii, p. 120.]

Mayandur, on a small river (B), Bendor (DEB); perhaps the port of BEDNUR, which itself lies inland.

Bracalor (BL), Brazzalor (B, and A. Corsali), Bracelor (DEB), Baçelor (S), Abúsaror (IB), Basarúr (Abulf.); BARCELOR. A small city on a gulf, abounding in coco-trees (IB). (A Dutch Factory in the seventeenth century.)

Bacanor (BL, DEB, S), Bracanor (B), Fakanúr, a large place on an estuary, with much sugar cane, under a pagan prince called Basadewa (IB), Fagnúr (Rashíd), Jai-faknúr (Firishta), probably the Maganúr of Abdurrazzak, and the Pacamuria of N. Conti; BACCANOR. There was a great export of rice in ships of Hormuz, Aden, Sohar and Malabar from both Barcelor and Baccanor (B). [Bārkūr, South Kanara District.]

Carcara and Carnate (DEB), Carnati (P. Vincenzo).

Mangalor (B, DEB, S, Abdurrazzak), Manjarúr (IB and Abul.), Manganor of the *Catalan Map*, MANGALORE. Probably Mangaruth, one of the pepper-ports of Cosmas, but the Mandagara of Ptolemy and the Periplus must have been much further north. (It is curious that Ptolemy has also a Manganor, but it is an inland city.) On a great estuary called Al-Dunb, the greatest on the coast; hither came most of the merchants from Yemen and Fars; pepper and ginger abundant; under a king called

Ramadewa (IB). A great place on a great river; here the pepper begins; the river bordered with coco groves; a great population of Moors and Gentiles; many handsome mosques and temples (B). Fifty or sixty ships used to load rice here (Varthema). Fallen off sixty years later, when C. Federici calls it a little place of small trade, but still exporting a little rice. [South Kanara District; to-day coffee is the chief article of export. See Buchanan, iii, p. 22.]

Maiceram (S), Mangeiron (DEB), Mangesairam (Linschoten), MANJESHWARAM. Nancaseram of Rennell? [Manjéswara, of Buchanan, iii, p. 20.]

Cumbala (B, DEB), Cumbola (BL), Cambulla (S), Coloal of Rennell? KUMBLAH. Exported rice, especially to the Maldives. [Cumly? of Buchanan, iii, p. 15, "situated on a high peninsula in a salt water lake, which is separated from the sea by a spit of sand."]

Cangerecora, on a river of the same name (DEB), CHANDRAGIRI? ["Chandra-giri is a large square fort, situated high above the river on its southern bank. It was built by Sivuppa Nayaka, the first prince of the house of Ikeri that established his authority in this part of Canara." Buchanan, iii, p. 15.]

Cote Coulam (S), Cota Coulam (DEB), Cote Colam (BL).

Nilexoram (S), Nilichilam (DEB), Ligniceron (P. Vincenzo), probably Barbosa's "port on the Miraporam River," which he describes as the next place to Cote Coulam, "a seaport of Moors and Gentiles, and a great place of navigation." Though the name has been excluded by the defects and caprices of our modern maps, this is the NILESHWERAM, NELISURAM, or NELLISEER of Rennell and others, which has been identified by Rennell with the *Nelcynda* of the Ancients. [Is it represented to-day by the village of Nīleshwar, south of Kāsaragod, South Kanara District?] There can be little doubt that the river on which it stands was that on which was situated the kingdom of Ely of Marco Polo, Hili of Rashíd and Ibn Batuta, Elly of the *Carta Catalana* (which marks it as a Christian city), and Helly or Hellim of *Conti*, who is, as far as I know, the last author who mentions a city or country of this name. We have perhaps another trace of *Eli* or *Hili* in the *Elima* of the Ravenna Geographer, which he puts in juxtaposition with *Nilcinna*. (*Berlin* ed., 1860, p. 42.) The name has continued to attach itself to a remarkable isolated or partially isolated mountain and promontory on the coast, first in the forms of Cavo de Eli (Fra Mauro), Monte d'Ili (Fra Paolino), Monte de Lin (DEB), Monte di Li (P. Vincenzo), and then in the corruption Mount Delly, or, as Rennell has it, Dilla. The name was also, perhaps, preserved in the RAMDILLY of Rennell, a fort on the same river as Nileshwaram, but lower in its course, which, before debouching near the north side of the mountain, runs parallel to the coast for ten or twelve miles. There is also a fort of Deela mentioned by P. Vincenzo and Rennell, immediately *north* of Nileshwaram. But all these features and names have disappeared from our recent maps, thanks, probably, to the Atlas of India, in which, if I am not mistaken, Mount Delly even has no place. However correct may be the trigonometrical skeleton of those sheets of that publication which represent the coast in question, I think no one can use them for topographical studies of this kind without sore misgivings as to the filling in of details. The *mountain* is mentioned by Abulfeda as "a great hill projecting into the sea, visible to voyagers a long way off, and known to them as Rás Haili," but he does not speak of the city or country. Barbosa says "Monte D'Ely stands in the low country close by the shore, a very lofty and round mountain, which serves as a beacon and point of departure for all the ships of Moors and Gentiles that navigate the Indian sea. Many springs run down from it, which serve to water shipping. It has also much wood, including a great deal of wild cinnamon" (BL). Marco Polo [see Yule-Cordier's ed., ii, pp. 385, 386*n*.] calls Ely an independent kingdom, 300 miles west of Comari (C. Comorin); it had no harbour but such as its river afforded; the king was rich, but had not many people; the natives practised piracy on such ships as were driven in by stress of weather; the ships of Manzi (S. China) traded thither, but expedited their lading on account of the insufficiency of the ports Ibn Batuta speaks of Hili as a large city on a great estuary, frequented by large ships, and as one of the three (four) ports of Malabar which the Chinese junks visited. Pauthier observes in his *Marco Polo,* "Ely est nomée par Ptolemée 'Αλόη." But the Aloe of Ptolemy is an inland city, which must make the identification very questionable. If Nileshweram be Nelcynda, then probably we have a trace of Ely in the ELA*bacare* of the Periplus. But the passage seems defective (see Hudson, i, 33).

Mount Delly is mentioned by several authors as in their time the solitary habitat of the true cardamom. Can there be a connexion between the name Hili, Ely, and the terms Elachi, Ela, and Hil (the form in Gujarat and the Deccan according to Linschoten) by which the cardamom is known in India? ["The correct name is Mount d'Eli (the Monte d'Ely of the Portuguese), from the ancient Malabar State of Ely or Heli, belonging to the Kolattiri Rājās, one of whose seats is near the northern slopes of the hill." 885 feet in height. *Gaz. India.*]

Maranel, a very old place, peopled with Moors, Gentoos, and Jews, speaking the country language, who have dwelt there for a very long time (BL), Marabia (DEB, P. Vincenzo). The Heribalca of (s) appears to be the same place, but the name looks corrupt. It is probable that the *balca* (for Balea) belongs to the next name, and then the *Heri* may be a trace of the lost *Hilí*. [See *Marco Polo*, II, p. 387.]

Balaerpatam, where the King of Cananor resided and had a fortress (BL), Bolepatam (DEB), Patanam (s, but, if the conjecture under the last head be correct, *Balea*patanam), BALEAPATNA of Rennell. Fra Paolino will have it to be the Balipatna of Ptolemy, and the Palaepatma of the Periplus. It would seem, however, that the ancient port must be sought much further north. (An English Factory in the seventeenth century.) [Valya-pattanam of Buchanan, ii, p. 555?]

CANANOR (B, DEB, S). Export trade to Cambay, Hormuz, Coulon, Dabul, Ceylon, Maldives, etc. Many merchants and infinity of shipping (B). A great and fine city, of great trade; every year two hundred ships of different countries took cargoes here (Varthema). Probably the Jurfattan of Ibn Batuta three parasangs from Manjarur (and therefore the Jarabattan of Edrisi, though misplaced by him, and perhaps the Harrypatan, for Jaripatan, of Firishta in Briggs, iv, 532), the residence of the King called *Kowíl*, one of the most powerful in Malabar, who possessed many ships trading to Aden, Hormuz, etc. The identification is confirmed by the fact that the Rajas of Cananor were really called *Kola-tiri* and their kingdom *Kola-nada* (Fra Paolino, pp. 90–1). In the time of C. Federici it had become "a little city," but one from which were exported the whole supply of cardamoms, with a good deal of pepper, ginger, areca, betel, coco-nuts, molasses, etc. [Canura, see Buchanan, ii, p. 553.]

Tarmapatam (B, S), Tramapatam (DEB), Tremopatam (BL), Tromapatam (Varth.), DHARMAPATAM; Darmaftun (for Darmafattan) of Rowlandson's *Tohfut-ul-Mujahideen* (p. 52). A great city of Moors who are very rich merchants and have many great ships; many handsome mosques (BL). Probably the Darapattan of Firishta (U.S.) and the Dehfattan of IB, which he represents as a great town with gardens, etc., on an estuary, under the same king as Jurfattan.

Terivagante (B), Firamuingate (BL), Tirigath (P. Vincenzo); TELLICHERRI? (Eng. Factory in seventeenth century) across the river from the last place (B), as were also Manjaim and Chamobai. ["Tellichery, Mahé, and Durmapatam (Dharma-pattam), form a circle under the management of Mr. Strachy." Buchanan, ii, p. 517.]

Manjaim and Chamobai (BL), Mazeire and Chemobai (B), Maim and Chomba (DEB), Mulariam and Camboa (S), Maino and Somba (P. Vincenzo), both places of the Moors, and of much navigation and trade (B), viz., MAHE and CHOMBE.

Pudripatam (B), Pedirpatam (BL), Pudipatanam (S), Puripatanam (DEB), the Peudifetania and Buffetania of Conti, the Budfattan of IB, and probably the Pudopatana of Cosmas (see preceding note). In Ibn Batuta's time it was under the same prince as Jurfattan (which we have identified with Cananor), was a considerable city on a great estuary, and one of the finest ports on the coast. The inhabitants were then chiefly Brahmins, and there were no Mahomedans. In Barbosa's time again it is still a place of much sea trade, but is become "a place of Moors." The name is not found in modern maps, but it must have been near the WADDAKARRE of Keith Johnston's.

Tircori (B), Tericori (S); TIKODI; Corri of Rennell?

Panderani (B), Colam Pandarani (S), Pandarane (DEB and Varthema), Pandanare (BL), Fandaraina (Edrisi and IB), Fenderena (Fra Mauro), Fundreeah of Rowlandson (u.s., p. 51), Fundarene of Emmanuel King of Portugal (in a letter quoted in Humboldt's *Exam. Critique*, v. 101), Fantalaina of the Chinese under the Mongals (Pauthier's *Polo*, p. 532) Bandinana (for Bandirana) of Abdulrazzak, Banderana of Balthazar Spinger (*Iter Indicum*, 1507, in *Voyage Littéraire* de deux Bénedictins, 1724, p. 364), Flandrina of Odoric (*supra*, II, p. 133). A great and fine place with gardens, etc., and many Mahomedans, where such Chinese junks as stayed over the monsoon in Malabar were wont to lie (IB). A place entirely of Moors, and having many ships (B). But then in decay, for Varthema calls it "a poor enough place, and having no port." Opposite, at about three leagues distance, was an uninhabited island. This must have been the Sacrifice Rock of the maps. The place itself is not mentioned, to my knowledge, after Barbosa's time.

Coulete (DEB), Coulandi (P. Vincenzo), Coilandy (Rennell); KOILANDI. [Coilandy of Buchanan, ii, p. 515.]

Capucar (B), Capocar (S), Capocate (DEB), Capucate (BL and P. Vincenzo), Capogatto, where there was a fine palace in the old style (Varthema). It has disappeared from our maps.

CALICUT (B, S, DEB), Cholochut of Fra Mauro, Kálikút, one of the great ports frequented by the Chinese junks, and the seat of the Samuri King (IB). From Spinger, quoted above, we learn that the Venetian merchants up to 1507 continued to frequent Calicut for the purchase of spices to be carried by the Red Sea, though the competition of Portuguese and *Germans* by the Cape was beginning to tell heavily against them. ["The proper name of the place is Colicodu," or the cock-crowing. Buchanan, ii, p. 474.]

Chiliate (BL), Chalia or Calia (S), Chale (DEB and Linschoten), Ciali (P. Vincenzo), Shaliyat (Abulfeda and IB). Ibn Batuta stopped here some time and speaks of the stuffs made there which bore the name of the place. This stuff was probably *shali*, the name still given in India to a soft twilled cotton, generally of a dark red colour. The Portuguese had a fort at Shalia.

Beypúr, [for some years] the terminus of the Madras Railway

[on the west coast], is not mentioned by any of the old travellers that I know of, till Hamilton (about 1700). Tippu Sultan tried to make a great port of it. (See Fra Paolino, p. 87.)

Paremporam (s), Purpurangari (B), Propriamguari (BL), Parangale (DEB), Berengari (P. Vincenzo); PEREPEN ANGARRY of some maps, Perpenagarde of Rennell.

Paravanor (B), Parananor (BL); Parone of Rennell?

Ytanor (B), Banor (BL), Tanor (s and DEB), TANORE or Tannúr. These two places had great trade and were the residence of great merchants (B). This was an ancient city with many Christian inhabitants, and the seat of an independent Raja, but in the end of last century had become a poor village.

Panamè (B), Panane (s and DEB), PONANI. Many rich merchants owning many ships; the place paid the King of Calicut a large revenue from its customs (B). (French and English Factories, seventeenth century.)

Beliamcor (s), Baleancor (DEB), BALLIANGOT of Rennell, and probably the Meliancota or Maliancora of Conti, "quod nomen magnam urbem apud eos designat, viii milliaribus patens."

Chatua (BL and DEB), Catua (B), Chetua (s), Chitwa (Rennell), Cettuva (F. Paolino); CHAITWA.

PALUR mentioned here by P. Vincenzo and F. Paolino. I do not know if this is Parúr, mentioned by Claudius Buchanan as the site of the oldest church in Malabar; but it is probably the Paliuria of Conti.

Aykotta, at the mouth of the river of Cranganor, was pointed out by tradition of the native Christians as the place where St. Thomas first set foot in India.

CRANGANOR (BL, S, DEB), Crangalor (B), said to be properly Kodangulor; Carangollor of P. Alvárez, where dwelt Christians, Moors, Jews and Cafirs, the Shikali of Abulfeda, Cyngilin of Odoric, etc. (*v. supra*, II, p. 133); according to some accounts one of the oldest royal cities in Malabar, one of the greatest centres of trade and the first place of settlement successively of Jews, Christians, and Mahomedans on this coast. It would seem to have been already in decay as a port in the time of Barbosa, who only says that the King of Cochin drew some duties from it. Sixty years later Federici speaks of it as a small Portuguese fort, a place of little importance. In 1806 Cl. Buchanan says: "There was formerly a town and fort at Cranganore...but both are now in ruins." It continued, however, to be the seat of a R. C. Archbishop.

COCHIN (B, S, DEB), Cochim (BL), Gutschin of Spinger, Cocchi of G. Balbi; properly Kachhí. ["The tradition is that Cochin was originally a small town on the banks of a small river (*Kocchi*, 'little')." *Gaz. India.*] It was not a place of any trade previous to the fourteenth century. In the year 1341 an extraordinary land-flood produced great alterations in the coast at Cochin, and opened a capacious estuary, but the place seems to have continued of no great consideration till the arrival of the Portuguese, though now it is the chief port of Malabar. It is the Cocym of Conti, the first author, as far as I know, who mentions it. The circumstances just stated render it in the highest degree improbable that Cochin should have been the *Cottiara* of the Ancients, as has often been alleged.

Porca (B, DEB), Porqua (BL); PARRAKAD. Formerly the seat of a small principality. Barbosa says the people were fishermen and pirates. Fra Paolino in the last century speaks of it as a very populous city full of merchants, Mahomedan, Christian, and Hindu. (Dutch Factory in seventeenth century.)

Calecoulam (B and DEB), Caicolam (S), KAYAN KULAM. A considerable export of pepper; the residence of many Christians of St. Thomas (B). A very populous town sending produce to Parrakad for shipment (F. Paolino). (Dutch Factory in seventeenth century.)

Coilam (BL), Coulan (B), Colam (S), Colom (G. d'Empoli), Colon (Varthema and Spinger), Kaulam (Abulfeda and IB), Coilon or Collun (M. Polo), Coloen (Conti); Kaulam-Malè of the merchant *Suleiman* (A.D. 851), (see II, p. 129 *supra*); the Columbus, Columbum, Colombo, Colonbi of Jordanus and Marignolli, Pegolotti, *Carta Catalana*, Fra Mauro, etc.; the modern QUILON.

Polo speaks of the Christians, the brazil-wood and ginger, both called *Coiluny* after the place (compare the *gengiovo Colombino* and *verzino Colombino* of Pegolotti and Uzzano), the pepper, and the traffic of ships from China and Arabia. Abulfeda defines its position as at the extreme end of the pepper country towards the east ("at the extremity of the pepper-forest towards the south," says Odoric), whence ships sailed direct to Aden; on a gulf of the sea, in a sandy plain adorned with many gardens; the brazil tree grew there, and the Mahomedans had a fine mosque and square. Ibn Batuta also notices the fine mosque, and says the city was one of the finest in Malabar, with splendid markets, rich merchants, etc. It continued to be an important place to the beginning of the sixteenth century, when Varthema speaks of it as a fine port, and Barbosa as a "very great city," with a very good haven, with many great merchants, Moors, and Gentoos, whose ships traded to all the eastern ports as far as Bengal, Pegu, and the Archipelago. But after this its decay must have been rapid, and in the following century it had sunk into entire insignificance. Throughout the middle ages it appears to have been one of the chief seats of the St. Thomas Christians.

There were several ports between Quilon and Cape Comorin, but my information about them is too defective to carry the list further.

THE TRAVELS OF IBN BATUTA IN CHINA,

PRECEDED BY EXTRACTS RELATING TO BENGAL AND HIS VOYAGE THROUGH THE ARCHIPELAGO.

HAVING sailed at last (from the Maldives) we were at sea for forty-three days, and then we arrived in Bengal. This is a country of great extent, and one in which rice is extremely abundant. Indeed I have seen no region of the earth in which provisions are so plentiful, but the climate is muggy, and people from Khorásán call it *Dúzakhast búr ni'amat*[1], which is as much as to say, *A Hell full of good things!*

He then proceeds to give a number of details as to the cheapness of various commodities, from which we select a few:

Mahomed al Masmúdí the Moor, a worthy man who died in my house at Delhi, had once resided in Bengal. He told me that when he was there with his family, consisting of himself, his wife and a servant, he used to buy a twelvemonth's supply of food for the three of them for eight dirhems. For he bought rice in the husk at the rate of eight dirhems for eighty rothl, Delhi weight; and when he had husked it he still had fifty rothl of rice or ten kantárs[2].

[1] Should be (*Pers.*) *Dúzakh ast pur-i ni'amat!* "*It is* a Hell full of wealth." This is much the way in which Sultan Baber speaks of India, concluding with the summary that "the chief excellence of Hindustan is that it is a large country, and has abundance of gold and silver" (p. 333), and such I fear have been the sentiments of many others from further west.

[2] In a passage omitted he explains that an Indian dínár was equal to eight dirhems of silver (see Note A *preceding*), and that

I have seen a milch cow sold in Bengal for three silver dínárs (the cattle of that country are buffaloes). As for fat fowls, I have seen eight sold for a dirhem, whilst small pigeons were to be had at fifteen for a dirhem. ...A piece of fine cotton cloth of excellent quality, thirty cubits in length, has been sold in my presence for two dínárs (of silver). A beautiful girl of marriageable age I have also seen sold for a dínár of gold, worth two and a half gold dínárs of Barbary. For about the same money I myself bought a young slave girl called Ashura, who was endowed with the most exquisite

a rothl of Delhi was equal to twenty rothl of Barbary. The editors in a note on a previous passage say that a rothl and a half of Barbary was equal to a kilogramme, which (taken exactly) would make the Delhi rothl of that day equal to 28·78 *lbs. avoirdupois.* In another place (ii, 74) he applies the more appropriate term *mann* (or *maund,* as in Anglo-India) to the Delhi weight, and says it was equal to twenty-five rothl of Egypt. The former calculation is corroborated with an exactness which must be partly fortuitous by a deduction from a statement in the *Masālak-al-Absār.* According to this work the current weights of Delhi were the *sir,* and the *mann* of forty *sirs,* precisely the terms and rates now current in Hindustan, but with different values. For the *sir* it is said was equal to seventy *mithkáls.* According to Amari the mithkal is 4·665 *grammes,* a datum which gives the *sir* = ·72 *lb.,* and the *mann* = 28·80 *lbs.* The modern "Indian maund" is a little over 82 lbs., and all the local maunds in the Bengal Presidency at this day approximate to that. We have seen (Note A, p. 58 *supra*) that the dínár probably represents the rupee. The quantity of unhusked rice purchased for the rupee in Ibn Batuta's time would therefore be about 2,300 lbs., equal to 28 modern maunds, about nine times as much for the money as I can remember ever to have heard of in our own time.

Mr. Thomas in one of his pamphlets referred to above (*Coins of the Patan Sultans,* etc., p. 137) gives the maund of that day as consisting of forty sirs of twenty-four tolas each. Taking these tolas even at the present rate of 180 grains (and they were probably less, see *Initial Coinage of Bengal,* p. 10) this would give the maund of that day as equivalent to 24·680 lbs., instead of 28·8 as deduced from the data quoted here.

With regard to Bengal cheapness I may add that Hamilton, writing at the end of the seventeenth century, says that an acquaintance of his bought at Sundiva (an island near Chittagong) 580 lbs. of rice for a rupee, eight geese for the same money, and sixty good tame poultry for the same. (*New Account of the East Indies,* ed. 1744, ii, 23.)

beauty. And one of my comrades bought a pretty little slave, called Lúlú (*Pearl*), for two golden dínárs[1].

The first city of Bengal which we entered was called SADKÁWÁN, a big place on the shore of the Great Sea[2]. The river GANGES, to which the Hindus go on pilgrimage, and the river JUN[3] unite in that neighbourhood before

[1] [Marco Polo writes: "The people have oxen as tall as elephants, but not so big. They live on flesh and milk and rice. They grow cotton, in which they drive a great trade, and also spices such as spikenard, galingale, ginger, sugar, and many other sorts. And the people of India also come in search of the eunuchs that I mentioned, and of slaves, male and female, of which there are great numbers, taken from other provinces with which those of the country are at war; and these eunuchs and slaves are sold to the Indian and other merchants who carry them thence for sale about the world." (*Marco Polo*, ii, p. 115 and note.)]

[2] Both Chatgánw (or Chittagong) and Satgánw (on the Húgli, some twenty-five to twenty-eight miles above Calcutta) were important havens when the Portuguese arrived in India, and the name here might, from the pen of an Arab, represent either of them. But Chittagong only of the two is near the shore of the ocean, and we know moreover that it was in this part of Bengal that Fakhruddín set up his authority. Hence Ibn Batuta must have landed at Chittagong. [The District of Chittagong "was probably first conquered by the Muhammedans during the period of Afghán supremacy in Bengal, between the thirteenth and sixteenth centuries. The Portuguese historian, Faria de Souza, states that in 1538, the Viceroy of Goa despatched an envoy to the Afghán King of Bengal, who landed at Chittagong, and proceeded thence to the capital at Gaur." (*Gazetteer of India*.)]

[Yule (*Hobson-Jobson*, s.v. *Chittagong*) identifies Sadkáwán or Sudkāwān with Chittagong, but this is doubtful; we read in the *Ayeen Akbery* (translated by F. Gladwin, ii, 1800, *Soobah of Bengal*, p. 11): "Satgong. There are two emporiums, a mile distant from each other; one called Satgong, and the other Hoogly, with its dependencies; both of which are in the possession of the Europeans. Satgong is famous for pomegranates." Sātgāon, to-day a ruined town in Hooghly District, "was the mercantile capital of Bengal from the days of Hindu rule until the foundation of Hooghly by the Portuguese. In 1632, when Hooghly was declared a royal port, all the public offices were withdrawn from Sātgāon, which rapidly fell into ruins." (*Imp. Gaz. India*.) The pilgrim Yi tsing arrived in Eastern India at Tan-mouo-li-ti (Tāmraliptī) which Chavannes, p. 71, identifies, like J. Fergusson (*J. R. As. Soc.*, N.S., vi, 1873, pp. 243 seq.), with Sātgāon. "The Gung, says the *Ayeen Akbery*, ii, p. 5, after having divided into a thousand channels, joins the sea at Satagong." See G. Ferrand, *Textes relat. à l'Ext. Orient*, ii, p. 434 *n.* Herr v. Mžik is in favour of Chittagong.]

[3] *Jún* is the name which our traveller applies to the Jumna. But it is difficult to suppose that even Ibn Batuta's loose geography

falling into the sea. The people of Bengal maintain a number of vessels on the river, with which they engage in war against the inhabitants of LAKHNAOTI[1]. The King

could conceive of the Jumna, whose banks he had frequented for eight years, as joining the Ganges *near the sea*. That now main branch of the Brahmaputra which flows into the Ganges near Jafargunge is called the *Janai*, and I have heard it called by natives *Jumna*, though this I supposed to be an accidental blunder. Whatever confusion existed in our traveller's mind, I suppose that it was the junction of the Ganges and Brahmaputra of which he had heard.

[1] *Lakhnaoti* is the same as Gaur, long the capital of the Mahomedan governors and sultans in Bengal, the remains of which are scattered over an extensive site near Maldah. Firishta distinguishes the three provinces into which Bengal was divided at this time as Lakhnaoti, Sunárganw, and Chatgánw (Briggs, i, 423). It would seem that by *Bengal* Ibn Batuta means only the two latter. The last, as appears from a quotation by Mr. Thomas (*Initial Coinage*, p. 65), should be *Satganw*, a much more probable division. This has been loosely indicated in the Sketch Map to Ibn Batuta's Bengal Travels. [Lakhnaoti is a corruption of Lakshmanáwati, which seems to have been the ancient name of this city. "The ascertained conquest of Gaur begins with its conquest in 1204 A.D. by the Mohammedans, who retained it as the chief seat of their power in Bengal for more than three centuries.... When the Afghán kings of Bengal established their independence, they transferred the seat of government to Panduah, a Hindu outpost of Gaur, also in Maldah district.... Panduah was soon afterwards deserted, and the royal residence re-transferred to Gaur, which continued, under the name of Janatábád, to be the capital of Bengal so long as its Muhammedan kings retained their independence." (Hunter, *Gazetteer of India*.) Gaur was sacked by Sher Sháh and his Afgháns in 1537.] ["In 1199 Muhammad Bakhtiyár Khiljí was appointed to lead the first Musalmán invasion into Bengal. The Muhammedan conquest of Behar dates from 1200, and the new power speedily spread southwards into the Delta. From about this date until 1336, Bengal was ruled by governors appointed by the Muhammedan Emperors in the North. From 1336 to 1539, its Musulmán governors asserted a precarious independence, and arrogated the position of sovereigns on their own account." (*Gazetteer of India*.)] [*Gaur*, or, more commonly, *Gour*, the name of a medieval city in Bengal, of which the scattered remains cover a large area in the district of Maldah, commencing not far south of the modern civil station of that name. The name Gaur is a form of the ancient *Gauḍa* (meaning the country "of sugar"), a term which was applied to a large part of modern Bengal, and specifically to that part in which these remains lie.... The most eminent [King] of the [last dynasty, that of the Senas, or of the Vaidyas, eleventh century], by name Lakshmanasena, who flourished at the end of the century...is said by tradition to have founded the royal city in Gauḍa which in later days reverted to a form of this

of Bengal was the Sultan Fakhruddín, surnamed Fakhrah, a prince of distinction who was fond of foreigners, especially of *Fakirs* and *Súfís.*

The traveller then recapitulates the hands through which the sceptre of Bengal had passed from the time of the Sultan Nasiruddín [1323–6] (the Bakarra Khan of Elphinstone's *History*), son of Balaban King of Delhi. After it had been held successively by two sons of Nasiruddín, the latter of these was attacked and killed by Mahomed Tughlak[1].

Mahomed then named as governor of Bengal a brother-in-law of his own, who was murdered by the troops. Upon this Ali Sháh, who was then at Lakhnaoti, seized the kingdom of Bengal. When Fakhruddín saw that the royal authority had thus passed from the family of the Sultan Nasiruddín, whose descendant he was, he raised a revolt in Sadkáwán and Bengal, and declared himself independent. The hostility between him and Ali Sháh was very bitter. When the winter came, bringing rain and mud, Fakhruddín would make an attack upon the Lakhnaoti country by the river, on which he could muster great strength. But when the dry season returned, Ali Sháh would come down upon Bengal by land, his force that way being predominant[2].

* * * * *

ancient name (Gaur), but which the founder called after his own name *Lakshmanavati*, or as it sounded in the popular speech *Lakhnaoti*....The first specific notice of the city of Gaur, from actual knowledge, is contained in the Persian history called *Tabaqât-i-Násiri*. The author, Minháj-i-Saráj, visited Lakhnaoti in 1243. H. Yule in *Encycl. Britannica*.]

[1] The second of these princes, Ghaiassuddín Bahádur Búrah, is entirely omitted by Firishta, but the fact of his reign has been established by a coin and other evidence, in corroboration of Ibn Batuta (Defr. and Sang. Preface to vol. iii, p. xxv). Some notes of mine from Stewart's *History of Bengal* appear to show that the reign of Bahádur Sháh is related in that work.

[2] These events are thus related by Stewart from Firishta and other Persian authorities:

Mahomed Tughlak soon after his succession appointed Kadir Khan to the government of Lakhnaoti, and confirmed Bairam

When I entered Sadkáwán I did not visit the Sultan, nor did I hold any personal communication with him, because he was in revolt against the Emperor of India, and I feared the consequences if I acted otherwise.

Khan in that of Sunárganw. These two chiefs governed their respective territories for some fourteen years with much equity. In 1338 Bairam Khan died at Sunárganw at the time when Sultan Mahomed was busy with the transfer of his capital to Daulatābād. Fakhruddín, the armour bearer of Bairam Khan, took the opportunity not only to assume the government, but to declare himself independent under the title of Sultan Sikandar. The Emperor ordered his expulsion by Kadir Khan, who marched against the rebel from Lakhnaoti, defeated him, and took possession of Sunárganw. There was a large sum in the treasury there, which Kadir Khan was preparing to forward to Delhi. Fakhruddín made known to the troops of Kadir Khan, that if they would kill their master and join him, he would distribute the treasure among them. They consented; Kadir Khan was slain, and Fakhruddín again took possession of Sunárganw, where he fixed his capital, proclaiming himself sovereign of Bengal, coining and issuing edicts in his own name. This was in 1340. He then sent an army to seize Lakhnaoti, but it was resisted and defeated by Ali Mubarak, one of the officers of the deceased governor, who, on this success, applied to the emperor for the government, but assumed it without waiting a reply, under the name of Alauddín, marched against Fakhruddín, took him prisoner, and put him to death, after a reign of only two years and five months, in 1342–3. A year and five months later, Ali Mubarak was assassinated by his foster-brother, Iliyas, who took possession of the kingdom under the title of Shamsuddín, and established his capital at Pandua (now a station on the railway between Calcutta and Burdwan, where there are some curious remains of the Mahomedan dynasty). See Stewart's *History of Bengal*, pp. 80–4.

We see from Ibn Batuta, that the date assigned to the death of Fakhruddín by the historians is much too early. For the traveller's visit to Bengal appears to have occurred in the cold weather of 1346–7, so that Fakhruddín was reigning at least four years later than Stewart's authorities represent. The Ali Sháh of Ibn Batuta is no doubt the Ali Mubarak of Stewart. The light thrown by Mr. Thomas on the history of the early sovereigns of Bengal from his numismatic and other researches corrects in various points the authorities (loose in this matter) followed by Stewart. Following the former, we have as the first Sultan mentioned by Ibn Batuta*

1. NASIR-UD-DÍN MAHMUD, called also *Baghrá Khan*, the son of the Emperor Balban. From A.H. 681 (A.D. 1282). It is not known how or when his reign terminated.

2. RUKN-UD-DÍN KAI-KAUS—Supposed doubtfully to be a son of the preceding, being known only from coins dating A.H. 691–5 (A.D. 1292–6).

* Several Governors of Bengal before this had assumed royal titles and declared independence.

Quitting Sadkáwán I went to the mountains of KAMRÚ, which are at the distance of a month's journey. They form an extensive range, bordering on China and also on the country of TIBET, where the musk-antelopes are found. The inhabitants of those regions resemble the Turks [*i.e.* the Tartars] and are capital people to work, so that as a slave one of them is as good as two or three of another race[1].

3. SHAMS-UD-DÍN FIRUZ, son of Násiruddín, reigning at Lakhnaoti, probably from A.H. 702 (A.D. 1302) up to 722–3 (1322–3).

4. SHAHAB-UD-DÍN BUGHRAH SHÁH, son of the preceding, expelled after a brief reign in A.H. 724 (1324), by

5. GHIAS-UD-DÍN BAHADUR SHÁH, surnamed according to Ibn Batuta *Búrah*, "meaning in the language of India *Black*" (?), another son of Shamsuddín. It is a difficulty about this prince that coins of his are found of A.H. 710–12 (possibly, Mr. Thomas thinks, from "originally imperfect die-rendering" for 720–2), and certainly of the latter dates. On the application of Shahabuddín, Tughlak Sháh intervened, and carried Bahádur Búrah captive to Delhi. Mahomed Tughlak on his accession restored him to power, but some years later was displeased with him, and marched an army against him. The Bengal prince was beaten, killed and *skinned*, *circa* 733 (A.D. 1332).

It was on this occasion apparently that Mahomed left *Kadr Khán* in charge of Lakhnaoti, and *Tátár Khan*, surnamed *Báhram Khán*, an adopted son of his father Tughlak Sháh, in charge of Sunárganw. On the death of Báhram Khán (737 or 739),

6. FAKHRUDDÍN MUBARAK his *silah-dar* ("armour bearer") took possession of the government and proclaimed independence. He retained his hold on Sunárganw and its dependencies, as his coins show, till 751 (A.D. 1350). Meanwhile

7. ALI SHÁH, erroneously styled by Stewart's authors (as at p. 85) *Ali Mubarak*, on the death of Kadr Khan (*circa* 742) assumed sovereignty in Western Bengal under the title of *Ala-ud-dín*. After 746 (the last date of his coinage) he was assassinated by Hájji Iliyás.

8. IKHTYYAR-UD-DÍN, *Ghazi Shah*, whose coins show him reigning at Sunárganw 751–3 (A.D. 1350–1), appears to have been a son of Fakhruddín. At the latter date he is displaced by Hájji Iliyás under the name of

9. SHAMS-UD-DÍN ILIYÁS SHÁH. This chief had coined money at Firuzabád (at or near Pandua) as early as 740; about 746–7 (1345–6) he had killed and succeeded 'Alá-uddín in Lakhnaoti, and now he conquered Sunárganw, so that he appears to have ruled all Bengal. His reign extends to the end of 759 (1358). We are not concerned to follow these sovereigns further.

[1] A discussion as to the direction of this excursion to *Kámrú* will be found in Note E at the end of this paper.

My object in going to the hill country of Kamrú was to see a holy personage who lives there, the Shaikh Jalaluddín of Tabriz[1]. This was one of the most eminent of saints, and one of the most singular of men, who had achieved most worthy deeds, and wrought miracles of great note. He was (when I saw him) a very old man, and told me that he had seen the Khalif Mosta'sim Billah the Abasside at Baghdad, and was in that city at the time of his murder[2]. At a later date I heard from the shaikh's disciples of his death at the age of one hundred and fifty years. I was also told that he had fasted for some forty years, breaking his fast only at intervals of ten days, and this only with the milk of a cow that he kept. He used also to remain on his legs all night. The shaikh was a tall thin man, with little hair on his face. The inhabitants of those mountains embraced Islam at his hands, and this was his motive for living among them.

Some of his disciples told me that the day before his death he called them together, and after exhorting them to live in the fear of God, went on to say: "I am assured that, God willing, I shall leave you to-morrow, and as regards you (my disciples) God Himself, the One and Only, will be my successor." Next day, just as he was finishing the noontide prayer, God took his soul during the last prostration. At one side of the cave in which he dwelt they found a grave ready dug, and beside it a winding sheet with spices. They washed his body, wound it in the sheet, prayed over him, and buried him there.

When I was on my way to visit the shaikh, four of

[1] Further on he is styled *Shirázi*, instead of *Tabrizi* (iii, 287).

[2] The Khalif Mosta'sim Billah was put to death by Húlakú, after the capture of Baghdad in 1258, therefore eighty-eight years previous to this visit. [See *Marco Polo*, i, p. 67 *n.*]

his disciples met me at a distance of two days' journey from his place of abode. They told me that the shaikh had said to the fakirs who were with him: "The Traveller from the West is coming; go and meet him," and that they had come to meet me in consequence of this command. Now he knew nothing whatever about me, but the thing had been revealed to him.

I set out with these people to go and see the shaikh, and arrived at the hermitage outside his cave. There was no cultivation near the hermitage, but the people of the country, both Musulman and heathen, used to pay him visits, bringing presents with them, and on these the fakirs and the travellers [who came to see the shaikh] were supported. As for the shaikh himself he had only his cow, with whose milk he broke his fast every ten days, as I have told you. When I went in, he got up, embraced me, and made inquiries about my country and my travels. I told him about these, and then he said: "Thou art indeed the Traveller of the Arabs!" His disciples who were present here added: "And of the Persians also, Master!"—"Of the Persians also," replied he; "treat him then with consideration." So they led me to the hermitage and entertained me for three days.

The day that I entered the shaikh's presence he was wearing an ample mantle of goat's hair which greatly took my fancy, so that I could not help saying to myself "I wish to God that he would give it me!" When I went to take my leave of him he got up, went into a corner of his cave, took off this mantle and made me put it on, as well as a high cap which he took from his head, and then himself put on a coat all covered with patches. The fakirs told me that the shaikh was not in the habit of wearing the dress in question, and that he only put it on at the time of my arrival, saying to them:

"The man of the West will ask for this dress; a Pagan king will take it from him, and give it to our Brother Burhán-uddín of Ságharj to whom it belongs, and for whom it was made!" When the fakirs told me this, my answer was: "I've got the shaikh's blessing now he has put his mantle on me, and I'll take care not to wear it in visiting any king whatever, be he idolater or be he Islamite." So I quitted the shaikh, and a good while afterwards it came to pass that when I was travelling in China I got to the city of Khansá[1]. The crowd about us was so great that my companions got separated from me. Now it so happened that I had on this very dress of which we are speaking, and that in a certain street of the city the wazir was passing with a great following, and his eye lighted on me. He called me to him, took my hand, asked questions about my journey, and did not let me go till we had reached the residence of the sultan[2]. I then wanted to quit him; however he would not let me go, but took me in and introduced me to the prince, who began to ask me questions about the various Musulman sovereigns. Whilst I was answering his questions, his eyes were fixed with admiration on my mantle. "Take it off," said the wazir; and there was no possibility of disobeying. So the sultan took the dress, and ordered them to give me ten robes of honour, a horse saddled and bridled, and a sum of money. I was vexed about it; but then came to my mind the shaikh's saying that a Pagan king would take this dress from me, and I was greatly astonished at its

[1] Quinsai, Cansay, etc., of our European travellers, see II, p. 192, III, pp. 149, 229, etc.

[2] The viceroy, as appears more clearly below. But some of the viceroys under the Mongols seem to have borne the title of Wang or King [for instance, Hien Yang Wang, prince of Hien Yang, title given to the Seyyid Edjell], so that Ibn Batuta may not be altogether wrong in calling him *Sultan*.

being thus fulfilled. The year following I came to the residence of the King of China at Khánbáliq, and betook myself to the Hermitage of the Shaikh Burhán-uddín of Ságharj. I found him engaged in reading, and lo! he had on that very dress! So I began to feel the stuff with my hand. "Why dost thou handle it? Didst ever see it before?" "Yes," quoth I, "'tis the mantle the Sultan of Khansá took from me." "This mantle," replied the shaikh, "was made for me by my brother Jalaluddín, and he wrote to me that it would reach me by the hands of such an one." So he showed me Jalaluddín's letter, which I read, marvelling at the shaikh's prophetic powers. On my telling Burhán-uddín the first part of the story, he observed: "My brother Jalaluddín is above all these prodigies now; he had, indeed, supernatural resources at his disposal, but now he hath past to the mercies of God." "They tell me," he added, "that he used every day to say his morning prayers at Mecca, and that every year he used to accomplish the pilgrimage. For he always disappeared on the two days of Arafat and the feast of the Sacrifices, and no one knew whither[1]."

When I had taken leave of the Shaikh Jalaluddín I proceeded towards the city of HABANK, which is one of the greatest and finest that is anywhere to be found. It is traversed by a river which comes down from the mountains of Kamrú, and which is called the Blue River. By it you can descend to Bengal, and to the Lakhnaoti country. Along the banks of this river there are villages, gardens, and water-wheels to right and left, just as one sees on the banks of the Nile in Egypt. The people

[1] Lady Duff Gordon made acquaintance in Egypt with a very holy shaikh, who, though dwelling on the Nile, was believed by the people to perform his devotions daily at Mecca (quoted in the *Times*, Sept. 15, 1865).

of these villages are idolaters, but under the rule of the Musulmans. The latter take from them the half of their crops, and other exactions besides. We travelled upon this river for fifteen days, always passing between villages and garden lands; it was as if we had been going through a market. You pass boats innumerable, and every boat is furnished with a drum. When two boats meet, the drum on board each is beaten, whilst the boatmen exchange salutations. The Sultan Fakhruddín before-mentioned gave orders that on this river no passage money should be taken from fakirs, and that such of them as had no provision for their journey should be supplied. So when a fakir arrives at a town he gets half a dínár. At the end of fifteen days' voyage, as I have said, we arrived at the city of SUNUR KÁWÁN[1]....

[1] Sunárganw (*Suvarna-gramma*, or Golden Town) has already been mentioned as one of the medieval capitals of Bengal. Coins struck there in 1353 and 1357 are described by Reinaud in *Jour. Asiat.*, iii, 272. It lay a few miles S.E. of Dacca, but I believe its exact site is not recoverable in that region of vast shifting rivers. It appears in Frau Mauro's map as *Sonargauam*, and must have continued at least till the end of the sixteenth century, for it is named as a district town in the *Ayin Akbari*, and retains its place in Blaeu's great Atlas (*Amst.* 1662, vol. x) as *Sornaquam*.

I formerly thought this *Sornagam* must be the CERNOVE of Conti. But the report of a paper on Bengal Coins by Mr. Edward Thomas (*Athen.*, Feb. 3, 1866) informs us that Lakhnaoti (Gaur) was renovated some time in the fourteenth century by the name of SHAHR-I-NAU (New City). Here we have *Cernove*, and still more distinctly the SCIERNO of Fra Mauro. Shahr-i-nau, I find, is also mentioned by Abdul-razzak (*India in the fifteenth cent.*, p. 6). [On Cernove and Shahr-i-nau, see Yule, s.v. *Gaur* in *Encyclop. Britan.* and *supra*, I, p. 124*n*.]

Sunárganw must dispute with Chittagong the claim to be that "city of Bengala" which has so much troubled those interested in Asiatic medieval geography, and respecting which Mr. Badger has an able disquisition in his preface to Varthema. That there ever was a town *properly* so-called, I decline to believe, any more than that there was a city of the Peninsula *properly* called Ma'bar (v. *supra*, III, p. 67), or that Canton was *properly* called Mahachin (II, p. 180); but these examples sufficiently show the practice which applied the name of a country to its chief port. The name becomes a blunder only when found side by side with the proper name as belonging to a distinct place. [Ma Huan at the beginning of the fifteenth century visiting Bengala (Pang-ko-la) anchors at Cheh-

On our arrival there we found a junk which was just going to sail for the country of Java, distant forty days' voyage.

ti-gan (Chittagong) and lands at Sona-urh-kong (Sunárganw). (*J.R.A.S.* 1895, p. 529.) Mr. John Beames, *l.c.*, p. 898, remarks that Cheh-ti-gan corresponds precisely to Chittagong (Chatgánw). At that place a traveller proceeding to the interior would transfer himself from a sea-going vessel to a country boat to go up the Meghna, just as the Chinese pilgrims describe. The distance, 166 miles to Sonārgáon, is also very nearly correct. Sonārgáon, however, is not "Suvarna-gramma, or Golden Town," but Suvarnakāra-grāma, or Goldsmith's Village. The site is not unknown, as Mr. Phillips supposes. It is on the Meghna, about twelve miles east of Dacca. A very interesting account of the ruins and remains at this place by Dr. Wise will be found in the Bengal Asiatic Society's Journal, vol. xliii, p. 82.—Phillips, *J.R.A.S.*, 1896, gives the following description from the Chinese work *Yuen-chien-lei-han*: "Sona-urh-kiang, Sonārgáon, is a walled city, where much trade is carried on; beyond which [no direction given] there is the city of Pan-tu-wa, in which the king of the country [Bengal] resides."] *Bengala* appears as a city in the curious and half obliterated *Portulano Mediceo* of the Laurentian Library (A.D. 1351), and also in the Carta Catalana of 1375. By Fra Mauro *Bengalla* is shown in addition to Sonargauam and *Satgauam* (probably Chittagong). Its position in many later maps, including Blaeu's, has been detailed by Mr. Badger. But I may mention a curious passage in the travels of V. le Blanc, who says he came "au Royaume de Bengale, dont la principalle ville est aussi appellée *Bengale* par les Portugais, et par les autres nations; mais ceux du pais l'appellent Batacouta." He adds that ships ascend the Ganges to it, a distance of twenty miles by water, etc. Sir T. Herbert also speaks of "Bengala, anciently called *Baracura*," etc. (Fr. transl., p. 490). But on these authorities I must remark that Le Blanc is almost worthless, the greater part of his book being a mere concoction, with much pure fiction, whilst Herbert is here to be suspected of borrowing from Le Blanc; and there is reason to believe, I am sorry to say, that the bulk of Sir Thomas's travels *eastward of Persia* is factitious and hashed up from other books. One of the latest atlases containing the city of Bengala is that of *Coronelli* (Venice 1691); and he adds the judicious comment, "*creduta favolosa*." [Geo. Phillips in his Introductory Notice to Ma Huan's account of Bengala writes (*J.R.A.S.*, 1895, p. 528): "I cannot conclude these introductory remarks to my paper without paying a tribute to the late learned geographer, Sir Henry Yule, in the wonderful exactness with which he has elucidated the travels of Ibn Batuta in Bengal in a sketch map given in his work *Cathay, and the way thither*. Nothing clearer could be given to show the Chinese traveller's route to the kingdom of Bengala: thereon is seen marked Chittagong, where the Chinese envoy landed, and the river up which he travelled until he reached Sona-urh-kong, called Sonarcawan by the Arab traveller; the position of Bengala as lying to the westward of Chittagong, and not to the eastward as placed by some

On this junk he took his passage, and after fifteen days they touched at BARAH NAGÁR, where the men had mouths like dogs, whilst the women were extremely beautiful. He describes them as in a very uncivilised state, almost without an apology for clothing, but cultivating bananas, betel-nut, and pawn. Some Mahomedans from Bengal and Java were settled among them. The king of these people came down to see the foreigners, attended by some twenty others, all mounted on elephants. The chief wore a dress of goatskin with the hair on, and coloured silk handkerchiefs round his head, carrying a spear[1].

early geographers, is here clearly defined, and fully agrees with the position given to it by our Chinese traveller."]

["Sonārgaon—Ancient Muhammedan capital of Eastern Bengal...in the Nārāyanganj sub-division of Dacca District,... near the banks of the Meghnā, 15 miles east of Dacca city. Sonārgaon was the residence of the Muhammedan governors of Eastern Bengal from 1351 to 1608, when the capital of the whole province was transferred to Dacca. The only remaining traces of its former grandeur are some ruins in and near the insignificant village of Pānām, about six miles east of Nārāyanganj.... While Sonārgaon was the seat of government, it was a place of considerable importance and was famous for its cloths and muslins; it was the eastern terminus of the grand trunk road made by Sher Shāh." (*Imp. Gaz. India.*)]

[1] Lee takes Barah Nagár for the Nicobar Islands, Dulaurier for the Andamans. With the people of the latter there does not seem to have been intercourse at any time, but the Nicobars might be fairly identified with the place described by our traveller, were it not for the elephants which are so prominent in the picture. It is in the *highest* degree improbable that elephants were ever kept upon these islands. Hence, if this feature be a genuine one, the scene must be referred to the mainland, and probably to some part of the coast of Arakan or Pegu, where the settlements of the wilder races, such as the Khyens of the Arakan Yoma, might have extended down to the sea. Such a position might best be sought in the neighbourhood of the Island Negrais (NAGARIT of the Burmese), where the extremity of the Yoma Range does abut upon the sea. And it is worth noting that the sea off Negrais is called by Caesar Frederic and some other sixteenth century travellers, "the Sea of BARA." The combination of *Bara-Nagarit* is at least worthy of consideration. The coloured handkerchiefs on the head are quite a characteristic of the people in question; I cannot say as much for the goat-skins. ["It is just possible that the term *Barra de Negrais*, which frequently occurs in the old writers (*e.g.* see Balbi, Fitch, and Bocarro) is a misinterpretation of the old name used by Ibn Batuta." *Hobson-Jobson*, s.v. *Negrais, Cape.*]

Dulaurier, however, points out that *Barah Nagár* may represent the Malay *Bárat* "West," and *Nagárá* "City or Country." This

In twenty-five days more they reached the island of Java, as he calls it, but in fact that which we call SUMATRA[1].

It was verdant and beautiful; most of its trees being coco-palms, areca-palms, clove-trees, Indian aloes, jack-

is the more worthy of notice as the crew of the junk were probably Malays, but the interpretation would be quite consistent with the position that I suggest. I take the dog's muzzle to be only a strong way of describing the protruding lips and coarse features of one common type of Indo-Chinese face. The story as regards the beautiful women of these dog-headed men is exactly as Jordanus had heard it (*Fr. Jord.*, p. 44; and compare *Odoric*, II, p. 168). This probably alludes to the fact that among some of these races, and the Burmese may be especially instanced, considerable elegance and refinement of feature is not unfrequently seen among the women; there is one type of face almost

Italian, of which I have seen repeated instances in Burmese *female* faces, never amongst the men. A like story existed amongst the Chinese and Tartars, but in it the men *were* dogs and not dog-faced merely; this story however probably had a similar origin (see King Hethum's *Narr.* in *Journ. As.*, sér. ii, tom. xii, p. 288, and *Plano Carpini*, p. 657). I give an example of the type of male face that I suppose to be alluded to; it represents however two heads of the *Sunda* peasantry in Java, as I have no Burmese heads available. [See *supra*, II, p. 168, and Cordier's *Odoric*, pp. 206–17.] [Marco Polo tells us (ii, p. 309) that the men of the "island of Angamanain have heads like dogs, and teeth and eyes likewise; in fact, in the face they are all just like mastiff dogs." See long note, *Marco Polo*, ii, pp. 309–12.]

[1] The terms *Jawa, Jawi*, appear to have been applied by the Arabs to the islands and productions of the Archipelago generally (Crawf. *Dict. Ind. Islands*, p. 165), but certainly also at times to Sumatra specifically, as by Abulfeda and Marco Polo (*Java Minor*). There is evidence, however, that even in old times of

trees[1], Mangoes, Jámun[2], sweet orange trees, and camphor-canes.

The port which they entered was called SARHA, four miles from the city of SUMATRA or Sumutra, the capital of the king called Al-Malik Al-Zahir, a zealous disciple of Islam, who showed the traveller much hospitality and attention.

Ibn Batuta remained at the Court of Sumatra, where he appears to have found officials and brethren of the law from all parts of the Mahomedan world, for fifteen days, and then asked leave to proceed on his voyage to China,

Hindu influence in the islands Sumatra bore the name of Java or rather *Yava* (see Friedrich in the *Batavian Transactions*, vol. xxvi, p. 77, and *preced.* and *Marco Polo*, ii, p. 294 *n.*). *Javaku* is a term applied to the Malays generally, in the Singhalese Chronicles. See Turnour's *Epitome*, p. 45.

[1] *Shaki and Barki.* For details on which see *Fr. Jord.*, p. 13, and *supra*, III, p. 237. [See Cordier's *Odoric*, pp. 518–19 and *Hobson-Jobson*.] ["Of these fruits are those termed the *Shaki* and *Barki*, the trees of which are high, and their leaves are like the Jawz (or Indian Nut): the fruit grows out from the bottom of the tree, and that which grows nearest to the earth is called the Barki; it is extremely sweet and well flavoured in taste; what grows above is the Shaki. Its fruit resembles that of the great gourd, its rind the skin of an ox (leather?). When it grows yellow in the autumn, they gather and divide it: and in the inside of each is from one to two hundred seeds. Its seed resembles that of a cucumber, and has a stone something like a large bean. When the stone is roasted, it tastes like a dried bean. These, *i.e.* the Shaki and Barki, are the best fruits found in Hindústan." (Lee, *Ibn Batuta*, p. 105.)]

[2] The French editors render this *Jambu*, but the *Jámun* which is meant here is quite another thing. On two former occasions (ii, 191; iii, 128) our traveller describes the fruit as being like an *olive*; which would be as like the Jambu or Rose-apple as a hawk is like a handsaw. The *Jámun*, which is common in Upper India and many other parts of the east, is really very much like an olive in size, colour and form, whilst the *Jambu* is at least as large as a duck's egg, in the different varieties exhibiting various shades of brilliant pink and crimson softening into white.

Erskine, in a note to Baber, notices the same confusion by a former commentator, and the source of it appears to be that the *Jámun* is called by botanists *Eugenia Jambolana*, the Rose-apple *Eugenia Jambu*, from which one must conclude them to be akin, though neither fruits nor trees have any superficial likeness (Baber's *Memoirs*, p. 325). [*See Jamboo* and *Jamoon* in *Hobson-Jobson*.] ["They also have the Jummūn, which is a high tree: the fruit resembles that of the olive, and is black; as does likewise its stone." (Lee, *Ibn Batuta*, p. 105.)]

as the right season had arrived. The king ordered a junk to be got ready, supplied the traveller with all needful stores, and sent one of his own people to accompany him and look after his comfort[1].

After sailing, he says, for one and twenty days along the coasts of the country belonging to Al-Malik Al-Zahir, they arrived at MUL-JAWA[2], a region inhabited by Pagans, which had an extent of some two months' journey, and produced excellent aromatics, especially the aloes-wood of KAKULA[3] and KAMARA, places which were both in that country.

1 Respecting Al-Malik Al-Zahir, son of Malik-al-Sálah, first Mahomedan King of Sumatra, see Dulaurier. The port of Sarha is identified by this scholar with *Jambu Air*, a village of the Batta coast between Pasei and Diamond Point. In that case the city of Sumutra or Samudra, which has given a name to the great Island, cannot have been so far west as Samarlanga (see *supra*, II, p. 149; *Journ. Indian Archip.*, ii, 610; *Journ. As.*, sér. iv, tom. ix, p. 124; *Id.*, tom. xi, p. 94).

2 See in Note F, at the end of the narrative, the editor's reasons for supposing Mul-Jawa to be a continental country on the Gulf of Siam.

3 *Kakula* is mentioned by Edrisi also, as a city towards China, standing upon a river which flowed into the Indian Ocean. Its people, according to that geographer, raised much silk, whence the name of *Kakali* was given to a kind of silk stuff (Jaubert's *Edrisi*, i, 185). [We shall remark that cardamome = قَاقُلَّة *qaqolla.*] [Van der Lith places Qaqola at Sumatra, north of the Battak Country, *Merveilles de l'Inde*, pp. 237–41 *n*. He says, p. 241, that camphor is one of the products of Qaqola, and of Sumatra, it is not a product of Cambodia nor of Java, therefore one must admit that Ibn Batuta saw aloes wood at Qaqola imported from Khmer. The notes of Van der Lith are generally poor for a geographer. Pelliot thinks that the *Ko kou lo* of Kia Tan is probably identical with the Qaqola of Ibn Batuta, and that it is situated on the west coast of the Malay Peninsula and not on the east coast as suggested by Hirth and Rockhill. *T'oung pao*, July, 1912, p. 455.]

The position of *Kumára* or *Komar*, the place from which the Kumari aloes came, has been inextricably confused by the Arabian geographers, for whilst some applications of the name point distinctly to the region of Cape *Comorin*, other authorities as well as Ibn Batuta place it in the vicinity of the Archipelago, and others again appear to confound it with *Kamrú* or Assam. Mr Lane considers Sindbad's Komari to have been on one or other shore of the Gulf of Siam, and this quite agrees with the view taken by the editor of the position of Mul-Jawa. Abulfeda also places Komar to the west of *Sanf* or Champa, with a short day's voyage between the countries. If his Sanf, as is probable, includes Cambodia, this also would indicate the northern part of the Malay Peninsula.

The port which they entered was that of Kakula, a fine city with a wall of hewn stone wide enough to admit the passage of three elephants abreast. There were war junks in the harbour equipped for piratical cruising, and also to enforce the tolls which were exacted from foreign vessels. The traveller saw elephants coming into the town loaded with aloes-wood, for the article was so common as to be popularly used for fuel. Elephants were also employed for all kinds of purposes, whether for personal use or for the carriage of goods; everybody kept them, and everybody rode upon them.

The traveller was presented to the Pagan king, in whose presence he witnessed an extraordinary act of self-immolation[1], and was entertained at the royal expense for three days, after which he proceeded on his voyage.

But in connexion with Mul-Jawa, where there was a market for the productions of the Archipelago, he takes occasion to state "what he knew of these from actual observation, and after verifying that which he had heard," and these statements it is well to quote at length, as throwing light on some of our author's qualifications as a traveller.

On Incense.

The incense tree is small, and at most does not exceed a man's height. Its branches resemble those of a thistle or artichoke; its leaves are small and narrow; sometimes they drop and leave the tree bare. The incense is a resinous substance found in the branches of the tree. There is more of this in the Musulman countries than in those of the Infidels[2].

[1] See *Fr. Jordanus*, p. 33 *note*.

[2] It is *Benzoin* of which he speaks here under the name of *Luban*, i.e. *Olibanum* or incense. The resin is derived from the *Styrax Benzoin* by wounding the bark. After ten or twelve years produce the tree is cut down, and a very inferior article is obtained by scraping the bark. It is imported in large white masses, resembling white marble in fracture. The plant which, as he says, is of moderate size, is cultivated chiefly in the Batta country of Sumatra, not far from the dominions of his friend Malik-al-Zahir; hence probably his reference to the country of

On Camphor.

As for the trees which furnish camphor they are canes like those of our countries; the only difference being, that in the former the joint or tube between the knots is longer and thicker. The camphor is found on the inside of each joint, so that when the cane is broken you see within the joint a similar joint of camphor. The surprising thing about it is that the camphor does not form in these canes till after some animal has been sacrificed at the root. Till that be done there is no camphor. The best, which is called in the country *Al-Hardálah*, viz., that which has reached the highest degree of congelation[1], and a drachm dose of which will kill a man by freezing his breath, is taken from a cane beside which a human victim has been sacrificed[2]. Young elephants may, however, be substituted with good effect for the human victim[3].

the Musulmans (Crawf., *Dict. Ind. Islands*; Macculloch's *Comm. Dict.*). The word *Al-Arshak* or *Harshaf*, which Defrémery translates "thistle or artichoke," is said by Dulaurier to mean "the plant called *Cynara Scolimus*."

[1] ["Is exceedingly cooling," Lee, p. 202.]

[2] ["This is called with them the Khardana; it is that, at the roots of which a man has been sacrificed." (Lee, *Ibn Batuta*, pp. 202–3.)]

[3] Dulaurier quotes an analogous practice in Tong King [from Marini]. [Chau Ju-kua calls benzoin *Ngan-si hiang* and says it comes from San-fo-ts'i; Ngan-si was Parthia, and Hirth and Rockhill, p. 201, consider that Ngan-si "may be held to be identical with Persia." The *Pen-ts'au kang mu* calls benzoin *cho pei lo* read by Hirth and Rockhill *Kiu-pei-lo*, which they think is but a transcription of Sanskrit *khadira* or *kunduru*. Pelliot reads *guggula* instead of *khadira* and comes to the conclusion that Chau Ju-kua means, not the product of Malaysia, but some stuff extracted from *Balsamodendron africanum* (*T'oung pao*, July 1912, p. 480). Chau Ju-kua writes that *Ngan-si hiang* "resembles the edible part of a walnut in shape and colour, but it is not fit to burn as incense; however, it brings out other scents, for which reason there is a demand for it for mixing purposes" (p. 201).] [Linschoten remarks "that benzoin from Sumatra and Java is not so good as that from Siam and Malacca." But this applies probably to the sweet benzoin, *Kin yen hiang*;

On the Indian Aloes-wood.

The Indian aloes is a tree like the oak, excepting that it has a thin bark. Its leaves are precisely like those of the oak, and it produces no fruit. Its trunk does not

cf. Chau Ju-kua, pp. 198–9, very likely the incense of Ibn Batuta. Benzoin was known to the Arabs under the name of Java incense, *luban jawi*, from which the Portuguese, according to Engelmann and Dozy, *Glossaire des mots espagnols et portugais dérivés de l'arabe*, second ed., p. 239, coined the word *Benzavi*, *Benzoin*. See Heyd, ii, pp. 580–1. *Marco Polo*, ii, pp. 396–7 *n*.]

The description here given of the production of camphor has no resemblance to the truth, and I suspect that he may have confounded with camphor either something that he had learned about the *Tabashir* [Chinese, *chu hwang*, *chu hao*] or siliceous concretion found in bamboo-joints, called by Linschoten *Saccar-Mambu* (bamboo-sugar), or *Spodium*, if that be not the same thing. For this last is explained by Cesare Federici to be "a congelation in certain canes," and in the work of Da Uzzano (*supra*, III, p. 142) there is mention several times of *Ispodio di Canna*. (The *Spodium* of Marco Polo is a different substance; as he describes it, a metallic slag.) [طباشير *Thabâshîr* is found on all the coast of India, according to Ali ibn Mohammed quoted by Ibn el-Baïthar, but it is more abundant at Sindapur, in the territory of Heili هيلى where black pepper is found. (*Notices et Ext.*, xxv, p. 399.)]

"The Malay camphor tree *Dipterocarpus Camphora* or *Dryabalanops Camphora* of botanists, is a large forest tree, confined, as far as is known, to a few parts of the islands of Sumatra and Borneo, but in these abundant. The oil, both in a fluid and solid state, is found in the body of the tree where the sap should be" (Crawfurd's *Dict. of Ind. Isl.*). The description in the text is yet more inapplicable to the Chinese camphor, obtained by distillation from the *Cinnamomum Camphora*.

Far nearer the truth is the description of Kazwini the Arabian geographer. He says the camphor is drawn both in a liquid state and in gummy particles from the branches and stem of a tree large enough to shade one hundred men. He had heard that a season of thunder and earthquakes was favourable to the production. Like Marco Polo he speaks of the camphor of *Fansûr* as the best; supposed to be the modern *Bârûs* on the west side of Sumatra (Gildem., pp. 194, 209). [See *Marco Polo*, ii, pp. 302–4; *Hobson-Jobson*; Heyd, pp. 590–5.]

The word *Hardâlah*, which Ibn Batuta applies to a species of camphor, does not seem to be known. I suspect he may have made a still further embroilment, and that what he has got hold of is the Malay *Artâl*, corresponding to the Hindustani *Hartâl*, "orpiment; native sulphuret of arsenic."

[Hirth and Rockhill, p. 194 *n*., derive the Chinese name of camphor which comes from P'o-li, Perak or thereabouts, *ku-pu-p'o-lü* from *kapur* = *ku-pu* and from *p'o lu*. Pelliot (*T'oung pao*,

grow to any great size; its roots are long, and extend far from the tree; in them resides the fragrance or aromatic principle.

In the country of the Mahomedans all trees of aloes-wood are considered property; but in the infidel countries they are generally left uncared for. Among them, however, those which grow at Kákula are cared for, and these give the aloes of the best quality. Such is the case also with those of Kamára, the aloes-wood of which is of high quality. These are sold to the people of Java (Sumatra) in exchange for cloths. There is also a special kind of Kamári aloes which takes an impression like wax. As for that which is called *'Athás*, they cut the roots, and put them under ground for several months. It preserves all its qualities, and is one of the best kinds of aloes[1].

July, 1912) makes the remark that in the pilgrim Yi-tsing's list camphor is in Chinese *p'o lu kao* and in Sanskrit *k'ie-lo-so* and asks if the original is not *karpūrarasa*. Chau Ju-kua writes: "The camphor which forms crystals is called 'plum flower camphor,' because it resembles the plum flower; an inferior quality is called 'gold foot camphor'; broken bits are called 'rice camphor'; when these are mixed up with splinters, it is called 'grey camphor'; after all the camphor has been removed from the wood, it is called 'camphor chips.' Nowadays people break these chips into small bits and mix them with sawdust, which mixture they place in a vessel of porcelain, covered by another vessel, the openings being hermetically closed; when baked in hot ashes, the vapour formed by the mixture condenses and forms lumps, which are called 'collected camphor.'" (Pp. 193–4.)]

[1] According to Crawfurd the tree yielding *Agila*, eagle-wood or aloes-wood, has not been ascertained, but probably belongs to the *Leguminosæ*. There can be no doubt, he adds, that the perfumed wood is a result of disease in the tree, produced by the thickening of its sap into a gum or resin. The name *Aloes* ('Αλόη in *Cosmas*, p. 336) is probably a corruption of the Arabic name with article *Al-'U'd*, "The Wood" (*par excellence*). It has nothing to do with any kind of aloe properly so called. The name *Agila*, which has been modified or erroneously translated into *Aquila*, *Eagle-wood*, *Adler-holz*, etc., is believed to be a corruption of *Aguru*, one of the Sanskrit terms for the article. Both Kákuli and Kumári aloes are mentioned by Avicenna among the good kinds, but not as standing highest. He names as the best the *Mandali*, and the *Hindi Jibali* or Indian mountain aloes; the *Samandúri*; the *Kumári*; the *Sanfi* (from *Champa*); the *Kákuli*; and the Chinese kind termed *Kazmúri*. Gerarde, in his "Herball,"

On the Clove.

The trees that bear cloves grow to a great age and size. They are more numerous in the country of the infidels than in that of the Mahomedans; and they are

speaks of three kinds of lign-aloes as known in England in his time, differing greatly in quality and price. Gützlaff also in our day speaks of three kinds in the markets of Cochin-China.

[Gharu wood or *Ch'ön hiang* ("sinking-incense") is "called in Malay and Javanese *kalambak* or *kalambah*, also *gharu* or *kayu gharu*, gharu wood, a corruption of the Sanskrit *agaru*, which in turn is the original form from which the Portuguese formed the name of *páo d'aguila*." (Hirth and Rockhill, p. 205 *n.*) The pilgrims who visited the celebrated temple of Multan in the region of the Indus brought with them as an offering some eagle-wood called *kamruny* from the place it came from, Kamrun, ancient kingdom of Kamrupa, Western Assam. See Heyd, pp. 581–5.]

[Chau Ju-kua says, p. 204, "Chön-hiang comes from different places. That coming from Chön-la (Cambodia) is the best; the second quality is that of Chan-ch'öng (Tong King), and the poorest qualities are those of San-fo-ts'i and Shö-p'o."]

[It is probable that the first Portuguese who had to do with eagle-wood called it by its Arabic name, *aghāluhy*, or malayālam, *agila*; whence *páo d'aguila*, "aguila wood." It was translated into Latin as *lignum aquilae*, and after into modern languages, as *bois d'aigle*, *eagle-wood*, *adlerholz*, etc. (A. Cabaton, *les Chams*, p. 50.) M. Groeneveldt (*Notes*, pp. 141–2) writes: "*Lignum aloes* is the wood of the *Aquilaria agallocha*, and is chiefly known as *sinking-incense*. The *Pen-ts'au Kang-mu* describes it as follows: '*Sinking incense*, also called *honey-incense*. It comes from the heart and the knots of a tree and sinks in water, from which peculiarity the name *sinking-incense* is derived....In the Description of Annam we find it called *honey-incense*, because it smells like honey.' The same work, as well as the *Nan-fang Ts'au-mu Chuang*, further informs us that this incense was obtained in all countries south of China, by felling the old trees and leaving them to decay, when, after some time, only the heart, the knots, and some other hard parts remained. The product was known under different names, according to its quality or shape, and in addition to the names given above, we find *fowl bones*, *horse-hoofs*, and *green cinnamon*; these latter names, however, are seldom used." H.C., in *Marco Polo*, ii, pp. 271–2 *n.*]

["The fine eagle-wood of Champa is the result of disease in a leguminous tree, *Aloexylon Agallochum* or *cây dó*, whilst an inferior kind, though of the same aromatic properties, is derived from a tree of an entirely different order, *Aquilaria Agallocha*, and is found as far north as Silhet." *Marco Polo*, ii, p. 272 *n.*]

The term *'Athás*, according to Dulaurier, is not known elsewhere in this application; the word in Arabic means *sneezing*; perhaps it indicates an effect, like the Scotch *sneeshin* for snuff? (See Gildemeister, pp. 64–7; *J. R. G. S.*, xix, 102; Gerarde, p. 1623; Maltebrun in his Trans. of Barrow's *Cochin China*, ii, 351; Varthema's *Travels* with Mr. Badger's notes.)

in such profusion that they are not regarded as property. What is imported into our country consists of the wood (or twigs)[1]; what the people of our countries call the *Flower of Clove* consists of those parts of the flowers which fall, and which are like the flowers of the orange tree. The fruit of the clove is the nutmeg, which we know as the *sweet nut*. The flower which forms on it is the mace. And this is what I have seen with my own eyes[2].

[1] ["That part of it which is taken into different countries is the *idan* (wood)." (Lee, *Ibn Batuta*, p. 203.)]

[2] And yet it is thick with misstatements. The legend that cinnamon is the bark, the clove the flower, and the nutmeg the fruit, of one and the same tree, has come down to our day in Upper India, for I have been asked by a respectable Mahomedan at Delhi if it were not so; and Ibn Batuta is much more likely to have picked up this bit of economic botany in the Delhi Bazar than in the Moluccas as Lassen will have it. Strange to say Dulaurier seems to accept the traveller's statement of the nutmeg being the fruit of the clove tree (*Journ. Asiat.*, sér. iv, tom. ix, p. 248; Lassen, iv, 890). The notion that the clove was the flower of the nutmeg appears also to have prevailed in Europe, for it is contradicted in a work of the sixteenth century (Bodæ, *Comment. in Theophrastum*, p. 992). Mandeville says in this case simply and correctly: "Know well that the nutmeg bears the maces, for right as the hazel hath a husk in which the nut is inclosed till it be ripe, so it is of the nutmeg and the maces" (p. 233). [Clove is the fruit of *Eugenia caryophyllata*.]

What our author says however about the clove imported into the west consisting of the wood or branches is curious. A marginal note on the MS. translated by Lee observes: "This is perhaps what physicians call *Kirfat-ul-Karanful* or bark of clove." However that may be, no doubt it was the same as the *Fusti di Gherofani* of Pegolotti and Uzzano (see note *supra*, III, p. 168). The term *flower of clove* cited in the text is also used by those writers.

I may note here that the *Diction. de Trévoux*, under the words *Noix Giroflée* or *Noix de Madagascar*, describes a nut of that island as *Nux Caryophyllacea*; "La seconde écorce de cet arbre étant séchée ressemble en figure à la canelle, mais elle a le gout du girofle: on l'appelle *Canelle Giroflée*." I have not met with any recent description of this, which would appear to be the *Kirfat-ul-Karanful* just mentioned.

[Chau Ju-kua writes, p. 209: "*Ting hiang* [cloves] come from the countries of Ta-shï and from Shö-p'o. They are called *ting hiang* or 'nail-incense' because they resemble in shape the Chinese character *ting* ('a nail'). They have the property of removing bad smells from the mouth, and high officials at Court put cloves into their mouths when they have to lay matters before the Emperor. The large ones are called *ting hiang mu*, and

After leaving Kakula they sailed for thirty-four days, and then arrived at the Calm or Pacific Sea (*ul Bahr-ul Káhil*), which is of a reddish tint, and in spite of its great extent is disturbed by neither winds nor waves. The boats were brought into play to tow the ship, and the great sweeps of the junk were pulled likewise[1]. They were thirty-seven days in passing this sea, and it was thought an excellent passage, for the time occupied was usually forty or fifty days at least. They now arrived at the country of TAWÁLISI, a name derived, according to Ibn Batuta, from that of its king.

It is very extensive, and the sovereign is the equal of the King of China. He possesses numerous junks with which he makes war upon the Chinese until they sue for peace, and consent to grant him certain concessions. The people are idolaters; their countenances are good, and they bear a strong resemblance to the Turks. They are

this is the same as *ki-shö-hiang*, though some say that *ki-shö-hiang* is the stone of the Persian date." Hirth and Rockhill add, p. 209 *n.*: "In the first part of this work, Chau has stated that cloves were a product of Eastern Java and its dependencies, the same region which produced sandal-wood, in other words the Moluccas. He refers also to the trade in cloves in Ceylon and in Malabar, whither they were brought by foreign traders. (*Fan Shang.*) Our author was, therefore, better informed on this subject than Marco Polo who, though stating in one passage (ii, 254) that they were a product of Java, adds in another (ii, 289) that they grew also on the island of Necuveran (Nicobar Islands). Ibn Batuta, iv, 243, confounded the cinnamon and the nutmeg-tree with cloves. De Candolle, *Origine des plantes cultivées*, 128, thinks that cloves, a product of the *Caryophyllus aromaticus*, Linné, are indigenous to the Molucca Islands."—*Ting hiang* are sometimes called *fowl-tongue incense*, not to be confounded with *fowl-bone incense*, a kind of lignum aloes. Groeneveldt, p. 143.]

[1] Polo mentions the practice of towing the large Chinese ships by their row-boats (iii, 1). ["It is on account of the calm state of this sea, that three other vessels are attached to each of the Chinese junks, by which these junks, together with their own cargoes, are carried forward by oars. Of these there are twenty large ones, which may be compared to the masts of ships. To each oar thirty men are appointed, and stand in two rows. By this means they draw the junks along, being connected by strong ropes like 'cables.'" Lee, *Ibn Batuta*, p. 205.]

usually of a copper complexion, and are very valiant and warlike. The women ride, shoot, and throw the javelin well, and fight in fact just like the men. We cast anchor in one of their ports which is called KAILÚKARI. It is also one of their greatest and finest cities, and the king's son used to reside there. When we had entered the harbour soldiers came down to the beach, and the skipper landed to speak with them. He took a present with him for the king's son; but he was told that the king had assigned him the government of another province, and had set over this city his daughter, called Urdujá[1].

The second day after our arrival in the port of Kailúkari, this princess invited the *Nákhodah* or skipper, the *Karáni* or purser[2], the merchants and persons of note, the *Tindail* or chief of the sailors[3], the *Sipahsalár* or chief

[1] ["The magistrate of this place is a daughter of the King Wahī Ardūjā." Lee, *Ibn Batuta*, p. 206.] [Cf. *supra*, III, p. 192.]

[2] This word *Karáni*, says Dulaurier, which Ibn Batuta translates by *Kátib* or clerk, is probably Persian, but of Mongol origin. The word is still in universal Anglo-Indian use, at least in the Bengal Presidency, as applied to writers in public offices, and especially to men of half-blood, for whom it has become almost a generic title; (vulgo *Cranny*). ["*Cranny*." "In Bengal commonly used for a clerk writing English, and thence vulgarly applied generically to the East Indians, or half-caste class, from among whom English copyists are chiefly recruited. The original is Hind. *karānī*, *kirānī*, which Wilson derives from Skt. *karan*, 'a doer.' *Karana* is also the name of one of the (so-called) mixt castes of the Hindus sprung from a Sudra mother and Vaisya father, or (according to some) from a pure Kshatriya mother by a father of Kshatriya origin. The occupation of the members of this mixt caste is that of writers and accountants." (*Hobson-Jobson*.)]

["*Nacoda*, *Nacoder*, etc., Pers. *nā-khudā* (*navis dominus*), 'a skipper'; the master of a native vessel. (Perhaps the original sense is rather the owner of the ship, going with it as his own supercargo)." (*Hobson-Jobson*.)]

[3] "*Tindail* or chief of the *Rajál*," which Defrémery renders "foot-soldiers," but I have ventured to follow Dulaurier in rendering it chief of the "sailors," both because this seems to be demanded by the context, and because the word *Tindail* is still in use in India, with usual (though not universal) application to a petty officer of native seamen.

["*Tindal*. Malayāl. *taṇḍal*, Telug. *taṇḍelu*, also in Mahr. and other vernaculars *ṭaṇḍel*, *ṭaṇḍail*. The head or commander of a

of the archers, to partake of a banquet which Urdujá had provided for them according to her hospitable custom. The skipper asked me to accompany them, but I declined, for these people are infidels and it is unlawful to partake of their food. So when the guests arrived at the Princess's she said to them: "Is there anyone of your party missing?" The captain replied: "There is but one man absent, the *Bakshi*[1] (or Divine), who does not eat of your dishes." Urdujá rejoined: "Let him be sent for." So a party of her guards came for me, and with them some of the captain's people, who said to me: "Do as the Princess desires."

So I went, and found her seated on her great chair or throne, whilst some of her women were in front of her with papers which they were laying before her. Round about

body of men; but in ordinary specific application a native petty officer of lascars, whether on board ship (boatswain) or in the ordnance department, and sometimes the head of a gang of labourers on public works." (*Hobson-Jobson*.)]

["*Sipahsalár*. A General-in-chief; Pers. *sipāh-sālār*, 'army leader.'" (*Hobson-Jobson*.)]

[1] Defrémery translates *Bakshi* "le Juge," taking *Kazi* as the explanation given by Ibn Batuta [or lawyer, learned man]. But the alternative reading *Fakiah* (Theologian) appears to be more probable. The word *Bakshi* is the Turkish and Persian corruption of *Bhikshu*, the proper Sanskrit term for a Buddhist monk; many of which class came to Persia with Hulákú and his earlier successors, whence the word came to be applied generally as meaning a *literatus*, a scribe, a secretary, and even according to Baber a surgeon. According to Burnes in modern Bokhara it indicates a *bard*. Under the Mahomedan sovereigns of India it came to mean an officer who had charge of registering all that concerned the troops, the assignation of quarters, etc. And hence probably has arisen by a gradual transfer its present meaning in the native army of India, viz., *Paymaster* (Quatremère's *Rashiduddín*, pp. 184–98; see also *supra*, II, p. 250). Quatremère points out the occurrence of the term in the Byzantine historian Pachymeres under the form Μπαξις. Ibn Batuta may have resumed the religious costume which he wore before his appointment to the embassy—indeed he appears to have worn the mantle given him by the hermit Jalaluddín,—and his sanctimonious excuse for not dining with the princess made the application of the term natural. [On *Bakhçhy*, a Buddhist priest, see Cordier's *Odoric*, p. 462, and *Cathay*, *supra*, II, p. 250.]

were elderly ladies, or duennas, who acted as her counsellors, seated below the throne on chairs of sandalwood. The men also were in front of the Princess. The throne was covered with silk, and canopied with silk curtains, being itself made of sandalwood and plated with gold. In the audience hall there were buffets of carved wood, on which were set forth many vessels of gold of all sizes, vases, pitchers, and flagons. The skipper told me that these vessels were filled with a drink compounded with sugar and spice, which these people use after dinner; he said it had an aromatic odour and delicious flavour; that it produced hilarity, sweetened the breath, promoted digestion, etc., etc.

As soon as I had saluted the princess she said to me in the Turkish tongue *Husn misen yakhshi misen* (*Khúsh mísan? Yakhshi mísan?*) which is as much as to say, Are you well? How do you do[1]? and made me sit down beside her. This princess could write the Arabic character well. She said to one of her servants *Dawát wa batak katur*, that is to say, "Bring inkstand and paper." He brought these, and then the princess wrote *Bismillah Arrahmán Arrahím* (In the name of God the merciful and compassionate!) saying to me "What's this?" I replied "*Tanzari nám*" (Tangri nam), which is as much as to say "the name of God"; whereupon she rejoined "*Khushn,*" or "It is well." She then asked from what country I had come, and I told her that I came from India. The princess asked again, "From the Pepper country?" I said "Yes." She proceeded to put many questions to me about India and its vicissitudes, and these I answered. She then went on, "I must positively go to war with

[1] Ibn Batuta had picked up these words on a former occasion when addressed to him by Alauddín Tarmashírín, Khan of Chagatai; but he then says they mean "*Are you well? You are an excellent man!*" (iii, 33).

that country and get possession of it, for its great wealth and great forces attract me." Quoth I, "You had better do so." Then the princess made me a present consisting of dresses, two elephant-loads of rice, two she buffaloes, ten sheep, four rothls of cordial syrup[1], and four *Martabans*, or stout jars[2], filled with ginger, pepper, citron and mango, all prepared with salt as for a sea voyage.

The skipper told me that Urdujá had in her army free women, slave girls, and female captives, who fought just like men; that she was in the habit of making incursions into the territories of her enemies, taking part in battle, and engaging in combat with warriors of repute. He also told me that on one occasion an obstinate battle took place between this princess and one of her enemies; a great number of her soldiers had been slain, and her whole force was on the point of running away, when Urdujá rushed to the front, and forcing her way through the ranks of the combatants till she got at the king himself with whom she was at war, she dealt him a mortal wound, so that he died, and his troops fled. The princess returned

[1] *Jaláb.*

[2] The word *Martaban* is unfamiliar to Dulaurier, who quotes from Father Azár a Maronite, that it means "a casket or vase for keeping medicines and comfits, etc." But the word is obviously used for the great vessels of glazed pottery, called Pegu or Martaban jars from the places where they were purchased, and which retained a wide renown up to the present century. "They make in this place" (Martaban), says Barbosa, "quantities of great porcelain jars, very big, strong, and handsome; there are some of them that will hold two hogsheads of water a piece. They are coated with a black glaze, are in great esteem among the Moors, bearing a high price among them, and they export them from this place with a great deal of benzoin" (*Livro de Duarte Barbosa*, p. 367). Linschoten speaks to the same effect, adding that they were used on the Portuguese Indiamen for storing oil and water. So also du Jarric: "Vasa figlina quæ vulgo *Martabania* dicuntur per Indiam nota sunt....Per orientem omnem, quin et Lusitaniam horum est usus" (Linsch., c. xvii; Jar., iii, pt. ii, p. 389). ["The *martaban* is a small deep jar with an elongated body, which is used by Hindus and Muhammadans to keep pickles and acid articles." (Hallifax, *Mono. of Punjab Pottery*, p. 9.)]

with his head carried on a spear, and the king's family paid a vast sum to redeem it. And when the princess rejoined her father he gave her this city of Kailúkari, which her brother had previously governed. I heard likewise from the same skipper that various sons of kings had sought Urdujá's hand, but she always answered, "I will marry no one but him who shall fight and conquer me!" so they all avoided the trial, for fear of the shame of being beaten by her[1].

We quitted the country of Tawálisi, and after a voyage of seventeen days[2], during which the wind was always favourable, we arrived in CHINA.

This is a vast country; and it abounds in all sorts of good things, fruit, corn, gold and silver; no other country in the world can rival China in that respect. It is traversed by the river which is called *Ab-i-Haiyah,* signifying the Water of Life. It is also called the river SÁRÚ[3], just like the Indian river. Its source is among the mountains near the city of KHÁNBÁLIQ, which are known by the name of *Kuh-i-Búznah* or Monkey Mountains. This river runs through the heart of China, for a distance of six months' journey, reaching at last Sín-ul-Sín[4]. It is bordered throughout with villages, cultivated plains, orchards, and markets, just like the Nile in Egypt; but this country is still more flourishing, and there are on the banks a great number of hydraulic wheels. You find in China a great deal of sugar as good as that of Egypt, better in fact;

[1] On *Tawálisi,* see Note G at the end of the Narrative.

[2] ["Seven," Lee, *Ibn Batuta,* p. 207.]

[3] ["River of Sibar," Lee, p. 207.]

[4] See remarks on Ibn Batuta's notion of the great River of China in the introductory notices. *Sarú* is no doubt, as explained by Defrémery, intended for the Mongol word *Sárú* or *Sári* yellow, a translation of the Chinese Hwang-Ho, whilst the Indian River is that of which he has spoken in previous passages of his book (c. ii and iii, 437) as the *Sarúr* or *Sarú,* viz., the Sarjū, Sarya, or Gogrā.

you find also grapes and plums. I used to think that the plum called *Othmani*, which you get at Damascus, was peerless; but I found how wrong I was when I became acquainted with the plum of China. In this country there is also an excellent water-melon which is like that of Khwárezm and Ispahan. In short all our fruits have their match in China, or rather they are excelled. There is also great store of wheat, and I never anywhere saw it finer or better. One may say just the same of the peas and beans.

Porcelain is made in China nowhere except in the cities of ZAITÚN and SIN-KALÁN. It is made by means of a certain earth got from the mountains of those provinces, which takes fire like charcoal as we shall relate hereafter. The potters add a certain stone which is found in that country; they burn it for three days, and then pour water on it, so that the whole falls to powder, and this they cause to ferment. That which has been in fermentation for a whole month, neither more nor less, gives the best porcelain; that which has not fermented for more than ten days gives one of inferior quality[1]. Porcelain in China is of about the same value as earthenware with us, or even less. 'Tis exported to India and elsewhere, passing from country to country till it reaches us in Morocco. 'Tis certainly the finest of all pottery-ware[2].

[1] ["The best of it, for five and thirty days; that which is inferior, for fifteen, ten, or fewer." Lee, p. 208.]

[2] Marco Polo also mentions the porcelain manufacture in connexion with his account of Zaitún, as being found at Timinguy (according to Pauthier's edition Tyunguy), a city in the neighbourhood. This Pauthier supposes to be *Tek-hua*, a town about sixty miles north of T'swan-chau or Zaitún, where, according to the Imperial geography, vases of white china were anciently manufactured, which enjoyed a great reputation. (*Marc Pol*, p. 532; *Marco Polo*, ii, p. 242 *n.*)

The china-ware of Fu-kien and Canton is now of a very ordinary description, the manufacture of real porcelain being

The cocks and hens of China are very big, bigger in fact than our geese[1]. The hen's egg also there is bigger than our goose eggs; whilst their goose on the other hand is a very small one. I one day bought a hen which I wanted to boil, but one pot would not hold it, and I was obliged to take two! As for the cocks in China they are as big as ostriches! Sometimes one sheds his feathers and then the great red object is a sight to see! The first time in my life that I saw a China cock was in the city of Kaulam. I had at first taken it for an ostrich, and I was looking at it with great wonder, when the owner said to me: "Pooh! there are cocks in China much bigger than that!" and when I got there I found he had said no more than the truth.

The Chinese are infidels and idolaters, and they burn their dead after the manner of Hindus[2]. Their king is a Tartar of the family of Tankíz Khan[3]. In each of their cities a special quarter is assigned to the Mahomedans, where these latter dwell by themselves, and have their mosques for prayer, and for Friday and other services. They are treated with consideration and respect. The flesh of swine and dogs is eaten by the Chinese pagans, and it is sold publicly in their markets. They are generally well-to-do opulent people, but they are not sufficiently particular either in dress or diet. You will see one of their great merchants, the owner of uncountable treasure,

confined to King-te chen in the province of Kiang-si. I have no account of the manufacture, such as enables me to trace the basis of anything here related by Ibn Batuta, but it looks like crude gossip; as if he had heard of the porcelain clay of China, and of the Coal of China, and had, like one of Dickens's illustrious characters, "combined the information." See *Marco Polo*, ii, p. 243 *n*.

[1] See *Odoric*, II, p. 186.

[2] This has already been noticed at III, p. 99, *supra*. Though no longer the practice, we see by Marco Polo and other authors that it was formerly very general in some parts of China.

[3] So Ibn Batuta always calls Chinghiz; I know not why.

going about in a dirty cotton frock[1]. The Chinese taste is entirely for the accumulation of gold and silver plate. They all carry a stick with an iron ferule, on which they lean in walking, and this they call their third leg.

Silk is very plentiful in China, for the worms which produce it attach themselves to certain fruits on which they feed, and require little attention. This is how they come to have silk in such abundance that it is used for clothing even by poor monks and beggars. Indeed, but for the demand among merchants, silk would there have no value at all. Among the Chinese one cotton dress is worth two or three of silk.

They have a custom among them for every merchant to cast into ingots all the gold and silver that he possesses, each of these ingots weighing a hundredweight, more or less, and these he places over the gate of his house. The man who has accumulated five such ingots puts a ring on his finger; he who has ten puts two rings; he who has fifteen is called *Satí*[2], which amounts to the same thing as *Káramí* in Egypt. An ingot is in China called *Barkálah*[3, 4].

[1] "The great sin of the Chinese costume is the paucity of white linen and consequently of washing" (Davis's *Chinese*).

[2] ["He who possesses fifteen such, is named El Sashi; and the piece itself they call a Rakala." (Lee, p. 209.)]

[3] *Pers.* Pargálah, *frustum, segmentum* (Meninski). *Satí*, again, is probably the Indian word *Set*, or *Cheti* as it is called by some old travellers. The *Káramí* merchants were a sort of guild or corporation in Egypt, who appear to have been chiefly occupied in the spice trade. Quatremère gives many quotations mentioning them, but without throwing much light on the subject (see *Not. et Extraits*, xii, 639, and xiv, 214). It is a common story in India, of rich Hindu bankers and the like, that they build gold bricks into the walls of their houses.

The *Masālak-al-Absār* relates that in some of the Indian islands there are men who, when they have succeeded in filling one pot with gold, put a flag on their house-top, and another flag for each succeeding potful. Sometimes, it is said, as many as ten of these flags are seen on one roof. And in Russia, according to Ibn Fozlan, when a man possessed 10,000 dirhems, his wife wore one gold chain, two gold chains for 20,000 dirhems, and so on. (*Not. et Extraits*, xiii, p. 219; *Ibn Fozlan* by Fraehn, p. 5.)

[4] ["Are termed a shat." Lee, p. 209.]

The people of China do not use either gold or silver coin in their commercial dealings. The whole amount of those metals that reaches the country is cast into ingots as I have just said. Their buying and selling is carried on by means of pieces of paper about as big as the palm of the hand, carrying the mark or seal of the Emperor. Twenty-five of these bills are called *bálisht*[1], which is as much as to say with us "*a dínár*[2]." When anyone finds

[1] ["In historical works, such as the *Jahán Kushái*, the *Jami-ut-Tawárikh*, and others, a *bálish* is thus described: 'A *bálish* is 500 *mitkhál* [of silver], made into a long brick with a depression in the middle.'" *Tarikh-i-Rashidí*, p. 256. These ingots are called *Yuen Pao* or *Sycee*.]

[2] I do not understand the text to mean that a *balisht* is precisely worth a *dínár*, but that it is the unit in which sums are reckoned by the Chinese as the dínár is with the Mahomedans. Paper money has been spoken of at III, p. 149, and at II, p. 196 some speculations were ventured on the origin of the term *Balisht* or *Balish*. I have since been led to believe that it must be a corruption of the Latin *follis*.

The common meaning of that word is a *bellows*; but it was used also by late classical writers for a leather money-bag, and afterwards (in some sense) for money itself, "just as to this day the Italians apply the term *purse* to a certain sum of money among the Turks" (Facciolati, Lipsiæ, 1839). Further, the term *follis* was also applied to a certain "pulvillus, sedentibus subjectus, qui non tomento aut plumâ inferciebatur, sed vento inflabatur," or, in short, to an *air-cushion*.

Now we have seen (II, p. 196) that *Balish* was also applied to a kind of cushion, as well as to a sum of money, such as in later days the Turks called a *purse*. This double analogy would be curious enough as a coincidence, even if we could find no clearer trace of connexion between the terms; but there seems ground for tracing such a connexion.

Follis was applied to money in two ways under the Byzantine Emperors.

In its commoner application (φόλλις, φύλλη, etc.) it was a copper coin, of which 288 went to the gold solidus; and in this sense probably had no connexion with the original Latin word. But *follis* was also used as a term for *a certain quantity of gold*, according to one authority the weight of 250 denarii, and was especially applied to a sort of tax imposed on the magnates by Constantine, which varied from two to eight pounds of gold, according to rank and income (see Ducange, *De Inferioris Aevi Numismatibus*, in Didot's ed. of the Dict., vii, pp. 194–5).

If the denarii mentioned here were gold denarii or solidi, then we have the Byzantine FOLLIS = 250 *mithkáls*, just as the BALISH of the Turks and Tartars in later days was = 500 *mithkáls*. The

that notes of this kind in his possession are worn or torn he takes them to a certain public office analogous to the Mint of our country, and there he gets new notes for his old ones. He incurs no expense whatever in doing this, for the people who have the making of these notes are paid by the emperor[1]. The direction of the said public office is entrusted to one of the first *amírs* in China. If a person goes to the market to buy anything with a piece of silver, or even a piece of gold, they won't take it; nor will they pay any attention to him whatever until he has changed his money for *bálisht*; and then he can buy whatever he likes.

All the inhabitants of China and Cathay in place of charcoal make use of a kind of earth which has the consistence and colour of clay in our country[2]. It is transported on elephants, and cut into pieces of the ordinary size of lumps of charcoal with us, and these they burn. This earth burns just like charcoal, and gives even a more powerful heat. When it is reduced to cinders they knead these up into lumps with water, and when dry they serve to cook with a second time. And so they go on till the stuff is entirely consumed. It is with this earth that the Chinese make their porcelain

probability that the latter word is as directly the representative of the former as *Dínár* and *Dirhem* are of the (gold) Denarius and Drachma seems very strong, and probably would not derive any additional support from the *cushions* with which both words have been connected.

Follis, again, in the sense of a copper coin, appears to be the same word as the Arab. *fals*, spoken of at II, p. 196, found also formerly in Spain as the name of a small coin *foluz*. And *follis* also in this sense, through the forms *Follaris* and *Folleralis* which are given in Ducange, is the origin of the *folleri* of Pegolotti (*supra*, III, p. 159).

[1] See a different account at III, p. 98 *supra*, and in M. Polo, ii, pp. 426–30.

[2] ["With respect to the earth they lay up, it is mere tempered clay, like the dry clay with us." (Lee, p. 209.)]

vases, combining a certain stone with it, as I have already related[1].

The people of China of all mankind have the greatest skill and taste in the arts. This is a fact generally admitted; it has been remarked in books by many authors, and has been much dwelt upon[2]. As regards painting, indeed, no nation, whether of Christians or others, can come up to the Chinese; their talent for this art is something quite extraordinary. I may mention among astonishing illustrations of this talent of theirs, what I have witnessed myself, viz., that whenever I have happened to visit one of their cities, and to return to it after awhile, I have always found my own likeness and those of my companions painted on the walls, or exhibited in the bazaars. On one occasion that I visited the Emperor's own city, in going to the imperial palace with my comrades I passed through the bazaar of the painters; we were all dressed after the fashion of Irák. In the evening on leaving the palace I passed again through the same bazaar, and there I saw my own portrait and the portraits of my companions painted on sheets of paper and exposed on the walls. We all stopped to examine the likenesses, and everybody found that of his neighbour to be excellent!

I was told that the Emperor had ordered the painters to take our likenesses, and that they had come to the palace for the purpose whilst we were there. They studied us and painted us without our knowing anything of the

[1] The coal of China is noticed by Marco Polo (i, p. 442), and by Rashíd (*supra*, III, p. 118). According to Pauthier, its use was known before the Christian era.

[2] Already in the tenth century, it was remarked by an Arab author: "The Chinese may be counted among those of God's creatures to whom He hath granted, in the highest degree, skill of hand in drawing and the arts of manufacture" (Reinaud, *Relation*, etc., i, 77).

matter. In fact it is an established custom among the Chinese to take the portrait of any stranger that visits their country. Indeed the thing is carried so far that, if by chance a foreigner commits any action that obliges him to fly from China, they send his portrait into the outlying provinces to assist the search for him, and wherever the original of the portrait is discovered they apprehend him[1].

Whenever a Chinese junk is about to undertake a voyage, it is the custom for the admiral of the port and his secretaries to go on board, and to take note of the number of soldiers, servants, and sailors who are embarked. The ship is not allowed to sail till this form has been complied with. And when the junk returns to China the same officials again visit her, and compare the persons found on board with the numbers entered in their register. If anyone is missing the captain is responsible, and must furnish evidence of the death or desertion of the missing individual, or otherwise account for him. If he cannot, he is arrested and punished.

The captain is then obliged to give a detailed report of all the items of the junk's cargo, be their value great or small. Everybody then goes ashore, and the custom-house officers commence an inspection of what everybody has. If they find anything that has been kept back from their knowledge, the junk and all its cargo is forfeited[2].

[1] A travelling Jew, whom Wood met on his Oxus journey, told him that before strangers are permitted to enter Yarkand, "each individual is strictly examined; their personal appearance is noted down in writing, and if any are suspected, an artist is at hand to take their portraits" (p. 281). This is one of the many cases in which the Chinese have anticipated the devices of modern European civilisation. Just as this was written, I read in the *Times* of the arrest at New York of the murderer Müller by the police provided with his photograph despatched from England.
I here omit a not very relevant interpolation by Ibn Juzai, the Moorish editor.

[2] This is no doubt the practice referred to by Odoric, *supra*, II, p. 132.

This is a kind of oppression that I have seen in no country, infidel or Musulman, except in China. There *was*, indeed, something analogous to it in India; for there, if a man was found with anything smuggled he was condemned to pay eleven times the amount of the duty. The Sultan Mahomed abolished this tyrannical rule when he did away with the duties upon merchandise.

When a Musulman trader arrives in a Chinese city, he is allowed to choose whether he will take up his quarters with one of the merchants of his own faith settled in the country, or will go to an inn[1]. If he prefers to lodge with a merchant, they count all his money and confide it to the merchant of his choice; the latter then takes charge of all expenditure on account of the stranger's wants, but acts with perfect integrity. When the guest wishes to depart his money is again counted, and the host is obliged to make good any deficiencies.

If, however, the foreign trader prefers to go to an inn, his money is made over in deposit to the landlord, who then buys on his account whatever he may require, and if he wishes it procures a slave girl for him. He then establishes him in an apartment opening on the court of the inn, and undertakes the provision of necessaries for both man and woman. I may observe here by the way that young slave girls are very cheap in China; and, indeed, all the Chinese will sell their sons as slaves equally with their daughters, nor is it considered any disgrace to do so. Only, those who are so purchased cannot be forced against their will to go abroad with the purchaser; neither, however, are they hindered if they choose to do so. And if the foreign trader wishes to marry in China he can very easily do so. But as for spending his money

[1] The word is *Fanduk*. See note on *Fondacum*, *supra*, III, p. 229.

in profligate courses that he cannot be allowed to do! For the Chinese say: "We will not have it said in the Musulman countries that their people are stript of their property in China, and that ours is a country full of riotous living and harlotry."

China is the safest as well as the pleasantest of all the regions on the earth for a traveller. You may travel the whole nine months' journey to which the empire extends without the slightest cause for fear, even if you have treasure in your charge. For at every halting place there is a hostelry superintended by an officer who is posted there with a detachment of horse and foot. Every evening after sunset, or rather at nightfall, this officer visits the inn accompanied by his clerk; he takes down the name of every stranger who is going to pass the night there, seals the list, and then closes the inn door upon them. In the morning he comes again with his clerk, calls everybody by name, and marks them off one by one. He then despatches along with the travellers a person whose duty it is to escort them to the next station, and to bring back from the officer in charge there a written acknowledgment of the arrival of all; otherwise this person is held answerable. This is the practice at all the stations in China from Sín-ul-Sín to Khánbáliq. In the inns the traveller finds all needful supplies, especially fowls and geese. But mutton is rare.

To return, however, to the particulars of my voyage, I must tell you that the first Chinese city that I reached after crossing the sea was ZAITÚN[1]. Although *Zaitún*

[1] Were there doubt as to the identity of Zaitún, Abulfeda's notice would settle it. For he tells us expressly that Zaitún is otherwise called *Shanju* (Chin-cheu, the name by which Ts'wan-chau was known to the early Portuguese traders, and by which it still appears in many maps).

[New arguments in favour of Zaitún = Ts'wan-chau and not Chang-chau have been brought forward by P. Greg. Arnáiz and

signifies *olives* in Arabic, there are no olives here any more than elsewhere in India and China; only that is the name of the place. It is a great city, superb indeed, and in it they make damasks of velvet as well as those of satin, which are called from the name of the city *Zaituníah*[1]; they are superior to the stuffs of Khansá and Khánbáliq. The harbour of Zaitún is one of the greatest in the world, —I am wrong: it is *the* greatest! I have seen there about one hundred first-class junks together; as for small ones

Max Van Berchem in a valuable paper on the Arab inscriptions of Ts'wan chau printed in the *T'oung pao*, Dec., 1911. Chang-chau, of a more recent origin than Ts'wan-chau, has no mosque. Arnáiz and Van Berchem give a full description of the mosque of Ts'wan-chau which was built in the year 400 of the Hegira (1009–10 A.D.) and repaired in 710 (1310–11) according to one of its inscriptions, the most ancient of China, since the inscription of the mosque of Canton is dated 751 (Sept., 1350). Arnâiz has fully answered the objections of Geo. Phillips. See *Marco Polo*, ii, pp. 234 *seq.*, and Odoric, II, p. 183.

[M. Gabriel Ferrand, an Arabic friend of mine, says that the word should be spelt *Zitún* and not Zaitún. The Arabs transcribe the Chinese *tze* by *zi*, i.e. *Man tze* = Manzi. Zaitún like the Chinese *Tze t'ung* means an olive, and naturally commended itself better to an Arabian ear than Zītún.]

[1] The words translated after Defrémery as *velvet* and *satin* are *kimkhwâ* and *atalas*. There may be some doubt whether the former word should be rendered *velvet*, as it is the original of the European *cammocca* and the Indian *kinkhwáb*, of which the former seems to have been a damasked silk, and the latter *is* a silk damasked in gold (see III, p. 155 *supra*). The word *Atalas* seems to correspond closely to the Italian *raso*, as it signifies both a *close-shaven face* and a *satin texture*. It has been domesticated in Germany as the word for satin (*Atlass*), and is used also in old English travels. I have a strong suspicion that the term *Zaituniah* in the text is the origin of our word *satin*. The possible derivation from *seta* is obvious. But among the textures of the fifteenth century named in the book of G. Uzzano (*supra*, III, p. 142) we find repeated mention of *Zetani, Zettani vellutati, Zettani broccati tra oro*, etc., which looks very like the transition from *Zaituni* to *satin*, whilst the ordinary word for silk is by the same author always spelt *seta*. The analogous derivation of so many other names of textures from the places whence they were imported may be quoted in support of this, e.g., *Muslin* (Mosul), *Damask* (Damascus), *Cambric* (Cambray), *Arras Diaper* (d'Ypres), *Calico* (Calicut); whilst we know that Genoese merchants traded at Zaitún (*supra*, III, p. 73). I see that F. Johnson's *Dict.* distinguishes in Persian between "*Kamkhá*, Damask silk of one colour," and "*Kimkhá*, Damask silk of different colours."

they were past counting. The harbour is formed by a great estuary which runs inland from the sea until it joins the Great River.

In this, as in every other city of China, every inhabitant has a garden, a field, and his house in the middle of it, exactly as we have it in the city of Segelmessa. It is for this reason that the cities of the Chinese are so extensive. The Mahomedans have a city by themselves.

The day after my arrival at Zaitún[1] I saw there the nobleman who had been in India as ambassador with the presents for the Sultan, who had set out (from Dehli) in company with me, and whose junk had been wrecked. He saluted me, and gave information about me to the chief of the council, who in consequence assigned me quarters in a fine house. I then had visits from the Kazi of the Mahomedans, Tájuddín of Ardebil, a virtuous and generous person; from the Shaikh of Islam, Kamáluddín Abdallah of Ispahan, a very pious man; and from the chief merchants of the place. Among these I will mention only Sharíf-uddín of Tabriz, one of the merchants to whom I ran in debt from my first arrival in India, and the one of my creditors who acted most like a gentleman; he knew the whole Koran by heart, and was a great reader[2]. As these merchants are settled there in a land of unbelievers, of course they are greatly delighted when they see a Musulman come to visit them, and when they can say: "Ah, here comes one from the lands of Islam!" and they give him alms of all that they have, according to the law,

[1] ["On the day of my arrival." Lee, p. 212.]

[2] It is of very great interest to note that all the Mahomedans named by Ibn Batuta are Persian; he has omitted to mention Aḥmad ibn Muḥammad, from Jerusalem?, surnamed the pilgrim Ruku (al dîn?) of Shiraz who built in 1310 the new portico of the mosque. It is the more interesting that the Mahomedans mentioned by Ibn Batuta in other towns of China came from Soghdiana, Mesopotamia, Egypt and Morocco, but not from Persia proper. [See *T'oung pao, l.c.*, p. 716.]

so that the traveller becomes quite rich like one of themselves. Among the eminent shaikhs at Zaitún was Burhan-uddín of Kazerún, who had a hermitage outside of the town. It was to him that the merchants used to pay their offerings for the Shaikh Abu Ishak of Kazerún[1].

When the chief of the council had learned all particulars about me, he wrote to the Ḳán, i.e. the Emperor, to inform him that I had arrived from the King of India. And I begged the chief that whilst we were awaiting the answer he would send some one to conduct me to Sín-ul-Sín, which these people call Sin-Kalán, which is also under the Kán, as I was desirous to visit that part of the country. He consented, and sent one of his people to accompany me. I travelled on the river in a vessel which was much like the war galleys in our country, excepting that the sailors rowed standing and all together amidships, whilst the passengers kept forward and aft. For shade they spread an awning made of a plant of the country resembling flax, but not flax; it was, however, finer than hemp[2].

[1] Kazerún, once a considerable place, now in decay, lies in a valley on the road from Bushire to Shiraz. The Shaikh Abu Ishak of Kazerún was a sort of patron saint of the mariners in the India and China trade, who made vows of offerings to his shrine when in trouble at sea, and agents were employed at the different ports to board the vessels as they entered, and claim the amounts vowed, which generally came to large sums. Applicants to the shrine for charity also used to receive circular notes payable by parties who had vowed. When the recipient of such a note met anyone owing an offering to the shrine he received the amount on presenting his bill endorsed with a discharge. (*Ibn Batuta*, ii, 90–1.)

[2] Perhaps grass-cloth.

["By the beginning of the seventh century the foreign colony at Canton, mostly composed of Persians and Arabs, must have been a numerous one, for Islam seems to have been brought there between 618 and 626. There is even some evidence for believing that the Moslim had also settlements at that time in Ts'wan-chau and Yang-chau; Ts'wan-chau, however, became of importance in their China trade only in the ninth century. By the middle of the eighth century the Mohamedans at Canton—which they called Khanfu,—had become so numerous that in

We travelled on the river for twenty-seven days[1]. Every day a little before noon we used to moor at some village, where we bought what was needful, and performed our midday prayers.

In the evening we stopped at another village, and so on until we arrived at Sin-Kalán[2], which is the city of Sín-ul-Sín. Porcelain is made there, just as at Zaitún, and it is there also that the river called *Ab-i-Haiyáh* (or water-of-life) discharges itself into the sea, at a place which they call the confluence of the seas. Sín-ul-Sín is one of the greatest of cities, and one of those that has the finest of bazaars. One of the largest of these is the porcelain bazaar, and from it china-ware is exported to the other cities of China, to India, and to Yemen.

In the middle of the city you see a superb temple with nine gates; inside of each there is a portico with terraces where the inmates of the building seat themselves. Between the second and third gates there is a place with rooms for occupation by the blind, the infirm or the crippled. These receive food and clothing from pious foundations attached to the temple. Between the other gates there are similar establishments; there is to be

758, when, for some reason which has not come down to us, Arab and Persian pirates sacked and burnt the city and made off to sea with their loot, some 5000 resident foreign traders were killed by them." (Hirth and Rockhill, pp. 14–15.)]

[1] It is very possible that there may be continuous inland navigation from Zaitún to Canton, parallel to the coast, but I cannot ascertain more than that there is such from Fu-chau, and I presume from Ts'wan-chau or Zaitún to Chang-chau. If this does not extend further, his journey "by the river" must have been up the Min river; then, after crossing the mountains into Kiang si, re-embarking and following the Kan-Kiang up to the Mei ling Pass, and so across that to the Pe-Kiang, leading to Canton; the latter part of the route being that followed by Macartney and Amherst on their return journeys, as well as by the authors of many other published narratives.

On Sin-Kalán or Sín-ul-Sín and its identity with Canton, see *supra*, pp. II, 179; III, 126, 249; and *supra*, 25.

[2] [Sīn-Kīlan. Lee, p. 213.]

seen (for instance) a hospital for the sick, a kitchen for dressing their food, quarters for the physicians, and others for the servants. I was assured that old folks who had not strength to work for a livelihood were maintained and clothed there; and that a like provision was made for destitute widows and orphans. This temple was built by a King of China, who bequeathed this city and the villages and gardens attached, as a pious endowment, for this establishment. His portrait is to be seen in the temple, and the Chinese go and worship it[1].

In one of the quarters of this great city is the city of the Mahomedans, where they have their cathedral mosque, convent, and bazaar; they have also a judge and a Shaikh, for in each of the cities of China you find always a Shaikh of Islam, who decides finally every matter concerning Mahomedans, as well as a Kâzi to administer justice. I took up my quarters with Auhad-uddín of Sinjár, one of the worthiest, as he is one of the richest, of men. My

[1] Canton has undergone many changes, and no temple now appears to correspond precisely with that described. It was however perhaps that called *Kwang hiao sze* (Temple of Glory and Filial Duty), near what is now the N.W. corner of the city. It was built about A.D. 250, and has often been restored. It possesses about 3500 acres of land for the support of its inmates. There is a retreat for poor aged infirm and blind people called Yangtséquen, which stands outside the walls east of the city, but neither this nor the other charitable institutions appear to be of old date, nor do there seem to be any such now attached to the temples (see *Chinese Repository*, vol. ii, pp. 145 *seq.*). [The *Kwang hiao sze* has nothing to do with the Mahomedans; it contains three colossal effigies of Buddha.

"The city of Canton with its environs has five important mosques....The 'Mosque of Holy Remembrance' is the largest and most ancient of all the five mosques in Canton....The mosque was destroyed by fire in 1343 A.D. and was rebuilt in 1349–51 A.D. by a certain Emir Mahmoud....In this mosque of the Holy Remembrance the most important Records are on two monuments dated respectively 1351 A.D. and 1698 A.D. The tablet dated 1351 A.D. has a bilingual inscription in Arabic and Chinese and records the rebuilding of the premises." (Marshall Broomhall, *Islam in China*, pp. 109 *seq.*) This mosque is called the *Kwang t'a* or *Kwang t'ap* and is probably the one referred to by Ibn Batuta.]

stay with him lasted fourteen days, during which presents from the kâzi and the other Mahomedans flowed in upon me incessantly. Every day they used to have a fresh entertainment, to which they went in pretty little boats of some ten cubits in length, with people on board to sing.

Beyond this city of Sín-ul-Sín there are no other cities, whether of infidels or Musulmans. Between it and the Rampart, or Great Wall of Gog and Magog, there is a space of sixty days' journey as I was told. This territory is occupied by wandering tribes of heathen, who eat such people as they can catch, and for this reason no one enters their country or attempts to travel there. I saw nobody in this city who had been to the Great Wall, or who knew anybody who had been there[1].

During my stay at Sin-Kalán I heard that there was at that city a very aged shaikh, indeed that he had passed his two hundredth year[2]; that he had neither ate nor

[1] This is an instance of Ibn Batuta's loose notions of geography. He inquires for the Wall of China from his co-religionists at the wrong extremity of the empire, as if (on a smaller scale) a foreigner should ask the French Consul at Cork for particulars of the Wall of Antoninus. Had he inquired at Khánbaliq (if he really was there) he might have received more information.

The Rampart of Gog and Magog (*Yájúj and Májúj*) was believed to have been erected by Alexander the Great to shut up the fierce nations of the north and bar their irruptions into civilized southern lands. It is generally referred to Derbend on the Caspian, but naturally came to be confounded with the Wall of China. Edrisi (ii, 416) gives an account of the mission sent by the Khalif Wathek Billah to explore the Rampart of Gog and Magog. See the Reduction of the Catalan Map, N.E. corner. [Cf. *Marco Polo*, i, p. 57 *n*.]

[2] Supernatural longevity is a common attribute of Mahomedan saints. Ibn Batuta himself introduces us to several others whose age exceeded one hundred and fifty years, besides a certain *Atha Awalía* in the Hindu Kush who claimed three hundred and fifty years, but regarding whom the traveller had his doubts. Shah Madar, one of the most eminent Indian saints, is said to have been born at Aleppo in 1050–1, and to have died at Makanpur near Ferozabad, Agra, where he was buried, in 1433, having had 1442 sons, spiritual it may be presumed! (Garcin de Tassy, *Particularités de la Rel. Mus. dans l'Inde*, p. 55). And John

drank nor had anything to say to women, although his vigour was intact; and that he dwelt in a cave outside the town, where he gave himself up to devotion. So I went to his grotto, and there I saw him at the door. He was very thin; of a deep red or copper-tint, much marked with the traces of an ascetic life, and had no beard. After I had saluted him he took my hand, blew on it, and said to the interpreter: "This man belongs to one extremity of the world, as we belong to the other." Then he said to me: "Thou hast witnessed a miracle. Dost thou call to mind the day of thy visit to the island where there was a temple, and the man seated among the idols who gave thee ten pieces of gold?" "Yes, in sooth," answered I. He rejoined, "I was that man[1]." I kissed his hand; the shaikh seemed a while lost in thought, then entered his cave, and did not come back to us. One would have said that he regretted the words that he had spoken. We were rash enough to enter the grotto in order to surprise him, but we did not find him. We saw one of his comrades, however, who had in his hand some paper bank-notes, and who said to us: "Take this for your entertainment, and begone." We answered: "But we wish to wait for the shaikh." He answered: "If you were to wait ten years you would not see him. For 'tis his way never to let himself be seen by a person who has learned one of his secrets." He added: "Think not that he is absent; he is here present with you!"

Greatly astonished at all this I departed. On telling my story to the kâzi, the Shaikh of Islam and (my host)

Schiltberger tells us of a saint at Hore in Horassan (Herat in Khorāsān) whom he saw there in the days of Timur, whose name was Phiradam Schycch, and who was three hundred and fifty years old (*Reisen*, p. 101).

[1] This refers to a mysterious incident that occurred to Ibn Batuta at a small island on the western coast of India just before he got to Hunawúr (see *supra*, p. 24).

Auhad-uddín of Sinjár, they observed: "This is his way with strangers who visit him; nobody ever knows what religion he professes. But the man whom you took for one of his comrades was the shaikh himself." They then informed me that this personage had quitted the country for about fifty years and had returned only a year previously. The king[1], the generals, and other chiefs went to see him, and made him presents in proportion to their rank; whilst every day the fakirs and poor monks went to see him, and received from him gifts in proportion to the deserts of each, although his cave contained absolutely nothing. They told me also that this personage sometimes related histories of past times; he would speak, for example, of the prophet (upon whom be peace!), and would say with reference to him: "If I had but been with him, I would have helped him." He would speak also with veneration of the two Khalifs, 'Omar son of Alkattab and 'Ali son of Abu Tálib, and would praise them highly. But, on the other hand, he would curse Yazíd the son of Mu'áwiyah, and would denounce Mu'áwiyah himself[2]. Many other things were told me about this shaikh by the persons named above.

Auhad-uddín of Sinjár told me the following story about him: "I went once (said he) to see the shaikh in his cave. He took hold of my hand, and all at once I imagined myself to be in a great palace where this shaikh was seated on a throne. Methought he had a crown on his head; on each side of him were beautiful handmaidens; and there were canals about into which fruit was constantly dropping. I imagined that I took up an apple to eat it,

[1] *I.e.* the viceroy.

[2] Omar and Ali, the second and fourth successors of Mahomed. Yazíd Bin Mu'áwiyah, the second Khalif of the Ommiades, who caused the death of Ali on the plain of Kerbela, is always mentioned with a curse by the Shias (D'Herbelot).

and straightway as I did so I found myself again in the grotto with the shaikh before me, laughing and ridiculing me. I had a bad illness which lasted several months; and I never would go again to see that strange being[1]."

The people of the country believe the shaikh to be a Musulman, but nobody ever saw him say his prayers. As regards abstinence from food, again, he may be said to fast perpetually. The kâzi told me: "One day I spoke to him about prayer, and his answer was: 'Thinkest thou that thou knowest, thou! what *I* do? In truth, I trow my prayer is another matter from thine!'" Everything about this man was singular[2].

The day after my visit to the shaikh I set out on my return to the city of Zaitún, and some days after my arrival there an order was received from the Kán that I was to proceed to the capital, with arrangements for my honourable treatment and for defraying my expenses. He left me free to go by land or by water as I chose; so I preferred going by the river.

They fitted up a very nice boat for me, such as is used for the transport of generals; the Amír sent some of his suite to accompany me, and furnished provisions in abundance; quantities also were sent by the kâzi and the Mahomedan merchants. We travelled as the guests of the sultan, dining at one village, and supping at another; and after a passage of ten days we arrived at KANJANFÚ. This is a large and beautiful city surrounded by gardens, in an immense plain. One would say it was the plain of Damascus[3]!

[1] A capital case of mesmeric influence in the Middle Ages.

[2] The holy man in Egypt, described by Lady Duff Gordon (*supra*, p. 90), "never prays, never washes, he does not keep Ramadán, and yet he is a saint."

[3] This I have little doubt is Kien ch'ang fu in Kiang si, to which a water communication conducts all the way from Fu-chau,

On my arrival the kâzi, the shaikh of Islam, and the merchants came out to receive me, with flags and a band of musicians, with drums, trumpets, and horns. They brought horses for us, which we mounted, whilst they all went on foot before us except the kâzi and the shaikh, who rode with us. The governor of the city also came out with his retinue to meet us, for a guest of the emperor's is highly honoured among those people. And so we entered Kanjanfú[1]. This city has four walls. Between the first and the second wall live the slaves of the sultan, those who guard the city by day as well as those who guard it by night. These last are called *baswánán.* Between the second and third wall are the cavalry, and the amír who commands in the city. Inside the third wall are the Mahomedans, so it was here that we dismounted at the house of their shaikh, Zahír-uddín ul Kurláni. The Chinese lived inside the fourth wall, which incloses the biggest of the four towns. The distance between one gate and the next in this immense city of Kanjanfú is three miles and a quarter. Every inhabitant, as we have described before, has his garden and fields about his house[2].

One day when I was in the house of Zahír-uddín ul Kurláni there arrived a great boat, which was stated to be that of one of the most highly respected doctors of the law among the Musulmans of those parts. They asked leave to introduce this personage to me, and accordingly

and probably from Zaitún, excepting for a space of 190 li (some fifty or sixty miles) in the passage of the mountains between T'sung nang hien in Fu-kien, and Yan chan hien in Kiang si (Klap., *Mém. Rel. à l'Asie*, vol. iii). Kien ch'ang fu is described by Martini as a handsome and celebrated city, with a lake inside the walls and another outside. It was noted in his time for the excellence of its rice-wine.

[1] [Fanjanfūr. Lee, p. 215.]

[2] This must at all times have been a great exaggeration.

he was announced as "Our Master Kiwámuddín the Ceutan[1]." I was surprised at the name; and when he had entered, and after exchanging the usual salutations we had begun to converse together, it struck me that I knew the man. So I began to look at him earnestly, and he said, "You look as if you knew me." "From what country are you," I asked. "From Ceuta." "And I am from Tangier!" So he recommenced his salutations, moved to tears at the meeting, till I caught the infection myself. I then asked him: "Have you ever been in India?" "Yes," he said; "I have been at Delhi, the capital." When he said that I recollected about him, and said, "Surely you are Al-Bushri?" "Yes, I am." He had come to Delhi with his maternal uncle, Abú'l Kásim, of Murcia, being then quite young and beardless, but an accomplished student, knowing the *Muwattah* by heart[2]. I had told the Sultan of India about him, and he had given him 3000 dínárs, and desired to keep him at Delhi. He refused to stay, however, for he was bent on going to China, and in that country he had acquired much reputation and a great deal of wealth. He told me that he had some fifty male slaves, and as many female: and indeed he gave me two of each, with many other presents. Some years later I met this man's brother in Negroland. What an enormous distance lay between those two[3]!

[1] "Ul-Sabtí."

[2] The *Muwattah* (the name signifies, according to Defrémery, "Appropriated," but D'Herbelot translates it "Footstool") was a book on the traditions, held in great respect by the Mahomedans, who called it *Mubárak*, or Blessed. It was composed by the Imám Málik Bin Ans, one of the four chiefs of Orthodox sects. (D'Herbelot.)

[3] This meeting in the heart of China of the two Moors from the adjoining towns of Tangier and Ceuta has a parallel in that famous, but I fear mythical story of the capture of the Grand Vizier on the Black Sea by Marshal Keith, then in the Russian service. The venerable Turk's look of recognition drew from the

I stayed fifteen days at Kanjanfú, and then continued my journey. China is a beautiful country, but it afforded me no pleasure. On the contrary, my spirit was sorely troubled within me whilst I was there, to see how Paganism had the upper hand. I never could leave my quarters without witnessing many things of a sinful kind; and that distressed me so much that I generally kept within doors, and only went out when it was absolutely necessary. And during my whole stay in China I always felt in meeting Musulmans just as if I had fallen in with my own kith and kin. The jurist Al-Bushri carried his kindness towards me so far that he escorted me on my journey for four days until my arrival at BAIWAM KUTLÚ[1]. This was a small city inhabited by Chinese traders and soldiers. There were but four houses of Musulmans there, and the owners were all disciples of the jurist above mentioned. We took up our quarters with one of them, and stayed three days. I then bade adieu to the doctor, and proceeded on my journey.

As usual, I travelled on the river, dining at one village, supping at another, till after a voyage of seventeen days we arrived at the city of KHANSÁ[2]. (The name of this city is nearly the same as that of Khansá, the poetess[3],

Marshal the same question that Al-Bushri addressed to Ibn Batuta, and the answer came forth in broad Fifeshire dialect—"Eh man! aye, I mind you weel, for my father was the bellman of Kirkaldy!"

[1] [Bairam Katlu. Lee, p. 216.] The name looks Turkish rather than Chinese and may be connected with that of *Baiam*, the great general and minister of Kúblái. It is possible, however, that the Baiwam may represent *Poyang*, the old name of Yao-chau, on the Poyang Lake, which I suppose had its name from this city (Martini in Thévenot, p. 109). The position would be very appropriate.

[2] Cansay of Odoric, etc., King-sze or Hang-chau fu; see II, p. 192, III, pp. 115, 229, etc., *supra*.

[3] All I can tell of this lady is from the following extract: "Al-Chansa, the most celebrated Arabic poetess, shines exclusively in elegiac poetry. Her laments over her two murdered brothers,

but I don't know whether the name be actually Arabic, or has only an accidental resemblance to it.) This city is the greatest I have ever seen on the surface of the earth. It is three days' journey in length, so that a traveller passing through the city has to make his marches and his halts! According to what we have said before of the arrangement followed in the cities of China, every one in Khansá is provided with his house and garden[1]. The city is divided into six towns, as I shall explain presently.

When we arrived, there came out to meet us the Kâzi of Khansá, by name Afkharuddín, the Shaikh of Islam, and the descendants of 'Othmán Bin Affán the Egyptian, who are the most prominent Mahomedans at Khansá. They carried a white flag, with drums, trumpets, and horns. The commandant of the city also came out to meet me with his escort. And so we entered the city.

It is subdivided into six towns, each of which has a separate enclosure, whilst one great wall surrounds the whole. In the first city was posted the garrison of the city, with its commandant. I was told by the Kâzi and others that there were 12,000 soldiers on the rolls. We passed the night at the commandant's house. The next day we entered the second city by a gate called the Jews' Gate. This town was inhabited by Jews, by Christians, and by those Turks who worship the sun; they are very numerous. The Amír of this town is a Chinese, and we passed the second night in his house. The third day we made our entrance into the third city, and this is occupied by the Mahomedans. It is a fine town, with the bazaars

Muawiya and Sachr, are the most pathetic, tender, and passionate, yet no translation could convey the fulness of their beauty. To be appreciated they must be read in the majestic, soft, sonorous words of the original." (*Saturday Review*, June 17, 1865, p. 740.)

[1] This agrees but ill with Odoric's "*non est spansa terræ quæ non habitatur bene.*" There are several very questionable statements in Ibn Batuta's account of the great city.

arranged as in Musulman countries, and with mosques and muezzins. We heard these last calling the Faithful to prayer as we entered the city. Here we were lodged in the house of the children of 'Othmán Bin Affán, the Egyptian. This 'Othmán was a merchant of great eminence, who took a liking to this town, and established himself in it; indeed it is named after him *Al'Othmániyah.* He bequeathed to his posterity in this city the dignity and consideration which he had himself enjoyed; his sons follow their father in their beneficence to religious mendicants, and in affording relief to the poor. They have a convent called also Al'Othmániyah, which is a handsome edifice, endowed with many pious bequests, and is occupied by a fraternity of Súfís. It was the same Othmán who built the Jáma' Masjid (cathedral mosque) in this city, and he has bequeathed to it (as well as to the convent) considerable sums to form a foundation for pious uses.

The Musulmans in this city are very numerous. We remained with them fifteen days, and every day and every night I was present at some new entertainment. The splendour of their banquets never flagged, and every day they took me about the city on horseback for my diversion. One day that they were riding with me we went into the fourth city, where the seat of the government is, and also the palace of the great Amír Kurtai. When we had passed the gate of the town my companions left me, and I was received by the Wazír, who conducted me to the palace of the great Amír Kurtai. I have already related how this latter took from me the pelisse which had been given me by the Friend of God, Jalal-uddín of Shíráz. This fourth town is intended solely for the dwellings of the emperor's officers and slaves; it is the finest of all the six towns, and is traversed by three streams of water. One of these is a canal from the great river, and by it the supplies of food and of stones for burning are brought in small boats; there are also pleasure boats to be had upon it. The citadel is in the middle of the town; it is of immense extent, and in the centre of it is the palace of the government. The citadel surrounds this on all sides, and is provided with covered sheds, where artisans are seen employed in making magnificent dresses, arms, and engines of war. The Amír Kurtai told me that there were 1600 master-workmen, each of whom had under his direction three or four apprentices. All are the Kán's slaves; they are chained, and live outside the fortress. They are allowed to frequent the bazaars of the town, but not to go beyond the gate. The Amír musters them daily, and if any one is missing their chief is responsible. It is customary to remove their fetters after ten years' service, and they have then the option of either continuing to serve without fetters or of going where they will, provided they do not pass beyond the frontier of the Kán's territory. At the age of fifty they are excused all further work, and are maintained at the cost of the State. But indeed in any case every one, or nearly every one, in China, who has reached that age, may obtain his maintenance at the public expense[1]. He who has reached the age of sixty is regarded by the Chinese as a child, and is no longer subject to the penalties of the law. Old men are treated with great respect in that country, and are always addressed as *Athá* or "Father[2]."

The Amír Kurtai is the greatest lord in China[3]. He

[1] See above, III, p. 92, and *M. Polo*, i. 39.

[2] See above, II, p. 201.

[3] [Emir Karti. Lee, p. 218.] I cannot identify this Prince in the translated Chinese histories. *Kurtai* is however a genuine Tartar name, and is found as the name of one of the Mongol generals in the preceding century (D'Ohsson, ii, 260). [Amír

offered us hospitality in his palace, and gave an entertainment such as those people call *Thuwai*[1], at which the dignitaries of the city were present. He had got Mahomedan cooks to kill the cattle and cook the dishes for us, and this lord, great as he was, carved the meats and helped us with his own hands! We were his guests for three days, and one day he sent his son to escort us in a trip on the canal. We got into a boat like a fire-ship[2], whilst the young lord got into another, taking singers and musicians with him. The singers sang songs in Chinese, Arabic, and Persian. The lord's son was a great admirer of the Persian songs, and there was one of these sung by them which he caused to be repeated several times, so that I got it by heart from their singing. This song had a pretty cadence in it, and thus it went:

Tá dil ba mihnat dádím,
Dar bahri-i fikr uftádím,
Chún dar namáz istádím,
Kawí bamihráb anderím[3].

Kurtai. Schefer, *Relat. des Musulmans avec les Chinois*, p. 23, calls him Qir Thay. Cf. Huart, *J. As.*, May–June, 1913, p. 701, says it should be Ḳaraṭai, name of several Turkish families.]

[1] *Thoï* or *Tuwi* is a word believed to be of Turki origin, used frequently by Rashíd and other medieval Persian writers for a *feast* or *fête* (see Quatremère's *Rashideddin*, pp. 139–40, 164, 216, 414; see also a previous passage of *Ibn Batuta*, iii, 40).

[2] *Harráqah*. "Navis incendiaria aut missilibus pyriis instructa" (Freytag). I do not understand what is meant by the comparison. It cannot refer to the blaze of light, because this was in the daytime. But perhaps Ibn Batuta applies the word only in the sense of some kind of state barge, for he uses the same title for the boat in which he saw the Il-Khan Abu Said with his Wazīr taking an airing on the Tigris at Baghdad (ii, 116).

[3] The "pretty cadence" is precisely that of:

We won't go home till morning,
We won't go home till morning,
We won't go home till morning,
Till daylight doth appear!

It may be somewhat freely rendered:

My heart given up to emotions,
Was o'erwhelmed in waves like the ocean's;
But betaking me to my devotions,
My troubles were gone from me!

Crowds of people in boats were gathered on the canal. The sails were of all bright colours, the people carried parasols of silk, and the boats themselves were gorgeously painted. They skirmished with one another, and pelted each other with oranges and lemons. In the evening we went back to pass the night at the Amír's palace, where the musicians came again and sang very fine songs.

That same night a juggler, who was one of the Kán's slaves, made his appearance, and the Amír said to him: "Come and show us some of your marvels." Upon this he took a wooden ball, with several holes in it through which long thongs were passed, and (laying hold of one of these) slung it into the air. It went so high that we lost sight of it altogether. (It was the hottest season of the year, and we were outside in the middle of the palace court.) There now remained only a little of the end of a thong in the conjuror's hand, and he desired one of the boys who assisted him to lay hold of it and mount. He did so, climbing by the thong, and we lost sight of him also! The conjuror then called to him three times, but getting no answer he snatched up a knife, as if in a great rage, laid hold of the thong, and disappeared also! By and by he threw down one of the boy's hands, then a foot, then the other hand and the other foot, then the trunk, and last of all the head! Then he came down himself, all puffing and panting, and with his clothes all bloody, kissed the ground before the Amír, and said something to him in Chinese. The Amír gave some order in reply, and our friend then took the lad's limbs, laid them together in their places, and gave a kick, when, presto! there was the boy, who got up and stood before us[1]! All this astonished me beyond measure, and I had

[1] In a modern Indian version of this trick, which I lately heard described by an eye-witness, the boy was covered with a

an attack of palpitation like that which overcame me once before in the presence of the Sultan of India, when he showed me something of the same kind. They gave me a cordial, however, which cured the attack[1]. The Kâzi Afkharuddín was next to me, and quoth he: "Walláh! 'tis my opinion there has been neither going up nor coming down, neither marring nor mending; 'tis all hocus pocus!"

The next day we entered the gate of the fifth city, which is the biggest of all the six, and is inhabited by the Chinese. It has splendid bazaars and capital artificers, and it is there that they make the textures called *khansáwiyah.* Among the fine things made here also are the plates and dishes called *Dast.* They are composed of cane, the fibres of which are platted together in a wonderful manner, and then covered with a brilliant coat of red lacker. Ten of these plates go to a set, one fitting inside the other, and so fine are they that when you see

basket and desired to descend into the earth. On his refusal, the conjuror rushed at the basket and pierced it violently in all directions with a spear, whilst blood flowed from under it, and the boy's dying groans were heard. On removing the basket there was of course nothing to be seen, and presently the boy made his appearance running from the gate of the *compound* in which the performance took place. The vanishing *upwards* certainly renders Ibn Batuta's story much more wonderful. A like feature is found in some extraordinary Indian conjurors' tricks described by the Emperor Jihanghir in his memoirs.

[1] On the occasion referred to (iv, 39), Ibn Batuta, when visiting Mahomed Tughlak, finds two Jogis in the king's apartments, one of whom whilst sitting cross-legged rises in the air. His comrade then pulls out a shoe and raps on the ground with it. The shoe immediately mounts in the air to the neck of the elevated Jogi, and begins tapping him on the nape of the neck; as it taps he gradually subsides to the ground. The traveller, unused to such operations of "levitation" and spirit-rapping, faints away in the king's presence.

Ricold de Monte Croce ascribes such practices to the *Boxitæ* (*Bakshis* or Lamas). One of them was said to fly. The fact was, says Ricold, that he did not fly, but he used to skim the ground without touching it, and when he seemed to be sitting down he was sitting upon nothing! (p. 117).

A Brahman at Madras some forty or fifty years ago exhibited himself sitting in the air. In his case, I think, mechanical aids were discovered, but I cannot refer to the particulars.

them you would take the whole set for but one plate. A cover then goes over the whole. There are also great dishes or trays made with the same cane-work. Some of the excellent properties of such dishes are these: they don't break when they tumble, and you can put hot things into them without spoiling or in the least affecting their colour. These plates and dishes are exported from China to India, Khorāsān, and other countries[1].

We passed a night in the fifth town as the guests of the commandant, and the next day we proceeded to enter the sixth by a gate called that of the *kishtiwánán*, or boatmen. This town is inhabited only by seamen, fishermen, caulkers, carpenters (these last they call *dúdkárán*), by the *sipahis*, *i.e.* the archers, and by the *piyádahs*, *i.e.* the foot-soldiers[2]. All of them are the emperor's slaves; no other class live with them, and their numbers are very great. The town of which we speak is situated on the banks of the Great River, and we stayed the night there, enjoying the hospitality of the commandant. The Amír Kurtai had caused a boat to be fitted up for us, and equipped with everything needful in the way of provisions and otherwise. He also sent some of his

[1] Lackered ware is still made in Burma quite in the way that the traveller describes, and so it is doubtless in China. Indeed the cane dishes are mentioned by the Archbishop of Soltania (*supra*, III, p. 99).

[2] Here as usual with Ibn Batuta one would suppose that these words were the vernacular Chinese instead of being Persian. If we could depend upon him thoroughly in such matters, the use of these words would indicate that Persian was the language of the Mahomedan communities in China. *Dúdkárán* is for *Durúdgarán*, carpenters. The explanations "archers" and "foot-soldiers" (*ul-rajál*) are Ibn Batuta's own, and the use of the latter word is perhaps unfavourable to the translation at p. 104. [To Ch. Schefer, *Relat. des Musulmans avec les Chinois*, p. 24, it seems that they were Persian artisans sent from Iraq, Khorāsān and Transoxiana by the Mongols and who had not yet been liberated. "Ibn Batuta les désigne sous les noms persans de *Kechtiouanan* (pilotes) et *Doroudgueran* (menuisiers). Les archers ou gens de trait étaient appelés *Sipahièh* et les gens de pied, *Piadèh* (piétons)."]

people to accompany us, in order that we might be received everywhere as the emperor's guests, and so we quitted this city, the province under which is the last of those of China, and proceeded to enter CATHAY[1].

Cathay is the best cultivated land in the world; in the whole country you will not find a bit of ground lying fallow. The reason is, that if a piece of ground be left uncultivated, they still oblige the people on it, or if there be none the people nearest to it, to pay the land-tax. Gardens, villages, and cultivated fields line the two banks of the river in uninterrupted succession from the city of Khansá to the city of KHÁNBÁLIQ, a space of sixty-four days' journey.

In those tracts you find no Musulmans, unless as mere passengers, for the localities are not adapted for them to fix themselves in, and you find no regular cities, but only villages, and plains covered with corn, fruit trees, and sugar cane. I do not know in the whole world a region to be compared to this, except that space of four days' march between Anbār and 'Anah. Every evening we landed at a different village, and were hospitably received[2].

And thus at last we arrived at Khánbáliq, also called KHÁNIKÚ[3]. It is the capital of the Kán or great Emperor,

[1] *Khithá*. Here Ibn Batuta makes China (*Sín*) correspond to *Mangi*, or the Sung empire, first reduced under the Mongols by Kúblái. In other passages he appears to use Sín for the whole empire, as (in iii, 17) where he speaks of Almáliq as situated at the extremity of Mā-warā-n-Nahr, near the place where China (*Sín*) begins.

[2] *Anbār*, on the Euphrates abreast of Baghdad; *'Anah*, about 120 miles higher up. The alleged absence of cities on the banks of the canal is so contrary to fact, that one's doubts arise whether Ibn Batuta could have travelled beyond Hang-chau.

[3] Of this name *Khánikú* I can make nothing. *Khánkú* indeed appears in Abulfeda several times as the alternative name of Khansá, but is in that case an evident mistake (one dot too many), for the *Khánfu* of Abu Said in Reinaud's *Relations*, the Ganpu of Marco, the Kánphú of the Chinese, which was the seaport of Khansá or Hang-chau, and stood upon the estuary of

who rules over China and Cathay. We moored, according to the custom of these people, ten miles short of Khánbáliq, and they sent a report of our arrival to the admirals, who gave us permission to enter the port, and this we did. At last we landed at the city, which is one of the greatest in the world, and differs from all the other cities of China in having no gardens inside the walls; they are all outside, as in other countries. The city or quarter in which the emperor resides stands in the middle like a citadel, as we shall tell hereafter. I took up my quarters with the shaikh Burhán-uddín of Ságharj, the individual to whom the Sultan of India sent 40,000 dínárs, with an invitation to go to his dominions. He took the money indeed, and paid his debts with it, but declined to go to the King of Delhi, and directed his course towards China. The Kán put him at the head of all the Musulmans in his empire, with the title of *Sadr-ul-Jihán*, or Chief of the World[1].

The word *Kán* (*Qán*) among the Chinese is a generic term for anyone governing the empire; in fact, for the kings of their country, just as the lords of the Lúr country

the Che Kiang, about twelve leagues from the great city (Klapr. *Mém.* ii, 200). [*Khaniku*, Ḫāniku, is the adjective taken as a substantive *Xan* + *qu*, "this of the Emperor, the imperial" (= *Xan-baliq*). Cl. Huart, *Jour. Asiat.*, May–June, 1913, p. 701.]

[1] As Ibn Batuta relates elsewhere (iii, 255) this celebrated preacher gave as his reason for refusing to visit India: "I will not go to the court of a king who makes philosophers stand in his presence." Curiously enough the story is also told in the *Masālak-al-Absār*, of which extracts have been translated by Quatremère. According to that work, Burhán-uddín of Ságharj was Shaikh of Samarkand, and Sultan Mahomed of Delhi, hearing much of his fame, sent him 40,000 *tankahs* (we here see corroboration that the Indian *dínár* of Ibn Batuta is the *tankah* of other authors) with an invitation to his court. The messenger on his arrival at Samarkand found the Shaikh had set out for China, so he gave the money to a young slave-girl of his, desiring her to let her master know that his presence was greatly desired by the King of Delhi (*Notices et Extraits*, xiii, 196). [Schefer, *l.c.*, p. 24, translates *Sadri Djihan*, "Supreme Judge of the World."]

are called *Atábek*. The proper name of this sultan is *Páshái*, and there is not among the infidels on the whole face of the earth so great an empire as his[1].

The palace of the monarch is situated in the middle of the city appropriated to his residence. It is almost entirely constructed of carved wood, and is admirably laid out. It has seven gates. At the first gate sits the *Kotwál*[2], who is the chief of the porters, whilst elevated platforms right and left of the gate are occupied by the pages called *Pardadáriyah* (curtain-keepers), who are the warders of the palace gates. These were 500 in number, and I was told that they used to be 1000. At the second gate are stationed the *Sipáhis*, or archers, to the number of 500; and at the third gate are the *Nizahdars*, or spearmen, also 500 in number. At the fourth gate are the *Teghdáriyah* (sabre-men), men with sabre and shield. At the fifth gate are the offices of the ministerial departments, and these are furnished with numerous platforms[3]. On the principal one of these sits the wazīr, mounted on an enormous sofa, and this is called the *Masnad*. Before

[1] *Atábek* was the title borne by various powerful Amírs at the court of the Seljukidæ, which they retained after becoming independent in different provinces of Irak, Azerbaiján, etc. The title is said to mean "The Prince's Father." It was also held at the Court of Delhi under the translated form *Khán Baba* (Elph. *Hist. of India*, ii, 216). Ibn Batuta had visited one of the Atábeks, Afrasiab, in Luristan, on his way from Baghdad to Ispahan. By *Páshái*, I suspect he only means the Persian *Pâdsháh*. The real name of the emperor at this time was Togon Timur, surnamed Ukhagatu, called by the Chinese Shun Ti.

[2] ["Les emplois des fonctionnaires étaient désignés par des mots persans. Le gouverneur est désigné par le mot *Koutoual*; les huissiers étaient appelés *Perdehdarièh*, les archers, *Sipahièh*, les gens armés de lances, *Nizéhdarièh*, et les porte-glaives *Tighdarièh*." (Schefer, *l.c.*, p. 24.)]

[3] The word is *Saqífah*, which is defined in the dictionary *Locus discubitorius ad instar latioris scamni constructus ante ædes*, and translated in the French *Estrade*. I suppose it here to represent an open elevated shed or pavilion, such as appears to be much affected in the courts of Chinese and Indo-Chinese palaces.

the wazīr is a great writing-table of gold. Opposite is the platform of the private secretary; to the right of it is that of the secretaries for despatches, and to the right of the wazīr is that of the clerks of the finances.

These four platforms have four others facing them. One is called the office of control; the second is that of the office of *Mustakhraj*, or "Produce of Extortion," the chief of which is one of the principal grandees. They call *Mustakhraj* the balances due by collectors and other officials, and by the amírs from the claims upon their fiefs. The third is the office of appeals for redress, where one of the great officers of state sits, assisted by secretaries and counsel learned in the law. Anyone who has been the victim of injustice addresses himself to them for aid and protection. The fourth is the office of the posts, and there the head of the news department has his seat[1].

At the sixth gate of the palace is stationed the king's body guard, with its chief commandant. The eunuchs are at the seventh gate. They have three platforms, the first of which is for the Abyssinians, the second for the Hindus, the third for the Chinese. Each of these three classes has a chief, who is a Chinese.

When we arrived at the capital Khánbáliq, we found that the Kán was absent, for he had gone forth to fight Firuz, the son of his uncle, who had raised a revolt against him in the territory of KARAKORÚM and BISHBÁLIQ, in Cathay[2]. To reach those places from the capital there

[1] In the whole of this description, with its Persian technicalities, it is pretty clear that Ibn Batuta is drawing either on his imagination, or (more probably) on his recollections of the Court of Delhi, and hence we have the strongest ground for suspecting that he never entered the palace of Peking, if indeed he ever saw that city at all. In iii, 295, he has told us of an office at the *Court of Delhi* which bore the name of *Mustakhraj*, the business of which was to extort unpaid balances by bastinado and other tortures.

[2] *Karakorúm*, the chief place successively of the Khans of Kerait, and of the Mongol Khans till Kúblái established his

is a distance to be passed of three months' march from the capital through a cultivated country. I was informed by the Sadr-ul-Jihán, Burhán-uddín of Ságharj, that when the Kán assembled his troops, and called the array of his forces together, there were with him one hundred divisions of horse, each composed of 10,000 men, the chief of whom was called *Amír Túmán* or lord of ten thousand[1]. Besides these the immediate followers of the sultan and his household furnished 50,000 more cavalry. The infantry consisted of 500,000 men. When the emperor had marched, most of the amírs revolted, and agreed to depose

residence in China. [See long note *Marco Polo*, i, p. 227.] *Bishbáliq* (*i.e.* "Pentapolis") lay between Karakorúm and Álmáliq; and had in ancient times been the chief seat of the Uighúr nation. It is now, according to Klaproth, represented by Urumtsi. [Klaproth in his dissertation on the *Détermination de l'emplacement de Bishbalik* (*Mém. relatifs à l'Asie*, ii, pp. 355–63) identified Bishbáliq with Pei t'ing of the T'ang period and Urumtsi, and his theory has been accepted since by all the Orientalists. M. Chavannes (*Tou-kiue occidentaux*, p. 11, note) shows from the *Si-yu shui tao ki* that Pei t'ing is but *Kin-man*. Kin-man which was according to the *Kiu T'ang shu* during the After Han the Posterior Royal Court (of the kingdom) of Kiu shi included five towns and its usual name was *Wu ch'eng che ti* which from a slab found there was 20 li N. of Pan hwei tien (or Tsi mu sa), viz., 90 li S.W. of Guchen; on the site of the ancient sub-prefecture of Kin-man is the place called Hu pao tze. Pei t'ing or Kin-man is not on the road from Turfan to Urumtsi by the Daban shan Pass, but on a more eastern road which runs from Turfan up to (near) Guchen. Bishbáliq (Five towns) = Pei t'ing = Kin-man = Hu pao tze, about 20 li N. of actual Pao hwei tien; thus it is not Urumtsi.—"Grum Gržimailo (*Opisanie puteshestv'ya v Zapadnij Kitai*, i, 221–2) was the first (in 1896) to express the opinion that the town (of Bishbáliq) was more to the east (than Urumtsi) and situated on or near the site of the present Guchen; in the second vol. of the same work (1899, pp. 42–3) this opinion was more strongly supported by a reference to the work *Meng-ku-yu-mu-ki* translated in 1895 by Popov....; in 1908 Dolbezev found that in the region indicated by the Chinese (near the village Hu pao tze, about 10 kilom. N. of the town of Tsi-mu-sa) were indeed ruins (called to-day P'o chöng tze) of a rather important town (4 kilom. pourtour)...it was during the seventh century that the Chinese names Kin-man and Pei t'ing appeared....During the thirteenth century Bishbáliq was then near Kara Khodja (Turfan), capital of a uighúr prince with the title of Idiqut and a vassal of the Gurkhan of the Kara Khitāi." *Encycl. de l'Islam*, W. Barthold, s.v. *Bishbaliḳ*.]

[1] *Tuman*. See *supra*, III, p. 199.

him, for he had violated the laws of the *Yasák*, that is to say, of the code established by their ancestor Tankíz Khán, who ravaged the lands of Islam[1]. They deserted to the camp of the emperor's cousin who was in rebellion, and wrote to the Kán to abdicate and be content to retain the city of Khansá for his apanage. The Kán refused, engaged them in battle, and was defeated and slain[2].

This news was received a few days after our arrival at the capital. The city upon this was decked out, and the people went about beating drums and blowing trumpets and horns, and gave themselves over to games and amusements for a whole month. The Kán's body was then brought in with those of about a hundred more of his cousins, kinsfolk, and favourites who had fallen. After digging for the Kán a great *Náwús* or crypt[3], they spread it with splendid carpets, and laid therein the Kán with his arms. They put in also the whole of the gold and silver plate belonging to the palace, with four of the Kán's young slave girls, and six of his chief pages holding in their hands vessels full of drink. They then built up the

[1] The *Yasa* or ordinances which Chinghiz laid down for the guidance of his successors may be seen more or less in Pétis de la Croix, D'Ohsson, Deguignes, in V. Hammer's *Golden Horde*, and in *Univers Pittoresque* (Tartarie, p. 313). The word is said to mean any kind of ordinance or regulation. Baber tells us in his Autobiography: "My forefathers and family had always sacredly observed the Rules of Chinghiz. In their parties, in their courts, their festivals, and their entertainments, in their sitting down, and in their rising up, they never acted contrary to the Institutions of Chinghiz" (p. 202).

[2] The Emperor Togon Timur or Shun Ti, who was on the throne at the time of Ibn Batuta's visit (1347), had succeeded in 1333, and continued to reign till his expulsion by the Chinese and the fall of his dynasty in 1368. Nor can I find in Deguignes or De Mailla the least indication of any circumstance occurring about this time that could have been made the foundation of such a story.

[3] Defrémery says from the Gr. *ναός*. Meninski gives *Náwús* (or *Náús*). "Cœmeterium, vel delubrum magorum."

door of the crypt and piled earth on the top of it till it was like a high hill. After this they brought four horses and made them run races round the emperor's sepulchre until they could not stir a foot; they next set up close to it a great mast, to which they suspended those horses after driving a wooden stake right through their bodies from tail to mouth. The Kán's kinsfolk also, mentioned above, were placed in subterranean cells, each with his arms and the plate belonging to his house. Adjoining the tombs of the principal men among them to the number of ten they set up empaled horses, three to each, and beside the remaining tombs they impaled one horse a-piece[1].

[1] This appears to be a very correct account of Tartar funeral ceremonies, though Ibn Batuta certainly did not witness those of a defunct *emperor*. As far back as the days of Herodotus we are told that the Scythians used to bury with their king one of his concubines, his cup-bearer, a cook, groom, lacquey, messenger, several horses, etc., and a year later further ceremonial took place, when fifty selected from his attendants were strangled, and fifty of his finest horses also slain. The bowels were taken out and replaced with chaff. A number of posts were then erected in sets of two pairs each, and on every pair the half felly of a wheel was set arch-wise; "then strong stakes are run lengthwise through the bodies of the horses from tail to neck, and they are mounted on the fellies so that the felly in front supports the shoulders of the horse while that behind sustains the belly and quarters, the legs dangling in mid air; each horse is furnished with a bit and bridle," etc. The fifty strangled slaves were then set astride on the horses, and so on.

When one Valentine was sent on a mission to the Turkish chiefs by the Emperor Tiberius II about 580, it is related that he witnessed a ceremonial at the tomb of a deceased chief when Hun prisoners and horses were sacrificed.

Huc and Gabet assert that like practices are maintained among Tartar tribes to the present day, large amounts of gold and silver, and many slaves of both sexes, being buried with the royal body, the slaves being killed by being made to swallow mercury till choked, which is believed to preserve their colour!

But the most exact corroboration of Ibn Batuta's account is to be found in the (almost) contemporary narrative of Ricold of Monte Croce. After speaking of the general practice of burying food and raiment with the dead, he goes on: "Magni etiam barones omnibus hiis addunt equum bonum. Nam armiger ejus ascendit equum, cum ipsi parant se ad sepeliendum mortuum, et fatigat equum currendo et revolvendo usque ad lassitudinem, et postea lavit equo caput cum vino puro et forti, et equus cadit, et ipse

It was a great day! Every soul was there, man and woman, Musulman and infidel. All were dressed in mourning, that is, the Pagans wore short white dresses, and the Musulmans long white dresses. The Kán's ladies and favourites remained in tents near the tomb for forty days; some remained longer; some a full year. A bazaar had been established in the neighbourhood, where all necessary provisions, etc., were for sale. I know no other nation in our time that keeps up such practices. The pagans of India and China burn their dead; other nations bury them, but none of them thus bury the living with the dead. However honest people in Súdán have told me that the pagans of that country, when their king dies, dig a great pit, into which they put with him several of his favourites and servants together with thirty persons of both sexes, selected from the families of the great men of the state. They take care first to break the arms and legs of these victims, and they also put vessels full of drink into the pit.

An eminent person of the tribe of Masúfah, living among the Negroes in the country of Kúber[1], who was much held in honour by their king, told me that when the king died they wished to put a son of his own into the tomb with some other children belonging to the country. "But I said to them," continued this eminent

exenterat eum, et evacuat omnia de ventre equi, et implet herba viridi, et postea infigit palum magnum per posteriora, et facit palum exire usque ad os, et ita dimittit equum impalatum, et suspendit eum et mandat ei, quod sit paratus, quandocumque vult dominus surgere, et tunc cooperiunt mortuum in sepultura. Cum vero moritur imperator, adduntur prædictis omnes lapides preciosi et etiam magni thesauri. Et consueverunt etiam sepelire cum domino mortuo usque viginti servos vivos, ut essent parati servire domino, cum voluerit surgere." Such proceedings took place at the burial of Hulákú.

(Rawlinson's *Herodotus*, bk. iv, c. 71–2, and notes; Deguignes, ii, 395–6; *Peregrin. Quatuor*, p. 117; see also *M. Polo*, ii, 54; *Rubruquis*, p. 337; and *Plano Carpini*, p. 629.)

[1] I suppose the *Gober* of Dr. Barth's map, near Sakatu.

person, "how can you do this, seeing the boy is neither of your religion nor of your country? And so I was allowed to ransom him with a large sum of money."

When the Kán was dead, as I have related, and Firuz, the son of his uncle, had usurped the supreme power, the latter chose for his capital the city of KARAKORÚM, because it was nearer to the territories of his cousins, the kings of Turkestan and Mā-warā-n-Nahr[1]. Then several of the amírs who had taken no part in the slaughter of the late Kán revolted against the new prince; they began to cut off the communications, and there was great disorder.

Revolt having thus broken out, and civil war having been kindled, the Shaikh Burhán-uddín and others advised me to return to (Southern) China before the disturbances should have arisen to a greater pitch. They went with me to the lieutenant of the Emperor Firuz, who sent three of his followers to escort me, and wrote orders that I should be everywhere received as a guest. So we descended the river to Khansá, Kanjánfu and Zaitún. When we reached the latter place, I found junks on the point of sailing for India, and among these was one belonging to Malik-ul-Záhir, Sultan of Java (Sumatra), which had a Mahomedan crew. The agent of the ship recognised me, and was pleased to see me again. We had a fair wind for ten days, but as we got near the land of Tawálisi it changed, the sky became black, and heavy rain fell. For ten days we never saw the sun, and then we entered on an unknown sea. The sailors were in great alarm, and wanted to return to China, but this was not possible. In this way we passed forty-two days, without knowing in what waters we were.

[1] Here two Mongol dynasties reigning in Central Asia seem to be spoken of (see III, p. 132, *supra*, and note at the end of this, p. 160).

On the forty-third morning after daybreak we descried a mountain in the sea, some twenty miles off, and the wind was carrying us straight for it. The sailors were surprised and said: "We are far from the mainland, and in this sea no mountain is known. If the wind drives us on this one we are done for." Then every one betook himself to humiliation and repentance, and renewal of good resolutions. We addressed ourselves to God in prayer, and sought the mediation of the prophet (upon whom be peace!).

The merchants vowed to bestow alms in abundance, and I wrote their vows all down in a list with my own hand. The wind lulled a little, and when the sun rose we saw the mountain aloft in the air, and the clear sky between it and the sea[1]. We were in astonishment at this, and I observed that the sailors were weeping and bidding each other adieu, so I called out: "What is the matter?" They replied: "What we took for a mountain is the Rukh! If it sees us it will send us to destruction." It was then some ten miles from the junk. But God Almighty was gracious unto us, and sent us a fair wind,

[1] Such an appearance is a well known effect of mirage, or abnormal refraction. As to the *Rukh* see Mr. Major's Introduction to *India in the 15th century*, p. xxxvi *seq.*, and a learned discourse in Ludolf's *Comment.* on his own *Historia Ethiopica*, pp. 163–4; also a cut from a Persian drawing in Lane's *Arabian Nights*, ii, 90. The most appropriate reference here however is perhaps to Pigafetta, who was told (possibly by descendants of Ibn Batuta's Malay crew) that in the sea of China *sotto Giava maggiore* there was a very great tree called *Campangunghi*, in which dwelt the birds called *garuda*, which were so big that they could fly away with a buffalo, or even with an elephant. No ship could approach the place within several leagues, on account of the vortices, etc. (*Primo Viaggio intorno del Mondo*, p. 174). *Garuda* is a term from the Hindu mythology for the great bird that carries Vishnu; its use among the Malays is a relic of their ancient religion, and perhaps indicates the origin of the stories of the *Rukh*. To an island of the Indian Sea also Kazwini attributes a bird of such enormous size, that, if dead, the half of its beak would serve for a ship (Gildemeister, p. 220). [See long note in *Marco Polo*, ii, pp. 415 *seq.*]

which turned us from the direction in which the Rukh was; so we did not see him (well enough) to take cognizance of his real shape.

Two months from that day we arrived at Java (Island of Sumatra), and landed at (the city of) Sumatra. We found the Sultan Malik-ul-Záhir had just returned from one of his campaigns, and had brought in with him many captives, out of whom he sent me two girls and two boys. He put me up as usual, and I was present at the marriage of his son to the daughter of his brother.

I witnessed the ceremony. I remarked that they had set up in the middle of the palace yard a great seat of state, covered with silk stuffs. The bride arrived, coming from the inner apartments of the palace on foot, and with her face exposed, so that the whole company could see her, gentle and simple alike. However it is not their usual custom to appear in public unveiled in this way; it is only done in the marriage ceremony[1]. The bride proceeded to the seat of state, the minstrels male and female going before her, playing and singing. Then came the bridegroom on a caparisoned elephant, which carried on its back a sort of throne, surmounted by a canopy like an umbrella. The bridegroom wore a crown on his head; right and left of him were about a hundred young men, of royal and noble blood, clothed in white, mounted on caparisoned horses, and wearing on their

[1] I suspect this apologetic assertion is not founded on fact. The Mahomedan proselytizers among the Malays and Indo-Chinese races have never been able to introduce the habitual use of the veil, and the custom of female seclusion. At Amarapura, in 1855, the Mahomedan soldiers of our Indian escort were greatly shocked at the absence of these proprieties among the Burmese professors of their faith; and at the court of the Sultan of Java, in 1860, I had the honour of shaking hands with more than half a dozen comely and veilless ladies, the wives and daughters of His Majesty. I was told that at times they even honoured a ball at the Dutch Residency with their presence.

heads caps adorned with gold and gems. They were of the same age as the bridegroom, and all beardless.

From the time when the bridegroom entered, pieces of gold and silver were scattered among the people. The sultan was seated aloft where he could see all that passed. His son got down from the elephant, went to kiss his father's foot, and then mounted on the seat of state beside his bride. They then brought pawn and betel-nut; the bridegroom took them in his hand and put them into the bride's mouth, and she did the same by him. Next he put a pawn-leaf first into his own mouth and then into hers, and she did in like manner[1]. They then put a veil over the bride, and removed the seat of state into the interior of the palace, whilst the young couple were still upon it; the company took refreshments and separated. Next day the sultan called the people together, and named his son as his successor on the throne. They took an oath of obedience to him, and the future sovereign distributed numerous presents in money and dresses.

I spent two months in this island of Java, and then embarked again on a junk. The sultan presented me with a quantity of aloes-wood, camphor, cloves, and sandal-wood, and then gave me leave to depart. So I sailed, and after forty days I arrived at Kaulam. Here I put myself under the protection of Al-Kazwini, the judge of the Mahomedans. It was the month of Ramazan, and I was present at the festival of breaking the fast in the chief mosque of the city. The custom of the people there is to assemble on the eve of the feast at the mosque, and to continue reciting the praises of God till morning,

[1] This is a genuine Malay custom, marking the highest degree of intimacy between the sexes. Dulaurier quotes several examples in illustration from Malay poems.

and indeed till the moment when the prayer appropriate to the feast begins. Then this prayer is offered, the preacher pronounces a discourse, and the congregation disperses.

From Kaulam I went to Calicut, where I remained some days. I intended at first to return to Delhi, but on second thoughts I had fears as to the consequences of such a step. So I embarked again, and after a passage of 28 days, I arrived at ZHAFÁR[1]. This was in the month of Moharram, of the year 48 (April or May, 1347)[2]. I

[1] *Zhafár* or *Dhafár*, one of the now decayed ports of Arabia, on the coast of Hadhramaut. It is spoken of by Marco Polo as a beautiful, large, and noble city (ii, p. 444), but probably from report only. Ibn Batuta seems chiefly struck by the flies and stench in the bazaar (ii, 196).

[2] At p. 36 I have pointed out generally that this date is inconsistent with previous statements. Let me sum up the intervals assigned to the different sections of his expedition to China:

Those previous statements would make the time of his second visit to the Maldive Islands fall at least as late as August, 1346. He is 43 days on the voyage thence to Chittagong, and 40 days on that from Sonárganw to Sumatra. It is not stated how long was the intervening time spent in Bengal, but he waited at Sumatra a fortnight, "till the right season for the voyage to China had arrived," and this must have been the termination of the N.E. monsoon, about March, 1347; or the commencement of the S.W. monsoon, a little later. The voyage to China occupies times as follows: To Mul-Jawa 21 days, stay there 3; to the Calm Sea 34, on that sea to Tawálisi 37, stay there say 3; to Zaitún 17, total 115 days, and time of arrival about July or August. The interval occupied by his journey in China may be thus estimated: stay at Zaitún probably not less than 10 days, voyage to Canton 27, stay there 14, back say 27, stay again at Zaitún say 4: journey to Kanjánfu 10, stay there 15; to Baiwam Kotlu 4, to Khansá 17, stay at Khansá at least 20; to Khánbáliq 64, stay there not specified, but probably not less than 60 days: voyage back to Zaitún say the same as before, omitting stoppages, *i.e.* 95 days. This makes the whole time over which his travels in China extended 367 days, and would bring the season of his sailing for India again to July or August. His voyage as far as Sumatra then occupies 112 days, he passes about 60 days there, is 40 days in sailing to Kaulam, stops a while, say 15 days, at Kaulam and Calicut, and reaches Zhafár in a voyage of 28, in all 255 days, which brings us to March or April, agreeing with the time assigned in the text for his arrival at Dhafár, but April in 1349, not April in 1347. The former date is, however, quite inconsistent with that assigned for his arrival in his native

took up my quarters with the city preacher, 'Isa Ibn Thâtha.

country (November, 1349); nor would perhaps even April, 1348, allow the traveller of those days to accomplish all that Ibn Batuta did in the interval, especially as he gives several consistent intermediate dates between his arrival at Dhafár and his reaching Fez.

Without going into tedious details, I think it probable that his visit to Bengal must, in spite of the data to the contrary, be put one year back, viz., to the cold weather of 1345–6, and that the time occupied in his Chinese travels, including the voyage thither and back, must be cut down by a whole year also. This may be considered in connexion with the doubts expressed as to his having really visited Peking.

NOTE E. (SEE PAGE 86.)

ON THE KAMRÚ OF IBN BATUTA (THE RESIDENCE OF THE SHAIKH JALÁL-UDDÍN), THE BLUE RIVER, AND THE CITY OF HABANK.

It has, I believe, been generally assumed that the country of Kamrú visited by Ibn Batuta was *Assam*, and that the Blue River by which he returned to the Ganges Delta was the Brahmaputra. And I gather that M. Defrémery (iv, 215) takes this view.

It appeared to me however when I took up the subject that there was some reason to believe that the district visited was SILHET, and that the river in question was one branch or other of the great Silhet River, the *Barak* or the *Surma*. This was first suggested by the statement in the text that Shaikh Jalál-uddín had converted a large number of the inhabitants to the Mahomedan faith; for it is a fact that in Silhet, though so remote from the centres of Mahomedan influence, there is an unusually large proportion of the peasantry who profess that religion. It seemed however probable that if Silhet *were* the site of Jalál-uddín's missionary exertions, some trace of his memory would be preserved there. And of this I speedily found indications in two English works, whilst at the same time I forwarded through a valued friend, who had a correspondent at Silhet, some brief queries for answer on the spot.

In the interesting narrative of Robert Lindsay, who was one of the first English residents or collectors of Silhet (*Lives of the Lindsays*, iii, 168), we find that on his first arrival there he was told "that it was customary for the new resident to pay his respects to the shrine of the tutelar saint SHAW JULOLL. Pilgrims of the Islam faith flock to the shrine from every part of India, and I afterwards found that the fanatics attending the tomb were not a little dangerous," etc. An article on Silhet, by Captain Fisher, in the *J.A.S. Bengal* for 1840 (ix, Pt. II, pp. 808–43), also speaks of Sháh Jalál's shrine, and of his being traditionally regarded as the conqueror of the country for the Mahomedans. ["The town of Sylhet existed in the time of Akhbar, and as this is known to date from the Mosque built over the tomb of Sha Gelaal, its patron saint, who conquered it from a native Raja, we may assume that the current tradition, which assigns its erection to the middle of the thirteenth century, is correct." P. 840.]

Kámrúb, Kámrún, or Kámrú, corrupted from the Sanscrit *Kámarúpa* or Kamrup, was vaguely known to the Arab geographers as the name of a mountainous country between India and China, noted for its production of a valuable aloes-wood (see Gildemeister, pp. 70, 191; and Reinaud, *Rel. des Voyages*, etc., p. 41). Though the seat of the ancient Hindu Government of Kamrup was probably in Assam, a central district of which still preserves the name, we are informed by Captain Fisher (with no view to such a question as the present) that "it is known that Kamrup extended to the southward as far as the confluence of the Megna with the Brahmaputra" (*i.e.* to the vicinity of Dacca; *o.c.*, p. 829). He adds that there are still in Silhet some Musulman families who are the descendants of Rajas once under the dynasty of Kamrup, and who were forced to conform to Mahomedanism on the change of masters. Of these, a principal one is the Raja of Baniachong (a place between the Barak and Surma, about forty miles S.W. of Silhet). The first invasion of Kamrup by the Mahomedans took place in 1205–6 under Mahomed Bakhtiyar Khilji, Governor of Bengal; a second in 1253–7 under another Governor called Toghral Beg Malik Yuzbek (see Stewart's *History of Bengal*, pp. 45 *seqq.*). Both these invasions ended in disaster; but, as far as can be understood, both appear to have been directed through the Silhet territory, and then across the passes of the Kasia or Jaintia Hills into Assam. In the accounts of both invasions mention is made of a great river called *Bangamati*, on which stood a chief city which was captured by Bakhtiyar Khilji. This name is not now applied to any river in that quarter; but it seems highly probable that it may be connected with the *Habank* (*Habanga*) of Ibn Batuta, and that this was situated at or near Silhet, perhaps at the place now called BANGA, at the bifurcation of the Surma and Barak, twenty or thirty miles above Silhet. The Bangamati is described in the account of the Khilji's campaign as "three times as big as the Ganges." But this might easily be accounted for if (as is very possible) the rivers of Silhet then chanced to occupy a more concentrated channel than at present, or if (as Captain Fisher suggests) the annual inundation had not quite subsided. This inundation, when at its height, as I have seen it from the Kasia Hills, appears like a vast estuary, covering the whole plain, eighty miles in width, between the Kasia and the Tipura Hills.

So far I had written when the answer arrived from my friend's correspondent, the Rev. W. Pryse of the Silhet mission. My questions had related to Jalál-uddín and Habank, and whether any traces of a city existed at Banga. Mr. Pryse states that the name of *Jalalludin Tabrizi* was known to the learned Mahomedans at Silhet only as that of a Pír or Saint in Hindustan, but not locally either in Silhet or Cachar. He then proceeds:

"SHÁH JELALL, according to tradition, came to Silhet about the middle of the fourteenth century (A.D.) accompanied by a hundred and eighty Arab *Pírs* [Holy Men] from Yemen. There is a Persian MS. called 'Suhayli-Yemen' still partly in existence at Sháh Jelall's Musjid here, which I have seen, but unfortunately the date and a large portion of the MS. are not legible, from the effect of the climate. Shah Jelall's tomb once was, but is not now, a place of pilgrimage.

"HABANG is the name of a small Tillah[1] in the Pergunnah of Dinarpore south of Hubbigunge in this Zillah, running along the eastern or left bank of the Barak or Koosiara River. In tradition it is noted for its *Pírs*, under the name of 'Habangia Tillah,' or, as pronounced in the neighbourhood, 'Hapaniya Tillah'. . . .

. "Chor Goola Tillah, to the south-east of Latoo, some ten or twelve miles S.E. of Banga Bazar (which still exists just at the separation of Soorma and Koosiara Rivers, on the western confines of Cachar), was formerly noted for its *Pírs*. An old fellow still resides there in the midst of the jungles on the bank of the beautiful Svind *Bheel* (lake). The illiterate Moslems around have a tradition that the *Pírs* there make the tigers their playmates and protectors, and that boats ready-manned start up from the lake ready for their use whenever they wish.

"*Banga Bazar* is a modern village. The hillocks and jungles to the eastward are the resort of the Pírs.

* * * * * * * * *

"I think it probable that all the eastern portion of the Zillah of Silhet was uninhabited when Mullik Yuzbek first entered the valley in 1253. Hence we find that the Hindus preponderate in the population of the western half, and the Moslems in that of the eastern half."

A later note from the same gentleman adds: "I have found four celebrated spots in this Zillah at which report says Sháh Jelall settled some of the *Pírs* who accompanied him, viz., Silhet, Latoo, Hapaniya Tillah in Toroff, and HABANG Tillah on the south-eastern bank of the Chingra Khal river, about six miles north-west from Silhet, and about four miles north from the village of Akhalia. At present nothing is to be found in any of these places excepting Silhet, where there is a mosque kept in repair by government. I believe the Habang Tillah on the Chingra Khal must be the one Col. Y. spoke of."

These interesting notes appear to me to render it *certain* that Silhet was the field of our traveller's tour. That Shaikh Jalál-ud-dín's name has got shortened by familiar use is of no importance

[1] *Tíla* is the word commonly applied in Eastern Bengal to low and often isolated hills starting up from the plain. At the town of Silhet there are several such, on which the houses of the European officials are built.

against this view—*Sháh* is a title often applied to eminent Mahomedan saints—whilst we learn that tradition still regards him as a saint and a leader of saints; that the date assigned to him corresponds fairly with that derivable from Ibn Batuta, for the *death* of Jalál-uddín must have occurred close upon the middle of the fourteenth century, shortly after Ibn Batuta's visit, *i.e.* in 1347 or 1348 (see *supra*, pp. 87, 90); and that the name of Habank still survives, and has a legendary fame. If no remains of Ibn Batuta's great city exist, that is small wonder. Neither climate nor materials in Bengal are favourable to the preservation of such remains, and I know of no medieval remains in Bengal Proper except at Gaur and Pandua.

The name of *Al-Azrak,* which our author applies to the river which he descends from Habank, is the same as that (*Bahr-al-Azrak*) which we translate as the *Blue Nile* of Abyssinia. Ibn Batuta applies the same name to the River Karun in Khuzistan (ii, 23). A Persian title of like significance (*Nil-Ab*) is applied by Musulman writers to the Indus, and also it would appear to the Jelum (see *Jour. A. S.*, ix, 201; *Sadik Isfahani*, p. 51; Dow's *Firishta*, i. 25), and the name here may therefore have been given arbitrarily. According to Wilkinson, however, *Azrak* signifies *black* rather than *blue* (Rawlinson's *Herod.*, ii, 25); and it is possible that the name of the River *Surma,* suggesting the black collyrium so called, may have originated the title used by Ibn Batuta.

I doubt if water-wheels are at present used for irrigation, as described by the traveller, in any part of Bengal Proper, though common in the Upper Provinces.

I should strongly dissent from Mr. Pryse's idea that Eastern Silhet was uninhabited in the 13th century. But I think it is highly probable that the inhabitants were not Hindus, but of Indo-Chinese race, like those occupying the adjoining hills and part of Cachar. This is implied in Ibn Batuta's account of the people, though in strictness he speaks only of the hill people. These, however, in the adjoining mountains, have not been converted to Mahomedanism. They retain their original character, and have the Mongolian type of features in the highest development. As regards their powers of work, of which the traveller speaks so highly, I may observe that, when I was in that region, porters of the Kasia nation used often to carry down from the coal mines of Cherra Punji to the plains, a distance of eleven miles, loads of two maunds or 165 lbs. of coal. Their strength and bulk of *leg* were such as I have never seen elsewhere.

On the map at the end of this book I have inserted a sketch from such imperfect materials as are available, to make Ibn Batuta's travels in Bengal more intelligible. No decent map of Silhet yet exists, but my friend Colonel Thuillier informs me that the survey is finished, so a correct representation of that remarkable country may be expected before long. [Maps of the Silhet District, etc., have since been published by the Government of India.]

NOTE F. (SEE PAGE 96.)

ON THE MUL-JAVA OF IBN BATUTA.

This *Mul-Java* is made by all the commentators, professed or incidental (see Lee, Dulaurier, Defrémery, Gildemeister, Walckenaer, Reinaud, Lassen), to be the Island of Java[1], and by help of Sanscrit the appellation is made with more or less of coercion to signify "*Primitive* or *Original* Java." Setting aside the questionable application of Sanscrit etymologies to explain names which were probably conferred by Arab sailors, surely it is not hard to see that if by Mul-Java, where elephants were kept by every petty shopkeeper, and eagle-wood was used to serve the kitchen fires, the traveller did mean JAVA, then he lied so egregiously that it is not worth considering what he meant. There are *no* elephants in Java, except such few as are imported to swell the state of the native princes—at present, perhaps, considerably fewer than we could muster in England—and there is no eagle-wood.

These circumstances taken alone would lead us to seek for the country in question on some part of the Continent bordering the Gulf of Siam, probably in or near Cambodia. *There* elephants are still almost as common as Ibn Batuta represents them, and the country is also, and has been for ages, the great source of supply of aloes or eagle-wood. When formerly suggesting this view (in a note on *Jordanus*, p. 33), I applied to a learned Arabic scholar to know if there were no term like *mul* in that language which might bear some such sense as *Terra-firma*. The answer was unfavourable. But I have since lighted on a solution. In vol. xxix of the *Jour. of the R.G.S.*, p. 30, Capt. Burton mentions that the Arabs having in latter times confined the name of Zanjibar to the island and city now so called, they generally distinguish the mainland as *Bar-el*-MOLI, or "Continent," in opposition to *Kisiwa* "Island." And below he adds: "The word *Moli*, commonly used in the corrupt Arabic of Zanjibar, will

[1] [Lee remarks, *Ibn Batuta*, p. 201, about Mul-Java: "This is, no doubt, the Java of our maps." Dulaurier, *Journ. Asiat.*, i, 1847, makes it "la Java du Commencement," "Java principale"; Kern, "la primitive Djavua." V. der Lith, *Merveilles de l'Inde*, p. 238, writes that *Moul* seems to be derived from the Sanscrit *moula* which means beginning, origin, root, and that there is no reason to seek for this Java outside of Sumatra.]

vainly be sought in the Dictionaries." *Mul-Java* then is Java of the Main.

It is true that in the only other place where I have been able to find this name used, a passage quoted by D'Ohsson from the Mongol History in the Persian language, called *Tarikh-i-Wassaf*, it is stated that in 1292 Kúblái Khan conquered "the *Island* of Mul-Java," which is described as lying in the direction of India, and as having a length of 200 farsangs, and a breadth of 100. It is added that the sovereign of this country, *Sri Rama* by name, died on his way to pay homage to Kúblái, but his son arrived, and was well received, obtaining the confirmation of his government on condition of rendering a tribute of gold and pearls (D'Ohsson, ii, 465)[1]. As regards the use of the word *island* here, it is to be remembered that the Arabs used the word *Jazírah* also for a peninsula, as we have already had occasion to observe. Thus Abulfeda calls the Spanish Peninsula *Jazirat-ul-Andalus*, and Ibn Jubair applies the plural *Jazair* to what we by a kind of analogy call the Two Sicilies (Reinaud's *Abulfeda*, ii, 234; *Jour. Asiat.*, Jan., 1846, p. 224; see also Gildemeister, p. 59). Let it be remembered also that the terms *Jawa*, *Jawi*, with the Arabs were applied not merely to the specific islands of Java and Sumatra, but "to the whole Archipelago, its language, and inhabitants" (Crawfurd's *Dict. of I. Islands*, p. 165). To what region then would the full appellation *Jazirah Mul Jáwa*, or "Peninsula of Java of the Main," apply so aptly as to what we call the *Malay Peninsula*, which, I may observe, Crawfurd in all his works on the Archipelago treats as essentially part of that region? And turning to the fragments of hazy history preserved by the Malays, we find as one of the early kings over the Malay or Javanese settlers in the peninsula, SRI RAMA Vikrama. The reign of this king indeed, according to Lassen's interpretation of the chronology, is placed 1301–14, some years too late for the date in Wassaf, but the Malay dates are very uncertain (see Lassen, iv, 542; and Crawfurd, *o.c.* 243). I have little doubt, then, that the Peninsula was the Mul-Java of the two authors, though possibly the extension of the name towards Siam and Cambodia may not have been very exactly limited, for we know from Barros that the king of Siam claimed sovereignty over the Peninsula even to Singapore, and it may still have been in the former quarter that Ibn Batuta landed. Even if this be not admissible, I may remark that we know little now of the eastern coast of the Peninsula or regarding the degree of civilisation to which it may have attained in former days. The elephant, however, abounds in its northern forests, and is still commonly domesticated. The aloes-wood also is found there, though lower

[1] [See *The Expedition of the Mongols against Java in* 1293 A.D., by W. P. Groeneveldt. *China Review*, iv, pp. 246–54.]

in repute than that of Cambodia (see Crawfurd in vv. *Elephant* and *Agila*).

[Van der Lith places Qâqola in Sumatra, north of the Battak country (*Merveilles de l'Inde*, pp. 237–41). He says, p. 241, that camphor is one of the products of Qâqola and of Sumatra; it is not a product of Cambodia or Java; therefore one must admit that Ibn Batuta saw aloes-wood at Qâqola imported from the Khmer kingdom.]

["From the circumstance of his [Ibn Batuta] not mentioning *Fanṣūr* we may deduce that his *Ḳākula* is not Angkola (W. Sumatra), as Van der Lith has wildly conjectured. Had Ibn Batuta been on the coast conterminous to the inland district of Angkola, he could scarcely have omitted to speak of Bārūs, which lies close by. Nor is it likely that *Mul-Jāwah*, the country where the port of *Ḳākula* was situated, is Java, as has been no less wildly fancied. All indications concur in pointing to places on the east coast of the Malay Peninsula, with names ringing like distant echoes of the Ptolemaic Kōli (if not exactly *Takōla* or *Kokkonagara*) and *Perimula* (= [*Peri-*] *Mula-Java*?). The triple coincidence in the events of (1) stone walls surrounding the city, (2) abundance of elephants, which are employed also in warfare, and (3) scarcity of horses in the country, occurring in almost the same words in the accounts of (i) Ḳāḳula by Ibn Batuta and (ii) *Ko-lo* by Ma Twan-lin, seems to point to the unmistakable identity of the two places, and therefore, confirm the location of *Ḳākula* on the east coast of the Malay Peninsula at either Kelantan or Lîgor." (Gerini, *Researches on Ptolemy's Geog.*, p. 444 *n.*)]

At p. 96 I have quoted from Abulfeda a slight indication of the position of Kumára, which Ibn Batuta represents to have been a city belonging to Mul-Java, as at the northern end of the Malay Peninsula. It may however have been on the other side of the Gulf of Siam, and in that case it is possible that the name may be connected with *Khmer*, the ancient native name of the kingdom of Cambodia (see Pallegoix, *Des. du Royaume Thai ou Siam*, i. 29, and Mouhot's *Travels*, i, 278).

NOTE G. (SEE PAGE 108.)

ON THE TAWÁLISI OF IBN BATUTA.

This *Tawálisi* is a great difficulty. The French translators say: "The Isle of Celebes, or rather perhaps Tunkin"; Dulaurier, "The coast of Camboja, Cochin-China, or Tunkin"; Lassen, "By this name no place can be meant but Tonkin"; whilst Walckenaer identifies it with *Tawal*, a small island adjoining Bachian, one of the Moluccas. This last suggestion seems to have been based on the name only, and all have been made in connexion with the assumption that the Mul-Jawa of our author is Java, which we have seen that it cannot be.

It seems to me impossible that Tawálisi should be Cambodia, Cochin-China, or Tong-King, for two conclusive reasons: (1) that the voyage from Mul-Jawa to Tawálisi occupies seventy-one days, and is considered by our traveller's shipmates an unusually good passage; (2) that the last thirty-seven days of this time are spent on the passage of the *Bahr-al-Káhil*, disturbed by neither winds nor waves, a character which in this case we should have to attach to the China Sea, the very metropolis of Typhoons.

But I do not find it easy to get beyond a negative. Indeed, considering that *Killa-Karai* is the real name of a port in South India, and that *Urdujá* is a name which our author in a former part of his travels has assigned to one of the Queens of Mahomed Uzbek Khan on the Volga, and has explained to mean in Turkish "Born in the Camp," whilst the Lady of Tawálisi herself is made to speak not only to the traveller but to her own servants a mixture of Turkish and Persian, a faint suspicion rises that Tawálisi is really to be looked for in that part of the atlas which contains the Marine Surveys of the late Captain Gulliver.

Putting aside this suspicion, no suggestion seems on the whole more probable than that Tawálisi was the kingdom of Soolo or Súlúk, N.E. of Borneo. "Owing to some cause or other," says Crawfurd, "there has sprung up in Soolo a civilisation and power far exceeding those of the surrounding islanders. A superior fertility of the soil, and better means of maintaining a numerous and concentrated population, has probably been the main cause of this superiority; but whatever be the cause, it has enabled this people not only to maintain a paramount authority over the whole Archipelago (*i.e.* the so-called Soolo Archipelago), but to extend it to Paláwan and to the northern coasts of Borneo and islands adjacent to it." Adopting this view, we should have the *Bahr-al-Káhil* in the sea between Java, Borneo and Celebes, where hurricanes are unknown, and stormy weather is rare. And, the time mentioned by Ibn Batuta, if we suppose it occupied in the voyage from the upper part of the Gulf of Siam through the Java Sea and Straits of Macassar to Soolo, a distance of some 2200 nautical miles, over a great part of which the ship had to be towed, would seem much less improbable than if the course were to Cochin-China or Tong-King. The naval power of Tawálisi is one of the most prominent features in the narrative, and the Soolo people have been noted throughout the seas of the Archipelago for the daring exploits of their piratical fleets from our earliest acquaintance with those regions. It would seem also from Ibn Batuta's expression, "the load of two elephants in rice," that elephants were used in Tawálisi. Now the elephant is alleged by Dalrymple to exist in Soolo, and though Crawfurd doubts the fact, there seems no sufficient reason for his doubts. It is *known*, moreover, to exist in the adjoining part of Borneo, which may have belonged to Soolo then as it does now, and though not used now it was found in a domesticated state at Brunei by Magellan's party in 1521. These are the only portions of the Archipelago east of Sumatra in which the elephant is known.

However, I by no means put forth this hypothesis with any great confidence. The statement that the Sovereign was the equal of the King of China would certainly be preposterous; but so it would in almost any conceivable identification of Tawálisi, unless we take it for Japan. To this there are objections still more serious.

I suspect this kingdom of Soolo, or *Súlúk*, as the Malays call it, may be also the *Lohac* of Marco Polo which has so much troubled commentators (iii, 7). This was an extensive region, lying 500 miles south-east of Sondur and Condur (Pulo Condore), inhabited by pagans, with a language of their own, under a king tributary to no one, being in a very inaccessible position, producing much brazil-wood and great abundance of gold, having elephants in its forests, and supplying all the east with *porcelains* or cowry-shells for currency. The position answers to that of Soolo with fair accuracy; cowries are said to be found in quantities there only of all the Indian islands; the elephant, as we have seen, is reported to exist there, and certainly does exist in the adjoining territory of Borneo, belonging to Soolo; its "much gold" is spoken of by Barbosa. Pauthier, indeed, in his new edition of Polo from ancient French MSS. reads *Soucat* instead of Lohac, and identifies it with *Sukadana*, on the S.W. of Borneo. But neither elephants nor cowries appear to be found in that part of Borneo; and as the native name of Soolo is *Sug*, that *may* have been the name indicated, if Soucat be the right reading. Let me add, however, that Soolo is said to have been at one time subject to Sukadana, and this circumstance might perhaps help to reconcile Pauthier's suggestion with the facts.

Confining ourselves to the indications afforded by the *names* as given by Ibn Batuta, besides the *Tawal* of Walckenaer we have (as noticed at p. 90) a place marked as *Talysian*, on the east coast of Borneo, and one of the chief Soolo islands called *Tawi-tawi*. As regards *Kailukari*, the Atlas of Mercator and Hondius shows on the west coast of Celebes a place called *Curi-curi*, which may perhaps be the same that we now find as *Kaili*, a district carrying on a good deal of trade with Singapore, Java, etc. There is also a place called *Kalakah*, on the north-eastern coast of Borneo. The port of Tawálisi is called *Kailúka* in Lee's version, but no importance can be attached to this. (See Crawfurd's *Dict. Ind.*

Islands, Articles, *Solo*, *Elephant*, *Kaili*, *Cowry*; ditto *Malay Dict.* p. 72; Pauthier's *Polo*, p. 563.) [*Marco Polo*, ii, pp. 277–80.]

We should not omit to call attention to a certain resemblance between the *Tawálisi* of our author and the *Thalamasin* of Odoric.

[G. J. Dozy, quoted by Van der Lith, p. 245 *n.*, is of opinion that the Tawálisi of Ibn Batuta must be looked for in the Philippine Islands.]

NOTE H. (SEE PAGE 145.)

REGARDING THE HISTORY OF THE KHANS OF CHAGATAI.

In this passage Ibn Batuta appears to speak of Turkestan and Mā-warā-n-Nahr as separate kingdoms. Whether he so intends or not it is the case that the CHAGATAI or Middle Empire of the Mongols was by this time divided; and as I know no book that contains a coherent sketch of the course of events in that empire, I will here put together what I have gathered from such scattered sources as are accessible[1].

The tract assigned by Chinghiz, in the distribution of his provinces, to his son Chagatai, embraced Mā-warā-n-Nahr [or Transoxiana] and part of Khwarizm, the Uighúr country, Kashgar, Badakhshán, Balkh, and the province of Ghazni to the banks of the Sindh[2]; or in modern geography, the kingdoms of Independent Tartary with the exception of Khiva or the greater part of it, the country under the Uzbeks of Kunduz, Afghanistan, and the western and northern portions of Chinese Turkestan, including Dzungaria. Bishbáliq, north of the T'ien Shan, was at first the headquarters of the Khans, but it was afterwards transferred to Almaliq[3].

[1] [The following work gives the history then wanted: *The Tarikh-i-Rashidi of Mirza Muhammad Haidar, Dughlát. A History of the Moghuls of Central Asia.* An English version, edited, with Commentary, Notes, and Map, by N. Elias. The translation by E. Denison Ross. London, Sampson Low, 1895, 8vo. pp. xxiii + 535.]

[2] Defrémery's Extracts from *Khondemir* in *Journal Asiatique*, sér. iv, tom. xix, pp. 58 *seqq.* [Chagatai's "central kingdom, Mávará-un-Nahr, or Transoxiana, was situated chiefly between the rivers Sir and Amu (the Jihun or Oxus), but included, in its extension towards the north-east, the hill ranges and steppes lying beyond the right bank of the Sir, east of the Kipchák plains, and west of lakes Issigh-Kul and Ala-Nor. Towards the east, the Chagatai domain took in the greater part of the region now known as Chinese (or Eastern) Turkestan, Farghána (or Khokand) and Badakhshán; while towards the south it embraced Kunduz, Balkh, and, at the outset, Khorasán—a country which, at that time, spread eastward to beyond Herat and Ghazni, and southward to Mekrán." (*Tarikh-i-Rashidi*, Int. p. 30.]

[3] As early as the time of Chagatai himself, however, his summer camp was in the vicinity of Almaliq. And when Húlakú was on the

In the space of about one hundred and twenty years no less than thirty descendants or kinsmen of Chagatai are counted to have occupied his throne, and indeed revolutions, depositions, murders, and usurpations seem to have succeeded each other with a frequency unusual even in Asiatic governments[1].

march from Karakorúm to destroy the Assassins (A.D. 1254) the Princess Regent Organah, widow of Kara Húlakú grandson and successor of Chagatai, came out from Almaliq to receive him with due honour. Hence it would appear that Almaliq was one at least of the capitals from a very early date. In the following century, about 1330–4, we find Ibn Batuta observing that it was the proper capital of the kings of this dynasty, and that one of the charges brought against the Khan Tarmashirin, which led to his supersession, was that he always remained in Mā-warā-n-Nahr, and for four years running had not visited Almaliq and the eastern dominions of his family. In the time of the immediate successors of Tarmashirin also, when Almaliq was visited by the Archbishop Nicolas [of Khánbáliq] (about 1335–6), and by Marignolli (1341), it appears to have been the residence of the sovereigns of Chagatai (Quatremère's *Rashid.*, p. 146; *Ibn Bat.*, iii, 41; *supra*, III, pp. 13, 213).

["Another famous town was Almaligh, which is known at the present day. The tomb of Tughluk Timur Khan is there, together with [other] traces of the city's prosperity. The dome of the Khan's tomb is remarkable, being lofty and decorated; while on the plaster, inscriptions are written.... As far as I can recollect the date inscribed on that dome was seven hundred and sixty and odd." (*Tarikh-i-Rashidi*, p. 364.) Tughluk Timur died about 764 A.H. = 1363 A.D.]

It was during the government of the above-mentioned Organah that Rubruquis passed through the country, and probably what he states of the region being called *Organum* originated in some misapprehension of this (see Rubr., p. 281).

[1] See for example at III, p. 35, *supra*, where some obscure points in the chronology of those kings have already been discussed. [Here is a list of the princes of Mā-warā-n-Nahr from Mr. Stanley Lane Poole's *Muhammadan Dynasties* (p. 242) and reproduced in the Introduction of the *Tarikh-i-Rashidi*, p. 49:

			A.H.	A.D.
1.	Chaghatai	Began to reign	624 =	1227
2.	Kara Huláku		639 =	1242
3.	Isu Mangu		645 =	1247
	Kara Huláku (*restored*)		650 =	1252
4.	Orgánah Khátun		650 =	1252
5.	Algu		659 =	1261
6.	Mubárak Shah		664 =	1266
7.	Barák Khan		664 =	1266
8.	Nikpai		668 =	1270
9.	Tuka Timur		670 =	1272
10.	Davá Khan		*c.* 672 =	*c.* 1274
11.	Kunjuk Khan		706 =	1306
12.	Taliku		708 =	1308
13.	Kabak Khan		709 =	1309
14.	Isán Bugha		709 =	1309
	Kabak Khan (*restored*)		*c.* 718 =	1318
15.	Ilchikadi		721 =	1321
16.	Davá Timur		721 =	1321
17.	Tarmashirin		722 =	1322
	Sanjar?		730-4? =	1330–4?
18.	Jinkishai		734 =	1334
19.	Buzun		*c.* 735 =	*c.* 1335

At an early date however in the history of the dynasty, the claims of Kaidu to the Supreme Kaanship, of which Kúblái had effective possession, seem to have led to a partition of the Chagatai territory. For Kaidu, who was of the lineage of Okkodai[1], not of Chagatai, whilst claiming in the higher character of Supreme Khakan to exercise superiority over the appanage of Chagatai and to nominate its proper khans, held also under his own immediate sway a large tract, the greater part of which belonged apparently to the former appanage as originally constituted. It is not very clear what were the limits between Kaidu's territory and that of the Chagatai Khans, and indeed the two must have been somewhat interlocked, for Kaidu and Borák Khan of Chagatai at one time exercised a sort of joint sovereignty in the cities of Bokhara and Samarkand. But it may be gathered that Kaidu's dominions included Kashgar and Yarkand, and all the cities bordering the south side of the T'ien Shan as far east as Karakhoja, as well as the valley of the Talas river, and all the country north of the T'ien Shan from Lake Balkash eastward to the Chagan Nur, and in the further north between the Upper Yenisei and the Irtish[2]. Khotan appears to have belonged to the Great Kaan, but Borák Kaan got possession of it in the beginning of his reign, and I do not know if it was recovered by Kúblái[3], or if it passed into the hands of Kaidu.

During a great part of Kaidu's struggles he found a staunch ally in Dua the son of Borák, whom he had set upon the throne of Chagatai in 1272[4]. After Kaidu's death in 1301, his son and successor Shabar joined with Dua in making submission to Timur the successor of Kúblái; but before long, the two former princes having quarrelled, Dua seized the territory of Shabar, and thus

			A.H.	A.D.
20.	Isun Timur	Began to reign	c. 739 =	c. 1339
	Ali (of Oktai stock)		c. 741 =	c. 1340
21.	Muhammad		c. 743 =	c. 1342
22.	Kazán		744 =	1343
	Danishmanja (of Oktai stock)		747 =	1346
23.	Buyan Kuli		749 =	1348
			—760	—1358

Anarchy and rival chiefs until the supremacy of Timur in 771 A.H. = 1370 A.D.]

[1] He was son of Kashin, son of Okkodai.

[2] See D'Ohsson, ii, 361, 450–2, 516; iii, 427; *Notices et Extraits*, xiv, 224; *Polo* in Pauthier's ed. and notes, pp. 137, 163, 241, 253, 716 *et seqq.*, also the version of a Chinese sketch of Asia under the Mongols on the Map at the end of that work. Khondemir appears to have written the History of Kaidu, which would I presume throw exacter light upon the limits of his dominions. But this does not seem to have been translated (see Defrémery, *op. cit.* p. 267, and *Marco Polo*, ii, pp. 457 *seq.*).

[3] Defrémery, *op. cit.* p. 250. Marco says of Khotan, "Ils sont au grand Kaan" (Pauthier, 143).

[4] So D'Ohsson. Khondemir puts Dua's accession in 1291, but notices that other accounts gave a different statement (Defrémery, p. 265).

substantially reunited the whole of the original appanage of Chagatai, as it had been before the schism of Kaidu[1].

This state of things does not appear however to have endured long; for within a few years a new schism took place, of which the history is very obscure.

The people of Eastern Turkestan and the other regions in that direction which had been subject to Kaidu, probably preferred to be under a separate rule from that of Transoxiana; for we are told by Abulghazi[2] that the people of Kashgar and Yarkand, the inhabitants of the Alatagh and the Uighúrs, "finding none of the posterity of Chagatai (qu. Okkodai?) among them to fill the vacant throne," called to be their Khan Imil Khwaja the son of Dua Khan[3]. This prince was succeeded in 1347 by his son Tughlak Timur. Thus was established a new *Eastern* branch of the Chagatai dynasty.

The kingdom so formed was that which is known to the Persian historians of Timur and his successors as *Moghulistan* (not to be confounded with the true Mongolia to the eastward), or the Ulús of Jatah (or in French spelling *Djéteh*, the Gète country of Pétis de la Croix). Their winter capital was perhaps originally at Kashgar or Yarkand, and afterwards at Aqsu, and their summer quarters north of the T'ien Shan[4]. In the history of Timur who took the royal residence in 1389 it is called AYMUL GUJA[5]. This is perhaps the *Imil*, on the banks of the river so called flowing into Lake Ala-Kul, which was the original capital of the K'itan refugees who founded the empire of Kara K'itai (*supra*, III, p. 21), and which John de Plano Carpini on his journey to the court of Kuyuk Khan names as Omyl. It is perhaps represented at the present day, as D'Avezac suggests, by the Chinese frontier town of Chuguchak or Tarbagatai[6]. It is difficult however to under-

1 D'Ohsson, ii, 518 *seq.*

2 Cited in the *Universal History* (Fr. Trans.), tom. xvii, 619 *seqq.* Deguignes, i, 289.

3 As the history is given by Abul Ghazi, this Imil Khwaja is *identical* with that son of Dua who succeeded to the throne of Chagatai under the name of Isanbuga Khán in 1309; and the story as told would seem to imply that he gave up reigning in Transoxiana to reign in Eastern Turkestan. If this be true, the establishment of this schism must have occurred some time before 1321, as Gabak or Kapak, the successor of Isanbuga on the throne of Chagatai, died in that year, the date of his accession not being recorded. According to Khondemir, however, Isanbuga reigned over Chagatai till his death, and Imil Khwaja would seem to be a brother (see Defrémery, pp. 270 and 280).

4 See *Russians in Central Asia*, p. 69.

5 In *H. de Timur Bec* by Pétis de la Croix, vol. ii; also in the *Univ. Hist.* as above, p. 622 *seqq.*

6 D'Avezac, *Not. sur les anciens Voyages en Tartarie*, etc., in *Rec. de Voyages*, iv, 516. The capital of Kara K'itai when at the height of its power was *Bala Sagun*. I cannot ascertain the proper position of this; but it was, I believe, different from Imil, and lay between Bishbáliq and Karakorúm. [*Balasaghoun*. Dr. Bretschneider (*Med.*

stand such a disposition of the frontier between the two branches of the Chagatai empire as should have permitted the capital of that one which ruled over Kashgar and Uighuria to be in the site

Res.) has a chapter on Kara K'itai (i, 208 *seq.*), and in a long note on Bala Sagun, which he calls Belasagun, he says (p. 226) that "according to the *Tarikh Djihan Kushai* (D'Ohsson, i, 433) the city of Belasagun had been founded by Buku Khan, sovereign of the Uighúrs, in a well-watered plain of Turkestan and rich pastures. The Arabian geographers first mention Belasagun, in the ninth or tenth century, as a city beyond the Sihun or Yaxartes, depending on *Isfidjab* (Sairam, according to Lerch), and situated east of Taras. They state that the people of Turkestan considered Belasagun to represent 'the navel of the earth' on account of its being situated in the middle between east and west, and likewise between north and south. (Sprenger's *Postr. d. Or.*, *Mavarannahar.*)" Dr. Bretschneider adds (p. 227): "It is not improbable that ancient Belasagun was situated at the same place where, according to the T'ang history, the khan of one branch of the Western T'u küe (Turks) had his residence in the seventh century. It is stated in the *T'ang shu* that *Ibi Shabolo Shehu Khan*, who reigned in the first half of the seventh century, placed his ordo on the northern border of the river *Sui ye*. This river and a city of the same name are frequently mentioned in the T'ang Annals of the seventh and eighth centuries, in connection with the warlike expeditions of the Chinese in Central Asia. *Sui ye* was situated on the way from the river *Ili* to the city of *Ta-lo-sz'* (Talas). In 679 the Chinese had built on the Sui ye river a fortress; but in 748 they were constrained to destroy it. (Comp. Visdelou in *Suppl. Bibl. Orient.*, pp. 110–114; Gaubil's *Hist. de la Dyn. des Thang* in *Mém. conc. les Chinois*, xv, pp. 403 *seq.*)" The *Djihan Kushai* (*Tarikh-i-Rashidi*, p. 361) mentions among the towns in Moghulistan "Balá Sakun, which in the *Suvar-i-Akálim* is reckoned among the cities of Khitái, and called 'Khán Baligh'; while in Moghulistan and Kara K'itai they have written the same 'Balá Sákun.'"

N. Elias in a long note on Bala Sakun (*l.c.*, p. 361) says: "There is every reason to believe that the Bála-Sákun spoken of in this passage was situated on or near the head waters of the Káragáty branch of the River Chu in Moghulistan, and that it was, up to the first quarter of the twelfth century, the capital of the Ilak Khans, or the so-called Afrásiábi Turks; while later it became, for a time the chief town of Kara-K'itai." Chavannes, *Tou-kiue occidentaux*, p. 86 *n.*, gives Bālaçaghoun = Tokmak. In Prof. V. Grigoriev's paper on *The Kharakhanides in Mā-warā-n-Nahr* there is a translation of the Chronicle of the Astrologer Munedjim-Bashi (b. *c.* 1630) which begins as follows: "Of the Khans of Turkestan. These Khans claimed to be descended from Afrasiab. Twenty of them reigned in all. The capital of their dominions was at first the city of Balasagun, but afterwards Bukhara and Samarkand. They began to rule over Mávará-n-Nahr in the year 383 (993 A.D.), and their dynasty came to an end in 609 (1212). Their main possessions were: 1. *Bala Sagun*, which was their capital, situated at the beginning of the 7th climate in 102° of longitude and 48° of latitude, not far from Kashgar, and considered from of old the boundary city of Turkestan; 2. *Kashgar*, the capital of Turan...; 3. *Khotan*...; 4. *Karakorum*; 5. *Taraz*...; 6. *Farab*; all three important cities." Prof. Grigoriev, in his note, besides mentioning the position of Bala Sagun as given by Al-Biruni, quotes from Hadji Khalfa, in his *Jihán Numá* the longitude as 101° and the latitude as 47½°. Eugene Schuyler, *Geog. Mag.*, Dec. 1, 1874, p. 389.—See *supra*, I, p. 60 *n.*]

Omyl. In a note to Carpini, Rockhill writes, p. 16 *n.*: "The original town of Imil, on the river which still bears that name, and which flows into the Ala-Kul, passing south of the town of Chuguchak, was built by the Kara Khitai somewhere about 1125. Imil was Kuyuk's appanage (*ulus*)."]·

just indicated, whilst that of the other branch ruling over Mā-warā-n-Nahr was situated at Almaliq. If the site assigned to Aymul be correct, probably it was not the headquarters of the eastern branch till the western branch of Chagatai in its rapid decay had lost its hold on the valley of the Ili.

Kazán Khan, slain in 1346 or 1348, was the last effective Khan of the main branch of Chagatai. After his time the titular Khans were mere puppets in the hands of the great Amírs, who set them up one year and probably murdered them the next. And so things continued until one of those Amírs, the famous TIMUR, became predominant. Even he in the height of his conquests continued to maintain titular successors to the throne of Chagatai, and to put their names at the head of State papers. Sultan Mahomed Khan, the last of these, died on one of Timur's campaigns in Anatolia, in 1403[1].

In 1360, and again in 1361–2, whilst Mā-warā-n-Nahr was in the state of anarchy to which we have alluded, Tughlak Timur invaded and subdued the country, leaving on the second occasion his son Elias Khwaja as his representative at Samarkand. Thus the whole empire would seem again to have been united; but it was only for a brief space. For in 1363–4, about the time of the death of Tughlak Timur, the amírs Husain and Timur revolted and expelled Elias. He escaped to his paternal dominions, but some time afterwards his life was taken by Kamaruddín Dughlak, of a powerful family which about this time became hereditary rulers of Kashgar. He seized the khanate, and put to death all the other children of Tughlak Timur on whom he could lay hands.

At a date which is uncertain, but probably about 1383, Khizr Khwaja, a son of Tughlak Timur, whose life had been rescued in infancy by the exertions of Khudáidád, son of Kamaruddín's brother Bulaji, the Amír of Kashgar, was through the same good offices seated on the throne of Moghulistan (or Eastern Chagatai), and he was its sovereign when Timur made his crushing campaign against the people of that country in 1389, taking the capital, and driving the Khan out of his dominions. Peace, however, was made eventually, and Timur married a daughter of Khizr Khwaja[2].

The latter at his death was succeeded by his son Mahomed Khan, and he by his grandson Wais or Awis Khan[3]. This prince, who throughout his reign was engaged in constant and unsuccessful wars with the Kalmaks, his eastern neighbours, at his death left

[1] *Univ. Hist.*, u.s.; Defrémery, pp. 281–2. Deguignes says it was not till after Timur's death that khans ceased to be nominated.

[2] Defrémery, p. 283; *Univ. Hist.*, u.s.; *Notices et Extraits*, xiv, p. 474 *seqq.*

[3] The extract from *Haft Iklim* in the *Not. et Ext.* just quoted mentions a Shir Mahomed between Mahomed and Awis. Awis Khán is noticed apparently as the reigning chief, and at war with a Shir Mahomed Oglan, in the narrative of Sháh Rukh's embassy to China (*Not. et Ext.*, xiv, Pt. i, p. 388).

two sons, Isanbuga and Yúnus, each of whom was backed by a party in claiming the succession. Those who favoured Yúnus took him to Mirza Ulugh Beg, the grandson of Timur (the celebrated astronomer prince), then governing at Samarkand, to seek his support; but he refused this, and sent Yúnus off into Western Persia, where he remained in exile for eighteen years. When Mirza Abu Said of the house of Timur (1451–68) had established himself at Samarkand, Isanbuga Khan invaded Farghána. Abu Said in retaliation sent for the exiled Yúnus, conferred on him the Khanate of Moghulistan, and dispatched him with an army into that country, where he succeeded in establishing himself[1]. During his reign a numerous army of Kalmaks entered his territory. Yúnus, in attempting to resist them, was completely defeated, with the loss of most of his amírs, and fled with the remains of his army to the Jaxartes. Here he seems to have established what remained of his authority at Tashkand, and at the same place his son and successor Mahmud, called by the Mongols Janikah, was crowned[2]. It would appear that Yúnus left behind another son, Ahmed, in Moghulistan, where he maintained himself for a time. Eventually both these brothers fell into the hands of Mahomed Khan Shaibani, otherwise called Shaibek, the founder of the Uzbek power in Transoxiana, and Mahomed was in the end put to death by that chief[3]. I can trace no information regarding later Chagatai Khans; indeed I presume that the Kalmaks about this time took possession of the country north of the T'ien Shan, and that the line of Khans survived no longer as such. A son [Saïd] of Ahmed however succeeded in founding a dynasty in Kashgar [1513], which maintained itself on the throne there for more than a century and a half[4].

[1] Defrémery, pp. 284–5. According to a quotation of Quatremère's from Haidar Mahomet, Yúnus Khán did not mount the throne till A.H. 873 = 1468, the last year of Abu Said (*Journ. des Savans* for 1839, p. 24).

[2] ["Sultán Yunus Khán was seized with paralysis, was bedridden for nearly two years, and died, suffering, at the age of seventy-four. No other Chaghatai Khákán ever reached such an advanced age; most of them, indeed, died before they reached the age of forty. The Khán was born in 818 and died in 892. He was buried near the tomb Puránvár Shaikh, Kháwand-i-Tahur [Master of Purification], in Tashkand; and a large mausoleum was built over the spot, which stands to this day and is very renowned." (*Tarikh-i-Rashidi*, pp. 114–15.)]

[3] [Mahmud Khán was put to death by Sháhi Beg Khán on the banks of the river of Khojand (914 A.H. = 1508–9). His brother Sultán Ahmad Khán, son of Yúnus, died in the winter of 909 (1503–4) of paralysis in Moghulistan. See the *Tarikh-i-Rashidi* for the end of the dynasty.]

[4] See Introduction to the Journey of Goës, *infra*. Deguignes says he had not been able to obtain any distinct information as to the rise of the power of the Kalmaks; nor can I find it in any later book within reach. [Ismael, the last of the Chaghatai princes of Kashgar, was dethroned in 1678 by the Kalmaks, who established as governor of the country Hidayat-allah, better known as Hazrat Afak.]

VII

THE JOURNEY OF BENEDICT GOËS FROM AGRA TO CATHAY

VII

THE JOURNEY OF BENEDICT GOËS FROM AGRA TO CATHAY

INTRODUCTORY NOTICE

THE traveller whom we are now about to follow over one of the most daring journeys in the whole history of discovery, belongs to a very different period from those who have preceded him in this collection. Since the curtain fell on Ibn Batuta's wanderings two hundred and fifty years have passed away. After long suspension of intercourse with Eastern Asia, the rapid series of discoveries and re-discoveries that followed the successful voyage of Da Gama have brought India, the Archipelago, China, and Japan into immediate communication with Europe by sea; the Jesuits have entered on the arena of the forgotten missions of the Franciscans, and have rapidly spread their organisation over the east, and to the very heart of each great eastern empire, to the courts of Agra, Peking, and Miako. Cathay has not been altogether forgotten in Europe, as many bold English enterprises by sea, and some by land, during the sixteenth century, testify; but to those actually engaged in the labours of commerce and religion in the Indies it remains probably but as a name connected with the fables of Italian poets, or with the tales deemed nearly as fabulous of old romancing travellers. The intelligence of the accomplished men, indeed, who formed the Jesuit forlorn in Northern China, soon led them to identify the great empire in which they were labouring with that Cathay of which their countryman Marco had told such wonders; but this conviction had not spread to their brethren in India, and when the leaders of the Mission at the Court of Akbar heard from Musulman travellers of a great and rich empire called KHITAI, to be reached by a long and devious course through the heart of Inner Asia, the idea seized their imaginations that here was an ample and yet untouched field awaiting the labours of the Society, if the way could but be found open; and this way they determined to explore.

The person selected for this venturesome exploration was BENEDICT GOËS[1]. Before he started on his journey

[1] The information regarding Goës, in addition to what is gathered from the narrative of his journey, is furnished by P. du Jarric, whose work I have seen only in the Latin translation entitled "*R. P. Iarrici Tholosani, Societat. Jesu, Thesaurus Rervm Indicarvm*, etc., *a Matthia Martinez a Gallico in Latinum sermonem translatum*; Coloniæ Agrippinæ, 1615." In the two copies that I have seen of this book (possibly therefore in all copies) there has been strange confusion made in binding the sheets. It consists of four volumes, numbered i, ii, iii, pt. 1; iii. pt. 2; and in each of three volumes out of these four are introduced numerous sheets belonging to the other two. The information regarding Goës is in vol. ii, pp. 530 *seqq.*; and in vol. iii, pt. 1, pp. 201 *seqq.*

[Peter du Jarric, S.J., was born at Toulouse in 1566 and he died at Saintes on the 2nd March, 1617, or 28th Feb., 1618.]

[Prof. Pelliot draws my attention to a passage in Padre Ant. Govea's *Histoire orientale*, Brussels, 1609, p. 18, in which it is related that a layman Diego d'Almeida, after the departure of Goës, informed the Archbishop of Goa, that Tibet was not to be confounded with Cathay; he, Diego d'Almeida, had resided two years in Tibet which is only separated from great Mogor by very high mountains, and is inaccessible save at certain times of the year on account of snow; the difficulty of going to Tibet, not being the distance, but the road practicable only during the good season, *i.e.* when the heat had melted the snow.]

[The Portuguese writer José de Torres in a somewhat romantic paper published in 1854 and entitled *Bento de Goes* (Ponta Delgada), calls our traveller Luiz Gonçalves, whose name would have been changed into Bento de Goes when he entered the Society of Jesus. This name Luiz Gonçalves seems not only to be ignored by the chief authorities mentioning the traveller but is also unknown in the Archives of the S. J., where, in the list of the

doubts had been suggested whether this Cathay were not indeed the very China in which Ricci and his companions were already labouring with some promise of success; but these doubts were overruled, or at least the leader of the Agra Mission was not convinced by them, and he prevailed on his superiors still to sanction the exploration that had been proposed.

The gallant soldier of the Society, one not unworthy to bear the Name on which others of that Company's deeds and modes of action have brought such obloquy, carried through his arduous task; ascertained that the mysterious empire he had sought through rare hardships and perils was China indeed; and died just within its borders. "Seeking Cathay he found heaven," as one of his brethren has pronounced his epitaph. And thus it is that we have thought his journey a fitting close to this collection; for with its termination CATHAY may be considered finally to disappear from view, leaving CHINA only in the mouths and minds of men. Not but that Cathay will be found for some time longer to retain its place as a distinct region in some maps and geographical works of pretension, but from that time its appearance could only condemn the ignorance of the authors.

Benedict Goës was born at Villa Franca do Campo, in the island of St. Michael (Azores), about 1561[1]. I find no particulars of his rank in life or early history, nor any

missionaries of the Goa province in the year 1588, when Goës joined the Society, the following entry exists under the date 31st December: *Benito de Goes, Portugues, de la Isla de Sant Miguel, de la Villa Franca, obispado de Angra, de 26 años, de nueve meses de la Compa.* There is apparently no basis for José de Torres' story. These particulars I draw from a very interesting paper by the Rev. C. Wessels, S.J., pp. 10–11, mentioned in the Bibliography, *infra.*]

[1] [Sommervogel says 1562, which is probable, and Father M. C. Baratta 1552. On the 11th April 1907 the third centenary of the death of Goës was celebrated and a monument was erected at Villa Franca.]

statement of the circumstances under which he originally went to India, but in his twenty-sixth year we first meet him as a soldier on board the Portuguese fleet on the coast of Travancore, a high-spirited and pleasure-loving young man. The dignity and culture of his character, as it shows in later life, seems to imply that he had been educated for a higher position than that of a common soldier; and it is probable that, like many a wild youth since, he had enlisted for the Indies in consequence of some youthful escapade. Happening, we are told, to enter a church near COLECHEA[1], and kneeling before an image of the Madonna and Child, he began to reflect seriously on his past life, and was seized with such remorse that he almost despaired of salvation. This spiritual crisis ended in his making full confession of his sins to a Jesuit priest, and eventually in his entering the Order as a lay coadjutor[2]. This position he held for the rest of his career, always modestly refusing to take orders, though often pressed to do so by his superiors in the Society.

In the end of 1594 a detachment of missionaries was sent to the Court of Akbar, at the request of the great king himself, whose oscillating convictions appear often to have been strongly in favour of Christianity[3]. The head

[1] *Kolechi*, a small port of Travancore, which Fra Paolino will have to be the Colchi of the Periplus. It has dropped out of our modern maps.

[2] [In 1588.]

[3] The inquiries of Akbar about Christianity dated from the visit of Antony Capral, whom he received as envoy from Goa in 1578. Hearing then of a Christian priest of eminent virtue in Bengal, he sent for him to Futtehpur Sikri (which du Jarric calls *Patefula*), and made him argue with the Mullahs. Moved by what this anonymous father said, the king wrote to Goa, begging that two members of the Jesuit Society might be sent to him with Christian books. This of course caused great delight and excitement, and the Provincial sent off Rudolf Aquaviva, a man of illustrious family (afterwards murdered by the natives of Salsette near Goa [on the 17th July, 1583; born in 1557]), and Antony of

of the mission was Jerome Xavier[1] of Navarre, a relation of the great Francis, and his comrades were Goës and the priest Emanuel Pinheiro[2], also a Portuguese. They proceeded first to CAMBAY, where they were well received by Sultan Murad, Akbar's second son, and provided with carriage and money for their journey to LAHORE, where the Padshah then held his court. Travelling with a Kafila by AHMEDĀBĀD and PATTAN, and then across the great Indian Desert, they reached Lahore on the 5th May, 1595, and were made most welcome by Akbar, who at the same time gladdened their hearts by his display of reverence to images of the Saviour and the Virgin Mary, the gift of a former missionary at his court.

Goës appears to have acquired the esteem of the king

Monserrate [died at Salsette in 1600]. They were most honourably received by Akbar, and great hopes of his conversion were raised. The celebrated Abul Fazl and other eminent men of the Court also showed great interest in the subject; but nothing material resulted. Some years afterwards, in 1590, Akbar's thoughts again turned to Christianity, and at this time, according to the statement of the Jesuits (I know not how far well founded), he ordered a general destruction of mosques and minarets, and forbade circumcision before the fifteenth year. He again applied for instructors, and in 1591 three brethren were sent to Lahore, but after a while, seeing no hope of good, they returned to Goa. Hence on this third occasion the mission was despatched without any great alacrity or sanguine expectations. It is probable that Akbar had arrived at no decided convictions in religion, excepting as to the rejection of Mahomedanism. He seems to have projected a new eclectic kind of Theism, in which adoration was to be addressed to the sun, as an emblem of the Creator. At the same time he never seems to have lost a certain hankering after Christianity, or ceased to display an affectionate reverence for the Christian emblems which he had received from his Jesuit teachers.

[1] [Jerome Ezpelata took the name of his relation, the great Xavier; entered the noviciate of the Jesuits at Alcala, on the 7th May, 1568. He went to India, was rector at Bassein and Cochin, superior of the convent of Goa; preached at Lahore, where he was nearly stoned to death; he returned finally to Goa in 1617, when he was appointed Archbishop of Angamale; he died on the 17th of June in the same year.—Sommervogel.]

[2] [Emanuel Pinheiro, born at Puente Delgada (island of S. Miguel) in 1556; embarked for India in 1592, and died at Goa, about 1618.—Sommervogel.]

in an especial degree, and with Xavier accompanied him on his summer journey to Kashmir. One Christmas too, we are told, Goës constructed a model of the manger and stable of Bethlehem, after the fashion still kept up in Southern Europe, whilst some of the pupils of the mission acted a Pastoral Eclogue in the Persian tongue on the subject of the Nativity, things that greatly pleased both Musulmans and Hindus, but especially the latter.

Whilst the Court was still at Lahore (which Akbar quitted for Agra in 1598) the circumstance occurred which turned the attention of Jerome Xavier to the long-lost Cathay (as he fancied it), and excited his imagination in the manner already alluded to. This circumstance is thus related by du Jarric:

"One day as Xavier was at the palace and engaged with the king, there presented himself a Mahomedan merchant of some sixty years of age. After he had made his salutations to the king, in answer to a question whence he was come, he said that he was lately arrived from the kingdom of XETAIA. This Xavier supposed to be the same as the Cathay spoken of by Marco Polo the Venetian in his Travels, and by Hayton the Armenian in his History, and which later writers have determined to be in Tartary, or not far from it. And when the king inquired for further particulars about that empire, and as to the length of the merchant's residence there, he replied that he had been thirteen years at the metropolis of the country, which he called Kambalu. . . . This he said was the residence of the kings, who were most powerful sovereigns. For, indeed, their empire included one thousand five hundred cities; some of them immensely populous. He had often seen the king, and it was his practice never to give any reply, favourable or unfavourable, to a request, but through the eunuchs who stood by him, unless, indeed, he was addressed in writing. King Akbar asking how he had got admission into the empire, he replied that it was under the character of an ambassador from the King of *Caygar* (KASHGAR). On arriving at the frontier he was detained by the local governor, who after inspecting the seals of the letters which he carried, sent off a despatch to the king by swift horse-post. The answer giving permission for the party to proceed came back within a month. In going on to the capital they changed horses at every stage, as is practised in Europe, and thus got speedily over the ground, although the distance is very great; for they accomplished one hundred Italian miles every day. On the whole journey they met with no affront or unfair treatment, for the local judges administered justice to all, and thieves were punished with great severity. When asked about the aspect of the natives, he said that they were the whitest people he had ever seen, whiter even than the *Rumis*, or Europeans. Most of the men cherished a long beard....The greater number were *Isauites, i.e.* Christians (for thus Christians are called after Jesus, just as if you were to say Jesuits!). When asked if they were all Isauites, he said, by no means, for there are many *Mussauites* (*i.e.* Jews, for Moses in the tongue of those people is called *Mussau*), and there are also some Mahomedans. But is the king a Mahomedan? asked Akbar. Not yet, said the merchant, but it is hoped that he will soon be so. The colloquy was then interrupted, the sovereign graciously naming another day for the reception of the merchant, in order to ask further questions about this empire. But Xavier getting impatient, out of eagerness to learn more, went to see the merchant in order to get more precise information about the religion of the inhabitants. The merchant repeated his statement that they were, for the most part, Christians, and that he had been on terms of great intimacy with several of them. They had temples, some of them of vast size, in which were images both painted and sculptured, and among others figures of the crucified Saviour, which were held by them in great reverence. A priest was set over every temple, who was treated with great respect by the people, and received presents from them....He also mentioned the continence of those priests, and the schools in which they brought up young people for holy orders....The fathers moreover wore black frocks, and caps like Xavier's, only a little bigger. In saluting any one by the way they did not uncover, but joined hands across the breast, interlacing the fingers....The king often went to the temples, and must, therefore, be a Christian," etc., etc.

Xavier lost no time in communicating this intelligence to the Provincial of his Order; and after arriving with the king at Agra sent the results of further inquiry made there from persons who had been to Cathay. Some people alleged that there was a way to Cathay by BENGAL and the kingdom of GARAGHAT[1], at the extremity of the Mogul territories. But merchants, who were sure to know the shortest routes, were in the habit of going from

[1] *Ghorāghāt* ("the horse-ferry") is a town and zemindari in the Bogra district of Bengal, and is mentioned as such in the *Ayin Akbari*. But the *kingdom* alluded to must be that of *Kúch Bihár*, which in the time of Akbar retained independence, and extended from the Brahmaputra westward to Tirhut, from the Himalaya south to Ghoraghat. In 1661 it was conquered by Mir Jumla (see Hamilton's *Gazetteer, in vv. Ghoraghat* and *Cooch Bahar*). Kúch Bihár still exists, with a modified independence, and very much restricted limits. It is remarkable that there should have been any talk of a route to China this way in the reign of Akbar. It probably lay through Lhása. We have seen (*ante*, III, p. 131) that Rashíduddín recognised an overland route by Bengal and the borders of Tibet. And some years after Akbar's time, the two Jesuits, Grueber and Dorville, found their way from China *via* Lhása and Katmandu to Patna (Kircher, *China Illustrata*, pp. 64 *seqq.*).

Lahore to Kashmír, and thence by the kingdom of REBAT[1], the king of which was in alliance with the Mogul, they went straight to Kashgar, from which it was said there was a direct and easy route to the first mercantile city of Cathay, a place which the merchants asserted to be inhabited by Christians. Xavier was now quite satisfied that the country in question was indeed the Cathay of Polo, and the Christian king the representative of the famous Prester John. He sounded the king on the subject of an exploratory mission, and found him disposed to assist it cordially. All this was duly communicated to the Provincial, and through him it would appear to the higher powers in Europe.

In 1601 the encouragement of those higher powers had been received in India, and the Provincial turned his attention to the selection of a fit man for the expedition. Now it happened that Xavier and Goës had accompanied King Akbar some time previously on his expedition into the Dekkan. After the conquest of Kandesh, Akbar on some pretext sent an embassy to Goa, partly it was supposed in order to spy out the land with a view to extending his conquests in that quarter. And with this embassy he sent Goës in charge of some children of Portuguese parentage who had been found in Burhanpur and other captured fortresses.

In Goës the Provincial discerned the very man that he wanted; his judgment, courage, and skill in Persian marking him out as especially qualified for such an

[1] I do not know what the name *Rebat* is intended for (proper names in du Jarric being often sadly mangled); perhaps for *Tibet*. The kingdom intended must be either Ladakh or Balti, which were known in those days as Great and Little Tibet. [Father Oranus has *Tebat*. There is no doubt that *Tibet* is meant. In a letter of the 26th July, 1598, quoted in R., p. 528 *n.*, Father Jerome Xavier writes: Mihi quoque dum in Caximire agebam, nunciatum est esse in regno Rebat multos cristianos et ecclesias cum sacerdotibus et episcopis. Cf. Hay, p. 797.]

enterprise. Goës readily accepted the duty, and in the following year (1602) arrived at Agra to make arrangements for his journey. Akbar praised his zeal, and contributed the value of four hundred pieces of gold to the expenses of the journey, besides giving the passports mentioned in the narrative.

After successfully accomplishing his journey, as has been already mentioned, Goës was detained for some seventeen months at the frontier city of Suchau, and there died a few days after the arrival of the native Christian whom Ricci and his comrades at Peking had sent to his aid and comfort[1]. The narrative of his journey was put together, apparently by Ricci himself, from some fragment of Benedict's note-book, along with the oral statements of his faithful comrade Isaac the Armenian,

[1] Matthew Ricci was born at Macerata, in the March of Ancona, 6th Oct., 1552. He entered the Jesuit Society in 1571. Being sent to India, he reached Goa in 1578, but speedily left it for Macao on being chosen by Father Valignani, the founder of the Jesuit Mission in China, as one of his aids. Not till 1583, however, were they able to establish themselves in the Canton territory. Ricci's great object for a long time was to get to Peking, and he did reach it in 1595, but was obliged, by an accidental excitement among the Chinese, to withdraw to Nanking. In 1600 he was enabled to go again, carrying presents, which had come from Europe for the Emperor. He was admitted; and having acquired the Emperor's favour, he devoted himself to the mission at the capital. Some striking conversions were made; and Ricci's science and literary works in Chinese gained him much esteem among the most eminent persons at Peking. He died 11th May, 1610, leaving Longobardi to succeed him. The chief literary men of the city attended his funeral. His name appears in the Chinese annals as *Li Ma-teu*. The principles of Ricci as a missionary appear to have been to stretch conciliation as far as possible; and to seek the respect of the educated Chinese by the display of superior scientific attainments. As regards the former point, he is accused of having led the way in those dubious concessions which kindled the disputes that ended in the downfall of the missions. He was the first European to compose books in Chinese. His works of this kind were fifteen in number, and one of them is said to have been included in a collection of the best Chinese writers ordered by the Emperor K'ien-lung (see Rémusat's article in *Biog. Universelle* [H. Cordier, *Bib. Sinica*, col. 1090–1092 and *Imprimerie Sino-européenne*.—See Bibliography, *infra*]).

and was published after the death of Ricci, with other matter that he had compiled concerning China and the mission history, in the work of Trigautius (Trigault) entitled *De Christianâ Expeditione apud Sinas.* From this our translation has been made, but some additional particulars given by du Jarric from the Indian reports, and from the letters which Goës was occasionally during his journey able to send back to his superiors at Agra or Goa, have been brought forward in the notes. Altogether it is a miserably meagre record of a journey so interesting and important; and had Benedict's diary, which he is stated to have kept in great detail, been spared, it would probably have been to this day by far the most valuable geographical record in any European language on the subject of the countries through which he travelled, still so imperfectly known.

There are some perplexities about the chronology of the journey as given in Trigault, which doubtless arise out of the manner in which the narrative was thus compiled. It is in some respects inconsistent with itself as well as with the statements in du Jarric.

Thus, according to du Jarric, Goës left Agra 31st October, 1602, whilst Trigault makes it 6th January, 1603. This is not of importance however, as they agree substantially regarding the time of his final start from Lahore.

But again. The narrative in Trigault professes to give, sometimes in precise, sometimes in round numbers, the intervals occupied by the various portions of the journey and its tedious halts. But if these be added together, even without allowance for two or three omissions, we find that the sum carries us a whole year beyond the time deducible from du Jarric, and in fact would throw Benedict's death a year later than the date which Trigault himself (or rather Ricci) fixes[1]. This is shown in detail below, but here I may explain that the chief inconsistency is found in the time alleged to have been spent between Lahore and Yarkand. According to Ricci's details this period extends from February 1603 to November 1604, whereas both du Jarric's data and Ricci's own *absolute* statement make the traveller reach Yarkand in November 1603, which unquestionably is the correct date. And as Ricci's *details* allege a positive halt of *eight months* at Kabul, it is evident that there must have been some singular kind of misunderstanding either of Benedict's notes, or of Isaac's language, or of both. Isaac, it will be seen, could speak nothing more intelligible than Persian,

[1] The following *absolute* dates are given by Trigault: Goës left Agra 6th January, 1603; left Lahore in Lent (which in 1603 began on 18th February); reached Yarkand November, 1603; left Yarkand November, 1604; reached Suchau in the latter part of 1605; his letters did not reach Peking till November, 1606; John Ferdinand started 11th December, and reached Suchau in the end of March, 1607; eleven days later Benedict died.

The following *absolute* dates are given by du Jarric: Goës left Agra 31st October, 1602; reached Lahore 8th December; left Lahore in middle of February, 1603; wrote from Yarkand in February and August, 1604; set out from Yarkand 14th November 1604; left Chalis 17th October, 1605; died 11th April, 1607.

The following are the *details* of time occupied in the journey, as given by Trigault (and full of error): Left Lahore in Lent [say first day of Lent, or 18th February], 1603; took to Attok thirty days, halted there fifteen, and across the Indus five; Peshâwar two *months*, halt there twenty days; go on a time not specified, halt twenty days; to Ghideli twenty-five days; to Kabul twenty days. [*This would bring him to* Kabul *on the 2nd of September*, 1603, *at the earliest.*] Halts at Kabul eight *months* [*and therefore leaves it about* 1st *May*, 1604]. To Charekar not specified; to Parwān ten days, halt there five; to Aingharan twenty; to Kalcha fifteen; to Jalalābād ten; to Talikhan fifteen, halt there one month [*which brings us at least to the* 15*th August*, 1604]. To Cheman, and halt there, not specified; Defiles of Badakhshan eight days, halt ten; Charchunar one day, halt five days; to Serpanil ten days; to Sarchil twenty, halt two; to Chechalith two; to Tanghetar six, at least; to Yaconic fifteen days; to Yarkand five days [*which brings him to Yarkand therefore on 7th November*, 1604, *at the earliest, or just* a year *later than the true date*]. It is not worth while to carry the matter further, and indeed the essential error is contained in that section of the journey which we have given here.

and John Ferdinand, the Chinese convert who came to seek the party at Suchau, could not communicate with him *at all* until he had himself acquired a little Persian. This language the missionaries at Peking probably knew nothing of, and it is not therefore wonderful if misunderstanding occurred.

What the nature of this misunderstanding must have been, in some instances at least, can I think be deduced from one case in which the misstatement of the time is obvious. The journey from Attok to Peshâwar is said to have occupied *two months*. Now, as the distance is about thirty miles, this is absurd. It is, therefore, not improbable that it may have been entered in Goës' notes as "II *mensil*" (Pers. *manzil*, a stage or march), and that this was understood by the Italians as "II *menses*."

[The autograph Italian manuscript of Matteo Ricci's Commentaries still exists in the Ricci family at Macerata, and it has been edited by Father Tacchi Venturi, S.J. (see *infra*, Bibliography) for the centennial anniversary of the celebrated missionary, the commemoration of which took place in his native city in 1910. I have carefully compared this text with Trigault's version and made some corrections. In spite of the defects of the Latin translations, the errors in the proper names are less numerous than I anticipated.—H.C.]

The chief obscurities attending the route of Goës, concern that section of his journey which lies between Kabul and Yarkand. In the first part of this section, embracing the passage of the Hindu Kush, the country is to a certain degree known, but there are several places named prominently by Goës which cannot be identified with any certainty. This is also the case in the second portion of this section of the journey, embracing the ascent through Badakhshan to the Plateau of Pamir, and the descent to Yarkand, where moreover we are in a country still most imperfectly known; for, since Marco Polo, Goës is the only European traveller across it of whose journey any narrative has seen the light[1].

[1] The following note from a recent work, called *The Russians in Central Asia*, consisting of various papers translated from the Russian by Messrs. Michell, shows that valuable matter, in illustration of these regions, *does* exist (I believe in the military archives at St. Petersburg): "In a paper on the Pamir and the upper course of the Oxus, read last year before the Russian Geographical Society by M. Veniukof, he says: 'The chaos of our geographical knowledge relating to the Pamir table-lands and the Bolor was so great that the celebrated geographer Zimmermann, working under the superintendence of Ritter, was able to produce only a very confused and utterly incomprehensible map of this region. The connecting link was wanting; it was necessary that some one should carry out the plan conceived by the Russian Government in the beginning of this century, by visiting and describing the country. Fortunately, such an additional source of information has been found,—nay, even two, —which mutually corroborate and amplify each other, although they have nothing further in common between them. I here allude to the "Travels through Upper Asia, from Kashgar, Tashbalyk, Bolor, Badakhshan, Vakhan, Kokan, Turkestan, to the Kirghiz Steppe, and back to Cashmere, through Samarkand and Yarkand," and to the Chinese Itinerary, translated by Klaproth in 1821, leading from Kashgar to Yarkand, Northern India, Dairim, Yabtuar, Badakhshan, Bolor, Vakhan, and Kokan, as far as the Karatau mountains. The enumeration alone of these places must, I should imagine, excite the irresistible curiosity of all who have made the geography of Asia their study. These fresh sources of information are truly of the highest importance. As regards the *Travels*, it is to be inferred from the preface, and from certain observations in the narrative, that the author was a German, an agent of the East India Company, despatched in the beginning of this or the end of the last century, to purchase horses for the British army. The original account forms a magnificent manuscript work in the German language, accompanied by forty sketches of the country traversed. The text, also, has been translated into French in a separate manuscript, and the maps worked into one itinerary in an admirable style. The Christian name of the traveller, George Ludwig von ———, appears over the preface, but the surname has been erased. Klaproth's *Itinerary* is so far valuable as the physical details are extremely circumstantial; almost every mountain is laid down, and care taken to indicate whether it is wooded or snow-capped; while equal care is taken to show whether the inhabitants are nomads or a stationary people. Ruins, bridges, and villages are also intelligibly designated; so that, although the same scale is not preserved throughout, its value, lucidity, and minuteness, are not thereby deteriorated.'"

I may add to the preceding notice that Professor H. H. Wilson,

It is not quite clear which of the passes was followed by Goës in crossing the Hindu Kush. Some account of these will be given in a supplementary note at the end of the narrative[1]. Here I will content myself with observing that as the traveller is mentioned to have visited Parwān as well as Charekar, it may seem most probable that he crossed by the Pass of Parwān, which Wood attempted unsuccessfully in 1837. Indeed, if Parwān is correctly placed in the only map I have seen which shows it (J. Walker's), it would be out of the way of a party going by any other Pass[2]. From Parwān till he reaches Talikhan on the borders of Badakhshan, none of the names given can be positively determined; Calcia and Jalalābād, the most prominent of them, are named

in his remarks on Izzet Ullah's Travels (see *J. R. A. S.*, vii, 294), mentions a Russian officer, Yefremoff, who was last century captured by the Kirghiz, but made his escape, and travelled by Kokand and Kashgar, across Tibet to Calcutta, and so home to St. Petersburg, where he arrived in 1782, and published his travels. Meyendorff, also, in his *Voyage d'Orenbourg à Bokhara*, speaks of the travels of Raphael Danibeg, a noble Georgian, which were translated from his native language into Russian, and printed in 1815. This gentleman travelled from Kashmir to Yarkand, Aqsu, Kulja, and Semipalatinsk. The same work contains a route from Semipalatinsk to Kashmir, by a Tajik of Bokhara. [Of course, new information has been brought to light by recent travellers, and one may refer on the subject to the third edition of *Marco Polo*.]

[1] See Note I at the end.

[2] The first notice which du Jarric gives of Goës, after mentioning his departure from Lahore, is that "after going 102 coss, each equal to an Italian mile, he wrote to Pinheiro from the province of *Gazaria* that he was struggling with severe cold on the passage over mountains covered with snow." The 102 coss must have been estimated from Kabul, not from Lahore, as the passage would literally imply, and the snow mountains of Gazaria must have been the Hindu Kush occupied by the *Hazara* tribes; (they are called *Kezareh* by Meyendorff, *Voyage à Bokara*, p. 140). At present the Hazaras, according to Wood (p. 199), do not extend further east than the Valley of Ghorbund; but Leech's Report on the Passes shows that they are found on the passes immediately above Parwān, and that they formerly extended to the mountains adjoining the Khawak Pass, the most easterly of all. I hope to add a sketch map such as will make Goës' route, and the doubts attending it, more intelligible.

so far as I know by no other traveller or geographer. Some remarks regarding them will however be found in the notes on the narrative.

From Talikhan also to the high land of Pamir we have a similar difficulty in identifying names except that descriptive one *Tangì-i-Badakhshan* ("the Straits of Badakhshan") which sufficiently indicates the character of the country. But I think there can be little doubt that the route of Goës was substantially the same as that followed by Captain John Wood of the Indian Navy on his famous journey to the source of the Oxus. Badakhshan and the adjoining districts of Tokharestan, inhabited by a race of Tajik lineage and Persian speech, would seem in the middle ages not merely to have enjoyed that fame for mineral productions (especially rubies and lapis lazuli) of which a shadow still remains, but at least in their lower valleys to have been vastly more populous and productive than they are now. The "Oriental Geography" of the tenth century translated by Ouseley, and Edrisi in the twelfth century, both speak of these as fruitful and well-peopled regions flourishing with trade and wealth. Marco Polo in the thirteenth century speaks of Talikhan and the adjoining districts in similar terms. Not long before his time the chief fortress of Talikhan held Chinghiz and his Tartar host at bay for six months [1221][1]. The

[1] D'Ohsson, i, 273. There was another Talikhan in Khorāsān, between Balkh and Merv (see tables of *Nasíruddín* in Hudson, iii, 107). And the authors of the Modern Universal History appear to have taken this for the city besieged by Chinghiz (*French Trans.*, iii, 356). But the narrative shows that it was Talikhan in Tokharestan, on the border of Badakhshan [province of Kataghan or Kunduz. See *Marco Polo*, i, p. 154 *n*.]. Edrisi describes both cities, but curiously his French translator, M. Jaubert, takes both for the same (i, 468, 476). [There were in fact *three* places so called; that in Badakhshan, that in Khorāsān, and a third in Daylam, the hill-country adjoining Kazbin. This *last* is the duplicate of Nasíruddín's Tables and not that in Khorāsān. (See Quatremère's *Rashid*, pp. 214, 278.)]

savage conqueror left not a living soul in the garrison, nor one stone upon another. And the present town of Talikhan, the representative of the place defended by this strong and valiant garrison, is a paltry village of some four hundred clay hovels[1]. Faizabad, the chief city of Badakhshan, once famous over the east, was, when Wood passed through the country, to be traced only by the withered trees that had once adorned its gardens, and the present capital of the country (Jerm) was but a cluster of hamlets, containing altogether some fifteen hundred souls[2]. Enduring decay probably commenced with the wars of Chinghiz, for many an instance in eastern history shows the permanent effect of such devastations. And here wave after wave of war passed over a little country, isolated on three sides by wild mountains and barbarous tribes, destroying the apparatus of culture which represented the accumulated labour of generations, and with it the support of civilisation and the springs of recovery. Century after century only saw progress in decay. Even to our own time the process of depopulation and deterioration has continued. In 1759 two of the Khwajas of Kashgar [Burhán-uddín (Boronitu) and K'odzishan (Huo-tsichan), descendant from Hazrat Afak], escaping from the dominant Chinese, took refuge in Badakhshan, and were treacherously slain by Sultan Sháh who then ruled that country[3]. The holy men are said in their dying moments to have invoked curses on Badakhshan and prayed that it might be three times depopulated. And, in fact, since then it has been at least three times ravaged; first, a few years after the outrage by Ahmed Sháh Durani of Kabul, when the

[1] Wood, p. 241.

[2] Ditto, p. 254.

[3] *Russians in Central Asia*, p. 186 *seqq.*; Wood, p. 250; Ritter, vol. vii; Burnes, iii, 192.

treacherous Sultan Sháh was put to death; in the beginning of this century by Kokan Beg of Kunduz; and again in 1829 by his successor Murad Beg, who swept away the bulk of the remaining inhabitants, and set them down to die in the marshy plains of Kunduz.

In the time of Goës the country was probably in a middle state, not fallen so low as now, but far below what it had been in days before the Tartar invasion. Akbar had at this time withdrawn all attempt at holding territory north of the Indian Caucasus, and the Uzbeks, who in the end of the fifteenth century had expelled the house of Timur and settled in Bokhara, seem to have been in partial occupation.

Of routes over the Bolor Tagh and high table-land of Pamir between Badakhshan and Kashgar, the only notices accessible are those of the Chinese pilgrims of the early centuries[1], the brief but pregnant sketches of Marco Polo, so singularly corroborated even to minutiæ in our own day by Captain Wood, and these fragmentary memoranda of Benedict Goës. It seems impossible absolutely to determine the route followed by Marco, but from his mentioning a twelve days' march along the lofty plain it seems probable that he followed, as certainly the ancient Chinese pilgrims did, a course running north from the head of the Oxus valley over the plateau to the latitude of Tashbáliq before descending into Eastern Turkestan. Goës and his caravan, on the other hand, following what is probably the usual route of later days, would seem to have crossed athwart the Pamir, in the direction of the sources of the Yarkand river, and passing two or more of the ridges that buttress the Bolor on the

[1] Of these, extracts are given in Ritter, vii, 493 *seqq.* I have no access at present to Hiuen Tsang. [See our itinerary in *Marco Polo*, i, pp. 175, 182. H. C.]

east, to have descended on Yanghi-Hissar, a city intermediate between Kashgar and Yarkand. A modern caravan route, laid down by Macartney in the map attached to Elphinstone's "Caubul," seems evidently to represent the same line as that taken by our traveller's party, and both representations appear to suggest the view of its general course which has just been indicated.

The country in which Goës found himself after the passage of these mountains has been equally shut up from European[1] access since the days of the great Mongol empires, but has become better known from Chinese sources, having been for long intervals and from a very early date under the influence of the Chinese. This region, perhaps best designated as Eastern Turkestan, but named in maps of the last century (I know not why) as "Little Bokhara," forms a great depressed valley of some four hundred miles in width from north to south, supposed by Humboldt from botanical inductions not to exceed twelve hundred feet in the absolute elevation of its lower portions. It is shut in on three sides by mountain ranges of great height, viz.: on the north by the T'ien Shan or Celestial Mountains of the Chinese, separating it from the plains of the Ili, on the south by the Kwen-Lun propping the great plateau of Tibet, and on the west by the transverse chain of the Bolor dividing it from Western Turkestan. The greater part of the surface of this depression is desert, of clayey soil and stony surface towards the foot of the mountain ranges, and of sand in the interior, which eastward accumulates into ranges of shifting sand hills. Though the air is of exceeding dryness and rain is rare, the amount of water which flows

[1] [What was exact in 1866 is not so now, as will be seen by the recent voyages quoted in the following pages of this new edition of *Cathay*.]

down from the snowy mountains on three sides of this valley must be considerable. The rivers carrying this drain into the central channel of the Ergol or Tarim, which is absorbed by Lake Lop on the eastern verge of the tract, and has no further outlet, except in the legends of the Chinese which connect it by subterranean issues with the Hwang Ho. The lateral rivers afford irrigation, and patches of more or less fertile soil border the bases of the three ranges, in which cities have risen, and settled states have existed from time immemorial. Similar oases perhaps once existed nearer the centre of the plain, where Marco Polo places the city of Lop, and across which a direct road once led from the Chinese frontier to Khotan[1]. From Khotan, as from the western cities of Kashgar and Yarkand, the only communication with China now followed seems to lie through the towns that are dotted along the base of the T'ien Shan[2].

Chinese scholars date the influence of the empire in the more westerly of these states from the second century B.C. In the first century after our era they were thoroughly subjected, and the Chinese power extended even beyond the Bolor to the shores of the Caspian[3]. The Chinese authority was subject to considerable fluctuations, but under the T'ang in the seventh century we find the country east of the mountains again under Chinese governors (whose seats are indicated as Bishbáliq, Khotan, Karashahr, and Kashgar)[4], till the decay of

[1] This road is said to have been abandoned on account of the Kalmak banditti who haunted it. It seems to have been followed, as an exceptional case, by Shah Rukh's ambassadors on their return from China (see *Not. et Extraits*, xiv, pt. 1, p. 425; also p. 476).

[2] Chiefly derived from *Russians in Central Asia*.

[3] [The Chinese Power *never* extended to the shores of the Caspian. The Chinese general Pan Ch'ao, who during the first century of our era carried his arms to the west, never went so far. See *supra*, 1, p. 40.]

[4] Pauthier, *Chine Ancienne*, p. 296.

that dynasty in the latter part of the ninth century, and those divisions of the empire which followed, and endured till the conquest of all its sub-divisions by Chinghiz and his successors. These latter held supremacy, actual or nominal, over Eastern Turkestan as part of the early conquests of their house. They fell in China, and their Chinese successors of the Ming dynasty had little power beyond the frontiers of China proper, or at most beyond the territory of Kamil[1]. The western states remained subject more or less nominally to the Khans of the eastern branch of Chagatai, whose history has been briefly traced in a previous page of this book. The government of Kashgar [office of *Ulusbegi*] had always since the days of Chinghiz been conferred on a chief officer of the Khan's court. Tughlak Timur, on his accession, bestowed it on the Amír Tulik, who was succeeded by Bulaji, both being brothers of Kamaruddín, who slew Elias the son of Tughlak Timur and usurped the Khanate. Bulaji was succeeded by his son Khudáidad, of whom we have already heard (*supra*, p. 165). This prince ruled for many years prosperously and beneficently, holding quasi-regal power over Kashgar, Khotan, Aqsu, Bai and Kucha[2], devoting

[1] The circumstance cited in a note at III, p. 132, *supra*, shows that, in 1419, the Chinese power did not extend to Turfan and Karakhoja. In 1605, as we shall see presently, it did not even include Kamil.

[2] "*Mai* and *Kush*," but I suppose the names in the text are those intended. For *Kucha* or *Kuchia*, see a note on Goës' journey further on. *Bai* is a town at the foot of the T'ien Shan, between Aqsu and Kucha, 137 miles N.E. of the former, famous now for its sheep-farming and felt manufacture. It is identified by Hugh Murray with the *Pein* of Polo; an identification followed by Pauthier, who however quotes Murray's remark, that it had "defied conjecture" (*hitherto*), without noticing that Murray had himself made the identification.

The mention of Bai here as a province coupled with Kashgar, Khotan, and Aqsu, adds strongly to the probability that it is really the *Pein* of Marco. There is a difficulty in the fact that the chief circumstance he notes about Pein is the production of jasper, *i.e.* jade, in its river; and I can find no notice of this mineral being

much of his revenue to pious objects, especially the redemption of Musulman captives carried off by the Mongols in their raids on Mā-warā-n-Nahr. His rule lasted under the reign of four successive Khans of Eastern Chagatai. In his old age he made the pilgrimage and died at Medina[1]. His son Mahomed Sháh inherited his honours, but the territories of Kashgar and Khotan had been annexed by Timur, and remained for some time subject to the descendants of that conqueror, who were in the habit of confiding those provinces to one of their own chief officers. Whilst it was administered by these, Said Ali, the son of Mahomed, made repeated attempts to recover his grandfather's dominions, and at length succeeded. It is needless to follow the history of this dynasty in further detail. During their time the country seems sometimes to have been divided into different states, of which Kashgar and Khotan were the chief, and sometimes to have been united under the prince of Kashgar. The last prince of the dynasty, Abubakr Khán, was also one of the most powerful. He reigned for forty-eight

found in the *northern* affluents of the Tarim, though Timkowski does mention *wrought* jade as a staple of Aqsu. Hence Ritter seeks Pein on the road from Yarkand to the Karakorúm Pass, where Izzet Ullah mentions a quarry of jade, near which there is a station called Terek-lak-*Payin*. The last word, however, I believe merely means "Lower," and the position scarcely can answer Polo's description. It is possible that the province or district of Bai may have extended south of the Tarim Kul so as to embrace a part of the jaspiferous rivers of Khotan (Murray's *Polo*, ii, 32; Pauthier's, p. 145; Timkowski, i, 391; Ritter, vii, 382; *Russ. in Cent. Asia*, p. 160). *Khatiyan* and *Bahi* are mentioned in juxtaposition also by the early Arab traveller, Ibn Mohalhil, and probably indicate these same two provinces (see notes to Preliminary Essay). [Bai has nothing to do with Pein, which is on the road from Khotan to Niya. Cf. *Marco Polo*, i, p. 192 *n.*; ii, 595 *n.* Bai is on the road from Kucha to Aulie-ata; it was the Chinese *A-si-you*. Cf. Chavannes, *Tou-kiue occidentaux*, p. 8.]

[1] According to *Notices et Extraits* (quoted below), Khudaidad ruled for *ninety* years. He is mentioned by Sháh Rukh's envoys to China, as coming to meet them near the Mongol frontier (*Not. et Extraits*, xiv, pt. i, p. 388).

years, and made considerable conquests beyond the mountain ranges. He it was also who transferred the seat of government to Yarkand. But about 1515, Abu Said, son of Ahmed, son of Yúnus Khán of Eastern Chagatai, being a refugee in Farghāna, organized an expedition against Kashgar and Yarkand, which he succeeded in capturing, adding afterwards to his conquests parts of Badakhshan, of Tibet, and of Kashmir[1]. When Goës travelled through the country, the king, Mahomed Khán, whom he found upon the throne of Kashgar (of which Yarkand was now the capital), appears to have been a descendant of this Abu Said[2]. His power, we gather from Goës, extended at least over the territory of Aqsu, and probably in some degree over the whole country at the base of the T'ien Shan to the Chinese frontier, including Kamil; for what Goës calls the kingdom of Cialis or Chalis, embracing Karashahr and Kamil with the intermediate towns of Turfan and Pijan, was ruled by a son of the prince who reigned at Yarkand. Khotan appears under a separate sovereign, sister's son to the king at Yarkand, and perhaps subsidiary to him.

The rulers of Eastern Turkestan had always been Mahomedan from the time of Tughlak Timur, who was, we are told, the first Mahomedan sovereign of Kashgar of the lineage of Chinghiz. Buddhism, indeed, was found still prevalent in the cities of Turfan and Kamil at the time of the embassy of Sháh Rukh in 1419, and probably did not become extinct much before the end of the century. But in the western states Islam seems to have been universal from an earlier date and maintained with

[1] See *Notices et Extraits*, as quoted at p. 193, *infra*.

[2] He was probably the *Mahomed Sultan*, sixth son of Abdul Rashíd Khán, who is mentioned in Quatremère's extracts (see p. 193) as governing the city of Kashgar during the reign of his brother Abdulkerim, towards the end of the sixteenth century.

fanatical zeal[1]. Saintly teachers and workers of miracles, claiming descent from Mahomed, and known as Khwajas or Hojahs, acquired great influence, and the sectaries attached to the chief of these divided the people into rival factions, whose mutual hostility eventually led to the subjugation of the whole country. For late in the seventeenth century, Hojah Appak, the leader of one of those parties called the White Mountain, having been expelled from Kashgar by Ismail Khán the chief of that state, who was a zealous supporter of the opposite party or Black Mountain, sought the aid of Galdan Khán, sovereign of the Eleuths or Kalmuks of Dzungaria. Taking the occasion so afforded, that chief in 1678 invaded the states south of the T'ien Shan, carried off the Khán of Kashgar and his family, and established the Hojahs [Hidayat Allah Hazrat Afak] of the White Mountain over the country in authority subordinate to his own [1678]. Great discords for many years succeeded, sometimes one faction and sometimes another being uppermost, but some supremacy always continuing to be exercised by the Khans of Dzungaria. In 1757 the latter country was conquered by the Chinese, who in the following year, making a tool of the White party which was then in opposition, succeeded in bringing the state of Turkestan also under their rule. So they have continued until the present day, the details of administration resting chiefly with the native authorities, but with Chinese officials in supervision, and Chinese garrisons in the chief towns and on the frontiers, the whole being

[1] According to the Mecca pilgrim, whose statements are given in the *Jour. As. Soc. Bengal*, vol. iv (I borrow from Ritter, vii, 353), there are now many Buddhist priests and temples at the capital of Khotan. But the presumption is that these have been re-established since the revival of Chinese domination in the last century. Islam seems to have been extensively prevalent in those regions for centuries previous to the Mongols' rule, though probably the rise of the latter gave a lift to other religions.

under the general government of the Ili province established at Kulja on the river so called, not far from the ancient Almâliq. Rebellions, however, have been very frequent and serious during the last sixty years, and a great one is now in progress of which we know little as yet[1].

I am not in a position to say much as to the bibliography of Goës' journey. It is translated or related, I believe, in Purchas, but I have no access to a copy of the Pilgrims. An abstract of it is given in the *China Illustrata* of the garrulous old Jesuit Athanasius Kircher (pp. 62–4, Amsterdam, 1667), and a somewhat abridged version,

[1] Chiefly from the *Russ. in Cent. Asia*. The history of these regions, from the fall of the Mongol dynasty in China to the events which led to the revival of the Chinese power in the eighteenth century, seems only obscurely known. The chief existing record of the history, up to the middle of the sixteenth century, is stated to be the work called *Tarikh-i-Rashidi*, written by Mirza Mahomed Haidar Kurkan, Wazír of Abdul Rashíd Khan of Kashgar, who came to the throne, according to Quatremère, A.H. 950 = A.D. 1543 (Valikhanoff says 1554), and reigned for thirty-three years. According to Capt. Valikhanoff, the second part of this history describes the personal adventures of the author, communicating much information respecting the mountain ranges and countries adjoining Kashgar, and should contain very interesting matter. The work seems to have been little meddled with in Europe. There is a long extract, however, by Quatremère, in vol. xiv of the *Notices et Extraits*, pp. 474–89, from the Persian geography called *Haft Iklím* (Seven Climates), but which is derived from the *Tarikh-i-Rashidi*, and partly it would seem from a somewhat later source, as Abdul Rashíd's son, Abdul Kerim, is spoken of as then reigning. This extract has furnished most of the particulars in the preceding paragraphs of the text. Valikhanoff also speaks of a manuscript history of the Hojahs, down to the capture of Yarkand by the Chinese in 1758, called *Tiazkarai Hojaghian*, which he obtained at Kashgar. From this apparently he derives the particulars which he gives regarding those persons and their factions. (*R. in Cent. Asia*, pp. 69, 167 *seqq.*; *Notices et Extraits*, u.s.) [The *Tarikh-i-Rashidi* has been edited by N. Elias and translated into English by E. Denison Ross, Lond., 1895, 8vo, and is frequently quoted in this new edition of *Cathay*. After the annexation by the Chinese, the country called Sin Kiang was divided into *T'ien shan Pe Lu* and *T'ien shan Nan Lu*; at the head of the Chinese administration was placed since 1762 a military governor, *Tsiang Kiun*, who resided in the Chinese Kulja, Hwei Yuan, built in 1764; he had a number of subordinate administrators and the native chiefs *begs* (Po-k'o, Pâh-k'eh).]

with notes, in Astley's *Voyages*, which I have formerly read, but have not now by me. Ritter first in recent times took some pains to trace the route of Goës systematically, by the light of modern knowledge regarding these regions, such as it is. It will be seen by the notes that I have on various occasions ventured to differ from him.

BIBLIOGRAPHY

—Ex India Cataium Lustraturus mittitur è Nostra Societate Benedictus Goësius Lusitanus. (*De Christ. Exp. apud Sinas*, Aug. Vind., 1615, Liber v, Cap. 11, pp. 544 *et seq.*)

—Reliquum itineris Cataium usque quod Sinarum Regnum esse compertum est. (*Ibid.*, Cap. 12, pp. 551 *et seq.*)

—Fratris Nostri Benedicti mors intra Sinense regnum, postquam ad eum excipiendum è Nostris unus Pechino missus aduenisset. (*Ibid.*, Cap. 13, pp. 561 *et seq.*)

An abstract has been made by A. Kircher:

"Le chemin qu'a tenu le Père Benoit Goës de la Compagnie de Jésus: pour aller en Cathaie ou la Chine." (*Chine illustrée*, pp. 85–88.)

—Troisiesme Partie de l'Histoire des Choses plvs memorables advenves tant ez Indes Orientales, qu'autres païs de la descouuerte des Portugais...par le P. Pierre Dv Iarric Tolosain...à Bovrdeavs...CIↃDCXIIII. 4to.

Livre v:

Benoist de Goes de la Compagnie de Iesvs, est enuoyé pour faire la descouuerte du Catay: & ce qui lui advint en vne partie du chemin, pp. 145–155.

Benoist de Goes après beaucoup de trauaux & dangers, trouua finalement le Catay n'estre autre païs que la Chine, où il finit son voyage, & le cours de ceste vie, pp. 155–162.

Much of the information has been drawn from F. Guerreiro's *Relations*.

—The Report of a Mahometan Merchant which had beene in Cambalu: and the troublesome trauell of Benedictvs Goes, a Portugall Iesuite, from Lahor to China by land, thorow the Tartars Countreyes (Purchas, iii, Lib. ii, c. 4, pp. 310 *et seq.*).

—Vite // Di alcvni religiosi, // fratelli Coadivtori // della Compagnia // di Giesv, // scritte // da diversi avtori, // e nel volgare // italiano. // Tradotte da vn Religioso della medesima // Compagnia. // In Torino, M.DC.LXIIII. // Per Gio: Giacomo Rustis,

// con licenza de' Superiori, 8vo, 7 ff. n. numb., front., [Cesare Laurentio Fece], tit., etc.,+pp. 364.

Benedetto Goez, pp. 262–9. Born in 1552 in the island of St. Michael. By Father Marius Clement Baratta. According to Sommervogel, this work contains seventeen notices translated from *Claros Varones* of E. Nieremberg.

—A Long and Dangerous Journey from Lahor, a City of the Great Mogul, to China over Land, by Benedict Goez. (*Travels of Avril*, Lond., 1693, pp. 163–170.)

—Berigt van een // Mahometaans Koopman, // aangaande // Cambalu. // Mitsgaders de moeijelijke Reys van // Benedictus Goes, // Gedaan van Lahor over Land door // Tartaryen na China, // In 't Jaar 1598. en vervolgens. // Nu aldereerst uyt het Portugys vertaald, met nodige // Konst-Printen en een Register verrijkt. // [engrav.] // Te Leyden, // By Pieter Vander Aa, Boekverkoper, 1706. // Met Privilegie, fol., pp. 17.

(Map; 2 engrav. in text.)

—The Travels of Benedict Goëz, a Portugueze Jesuit, from Lahor in the Mogol's Empire, to China, in 1602.

In Astley's *Collection of Voyages*, iv, pp. 642–9.

—Father Pennequin wrote an elegy on Goës; the sixteenth of Book iii of his *Primum S.J. saeculum*, Atrebati, 1611, 4to.

—The Travels of Benedict Goëz, a Portugueze Jesuit, from Lahor in the Mogul's Empire to China, in 1602. (Pinkerton's *Coll. of Voyages*, vii, 1811, pp. 577–587—From Astley.)

—José de Torres wrote an historical novel having as a basis Goës' adventures, with the title *Bento de Goes*, printed at Ponta Delgada, in 1854.

—Ménologe de la Compagnie de Jésus par le P. Elesban de Guilhermy....Assistance de Portugal...Poitiers, 1867, 2 parts, 4to.

I–XI Avril, pp. 341–4 [Goës].

—Ferdinand Freiherrn von Richthofen. China...Erster Band, Einleitender Theil. Berlin, Dietrich Reimer, 1877.

Reise von Benedict Goës, pp. 666–8.

—Benoit de Goès, Missionnaire voyageur dans l'Asie centrale 1603–1607. Par le R. P. J. Brucker de la Compagnie de Jésus. Extrait des *Études religieuses*, Lyon, Imprimerie Pitrat aîné, 1879, 8vo, pp. 42.

—Bento de Goes (1607–1907), por Augusto Ribeiro. (*Bol. Soc. Geog. Lisboa*, Abril, 1907, pp. 137–148.)

—Bento de Goes, Explorador da Asia o seu Itinerario, por Ernesto de Vasconcellos. (*Bol. Soc. Geog. Lisboa*, Abril, 1907, pp. 148–151, carte.)

Centenary of Goës.

These two articles were printed in a pamphlet 8vo, pp. 23, with the title: Sociedade de Geographia de Lisboa.—No Centenario de

Bento de Goes (1607–1907) Homenagem da Sociedade de Geographia de Lisboa 11 de Abril de 1907....Lisboa, Typographia Universal, 1907.

—Bento de Goes, Explorador da Asia. O seu itinerario. Por Ernesto de Vasconcellos. (*Revista Portugueza*, 1907, 20 Abril, pp. 1–5.) Historia da sua viagem ao Cataio. Trad. de João Farmhouse. (*Ibid.*, pp. 6–16; 20 Maio, pp. 49–50.)

—Elogio Historico de Bento de Goes—Proferido no dia 11 de Abril de 1907, tricentenario da sua morte, por occasião do solemne Te Deum na matriz de S. Miguel Archanjo de Villa Franca do Campo, pelo Padre Manuel Ernesto Ferreira. Typ. A. Moderna, Rua do Castello, no. 1, Ponta Delgada, 1907.

—Opere storiche del P. Matteo Ricci S.I. edite a cura del Comitato per le Onoranze nazionali con prolegomeni note e tavole dal P. Pietro Tacchi Venturi S.I. Volume primo I Commentarj della Cina. Macerata, Filippo Giorgetti, 1911, large 8vo, pp. LXVIII+650+3ff. n. n., port., engrav., maps, facsim., etc.

See the three Chapters devoted to Goës in Book V:

Capitolo XII. Del Viaggio del fratello Benedetto di Gois della nostra Compagnia che fece per terra dall' India verso Levante, mandato da' suoi Superiori per scoprire il Gran Cataio, sino alla città regia del regno di Cascar. [Gennaio—novembre, 1603.] Pp. 526–537.

Capitolo XIII. Il resto del viaggio del fratello Benedetto di Gois della nostra Compagnia di Cascar sino al Cataio, che ritrovò esser l' istesso che la Cina. [Decembre 1603—novembre 1605.] Pp. 538–548.

Capitolo XIV. Della morte del fratello Benedetto di Gois, e come fu liberato dalle mani de' Saraceni Isac Armenio dal fratello Giovanni Fernandes, che era stato a Socceo di Pacchino. [Ultimi di decembre 1605—28 ottobre 1606.] Pp. 549–558.

In our notes we mention this text as R., or Ricci.

—Atti del VII Congresso geografico italiano, Palermo, 30 aprile—6 maggio 1910. La identificazione della Cina con il Cataio dovuta al P. Matteo Ricci (n. Macerata 1552—m. Pechino 1610) Geografo e Apostolo della Cina. Memoria del Prof. Ettore Ricci. Palermo, Virzì, 1911, 8vo, pp. 14.

Itinerary of Goes, pp. 8–10.

—Joseph Brucker. Pour le Centenaire du P. M. Ricci. Publications du P. Tacchi Venturi, du marquis Ricci Riccardi, de M. Laufer, etc. (*Études...par des Pères de la Compagnie de Jésus*, 20 avril, 1912, pp. 215–229.)

—Bento de Goes S.J. Een Ontdekkingsreiziger in Centraal-Azië (1603–1607) door C. Wessels, 8vo, pp. 46, 1 plate monument of Goës.

Overgedrukt uit *De Studiën* Tijdschrift voor Godsdienst Wetenschap en Letteren. Afl. no. 1 & 2, Jaargang 43, Deel LXXV.

Uitgegeven te Nijmegen door L. C. G. Malmberg, 1911, pp. 72–96, 229–248.

—Bergeron's *Voyages*, 1735 (Chap. XXVII of the *Traité de la Navigation*).

—*Histoire générale des Voyages*, vii, 1749, p. 410.

—Laharpe, *Abrégé des Voyages*, vi, Livre v, Chap. IV, pp. 420–438.

—*Biographie universelle*, Article by Eyriès.

—C. Ritter, *Asien*, I, 1 sect., § 22, p. 218; 2 sect., § 29, p. 362; v, Book iii, 1 sect., § 5, no. 2, pp. 391, 503–6.

THE JOURNEY OF BENEDICT GOËS TO CATHAY;

FROM CHAPTERS XI, XII, AND XIII OF THE WORK ENTITLED "DE CHRISTIANA EXPEDITIONE APUD SINAS, SUSCEPTA AB SOCIETATE JESU, EX P. MATTHÆI RICII COMMENTARIIS, ETC., AUCTORE P. NICOLAO TRIGAUTIO." AUGUST. VIND., 1615.

CHAPTER XI OF BOOK V

How the Portuguese, Benedict Goës, a member of our Society, is sent to find out about Cathay.

LETTERS from those members of the Society who were living at the court of the Mogul brought to Western India[1] some news regarding that famous empire which the Mahomedans called CATHAY, the name of which was once familiar to Europe through the story of Marcus Paulus the Venetian, but had in the lapse of ages so fallen out of remembrance that people scarcely believed in the existence of such a country. The substance of what the Fathers wrote from time to time was, that the empire of Cathay lay towards the east, somewhat further north than the kingdom of the Mogul; and that they had reason to believe that many professors of the Christian faith were to be found in it, with churches, priests, and

[1] Literally, "From the letters of the members dwelling at the court of *Mogor*, it was heard in *India*." With the missionaries of this age, and the Portuguese, *India* meant Goa and the Western Coast (just as with the Dutch now India means Java and Sumatra); Hindustan Proper and the dominions of the *Mogul* were called Mogor.

sacraments[1]. On this Father Nicolas Pimenta[2] the Portuguese, who was Visitor of the Society in the East Indies, became greatly taken up with the desire of establishing a field of labour for our Society among that people; all the more because it might well be supposed that Christians separated from their head by such vast distances must have fallen into sundry errors. Hence he thought it well to communicate on the matter both with the Pope and with His most Catholic Majesty[3]. And by the King's command, accordingly, despatches were sent to the Viceroy, then Arias Saldanha, desiring him to support the expedition proposed by the Visitor with both money and countenance; an order which he carried out, and more, as might indeed have been expected from the favourable disposition that he entertained both towards the propagation of the faith, and towards our Order in particular. The Visitor proceeded to select for the exploration one of our Brethren called Benedict Goës[4], a Portuguese by nation, and an eminently pious and sensible man, who from his long residence in the Mogul's territories, had an accurate knowledge of the Persian tongue, and a thorough acquaintance with Mahomedan customs, two qualifications which appeared to be indispensable for any one attempting this journey.

[1] [Ricci, p. 526: "Per via de' padri della Compagnia, che stanno nelle terre del Gran Mogore, si hebbe nova nell' India che quel celebre regno, che si noma il Gran Cataio, cui fama tanti anni sono arrivò in Europa per via di Marco Polo venetiano e di altri e poi se ne era persa la notizia, stava al levante più al settentrione dello stato del Mogore, e che molti Saraceni volevano là andare a far le loro faccende, dando per nova che quivi erano molti christiani con chiese e sacerdoti et altri riti de' nostri."]

[2] [Nicolas Pimenta, born at Santarem, on the 6th December, 1546, died at Goa on the 6th March, 1614, or, according to the *Catalogus brevis Provinciae Goanae*, quoted in Ricci, p. 526 *n.*, on the 6th March, 1613.]

[3] Philip III.

[4] [Written *Gois* by Ricci.]

Our brethren had heard indeed, by extracts of Father Matthew's letters from the capital of China, that Cathay was but another name for the Chinese empire[1], (a fact which has been established by various arguments in a previous part of this book). But as quite an opposite view was taken in the letters of the Fathers at the Mogul's court, the Visitor first wavered and then inclined to the opinions of the latter; for whilst he found it distinctly stated in regard to Cathay that a considerable number of Mahomedans were to be met with there, it had come to be considered an established fact that the follies of that sect had never found their way to China. Moreover, whilst it was denied that there ever had been a vestige of Christianity in China, the positive assertions of the Mahomedan eye-witnesses were held to put beyond question its existence in the country called Cathay. It was suggested that the name of an empire conterminous with China might have been extended also to the latter; and it was decided that the investigation should be carried out, so as both to remove all shadow of doubt, and to ascertain whether a shorter line of communication with China could not be established.

As regards the Christians who were held so positively to exist in Cathay (*i.e.* as we shall see by and by in *China*), either the Mahomedan informants simply lied, as they have a way of doing, or they were misled by some superficial indications. For as they themselves never pay respect to images of any kind, when they saw in the Chinese temples a number of images not altogether unlike our representations of the Mother of God and some of the Saints, they may possibly have thought that the

[1] [Ricci knew that China and Cathay were but one country; it is proved by his unpublished letter of the 13th October, 1596, mentioned in R., p. 528 *n.*]

religion of the country was all one with Christianity. They would also see both lamps and wax lights placed upon the altars; they would see those heathen priests robed in the sacred vestments which our books of ritual call *Pluvials*[1]; processions of suppliants just like ours; chaunting in a style almost exactly resembling the Gregorian chaunts in our churches; and other parallels of the same nature, which have been introduced among them by the devil, clumsily imitating holy things and grasping at the honours due to God. All these circumstances might easily lead a parcel of traders, especially if Mahomedans, to regard the people as professors of Christianity[2].

So our Benedict began to prepare for his journey, and assumed both the dress and the name of an Armenian Christian merchant, calling himself Abdula, which signifies *Servant of the Lord*, with the addition of *Isái* or the Christian[3]. And he got from the Mogul king, Akbar by

[1] [R., p. 528: "I sacerdoti con cappe e vestimenti far processioni."]

[2] So easily that the alternative supposition might have been spared. The like confusion has often occurred, and the Jesuits themselves have here shown why. According to Deguignes, the Chinese describe the sovereign and people of the (Eastern) Roman Empire as worshippers of *Fo*, or Buddha, and as putting his image on their coins: Da Gama, in his report of the various eastern kingdoms of which he heard at Calicut, describes the Buddhist countries of Pegu, etc., as Christian. Clavijo sets down the king and people of India as Christians of the Greek faith, and heard that the Emperor of Cathay was a Christian also. The Tartars, whom Josaphat Barbaro met at Tana, assured him that the inhabitants of Cathay were Christians, because "they had images in their temples as we have." Anthony Jenkinson's party were told at Bokhara, in 1559, that the religion of the people of Cathay was that of the Christians, or very nearly so (see also *supra*, III, p. 54, a note from Quatremère). When Dr. Richardson and Capt. Macleod, in their explorations of the states east of Burma, fell in with Chinese traders, these generally claimed them as of their own religion.

[3] Du Jarric says the name bestowed on him by Xavier was "*Branda* Abedula, *i.e.* Servant of the Lord." I do not know what the first word is meant for.

name, who was friendly to the brethren and above all to Benedict himself, sundry rescripts addressed to various Princes known to be either friends or tributaries of his. So he was to pass for an Armenian, for in that character he would be allowed to travel freely, whilst if known as a Spaniard he was certain to be stopped[1]. He also carried with him a variety of wares, both that he might maintain himself by selling them, and to keep up his character as a merchant. There was a large supply of these wares both from (western) India, and from the Mogul dominions, provided at the expense of the Viceroy of India, aided by contributions also from Akbar himself. Father Jerome Xavier, who had for many years been at the head of the Mogul mission, appointed two men acquainted with those countries to be the comrades of his journey. One, for Benedict's comfort, was a priest, by name Leo Grimanus, the other a merchant called Demetrius[2]. There were also four servants, Mahomedans by birth and former profession, but converted to Christianity. All of these servants however he discharged as useless when he got to LAHORE (the second capital of the Mogul), and took in lieu of them a single Armenian, Isaac by name, who had a wife and family at Lahore. This Isaac proved the most faithful of all his comrades, and stuck to him throughout the whole journey, a regular *fidus Achates*. So our brother took leave of his superior, and set out, as appears from the

[1] "He adopted the common Armenian costume, viz. a long frock and turban, with a scymitar, bow, and quiver, this being a dress usually worn by merchants, but yet such as marked him for a Christian" (Du Jarric). He allowed his hair and beard to grow long, as was the practice of merchants. He was often, however, on the journey, as his letters mentioned, taken for a *Saida* (Syad), or descendant of Mahomed (*Ib.*).

[2] The former is probably the same person who is mentioned by Du Jarric as "the subdeacon Leo Grymonius, a clever and experienced man," a Greek by nation, who was sent by Akbar on a mission to Goa about 1590 (ii, 529).

letter of instructions, on the sixth of January in the third year of this century (1603)[1].

Every year a company of merchants is formed in that capital to proceed to the capital of another territory with a king of its own, called CASCAR[2]. These all take the road together, either for the sake of mutual comfort or for protection against robbers. They numbered in the present case about five hundred persons, with a great number of mules, camels, and carts[3]. So he set out from Lahore in this way during Lent of the year just mentioned[4], and after a month's travelling they came to a town called ATHEC[5], still within the province of Lahore. After (a halt of) about a fortnight they crossed a river of a bowshot in width, boats being provided at the passage for the accommodation of the merchants[6]. On the opposite bank of the river they halted for five days, having received warning that a large body of robbers was threatening the road, and then after two months they arrived at another city called PASSAUR[7]: and there they

[1] The instructions were probably sent after him to Lahore, for we have seen that according to another and probably more correct statement he set out on the 31st October, and reached Lahore 8th December, 1602. As instructed, he did not put up at the church at Lahore, then occupied by the Jesuits Emanuel Pinheiro and Francis Corsi, but at the house of John Galisci, a Venetian (Du Jarric).

[2] Kashgar.

[3] [R., p. 530: "Quattrocento o cinquecento persone con cavalli, cameli e cariaggi."]

[4] Easter in 1603 was 30th March, N.S.

[5] Attock, on the Indus. [Attock Town (Atak) is a fort above the Indus "built by Akbar in 1581, to protect his empire against the inroads of his brother, Hakim Mirza, governor of Kābul; and he named it Atak-Banāras in contrast to Katak-Banāras, the fort which lay in the south-east corner of his empire." The District of Attock is in the Rāwalpindi Division of Punjab. (*Imp. Gazetteer of India.*)]

[6] [R., p. 530: "cavalli, cameli e mercantie."]

[7] Peshāwar. For two *months* read two *marches*, see p. 180, *supra*. These halts of twenty days, thirty days, all look suspicious. Some mistaken interpretation is probably at the bottom of the

halted twenty days for needful repose. Further on, whilst on their way to another small town, they fell in with a certain pilgrim[1] and devotee, from whom they learned that at a distance of thirty days' journey there was a city called CAPPERSTAM, into which no Mahomedan was allowed to enter, and if one did get in he was punished with death[2]. There was no hindrance offered to the entrance of *heathen* merchants into the cities of those people, only they were not allowed to enter the temples. He related also that the inhabitants of that country never visited their temples except in black dresses; and that their country was extremely productive, abounding especially in grapes. He offered our brother Benedict a cup of the produce, and he found it to be wine like our own; and as such a thing is quite unusual among the Mahomedans of those regions, a suspicion arose that perhaps the country was inhabited by Christians[3]. In

difficulty. [Peshāwar, since 1901 capital of the North-West Frontier Province, "is situated on a ridge overlooking the surrounding plain and the city, which lies near the left bank of the Bārā Stream, 13½ miles south-east of the junction of the Swāt and Kābul rivers, and 10½ miles from Jamrūd fort near the entrance of the Khyber Pass." In the time of Fa Hian it was the capital of the Ghandara Province. "In 1552 Humāyūn found the fortress in ruins, but had it repaired and entrusted it to a governor, who successfully defended it against the Afghāns under Khān Kajū. The town appears to have been refounded by Balgram, a contemporary of Akbar, and was much enlarged by General Avitabile, its governor under the Sikhs." (*Imp. Gaz. of India.*)]

[1] [R., p. 530: "un eremitano de idoli pellegrino."]

[2] [Under "the reign of the late Amír, when Afghān troops overran the country, and brought about its complete subjection. With the exception of the Rāmgulis, who held out for a considerable period, the Kāfirs, who were ill-armed, made but a feeble resistance, and have accepted the Muhamedan religion with little demur." (*Imp. Gaz. of India.*)]

[3] [R., p. 530: "Caferstam."] The "city called Capperstam" represents KAFIRISTAN [in Afghanistan], the hill-country occupied by the fair race called by the Mahomedans *Kafirs*, or infidels, of whom we still know extremely little. Some of them, at least, are called *Siyaposh*, or black-clothed (like the Scythian *Melanchlæni* of Herodotus, iv, 107), from their wearing black goat-skins. The abundance of grapes and wine among them is noticed by

the place where they met with that wanderer they halted for twenty days more, and as the road was reported to be infested with brigands they got an escort of four hundred soldiers from the lord of the place. From this they travelled in twenty-five days to a place called

Elphinstone (ii, 375) and Wood. Sultan Baber also says: "So prevalent is the use of wine among them, that every Kafir has a *Khig*, or leathern bottle of wine, about his neck; they drink wine instead of water" (p. 144). Timur, before entering Afghanistan on his march towards India, sent an expedition against the Siyaposh; and himself led one against another section of the Kafirs, the members of which, according to his historian, went quite naked. To reach these he crossed the snowy mountain *Kataur*. This is the name of one of the Kafir tribes in Elphinstone, and *Shah Kataur* is a title still affected by the Chief of Chitral, according to Burnes. Chinghiz also after his campaign in the region of the Hindu Kush, is stated to have wintered in the mountains of *Buya Kataur*. Thence he attempted to reach Mongolia by Tibet (probably by the passes of Karakorúm), but failed, and had to go round by Bamian. Akbar and Nadir Sháh also undertook expeditions against the Kafirs, both unsuccessfully. (*H. de Timur Bec*, iii, 14–21; D'Ohsson, i, 319; Elphinstone's *Caubul*, ii, 376, 381; Ritter, vii, 207.)

Kafiristan has lately been visited by two native missionaries, employed under the agents of the Church Missionary Society at Peshāwar, and some account of their experiences has been published, but it does not amount to much. The chastity and honesty of the people are lauded. Those of the same village entertain a strong feeling of kindred, so that neither fighting nor marrying among themselves is admissible. But the different tribes or villages are often at war with each other, and then to kill men or women of an alien tribe is the road to honour. They have no temples, priests, or books. They believe that there is one God, but keep three idols whom they regard as intercessors with him. One of these, called *Palishanu*, is roughly carved in wood, with silver eyes; he is resorted to in excess or defect of rain, or in epidemic sickness. Goats are sacrificed, and the blood sprinkled on the idol. Women must not approach it. The other two idols are common stones. Goats' flesh is the chief food of the people, and occasionally partridges and deer; but fowls, eggs, and fish are not used [though the rivers teem with fish]. They have no horses, donkeys, or camels, only a few oxen and buffaloes, and a few dogs. "They drink wine in large quantities, and very nasty it is, if what was brought down to Peshāwar may be taken as a specimen;" but none were seen drunk. Their drinking-vessels were of curiously wrought pottery, and occasionally of silver. They live to a great age, and continue hale till the day of death. "The men are somewhat dark, but the women are said to be as fair as Europeans, and very beautiful, with red cheeks." The men hardly ever wash either their clothes or their persons. In talking they shout with all their might. They bury their dead

GHIDELÌ[1]. In the whole of this journey the baggage and packs were carried along the foot of the hills, whilst the merchants, arms in hand, kept a look out for the robbers from the hill-top[2]. For these latter are in the habit of rolling stones down upon travellers, unless these are beforehand with them on the heights, and meeting violence by violence drive them away. At this place the merchants pay a toll, and here the robbers made

with coffins, in caves among the hills. (From *Christian Work*, September, 1865, p. 421.) ["The dead are disposed of in a peculiar manner. They are not buried, or burnt, but are deposited in large boxes, placed on the hill-side or in some more or less secluded spot." (*Imp. Gaz. of India.*)]

Leech, in his Report on the Passes of Hindu Kush, mentions that *smiths* are regarded by the Kafirs as natural bondsmen, and are occasionally brought for sale to the Musulman people of the valleys; also, that the oath of peace of the Kafirs consists in licking a piece of salt. This last was also the oath of the Kasias on the eastern frontier of Bengal, in whose country I spent some time many years ago.

1 George Forster was, on the 31st July, at Gandamak; on the 1st of August he rested at *Djeguid-Ali* (I am using a French version, and do not know how Forster spells it); next day he got to Kabul. I suspect that this *Djeguid-Ali* is the *Ghidelì* of Goës, and that both represent the *nomen infelix* of Jugdulluk (*Jour. from Bengal to Petersburg*, French version by Langlès, ii, 52). The preceding town, where Goës' party got an escort, was probably Jalalābād. The exaggerated interpretation of the times occupied in the march must be kept in mind, whatever be the cause of the error. According to the text, Goës was forty-five days $+x$ in getting from Peshāwar to Kabul. Forster's account makes him only seven days; Wood, with Burnes, was nineteen days, but with halts included. [On Major-General Walker's Map of Turkestan, 1878, Sheet No. 4, between Peshāwar and Jalalābād we find Girdi and Girdikas; it may be Ghidelì.]

[In one itinerary from Peshāwar to Kabul taken from Muhammad Abdul Kerim Moonshy's *Tarikhi Ahmed*, translated from the Persian by the late Ch. Schefer (*Recueil d'Itinéraires et de Voy. dans l'Asie centrale.* Paris, Ernest Leroux, 1878, pp. 361–6), we read that on the tenth day the traveller reaches Guendoumek (Gandamak), on the eleventh Djegdelèh, and on the fifteenth Kabul. "Djegdelèh, localité bien peuplée et qui constitue le domaine de la tribu afghane de Suleyman-Kheyl." I have little doubt that this Djegdelèh is the Ghidelì of Goës.]

[Jalalābād, in Afghanistan, 79 miles from Peshāwar and 101 from Kabul, was founded in 1570 by the Emperor Akbar.]

2 The neglect of this same practice of "crowning the heights" caused grievous disaster in those very passes, in the first attempt to relieve the "Illustrious Garrison" of Jalalābād in 1841.

an onslaught. Many of the company were wounded, and life and property were saved with difficulty. Our Benedict fled with the rest into the jungle, but coming back at night they succeeded in getting away from the robbers. After twenty days more they reached CABUL[1], a city greatly frequented for trade, and still within the territories subject to the Mogul. Here our friends halted altogether for eight months. For some of the merchants laid aside the intention of going any further, and the rest were afraid to go on in so small a body.

At this same city the company of merchants[2] was joined by the sister of that very King of Cascar, through whose territory it was needful to pass on the way to Cathay. The king's name is Maffamet Can[3]; his sister was the mother of another king, entitled the Lord of COTAN[4], and she herself was called Age Hanem[5]. *Age* is a title with which the Saracens decorate those who go on pilgrimage to the impostor's carcase at Mecca[6]. In

[1] [Kabul, capital of Afghanistan. "Kabul first became a capital when Bābar made himself master of it in 1504, and here he reigned for twenty years before his invasion of Hindustán. It passed on the death of Bābar to his younger son, Kāmrān, who, after several attacks on his brother Humāyūn, was defeated and blinded by him (1553). Humāyūn left it to his infant son, Mirza Hakim, on whose death, in 1585, it passed to the latter's elder brother, Akbar. From this time up to its capture by Nādir Shah (1738), it was held by the Mughal Emperors of India. From Nādir Shah it passed to Ahmad Shāh Durrāni, whose son, Timūr, made it the capital of his kingdom. It continued to be the capital during the Sadozai dynasty, and is so still under the now reigning Bāraksais." (*Imp. Gaz. of India.*)]

[R., p. 531: "con archi e freccie."]

[2] [R., p. 531: "[s']incontrò il fratel Benedetto con una sorella del re di Cascàr."]

[3] [R., p. 531: "Mafamet Cam."] [4] [R., p. 531: "Cotàm."]

[5] *Hajji-Khanum*, "The Pilgrim Princess." Du Jarric calls her *Ahehaxam*, *i.e.*, in the Turkish tongue, "*Beauty coming down from Mecca*" (?). The king's name is, of course, Mahomed Khán; his sister's son, the Lord of Khotan, south-east of Kashgar and Yarkand.

[6] [It is hardly necessary to recall that the Prophet was buried at Medina, not at Mecca.]

fact she was now on her return from that immense journey to Mecca, which she had performed for the sake of her blasphemous creed; and having run short of money she came to seek assistance from the merchants, and promised that she would honestly repay their advances with ample interest on reaching her territory. This seemed to our brother an opportunity not to be lost of obtaining the favour of the king of another kingdom, for now the efficacy of the Mogul's orders was coming to an end. So he made her an advance of about six hundred pieces of gold from the sale of his goods, and refused to allow interest to be stipulated in the bond. She would not, however, let herself be outdone in liberality, for she afterwards paid him in pieces of that kind of marble[1] which is so highly esteemed among the Chinese, and which is the most profitable of all investments that one can take to Cathay.

From this place the Priest Leo Grimanus went back [to Lahore], being unable to stand the fatigues of the journey; and his comrade Demetrius stopped behind in the town on account of some business. So our brother set out, attended by no one but the Armenian, in the caravan with the other merchants. For some others had now joined them, and it was thought that they could proceed with safety.

The first town that they came to was CIARAKÁR, a place where there is great abundance of iron[2]. And here

[1] [R., p. 532: "pietra di iaspe, molto fina, che è la migliore mercantia che di Cascar portano alla Cina."]

[2] *Chārikār* [on the Ghorband] at the head of the Koh-Daman valley, north of Kabul, famous in our own day for the gallant defence made there by Eldred Pottinger, and Haughton, during the Kabul outbreak (1841). It is mentioned by Ibn Batuta as *Charkh*. Leech, in his Report on the Passes, calls it *Charka*. [Chārίkār, in Afghanistan, at the mouth of the Ghorband Valley, about forty miles north of Kabul. "Iron ore is brought to Chārikār in great quantities from the Ghorband mines, and is worked up

Benedict was subjected to a great deal of annoyance. For in those outskirts of the Mogul's dominions no attention was paid to the king's *firman*, which had hitherto given him immunity from exactions of every kind. Ten days later they got to a little town called PARUÁN[1], and this was the last in the Mogul's territories. After five days' repose they proceeded to cross over very lofty mountains by a journey of twenty days, to the district called AINGHARÀN[2], and after fifteen days more they

for the Kābul market." (*Imp. Gaz. of India.*) It is the residence of the governor of Kohistan, a sub-province of Kabul.]

It is to be recollected that the names in the text are all spelt by Ricci after the Italian fashion.

[R., p. 532: "dove stettero venti giorni."]

[1] [R., p. 532: "Parvam, terra piccola e ultima dello stato del Mogore."] *Parwān*, in a nook of the Hindu Kush, has, from its position near the terminus of several of the chief passes, often been famous in Asiatic history. It is evidently the *Karwan* of Jaubert's Edrisi (a mistranscription for *Farwan*)—"The town of Farwán is of no great size, but a nice enough place with agreeable environs, thronged bazaars, and rich inhabitants. The houses are of clay and brick. It is situated on the banks of the river Banjhir (*Panjshir*). This town is one of the principal markets of India" (i, p. 477). At Parwān the army of Chinghiz was checked for the moment in 1221, being defeated by the Sultan Jalal-uddín of Khwarizm. And in an action near Parwān in 1840 took place the ominous misconduct of a regiment of Bengal cavalry, which caused the day to be lost, with the lives of several valuable officers, though Dost Mahomed Khan surrendered immediately afterwards.

[2] Here the great number of days occupied in the various portions of the journey is perplexing in the detail as well as erroneous in the total (as we have seen it to be). Goës and his party are made to take seventy-five days from Kabul to Talhan (the identity of which can scarcely be doubtful), a journey which could scarcely have occupied more than sixteen to twenty at most.

Wood, in his unsuccessful attempt to cross one of the Passes of Parwān (perhaps that followed by Goës), on the second day reached the village I-ANGHERAN, and Ahingaran [R., p. 532: "Aingaràm"] is also mentioned in Leech's Report as a village on one of the passes from Parwān at twenty-six miles from the entrance of the pass. But this place is on the *south* side of the mountains, whilst the Aingharàn of Goës is on the north. Either it has been confounded with *Andarab*, or, as is very possible, the name, which I suppose is *Ahan-gharán*, "The Iron-Mines," recurs. Indeed just before receiving the proof of this sheet I have observed the recurrence of the name in another locality, suggesting a different view of Goës' route over the mountains,

reached CALCIÀ. There is a people here with yellow[1] hair and beard like the people of the Low Countries, who occupy sundry hamlets about the country. After ten days more they came to a certain place called

for which I refer to the note on the Passes at the end. *Calcià* (Kalsha, Kalacha, Kilasiya?) is a great difficulty, as it was evidently a place of some importance, but no place of the name can be traced. *Khulum* however appears to have been in the possession of a family called Khallach or Killich, and it is possible that that town may be meant (see Elphinstone's *Caubul*, ii, 196; also Burnes, iii). I must not, however, omit to mention that on the north side of the Oxus in this longitude, occupying part of the hill-country east of Bokhara, there is a poor but independent people of Persian race called *Ghalchas*. Meyendorff calls them very swarthy, but Valikhanoff says expressly: "The Tajiks have dark complexions and hair, whilst fair people are found among the Ghalcha." This might explain the yellow-haired people mentioned by Goës, and his use of the expression *Calciensium Populos*.

["The population of Sarīkol, apart from the nomadic Kirghiz herdsmen who visit its grazing grounds, consists of hill Tājiks, who by physical appearance and language alike are unmistakably proved to belong to the so-called Galcha stock." Stein, i, p. 25. "The hillmen of Sarīkol at the present day form the extreme outpost of Irānian nationality towards the east." *Ibid.* p. 26.

"Finally, it may be pointed out in passing that an ethnic link between the Irānian Sarīkolis and the present population of those oases is, perhaps, to be found in the small and little known hill-tribe of the Pakhpos, who partly as herdsmen, partly as cultivators, dwell in the narrow valleys near the headwaters of the Tiznaf and Yarkand Rivers. Dr. Bellew, to whom we owe what scanty information has so far been recorded about this curious people, describes them as of 'pronounced Caucasian features' and very fair." Stein, p. 26.]

But I cannot well see how his Calcià should be beyond the Oxus, nor find any evidence of Ghalchas south of that river. *Gaoloshan* in the Chinese tables, which is nearer Calcià than any other name, is placed 1° 36′ west of Badakhshan and 0° 26′ north of it. This indication also points to the north of the Oxus, about twenty miles due north of Hazrat Imam (see Meyendorff, p. 132; *Russ. in Cent. Asia*, p. 65; Amyot, *Mémoires*, tom. i, p. 399). If Calcià, however, be Khulum, *Jalalābād* must then be sought between Khulum and Talikhan, about Kunduz or Aliabad, if not identical with one of these. [I should rather seek for Calcià at Khanabad between Kunduz and Talikhan.]

[1] [R., p. 532: "barba e capelli rossi."]

[Stein speaking of a friendly Sarikoli says: "With his tall figure, fair hair, and blue eyes, he looked the very embodiment of that *Homo Alpinus* type which prevails in Sarikol. I thought of old Benedict Goëz, the lay Jesuit, who when passing in 1603 from the Upper Oxus to 'Sarcil' or Sarikol, noted in the looks of the scanty inhabitants a resemblance to Flemings." *Ruins of Desert Cathay*, I, p. 89.]

GIALALABATH. Here are brahmans who exact a toll under a grant made to them by the King of Bruarata[1]. In fifteen days more they came to TALHAN, where they halted for a month, deterred by the civil wars that were going on[2]; for the roads were said to be unsafe on account of the rebellion of the people of Calcià[3].

From this they went on to CHEMÀN[4], a place under Abdulahan King of Samarkan, Burgavia[5], Bacharata,

[1] *Bruarata* is almost certainly a misreading for *Bacharata*, the term used further on for *Bokhara*. [R., p. 533: "*Bucarate*."]

[2] [R., p. 533: "in tumulto per la ribellione delli popoli di Calcià."]

[3] *Talhan* is the first terra firma in the narrative since quitting Parwān. It is doubtless Talikhan, about fifty miles east of Kunduz, and has been spoken of in the Introductory Notice (p. 184). It is mentioned by Marco Polo under the name of *Taican* (i, p. 153). [In the travels of Sidi Ali, son of Husaïn (*Journ. Asiat.*, October, 1826, p. 203), "Talikan, in the country of Badakhschan" is mentioned. It is still existing in the province of Kataghan or Kunduz, but it bears the former name (*Thâîḳân*) in the old Arab geographies.]

[Goës has now arrived at a point, Talikhan, of Marco Polo's route, and there seems little doubt that he is now marching in the footsteps of the Venetian traveller until he reaches the Pass of Chichchiklik, viz. the River Vardoj, the Pass of Ishkashm, the Panja, to Wakhán; Little Pamir at Bozai-Gumbaz joins with the Pamir-i-Wakhán at the Wakhijrui Pass, first explored by Colonel Lockhart's Mission. Hence the route lies by the old fort of Kurgan-i-Ujadbai at the junction of the two branches of the Tāgh-dum-bāsh Pamir (Supreme Head of the Mountains), the Tāgh-dum Pamir and Tāsh-Kurghān.]

[4] I cannot say what place this is. Hazrat *Imâm* on the Oxus appears too much out of the way. But Wood mentions, at the junction of the Kokcha with the Oxus, due north of Talikhan, a mountain which he calls *I-Khanam* (*Koh-i-Khanam?* "Hill of Khanam"): "Immediately below I-Khanam, on its east side, the ground is raised into low swelling ridges. Here, we were informed, stood an ancient city called Barbarrah, and there is a considerable extent of mud-walls standing which the Tajiks think are vestiges of the old city, but which are evidently of a comparatively modern era." It is possible that this was *Khanam*, and the *Cheman* of Goës. [R., p. 533: "Chescàn."] [Both on the Russian Map of Asiatic Russia in eight sheets (Sheet 5, 1883), and the Map of Turkestan of Major-General Walker, 1878 (Sheet No. 4, scale 1 in. = 32 miles), beyond Talikhan situated between Kunduz and Kishm, we find Teskan or Teshkán, probably our Chescàn, on the road to Faizabad.]

[5] *Burgavia* is probably a misprint for *Burgania* (as Astley in his version has indeed printed it), and intended for *Farghānah*.

and other adjoining kingdoms[1]. It is a small town, and the governor sent to the merchants to advise them to come within the walls, as outside they would not be very safe from the Calcià insurgents. The merchants, however, replied that they were willing to pay toll, and would proceed on their journey by night. The governor of the town then absolutely forbad their proceeding, saying that the rebels of Calcià as yet had no horses, but they would get them if they plundered the caravan, and would thus be able to do much more damage to the country, and be much more troublesome to the town; it would be a much safer arrangement if they would join his men in beating off the Calcià people. They had barely reached the town walls when a report arose that the Calcià people were coming! On hearing this the bragging governor and his men took to their heels[2]. The merchants on the spur of the moment formed a kind of entrenchment of their packs, and collected a great heap of stones inside in case their arrows should run short. When the Calcià people found this out, they sent a deputation to the merchants to tell them to fear nothing, for they would themselves escort and protect the caravan. The merchants, however, were not disposed to put trust in these insurgents, and after holding counsel together flight was determined on. Somebody or other made this design known to the rebels, upon which immediately they made a rush forward, knocked over the packs, and took whatever

The prince is then Abdulla Khan, King of Samarkand, Bokhara and F*a*rgha*n*a. The reigning sovereign at this time, according to Deguignes (i, 291–2) was Abdul Mumin of the Uzbek house of Shaibek, which had reigned for a century in Mā-warā-n-Nahr.

[1] [R., p. 533: "Re di Samarhan, Burgagne, Bucarate et altri regni vicini."]

[2] [R., p. 533: "Arrivò la compagnia presso ai muri, e venendo nova che quei di Calcià venivano con grande furia, il governatore abandonò la villa e con tutta la gente se ne fugitte in cavalli e cameli."]

they liked. These robbers then called the merchants out of the jungle (into which they had fled) and gave them leave to retire with the rest of their property within the empty city walls. Our Benedict lost nothing but one of his horses, and even that he afterwards got back in exchange for some cotton cloths[1]. They remained in the town in a great state of fear lest the rebels should make a general attack and massacre the whole of them. But just then a certain leading chief, by name Olobet Ebadascan, of the Buchara country, sent his brother to the rebels, and he by threats induced them to let the merchants go free[2]. Throughout the whole journey, however, robbers were constantly making snatches at the tail of the caravan. And once it befel our friend Benedict that he had dropped behind the party and was attacked by four brigands who had been lying *perdus*. The way he got off from them was this: he snatched off his Persian cap[3] and flung it at the thieves, and whilst they were making a football of it our brother had time to spur his horse and get a bowshot clear of them, and so safely joined the rest of the company.

[1] [R., p. 534: "il quale poi riscosse con due pezze di tela."]

[2] There are some doubtful points in reading this. In Trigault the sentence runs: "*Misit dux quidam e maximis, nomine* Olobet Ebadascan, *Bucharatis regione fratrem suum, qui* minus *Calcienses rebelles adegit ut negotiatores liberos abire permitterent,*" where Olobet Ebadascan ('Ala-Beg Ibadat Khan?) is treated as one name. Perhaps however the original ran, "Olobet e Badascan"—"a chief by name 'Alá-Beg (or Wali-Beg) of Badakshan, a country under Bokhara." In the latter clause I have supposed *minus* to be a misprint for *minis*; otherwise it must be "induced the less rebellious of the Calcha people," which would be awkward. [R., p. 534: "Stando i mercanti dentro delle mura con grande paura di essere ammazzati da quei ribelli, un grande capitano per nome *Olobeth*, mandò di Badasciàn, terra del Bucarate, suo fratello *Oscialbeth* a minacciare ai ribelli di Calcià se facessero nessun male a quella compagnia di mercanti; e per questo furno lasciati andare al loro cammino, ma con molte roberie in tutto esso."]

[3] [R., p. 534: "il turbante que portava nella testa a guisa degli armenij di tela della India."]

After eight days of the worst possible road, they reached the TENGHI BADASCIAN[1]. *Tengi* signifies a difficult road; and it is indeed fearfully narrow, giving passage to only one at a time, and running at a great height above the bed of a river[2]. The townspeople here, aided by a band of soldiers, made an attack upon the merchants, and our brother lost three horses. These, however, also he was enabled to ransom with some small presents. They halted here ten days, and then in one day's march reached CIARCIUNAR, where they were detained five days in the open country by rain, and suffered not only from the inclemency of the weather, but also from another onslaught of robbers[3].

From this in ten days they reached SERPANIL; but this was a place utterly desolate and without a symptom of human occupation; and then they came to the ascent of the steep mountain called SACRITHMA[4]. None but the stoutest of the horses could face this mountain; the rest had to pass by a roundabout but easier road. Here two of our brother's mules went lame, and the weary servants wanted to let them go, but after all they were got to follow the others. And so, after a journey of twenty days, they reached the province of SARCIL[5], where they found a number of hamlets near together. They halted there two days to rest the horses[6], and then in two days more reached the foot of the mountain called CIECIALITH. It was covered deep with snow, and during the ascent many were frozen to death, and our brother

[1] [R., p. 534: "Tenghi Badasciàn."]

[2] [R., p. 535: "sotto di esso correre un grande fiume sino a arrivare alla stessa città di Badasciàn."]

[3] [R., p. 535: "di Calcià."]

[4] [R., p. 535: "con mani e con piedi."]

[5] [R., p. 536: "Sarcòl."]

[6] [R., p. 536: "che venivano assai stanchi."]

himself barely escaped, for they were altogether six days in the snow here. At last they reached TANGHETÀR, a place belonging to the Kingdom of Cascar. Here Isaac the Armenian fell off the bank of a great river into the water, and lay as it were dead for some eight hours till Benedict's exertions at last brought him to.

In fifteen days more they reached the town of IAKÓNICH[1], and the roads were so bad that six of our brother's horses died of fatigue. After five days more our Benedict going on by himself in advance of the caravan reached the capital, which is called HIARCHAN[2], and sent

[1] [R., p. 536: "Jacorich."]

[Iakonich or Yakonich "manifestly contains the misspelt name of the large village Yaka-arik, south-west of Yarkand, passed on the route from Chichiklik." (Stein, *Ancient Khotan*, i, p. 40 *n.*) On the map of Great Tartary by Philipp Johann von Strahlenberg (1723) we find: Choteen, Kargalagga, Sarikol, Tamgeran, Jakonig, Ierken or Hiarchan.]

[2] Goës travelled like Hiuen Tsang from India to the Upper Oxus by way of Kabul and Badakhshan, then to Tash Kurghān (*i.e.* Sarcòl, Sarikol), Chichiklik, Tangheter (Tangitar), Yakonich (Yaka-aryk), Hiarchan (Yarkand). *Cf.* Stein, *Ancient Khotan*, p. 40.

"Taking into account the topographical indications furnished by the pilgrim's [Hiuen Tsang] own route and the distance and bearing recorded, I had previously arrived at the conclusion that the site of the hospice would have to be looked for on the Chichiklik Maidan, the plateau-like head of a high valley, where the main route from Tāsh-kurghān, the Sarīkol capital, to Kāshgar crosses the second great mountain range stretching south from the Muztāgh-ata massif. But it was only on my recent journey that I was able to examine this route and to verify the conjectured location. I found that the curious level plain about 2½ miles long and about 1½ miles across, at the head of the Shindī Valley, situated at an elevation of over 14,000 feet and bordered all round by snowy ridges, corresponds most closely to Hsüan-tsang's description. The accounts of my caravan men and my personal observations amply sufficed to convince me of the losses which this desolate upland of Chichiklik, exposed to the winds and snows, claims annually in animals and sometimes in men Most of it was still under snow when I passed here in June, 1906." (M. Aurel Stein, *Buddhist Local Worship in Central Asia*, pp. 840–1. Stein quotes the passage of *Cathay*, p. 562.)

["While all the other Pāmīrs are situated within the drainage area of the Oxus, the waters of the Tāghdumbāsh Pāmīr discharge themselves eastwards into the great Turkestān Basin. The river of which they are the main feeders, and which takes its best-known name from Tāsh-kurghān, the chief place it passes, breaks

back horses to help on his party with necessaries for his comrades. And so they also arrived not long after safe at the capital, with bag and baggage, in November of the same year 1603[1].

through the great meridional range flanking the Pāmīrs on the east, and ultimately joins the Yarkand river or Zarafshan. The collection of valleys which the river of Tāsh-kurghān drains, together with some minor alpine tracts adjoining them towards the Upper Yarkand River, constitutes the well-defined mountain district now known as Sarikol." Stein, i, pp. 22–23.]

[1] The places named in the preceding paragraphs continue to present some difficulty, but in a somewhat less degree than those lately encountered.

The *Tangi-i-Badakhshan*, "Straits or Defiles of Badakhshan,"—this precise expression is used in the *Akbar-Namah* as quoted by Quatremère. (*Not. et Ext.*, xiv, Pt. i, 222.)—I should look for them along the Oxus in Darwaz and Shagnan, where the paths appear, from what Wood heard, to be much more difficult and formidable than that which he followed, crossing from the Kokcha at Faizabad to the Upper Oxus in Wakhán, where again the latter river runs in a comparatively open valley. The title is well illustrated by Marco Polo's expressions: "En cest regne (de Balacian) a *maint estroit pas moult mauvois* et si fort que il n'ont doute de nullui" (Pauthier's Ed., p. 121). ["After our experiences across the Baroghil and Wakhjir the snow-beds encountered on the Chichiklik Maidan, relatively firm under a grey heavy sky, did not impress me so much as they might otherwise have done. Yet I could not help realizing the trials presented at other times by this bleak plateau close on 15,000 feet above sea, as I recalled here the account left by Benedict Goëz." Stein, *Ruins of Desert Cathay*, i, p. 99. From the Chichiklik Maidan he "entered the deep-cut defile eastwards, appropriately known as 'Tangi-tar,' *i.e.* 'the narrow gorge,' through which the winter route passes eastwards." *Ibid.*—This is exactly the route followed by Goës.] *Ciarciunar* is, I suppose, unquestionably the Persian CHAR CHINAR, "The four plane-trees." This (Chárchinár) is actually the name of an island in the Lake of Kashmir, formerly conspicuous for its four great plane-trees (see Forster's *Journey*). *Serpanil*, desolate and without human habitation, I take to be probably SIR-I-PAMIR, "The head or top of Pamir," the celebrated plateau from which the Oxus, Jaxartes, Rivers of Yarkand and Kashgar, and the Gilgit branch of the Indus derive their headwaters. The anomalous name *Sacrithma* may represent a station which appears in Macartney's map on the mountains near the head of the Oxus as SARIKBAEE. Wilford makes some wild work with this name Sacrithma, quoting Goës, in his essay on the "Isles of the West" in vol. viii of the *As. Researches*. The ridge to which Goës applies the name must be that which separates the Sirikul from the headwaters of the Yarkand River. *Sarcil* may then be, as Ritter surmised, the district of SARĪKOL near the said headwaters (see *Russ. in Cent. Asia*, p. 157; Ritter, vii, 489, 505; iii, 635). *Ciecialith* (*i.e.* Chechalith) is then without doubt that spur of the Bolor running out towards Yarkand, which appears on some recent maps of Asia as the CHICHECK TAGH, and in Klaproth's map cited by Ritter as *Tchetchetlagh*, immediately north of Sarikul. The passage of this great spur is shown very distinctly in a route laid down in Macartney's map (in Elphinstone's *Caubul*), only the author supposed it to be the main chain of the Kara Korum. Macartney terms the *Col* of which Goës gives so formidable an account, the *Pass of Chiltung*, and a station at the northern side of it CHUKAKLEE, which is probably the Chechalith of our traveller.

Tanghetàr I had supposed to be a mistranscription for *Yanghesar, i.e.* Ingachar or YANGI-HISAR, an important town forty-seven miles S.E. of Kashgar on the road from that city to Yarkand, an error all the more probable as we have Tusce for Yusce a little further on. *Tungeetar*, however, appears in Macartney's map, and immediately beyond he represents the road as bifurcating towards Kashgar and Yarkand. It must in any case be near Yengi-Hisar if not identical with it. *Iakonich* I cannot trace. [See *supra.*]

[Stein, *Ancient Khotan*, i, p. 42, remarks that Goës "appears to have spent not less than twenty-eight days in the journey from the hamlets of 'Sarcil' (Sarīkol, *i.e.* Tāsh-kurghān) to 'Hiarchan' (Yarkand)—a distance of some 188 miles, now reckoned at ten days' march."]

["Though Yarkand is in all probability a place of considerable antiquity, it is difficult to trace back its name or even its existence as a town of importance previous to the Mongol conquest in the thirteenth century.... Yarkand undoubtedly owes its old-established prosperity and its flourishing trade to its position at the point where the great routes from Khotan, Ladāk, and the Oxus are joined by those leading to Kashgar and the north-eastern part of the Tarim Basin. The abundance of local produce favours the growth of a large town population, and this, with its quasi-cosmopolitan colonies drawn from all parts of the Oxus Valley, from Ladāk, Baltistan, Afghanistan, and the border regions of China, reflects the true causes of Yarkand's importance." Stein, *Ancient Khotan*, i, pp. 87–8.]

Ritter is led by the slight resemblance of names to identify the Charchunar of Goës with Karchu, near the upper waters of the Yarkand, and this mistake, as it seems to me, deranges all his interpretation of the route of Goës between Talikhan and Sarīkol.

Goës in a letter from Yarkand to Agra spoke of the great difficulties and fatigues encountered in crossing this desert of *Pamech* (PAMIR), in which he had lost five horses by the cold. So severe was it, he said, that animals could scarcely breathe the air, and often died in consequence. As an antidote to this (which, of course, was the effect of attenuated atmosphere rather than of cold) the men used to eat garlic, leeks, and dried apples, and the horses' gums were rubbed with garlic. This desert took forty days to cross if the snow was extensive (Du Jarric). Forty days is the time assigned by Polo also to the passage of this lofty region (ii, 27).

CHAPTER XII OF BOOK V

The remainder of the Journey to Cathay, and how it is ascertained to be all the same as the Chinese empire.

HIARCHAN, the capital of the kingdom of Cascar[1], is a mart of much note, both for the great concourse of merchants, and for the variety of wares. At this capital the caravan of Kabul merchants reaches its terminus; and a new one is formed for the journey to Cathay[2]. The command of this caravan is sold by the king, who invests the chiefs with a kind of royal authority over the merchants for the whole journey[3]. A twelvemonth passed away however before the new company was formed, for the way is long and perilous, and the caravan is not formed every year, but only when a large number arrange to join it, and when it is known that they will be allowed to enter Cathay.

There is no article of traffic more valuable, or more generally adopted as an investment for this journey, than

[1] [R., p. 538: "La città di Hiarcàn molto grande." It is the kingdom called *So kiu* by the Chinese.]

[2] ["Though the political centre has shifted from Yarkand since the re-establishment of Chinese rule, the above description still holds good; and we may well conclude that the flourishing condition of the city which Marco Polo's account also indicates, was maintained from early times independent of political predominance." Stein, pp. 88–9.]

[3] Du Jarric, from the letters which Goës wrote from Yarkand in February and August, 1604, mentions that the chief whom he eventually accompanied paid the king two hundred bags of musk for the nomination. Four others were associated with him as envoys; and one hundred and seventy-two merchants, who purchased this privilege from the chief at a high price, insomuch that he cleared a large amount by the transaction.

lumps of a certain transparent kind of marble which we, from poverty of language, usually call jasper. They carry these to the Emperor of Cathay, attracted by the high prices which he deems it obligatory on his dignity to give; and such pieces as the Emperor does not fancy they are free to dispose of to private individuals. The profit on these transactions is so great that it is thought amply to compensate for all the fatigue and expense of the journey. Out of this marble they fashion a variety of articles, such as vases, and brooches for mantles and girdles, which when artistically sculptured in flowers and foliage certainly have an effect of no small magnificence. These marbles (with which the empire is now overflowing) are called by the Chinese Iusce[1]. There are two kinds of it; the first and more valuable is got out of the river of Cotàn, not far from the capital, almost in the same way in which divers fish for gems[2], and this is usually extracted in pieces about as big as large flints. The other and inferior kind is excavated from the mountains; the larger masses are split into slabs some two ells broad and these are

[1] The word as printed in Trigautius is *Tusce*, but this is certainly a mistake for Iusce, *i.e. Yu shé* or "Yu stone," the Chinese name of the oriental jade, the *Yashm* of Western Asiatics (see II, p. 221, *supra*).

The description in the text of the double source of supply of jade is perfectly in accordance with the Chinese authorities, one kind being fished up in boulder form by divers, from the rivers on each side of the chief city of Khotan, which are called respectively Yurung-Kash and Kara-Kash (White Jade and Black Jade), and the other kind quarried in large masses from the mountain called *Mirjai*, which is stated by a Chinese writer to be two hundred and thirty *li* (about seventy miles) from Yarkand. From the mention of a jade quarry by Mir Izzet Ullah, about half-way from the Kara Korum Pass to Yarkand, it is probable that the Mirjai mountain is to be sought thereabouts (see Ritter, vii, 380–9). Ritter will have the *Cansanghi Cascio* of our text to be a mistake for *Karangui-Tagh*, the name which he finds applied to the range in which the rivers of Khotan spring, probably a part of the Kuen-Lun. But the words are Persian, *Kán sang-i-Kásh*, "The mine of Kash (or Jade) Stone," *Kash* being the Turki word for that mineral.

[2] [R., p. 539: "perle e margarite."]

then reduced to a size adapted for carriage. That mountain is some twenty days' journey from this capital (*i.e.*, Yarkand) and is called CANSANGHI CASCIO[1], *i.e.* the Stone Mountain, being very probably the mountain which is so termed in some of the geographical descriptions of this empire[2]. The extraction of these blocks is a work involving immense labour, owing to the hardness of the substance as well as to the remote and lonely position of the place. They say that the stone is sometimes softened by the application of a blazing fire on the surface. The right of quarrying here is also sold by the king at a high price to some merchant, without whose license no other speculators can dig there during the term of the lease. When a party of workmen goes thither they take a year's provisions along with them, for they do not usually revisit the populated districts at a shorter interval.

Our brother Benedict went to pay his respects to the king, whose name was Mahomed Khan[3]. The present

[1] [R., p. 539: "Can Sanguicascio."]

[2] [R., p. 539: "e pare uno che si suol pingere in certi mappamondi novi nel regno di Cascàr col titulo di *mons lapideus.*"]

[3] [R., p. 539: "Fu a visitare il re di Cascàr per nome *Mahamethàn.*"] In orig. *Mahamethin*, for *Mahamethan*. A letter which Goës wrote to Xavier from Yarkand, 2d February, 1604, mentioned that the excitement created in the city by the announcement of the arrival of an Armenian *Rumi* who did not follow the Law of Islam, was so great that he thought it desirable to pay his respects to the king, and he was well received. The vizir having been attracted by a cross and a book of the Gospels (apparently a breviary) which he saw among the baggage, Benedict was desired to produce these at a second audience. The king received the book with much reverence, and directed Goës (to his great joy) to read a passage and explain its meaning. He turned up at a venture the anthem for Ascension Day, *Viri Galilæi, quid statis aspicientes in Cœlum?* and then, in deep emotion at an opportunity so unlooked for, proceeded to declare the glorious Ascension of the Saviour before those Mahomedans; adding also some remarks on the descent of the Spirit at Pentecost, and on the Advent of Christ to judgment. Opening the book a second time he read the 50th (our 51st) Psalm, and took occasion from it to speak of repentance. The bearded doctors of the law regarded one another with astonishment, and the king also expressed his surprise. The latter then requested to see the cross; and asked "To what quarter did

that he carried with him secured him a good reception, for it consisted of a pocket watch[1], looking glasses, and other European curiosities, with which the king was so charmed and delighted that he adopted the giver at once into his friendship and patronage. Our friend did not at first disclose his desire to go to Cathay, but spoke only of the kingdom of Cialìs, to the eastward of Cascar, and begged a royal passport for the journey thither. His request was strongly backed by the son of that pilgrim queen to whom he had lent six hundred pieces of gold [in Kabul][2]. And he also came to be on intimate terms with divers gentlemen of the court.

Six months had passed away when behold Demetrius, one of the original comrades of his journey, who had stayed behind at Kabul, arrived at Hiarchan. Benedict and Isaac the Armenian were greatly delighted at his arrival; but their joy was of short continuance, for very soon after this Demetrius caused our friend a great deal of trouble. At that time, with the king's leave, one of the merchants was elected mock emperor, whilst all the

the Christians turn in prayer?" To all, said Benedict, for God is everywhere. Did they use any washings and ceremonial ablutions? None corporeal, said he, like those of the Mahomedans, to wash away the stains of sin, for these were of no profit to the soul; but spiritual washings, by which souls are cleansed from sin's foulness: an answer which seemed to give satisfaction.

On another occasion (for he was often called to the palace) the king showed him papers inscribed in a certain round and vermiculate character, and asked what they were. Goës when he had read them (in what language is not stated) found them to treat of the Trinity, and took occasion therefrom to speak of the Divine greatness and Omnipotence, etc. So much did they all admire what he said, that in turn they began to ask, "And are these the men whom we have called Kafirs? Of a truth they acknowledge God as well as we." And the king said, "Surely it is a Mullah that is speaking!" (Du Jarric).

[1] [R., p. 539: "un horiulo di ferro per portare al collo."]

[2] This Prince of Khotan had come to Yarkand to meet his mother, and showed Benedict much courtesy and gratitude for the aid rendered her at Kabul. He also was greatly taken with the readings from the Scripture (*ib.*).

rest, according to a custom of theirs, paid homage to him and offered him presents. Demetrius, to save his pocket, held back; and as the emperor had the power of putting rebels against his authority in irons, or even of flogging them, Demetrius had great difficulty in escaping both penalties. Our Benedict, however, by his good management, arranged the whole matter, for his intercession and a small present got pardon for Demetrius. A greater peril also befel the party, when thieves broke into the house, and laid hold of the Armenian whom they tied up, putting a dagger to his throat to prevent his giving the alarm. The noise however roused Benedict and Demetrius, and the robbers made off.

On another occasion Benedict had gone away to get his loan repaid by the mother of the Prince of QUOTAN[1].

[1] [R., p. 540: "Cotān."] Khotan, which may be considered the most central and inaccessible state of all Asia, was a seat of very ancient civilisation, and was already in friendly relations with China in 140 B.C. In the fourth century of our era Buddhism was in high development here. Though much of the surface appears to be rugged mountain, it is interspersed with levels which are both fruitful and populous. At this time, like the other states of Eastern Turkestan, it was under a Mahomedan chief of Turkish or Mongol descent. Khotan is the subject of a short chapter in Marco Polo. In modern times its only European visitor has been Adolphus Schlagintweit, who never returned to tell his tale. [Khotan, also Kustána [Hiuen Tsang], Hwan-na, K'iu lan is the old kingdom of Yu t'ien; in the seventh century the king Fu-tu Hiung went to the court of the Chinese Emperor to pay him homage. His government was turned into the government of P'i sha, Fu-tu Hiung receiving the title of governor. Khotan was one of the Four Garrisons of the Chinese in Eastern Turkestan, the others being Su lei (Kashgar), Yen k'i (Karashahr) and K'iu-tze (Ku cha), in the seventh and eighth centuries. The Buddhist Government of Khotan was destroyed by Boghra Khán (about 980–90); it was temporarily restored by the Buddhist Kutchluk Khán, chief of the Naïmans, who came from the banks of the Ili, destroyed the Mahomedan dynasty of Boghra Khán (1209), but was in his turn subjugated by Chinghiz Khán. The remains of the ancient capital of Khotan were accidentally discovered, some forty-five years ago, at Yotkán, a village of the Borazân Tract, about eight miles to the west of the present Khotan. The sacred sites of Buddhist Khotan which Hiuen Tsang and Fa Hian describe, can be shown to be occupied now, almost without exception, by Mohamedan shrines forming the object of popular

Her capital was ten days' journey distant, and what with going and coming, a month had passed and he was still absent. So the Saracens took occasion by this to spread false reports of Benedict being dead, alleging him to have been put to death by priests of theirs for refusing to invoke the name of their false prophet. And now those initiated priests of theirs whom they call *Cashishes*[1],

pilgrimages. Dr. Sven Hedin followed the route Kashgar, Yangi-Hissar, Yarkand to Khotan, in 1895; he made a stay of nine days at Ilchi, the modern capital, the population of which is estimated at 5500 inhabitants (5000 Musulmans, 500 Chinese). The *Shui king* (sixth century) says that the kingdom of Yu t'ien has Si for its capital, that its soil produces a great quantity of jade and that it is situated 380 li eastward of Pi Shan.

Marco Polo, i, pp. 188–91 *n.*; Grenard, ii, pp. 191–2.—Stein, Sven Hedin, Chavannes, *Tou-kiue*, pp. 125–9; *Wei lio*, p. 564.]

[1] In orig. *Cascisces*. [R., p. 540: "*cazissi*."] *Kashísh* or *Kasís*, from a Syrian root signifying "*Senuit*," is the proper Arabic term for a Christian presbyter. It is the term (*Kashísha*) applied by the Syrian Christians of Malabar to their own presbyters (Buchanan, *Christ. Resear.*, pp. 97 *seqq.*); it will be found attached to the Syriac names of priests on the ancient monument of Si-ngan fu (see Pauthier's work on it, pp. 42 *seqq.*); and it is also applied by the Arabs to Catholic priests. Mount Athos, according to D'Herbelot, is called by the Turks *Kashish Daghi*, from its swarms of clergy. "By neither Christians nor Mahomedans," says my friend Mr. Badger, "is the word adopted to designate any minister of Islam." We have, however, many instances of its misapplication to Musulman divines by European travellers. And as I find the word given in Vieyra's *Portuguese Dictionary* (ed. Paris, 1862) in the form "Caciz—*A Moorish Priest*," it seems probable that this misapplication originated in the Peninsula. In like manner in India *Fakír* has come to be applied to the Hindu Jogis and other devotees, though properly a Mahomedan denomination. In fact, our own application of *priest* (*i.e.* presbyter) to ministers of pagan worship is in some degree parallel. Only as regards *Kashish* it is notable that it seems to have been regarded by European Christians as the specific and technical term for a Mahomedan divine, whereas it was in its proper oriental application the specific and technical term for a Christian presbyter.

It was in general use by the Catholic missionaries as the term for a Mullah; see Du Jarric's Jesuit history *passim* (*Cacizii*); P. Vincenzo the Carmelite (*Casis o con altro nome Schierifi*, p. 55), etc. In Mendez Pinto also we have "*hum* Caciz *seu Moulana que elles tinhão por santo*" (cap. v).

Gonzalez de Clavijo again speaks of "Moorish hermits called *Caxixes*," and in another passage of "a great *Caxix* whom they look upon as a saint" (Markham's *Trans.*, pp. 79, 114).

In the description of Khansa in the Mongol History of Wassaf (in Persian) it is said: "The city includes seven hundred temples

were endeavouring to lay violent hands upon his property, as that of one who was dead intestate and without an heir. This matter caused great distress to Demetrius and Isaac, both in their daily sorrow at the supposed death of their comrade, and in the danger of their own position. So their joy was twofold when after a while he turned up in safety. He returned with his debt paid in ample measure with pieces of that valuable stone of which we have spoken; and to mark his gratitude to God he made a large distribution of alms to the poor, a custom which he kept up throughout his whole journey.

One day when he had sat down with a company of Saracens at a dinner to which one of them had invited him, some fanatic burst in, sword in hand, and pointing his weapon at Benedict's breast desired him instantly to invoke the name of Mahomet. Our friend replied that no such name was wont to be invoked in the law which he professed, and that he must absolutely refuse to do so. The bystanders then came to his aid, and the madman was ejected. The same threats of death however, unless he would address prayer to Mahomet, are said to have been directed to him repeatedly, yet God ever delivered him until the end of his journey. On another day it happened that the King of Cascar sent for him, when the priests and theologians[1] of the accursed faith were present at the court, (they call their theologians *Mullàs*). Being then asked what faith he would profess, whether that of Moses, or of David, or of Mahomet, and in what direction he would turn his face in prayer? our friend replied that

resembling fortresses, each of which is occupied by a number of priests without faith and monks without religion (kashishán *be kesh wa Rahabín be dín*)" (see Quatremère's *Rashid.*, p. lxxxvii). Here the Persian author seems to apply to Pagans the terms both for "presbyter" and "monk" appropriated to Christians.

[1] [R., p. 541: "mullasi e cazissi."]

the faith he professed was that of JESUS, whom they called *Isai*, and that it mattered not to what quarter he turned in prayer, for God was everywhere. This last answer of his created a great discussion among them, for in prayer they make a point of turning to the west. At last they came to the conclusion that our law also might have some good in it[1].

Meantime a certain native named Agiasi[2] was nominated[3] chief of the future caravan of merchants. And having heard that our brother was a man of courage, as well as a merchant of large dealings, he invited him to a grand entertainment at his house, at which there was a great concert of music[4] after the manner of those people, as well as a dinner. After dinner the chief requested our brother to accompany the caravan all the way to Cathay. He indeed desired nothing better, but experience had taught him how to deal with Saracens, so he was glad that the proposal should come from the other side, and thus that he should seem to be granting rather than accepting a favour. So the king himself was prevailed on by the chief to make the request, and did accordingly ask Benedict to accompany the *Caruanbasa*[5] as they call the chief of the company. Benedict agreed to do so on

[1] At Yarkand there were one hundred and sixty mosques; and every Friday an official went about the bazaar reminding the people of the duties of the day. After this twelve men issued from the chief mosque armed with whips of hide, which they laid about those whom they found in the streets, absenting themselves from public prayer (Du Jarric). The same custom is mentioned by Ibn Batuta as existing at Khwarizm in his time, and he tried to introduce similar *Blue Laws* when judge in the Maldives. It still prevails in Bokhara (Burnes, ii, 243; Vambéry, p. 185). The pious Mahomed Tughlak enforced like regulations at Delhi when the whim took him, sometimes with death as his manner was.

[2] Hajji 'Aziz? [R., p. 541: "*Agi Afis.*"]

[3] [R., p. 541: "comprò."]

[4] [R., p. 541: "con molti canti, balli e stromenti."]

[5] [R., p. 541: "*Carvàn Bascì*, che vuol dire 'capitanio della compagnia di mercanti.'"]

condition that the king would grant him circular letters[1] for the whole course of the journey. His former comrades, belonging to the Kabul caravan, took offence at this, for, as has been said, it was always necessary on those occasions to travel in large numbers. So they counselled him against putting any trust in the natives, for these intended the thing only as a trap by which they might succeed in devouring his fortune, and his very life. Our friend however represented that he was acting in accordance with the King's expressed wishes, and had given his promise to the chief of the caravan, from which as an honest man he could not go back. In truth the fears which those merchants professed to entertain were not unfounded, for many of the natives of the country declared that those three Armenians (for so they called them, as being all of one faith[2]) would be murdered as soon as they set foot outside the city walls. And so Demetrius took fright, and a second time drew back from prosecuting the journey further, trying also to persuade our brother to go back. Benedict would not listen to him, saying that he had never yet let himself be deterred by fear of death from the duty of obedience, much less would he do so now in a business from which so much glory to God might be expected. It would be most unworthy conduct, he said, to frustrate the hopes of so many for fear of death; and to throw away all the expense that had been incurred by the Archbishop of Goa[3] and the Viceroy[4]. He hoped still to carry through the under-

[1] [R., p. 541: "una molto buona patente."]

[2] [R., p. 542: "(che pensavano esser i tre nostri per l' abito e nome con che si chiamavano)."]

[3] [Alessio di Gesù de Menezes.]

[4] [Arias Saldanha. R., p. 542: "e di essa se ne era data nuova al papa et al re di Spagna, e non pareva bene, inanzi all' arrivare al Cataio, ritornarsene nel mezzo del cammino senza nessuna conchiusione."]

taking by the help of Him who had thus far brought him prosperously, but in any case he would rather risk his life in the cause than draw back from his purpose[1].

So he girded up his loins for the journey, and bought ten horses for himself and his comrade and their goods, having already one more at his house. Meanwhile the chief of the caravan[2] went off to his home, which was some five days from the capital, to get ready for the journey, and after his arrival sent back a message to our friend to start as soon as possible, and to hasten the other merchants by his example. He was glad enough to do so, and set out accordingly, in the middle[3] of November, 1604, proceeding first to a place called IOLCI, where duties used to be paid and the king's passports to be inspected. After this, in twenty-five days, passing successively HANCIALIX, ALCEGHET, HAGABATETH, EGRIÁR, MESETELECH, THALEC, HORMA, THOANTAC, MINGIEDA, CAPETAL COL ZILAN, SARC GUEBEDAL, CANBASCI, ACONSERSEC and CIACOR[4], they

[1] [R., p. 542: "Il Demetrio, non gli bastando l' animo di patire tanti travagli e far tante spese, se ne ritornò a Lahor, lasciando parte della sua faccenda al fratello Benedetto."]

[2] [R., p. 542: "*Carvàn Basci.*"]

[3] [R., p. 542: "14 de novembre dell' anno 1604."]

[4] I cannot identify one of these places in any routes or maps of Central Asia except *Canbasci*, which appears in K. Johnston's map of Asia as *Kumbashi*, and is mentioned in the Russian Reports as one of the most important settlements of the Aqsu district (*Russians in Central Asia*, p. 160). Of the other names *Hancialix* translated from Ricci's spelling would be probably *Khan-Chalish*; *Sarc Guebedal* is probably the same name as *Saregabedal* which occurs further on; *Aconsersec* is possibly the *Saksak* of Berghaus's map; *Ciacor* is probably *Shakyar*, which indeed is the name of a town some 4° east of Aqsu, but which also appears to be common to many other places in the country, if it is not indeed a local form of the Persian *Shahr* (city). This is suggested by the fact that *Karashahr* appears in one of the routes in the book just quoted as *Karashagiar* (*R. in C. A.*, p. 527). The journey here is said to occupy twenty-five days, but the stages mentioned are sixteen. The latter is the number of stages according to the Chinese route in the *Russ. in Central Asia*, pp. 531–3, though none of the names correspond. It is also the number of stages assigned by the Tajik itinerary from Semipalatinsk to Kashmir which is

reached ACSU[1]. The difficulties of the road were great,

given in the appendix to Meyendorf's *Bokhara*. The Georgian Raphael Danibeg was thirteen days from Yarkand to Aqsu. (Meyendorf, pp. 314 *seq*. and 122 *seqq*.)

[It must be acknowledged that these identifications or rather non-identifications are unsatisfactory; we shall be more successful if we do not seek exclusively the route followed by Goës in the itineraries of to-day. Prof. Paul Pelliot, who has travelled along the same road, writes to me: "When leaving Yarkand, Goës followed what was *then* the usual caravan road to Aqsu; it differs in parts from the present-day road. We have an almost exactly situated spot in *Horma*; it is the *Hu-eul-man* of Chinese texts of the XVIIIth century. A battle was won there in 1756 by part of the army of Chao Hwei, in his fight in Turkestan against Huo-tsi-chan (K'o Dzi-chan). From chap. 18 of the *Si yü t'u che*, Hu-la-ma was situated 130 li south-west of Pa-eul-ch'u-k'o; this name, Barchuq, was borne at the time by Maralbashi. From Horma, Goës followed a road more easterly than the present one; this is proved by the stage *To antac* = Tewan-tâgh, the 'low hill'; it is to this day the name of a hilly spur to the east of the road Maralbashi—Aqsu. Then comes *Mingieda* = *Mingdjigda* the name of one *Elaeagnus* and *Capetalcol*, Capetal-col, which seems to be *Kaptar-köl*, the lac of pigeons. The stage *Čilàn*, *Zilan*, in Chinese Ts'i lan (jujube) is still marked on native maps. *Sare Guebedal* must be Sarygh-abdal, but I do not remember finding this name in this part of the country; it may be a duplicate name of the *Saregabedal* of the itinerary from Aqsu to Kucha. Cambasci has been already identified by Yule with Qum-bashi, on the Qum-aryq; I think this name a very old one and I believe I can find it under the Han and the T'ang dynasties; it is the Huen-ba-sheng mentioned in the biography of Ye-liu Hi-leang. (*Cf.* Bretschneider, *Mediaeval Researches*, i, p. 162.)"]

[1] *Aqsu*, a city of Chinese Tartary, lying to the south of the glacier pass over the Mus-Tagh (and according to the tables in *R. in C. A.*, p. 521) in long. 78° 58′, lat. 41° 9′. According to that authority it contains twelve thousand houses, though Timkowski states the number more probably at six thousand. It stands at the confluence of the Rivers Aqsu (white-water) and Kokshal; it is the central point of the Chinese trade, and from it diverge all the great routes towards China, the Ili country, and the cities both of Eastern and Western Turkestan. The tract immediately surrounding it is one of some fertility, producing a variety of fruits including grapes and melons, besides cereals and cotton. There is a manufacture of jade articles, and of embroidered deer-skin saddlery. Aqsu appears in the Chinese annals, according to Deguignes, as early as the second century B.C. under the Han dynasty, as having a Chinese Governor. Deguignes and D'Anville think it to be the *Auxacia* of Ptolemy. It was at one time the residence of the Kings of Kashgar and Yarkand. From Aqsu the high pass, called by the Chinese the "Pass of Glaciers," leads over that lofty part of the T'ien Shan called the *Muz-art*, or Icy Mountains to Kulja, the seat of the Chinese General Government of Dzungaria and Turkestan. (*Russ. in C. A.*, pp. 112, 119, 159;

either from the quantities of stones, or from the waterless[1] tracts of sand which they had to pass.

Acsu is a town[2] of the kingdom of Cascar, and the chief there was a nephew of the king's, and only twelve years of age. He sent twice for our brother. The latter carried him presents of sweetmeats and the like, such as would be acceptable to a child, and was most kindly received. A grand dance happening to be performed before them, the young prince asked Benedict how the people of his country used to dance? and so Benedict, not to be churlish with a prince about so small a matter, got up and danced himself to show the way of it. He also visited the prince's mother and showed her the royal rescript[3], which she looked on with great respect. To her he presented some little things such as women like, a looking glass, India muslin, and so forth. He was also sent for by the boy's governor who conducted the administration[4].

In this journey one of the pack horses belonging to our merchant fell into a very rapid river. In fact having broken the rope with which its feet (I know not why) were tied, it made off and crossed to the other side of the river. Benedict feeling the loss a serious one invoked

Timkowski, i, 391; Deguignes, i, 26; II, xxxix; Ritter, vii, 431, 449.)

[R., p. 543: "Hancialix, Alcegher, Habagateth, Egriár, Meselelec, Tallec, Horma, Toantac, Mingieda, Capetalcol, Cilàn, Sare Guebedal, Cambasci, Aconterzec, Ciacor, Acsù."]

[We find on Carey's Map: Menut, Ala Aighir, Shamál, Maralbashi (Barchuk), Charwagh, Tumchuk, Chadir Kul, Yaka Kuduk, Jaidi-urtang, Chilan, Well, Shor Kuduk, Sai-Arik, Ai kul, Chuktal, Asuk, Aksu.]

[1] [R., p. 543: "puoca acqua."]

[2] [R., p. 543: "città piccola."]

[3] [R., p. 543: "la patente de Hiacàn e passar franco senza pagar gabella."]

[4] [R., pp. 543–4: "Fu anco invitato dal maestro di quel putto, che in suo luogo governava lo stato, e lo trattò con grande amorevolezza."]

the name of Jesus; and the horse of its own accord swam back to join the others, and our friend, delivered from the anticipated misfortune, returned thanks for the benefit vouchsafed. On this part of the journey they crossed the desert which is called CARACATHAI, or the Black Land of the Cathayans, because 'tis said that the people so called long sojourned there[1].

At this town (Acsu) they had to wait fifteen days for the arrival of the rest of the merchants. At last they started, and travelled to OITOGRACH GAZO, CASCIANI, DELLAI, SAREGABEDAL, and UGAN, whence they got to CUCIA[2], another small town at which they halted a

[1] *Kara-K'itai* has already been spoken of and the origin of the name indicated in connection with an extract from Rubruquis (*supra*, III, pp. 19–21), and its people are mentioned by Plano Carpini under the translated name of *Nigri K'itai* (pp. 750–1). The extent of the territory to which the name applied probably varied considerably, but its nucleus or axis rather seems to have been the range of the T'ien Shan. Here it is applied to the desert south of that chain. The name has come down to modern times, for we find it applied in 1811 (*Khara-Kitat*) to a portion of the inhabitants of the Ili country (Klaproth, *Mag. Asiatique*, i, 209).

[2] None of these places except the last can be traced either in the Chinese routes given in the *Russians in Central Asia*, or in the route set down by Mir Izzet Ullah, Moorcroft's explorer. *Kucha* itself is a place of some importance, containing according to Timkowski's information about one thousand houses, and considered by the Chinese to be the key of this part of Turkestan. The Chinese route says "a very large town, composed of one hundred thousand (!) houses, occupied by Musulmans; six hundred Chinese soldiers." [From Kucha which he left on the 19th January, 1887, Dalgleish on his way to Aqsu passed Karaul, where passports are checked and examined, Toghrak Dung (20th January), Shilder Dawan Pass, Kizil (21st January), crossed a large stream which passes through a ravine in the mountains towards Shahyar, Sairam (22nd), a large straggling village with extensive cultivation, Bai (22nd January), small town with extensive cultivation, and a large bazaar, at five marches E.N.E. of Aqsu. On the map accompanying the paper we note the following names: Aqsu, Jam, Kara-yulgun, Tugrakdan, Yaka-arik, Kush-tam, Bai, Sairam, Kizil, Rabat Lodansa, Shilder Dawan, Toghrak Dunk, Karawal, Kucha, none of which have any resemblance with Benedict's names. Nor are we more successful with the Chinese itinerary given by Chavannes (*Tou Kiue occidentaux*, pp. 8–9) from the *T'ang Shu*: Kucha, Che kiue pass, Pe-ma-ho (White Horse River) near the village of Khodjo tulas, 60 li west of Kucha, plain of Kiu-p'i-lo (sandy desert of Hosol),

whole month to rest their cattle, for these were nearly done up, what with the difficulties of the road, the weight

bitter wells, town of Kiu-p'i-lo (Sairam), A-si-yen (Bai), Pohwan or Pu hwan (Wei jung, Kumo chou, near the river Se hoen, the kingdom of Pa lu ka of Hiuen Tsang), Siao she, river Hu lu, Ta she (Yu chu, Wen su chau, Aqsu).

Po hwan or rather Pa-lu-ka is identified by Watters, *China Review*, xix, p. 115, with Yurgun or Khara-Yurgun, while Chavannes takes it for Yaka arik; the river of Po hwan (Yaka arik) on Carey's map is the Muzart Su. The route is pretty clear but does not give any clue to our traveller's names; Chavannes, on the suggestion of F. Grenard, has altered his opinion and now believes (*Wei lio*, p. 37) that Ku-mo, Pa lu ka, Po hwan = Aqsu.]

[Here again, Prof. Paul Pelliot comes to the rescue: "From Aqsu, Goës did not go to Kucha by the present road of Bai and Sairam. The plain of Bai is in truth closed on the south by an important mountain range, though it has been omitted from our maps; this range is called Chöl-tâgh, the 'barren mountains'; practically it cannot be crossed by caravans. The Muzart Daria crosses it through a narrow gorge; the *ming-oï* (caves, grottoes) of Qyzyl is situated at the northern entrance of this gorge, and the no less interesting *ming-oï* of Qum turâ is to be found at the southern entrance. Up to the first half of the XIXth century, caravans going from Aqsu to Kucha took the route south of Chöl-tâgh as well as to-day's route viâ Bai and Sairam. It is this southern road, almost forsaken to-day, which was followed by Goës. The names of Oï-togrhaq and of Sarygh-Abdal, known to this day along this road, are sufficient proof of it. A last proof is to be found in the word *Ugan*. It was transcribed *Wei-kan* by the Chinese geographers of the XVIIIth century who gave this name to the Muzart Daria after it had flowed out of the Chöl-tâgh. The native form of the word is *Ögan*, and this name is still given to a canal joining the Muzart Daria to Qum turâ. To sum up the question, Goës from Horma to Aqsu followed a more easterly road, and from Aqsu to Kucha a more southern one than the present."]

[Kucha or Ku char = K'iu tze, at the foot of the T'ien shan, watered by two large rivers, is celebrated for its ruins excavated by various archaeological missions, Japanese, German, Russian and French (Pelliot), and visited by Sir M. Aurel Stein. The first diplomatic relations of Kucha with China date from the year 65 A.D., when its king paid a visit to the court of the Han Emperor; when Pan yong, son of the celebrated Chinese general Pan Ch'ao subjugated Yen k'i (Karashahr) in 127, seventeen kingdoms, including K'iu tze (Kucha), Su lé (Kashgar), Yu t'ien (Khotan), So kiu (Yarkand), submitted to the Conqueror. In 384 Pe chen was made king of Kucha by Lu kwang; in 658 Kucha, in lieu of Turfân, became the seat of the Protectorate of Ngansi which included Karashahr, Kashgar and Khotan; Kucha and these three places were the "Four Garrisons" of the Chinese in the eighth century: Chavannes, *Tou Kiue (Turcs) occidentaux*. Stein, *Ancient Khotan* and *Ruins of Desert Cathay*.]

[R., p. 544: "Oitograc, a Gasò, a Casciani, a Dellal, a Saregabedàl, a Ugan et arrivorno a Cucià."]

of the marble which they carried, and the scarcity of barley[1]. At this place our traveller was asked by the priests why he did not fast during their appointed time of fasting. This was asked in order that he might offer a bribe for exemption, or that they might extract a fine from him. And they were not far from laying violent hands on him, to force him into their place of worship[2].

Departing hence, after twenty-five days' journey they came to the city of CIALIS, a small place indeed, but strongly fortified. This territory was governed by an illegitimate son of the King of Cascar, who, when he heard that our brother and his party professed a different faith, began to utter threats, saying that it was too audacious a proceeding that a man professing another creed should intrude into that country, and that he would be quite justified in taking both his life and his property. But when he had read the royal letters which Benedict carried he was pacified, and after the latter had made him a present he became quite friendly. One night when this prince had been long engaged with the priests and doctors of his faith in one of their theological discussions, it suddenly came into his head to send for Benedict, so he despatched a horse for him and desired him to come to the palace. The strange hour at which this message came, and the harsh reception which they had at first experienced from the Prince, left little doubt with Benedict's party that he was sent for to be put to death. So having torn himself from his Armenian comrade, not without tears, and earnestly begging him to do his uttermost, if he at least should escape the present danger, to carry the news of his fellow traveller's fate to the members

[1] [R., p. 544: "con mancamento di mangiare."]

[2] [R., p. 544: "Et hebbe grande travaglio per uscire de loro mani e non fargli forza per andare alla loro meschita."]

of the Society, Benedict went off fully prepared to meet his death. On getting to the palace he was desired to engage in a discussion with the Doctors of the Mahomedan Law; and inspired by Him who has said, *It shall be given you in that hour what ye shall say*[1], he maintained the truth of the Christian religion by such apt reasoning that the others were quite silenced and defeated. The Prince constantly fixed his attention on our brother, expressing approval of everything that he said, and finally pronounced his conclusion that Christians were really *Misermans*[2], or True Believers, adding that his own ancestors had been professors of their faith[3]. After the discussion was over, Benedict was entertained at a sumptuous supper and desired to spend the night at the palace. And it was late next day before he was allowed to leave, so that Isaac quite despaired of his return. Indeed Benedict found him weeping grievously, for the long delay had fully convinced him of his master's death.

In this city[4] they halted three whole months, for the chief of the merchants did not wish to set out until a

[1] [This sentence is added to the text which runs (R., p. 545): "e seppe il fratello provare con tanto belli argomenti la verità della fede christiana che non seppero respondergli."]

[2] [R., p. 545: "*misermani*."]

[3] This is a curious trace of the ancient Christianity of several of the Mongolian and Turkish tribes.

[4] Ritter in one place suggests that *Cialis* of Goës may be Karashahr, but in another he will have it to be *Yulduz*, a place lying among the mountains of the T'ien Shan, celebrated for its beauty, its springs, meadows, and fine breezes, which was the encamping ground of Timur after his campaign of extermination against the Jats. Ritter had also previously identified Yulduz with the *Cailac* of Rubruquis.

The notion that Yulduz was Cialis seems to have been originated by Pétis de la Croix in his translation of Sharifuddín's *Life of Timur*. D'Anville also has identified Cialis with the Cailac of Rubruquis; both identifications seem to me to be wrong.

Yulduz lies in the mountains, a long way to the left of the great route along the foot of the T'ien Shan, which the caravan followed. Shah Rukh's ambassadors indeed pass Yulduz, on their way to Turfàn and Kamul. But it is clear that from Tashkand they took

large party should have collected, for the larger it was, the more profitable for him: and for this reason he would not consent on any account that individuals of the company should go on before. Our brother, however, weary of

a route *north* of the T'ien Shan, and were passing from the north to the south of the mountains when they touched at Yulduz.

The real position of Cialis must be either identical with Karashahr, as D'Anville thought, or close to it. The chief places noted in nearly all the routes and maps of this line of country are Aqsu, Kucha, Karashahr, Turfàn, Pijan, and Kamul. All these are mentioned by Goës except Karashahr, and where Karashahr should come, he gives us Cialis. D'Anville, indeed, observes that *Scialik* would mean, in Persian, the same as Karashahr, or Black Town (?). But the name seems to be not *Siyalis*, or *Siyalik*, but *Chalis*, or rather *Chálish*. This (*Jalish*) is mentioned by Sharifuddín as a place which Timur passed on his way to Yulduz; and by Haidar Razi, the historian of Turkestan, *Jalish* is spoken of as a city near Turfàn, both places being under a prince called Mansur Khan, who is mentioned about A.H. 938 (A.D. 1531), as marching by *Jalish* to attack Aqsu. Ramusio's friend, Hajji Mahomed, also mentions *Chialis* exactly where Karashahr should come, as may be seen by comparing his route with Izzet Ullah's:

Izzet Ullah.		*Hajji Mahomed.*	
Kamul to Turfàn .	13 days.	Kamul to Turfàn .	13 days.
Turfàn to KARASHAHR	9 ,,	Turfàn to CHIALIS	10 ,,
KARASHAHR to Kucha	10 ,,	CHIALIS to Kucha .	10 ,,

and this seems to put the identity of Cialis with Karashahr past question.

[Dalgleish gives:

Kamul to Turfàn .	15 days	(including days of departure and arrival, and one day's rest at Jigda).
Turfàn to Karashahr	28 ,,	(including days of departure and arrival and trip to Urumtsi
Karashahr to Kucha .	15 ,,	18 days, and a day's rest at Tokhlasun, including two days' rest at Kurla.)]

Karashahr, anciently called by the Chinese Yen-k'i, stands on the K'aidu river*, which irrigates the country round, and makes it yield plenty of fruit and corn. The Chinese route, elsewhere quoted, speaks of it as a large town inhabited by Chinese, with Kalmuks round them, and having a Chinese garrison of 500 men.

[The road from Kurla to Karashahr City, when leaving Sharshuk "runs N.E. the first six miles through desert to Dhungzil Langar. A little beyond are the ruins of the old city of Karashahr.

* [The K'aidu Gol falls into Lake Bagratch; it is the lower part of the Yulduz River.]

the delay and of the great expense which it involved, was eager to get away; and by means of new presents he at last persuaded the Prince to arrange measures for his departure. But this was so completely against the wish of the chief of the caravan and his party, that it put an end to the friendly terms on which Benedict had hitherto stood with them.

He was just preparing for his departure from the town of Cialis when the merchants of the preceding caravan arrived on their return from Cathay. They had made their way to the capital of Cathay as usual by pretending to be an embassy; and as they had been quartered in Peking at the same hostelry with the members

At 7½ miles the road passes Kalka Mazar, a little to the left. From Dhungzil road runs N. by E. to Karashahr, and the extensive level plain watered by the Karashahr river becomes a prairie, and is the home of a large body of Kalmaks. Before entering the city crossed the Karashahr river, now frozen" (Dalgleish, 17th Dec. 1885, p. 28, distance from Kurla to Karashahr, 27½ miles.] Chavannes, *Tou kiue*, p. 7, makes the remark that the present Karashahr is on the left bank of the K'aidu gol, while the history of the T'ang and Hiuen Tsang places the capital of Yen-k'i to the west of this river. The capital of Yen-k'i (Karashahr) is called A-ki-mi by Hiuen Tsang; it is the Wou yi (Wou k'i) of Fa hian (Watters, *Yuan Chwang*, i, p. 46; Chavannes, *Wei-lio*, pp. 564–5 *n.*). In 719, it took the place of Tokmak captured by the Tu kiue, in the Four Garrisons (Kucha, Kashgar, Khotan, Tokmak).]

As regards the *Cailac* of Rubruquis, it seems rather to be sought where D'Avezac has placed it in the vicinity of Lake Balkash, or at any rate, to the north of the T'ien Shan. It is mentioned by D'Ohsson as a town of the Karliq Turks, who lay in this direction, and is coupled with Imil and Bishbaliq, both cities north of the mountains. Sadik Isfahani also names Kaliq with Almaliq, Bishbaliq, etc. It is probably the Haulak or Khaulak of Edrisi, in a route given in his work (ii, 215), which brings it within eight days' journey of Akhsi, a city on the Jaxartes near Kokhand. It is perhaps the *Kainak* which Valikhanoff mentions as a place famous in the ancient Genoese trade, and still existing in Dzungaria, but he does not indicate where that is (Ritter, vii, 437, 439, 441–2; *H. de Timur Bec*, ii, 53–56; D'Anville, in *Acad. Inscript.*, xxxii, 589; *J. R. As. Soc.*, vii, 308; *Not. et Extraits*, xiv; Ramusio, *Esposizione*, in II, ff. 14–16; D'Ohsson, I, iii, 166; II, 516; *Sadik Isfahani*, p. 10; *Russ. in Cent. Asia*, pp. 62, 527). [Rockhill places Cailac a little west of the modern Kopal. (*Rubruck*, p. 139.)]

of our Society, they were able to give our brother most authentic information about Father Matthew and his companions, and in this way he learned to his astonishment that CHINA was the Cathay that he was in search of.

These were the same Saracens of whom it has been related in a preceding book, that they had dwelt for nearly three months under the same roof with our brethren. They were able to tell therefore how our brethren had made presents to the Emperor of sundry clocks, a clavichord, pictures, and other such matters from Europe. They related also how our brethren were treated with respect by all the dignitaries at the capital, and (mixing falsehood with truth) how they were often admitted to converse with the Emperor. They also described accurately enough the countenances of the members of the Society whom they had seen, but they could not tell their names, it being a Chinese custom to change the names of foreigners. They also produced the strangest corroboration of their story in a piece of paper on which something in the Portuguese language had been written by one of our brethren, and which the travellers had rescued from the sweepings of the rooms and preserved, in order that they might show it as a memorial to their friends at home, and tell them how the people that used this kind of writing had found their way to China. Our travellers were greatly refreshed with all this intelligence, and now they could no longer doubt that Cathay was but another name for the Chinese Empire, and that the capital which the Mahomedans called Cambalu was Peking, which indeed Benedict before leaving India had known, from the letters of our members in China, to be the view taken by them.

As he was departing, the prince granted him letters for his protection, and when a question arose under what name he wished to be described and whether he would have himself designated as a Christian? Certainly, said he, "for having travelled thus far bearing the name of Jesus, I would surely bear it unto the end[1]." It so chanced that this was heard by one of the Mahomedan priests, a venerable old man, who snatching off his cap flung it on the ground and exclaimed: "In verity and truth this man is staunch to his religion, for lo here in presence of thee a prince of another faith, and of all the rest of us, he has no hesitation in confessing his Jesus! 'tis very different with our people, for they are said to change their religion with their residence." And so turning to our traveller, he treated him with extraordinary courtesy. Thus even in the dark virtue is lustrous, and even from hostility and ill-will it extorts respect!

He set off at last with his comrade and a few others, and in twenty days came to PUCIAN[2], a town of the same kingdom, where they were received by the chief of the place with the greatest kindness, and supplied with the necessary provisions from his house. Hence they went on to a fortified town called TURPHAN[3], and there they

[1] [R., p. 547: "Rispose il fratello Benedetto che sì, e che scrivesse *Abdullà Isai*, cioè *Abdullà della legge di Giesù*, perchè come christiano, era passato per tutto quello cammino e come tale lo voleva finire."]

[2] [R., p. 547, "Pucciàn."]

[3] [R., p. 547: "Turfàn, città con muri e forte, dove stettero un mese."]

["Turfàn, like Hami, is near the southern slopes of the T'ien Shan, and is one of the largest towns of E. Turkestan. Climate very hot in summer and cold in winter. Water is produced from wells chiefly, and irrigation is carried on by means of underground canals." (Dalgleish, p. 53.)] It is the old kingdom of Kao ch'ang whose king had his capital at Kiao ho = Yar khoto. It was the seat of the Protectorate of Ngansi before it was transferred to Kucha (658), when the name of "Four Garrisons" appears probably for the first time. After the Tibetan invasion (760) the Chinese had but "Two Garrisons," one at Pei t'ing near Guchen and the other at Kucha, but these also disappeared in 787.]

halted a month[1]. Next they proceeded[2] to ARAMUTH[3],

[1] *Pijan* (*Pucian* of the text) and Turfàn appear in some way to have been transposed, for both Izzet Ullah and the Chinese routes agree with the maps in making Pijan lie considerably to the *east* of Turfàn. [Pichan is situated between Turfàn and Hami.] According to the tables of the Chinese survey, the former lies in lat. 42° 52′, long. 90° 28′; the latter in lat. 43° 4′, long. 89° 18′ (*Russ. in Cent. Asia*, p. 521). ["Pichan or Pachan is a large straggling village with several miles of cultivation. The bazaar is inside a mud fort. Population, Turks, with a number of Tunganis and Chinese." (Dalgleish, p. 53.)]

When Shah Rukh's ambassadors passed this way in 1419, most of the people of Turfán were still idolaters; there was a huge temple in the town, with a figure of Sakya Muni on the platform.

[2] [R., p. 547: "Partirno da Turfàn a 4 di settembre dell' anno 1605."]

[From Turfàn which he left on the 9th December, 1886, Dalgleish on his way to Kucha, passed over a rough and stony road to Dah-din (10th December), the valley becomes fertile, Tokhtasun (11th December) a small town within mud wall fort; visited Urumtsi; left Tokhtasun (29th December) for Su Bashi (30th December), then Eghar Bulak in ravine (30 December), Uzma Dhung, Kumish (1st January, 1887), Kara Kizil (2 January), Ushak Tal (3rd January), Tavilgo (4th January), Karashahr (5th January), river 200 yards wide, Kalka Mazar, Dhung Zil Langar, Shorshuk (6th January), Kurla (9th January), Shangkho (10–11th January), Charchi (12th January), small village end of the Kurla district, Ishma, small village (13th January), Chadar (14th), Yenghi Hissar large village (15th), Bugor, old stage in plain (16th), Yenghi abad (17th) very small village, Awat, Yaka arik, fair sized village (18th), Ush Kara Langar, Kucha (19th January, 1912).]

[3] *Aramuth*, according to Pétis de la Croix, is Kara Khoja (see *supra*, III, pp. 132–3), but I suspect he is speaking without authority, as he often does. Thus, when speaking of the forerunners of Timur's invasion of India, who, after crossing the Indus, reach *Uchh* before advancing against Multān, he notes "*Outchah*, ville à l'orient de l'Indus *au nord* de Multān," he is simply putting forth his own erroneous deductions from the text as a piece of independent knowledge. And when Pauthier quotes from the same author (*Polo*, p. 197), a professed extract from the *Yasa* of Chinghiz as corroborating, with extraordinary minuteness, certain statements of Marco, I suspect it will prove that Pétis de la Croix had merely borrowed the said statements from Polo himself (*H. de Timur Bec*, ii, 46). Shah Rukh's people reach *Kara-Khoja* in three days from Turfàn; in fourteen days more, *Ata-Sufi*; and in two days more, Kamul. [However Pétis de la Croix is probably right in this instance: after leaving Turfàn, Goës, like the ambassadors of Shah Rukh, passes Kara Khodja; see I, p. 272.]

[The itinerary of Dalgleish from Hami to Turfàn is the following: Hami (22nd November, 1886), good road, Sim Kargha (23rd), Tograchi (24th), Jigda village, Taranchi, Urda lik (27th Nov.), and thence to CAMUL[1], another fortified town. Here they stopped another month to refresh themselves and their beasts, being glad to do so at a town which was still within the limits of the kingdom of Cialìs, where they had been treated with so much civility.

From Camul they came in nine days to the celebrated northern wall of China, reaching it at the place called CHIAICUON[2], and there they had to wait twenty-five days for an answer from the Viceroy of the province. When they were at last admitted within the wall, they reached, after one more day's travelling, the city of SUCIEU[3]. Here they heard much about Peking and other names with which they were acquainted, and here Benedict parted with his last lingering doubt as to the identity in all but name of Cathay and China.

The country between Cialìs and the Chinese frontier

Sarik Kumish (28th), Shilder Kumish (29th), village of Chiktem (1st December), Korgha Utra (2nd), Pichan (3rd), Lemyin (5th), Suigim (5th), Suigim (6th Dec.), Turfàn (12th stage).]

[1] Kamil, Kamul, Komul, Qomul, Hami of the Chinese, and formerly called by them I-wu, an ancient city of the Uighúr country, has already been spoken of (*supra*, III, p. 265). It is the point of departure for crossing the desert into China, and near it the road from China branches, one line going north of the T'ien Shan, by Barkul, the Urumtsi district, and Kurkarausu to Ili; the other south of the mountains, by which Goës came. Kamul is the seat of the [Chinese Agent in this region, who bears the title of *Pan She Ta Tchen* and is of lesser rank than the *K'u lun Pan She Ta Tchen*, who resides at K'urun (Urga)]. The climate of Kamul appears to be very mild, for oranges are grown there (*R. in C. Asia*, p. 129). [*Kamul* is the Turkish name of the province called by the Mongols *Khamil*, by the Chinese *Hami*; the latter name is found for the first time in the *Yuen Shi*, but it is first mentioned in Chinese History in the first century of our era under the name of *I-wu-lu* or *I-wu* (Bretschneider, *Med. Res.*, ii, p. 20); after the death of Chinghiz, it belonged to his son Chagatai. From the Great Wall, at the pass of Kia yü, to Hami there is a distance of 1470 *li*. *Cf. Marco Polo*, i, 211 *n*.]

[2] *Kia-yu Kwan*, or the "Jade Gate," of the Great Wall, the Jaiguouden of Mír Izzet Ullah's route. *Kwan*, in Chinese, is a fort guarding a defile (Ritter, ii, 213; D'Ohsson, ii, 625; *J. R. As. Soc.*, vii, 283, *seqq*.). This place is probably the *Karaúl* of Shah Rukh's people.

[3] [R., p. 548, "Socceo."]

has an evil fame on account of its liability to Tartar raids, and therefore this part of the road is traversed by merchants with great fear. In the day time they reconnoitre from the neighbouring hills, and if they consider the road safe they prosecute their journey by night and in silence. Our travellers found on the way the bodies of sundry Mahomedans who had been miserably murdered[1]. Yet the Tartars rarely slay the natives, for they call them their slaves and shepherds, from whose flocks and herds they help themselves. These Tartars make use neither of wheat nor of rice, nor of any kind of pulse, for they say such things are food for beasts and not for men; they eat nothing but flesh, and make no objection to that of horses, mules, or camels. Yet they are said to be very long lived, and indeed not unfrequently survive to more than a hundred. The Mahomedan races who live on the Chinese frontier in this direction have no warlike spirit, and might be easily subdued by the Chinese, if that nation were at all addicted to making conquests.

In this journey it happened one night that Benedict was thrown from his horse and lay there half dead, whilst his companions who were all in advance went on in ignorance of what had happened. In fact it was not till the party arrived at the halting place that Benedict was missed. His comrade Isaac went back to seek him, but the search in the dark was to no purpose, until at last he heard a voice calling on the name of Jesus. Following the sound he found Benedict, who had given up all hope of being able to follow his companions, so that his first words were: "What angel has brought thee hither to rescue me from such a plight?" By help of the Armenian he was enabled to reach the halting place and there to recover from his fall.

[1] [R., p. 548: "per voler andare per li soli."]

CHAPTER XIII OF BOOK V

How our Brother Benedict died in the Chinese territory, after the arrival of one of our members who had been sent from Peking to his assistance.

TOWARDS the northern extremity of the western frontier of China the celebrated wall comes to an end, and there is a space of about two hundred miles through which the Tartars, prevented by the wall from penetrating the northern frontier, used to attempt incursions into China, and indeed they do so still, but with less chance of success. For two very strongly fortified cities, garrisoned with select troops, have been established on purpose to repel their attacks. These cities are under a special Viceroy and other officials deriving their orders direct from the capital. In one of these two cities of the province of SCENSI[1], which is called CANCEU, is the residence of the Viceroy and other chief officers; the other city called SOCIEU[2], has a governor of its own, and is divided into

[1] [Su chau and Kan chau are now in the Kan Su Province, but in the days of Goës, Kan Su was a part of the Shen si Province.]

[2] *Su chau*, the Succuir [and Sukchur] of Marco Polo [I, pp. 217–219] the *Sukchú* of [Rashíd ud-dín and of] Shah Rukh's embassy, and the *Sowchick* of Anthony Jenkinson's reports. [Su-chau had been devastated and its inhabitants massacred by Chinghiz Khan in 1226.] The Persian envoys describe it (1419) as a great city of a perfectly square form, with a strong fort. The bazaars were fifty cubits in width, kept clean and watered. There were four gates on each side, and behind (over?) each gate was a pavilion of two stories with a roof *en dos d'âne* after the Chinese fashion. The streets were paved with vitrified brick, and there were many great temples. See also Hajji Mahomed in Notes to Prelim. Essay.

Canceu is the still existing *Kan chau*, the *Canpichu* of Polo [I, pp. 219–23], the *Camexu* of Pegolotti, the *Kamchú* or *Kamjú*

two parts. In one of these dwell the Chinese, whom the Mahomedans here call Cathayans[1], in the other the Mahomedans who have come for purposes of trade from the kingdom of Cascar and other western regions. There are many of these who have entangled themselves with wives and children, so that they are almost regarded as natives, and will never go back. They are much in the position of the Portuguese who are settled at AMACAO[2] in the province of Canton, but with this difference, that the Portuguese live under their own laws and have magistrates of their own, whereas these Mahomedans are under the government of the Chinese. Indeed they are shut up every night within the walls of their own quarter of the city, and in other matters are treated just like the natives, and are subject in every thing to the Chinese magistrates. The law is that one who has sojourned there for nine years shall not be allowed to return to his country.

To this city are wont to come those western merchants, who, under old arrangements between seven or eight kingdoms in that quarter and the Empire of China, have leave of admission every sixth year for two-and-seventy persons, who under pretence of being ambassadors go and offer tribute to the Emperor. This tribute consists of that translucent marble of which we spoke before, of

of Rashíd and the Ambassadors (see *supra*, III, p. 128). The latter say it was nine posts from Sukchu, and was the seat of the *Dankshi* or chief governor of the frontier. They describe here a great temple, and one of those gigantic recumbent figures, representing Gautama in a state of Nirwana, which are still to be seen in Ceylon, Burma, and Siam. This one was fifty paces long, with figures of other divinities and *Bakshis* round about, executed with great vivacity. There was also a singular pagoda of timber, fifteen stories high, which turned upon a pivot. Here the envoys had to deposit their baggage, and received thereafter all supplies from the Chinese government.

[1] [R., p. 549: "nell' una stanno gli Catai, che da qui avanti chiamaremo col suo primo nome di Cinesi."]

[2] [R., p. 549: "città di Maccao."]

small diamonds, ultramarine, and other such matters; and the so-called ambassadors go to the capital and return from it at the public expense. The tribute is merely nominal, for no one pays more for the marble than the Emperor does, considering it to be beneath his dignity to accept gifts from foreigners without return. And indeed their entertainment from the Emperor is on so handsome a scale, that, taking an average of the whole, there can be no doubt that every man pockets a piece of gold[1] daily over and above all his necessary expenses[2]. This is the reason why this embassy is such an object of competition, and why the nomination to it is purchased with great presents from the chief of the caravan, with whom it lies. When the time comes the *soi-disant* ambassadors forge public letters in the names of the kings whom they profess to represent, in which the Emperor of China is addressed in obsequious terms. The Chinese receive embassies of a similar character from various other kingdoms, such as Cochin-China, Siam, Leuchieu, Corea, and from some of the petty Tartar kings, the whole causing incredible charges on the public treasury. The Chinese themselves are quite aware of the imposture, but they allow their Emperor to be befooled in this manner, as if to persuade him that the

[1] [R., p. 550: "ducato."]

[2] Martini and Alvarez Semedo speak in similar terms of the embassies, or pretended embassies, that came periodically to Peking from Central Asia. The latter says that their present to the Emperor always consisted of 1000 *arrobas*, or 1333 Italian pounds, of jade, 300 being of the very finest quality; 340 horses; 300 very small diamonds; about 100 pounds of fine ultramarine; 600 knives; 600 files. This was the old prescriptive detail which none might change. The cost price of the whole might be some 7000 crowns, but the Emperor's return present was worth 50,000 (p. 27; see also narrative from Busbeck in Notes to Essay at beginning of the first volume).

These sham embassies, disguising trading expeditions, were of old standing in China, going back at least to the days of the Sung Emperors. (Rémusat, in *Mém. de l'Acad.*, viii, 77–8.)

whole world is tributary to the Chinese empire, the fact being that China pays tribute to those kingdoms.

Our Benedict arrived at Socieu in the end of the year 1605, and it shows how Divine Providence watched over him, that he came to the end of this enormous journey with ample means, and prosperous in every way. He had with him thirteen animals, five hired servants, two boys, whom he had bought as slaves, and that surpassing piece of jade[1]; the total value of his property being reckoned at two thousand five hundred pieces of gold[2]. Moreover both he and his companion Isaac were in perfect health and strength.

At this city of Socieu he fell in with another party of Saracens just returned from the capital, and these confirmed all that he had already been told about our fathers at Peking, adding a good deal more of an incredible and extravagant nature; for example, that they had from the Emperor a daily allowance of silver, not counted to them, but measured out in bulk! So he now wrote to Father Matthew[3] to inform him of his arrival. His letter was intrusted to certain Chinamen, but as he did not know the Chinese names of our fathers, nor the part of the city in which they lived, and as the letter was addressed in European characters, the bearers were unable to discover our people.

At Easter however he wrote a second time, and this letter was taken by some Mahomedan who had made his escape from the city, for Mahomedans also are debarred from going out or coming in, without the permission of the authorities. In this letter he explained the origin and

[1] [R., p. 550: "e doi putti cattivi, che aveva comprati, e con la più fina pietra di iaspe che vi era."]

[2] [R., p. 550: "ducati d' oro."]

[3] [R., p. 551: "ai padri di Pacchino."]

object of his journey, and begged the fathers to devise some way of rescuing him from the prison in which he found himself at Socieu, and of restoring him to the delight of holding intercourse with his brethren, in place of being perpetually in the company of Saracens. He mentioned also his wish to return to India by the sea route[1], as usually followed by the Portuguese.

The fathers had long ere this been informed by the Superior's letters from India of Benedict's having started on this expedition, and every year they had been looking out for him, and asking diligently for news of him whenever one of those companies of merchants on their pretended embassy arrived at court. But till now they had never been able to learn any news of him, whether from not knowing the name under which he was travelling, or because the ambassadors of the preceding seasons really had never heard of him.

The arrival of his letter therefore gave great pleasure to the fathers at Peking. It was received late in the year, in the middle of November[2], and they lost no time in arranging to send a member of the Society to get him away some how or other and bring him to the capital. However on re-consideration they gave up that scheme, for the bringing another foreigner into the business seemed likely to do harm rather than good. So they sent one of the pupils who had lately been selected to join the Society but had not yet entered on his noviciate. His name was John Ferdinand, he was a young man of singular prudence and virtue, and one whom it seemed safe to entrust with a business of this nature. One of the converts acquainted with that part of the country was sent in company with

[1] [R., p. 551: "per via di Quantone."]

[2] [The letter was received, according to Ricci, writing to Acquaviva, not in the middle of November, but "nel principio del mese di novembre dell' anno 1606." See R., p. 551 *n.*]

him. His instructions were to use all possible means to get away Benedict and his party to the capital, but if he should find it absolutely impossible either to get leave from the officials or to evade their vigilance, he was to stop with our brother, and send back word to the members of the Society. In that case it was hoped that by help of friends at Court, means would be found to get him on from the frontier.

A journey of this nature might seem unseasonable enough at a time of the year when winter is at the height of severity in those regions; and the town at which Benedict had been detained was nearly four months'[1] journey from Peking. But Father Matthew thought no further delay should be risked, lest the great interval that had elapsed should lead Benedict to doubt whether we really had members stationed at Peking. And he judged well, for if the journey had been delayed but a few days longer the messengers would not have found Benedict among the living. They carried him a letter from Father Matthew, giving counsel as to the safest manner of making the journey, and two other members of the Society also wrote to him, giving full details about our affairs in that capital, a subject on which he was most eager for information.

Our Benedict in the meantime, during his detention at that city, endured more annoyance from the Mahomedans than had befallen him during the whole course of his journey. Also, on account of the high price of food in the place, he was obliged to dispose of his large piece of jade for little more than half its value[2]. He got for it

[1] [R., p. 552: "tre o quatro mesi."]

[2] [R., p. 552: "É in quella terra il vitto molto caro, et egli, se bene aveva molta mercantia, non aveva nessun danaro; per questo fu forzato a vendere tutta la pietra iaspe, che aveva, per la metade di quello che valeva."]

twelve hundred pieces of gold[1], a large part of which went to repay money which he had borrowed, whilst with the rest he maintained his party for a whole year. Meanwhile the caravan of merchants with their chief arrived. Benedict was obliged to exercise hospitality, and in course of time was reduced to such straits that he had to borrow money to maintain his party; this all the more because owing to his nomination as one of the seventy-two ambassadors he was obliged (again) to purchase some fragments of jade. He hid a hundred pounds of this in the earth to preserve it from any tricks of the Mahomedans, for without a supply of this article he would have been absolutely incapacitated from taking part in the journey to Peking.

John Ferdinand[2] left Peking on the eleventh of December in that year; and his journey also was attended with a new misfortune, for at SINGHAN[3], the capital of the province of SCIENSI, his servant ran away, robbing him of half his supplies[4] for the journey. Two months more of a fatiguing journey however brought him to Socieu, in the end of March 1607[5].

He found our Benedict laid low with a disease unto death. The very night before it had been intimated to him, whether by dream or vision, that on the following day one of the Society would arrive from Peking; and upon this he had desired his comrade the Armenian to go to the bazaar and buy certain articles for distribution among the poor, whilst at the same time he earnestly

[1] [R., p. 552: "ducati."]

[2] [John Fernandez, Christian name of the Chinaman Chong Ma-li, a lay brother, born in 1581; joined the Jesuits in 1610; he left for Su chau on the 12th December 1606.]

[3] [The great city of Si-ngan.]

[4] [R., p. 553: "dinari."]

[5] [R., p. 553: "l' ultimo giorno di marzo dell' anno seguente 1607."]

prayed God not to suffer the hopes raised by his dream to be disappointed. Whilst Isaac was still in the bazaar some one told him of the arrival of John Ferdinand from Peking, and pointed him out. The latter followed the Armenian home, and as he entered saluted our brother Benedict in the Portuguese tongue. From this he at once understood what the arrival was, and taking the letters he raised them aloft with tears of joy in his eyes, and burst into the hymn of *Nunc dimittis servum tuum, Domine.* For now it seemed to him that indeed his commission was accomplished, and his pilgrimage at an end. He then read the letters, and all that night kept them near his heart. The words that were spoken, the questions that were asked may be more easily conjectured than detailed.

John Ferdinand did his best to nurse him, hoping that with recovered strength he might yet be able to undertake the journey to Peking. But strength there was none; as indeed physician there was none, nor proper medicines; nor was there anything to do him good in his illness, unless it were some European dishes which John Ferdinand cooked for him. And thus, eleven days[1] after the latter's arrival, Benedict breathed his last; not without some suspicion of his having been poisoned by the Mahomedans.

These latter had fellows always on the watch, in order to pounce upon whatever the dead man might leave. This they did in the most brutal manner; but no part of the loss which they caused was so much to be deplored as the destruction of the journal of his travels, which he had kept with great minuteness. This was a thing the Mahomedans fell on with open jaws! For the

[1] [In his letter of the 22nd August 1608, Ricci says ten days instead of eleven. See R., p. 553 *n.*]

book also contained[1] acknowledgments of debt which might have been used to compel many of them to repay the sums which they had shamelessly extracted from him. They wished to bury the body after their Mahomedan ritual, but Ferdinand succeeded in shutting out their importunate priests, and buried him in a decent locality[2] where it would be practicable to find the body again. And these two, the Armenian and John Ferdinand, having no service-books, devoutly recited the rosary as they followed his bier[3].

It seems right to add a few words in commemoration of a character so worthy. Benedict Goës, a native of Portugal, a man of high spirit and acute intellect, on his first entrance into the society was sent as a volunteer to join the mission in the Mogul Empire. For many years he gave most active aid to that mission, instructing Mahomedans, Hindus, and converts as far as his own acquirements went, and gaining the love of all as he did so. Yet he was not a priest; but he was held in high esteem for his great good sense and other valuable qualities natural and acquired. Hence also he was admitted to

[1] [R., p. 554: "in lingua persiana."]

[2] [R., p. 554: "comprando una cassa di legno assai buona, lo sotterrò in un luogo netto."]

[3] ["Here at Su-chou," writes Stein, *Ruins of Desert Cathay*, ii, p. 292, "where he might well think himself near to his goal, and where, nevertheless, he came to be detained for sixteen weary months, the devoted Jesuit traveller succumbed in 1607 to disease and privations. I had thought of him and his plucky perseverance at all the points—Lahore, Peshawar, the Pamirs, Sarikol, Yarkand, and Khotan—where I had touched the line of his wanderings. And grateful I felt now to Fate which had allowed me to reach the site of his tragic end. There is nothing to suggest even approximately the spot where his wearied limbs were laid to rest by the young Chinese convert whom the Jesuit fathers had despatched from Peking to his relief, and who arrived just a few days before all earthly trouble was ended. But I hope that when the Catholic Mission at Su-chou shall have built its permanent chapel, means may be found to recall to those who worship in it the memory of Benedict Goëz."]

the intimate friendship of the Mogul Sovereign, and when this prince was despatching an embassy to Goa, along with his own envoy he sent Benedict also in the same character.

This king indeed entertained a project for the conquest of (Portuguese) India, and it may be ascribed to Benedict's prudence that war with so powerful a monarch was averted.

A short time before his death he wrote to warn our members at Peking never to put faith in Mahomedans, and also in deprecation of any future attempts to travel by the route which he had followed, as being both dangerous and useless.

A circumstance is well known in our Society which manifests the holy character of the man. Remarking how many years had past without the opportunity of confession and absolution, "I am dying," he said, "without this consolation, and yet how great is God's goodness! For He does not allow my conscience to be disturbed with anything of moment in the review of my past life[1]!"

A truly abominable custom prevailed among those merchants, that the property of anyone dying on the way should be divided among the rest of the company. On this account they laid hold of Isaac the companion of Benedict, and tied him up, threatening him with death unless he would call upon the name of Mahomed. Ferdinand, however, sent a memorial to the Viceroy at Canceu claiming Isaac's liberation. The Viceroy passed his orders on the petition, desiring the Governor of Socieu to decide according to right and justice, and to restore the youth's uncle to him with the property of the deceased[2].

[1] [This passage does not appear in Ricci.]

[2] [R., p. 555: "Per questo si risolse il fratello Giovanni di andare a Canceo, che sta tre giorni di cammino di Succeo, a dar libello al vicerè, chiedendoli che gli facesse ritornare Isac; chè

At first the governor was favourable to Ferdinand, but when some forty[1] of the Saracens joined together to bribe him, he then threatened to flog Ferdinand, and kept him three days in prison. The latter did not, however, a bit the more desist from his undertaking, but when he ran short of money to prosecute his suit, he sold all the clothes that he could do without to raise a small sum. He was detained for five months about this business, and yet had no means of communicating with the Armenian, from his ignorance of Persian; the other being equally unable to speak either Portuguese or Latin. When they were called before the Court, Ferdinand recited the Lord's Prayer, whilst Isaac repeated the name of Benedict Goës with a few words of Portuguese; and as nobody understood a word of what either of them said, the judge gave it as his opinion that they were talking in the Canton dialect, and understood each other perfectly! Latterly, however, Ferdinand learned in about two months to talk Persian, and so was able to converse with the Armenian.

Sometimes the Mahomedans raised objections from the extreme discrepancy of their physiognomies, which they said evidently betrayed one to be a Saracen and the other a Chinaman. But Ferdinand answered that his mother had been Chinese, and that he took the character of his features after her. Nothing, however, moved the judge so much as what occurred one day when Ferdinand declared before the Court that Isaac was heartily opposed to the Mahomedan religion, and that in any case if he really did belong to that faith he would never touch pork;

per poter far meglio questo si fece egli figliuolo di un fratello del fratello Benedetto e di Isac armenio, dando il suo cognome di *Cium* a ambedue, e il nome al modo della Cina, e venuto della provincia di Quantone."]

[1] [R., p. 555: "trenta o quaranta."]

and taking a piece of pork out of his sleeve he offered it to Isaac, and both of them began to eat it, to the intense disgust of the Mahomedans and to the amusement of the other spectators. Indeed when the Saracens saw this they gave up the case as hopeless, and went out of Court, spitting at Isaac as they went, and saying that he had been deluded by that Chinese impostor. For it was true that on the whole journey neither Isaac nor Benedict had ever eaten pork, in order not to give offence to the Mahomedans; or if they ever did so, at least it was in private. These circumstances moved the judge to decide in Ferdinand's favour, and to order all that Benedict had left to be restored to him[1]. Nothing was found, however, except the pieces of jade which had been buried[2]. From the proceeds of these debts were paid, and means furnished for the journey to Peking. But still there was not enough to cover the great expense of all those months of detention, so they had to borrow twenty pieces of gold on the security of some bits of jade which still remained. At last they both got to the brethren at Peking, to whom the whole affair had caused a good deal of anxiety[3]. They had now cause for both grief and joy; Benedict's loss was to be mourned, and the Armenian to be congratulated on his escape. Him they received as if he had been one of our

[1] [R., p. 556: "Con questo il giudice diede sententia che gli ritornassero i Saraceni il suo zio e quanto era restato del fratello Benedetto, e gli avrebbe tornato anco il putto cattivo; ma gli messero i Saraceni tanta paura se diceva voler ire col fratello che, avanti il giudice, disser voler restar con i Mori, e così il giudice non lo volse forzare a ire."]

[2] [R., p. 556: "Non si ritrovò altra cosa delle robe e denari che le quattro cento libre di iaspe molto cattivo, del quale vendettero più della metà e pagorno i debiti del fratello Benedetto, e l' altro volevano portare a Pacchino."]

[3] [R., p. 556: "Tutto questo tempo, che fu di otto mesi, sino alla arrivata del fratello Giovanni Ferdinando e Isac armenio, che fu a 28 di ottobre, stettero i padri di Pacchino con molta sollecitudine e paura."]

own body, for Benedict had spoken in strong terms of the faithful help which he had rendered throughout the journey.

Ferdinand brought to Peking a cross elegantly painted on gilt paper, the only one that Benedict had ventured to carry among those Mahomedans, and also the three rescripts of the three kings, viz. of Cascar, Quoten and Cialis, all which are now preserved as memorials in our house at Peking. There also are preserved the letters patent of Father Jerome Xavier, with other letters of his which had arrived during the journey, and letters likewise from Alexius Menezes, archbishop of Goa, and from the said Jerome, to the members of the society at Peking, in which they expressed themselves as feeling satisfied that Cathay could not be a long way from Peking, and that probably the two kingdoms had a common frontier.

Isaac the Armenian stopped a month at Peking, and during that time he communicated to Father Matthew from his own recollection, assisted by some papers of Benedict's, all that we have related in these three chapters. He was then despatched to MACAO by the road which our people are in the habit of using, and was there most kindly received by the Society and its friends. Having then sailed on his way back to India, the ship was taken by pirates[1] in the Straits of SINCAPURA, and the Armenian was plundered of all his trifling possessions and reduced to a wretched state of bondage. He was ransomed, however, by the Portuguese of Malacca, and went on to (Western) India. Hearing there of his wife's death, he proceeded no further towards the Mogul's territories, but settled at a certain town of the East Indies called

[1] [R., p. 557: "corsari olandesi."]

CIAUL, where he still survives at the date when this is written[1].

[1] Du Jarric's statement about Isaac is somewhat different. According to that writer he was taken by a *Dutch ship* on his way to Malacca. The captain was so struck by his history that he caused it all to be written down, and sent him to Malacca. Thence the fathers of the Society sent him on to Cochin and Goa, where he fell in with Father Pinheiro (who had been stationed at Lahore when Goës started on his journey). The Provincial of India gave Isaac one hundred *pardaos*, and he went with Pinheiro to Cambay (p. 226).

Chawul (Ciaul) is a port of the Konkan about thirty-five miles south of Bombay, which was an important place of trade in the sixteenth century.

[The end of the narrative in Ricci's text is as follows: "Et, essendosi Isac imbarcato per passare all' India e da lì ritornare al Mogore, dove stava sua moglie e figliuoli, fu presa la barca da' corsari olandesi nello stretto di Sincapure e, riscattato da quei di Malacca, arrivò pure al fine all' India, doppo sì gravi travagli."]

NOTE I. (SEE PAGE 182.)[1]

THE PASSES OF THE HINDU KUSH.

Wood, in his Journey to the Oxus[2], names only four such passes. Three of these are reached from Kabul through the valley of Koh-Damán north of that city, and diverge from each other near Charekar; viz., the Pass of PANJSHIR or KHAWAK, the Pass of PARWĀN, and the Pass of GHORBAND; but each of these in fact represents a group of several routes over the mountains. The fourth that he mentions is the Pass of HAJJIYAK[3], lying much further west, passing by Bamian, and usually, in modern times at least, approached from Kabul by the road running west from that city by Rustam Khail, south of the offshoots of the Indian Caucasus called the Pugman Range and Kohistan of Kabul.

If we turn to Sultan Baber we find the number of Passes raised to seven. Those which he names are *three* leading out of the Panjshir Valley, viz. (1) KHAWAK, (2) TÚL, (3) BAZARAK; then (4) the Pass of PARWĀN; and *three* described as in Ghorband. viz. (5) YANGI YULI or the "New Road," (6) KIPCHAK, and (7) SHIBRTU[4].

As Ritter understands this list it does not include the Hajjiyak at all. But we know that the Shibrtu route, which Baber says was the only one passable in winter, lies some twenty-five or thirty miles west of Bamian, and I have little doubt that the Kipchak of Baber is the Hajjiyak, which, leading by what was in old times the great and flourishing city of Bamian, must always have been a main line across the mountain barrier; and it is scarcely conceivable that Baber should have omitted it in his list. That both Kipchak and Shibrtu are mentioned by the king among the passes reached from Ghorband, is, I suppose, to be accounted for by the fact that a transverse route does pass along the whole length of the Ghorband Valley to the foot of the Hajjiyak Pass, whilst there is also a lateral communication from Bamian to Shibrtu.

The account in the *Ayin Akbari* is remarkable, as it seems partly copied from Baber and partly modified. This also mentions seven passes, viz. (1) Hawak (read *Khawak*), (2) Tool (*Túl*),

[1] See also the map facing page 529.

[2] *Journey to the source of the River Oxus*, 1841, p. 186.

[3] Called also Hajikak and Hajigak.

[4] Leyden and Erskine's *Baber*, p. 133 *seq.*

(3) Bajaruck (*Bazarak*), (4) not named, but probably Parwān; (5) "by the Hill of Kipchak, and this also is somewhat easy to pass. The sixth (6) is by the Hill of Sheertoo (read *Shibrtu*), but in the summer when the waters are out you must go by the route of Bahmian and Talakan (*Talikhan*). The seventh (7) is by the way of Abdereh. In winter travellers make use of this road, it being the only one passable in the depth of that season." This last route is, I presume, to be looked for in the Koh-i-Baba, still further west than Shibrtu, but I believe no existing map will help us to it.

The most complete notice of the Passes from the Panjshir and Ghorband Valleys is to be found in a Report by Major R. Leech of the Bombay Engineers, published at Calcutta by the Indian Government[1]. By help of this we make out the following list of the whole number, commencing with the most westerly:

PASSES FROM PANJSHIR.

1. Pass of ANJUMAN. This is a pass starting from Paryan near the head of the Panjshir Valley and crossing into Badakhshan direct. It probably descends the Kokcha Valley by the lapis-lazuli mines. Paryan is perhaps the *Perjan* of Sharifuddín (in P. de la Croix) which Timur passed in his expedition against the Kafirs. Leech's Reports mention traditions of Timur's doings in the Passes into Kafiristan that ascend from Paryan.

2. KHAWAK Pass, at the very head of the Panjshir Valley, crossing to the Valley of Anderab, which it descends to the town of that name. [Taken by Alexander to enter Bactriana.]

3. TÚL. This is a loop line to the Khawak Pass. It quits the latter about twenty miles short of the summit and rejoins it at Sirab about twelve or fourteen miles[2] beyond the summit in the descent to Anderab.

4. ZARYA ascends from Safed Chir on the Panjshir R. some six miles below Túl, and joins the last pass just before reaching Sirab.

5. From UMRAZ (or Murz of Wood's survey), fifteen miles further down the Panjshir, and about thirty-one miles from the entrance of the valley, three bad passes, called Shwa, Urza, and Yatimak, lead across the mountains joining the Bazarak Pass (No. 6) on the other side of the ridge. The two last of the three are seldom free from snow.

[1] I have only MS. extracts of this report, for which I am indebted to Dr. F. Hall, of the India Office Library.

[2] These distances in the Panjshir Passes I take from Wood's survey as embodied in a map by Mr. J. Walker. The distances here as given in Leech's report are inconsistent, and in fact impossibly small. In the Ghorband Passes I have to take Leech's distances.

6. BAZARAK. This quits the Panjshir at the village of that name, twenty-eight and a half miles from the mouth of the valley, and descends upon KHINJAN on the Anderab River.

7. SHATPAL. This starts from Gulbahar at the entrance to Panjshir Valley, and joins the Bazarak Road on the other side at Kishnabad or Kishtabad, twenty-one miles from Khinjan.

PARWĀN PASSES.

8. Pass of PARWĀN, from the town of that name, once a place of consequence (see p. 209), descends upon Bajga belonging to Anderab, apparently to the west of Khinjan. Baber says this pass is a very difficult one, and that between Parwān and the great *col* there are seven minor passes called the *Haft Bacha* (Seven young ones).

9. Pass of SALULANG (Sir-i-lung of Wood). This starts from Tutan Dara, six miles north-west of Charekar and descends, like the last, somewhere not far from Khinjan.

PASSES FROM GHORBAND.

10. KUSHAN. This is the pass which leads close under the great peak specially known as Hindu Kush. It starts from a point in the Ghorband valley about ten miles from Tutan Dara. Kushan lies some miles up the pass. It descends upon Khinjan like the two last, which it probably receives before reaching that place.

11. GWALIAN. This leaves the valley some twenty miles from Tutan Dara. It descends upon Gozan on the Anderab river.

12. GWAZYAR. This pass leaves the valley near the ruins of the old town of Ghorband, some twenty-four and a half miles from Tutan Dara. It leads to Kilagai, a small town on the road from Khinjan to Baghlan and Kunduz.

13. CHAR DARYA. This pass leaves the valley at about twenty-nine miles from Tutan Dara, and descends upon GHORI, a considerable town. It is passable for Kafilas of every description.

From this the road goes on along the valley of Ghorband, throwing off one or two minor passes, and eventually joins the Hajiyak road at the ruins of Zohak near Bamian.

14. The Pass of HAJJIYAK or Bamian.

15. SHIBRTU.

16. ABDEREH, for which my only authority is the *Ayin Akbari* as already quoted. These two last are beyond the limits to which the name Hindu Kush is applied.

Of these Passes Hajjiyak was that crossed on his celebrated journey by Burnes, the first European traveller who saw and described the great rock idols of Bamian; it was also that crossed by Wood on his journey northward to the Oxus. It was probably by this pass that Chinghiz crossed, for the siege of Bamian was one of the events of his campaign in these regions; and by it Hiuen Tsang travelled to India.

The Pass of Chardarya was crossed by Aurungzib. The Pass of Salulang was attempted by Capt. Wood[1], but unsuccessfully, owing to the lateness of the season. Timur on his expedition into India crossed the Hindu Kush by the Pass of Túl, and returned by that of Shibrtu. The Khawak Pass was crossed by Wood and Lord on their return from the Oxus. By this pass or one of its branches Ibn Batuta had crossed five hundred years before[2]; and we have already seen reason to believe that one of the passes into the Panjshir Valley was crossed by Friar Odoric on his return to Europe[3]. Hiuen Tsang also returned by Panjshir and Anderab on his way to China.

I have already observed that the mention by Goës of Parwān

[1] Wood himself calls it the Pass of Parwān, but it is evident from comparison with Leech's report that it was the Pass called in the latter Salulang.

[2] See p. 9 *ante*. Ibn Batuta after passing KUNDUZ and BAGHLAN (see map) arrived at Andar (ANDARAB), where he says a city formerly existed which had altogether disappeared. Starting for the Hindu Kush (the name which he uses) they met with hot springs, in which he washed, and lost the skin of his face in consequence. These were no doubt the hot springs of SIRAB, near where the Passes of Túl and Khawak diverge in the Upper Valley of Anderab, and which are mentioned by Wood as having temperatures of 108° and 124° *Fahr*. (*Journey*, p. 413). The Moor next mentions halting in a place called *Banjhir* (PANJSHIR) where there had been formerly a fine city on a considerable river descending from the mountains of Badakshan. All the country had been ruined by Chinghiz and had never recovered. He then arrived at the mountain of PASHAI (*supra*, p. 9). The Pashais are mentioned repeatedly by Leech as one of the most numerous tribes in the Panjshir valley and adjoining passes. These, I gather, are now Mahomedans, but as the name is mentioned also by Elphinstone as that of one of the Kafir tribes, no doubt part of them in the mountains have retained their heathenism and independence. He then reaches Parwān and Charkh (CHAREKAR, which Leech also calls *Charka*). It will be seen that these data leave nothing ambiguous in the traveller's route excepting the short alternative of the Khawak and Túl routes over the actual ridge of the Hindu Kush (see *Ibn Bat.*, iii, 82–8).

Edrisi speaks of the people of the towns of *Banjhir* and *Hariana* on the Banjhir (Panjshir River) as employed in mining silver, and those of the latter as notorious "for the violence and wickedness of their character." The position of this town of Panjshir does not seem to be known now (though Mahomedan coins exist struck in the ninth century), but the valley has retained its character to this day. "This fair scene," says Wood, "is chiefly peopled by robbers, whose lawless lives and never-ending feuds render it an unfit abode for honest men." *Hariana* is perhaps PARYAN, at which there are silver mines marked in Wood's survey. Edrisi also speaks of Andarab as a town surrounded by gardens, orchards, and vineyards, where they stored the silver from Panjshir and Hariana (i, 476 *seq.*).

[3] *Supra*, II, p. 10.

as occurring just before the entrance of their Kafila to the mountains involves strong probability that he crossed by the pass taking its name from that town. One of the minor difficulties of the narrative, however, is the application of the name *Aingharan* to the district which he reached after crossing the mountains. Now I find from Wood's survey, as embodied in J. Walker's map, that the name *Dara-i-Aingharan* is applied to two of the valleys in the vicinity of Bamian. It is a possible explanation, therefore, that the Kafila might from Parwān have struck up the Ghorband valley and crossed the Hajjiyak Pass. This circuitous route would also be more consistent with the great length of time assigned to the journey, and with the identification of Khulum as the Calcia of our traveller. None of these grounds, however, are stable enough to build upon with much confidence[1].

[1] In the preparation of this note I have had greatly to regret the want of access to the *Journal of the Asiatic Society of Bengal*, which contains a variety of valuable papers bearing on the subject.

[Since Sir Henry Yule wrote this note, the Hindu Kush has been explored and the following list of passes from the *Imperial Gazetteer of India* may prove useful for comparison: "The Hindu Kush is crossed by the following passes, going from east to west—the Karambar or Ishkamán, the Darkot, the Baroghil (at the eastern end of the range, elevation about 12,000 feet), the Yur, the Vost, the Nuksán, the Kharteza, the Dora, and in the extreme West of the main range the Bamián or Irak Pass, a great trade route into India from Central Asia. These passes lead from Chitral into Wakhán and Badakhshán. Of the Káfiristán passes little is known. The Kháwák Pass (13,200 feet) is the most important of the routes between Badakhshán and Káfiristán. From Deh-i-Parian in the Panjshir valley a pass leads by Anjúman to Badakhshán. The other principal passes are—the Thal, the Kháwák, the Bazárak, the Shatpal, the Parwān, the Saraláng, the Káoshán, the Gwálián, the Gwazgar, the Chárdar, the Gholáláy, the Faringal, and the Ghorband. Most of the passes are not difficult. Some are practicable for *káfilas* or caravans of laden carts. On some, snow lies for but three months in the year. Others are covered by perpetual snow. These are impracticable for laden animals, but foot-passengers slide over and down them on leathern aprons."]

NOTE II.

TITLES OF SOME BOOKS QUOTED IN THIS WORK BY ABBREVIATED REFERENCES.

ABULPHARAGIUS.—*Historia Compend. Dynastiarum*, etc., ab Ed. Pocockio. Oxon., 1663.

ACAD. means *Mém. de l'Acad. des Inscriptions et Belles-Lettres*.

ASSEMANI.—*Bibliotheca Orientalis*. When no volume is specified the reference is to vol. iii, part ii, containing the account of the Nestorian Church.

ASTLEY.—*A new general collection of Voyages and Travels*, etc. Printed for Thomas Astley. London, 4 vols., 1745–47.

BABER.—*Memoirs of the Emperor*; by Leyden and Erskine. 1826.

BALDELLI BONI.—*Il Milione di M. Polo*. Firenze, 1827, 4to.

BARBOSA (Lisbon ed.).—*Livro de Duarte Barbosa* in *Collecção de Noticias*, etc., publicada pela Acad. Real das Sciencias, Tomo II. Lisboa, 1812.

BEAZLEY, C. R.—*The Dawn of Modern Geography*. ii, Lond., 1901; iii, 1906, 8vo.

——.—*Plano Carpini and Rubruquis*, see I, p. 157.

BENJAMIN OF TUDELA, see *Early Travels in Palestine*.

BONAPARTE, Prince Roland.—*Documents de l'époque mongole des* XIII*e et* XIV*e siècles*. Paris, 1895, fol.

BRETSCHNEIDER, E.—*Knowledge possessed by the Ancient Chinese of the Arabs and Arabian Colonies*. Lond., 1871, ppt. 8vo.

——.—*Archaeological and Historical Researches on Peking*. Shanghai, 1876, 8vo.

——.—*Mediaeval Researches from Eastern Asiatic Sources*. London, 1888, 2 vols. 8vo.

BROWNE'S *Vulgar Errors*. Bohn's Edition.

CHABOT, J. B.—*Histoire de Mar Jabalaha III*. Paris, 1895, 8vo.

CHAU JU-KUA, see HIRTH, and I, p. 233.

CHAVANNES, Ed.—*Les Mémoires historiques de Se-ma Ts'ien*. Paris, I, 1895, et seq.

——.—*Trois généraux chinois de la dynastie des Han orientaux*. Ext. du *T'oung pao*. Leyde, 1906, ppt. 8vo.

——.—*Documents chinois découverts par Aurel Stein*. Oxford, 1913, 4to.

CHAVANNES, Ed.—*Un texte manichéen retrouvé en Chine*, in *J. Asiat.*, Nov.–Déc. 1911 ; Janv.–Avril, 1913 [with Pelliot].

——.—*Mission archéologique dans la Chine septentrionale.* I, Paris, 1913–5, 2 parts 8vo.

——.—*Documents sur les Tou-Kiue (Turcs) occidentaux.* St. Petersb., 1903, 8vo, and *T'oung pao*, 1905.

——.—*Les Pays d'Occident d'après le* Wei lio, in *T'oung pao*, 1905; *d'après le* Heou Han Chou, in *T'oung pao*, 1907.

CHINE (ANCIENNE), *Description Historique*, etc., etc., par M. G. Pauthier. Paris, 1837 (*L'Univers Pittoresque*).

—— (MODERNE), par Pauthier et Bazin. Ditto, ditto, 1853.

CIVEZZA, Marcellino da.—*Storia universale delle missioni francescane.* I–VI, Roma–Prato, 1857–1881, 6 vols. 8vo. See II, p. 88.

COEDÈS, George.—*Textes d'auteurs grecs et latins relatifs à l'Extrême-Orient depuis le* IVe *siècle av. J. C. jusqu'au* XIVe *siècle.* Paris, 1910, 8vo.

CONTI, Nicolò, see I, p. 266.

CORDIER, Henri.—*Bibliotheca Sinica.—Dict. bibliog. des ouvrages relatifs à l'Empire Chinois.* Paris, 1904–1908, 4 vols. 8vo.

——.—*Les Voyages en Asie au* XIVe *siècle du bienheureux frère* Odoric de Pordenone. Paris, 1891, large 8vo.

——.—*L'Extrême-Orient dans l'Atlas catalan de Charles V.* Paris, 1895, 4to.

——.—See YULE's *Marco Polo.*

COSMAS, see MCCRINDLE, J. W.

CRAWFURD.—*Descriptive Dictionary of the Indian Islands and adjacent countries.* London, 1856.

——.—*Grammar and Dictionary of the Malay Language.* London, 1852.

CUINET, Vital.—*La Turquie d'Asie.* Paris, 1890–4, 4 vols. 8vo.

D'AVEZAC.—*Notice sur les Anciens Voyages de Tartarie en général, et sur celui de Jean du Plan de Carpin en particulier.* (In vol. iv of *Recueil de Voyages et de Mémoires, publié par la Soc. de Géographie.* Paris, 1839.)

DAVIS.—*The Chinese*, new ed. in 3 vols., and a supplem. volume. C. Knight, 1844.

DEGUIGNES.—*Histoire générale des Huns.* Paris, 1756–8, 4 vols. 4to.

DELLA DECIMA, see III, p. 137.

DEVÉRIA, G.—*Origine de l'Islamisme en Chine*, in *Centenaire de l'Ecole des Langues orientales*, 1895.

——.—*Musulmans et Manichéens chinois*, in *Jour. Asiat.*, 1895, II, pp. 445–484.

D'OHSSON.—*Hist. des Mongols*, par le Baron C. La Haye et Amsterdam, 1834 and 1852, 4 vols. 8vo.

EARLY TRAVELS IN PALESTINE, edited by Thomas Wright. Bohn's Antiq. Library, 1848, 8vo.

EDRISI.—*La Géographie de*, traduite, etc., par P. Amédée Jaubert. Paris, 1836–1840.

ELIAS, E.—*The* Tarikh-i-Rashidi *of Mirza Muhammad Haidar. Transl. by* E. Denison Ross. London, 1895, 8vo.

ELLIOT, Sir H. M.—*Biographical Index to the Historians of Muhamedan India*, vol. i. Calcutta, 1849.

FERRAND, Gabriel.—*Relations de Voyages et Textes géographiques arabes, persans et turks relatifs à l'Extrême-Orient du* VIIe *au* XVIIIe *siècles.* Paris, 1913–4, 2 vols. 8vo.

GAMS, B.—*Series Episcoporum Ecclesiae catholicae.* Ratisbonae, 1873, 4to.—Suppt. 1886, 4to.

GANDAR, Dom.—*Le Canal Impérial*, Variétés sinologiques No. 4.—Shanghai, 1894, 8vo.

GILDEMEISTER.—*Scriptorum Arabum de Rebus Indicis Loci et Opuscula Inedita.* Bonn, 1838.

GOEJE, M. J. de, *Ibn-Khurdâdhbah*, see I, p. 137.

GROOT, J. J. M. de.—*Sectarianism and Religious Persecution in China.* Amst., 1903–1904, 2 vols. 8vo.

HAVRET, Henri.—*La Stèle chrétienne de Si-ngan fou.* Variétés sinologiques Nos. 7, 12, 20. Shanghai, 1895, 1897, 1902, 3 pts. 8vo.

HEYD, W.—*Histoire du Commerce du Levant au Moyen-Age.* Leipzig, 1885–6, 2 vols. 8vo.

F. HIRTH.—*China and the Roman Orient.* Shanghai, 1885, 8vo.

——.—Chau Ju-kua: *His Work on the Chinese and Arab Trade in the twelfth and thirteenth Centuries entitled* Chu-fan-chi. *Transl. from the Chinese* by F. HIRTH and W. W. ROCKHILL. St. Petersburg, 1912, 8vo.

Hobson-Jobson.—See YULE.

HUNTER, W.—*Imperial Gazetteer of India*, 1909, 26 vols. 8vo.

IBN-KHURDÂDHBAH, see I, p. 137.

IBN MUHALHIL, see I, p. 139.

JARRIC, DU. See IV, p. 170.

JOHNSON, Francis.—*Dict. Persian, Arabic, and English.* 1852.

JOUR. ASIAT.—*Journal Asiatique.*

J.A.S.B.—*Journal of the Asiatic Society of Bengal.*

J.R.A.S.—*Journal of the Royal Asiatic Society.*

J.R.G.S.—*Journal of the Royal Geographical Society.*

KLAPROTH.—*Mémoires relatifs à l'Asie.* Paris, 1824–25.

——.—*Tableaux Historiques de l'Asie*, etc. Paris, 1826.

KUNSTMANN, Prof. Friedrich, see II, p. 88.

LA PRIMAUDAIE, F. Elie de.—*Etudes sur le Commerce au Moyen Age.* Paris, 1848, 8vo.

LASSEN.—*Indische Alterthumskunde.* 1847–1862.

LE STRANGE, G.—*The Lands of the Caliphate.* Cambridge, 1905, 8vo.

LÉVI, Sylvain.—*Les missions de* Wang Hiuen-ts'e *dans l'Inde.* (*Journ. Asiatique*, 1900.)

LINSCHOTEN.—*Hist. de la Navigation de Jean Hugues de Linschot, Hollandois.* 3ième éd. Amsterdam, 1638. Sometimes the Latin edition, Hagæ Com., 1599, fol.

LUDOLF.—*Historia Æthiopica*, Francof. a. M., 1681. *Commentarius*, etc., 1691, and Suppt., 1693.

MCCRINDLE, J. W.—*The Christian Topography of* Cosmas, *an Egyptian Monk.* Lond., Hakluyt Soc., 1897, 8vo.

MA HUAN, see Geo. PHILLIPS in *J.R.A.S.*, 1895–6.

MAJOR, R. H.—*India in the Fifteenth Century*, see I, p. 266.

MANDEVILLE'S *Travels*, see *Early Travels in Palestine.*

MAR JABALAHA, see CHABOT.

MARQUART, J.—*Ibn Muhalhil*, see I, p. 139.—*Êranšahr nach der Geographie des Ps. Moses Xorenac'i.* I, 1901, pp. 206, 4to.

MARTINI.—Martinii *Atlas Sinensis.* In Blaeu's *Atlas*, vol. x, and in Thévenot's *Collection.*

MASPERO, Georges.—*Le Royaume de Champa.*—Leide, 1914, 8vo.

MAS'ÛDI.—Maçoudi, *Les Prairies d'Or*, par C. Barbier de Meynard et Pavet de Courteille. Paris, 1861 *seqq.* See I, p. 137.

MOOR'S *Notices of the Indian Archipelago.* Singapore, 1837.

MOSHEIM.—*Historia Tartarorum Ecclesiastica.* Helmstadi, 1741, 4to. The book is *not* by Mosheim, as the preface informs you; but written under his instructions by H. C. Paulsen.

OLLONE, Com^{t} d'.—*Recherches sur les Musulmans chinois.* Paris, 1911, 8vo.

PALLADIUS.—*Elucidations of Marco Polo's Travels in North-China drawn from Chinese Sources*, in *Journ. North China Branch R. A. S.*, x, 1876, pp. 1–54.

PAOLINO, Fra— di S. Bartolomeo, etc.—*Viaggio alle Indie Orientali.* Roma, 1796.

PAUTHIER.—*L'Inscription Syro-Chinoise de Si-ngan-fou*, etc. Paris, 1858, 8vo.

——.—*De l'Authenticité de l'Inscription Nestorienne de Si-ngan-fou*, etc. Paris, 1857, 8vo.

——.—*Histoire des Relations Politiques de la Chine avec les Puissances Occidentales.* Paris, 1859, 8vo.

——.—See POLO and CHINE.

PELLIOT, Paul. *Deux Itinéraires de Chine en Inde à la fin du* VIIIe *siècle.* Hanoi, 1904, 8vo.

——.—*Le Fou Nan*, in *Bul. Ecole Extrême-Orient*, Avril–Juin 1903.

——.—*Chrétiens d'Asie centrale et d'Extrême-Orient*, in *T'oung pao*, Dec. 1914, pp. 623–644.

Peregrinatores Medii Ævi Quatuor (Burchardus de Monte Sion, Ricoldus de Monte Crucis, [Pseudo] Odoricus de Foro Julii, Wilbrandus de Oldenborg). Recensuit J. C. M. Laurent, Lipsiæ, 1864, 4to.

Pigafetta.—*Il Primo Viaggio intorno del Mondo.* Milan, 1800.

Plano Carpini.—In tom. iv of the *Recueil de Voyages*, etc. (see D'Avezac). See Rockhill, Beazley and Pullé, I, pp. 156–7.

Polo, Marco. When quoted simply, the reference is to the fourth edition of that by Hugh Murray, or to Yule-Cordier's edition.

—— Pauthier's.—*Le Livre de Marco Polo*, par M. G. Pauthier. Paris, 1865, large 8vo.

—— Bürck's. Leipzig, 1845.

—— See Baldelli.

Pullé, G.—*Pian del Carpine*, see I, p. 157.

Quatremère's *Rashid*, see *Rashid*.

Quétif and Echard.—*Scriptores Ordinis Prædicatorum.* Paris, 1719, 2 vols. fol.

Radloff, W.—*Arbeiten der Orchon-Expedition.—Atlas der Alterthümer der Mongolei.* St. Petersburg, 1892, fol.

Rashid.—*Histoire des Mongols de la Perse*, par Raschid-el-din, traduite, etc., par M. Quatremère. Paris, 1836, fol.

Reinaud.—*Relations des Voyages faits par les Arabes dans l'Inde et à la Chine*, etc. Paris, 1845.

——.—*Relations politiques et commerciales de l'Empire Romain avec l'Asie Orientale*, etc. Paris, 1863, 8vo.

Relations, etc., see Reinaud.

Rémusat, Abel.—*Mélanges Asiatiques*, Paris, 1825; and *Nouveaux Mélanges Asiatiques.* Paris, 1829.

Ritter.—*Erdkunde.*

Ritter's Lectures.—*Gesch. der Erdkunde und der Entdeckungen...herausgegeben* von H. A. Daniel. Berlin, 1861.

Rockhill, W. W.—*Rubruck and Pian de Carpine*, see I, p. 156.

——.—Chau Ju-kua, see Hirth.

Rubruquis. In tom. iv of the *Recueil de Voyages*, etc. (see D'Avezac). See Rockhill, i, pp. 156–7 and Beazley.

Saint-Martin.—*Mémoires Historiques et Géographiques sur l'Arménie*, etc. Paris, 1818–19, 2 vols. 8vo.

Saint-Martin on Lebeau.—*Hist. du Bas Empire* (with notes and corrections by Saint-Martin). Paris, 1828.

Schefer, Ch.—*Relations des Peuples musulmans avec les Chinois*, in *Centenaire de l'Ecole des Langues Orientales*, Paris, 1895, 4to.

Schiltberger.—*Reisen des Johannes—aus München.* Von K. F. Neumann. München, 1859.

Schmidt, I. J.—*Geschichte der Ost-Mongolen*, etc., verfasst von Ssanang Ssetzen Chungtaidschi. St. Petersburg, 1829.

SEMEDO, P. Alvaro.—*Relazione della Cina.* Roma, 1643.

SSANANG SSETZEN. See SCHMIDT.

STEIN, Sir Aurel.—*Ancient Khotan.* Oxford, 1907, 2 vols. 4to.

——.—*Ruins of Desert Cathay.* Lond., 1912, 2 vols. 8vo.

——.—See CHAVANNES.

TIMKOWSKI.—*Travels of the Russian Mission through Mongolia to China*, etc. London, 1827, 2 vols. 8vo.

TURNOUR.—*Epitome of the History of Ceylon*, etc., *and the first twenty chapters of the Mahawanso.* Ceylon, Cotta Ch. Mis. Press.

VAN DER LITH and Marcel DEVIC.—*Livre des Merveilles de l'Inde, par le capitaine* BOZORG. Leide, 1883–1886, 4to.

VINCENZO MARIA.—*Viaggio all' Indie Orientali del* P. F.—— di S. Caterina da Siena, etc. Roma, 1672.

WADDING.—*Annales Minorum*, etc. (History of the Franciscan Order), see II, p. 85.

WANG HIUEN-TS'E, see Sylvain LÉVI.

YULE, Sir Henry.—*The Book of Ser Marco Polo*....Third ed. revised by Henri CORDIER. Lond., 1903, 2 vols. 8vo.

——.—*Hobson-Jobson. A Glossary of Colloquial Indian Words and Phrases.* New ed. by William CROOKE. Lond., 1903, 8vo.

NOTE III.

CORRECTIONS AND ADDITIONAL ILLUSTRATIONS.

VOLUME I.

Pp. xxii, 201; III, p. 186 *n*. *Read* Periegetes *instead of* Periergetes.

Pp. xxiii, 262. Letter of Sempad (1243); the letter was written between 1248, date of his departure, and 1250.

P. 8, note 1, line 3. *Read* Hau Han Shu *instead of* Han Han Shu.

P. 9, note 2, line 5. *Read* Chavannes *instead of* Chevannes.

P. 29. On Theophylactus, see Chavannes, *Tou-Kiue*, pp. 249 seq. On *Tabγač* = uighûr *tapqač*, see V. Thomsen, *Insc. de l'Orkhon*, 1896, p. 139.

P. 41. *Read* TSIN *instead of* TS'IN.

P. 60, line 6. Read *Samanids* instead of *Sassanids*. Read *Lun tsang* instead of *Lunt sang*; *Aṃcuvarman* instead of *Ançuvarman*.

P. 70, note. T'ai Tsung died during the fifth moon 549.

P. 101, note 1, line 1. Read *J. R. Geog. Soc.*, vol. xxviii *instead of* vol. xxvii.

P. 110, note 2. *Read* Izdbuzid *instead of* Idbuzid.

P. 193. On Kattigara, *see* Dr. A. Hermann in the Berlin Geog. Soc. *Zeitschrift*, N. 10, 1913, and the *Geographical Journal*, May 1914, p. 579. He places Kattigara on the northern borders of Annam, just where Richthofen and Hirth, on the authority of the Chinese annals, have placed the southern limit of the Chinese Empire at the time.

P. 205, note 3. *Titeupuli*. Prof. Chavannes, *Tou-Kiue*, p. 227 *n*., shows that *Ti-t'eou-pu-li* has never existed.

P. 378, note 4. Read CHENG TING FU *instead of* CH'ENG TING FU.

VOLUME II.

P. ix. *Add* Dr. Nob. Luigi Tinti Canonico Decano Prof. di Teologia e Pastorale nel Seminario vescovile di Portugruaro, Delegato del Vescovo di Concordia — Vita e Missioni nell' Indo-Cina del Beato Odorico da Pordenone dei Frati Minori (1285–1331). Con illustrazioni.) — Roma, Desclée, Lefebvre & Ci, 1901, 8vo, pp. 178 + 1 f. n. ch. ind. ill.

Gives (p. 161) a sketch of the sarcophagus as it stood before the XVIIIth cent., surmounted with a bust of Odorico, showing the project of restoration.

P. 71. See *Notice sur le grand et le petit Pou lu* [Baltistan and Gilghit] from the *T'ang Shu* in Chavannes' *Tou-Kiue*, pp. 149–154.

P. 199. Prof. PELLIOT has devoted an article to the Turkish name of wine in Odoric of Pordenone (*T'oung pao*, July, 1914, pp. 448–453). He thinks with Yule that *bigni* must be *bagni*, but Turkish, not Persian. "Ce qu'on boit au Tchö kiang, c'est surtout du vin de sorgho, et les crûs en sont célèbres dans toute la Chine. Précisément, c'est un produit un peu analogue, c'est-à-dire un produit de la fermentation de céréales, qui était désigné en Perse sous le nom de *bàgni*. Il me paraît donc probable... que *băgni* désigne les bières, vins de sorgho, vins de millet, bref toutes les boissons fermentées autres que le produit de la vigne et à l'exclusion des alcools distillés. Pour de telles boissons, simples ou composées, c'est d'Asie centrale que le nom de *băgni* aurait gagné le monde iranien."

P. 203. In the *Bul. de l'École d'Extrême-Orient*, XIV, No. 8, 1914, Prof. H. MASPERO in the narrative of an archaeological Mission through the Che Kiang Province has given an interesting description of the *Hia T'ien-chu sze* or *Ling-yin sze*, situated on the western side of the Si Hu.

P. 223. *Bogtak*. According to Prof. Pelliot, the word is found already in the list of Wei words contained in the *Nan Ts'i Shu* (VIth century).

P. 224. "Un grand préfet ou un autre officier qui va au palais du prince, entre et sort à droite du poteau dressé entre les deux battants des portes. Il évite de mettre le pied sur le seuil." *Li Ki*, Chap. I, K'iu li, Partie I, Art. II, 27, p. 17; transl. by Couvreur.

P. 241. *Tartar Lamb*.—Dr. B. LAUFER has made a new study of the question in his paper, *The Story of the Pinna and the Syrian Lamb* (*Journ. of American Folk-Lore*, April–June, 1915), and he has come to the following conclusion (p. 126): "The traditions of the Chinese have enabled us to study the development of the story in its various stages, from the beginning of the Christian era down to the thirteenth century, and to recognize its origin, growth and significance. We have seen that it takes its birth from the pinna, and that the Aristotelian doctrine of the fusion of vegetal and animal characteristics, applied to the life-habits of the pinna, is the very germ, the protoplasm, so to speak, which has called into existence the West-Asiatic notion of a vegetal lamb. This vegetal lamb therefore was evolved from a marine mollusk, never from a plant, and least of all from the cotton-plant. For this reason Yule was misguided in seeking for 'the plant about which these fables have gathered,' and in regarding it as a certain genus of ferns. Animal figures shaped by the Chinese from the rhizome of a fern greatly stirred the imagination of scholars in the eighteenth and nineteenth centuries, and were believed to have yielded the basis for the so-called Syrian lamb. It is the uncontested and great merit of H. Lee to have utterly destroyed these scientific fables, which, as usual, are more colossal and more baffling than the fables themselves, whose mystery they try to solve."

P. 245. Prof. PELLIOT suggests that Tozan was Tung-sheng chau. See *Journ. N. C. B. R. As. Soc.*, 1915, p. 28. Elsewhere (*T'oung pao*, Dec. 1914, p. 634) he says that it is pretty sure that Tozan is the Košang of Rabban Çauma, that Košang is an alteration of Tošang = Tung sheng = Tokto.

P.247. In *T'oung pao*, July, 1914, pp. 405–418, Dr. B. LAUFER raised the question: *Was Odoric of Pordenone ever in Tibet?* He says: "Tibet has left no profound or lasting impression upon his mind, because he rubbed elbows but superficially with its north-eastern borderland." He comes to the conclusion: "Odoric of Pordenone has never traversed Tibet proper, has never been at Lhasa,—a feat with which he has been unduly credited for so long and to which he himself lays no claim. The honor of being the first Europeans to have reached Lhasa is justly due to the two Jesuit Fathers Grueber and Dorville, who spent two months there in 1661."

P. 248. With regard to bread and wine in Tibet, Dr. LAUFER has, *l.c.*, p. 412: "Such a statement cannot possibly be advanced by any one who has had but the slightest contact with the Tibetan borderlands and the most superficial acquaintance with Tibetan people. First of all, there is nothing like bread in Tibet, where even the preparation of dough is unknown. Parched barley-flour mixed with tea or milk into a porridge forms the staple food, and the alcoholic beverage called *č'aṅ*, obtained from fermented barley, is neither wine nor beer, but a liquor *sui generis*. Even granted that Odoric simply committed a mistake in the choice of his words, and merely intended to say that food and drink abound in Tibet, his statement nevertheless remains very strange. The majority of Tibetans eke out a wretched living as poor shepherds or farmers, and earn enough to be kept from starvation; but emphasis on the food-supplies being as abundant as anywhere in the world is thoroughly out of place for a poor country like Tibet."

P. 248. Respecting the tents of black felt, Dr. LAUFER says: "Certainly the Tibetans understand the art of making felt; but the tents inhabited by the pastoral tribes of Tibet, throughout the country, are covered with a black cloth woven from yak-hair. In this respect, and in its quadrangular structure, the Tibetan tent represents a dwelling-type of its own, which is plainly distinguished from the Mongol circular felt tent. It is impossible to assume that in the days of Odoric there may have been Tibetan nomads living in felt tents, and thus come to the Friar's rescue. ...It is obvious beyond any doubt that Odoric's observation refers, not to Tibetan, but to Mongol tents."

P. 250: Dr. LAUFER writes, *l.c.*, p. 411: "The word *bakshi* is not, as stated by YULE (also *Marco Polo*, I, p. 314), connected with Skr. *bhikshu*. The Tibetans are acquainted with both words, translating the latter by the term *dge-sloṅ*, and writing the former *pag-ši* (Jäschke's spelling *pa-ši* is incorrect). The Tibetan dictionary *Li-šii gur k'aṅ*, fol. 23*a*, explains this word by *btsun-pa* ('respectable, reverend'), and states that it is derived from the language of the Turks (*Hor*). The word seems to be, indeed, of Turkish origin (VAMBERY, *Primitive Cultur*, p. 248, RADLOFF, *Wörterbuch der Türk-dialecte*, IV, col. 1445)."

P. 251. With regard to the word *Abassi*, Dr. LAUFER says; *l.c.*, p. 411: "Odoric plainly states that the word is of the Tibetan language, and it has to be sought, therefore, in Tibetan only. ...The Sa-skya hierarchs, who practically ruled Tibet in the age of the Mongols, bore the Tibetan title *ạ P'ags-pa* (eminent, excellent) and were spoken of as the *ạ P'ags-pa b La-ma*. This word, variously articulated *p'ags-pa, p'ag-pa, p'as-pa, p'a'-pa*, is the source of Odoric's *Abassi*." "This term," adds Dr. Laufer, "is neither a common title nor a title at all, but merely a personal name."

P. 251. With regard to the hair, Dr. LAUFER remarks, p. 413, that boar's tusks are generally employed by Tibetan women for making the parting of their hair; if Odoric had really crossed Tibet to Lhasa and beyond, he could not have failed to notice that quite different styles of hair-dressing prevail in other parts of the country.

P. 254. Prof. E. H. PARKER in a notice of this volume in the *Geographical Journal*, August, 1914, says: "As to the Tibetans drinking out of their ancestors' skulls, it may be pointed out that they do it even now; not to refer to other and remoter authorities, it is only necessary to quote the graphic account of Tibetan family life this very year, as given in the *North China Herald* for March 14, where the practice is plainly mentioned." I have not found the passage referred to in the number of the *N. C. Herald* for March 14.

VOLUME III.

P. 48. *Land of the Goths*. In a somewhat acerb anonymous article in *The Athenaeum* of Dec. 25, 1915, a critic, whom I could easily name, remarks that the MS. from which are drawn the *Documents relating to the Mission of the Minor Friars to China in the thirteenth and fourteenth Centuries, edited by the* Rev. A. C. Moule in the *J.R.A.S.*, July, 1914, reads "per terram Cothay";

I cannot but regret that these documents had not appeared before I had myself printed the letters, the proofs of which I lent to Mr. Moule, because I might have added this note (*J.R.A.S.*, *l.c.*, p. 550) evidently used by the *Athenaeum* reviewer: "Wadding transcribed this word *Gothorum*, and, in the second letter, *Kathan*. It probably stands (as M. Pelliot suggests) for Marco Polo's Toctai, the Chinese T'o-t'o, descended from Chingis' eldest son, Chu-ch'ih, Khan of Kipchak, whose capital was at Saraï, on the Volga, north of the Caspian Sea."

P. 52. *I have been thinking*...The text of the *J.R.A.Soc.*, July 1914, p. 552, reads: "Cogitauj uos non sine causa mirarj quod tot annis in provincia tam longinqua consistens nunquam meas litteras recepistis."

P. 52. *The Lord Kathan Khan.* The text of the *J.R.A.S.*, July, 1914, p. 552, reads: "domini Cothay Canis." See note *supra*, p. 269.

P. 58. The Rev. A. C. Moule, *J.R.A.S.*, July 1914, p. 557, remarks that Quinquagesima fell on 13th February in 1306.

P. 73. "Zayton which is about three weeks' journey distant from Cambaliech." The *J.R.A.S.*, July 1914, p. 566, has: "Zayton que distat a Cambaliech itinere mensium fere trium."

P. 119, note 1. Instead of "See *supra*, p. 214," read "See supra, II, p. 214."

P. 120. Instead of "See p. 265," read "See II, p. 231."

P. 127. In a paper on Karajang inserted in the *Journ. R. A. Soc.*, Oct. 1915, p. 781, Dr. LAUFER believes that YULE was correct in his conception, and that in accordance with his suggestion, *Jang* indeed represents the phonetically exact transcription of a Tibetan proper name. This is the Tibetan *ạ Jaṅ* or *ạ Jàns*, pronounced *Jang* or *Djang*. It will be remembered that YULE (*Marco Polo*, II, p. 72) analysed the word into *Ḳará-jáng*, in which the first element was the Mongol or Turki *Ḳárá* (black). *Jang* has not been explained; but probably it may have been a Tibetan term adopted by the Mongols, and the colours may have applied to their clothing. *Jaṅ* is a Tibetan tribal and geographical term. *Jaṅ* or *Jang* is the Tibetan designation of the Mo-so and the territory inhabited by them, the capital of which is Li-kiang fu.

P. 144. My friend, Prof. M. PROU, remarks that *Chiaveria* is not key-money. The *Clavarii* were the collectors of taxes; they had charge of the keys of the municipal safe. Du Cange has: "*Clavaria*, Munus *Clavarii*; Locus ubi *Clavarius* reponebat omnia ad *Clavariam* spectantia; *Clavarius*, Ital. *Chiavaio* et *Chiaivolo*, Cui claves fisci communis commissae sunt; *Clavariae Jus*, Vectigal, quod pro mercibus in regesta inscribendis pensitabatur." E. Levy, *Petit Dict. provençal-français*, p. 179, col. 1, gives: "*Clavaria*, s. f., trésorerie; édifice où se trouve la trésorerie; circonscription d'un trésorier, d'un receveur des revenus ecclésiastiques."

P. 144, note 6. The same friend suggests that *Lelda* might be read *leida*; we have in Provençal *leuda, leida, leda, lesda, lesna*. Cf. E. Levy, *Dict. provençal-français*, 1909, p. 224, col. 1, p. 225, col. 2: *leudier, leidier, lesdier*, percepteur de la leude.

P. 182, note. The *Athenaeum* critic remarks that Fu ting is found in chap. 132 of the *Yuen Shi*, Hiang shan in chap. 135, and Gemboga in chap. 123.

P. 186. The An ts'aï (Asii, Asiani) changed their name into A-lan-na (Alans) under the Posterior Han; during the second Wei, they called themselves *The su* [Su t'o] and Wen-na-sha. Cf. Rémusat, *Nouv. Mél. As.*, I. p. 239.

P. 187. The massacre of Alans took place at Chen ch'ao, a little north of the Kiang, not at Ch'ang chau (1275). Cf. Pelliot, *T'oung pao*, Dec. 1914, pp. 641–2.

P. 194, note. *Instead of* Ta yi chi lio, *read* Tao yi chi lio.

P. 237. Mangoes. *A'nbâ*, Mango. "C'est un arbre de l'Inde que l'on ne trouve que dans l'Inde et la Chine. Il a une tige épaisse, des branches et des feuilles pareilles à celles du noyer. Le fruit ressemble au *mokl* espagnol. Les Indiens le recueillent quand il est formé et le confisent dans de l'eau, du sel et du vinaigre. Il a un goût pareil à celui de l'olive. On en use à titre de condiment et il excite l'appétit. L'usage prolongé de ce fruit assainit l'odeur des transpirations et détruit la fétidité des émanations intestinales." (*Ibn el-Beïthar*, in *Not. et Ext.*, XXV, 1881, p. 471.)

Volume IV.

P. 20. Kanauj, in Farrukhābād District, United Provinces.

P. 190, note. *Instead of* A-si-you, *read* A-si-yen. Cf. p. 231. Prof. Chavannes has since altered his opinion.

P. 193. Fifth line from foot of page, *suppress* T'ien shan.

P. 222, note. *Read* K'iu *tan instead of* K'iu *lan*.

P. 228, note. *Read* Toan tac, *instead of* To antac.

P. 235. The *Cailac* of Rubruquis is the *Kayâlik* of ancient writers, the *Kiyâk* of the *Jahân Kushâi*. "It was situated, according to the most trustworthy critics, to the south-west of the Imil River, and near the modern Kopál." (N. Elias, *Tarikh-i-Rashidi*, p. 288.)

P. 239. *Kia-yü Kwan*, or the "Jade Gate." I should have referred to my note in *Marco Polo*, I, p. 193, in which I said: "According to the Chinese characters, the name of Kia-yü Kwan does not mean 'Jade Gate,' and as Mr. Rockhill writes to me, it can only mean something like 'barrier of the pleasant Valley.'"

INDEX

Names of Persons in CAPITAL letters. Subject Names in **thick letters.**
Titles of books in *italics.*

AARON, III, 209
Aas (The Alans), III, 185, 186; see Alans
Abadan, I, 86, 309
ABAGARUS, King, III, 226
ABAKA, Khan of Persia, I, 119, 120; III, 108; IV, 7
Abano, III, 195; see PETER of Abano
ABARANER, Thomas de, II, 104
Abari, I, 307
Abarim, I, 307
Abasa, I, 202
Abasci, Abascy, III, 223
Abassi (Lama), II, 250; IV, 269
Abassi de Khalifs, II, 250
Abasty, III, 222, 223
Abaz Country, III, 185
ABBA GREGORY, I, 222; II, 157
ABBAN, III, 252
Abbeys of the Idolaters (Buddhist), III, 94
—— in Scotland and England, III, 170
ABBOTT, Col. James, I, 243; II, 107; III, 82
Abbreviations used in reference to MSS. and editions of Odoric, II, 95; in reference to books quoted, IV, 260 *seq.*
ABD-ALLAH of Misr, Shaikh, IV, 2, 33
ABDALLATIF, II, 141
Abdeni, I, 309
Abdereh, IV, 256, 257
ABDIAS, Bishop, III, 252
ABDULAHAN, IV, 211
ABDULA ISÁf, travelling name of Goës, IV, 201, 237
ABDUL KERIM, IV, 191, 193
ABDULLA KHAN, IV, 212
ABDULMALIQ, Khalif, I, 49
ABDUL MEDJID, I, 318
ABDUL MUMIN, IV, 212
ABDUL RASHID KHAN, IV, 191, 193
ABDUR RAZZAK, I, 87, 179, 271, 291, 313; II, 133; III, 249
ABEL, I, 151; III, 244
Abeskun, II, 105
Ab-i-Haiyah, river, IV, 108, 121
Ab-i-Siyah (Kali Nadi), IV, 22
Abohar, IV, 12
Abragana, I, 195
ABRAHAM, cast into the Fire, Legend of, II, 121; land of, III, 225; buried in Ebron, III, 245, 265
ABRAHAM (Ngao-lo-han), II, 210
ABRAM, III, 239
Abserai, III, 84
ABU ABDALLAH, Mahomed, King of Granada, III, 230
Abubakhr, Castle, IV, 12
ABUBAKR (Báyán Fanchán), III, 122
ABUBAKR, Khan of Kashgar, IV, 190
ABUBEKR, III, 69
ABU DULAF, see IBN MUHALHIL
ABU ISHAK of Kazerun, Shaikh, IV, 120
ABU JAFAR al Mansúr, I, 91, 92
Abukir, I, 306
ABU'L ABBAS, I, 92
ABULFARAJ, Mahomed, I, 113
ABUL FAZL, I, 74; IV, 173
ABULFEDA, Notices of China, I, 145, 255–8
Abulustein, IV, 5
ABU SAID, Arab, I, 104
ABU SAID Bahádur Khan of Persia, I, 121; II, 104; III, 89, 90, 96, 108, 109, 160; IV, 133, 137, 166
ABU SAID, son of Yunus Khan of Eastern Chagatai, IV, 191
ABU ZAID of Siraf, I, 112, 125, 131, 132–5, 138, 197, 241; IV, 5
Abyssinia, I, 218, 219, 220, 222; II, 132, 157; III, 224; IV, 154; Transfer of Prester John stories to, III, 26–27; many Kings subject to Emperor of, III, 43; Power of the King to divert the Nile, III, 222; see Ethiopia
Acbatana, I, 43; see Ecbatana

Acesines, I, 24
ACHIKI, III, 128
Achin, I, 152; II, 146, 174
Achmetha, II, 102
Aconsersec, IV, 227
Aconterzec, IV, 229
ACQUAVIVA, IV, 245
Acre, III, 49
Ac-Sarai, III, 84
Acsu, see Aqsu
Actam, II, 105
Acta Sanctorum, II, 9, 12, 16, 21, 22, 24, 27, 28, 53, 80, 100, 117, 118, 125, 126, 271
Aczum, I, 217
ADALBERT, St., III, 264
'Adali, coin so called, IV, 60 *seq.*
ADAM, II, 171; III, 194, 197, 201, 226–8, 232–6, 238, 240, 242, 243, 245, 250, 254, 260; Foot, III, 242; Peak, II, 171, 172; III, 219, 232, 233; IV, 32
ADAM (King Tsing), I, 108, 111–113
ADAM, William, Archbishop, III, 37
Adanah, IV, 5
Aden, I, 87, 88, 217; II, 133; III, 68; IV, 3, 4, 65; Water Cisterns at, IV, 3
Adiabene, II, 109; III, 22, 23
Adil, II, 242, see Volga
ADORNO, Hieronimo, I, 124
Adua, I, 217
Aduh, IV, 21
Adule, I, 25, 217–9, 227, 229, 230
Aegae, II, 190
AELIAN, I, 243; II, 231
Aethiopos, I, 195
Afghanistan, I, 37, 154; IV, 160, 204, 205, 207, 217
Afghans, II, 263; IV, 204
AFKHARUDDÍN, IV, 130, 135
AFRAÇIAB, AFRASIAB, I, 9, 10, 60, 100; IV, 164
AFRASIAB, Atabek, IV, 139
Afrasiábi Turks, IV, 164
Agaos, I, 218
AGATHEMERUS, II, 160
Agau, in Abyssinia, I, 218, 219
AGE HANEM, IV, 207
AGGABODHI III, I, 71
AGGABODHI VI Sīlamegha, I, 72
Aggia, III, 163
AGIASI, IV, 225
Agila, IV, 100; see Aloes Wood
Agisymba, I, 187, 188
Agitarcan, Agitarchan (Astrakhan), I, 308; III, 84, 147
AGNOLO DI LOTTI of Antella, III, 143
Agnus scythicus, II, 242, 243
Agra, II, 230, 234; III, 262; IV, 21, 169, 174, 176, 178–180, 217
Agreboce, III, 161
Agrican (Astrakhan), III, 198
AGUDA, I, 148
Ahan-gharán, IV, 209
AHASUERUS, II, 102
AHEHAXAM, IV, 207
Ahingaran, IV, 209
AHMAD KHAN, AHMED, Son of Yunus, IV, 166, 191
Ahmedābād, III, 78; IV, 173
AHMED bin Ayas, IV, 10, 11
AHMED, Hagi, I, 290
AHMED, Khan of Persia, I, 120
AHMED SHAH, I, 282, 283
AHMED SHAH DURANI, IV, 185, 207
AHSAN SHAH, IV, 34
Ahwáz, II, 109, 110
Aias, Aiazzo, I, 307; II, 115; III, 139, 159, 160, 161, 164
Aidháb, I, 306; IV, 3
Aidin, IV, 5
Ai Kul, IV, 229
Ai lao, I, 161
Aingaràm, Aingharàn, IV, 180, 209, 259
Ain Sindi, I, 241
AIRI SHAKARWATI, IV, 32
AITKEN, P. H., II, 43
Ajazzo, see Aias
Ajudahan, IV, 12
Ajudin, IV, 12
Akadra, I, 196
AKBAR, AKHBAR, I, 110, 197; IV, 18, 23, 151, 170, 172–8, 201–5, 207
Akbar Namah, IV, 216
AKBO, I, 71
Akche (Turkish coin), III, 161
AKČURA OGHLI, I, 140
Akhalia, IV, 153
Akhsi, IV, 235
Akhsua, I, 315
AKHTAKI, III, 127
Akhtuba, III, 82
A-ki-mi, IV, 235
Akjar, I, 316
Akkerkuf, III, 262
Akoli, III, 125
Akserai, III, 84
Aksu, see Aqsu
Ak-tagh, I, 209
Ala Aighir, IV, 229
Alabandinum, I, 228
ALA-BEG IBADAT KHAN, IV, 213
Aladagh, I, 289

ALA-EDDIN, ALA-UDDIN, of Delhi, II, 115, 143, 197; III, 69, 70
Alafa, III, 72
ALAGAKKONARA, I, 76
Al-Ahsa, III, 65; IV, 5
ALAHUSH, III, 15
Alai, plateau, I, 192
Ala Kul, Lake, I, 288, 289; IV, 163, 164
Alamut, I, 153; II, 258
ALANASHUN, I, 69, 70
Alanean Mountains, III, 184
Alanethi, III, 185
Alani-Scythae, III, 184
A-lan-na, III, 186; IV, 271
Ala Nor, IV, 160
Alans, I, 119, 167, 212; II, 199, 225; III, 15, 179–187, 210, 215, 248; IV, 271
Alāpur, IV, 22
Ala-tagh, I, 288, 289; IV, 163
Ala Tau, I, 288
ALA-UDDÍN, of Delhi, see ALA-EDDIN
ALA-UDDÍN of Almaliq, III, 125
ALA-UDDÍN (Ali Mubarak), IV, 85
ALA-UDDÍN FANCHÁN, III, 126
ALA-UDDÍN MUSAÚD, I, 78
ALA-UDDÍN TARMASHÍRÍN, IV, 9, 106
ALA-UL-MULK, IV, 9
Alawei, I, 74
Al-Azrak (*Blue* River), IV, 154
Al-Baidha, III, 84
Albani, III, 186
Albarbarah, pieces of gold, IV, 9
Al-Bayadi, I, 306
ALBEHDYLL, D', III, 220
ALBERICUS TRIUM FONTIUM, I, 149
AL-BIRUNI, I, 22, 33, 74, 127, 149, 151, 241, 242, 254, 256; II, 139, 180; IV, 164
ALBIZZI of Pisa, Bartholomew, II, 7, 9
ALBOIN, II, 4
ALBUQUERQUE, III, 8, 224
AL-BUSHRI, a Ceutan in China, IV, I, 2, 39, 128, 129
Alcala, IV, 173
Alcarone, II, 100, 101
Alcegher, IV, 229
Alceghet, IV, 227
AL-CHANSA, IV, 129
Al-Dabah, I, 306
Aldabra, II, 166
Aleana, I, 43
A-LE-KO-NAR, I, 76
Alep, Aleppo, I, 188; II, 223; III, 199, 226; IV, 3, 37, 45
ALEXANDER THE GREAT, I, 14, 31, 189, 193, 220, 304; II, 102, 114; III, 7, 218, 219, 229; IV, 123, 256
ALEXANDER de Caffa, Bishop, III, 14
ALEXANDER III, Pope, III, 17
Alexandria, I, 187, 216, 224, 254, 264, 306; II, 100, 122, 231; III, 167, 223, 224; IV, 2, 4
ALEXIS I, Emperor, I, 47, 57
ALEXIS II, II, 99
ALEXIS III, IV, 7
ALEXIS IV, IV, 7
Al-Faliq, III, 24
ALGU, IV, 161
ALHACEN, I, 33
Alhama, IV, 39
Al-Hirah, I, 84
ALI, Khalif, I, 84, 246; IV, 3
ALI, of Okkodai Stock, III, 33–35; IV, 162
ALI MIRZA, Shaikh, II, 164
ALI MUBARAK, IV, 85, 86
ALI SHAH of Lakhnaoti, IV, 84–6
ALI SHAH JABALÁN, III, 108
Aliabad, IV, 210
Al-i-Afrasyab, I, 148
Alībāg, I, 254
ALI BEG the Balúch, III, 127
A LIE KU NA EUL, I, 76
Aliga, river, IV, 72
Aligarh, IV, 20, 21
Alimali, III, 87
Alimatu, III, 87
ALISOLDA, III, 32, 34
Al-Jîr, I, 85
Al-Katif, III, 65; IV, 5
AL-KAZWINI, IV, 148
Al-Kharlokh, I, 249
Al-Khawarnak, I, 83
Al-Kûfah, I, 84
Alla, III, 145
Alla Apostolica, III, 243
Allania, I, 305
ALLEN'S *Indian Mail*, II, 144, 145
Alligators, II, 182
Al-Maïd, I, 136
AL-MALIK AL-ZAHIR, IV, 95, 96
Almaliq, Almalik, Almaligh, I, 154, 163, 171, 289; III, 13, 24, 31, 33, 35, 85, 87, 88, 89, 125, 148, 156, 190, 212, 213, 216, 225; IV, 137, 141, 160, 161, 165, 193, 235
Almaty, I, 288
ALMEIDA, Diego d', IV, 170
Almonds, III, 165
AL-NISWY, I, 33, 256
Aloes, I, 227, 243, 253; III, 7,

195, 245; IV, 96, 97, 99–101, 156
ALOPANO, ALOPENO (Olopen), I, 109
A'los, I, 272
Al'Othmániyah, IV, 131
ALPHONSO XI, IV, 38
Al-Rami, II, 146
Al-Rāmnī (Sumatra), I, 127; see Lambri
Altai, I, 64, 205, 208, 209, 308
ALTAMSH, I, 131
Al-Ubullah, I, 84
A-LU-CHI, II, 248
Alum Mines of Phocaea Nova, III, 44
Alu Wihara, III, 233
ALVAREZ, I, 218
Al-Wakin, I, 135
Alzarone, II, 100, 101
Am, III, 236
Amacao (Macao), IV, 242
Amarah, II, 110
Amarapura, II, 152, 219; IV, 147
AMARI, I, 241
Amarkantak, III, 221
AMAT DI S. FILIPPO, I, 290; II, 61, 62, 90, 92; III, 4
Amazons, I, 265
Amba, III, 236
Ambalám, III, 237
Ambassadors threatened with death for refusing to *kotow*, I, 90
Ambastes, River, I, 195
Amburan (Mango), III, 236
Amburanus, III, 236–7
Ameri, II, 146
Amethyst, I, 226
AMHERST, Lord, I, 134; IV, 121
Amir, II, 122; IV, 26, 67
Amjari, IV, 23
Amjhera, IV, 23
AMMIANUS MARCELLINUS, I, 15, 16, 21, 127, 203; III, 23, 248
Amol, I, 315
Amouïeh, I, 287
Amoy, II, 168
Amritsar, II, 143
Amroha, IV, 18
AMRU, III, 23
Amulets rendering invulnerable, II, 157
Amur, III, 24
Amwari, IV, 22
An, I, 4
Anabad, III, 160
Anāchāranirṇaya, II, 140
'Anah, in India, I, 243
'Anah, on the Euphrates, IV, 137
Analecta Franciscana, I, 156
ANANDA, III, 127
ANAN-JESUS II, Patriarch, I, 108
Anatolia, IV, 165
Anbár, on the Euphrates, IV, 137
Ancestors' skulls, I, 254; IV, 269
Anchediva, IV, 24, 72
Ancona, III, 166
ANÇUVARMAN, I, 60
Andagan, Andegan, I, 286, 287
Andaman Islands, I, 127; II, 168; IV, 93
Andar, IV, 9, 258
Andarab, Anderab, IV, 9, 209, 256–8
Andijan, I, 191, 286
Andijára, I, 315
ANDRADE, F. d', I, 180
ANDREW the Frank, III, 179, 180
ANDREW, Friar, III, 19
ANDREW of Florence, III, 5
ANDREW of Perugia, Bishop of Zaitún, I, 169, 170; II, 22, 183; III, 10, 11, 28, 71, 96, 100
ANDRONICUS the Elder, I, 120; IV, 7, 8
ANDRONICUS the Younger, IV, 8
Androstachyn, I, 227
ANDRUTIUS of Assisi, Bishop, III, 10, 75
Angamale, IV, 173
ANGKA WIJAYA, III, 193
Angkola, IV, 157
Anhilawara, I, 310
An-hsi (Parthia), I, 23, 41, 43
Anjára, I, 315
Anjediva, IV, 72; see Anchediva
Anjuman, IV, 256, 259
Ankjy, I, 273
Ankolah, IV, 72
Ankuah, Chief City of Sila, I, 131
Annales des Voyages, Nouv., I, 12, 212
Annales des Voyages, I, 220
Annales ecclésiastiques, I, 166
Annales Minorum, II, 22; see WADDING
Annali di Geog. e di Stat., II, 105
Annam, I, 4, 135; II, 256
Annesley Bay, I, 217
Anniba, I, 194, 203
Annibi, I, 195
ANNIUS PLOCAMUS, I, 199
Anniva, I, 203; see Anniba
Ansee, I, 306
Anser cygnoides, II, 181
An si (Parthia), I, 23, 41, 43; see Asi
Ansi chow, I, 117
ANSUINO da Forli, II, 142
Ant, I, 43

Anta, I, 43
Antarctic, II, 160
ANTHONY of Padua, St., II, 12, 32, 119, 165, 166
Anthumusia, I, 216
Antiaris toxicaria, II, 158
Antioch, I, 43, 44, 55, 158, 220, 234; III, 18
Antiocheia, I, 216
Antiphonarium, III, 49
Antipodes, I, 27; III, 260, 261
Antivari, III, 37
ANTONINA, III, 230
ANTONIO FERNANDEZ, I, 237
ANTONY of Monserrate, IV, 172, 173
ANTONY of Parma, III, 5
An ts'ai, III, 186
Antu (Antioch), I, 43, 234
ANTUN, I, 51, 193
Antwerp, II, 154
Anurajapura, I, 71, 227; III, 233, 242
ANVILLE, d', I, 24, 194; II, 227; IV, 228, 233, 234
Aornos, I, 243; III, 219
Aorsi, III, 186
A-PAO-KI, I, 147
Apes, II, 202, 203; III, 260
Apocalypse, I, 304
Apocrypha, II, 102
APO Kagan, I, 206
Apollinopolis Parva, IV, 4
Apollonia, I, 221
APOLLONIUS, II, 190, 240
Apologos, I, 84
A-PO-LO-PA, I, 92
Apostolorum, ad modum, III, 243
Apple of Paradise, III, 236
A P'U CH'A FO, I, 92
Apulia, III, 166, 169
Aqkala, III, 162
Aqsu, I, 40, 58, 62, 194, 251, 293, 311; III, 55; IV, 163, 183, 189, 190, 191, 227, 228, 229, 230, 231, 234
AQUAVIVA, Rudolf, IV, 172
Aquileia, II, 4, 6, 14
'Arábah, I, 276
Arabia, I, 83, 92, 102, 104, 126, 197, 199, 200, 220, 221; III, 22; IV, 36, 149
Arabic terms in Italian, IV, 59
Arabs, I, 48, 59, 61, 83, 89, 90, 97, 100, 151
ARABSHAH, I, 272; II, 116
Arafat, III, 228
Arakan, III, 174
Arakka, I, 276
Aral, I, 210, 211, 247, 288, 304, 315; III, 180, 184
Aramuth, IV, 238
Ararat, II, 30, 34, 102; III, 40, 41, 163, 197, 234, 246
Arasht, I, 247
Arauraci, III, 161
Arawaks, II, 147
Araxes, I, 31; III, 84, 163, 164, 198
Arba, III, 245
Arbela, I, 119; III, 22, 23
Arbil (Arbela), III, 23
Arbo, I, 308
Arbor Secco, II, 102, 103
Archbishops, of Socotra, III, 7; of the Nestorians, III, 22, 23; appointed by the Pope to Cambalec, III, 9 *seq.*; of Soltania, III, 36, 37, 89; of Armagh, III, 204
Archæological Journal, I, 167
Archipelago, I, 224, 253; II, 26, 31; III, 180
Archivio Storico Italiano, I, 124; II, 83
Archivio Veneto, II, 82
Arctic Sea, I, 300; II, 160
ARDASHIR, ARDESHIR, I, 94
Aren Palm, II, 157
Arequipa, Desert, II, 262
ARES, I, 217
ARFAXAT, III, 248
Argell, I, 225
Argellion (Coco Nut), I, 225
ARGHÚN Khan of Persia, I, 120, 166, 167, 208; II, 104; III, 4, 108, 119
Argis, Sea of, I, 304, 308
Argives, III, 265
Argons, III, 120, 121
ARGUTINSKY, I, 164
Argyrē, II, 151
Aria, I, 190
ARIAS SALDANHA, Viceroy of Portuguese India, IV, 199
ARIOSTO, III, 197
ARISTOTLE, I, 14, 198, 199; III, 205, 213, 266
ARJASP, King of Tartary, I, 10
Arjish, I, 308
Arkâun (Asiatic Christians), III, 120
Armâbyl, I, 136
Armagh, III, 204, 205, 206
Armalec, III, 31, 87, 88, 148, 156, 190, 212, 213, 216; see Almaliq
Armalech, III, 33, 89; see Almaliq
Armalek, III, 85; see Almaliq
Armenia, I, 92, 94, 95, 101, 161, 163, 216, 307, 308; II, 11, 97,

100, 118; III, 16, 22, 23, 160, 246
Armenia, Kingdom of Lesser, III, 139
Armenian families of Chinese origin, I, 94
Armenians, I, 20, 93, 94; II, 258; IV, 226
Armuza, II, 112
ARNÁIZ, G., I, 88; IV, 117
Arno, III, 178
ARNOBIUS, *Adversus Gentes*, I, 102, 104
ARNOLD of Cologne, III, 5, 14, 46
Aromatic Cape (Guardafui), I, 212
ARPOG, I, 94
Arramaniya, I, 243
Ar-Rán, III, 23
ARRIAN, I, 145, 146, 189; II, 133
ARROWSMITH, I, 310; III, 23
Arsinoê, I, 221
ARSLAN, Alan Prince, III, 187
Artag, I, 152
Artocarpus integrifolia, II, 139; III, 237
Artois, III, 199
Arts, Chinese skill in the, IV, 114
Aruê Haris (the Rhinoceros), I, 222
Arys, III, 147
Arzan-al-Rum (Erzrum), II, 100
Arzerone, III, 162
Arzinga, III, 161
Arziron, II, 100
Arz-ul-Hind, II, 111
Ascension Feast at Venice, II, 178
ASCIAR, Lord of Kail, III, 68
Asfarah, I, 272
Asfiria, I, 143
Asfrole, the word, III, 166
Asham, II, 105
Ashkal, I, 246
Ashparah, I, 272; see Asparah
A-SHU, III, 133
Ashurada, II, 105
Asi, People called, I, 23; III, 185, 248; see An si
Asia, I, 221; III, 246
Asia, Central; see Central Asia
Asia Minor, II, 263; III, 186; IV, 5
Asia, Upper, IV, 182
Asiatic Researches, II, 173
A-si-yen, IV, 231, 271
A-si-you, IV, 190, 231, 271
Askhra, I, 143
Asmira, Asmiraea, Asmiraeus, I, 195, 203
Asmiraean Mountains, I, 194
ASOKA, I, 10
Aspacara, I, 195
Asparah, I, 272, 287, 288
Asper, III, 158, 159, 161
Asphaltites, Lake, II, 115
Aspidium Baromez, II, 242
Aspithra, I, 143, 195, 196
ASQUINI, Life of Odoric, II, 6, 8, 15, 16, 20, 24, 85
As-Sadir, I, 83
Assam, I, 79, 243, 253, 254; IV, 96, 101, 151, 152
ASSAMBEI, Lord, I, 178
Assassins, I, 153; II, 257, 258; IV, 161
ASSEMANI, I, 26, 101, 103, 104, 108, 109, 121, 127, 308; II, 107, 109, 118, 129, 132, 133, 136, 177; III, 17, 23
Aš-ŠIRKI, I, 2
Assisi, III, 81, 205
Assuan, I, 306
Assyria, I, 189, 198; III, 22, 225, 226, 265
ASTLEY'S *Voyages*, I, 179, 276, 280, 281, 282, 283, 286, 298; II, 23, 85, 184, 199, 205, 212, 238, 245; IV, 194
Astrabad, I, 190
Astracan, Astrakhan, I, 308; III, 82, 84, 146, 147, 198; IV, 7, 49; see Gittarchan
Astrologers at the Great Khan's Court, II, 239
Astronomy in India and China, I, 2
Asu (the Alans), III, 15, 185, 186, 248; see Alans
Asuk, IV, 229
A-sze, III, 248; see Alans
Atabek, title, IV, 139
Atak, IV, 203
Atak Banāras, IV, 203
Atalas, IV, 118
Ata Sufi, I, 272; IV, 238
Atcheh, Atjeh, I, 152; II, 146
Atha, Father, II, 200, 201; IV, 132
ATHANASIUS, St., I, 212, 221; II, 34, 100; III, 226
Athás (Alves), IV, 100, 101
Athec (Attok), IV, 203
Athenæum, The, IV, 269
Athil, Atil, Attila, I, 212, 245, 307; II, 242; IV, 6
Athos, Mount, IV, 223
Athur (Nineveh), III, 23
Atlass (Satin), IV, 118
Atropatenian Ecbatana, III, 232
Attock, Attok, I, 74, 242; IV, 180, 181, 203
Aú, IV, 21
AUGUSTINE, St., III, 44, 197, 243, 245, 249, 254, 260
AUGUSTUS, I, 18; III, 263

AUHAD-UDDÍN of Sinjár, IV, 122, 125
Aujan, II, 105
Aulie-Ata, I, 60; IV, 190
AURANGZIB, IV, 18, 258
Aurantia, II, 115
Aureus, I, 229
Aurungabad, I, 242
AUSTIN, *Map of Balti*, I, 310
Auxacia, I, 194; IV, 228
Auxacian Mountains, I, 194, 195
Auxacius, I, 203
Auxerre, II, 199
Auxumê, I, 213
Auxumites, I, 213
Ava, I, 151, 177, 183, 243, 266, 302; II, 106, 236; III, 221
AVALŌKITÊCVARA, III, 269
Avars, I, 208
Avelines, III, 97
Avellino, III, 97
AVEZAC, d', I, 152, 156; II, 9, 28, 87; III, 37; IV, 163, 235
AVIENUS, Rufus Festus, I, 183, 201; III, 219
Avignon, II, 12, 27; III, 81, 188, 190, 199, 200, 206, 207, 210, 216
AVITABILE, Gen. IV, 204
Awat, IV, 238
AWIS KHAN, A'WYS KHAN, I, 272; IV, 165
Awliya-Ata, I, 60; IV, 190
Axam, II, 105
Axoum, Axum, I, 184, 216–220, 222, 223
Axoumites, Axumites, I, 216, 218
Aydip, I, 306; see Aidhab
Ayin Akbari, I, 151; IV, 22, 176; on Passes of Hindu Kush, IV, 255, 257
Aykotta, IV, 78
A'yl, I, 272
AYMONIER, E., II, 164, 167
Aymul Guja, IV, 163, 165
Ayodhya, I, 124
AYUBITE, Sultans, I, 49
AYUR BALIBATRA, III, 10
AZÁR, II, 115
Azerbaidjan, I, 119; III, 22; IV, 139
Azes, III, 15; see Asu
Azetrechan, III, 147
Azimabad, II, 249
Azov, I, 179, 305; III, 81, 84, 150, 169, 225; IV, 6; see Tana

Babel, Tower of, II, 110; III, 209, 263
BABELON, *Monnaies grecques*, I, 229
BABER, BĀBAR, Sultan, I, 210; II, 139, 234, 262, 263; III, 237; IV, 18, 142, 205, 207, 255, 257
Babillonia, I, 306
Babirussa, I, 224
Babul, III, 263
Babylon, I, 34, 84, 216; II, 106, 110; III, 199, 241, 262, 263, 269; IV, 4
Babylonia, III, 252
Babylonian Record, I, 11
Bacanor, Baccanor, IV, 73
Baccadeo, III, 165
Baccam, II, 148
BACCHUS, III, 219
Bacharata, IV, 211
Bachian, IV, 157
BACHU NOIAN, I, 163
BACKER, Louis de, II, 72, 81, 82; III, 36
BACON, Roger, II, 23; III, 225, 240
Bactra, I, 190, 192, 286
Bactria, I, 4, 16, 17, 183; III, 252
Bactriana, I, 36, 65, 183, 192, 194; IV, 256
Bactrians, I, 104, 215, 220
Bacu, Bacuc, Bacuk, Sea of, II, 105, 211; III, 84, 224
Badakhshan, I, 36, 72, 191, 248, 286, 287, 303, 311, 313–5, 318; II, 188, 263; III, 21; IV, 160, 180–6, 191, 210, 211, 213, 215, 256, 258, 259
Bad-baft, I, 197
BADGER, Rev. G. P., I, 33, 124, 178, 255; II, 117, 166, 196, 223; III, 243; IV, 223
Badhaghis, I, 205
Badja, I, 129, 244
Badli, IV, 13
Ba'fu, I, 276
Bağā, I, 244
Bagbel, III, 263
Bagdag, III, 263
BAGHAR, I, 2
Bagharghar, I, 247
BAGHBAR ibn Kamād, I, 2
Baghbugh, Baghbúr, Baghbour (Emperor of China), I, 33, 141, 142, 143, 256; see **Facfur**
Baghdad, I, 34, 42, 119–121, 153, 170, 262, 304, 308; II, 10, 30, 102, 110, 112, 178; III, 23, 24, 108, 119, 125, 156, 199, 262, 263; IV, 3, 36, 87, 133, 137, 139
Baghlán, I, 315; IV, 257, 258
Baghrač, I, 246
Baghraj, I, 246

Bagh Shurá, I, 140, 141
Baglana, I, 242
Bağnak, I, 244, 245
Bagni, II, 199; IV, 267
Bagratch, Lake, IV, 234
Bagratidae, I, 246
Bahāwalpur, IV, 10
Bahi, I, 251; IV, 190
Bahmanabad, I, 255
Bahmian, IV, 256
Bahrain, Bahrein, I, 85; III, 68; IV, 5
Bahr-al-Azrak, IV, 154
Bahr-al-Kâhil, IV, 103, 158
BAHRAM, I, 115
BAHRÂM GÛR, I, 83
Bahri, I, 230
Bahr Kolzum, I, 221
BAHU I, II, 170
BAHU II, II, 170
BAHU III, II, 170; IV, 32
BAHU IV, II, 170
BAHU V, I, 76, 77; see BHUWANEKA
BAHU VI, I, 76, 77
Bai, I, 251; IV, 189, 190, 230, 231
BAIAN, BAIAM, III, 119; IV, 129
Baiburt, I, 307
Baikal, III, 246
BAIKOV, F. I., I, 181
Bainiel, I, 119
Bairam, III, 86; IV, 23, 64
Bairami, IV, 19
Bairam Katlú, IV, 129, 149
BAIRAM KHAN, IV, 85
BAISANGAR, I, 278, 280
Baiwam Kotlú, IV, 129, 149
Baja, I, 244
Bajah, cap. of the Faghfur, I, 143, 256
Bajalisah, IV, 22
Bajarma, III, 23
Bajaruck, IV, 256
BAJAZET, I, 174
Bajga, IV, 257
Bajnak (Pechinegs), I, 244, 246; see Baja, Badja
Bakanur, I, 309
Bakar, IV, 10
BAKER, Gen. W. E., III, 221
Bakhar, IV, 10
Bakhshy, Bakshi, II, 250, 251; IV, 105, 135, 242, 268
BAKHTIYAR KHILJI, I, 78, 79; IV, 152
Bak Sings, I, 8
Baku (the Caspian), II, 105; III, 84, 224, 225; see Bacu, Bacuc
BAKUI, Arabian geographer, I, 34; II, 104, 133, 139
BALAAM, I, 224
Balaçācāghun, Balāsāghūn, Bala Sagun, I, 60; III, 21; IV, 163, 164
Balacian, IV, 216
Balaclava, Balaklava, I, 305; III, 14
Balad-ul-Falfal, I, 226
Balaerpatan, IV, 76
Balara, IV, 13
Balarghui, III, 122
Balāsāghūn, see Balaçācāghun
BALBAN, Emperor, III, 132
BALBI, Gasparo, I, 81; II, 114, 140, 145, 174; III, 252
Balchimkin, I, 305
Baldach, I, 304, 308; see Baghdad
BALDAEUS, III, 219, 220
Baldassia, I, 303; see Badakhshan
BALDELLI BONI, I, 82, 122, 165, 301; II, 177, 192, 214, 219; III, 138, 195
BALGRAM, IV, 204
BALHARA, I, 241, 243
Balian, I, 315
Balis, Balish, II, 196–8, 210–211; III, 149, 154; IV, 112
Balkash, Balkhash, Lake, I, 288, 289; IV, 162, 235
Balkh, I, 98, 108, 110, 123, 182, 190, 191, 205, 271, 286, 287, 315; III, 22, 24; IV, 160, 184
Ballabhipura, I, 241
Ballabhiráa or raja, I, 241
Ballád-ul-Jibal, II, 257
Ballarò, Piazza, I, 241
Balledirucco, III, 170
Balliangot, IV, 78
Balmannac, Balmerino, Balmerynac, III, 170
Baltachinta, I, 305
Balti, I, 71, 310, 314; IV, 177
Baltic, III, 246
Baltistan, IV, 217, 267
Baluristan, I, 314
BALUZE, II, 85; III, 38
BALZANI, Count Ugo, II, 89
Bamblunah (Cairo), III, 263
Bamboo, II, 160, 161
Bamian, I, 98, 277; II, 153, 263; IV, 205, 255, 257–9
Bamir, I, 313
Bāmyin (Badaghis), I, 205
Banāt Na's, I, 245
Bandan, I, 176; II, 155
Bandar Kanching, II, 147
BANDI, III, 68
BANDINI, I, 123, 231
BANDURI, I, 46, 47, 245
Banga, IV, 152

Banga Bazar, IV, 153
Bangala, I, 302
Bangamati, IV, 152
Bangán, I, 285
Baniachong, IV, 152
Banjarmasin, Banjermasin, II, 156, 161
Banjhir, IV, 209, 258; see Panchshir
BANSHOA, I, 132, 133
Bantam, II, 155
Baptisms, in Tartary, II, 262; in Cathay, III, 46, 55, 74; in India, III, 57; of a Brahmin at Columbum, III, 257; of people at Kamul, conditions regulating, III, 266
Bara, III, 145
Barah Nagar, IV, 93
Barak, IV, 151–3
BARÁK KHAN, IV, 161
BARAKSAIS, IV, 207
Barámasí, III, 40
Bārā Stream, IV, 204
BARATTA, M. C., IV, 171
BARBARO, Josafat, I, 151, 178, 179, 269; II, 98, 104, 107, 108, 211; III, 185; IV, 201
Barbarrah, IV, 211
Barbary, I, 212, 213, 214, 217, 218
Barberyn, III, 231
BARBIER DE MEYNARD, I, 84, 135, 137, 248
BARBOSA, I, 86; II, 133, 174; III, 253; IV, 159
Barcelor, I, 309; IV, 73
Barchium, I, 306
Barchuk, Barchuq, IV, 228, 229
Barda'a, III, 23
BARDI, III, 140, 143
Bar-el-Moli, IV, 155
Bargelidoa, I, 310
Barkálah, IV, 111
BAR KALIQ, I, 119
Barki, IV, 95
Barkul, Lake, I, 35, 39, 58; III, 213; IV, 239
Bārkūr, IV, 73
Barley, IV, 232
Barmiciacche, Barmunacche, III, 170
Barnacle geese, II, 241–4
Baroch, I, 87, 227, 309; IV, 63
Baroghil, I, 61; IV, 216, 259
Baromez, II, 242
BARONIUS, III, 17, 18
Barrel of Horn, II, 187, 188
BARROS, II, 146, 160; IV, 156
BARROW, II, 197, 201, 212
BARTA of Edessa, I, 95
BARTH, A., II, 83, 142
BARTH, Dr., IV, 144
BARTHOLD, I, 60, 140
BARTHOLOMEW, Apostle, I, 101
BARTHOLOMEW, Bishop of Khanbaliq, III, 14
BARTHOLOMEW, Bishop of Maraga, III, 76
BARTHOLOMEW of Pisa (Albizzi), II, 258; III, 31
BARTHOLOMEW the Florentine, I, 178
BARTHOLOMEW of Santo Concordio, III, 58
BARTHOLOMEW of Tivoli, I, 306
BARTOLI, D., I, 237
Barus in Sumatra, IV, 157
Barygaza, I, 183, 227, 230
Basahí, IV, 13
Bascon, Sea of (Caspian), II, 105
Bashiar, I, 143
Bashkird, I, 307
Bashkirs, I, 308
Basil, II, 116
BASIL, Emperor, IV, 7
Basra, Basrah, Bassorah, I, 84, 85, 137, 309; II, 111, 112; III, 22, 23, 180, 228; IV, 3, 4, 36, 39
Bassano, II, 267
Bassein, I, 177; IV, 173
BASSET, René, II, 114
BASTARD, Count de, II, 70
BASTIAN, Dr., I, 111; II, 147
Baswánán, IV, 127
Batae, I, 195
Batak, Battaks, II, 149, 168, 173; IV, 157
Batang, II, 156
Bat-da-lik, I, 54
Batharekah, Bathric, Bathrik, Bathirak, I, 54
Bathenians, II, 257
Batkul, IV, 73
Bats, II, 116
Batta Country, IV, 97
Battecala, Bathecala, IV, 72, 73
Batthálah, IV, 32
BATU, I, 152, 154, 156, 158, 163, 208, 209, 289; III, 82, 119, 248
Batúma, I, 128
Baudas, I, 262; III, 156; see Baghdad
BAUDRAND, I, 182
Baurawa, I, 242
Bautes, Bautis River, I, 194, 203
Bawal, Bawul, III, 68, 70
Bawurah, I, 242
BAYAM, Baian, III, 119; IV, 129
BÁYÁN FANCHÁN, III, 122, 126
Bayazid, III, 162–4

Bazarak, IV, 255–7, 259
Bazarra, III, 145
Bdellium, III, 224
Beacon Towers in China, II, 233
BEAL, S., II, 157
BEAMES, John, I, 80
Beasts and Monsters, Strange, II, 229–30; III, 254
Beatification of Odoric, II, 15 *seq.*, 35 *seq.*
BEATRICE of Bavaria, II, 14
Beauty of Women, of China, II, 179; of Thafan, I, 242
BEAZLEY, C. R., I, 12, 157, 214, 232; II, 40, 225; III, 202
BEDE, III, 197
Bednur, IV, 73
Bedr, IV, 3
Beersheba, II, 130, 179
Begia, I, 306
BEHAIM, Martin, II, 154
Behar, I, 68
Beirami, IV, 19
Beitkul, IV, 72
Bejah, I, 230, 306
BEL, III, 263
Belal, III, 66
Bela-Sagun, see Balaçăcăghun
Beler, III, 84
Belgian, Desert of, I, 259, 262
Belgium, III, 206
Beliamcor, IV, 78
BELKIS, Arab Legend of Queen, III, 264, 265
BELL of Antermony, John, II, 199
BELLARMINE, III, 243
BELLEW, Dr., IV, 210
Bells, for petitioners at the Emperor's or Governor's gate, I, 131; in Churches at Zaitún, III, 229; an abomination to the Mahomedans, III, 230; IV, 6
Belsa, II, 188
BELTIS, III, 265
BELUS, III, 263, 264
BENAKETI, III, 131
Benbij, I, 307
Bencoolen, IV, 151
Bendor, IV, 73
BENEDICT X, Pope, III, 209
BENEDICT XI, Pope, III, 209
BENEDICT XII, Pope, III, 13, 28, 33, 34, 85, 187, 188
BENEDICT XIV, Pope, II, 17
BENEDICT the Pole, Friar, I, 156; III, 49; IV, 70
Bengal, I, 78–80, 124, 177, 184, 230, 303, 310; IV, 36, 67, 80, 149, 150, 153, 154, 176
Bengala, I, 79, 124, 303, 309; II, 180; III, 132
Bengalla, I, 177
Beni Suef, I, 306
BENJAMIN of Tudela, I, 45, 46, 47, 144; II, 102, 133, 251, 258
Bentam, II, 156
Bentotte, III, 231
BENTWORTH, R., III, 205
Benzab, I, 307
Benzoin, IV, 97–99
Berberah, I, 217
BERCHEM, Max van, IV, 118
Berchimam, I, 308
Berenicê, I, 221, 306
BERGERON, II, 250
BERGHAUS, II, 213; IV, 227
BERMAL, III, 69
BERNARD, I, 122; II, 214; see BERNARDINO della CHIESA
BERNARD of Gardiola, III, 76
BERNARDIGGI, Conrad, II, 13
BERNARDINO della CHIESA, I, 122; II, 214
BERNARDUS, Bishop of Khan Baliq, III, 14
BERNIER, I, 292
Bersi, III, 62
Berthas, I, 245
Beruwala, III, 231
Berwick, North, III, 170
Besadae, I, 185
Besh Tau, IV, 6
Besidae, I, 183, 184
Besidiae (Bisignano), III, 200
Beth-Garma, I, 189; III, 22, 23
Beth-Seleucia, III, 22, 23
Bethlehem, I, 44, 45, 162; III, 269; IV, 174
BETOUAL, I, 9
Betoumah, I, 128; II, 156
Beu, II, 248
BEYALÚN, IV, 7
Beypur, IV, 77
Bezoar, I, 246, 251; II, 162
Bhághalpúr, II, 163
Bhamo, I, 177
Bharoch, I, 230
Bharuch, III, 76
Bharukachha, III, 76
Bhatkal, IV, 73
Bhattiāna, IV, 12
Bhikshu, II, 250; IV, 105, 269
Bhind, IV, 22
Bhotiya, I, 184
BHUWANEKA BAHU I, II, 170; see BAHU
—— BAHU II, II, 170
—— BAHU V, I, 76, 77
Biana, IV, 21

BIANCHI, G., abbate, II, 14
—— Bishop of Udine, II, 16
BIANCO, Andrea, Map, II, 130; III, 85, 197
Bibliography of Cosmas, I, 231; of Odoric, II, 59–96; of Marignolli, III, 208; of Ibn Batuta, IV, 52–3; of Goës, IV, 194–7
Bibliotheca Sinica; see CORDIER, Henri
Bibliothèque de l'École des Chartes, II, 83
BICASSINI, Nicolas, III, 209
Bidr, I, 310
Biduini, II, 207
Bielaya, I, 308
Bielo Osero, III, 247
Bigni, II, 199; IV, 267
Bijalár, III, 131, 132
Bijder, I, 310
Bikan, I, 285
BIK KHWAJA THUSI, III, 126
Bilal, I, 82
BILAL DEO, IV, 24
Bilaur, I, 314
Bilugtu, I, 272
Bimlifatan, Bimlipatam, III, 132
Bindanajo, III, 144
Binh Thudu, II, 163, 164, 167
Bintang, II, 155, 156
Biographie universelle, II, 87
Biolanda, III, 171
BIOT, Ed., *Dict.*, II, 205, 208, 212, 213, 215
Bir, I, 307
Bira, I, 307
BIRCH, S., I, 10
Bird with two Heads, Origin of Story, II, 173
Birs Nimrud, II, 110; III, 262, 263
Biru, II, 156
Birypur, IV, 21
Bisades, I, 183, 184
Bishbaliq, I, 163, 195; III, 133; IV, 140, 141, 160, 163, 188, 235
Bishdagh, IV, 6
Bishop, Sovereign, in China (G. Lama), III, 93
Bishops appointed by the Pope to Cathay, III, 9–10; venerated in the East, III, 215
Bishop of the Saracens, II, 117; III, 86
Bisignano, III, 177, 200, 205, 206, 209
BITCHOURIN, II, 252
BITHYNI, I, 151
Bivalse, III, 171
Biyardáwal, IV, 35
Black Clothes of N. Chinese, I, 30, 31
Black Death, III, 254; IV, 37
Black Irtysh, I, 59
BLACK JOHN, III, 26
Black Mountain, IV, 192
Black Sea, I, 300, 305; II, 242; III, 81, 180, 190; IV, 6
Black and White City Walls in Tibet, II, 248
BLAEU, I, 291, 308
BLAGDEN, C. O., I, 129; II, 147
BLASISH, Ferd., II, 90
Blemmyes, I, 230
BLOCHET, E., I, 45; III, 112
Blow Tube for Arrows, II, 158
Blue Nile, IV, 154
Blue River, IV, 90, 151
Bocca, II, 222
BOCCACCIO, I, 173
Bocca Tigris, I, 173
Bó chánh quân, II, 163
BOCHANOS, I, 206
Bochara, see Bokhara
Bod, II, 247, 250
BOGHRA KHAN, I, 59, 60, 246; IV, 222
BOGLE, II, 251, 253
Bogra District, IV, 176
Bogtak, II, 223; IV, 267
BOHA-ADDÍN KANDÁRI, III, 126
Bohemia, III, 177, 199, 201, 209, 247
BOHN, I, 144; II, 34
Bohrahs, IV, 64
Bokhara, I, 23, 60, 71, 90, 101, 138, 139, 163, 181, 293, 296, 297; III, 121; IV, 9, 162, 164, 183, 186, 187, 201, 210, 211, 212, 213, 225, 228
Bokhara, Little, IV, 187
Bokju, I, 286
Bolar, III, 84
BOLDENSEL, II, 34
BOLESLUZKY, Matthias, III, 201
Bolgar, Bolghar, I, 307; III, 84; IV, 6
Bolgari, IV, 6
Bolin, IV, 8
BOLLAERT, II, 262
Bologna, II, 184; III, 200, 255
Bolor, I, 90, 98, 100, 150, 311, 313, 314, 316, 317; IV, 182, 187, 188, 216
Bolor Tagh, I, 35; IV, 186
Bombain, Cape, II, 114
Bombay, I, 220, 227, 254; II, 114; III, 78; IV, 254, 256
Bombycina, I, 198
BONAPARTE, Prince Roland, I, 166, 167

BONET, Jean, *Dict. annamite*, II, 234
BONET, Nicholas, III, 188, 189
BONIN, III, 53
BONSAET, III, 160; see ABU SAID
Book of the Estate of the Great Khan, III, 89
BORÁK KHAN, IV, 162
Borametz or Lamb-Plant, II, 241; see Agnus scythicus
Borassus flabelliformis, IV, 71
Borassus Gomuti, II, 157
Borazán Tract, IV, 222
Borchara, I, 297; see Bokhara
Borgar, I, 307
Borneo, I, 244; II, 10, 147, 156, 157, 161, 162, 168, 174; IV, 158, 159
Boro Bodor, II, 153
BORONITU, IV, 185
Borysthenes, III, 158
BOSELLI, II, 62
Bos grunniens, I, 223
Bostam, I, 190
Bostra, I, 43
Botenigo, II, 151
Botm, I, 315
Botterigo, II, 151
BOUILLEVAUX, II, 167
BOUSSAY, BOUSSAYE, III, 89, 90, 96; see ABU SAID
BOUVET, II, 209
BOVENSCHEN, A., II, 91
BOWRING, J., I, 277
Boxitae, IV, 135
Bozai Gumbaz, IV, 211
Bracalor, IV, 73
Brachmans, Bragmans, I, 214; II, 240; III, 245
BRADDELL, I, 124
BRADSHAW, Henry, II, 39
BRAHMA, III, 198, 222
Brahmaputra, I, 310; III, 198, 222; IV, 151, 152, 176
Brahmini Bulls, II, 138
Bramador, II, 262
Brambanan, IV, 71
Bramma, I, 195
Branchicha, I, 305
BRANDA ABEDULA, IV, 201
Branki, I, 305
Bransko, I, 305
BRANT, II, 99, 100, 102
Bras, Island, II, 146
Brass, I, 227
Brazil, Brazil Wood, II, 137, 148, 174; III, 62, 195, 252, 253
Bread in Tibet, I, 248; IV, 268
Brenta, II, 267
Breslau, I, 152
BRETSCHNEIDER, E., I, 98, 148, 164; II, 216, 219; IV, 164; *Arabs*, I, 33, 48, 60, 62, 64, 87, 89, 91, 92, 131, 164, 248; II, 172, 234, 243, 248, 258; III, 13; *Botan. Sin.*, II, 200; *Táng*, I, 89; *Notes and Queries*, I, 89, 95; *Peking*, II, 217, 220
BRIBTSUN, I, 60
Bricks dug for at Babylon, III, 261
Bridal Ceremonies, Malay, IV, 147
Bridge, Natural, I, 315, 318
Bridges of Cansay, I, 195; III, 229
BRIGGS, *Firishta*, I, 78; II, 135, 143
Brisom, I, 307
Broach, III, 76
Brocades, II, 106
BROCARD, III, 38
BROSSET, I, 164
Broussonetia papyrifera, I, 298
BROWN, Sir T., *Vulgar Errors*, II, 184, 208, 241
Bruarata, IV, 211
BRUCKER, J., I, 313
Brunei, IV, 159
BRUNET, *Manuel*, II, 59
Brussa, IV, 2
Brussels, II, 186
BRUT the Trojan, I, 151
BRYENNIUS CAESAR, I, 57
BUCAI, III, 119
BUCHANAN, F., IV, 72
BUCHANAN, Hamilton, III, 222
Buchara, IV, 213; see Bokhara
BUCHON, I, 299, 300
Buda, I, 122
BUDDHA, I, 66, 67, 68, 76, 164, 278; III, 233, 235; IV, 201
BUDDHA, Images of, III, 94, 232–3; Colossal, I, 164, 277, 294; II, 184
BUDDHA's Fort, III, 242
BUDDHAGOSA, I, 67
Buddh-Gaya, III, 242
Buddhism, introduced into China, I, 66; resemblance of rites to those of Catholicism, IV, 200–1; confounded with Christianity, IV, 201; in Turkestan, IV, 191; at Khotan, IV, 191
Buddhist Monks, their sanctity, I, 295; III, 57, 94, 233, 234, 242, 243, 260
—— Monastery at Cansay and strange exhibition there, I, 202; III, 260
—— Pilgrims from China to India, and their narratives, I, 74 *seq.*; IV, 17

Buffalo, I, 223
Buffetania, III, 40
Bugor, IV, 238
Bukhara, IV, 164; see Bokhara
BUKU KHAN, IV, 164
BULAJI, IV, 165, 189
Bulandshahr, IV, 21
Bulgarians, I, 221, 245, 246
Bulletin École franç. Ext. Orient, I, 5, 8, 66, 74, 75, 152, 157, 167, 168, 173
Bulletin Soc. Anth., II, 256
Bulletin Géog. hist. et desc., I, 300
Bulletin Soc. Géog., I, 127; II, 154
Bulletin Soc. Géog. commerciale, II, 204
Bull Stag, I, 223
BU MIN, I, 58
BUNBURY, I, 189; III, 186
Bundelkhand, IV, 21, 22
Buntus, II, 98
BUNYAN, John, II, 263
BUONO da Forli, II, 142
Bura, I, 143
BURCHARD, Friar, I, 307; II, 22; III, 7, 27, 38
BÜRCK, *Polo*, I, 141
Burdwan, III, 40
Burgania, IV, 211
Burgaria, I, 305
Burgavia, IV, 211
Burhánpur, IV, 64, 177
BURHÁN-UDDÍN, IV, 138, 141, 145, 185
BURHÁN-UDDÍN of Kazerun, IV, 120
BURHÁN-UDDÍN of Sagharj, IV, 89, 90
Burjbúrah, IV, 21
BURLEY, Walter, III, 205
Burma, Burmah, I, 53, 111, 177, 243, 273, 277, 280; II, 143, 219, 255; III, 80, 244, 256; IV, 136, 201, 242
Burmese, II, 162; III, 222
BURNELL, II, 134, 135
BURNES, I, 17, 250, 310, 313; II, 153, 234, 262–4; III, 23, 221; IV, 205, 206, 257
BURTON, II, 149, 155
BUSAÍD, III, 160; see ABU SAÍD
BUSBECK, Auger Gislen, de, I, 181, 274, 296, 298; II, 100; III, 48, 49; IV, 243
BUSCAREL, I, 167, 208
Busching's Mag., I, 255
Búsh, I, 306
BUSHELL, S. W., I, 71; II, 227
Bushire, IV, 120
Bussi, I, 306
BUTAN KHAN, III, 33, 34, 35
Butifilis, I, 309
Buya Kataur, IV, 205
BUYAN KULI, III, 34; IV, 162
Buyar, Lake, III, 20
BUZAN OGLU, III, 34
BUZUN, III, 34; IV, 161
Byland, III, 171
Byrám, I, 272
Byrampaut, IV, 19
Byssus, I, 202; II, 243
Byzantine History, Passage of, in Annals of China, I, 48
Byzantium, I, 44, 45, 56, 59, 147, 188, 189, 190, 204, 205, 207, 208, 211, 212, 216

Cabal, III, 131
CABATON, A., *Chams*, II, 167
CABOT, I, 181
Cabul, II, 234; IV, 207, 218, 226
Cachanfu, I, 292
Cachar, IV, 152, 153, 154
Cacianfu, I, 292
Caciz, the word, IV, 223
CADAMOSTO, A., I, 219; III, 259
Cade, I, 308
Cadegi Indi, I, 185
Cadeli, II, 240, 242
Cadi (Kazi), used by Odoric, II, 117
Cadini, III, 86
Cadungalor, II, 135
Cael, II, 129; see Cail
CAESAR, I, 199
Caferstam, IV, 204
Caffa, I, 293, 305; II, 105; III, 143, 155, 158, 159, 169, 190, 211, 224, 230; IV, 6
Cafiso, Measure so-called, III, 159
Caga (Gogo), III, 78; IV, 64
Cahyapos, II, 147
Cail, II, 129; III, 65, 68; IV, 35
Cailac, I, 287–9; IV, 233, 235, 271
CAIN, I, 151; III, 194, 242, 244, 245
Caindu, I, 249
Cairo, I, 306; III, 224, 229, 263; IV, 2, 4, 5; see Babylon
ÇAKTISIṂHA, I, 73
Cala Ataperistan, II, 106
Calabria, III, 169, 200
Calacresti, III, 163
Calah, III, 23
Calajan, I, 301
Calamina, II, 34
Calamit, I, 305
Calamy, II, 34
Calao, II, 173

Calcha, people, IV, 213
Calcia, IV, 183, 210–212, 259
Calcutta, II, 145, 249; III, 243; IV, 183, 256
Calder Abbey, III, 171
Calderea, III, 171
CALDWELL, Dr., II, 130
Calecoulam, IV, 79
Calicut, I, 78, 87; II, 133; III, 218, 249; IV, 2, 24, 26, 27, 36, 67, 77, 149, 201
CALIXTUS, Pope, III, 252
Callirrhoe, I, 308
Pseudo-Callisthenes, I, 183
CALLISTUS NICEPHORUS, I, 29
Calm Sea, IV, 103, 158
Camalls, III, 241
Camar, I, 300
Camara, II, 108
Cambalec, Cambalech, Cambaliech, Cambalu, Cambaluc (Khan baliq, Pe King), I, 172, 174, 175, 181, 265, 266, 269, 301; II, 10, 11, 118, 200, 202, 215, 216, 228, 235, 245, 270; III, 3, 5, 7, 9, 11, 13, 14, 22, 34, 46, 48, 51, 58, 71, 73, 75, 90, 97, 100, 101, 130, 149, 153, 181, 187–9, 191, 210, 213–6; IV, 236, 270
Cambaleschia (Cambalec), I, 175, 266
Cambasci, IV, 227, 228, 229
Cambay, I, 86, 309; III, 78, 229; IV, 3, 21, 22–24, 173, 254
Cambodia, I, 66, 77, 128; II, 32, 156, 157, 161, 164; III, 221; IV, 96, 101, 155–8
Camechu, III, 148; see Kan Chau
Cameleopard, I, 223
Camels, III, 241
Camexu, III, 148, 156; IV, 241; see Kan chau
Caminietz, I, 305
Cammucca, Camocas, Camocato, III, 99, 155; IV, 17
Campa, II, 163
Campangunghi, IV, 146
CAMPBELL, A. G., II, 147
Camphor, I, 244, 253, 267; II, 148, 153; III, 195; IV, 95, 96, 98–100
Campichu, I, 277; III, 148
Campicion, Canpicion, I, 291; III, 128
Campion, I, 291, 293, 294, 296
Campsay, Camsay, Cansa, Cańsai, Cansay, I, 171, 172; II, 192, 201, 202; III, 90, 97, 126, 148, 149, 229, 248, 260
Can-sanghi Cascio, IV, 219, 220
Camul, I, 249, 293; IV, 239
Camuzoni, III, 164
Canada, I, 305
Canal, of China, the great, II, 213; III, 115; IV, 136
Cananor, IV, 24, 76
Canara, II, 140
Canbasci, IV, 227; see Cambasci
Canbetum, I, 309
Canceo, Canceu, IV, 241, 250; see Kan chau
Candia, III, 158
CANDIDO, Giovanni, II, 90
CANDIDUS, Guido, Bishop of Udine, II, 16
ČANDRAGUPTA, I, 6, 73; see CHANDRAGUPTA
Canes, very long, II, 160
Cangerecora, IV, 74
Can Grande, II, 218
Cangue, I, 279
Canine Philosophers, III, 249
Canis Magnus, II, 217
Cannamela, I, 307
Cannanore, IV, 24, 76
Cannibal Islands, II, 14
Cannibalism, II, 149, 168, 253
Cannibals, II, 148
Cannibal Scythians, I, 196, 197
Canope, I, 245
Canpichu, IV, 241; see Kan chau
Cansio, I, 302
Cantar, III, 157
Canton, I, 39, 51, 86, 88, 89, 92, 112, 135, 143, 173, 180, 256, 258; II, 10, 133, 179, 180, 181, 187, 213, 231; III, 72, 115, 126, 128–130, 221, 249; IV, 25, 68, 109, 118, 120–3, 149, 242, 245, 251; Mosque, IV, 122
Cap of the great Khan, Precious, II, 271
Capelang, I, 177
Cape Notion, I, 195
Capetalcol, IV, 228, 229
Capetalcol Zilan, IV, 227
Cape Tribe, II, 147
Cappadocia, I, 221
Capperstam, IV, 204
CAPRAL, Antony, IV, 172
Capreri, I, 308
Capucar, IV, 77
Caracatai, I, 287, 288
Cara Catay, III, 19
Caracathai, IV, 230
Caracorum, III, 19; see Kara Korum
Caraian, III, 127, 131; IV, 62
Carajan, I, 302; II, 182

Caramela, I, 307
Caramoram, Caramuran, II, 213; III, 126
Caramoran, II, 212
Çarazan, I, 301
Čarčan, I, 246
Carcara, IV, 73
Carcha, III, 22
Cardamoms, II, 153; IV, 96
CARDOSO, III, 30
CAREY, IV, 229, 231
Caria, I, 228
CARLETTI, Francesco, I, 161, 192
Carligh, I, 249
Carmania, I, 199
Carnate, IV, 73
Carniola, II, 14
Carocam, I, 309
Caromoran, III, 224
CARPINI, Plano, John of, I, 156, 163, 164, 208, 209, 288; II, 9, 34, 40, 87, 98, 223, 224, 225, 252, 261; III, 18, 20, 49, 53, 185, 210, 216; IV, 70, 163, 164, 230
Carthage, III, 247, 255
Caruabansa, IV, 225
CARUS, emperor, I, 54
Carvan basci, IV, 225, 227
Carwar, IV, 72; see Kārwār
Casa Jacomi, III, 161
Casar Bochir, I, 306
Casbin, I, 293
Cascar, I, 238, 293; IV, 203, 207, 208, 215, 218, 220, 221, 224, 229, 232, 242, 253; see Kashgar
Cascat, I, 263
Caschar, I, 162
Casciani, IV, 230, 231
Cascito, III, 158
Casena, III, 160
Cashgar, III, 22
Cashishes, priest, IV, 223
Cashmere, IV, 182
Caspian Sea, I, 20, 41, 54, 100, 105, 150, 153, 183, 187, 196, 210, 213, 216, 288, 290, 293, 300, 304, 307, 308; II, 10, 105, 242; III, 22, 23, 82, 84, 180, 198, 225, 243, 246; IV, 188
Caspian Gates, I, 189, 190
Caspian Mountains, II, 240, 242
Caspis, Mountains, I, 304
Caspius, II, 243
Cassai, III, 148, 149; see Cansay
Cassan (Kashan), II, 34, 106
Cassan, II, 160–2
Cassay, III, 90, 97, 148; see Cansay
CASSINI, Maffeo, II, 15
CASSIUS, Avidius, I, 52
Cast Iron, Chinese, I, 17
Castorin, I, 227
Castra, I, 152
Castrovillari, III, 200
Cataea of ARRIAN, I, 145
Catalan Map of 1375, I, 81, 299, 302, 308; II, 129, 180, 208, 209, 212, 258; III, 78, 84, 85, 147, 194, 221, 223, 230, 250; IV, 4, 23
Catalogue Amsterdam, Sect. coloniale, II, 161
Cataracts, the, I, 216
Cataria, III, 164
Cathan, city of Pygmies, II, 207, 208
CATHANI, And., III, 43, 44
Cathay, Catay, Cathaia, I, I, 34, 146, 156, 162, 182, 258, 260, 261, 263, 266, 269; II, 34, 165, 177, 216, 231; IV, 174, 176, 235, 236
Cattigara, I, 143, 188, 191, 193, 194, 195; see Kattigara
Caubul, IV, 187, 217
Caucasus, I, 152; II, 199, 242; III, 184, 185, 248; IV, 6; see Caspian Mountains
Caugigu, III, 130
Caulking vessels, II, 212
ÇAUMA, Rabban, I, 116, 119, 121, 166; IV, 268
CAUTLEY, II, 166
Cauvey, IV, 63
CAVE, *Script. Eccles.*, II, 9; III, 206
Caveri, III, 66
Caviar, III, 158
Caxix, IV, 223
Cayda, see Kaidu
Caygar (Kashgar), IV, 175
Caynam (Hainan), I, 301, 303
Cecini, Cesani, Cesenae, Cesini, II, 218, 219
Celai, II, 144; III, 69
Celebes, II, 147, 156; IV, 157, 159
Cembalo, III, 14
Cembaro, I, 305
Cenan, I, 293
Censcalan, II, 179; see Canton and Sin Kilan
Central Asia, I, 63, 215, 300, 303, 313, 318; II, 263
Ceos, I, 198
Cernoue, Cernove, I, 124, 177; IV, 91
CESANA, Michael de, II, 12
Cesana, II, 12, 16
Cetey, I, 174
Cethym, III, 246

Ceuce, I, 238, 239
Ceuta, IV, I, 38, 39, 128
Ceylon, I, 67, 68, 70, 71, 72, 75–78, 86, 126, 127, 144, 176, 184, 199, 213, 214, 215, 226, 228, 253, 277; II, 10, 26, 31, 34, 106, 130, 134, 140, 141, 168, 169–172, 184; III, 62, 65, 68, 167, 192, 194, 196–9, 216, 219, 231–4, 242, 244, 245, 257, 259; IV, 32, 33, 242
Chabalech, I, 301
Chabassi, III, 237
CHABECH, King, I, 301
Chabēris, I, 228
Chabol, I, 300
CHABOT, J. B., I, 116, 121, 166, 167
Chacatays, I, 33
Chadar, IV, 238
Chadir Kul, IV, 229
Chagan, I, 167
Chagan Nur, II, 227; III, 132; IV, 162
Chagan Talas, I, 117
CHAGATAÏ, I, 33, 149, 153; III, 30, 31, 33–5, 85, 87, 132, 188, 190; IV, 160–6, 189–191, 239
CHAGGI MEMET, I, 290, 294; see HAJJI MAHOMED
Chaghan Jang, III, 131
Chá-i-Khitai, I, 292
Chaimul, I, 254
Chaitwa, IV, 78
Chakebaruhe, III, 237
Chakheraller, I, 318
Chăkka, III, 237
CHALCONDYLAS, Laonicus, I, 34, 250; III, 49
Chaldaea, I, 308; II, 34, 109, 110; III, 269
Chaldiran, I, 216
Chale, Chalia, II, 133
Chalis, I, 293; IV, 180, 191, 234; see Cialis
Chalish, IV, 234; see Cialis
Chalukyas, I, 243
Cham (Khan), I, 149, 262, 263
CHAM, III, 247
Chambalec, III, 34; see Cambalec
Chambalech, I, 301; see Cambalec
Chambers' Asiatic Miscellany, I, 179
Chamobai, IV, 76
Champa, I, 8, 128, 129, 135, 138, 143, 193, 253, 254; II, 10, 25, 31, 32, 34, 152, 156, 163, 165; III, 131; IV, 96, 101
Champāvati, I, 254
Chan (Khan), I, 235
Chana (Thana), II, 34; III, 207, 224
Chanbalech, I, 301; see Cambalec
Chan Ch'eng, I, 78
Chandana, I, 227
Chandar, I, 177
Chanderi, IV, 22
Chandra-giri, IV, 74
CHANDRAGUPTA, I, 6, 68, 70, 73
CHANDRAPIDA, I, 70
Chandu, II, 227; see Shang tu
Chanf, I, 128; see Champa
CHANGA, III, 255
Ch'ang an, I, 23, 31; see Ch'ang ngan and Si ngan fu
Chang Chau, I, 122, 123; II, 183; IV, 117, 118, 121, 271
CH'ANG CH'UN, III, 55
Chang Ho, II, 213
CHANG K'IEN, I, 4, 37–9, 41, 51, 65, 160
Ch'ang ngan, I, 23, 30, 31, 43, 61, 97, 105, 114, 116, 133, 237
CHANG SHE, II, 194
CHANG Sheu-tsie, II, 243
CHANG Shih-ch'êng, III, 12
CHANG TSUEN, I, 68
Chang ye, I, 38
Chank shells, I, 228
CHAN SI, III, 35
Chánwul, I, 254
Cháo, I, 114
Chao (Paper Money of China), I, 283; III, 150
CHAO HWEI, IV, 228
CHAO Ju-kwa, CHAU Ju-kwa, I, 43, 85, 86, 136, 225, 233; II, 168, 172; IV, 4, 98–102
CHAO T'O, I, 39
Character of Ibn Batuta, IV, 51
Characters, Chinese, I, 161, 259
Charax Spasinu, I, 43
Charcha, III, 23
Charchan, I, 58
Charchi, IV, 238
Char Chinar, IV, 216
Charchunar, IV, 180, 217
Chárdar, IV, 259
Char Darya, IV, 257, 258
CHARDIN, II, 102, 104, 107, 109
Charekar, IV, 9, 180, 183, 208, 255, 257, 258
Chargāh, I, 244
Chārikār, IV, 208; see Charekar
Charka, IV, 208, 258
Charkh, IV, 9, 208, 258
CHARLEMAGNE, II, 4
CHARLES IV, Emperor, II, 199; III, 204, 239, 255, 259

CHARLES V, Emperor, I, 181, 274, 304
CHARLES II, II, 189
CHARLES V, King of France, I, 299
CHARLES VI, King of France, III, 37
Charters of Malabar Christians, III, 254
CHARTON, Ed., I, 232; II, 71
Charwagh, IV, 229
Chasars, III, 169
Chasemgarah, III, 22
Chastac, I, 263
Chata, I, 162, 263; see Cathay
Chatao, I, 182; see Cathay
Chatgánw, IV, 82, 83, 92
Chatha, I, 263; see Cathay
CHATICEN TUNGII, III, 181
Chatta Irmak, III, 161
Chattarpúr, IV, 22
Chatua, IV, 78
Chatyr, III, 256
Chau, State of, I, 35
Chau, Dynasty, I, 96, 114
Chau chi, I, 105
CHAU Kung, I, 8
Chau Kwo, II, 216
Chaul, I, 227, 254
CHAVANNES, Ed., I, 37, 38, 41, 42, 44, 45, 50, 53, 55, 59, 64, 66, 75, 91, 106, 205, 206, 208, 209, 211, 248, 276; II, 139, 157, 243; IV, 141, 164, 190, 230, 231, 235, 266, 267, 271
Chawul, IV, 254
CHAY LING, I, 38
Chayre, I, 306
CHAYSCAN, I, 264
Chazene, III, 23
Cheapness, in China, II, 181; in Bengal, IV, 80 *seq.*
Chechalich, I, 318
Chechalith, Chechalit, I, 318; IV, 180, 216, 217
Chechi, I, 309
Chechuklik, I, 318
Cheghánián, I, 316
Cheh-Kiang, II, 177; see Che-Kiang
Che-Kiang, I, 39, 136; II, 177, 187, 188, 189, 192, 193; III, 128; IV, 138
CHEIKHO, Father, I, 108
Che kiue Pass, IV, 230
Chelim, II, 205
Che lin fu, II, 205
CHE LU-KU (YE LIU), I, 148; III, 21
Cheman, IV, 180, 211
Chemenfu, II, 227; III, 116
CHEN, I, 4
CH'EN, I, 30
Chenāb, IV, 10
Chen Ching, I, 4
CHENG HO, I, 76, 77, 80
CHENG T'IEN, I, 148
Cheng ting fu, I, 278; IV, 266
CH'ENG TSU, I, 76, 79, 87, 179; II, 134; see YONG LO
Ch'eng Tu, I, 65, 116, 139, 140; III, 126, 128
Cheng tung, II, 231; III, 128
CH'ENG WANG, I, 8, 10
Cheng-yuen Sin-ting-Shih-kiâo-muh-luh, I, 112
Chen Kiang, II, 213; see Chin Kiang
CHENNAPA, I, 81
Chennapapatam, Chennapattanam, Chennappapattanam, I, 81
Chennapatam, I, 81
CH'EN SUNG, I, 66
CHENTOLOPITI, I, 70
CHEN TSUNG, I, 56
CH'EN Yu-liang, III, 12
Cheria, Cheriah, I, 34
Cheribon, III, 193, 267
Cherra Punji, IV, 254
Chersonese, I, 193
CHERUMÁN PERUMAL, II, 134
CHESAUD, Aimé, I, 182
Chescan, IV, 211
Chesi, I, 308
Chesimo, I, 309
Chesmi, I, 177
Chestnuts, II, 246
Chetey, I, 174
Cheul, I, 227, 254
CHEVALIER, Ulysse, II, 92
CHE-YIH, II, 203
Chhessé, I, 195
Chiai Catai, I, 292
Chiaicuon, IV, 239
Chíalis, I, 293; IV, 234; see Chalish
CHIANSAM, III, 182
Chiao fu, I, 114
Chiaveria, III, 144; IV, 270
Chi chau, II, 188
Chichchiklik, Chichiklik, IV, 211, 215, 216
Chicheck Tagh, IV, 217
Chichintalas, I, 117
Chidebeo, II, 232–4
Chiêm-thành, II, 167
Chienciùn, I, 239
Ch'ien Han Shu, I, 23, 149; see *Ts'ien Han Chu*
Chí fú, I, 276
Chigin, I, 117

Chih-li, Chi-li, I, 114; II, 152; III, 12
Chi kin, I, 117
Chiktem, IV, 239
Chilan, I, 290
Chīlan, IV, 229
Chilaw, IV, 33
Children sold, II, 148
Chi len fu (Nanking), II, 35, 204
Chilerapha, II, 35
Chileso, II, 35
Chiliate, IV, 77
Chilosola, III, 170
Chiltung, Pass, IV, 217
CHILUKHIPALO, I, 70
Chimay, Lake, III, 221
Chimía, Símía, Límía, I, 296
Chimolo, I, 254
Chin, I, I, 5, 151, 179, 281; III, 68
CH'IN, I, 5
China, I, I, 2, 6, 7, 15; IV, 2
Chinapatam, I, 81
Chínár, II, 103
China Review, I, 9, 48, 78, 142; II, 232
Chinas, I, 2, 6
Chinasthána, I, 28
Chin Chau, Chin ceo, I, 169, 173, 257; II, 183; see Ts'iuen Chau and Zaitún
CHIN CIN, I, 241
CH'ÎN E, II, 206
Chine ancienne; see PAUTHIER
Chine moderne; see PAUTHIER
Chinese Junk, IV, 115
Chinese Recorder, I, 118; II, 213
CHING, Dynasty, I, 3
CHINGHIZ Khan, I, 33, 60, 115, 148, 149, 150, 155, 157, 170, 276; II, 100, 192, 197, 216, 221, 227, 228, 236, 246; III, 17, 20, 21, 25, 55, 82, 87, 110, 111, 113, 114, 132, 147, 180, 184, 186, 248; IV, 110, 142, 160, 184, 185, 189, 191, 205, 209, 222, 238, 239, 241, 258
Chingleput, I, 81
Chingra Khal, river, IV, 153
Chini, I, 269
Chini-Bachagán, III, 249
Chinista, I, 176
Chinistan, I, 28, 93
Chinkalan, I, 172; II, 179; III, 115, 126, 128; see Canton and Sín Kalán
Chin Kiang, I, 118; II, 212, 213; III, 15
Chin la, II, 164
Chinsang, II, 231–2; III, 119–121
Chin seang, II, 232
Chin Shu, I, 54
Chintabor, I, 309; IV, 65, 72
Chios, II, 153
Chipangu, III, 129
Chipre, I, 262
Chirchistallo, III, 171
Chiricchestede, III, 171
Chis, I, 309
Chi shun Chin-kiang chi, I, 118
Chitral, I, 314; IV, 205, 259
Chittagong, I, 177; II, 147; IV, 81, 82, 92, 149
Chittim, III, 246
Chiugin, I, 239
Chiva, I, 305
Chivil, I, 254
Chliatae, I, 210
Choban Keupri, III, 163
Cho chau, III, 117
Chocosse, III, 62
Choerelaphus, I, 224
Ch'o keng lu, II, 172, 217, 219, 220
Chola Kingdom, I, 72
Choliatae, I, 210, 211
Cholma, river, I, 307
Chōl-tâgh, IV, 231
Chombe, IV, 76
Chong Kouo, I, 75
CHONG Ma-li, IV, 247
Chonka, II, 186
Chön-la, IV, 101
Chorasmia, II, 224
Choreb, Mount, I, 221
Chor Goola Tillah, IV, 153
Chos, I, 306
CHOSROES, I, 29; II, 115
Chossa, I, 306
Chotan, I, 250, 251
Choteen, IV, 215
Chou Shu, I, 149
Chowries, I, 243
Christian, taken for a national title, I, 163
Christianity, Nestorian, see Nestorian and I, 101 *seq.*; in Socotra, I, 123, 226; III, 7; in Ceylon, I, 220, 226; traces of in Indo-Chinese countries, I, 123; ascribed to Chinese, I, 270; IV, 175, 200; often confounded with Buddhism, I, 49; III, 54; IV, 201
Christians in China, I, 89, 104; IV, 130; also see whole section on Nestorian Christianity in China, I, 101 *seq.*, and 235–241; among Tartars; see above section, also I, 163, 177; and PRESTER JOHN, Nestorian; of St. Thomas, II, 117, 130, 132,

135, 142; III, 63, 217, 251, 253, 257
CHRISTOPHER, St., II, 142, 184
Chronology, of Khans of Chagatai, III, 33 *seq.*; IV, 161; of Marignolli's Journey, III, 216; of Ibn Batuta's Voyage to China, IV, 35, 149; of Journey of Goës, IV, 180
Chryse, I, 183; II, 151
Chu, I, 161
Chu, River, I, 60, 288, 289; III, 21; IV, 164
Chubdan, I, 233
Chu Chau, II, 188
Chuche, I, 293
Chú Chu, III, 117
Chu Ch'uan, I, 161
Ch'ue keng lu; see *Ch'o keng lu*
Chu Fan chi; see CHAO Ju-kwa
Chuguchak, IV, 163, 164
Ch'ui lan, II, 168
Chukaklee, IV, 217
Chu Kiang, IV, 68
Chukiupo, I, 191
Chuktal, IV, 229
Chúl, I, 286; III, 213
Chūliā, IV, 29
Chulien, I, 72
CH'U-LO Kagan, III, 55
CHULOTA, I, 68
Chü-mi-t'o, I, 192
Chunar, I, 177
Chundur-fūlāt, I, 128
CHU NGAN, III, 15
Ch'ung K'ing, III, 113, 127, 128
Chung Shu, II, 231
Chung tu, I, 148, 150; II, 216; III, 114
Ch'un tsew Period, II, 216
Chu pu, I, 87
Churche, I, 281; III, 125, 128, 129, 148
Churches, Catholic, in Cathay, I, 169; in Cambalec, III, 46, 50, 55; in Tenduc, III, 47; at Zaitún, III, 72, 73, 229; at Almaliq, III, 212; in Malabar, III, 218
Churmansk, I, 307
Chus, IV, 4
Chusan Archipelago, II, 184; III, 269
Chutal, I, 250
Chutalān, I, 250
Chutanān, I, 250
CHU YING, I, 66
CHUYSCAN, I, 264, 174
CHU Yun-ming, I, 78
Ciacor, IV, 227, 229
Ciake Baruhe, III, 237
Cialis, IV, 191, 221, 232, 233, 234, 235, 239, 253; see Chalis, Chalish
Ciaṇba, II, 163
Ciandu, II, 227
Cianganor, III, 132
Ciarakar (Charekar), IV, 208
Ciarcunar, IV, 214, 216
Ciaul (Chawul), IV, 254
CIBRARIO, L., II, 196
CICERO, II, 252
CICOGNA, E. A., II, 57, 66
Ciecialith, IV, 214, 216
Čikil, I, 245
ÇĪLADĪTYA, I, 68, 69, 70
Čilan, IV, 228, 229
Cilicia, I, 161, 163, 221; II, 118
Çimesquinte (Samarkand), III, 39
Čin, I, 2
Cīna, I, 6
Činandjket, I, 140
Činastān, I, 215
Cīnasthāna, I, 28
Cincalam, Cincolam, I, 301; II, 180; see Sin Kilan
Cini, I, 151
Cinnamomum, I, 185
Cinnamon, I, 264; III, 62
CINQUINUS, Franc., II, 103
Cintabor, IV, 65
Cintacola, I, 180
Cipangu, I, 180
Circassians, I, 210, 223
CISTERCIANS, III, 171
Cisterns at Aden, IV, 3
Cities of China, vast number of, II, 178, 231; III, 228; gradation of their rank and appropriate titles, III, 118
Citracan (Astrakhan), III, 147
Cittadino Italiano, II, 90
Ciutat Sioene, I, 306
CIVEZZA, Marc. da, II, 50, 80, 81, 82, 87, 88, 92; II, 267, 272; III, 5, 11
Cividale, II, 3, 4; II, 14
CLARA, St., III, 231
CLAUDIAN, I, 21
CLAUDIUS, I, 198
CLAUSER, Conrad, I, 250
CLAVIJO, Ruy G. de, I, 33, 173, 174, 177, 178, 211, 264, 283, 293; II, 99, 103, 105, 233; III, 39, 85; IV, 201, 223
Clemenfu, II, 227; III, 116
CLEMENT V, Pope, III, 28, 75, 100, 168; III, 11
CLEMENT VI, Pope, III, 189

CLIFFORD, Hugh, II, 91
Climate of India, III, 59
Clove Country, I, 226, 228
Cloves, I, 227, 264; III, 168; IV, 101, 102
Clove Wood, III, 168
Clubbing System, Chinese, II, 194
Clysma, I, 27, 221
Coal, III, 118; IV, 114
Coale, I, 306
Côbalek, III, 85
Cocco Nagara, I, 196
Coccora Nagara, I, 196
Cochin, I, 237, 267; II, 129, 134, 135; III, 218; IV, 24, 78, 79, 173, 184
Cochin-China, I, 4, 8, 18, 77, 128, 214, 244; II, 163; III, 167, 255; IV, 157, 158, 243
Cocintana, I, 309
Cocintaya, I, 309
Cocks and hens in China, II, 186; IV, 110
Coconut tree, I, 225; III, 62, 236; palm fibre, texture from, III, 227, 241
Coda, I, 76
Codangalur, II, 135; III, 254
CODINUS, I, 47
COEDÈS, G., *Textes*, I, 186
Coilam, IV, 79; see Quilon
Coilandy, IV, 77
Coilum, II, 137; see Quilon
Coins, Indian, IV, 54–62
Coinuch, III, 84
Coir Cham, Coir Khan, III, 18, 22
Colchi, IV, 172
Coldingham, III, 170
Colechea, IV, 172
COLERIDGE, II, 227
Colidara, III, 159
Colom, II, 130, 218; see Quilon
Colombino, II, 137
Colombo, II, 137; see Quilon
Colomni, II, 137
Colon, II, 129; see Quilon
Columbo, I, 309; II, 130, 170; III, 216, 217, 231, 244; IV, 33; see Quilon
Columbum, II, 129, 130, 133, 137, 146, 191, 218, 220; III, 29, 31, 191, 216, 217, 218, 230, 249, 257, 258, 259, 268; IV, 29, 79
COLUMBUS, Christ., I, 179; III, 196
Columbus, III, 77, 217
Columns, set up by Marignolli at Columbum, III, 218; of Alexander, III, 218, 219; of Bacchus, III, 219
Comedae, Comedi, I, 190, 192
Comerchio, III, 144
Comerum, II, 108
Commercial Intercourse of Europe with China and India in 14th Century, I, 170
Community of Wives, II, 147
COMNEN, John, I, 245
Comorin, Cape, I, 213; II, 129, 141; III, 197, 198, 219
Comoro, Great, I, 138
Compostella, II, 178
Comuch, III, 84
Comum, II, 34, 35
CONCHAM, III, 18
Condor, I, 152
Condro, III, 164
Condur, I, 128; IV, 159
CONFUCIUS, I, 31; II, 224
Congo, III, 221
Conjurors, IV, 134
CONRAD II, II, 4
CONRADUS, III, 14
CONSTANS, I, 54
CONSTANTINE Ducas, I, 247
CONSTANTINE the Great, I, 229
CONSTANTINE, son of Heraclius, I, 54
CONSTANTINE IV, Pogonatus, I, 48
CONSTANTINE Porphyrogenitus, I, 212, 244, 245
Constantinia, IV, 8
Constantinople, I, 44, 47, 115, 120, 274, 293; II, 10, 31, 100; III, 48, 81, 155, 164, 165, 190, 211, 256; IV, 7
CONSTANTIUS, I, 221
CONTI, Nicolò, I, 87, 124, 151, 174–8, 266, 268, 303; II, 24, 151, 162, 166, 182; III, 8, 27, 40
COOLEY, W. D., I, 272; II, 86
Coppolanda, III, 171
COQUEBERT-MONTBRET, III, 39
CORA, John of, Archbishop of Soltania, I, 169; III, 36, 37 89; see JOHN of Cora
Corassam, I, 293, 295
Corbara, II, 12, 16
CORBARIUS, III, 205
Corea, I, 118, 131, 135–7, 148, 177, 257, 303; II, 237; III, 113, 125, 128; IV, 243
Corleone, I, 241
Cormorants, II, 188, 189
Cormos, II, 242
Cornaa, II, 34, 35
Coromandel, II, 141, 142, 165; III, 5, 65, 191, 252
CORREA, Gaspar, II, 134

Corrections and Additional Notes, IV, 266 *seq.*
CORSALIS, Andrew, I, 180; II, 154
CORSI, Francis, IV, 203
CORTES, F., I, 170
Cory, Cape, I, 191
Corypha umbraculifera, IV, 71
Cos, I, 14, 98, 199; IV, 4
Cosenza, III, 200
COSMAS, Friar, appointed archbishop of Cambalec, III, 13, 14
COSMAS Indicopleustes, I, 12, 24, 25, 26, 27, 28, 86, 104, 107, 176, 212, 213, 219–226, 231, 253; II, 14, 133; III, 76, 197, 259, 261
Cosmi, I, 159
Cosmin, I, 177
Cosmos, I, 209
Costrama, I, 307
Costuma, III, 145
Cotan, IV, 207, 219, 222; see Khotan
Cote Coulam, IV, 74
Cotroba, III, 22
Cotrone, III, 169
Cotta, III, 231, 233
Cotte Civitas, III, 244
Cottiara, IV, 79
Cottiaris, R., I, 195
Cotton, I, 202; III, 166
COTTONIAN Collection, III, 36
Coulang, III, 219
Coulete, IV, 77
Council of Lyons, I, 154
COUPLET, Ph., I, 123
COURT, Gén., I, 310
Court Ceremonial at Cambalec, II, 238
Couvade, III, 131
Cowries, I, 243
COYA JAAN, III, 231
Cracow, I, 152
Craft, vast amount of, on Chinese waters, II, 211
Cranganor, I, 82, 237; II, 10, 134, 135; III, 249, 254; IV, 78
CRASSUS, I, 18
Craven, III, 171
Cravenna, III, 171
CRAWFURD, I, 128, 185; II, 149, 151, 153, 155–7, 162, 221; IV, 156, 158, 159
Crecy, III, 199
Creman, I, 309
Cremation, II, 32, 166, 167
Cremi, I, 308
Crete, III, 169
Crimea, III, 14, 81, 84, 169; IV, 2
Crimson dye, quaint fable about, I, 160
Crim-Tartars, I, 283
Crit, I, 152; III, 19
Croce della Giudecca, Sta., II, 100
Cronaca delle Miss. francescane, II, 87
CROOK, Wm., I, 5
Crophi, I, 151
Cross, woods of the, discussed, III, 238
Crotona, III, 169
Crucifix in the Plantain, III, 236
Crynes, II, 113
CTESIAS, I, 14, 224; II, 168, 208; III, 263
Ctesiphon, I, 43, 120, 216
Cubebs, II, 153
Cucia (Kucha), IV, 230
Cuciã, IV, 231
Cueran, II, 168
Cumania, I, 305
Cumanian, III, 152
Cumbala, IV, 74
Cumberland, III, 171
Cummin, III, 166, 167
CUNNINGHAM, Gen. Sir A., I, 74, 191, 192, 313, 314, 316
Cupar, III, 170
Cupero, III, 170
Cups that fly through the air, II, 239
Curcuma longa, I, 292
Curi-curi, IV, 159
Currents, Southerly, from Indian Islands, II, 160
Curringhacherry, III, 218
CURTIUS, Quintus, I, 189
CURZON, Lord, I, 145, 190, 314, 317; II, 108
CURZON, Rob., II, 99, 100
Cus, II, 109
Cuthe, Aides-de-camp of Great Khan, II, 228
Cutrone, III, 169
CUVIER, I, 199
Cyagannor, III, 132
Cyatyr, III, 256
Cycni, II, 219
Cylbandj, I, 137
Cyn, III, 249
Cyncilim, II, 134; see Cynkali
Cyngilin, II, 133; see Cynkali
Cynkalan, II, 179; III, 248, 249; see Sin Kilan and Canton
Cynkali, I, 82; II, 133, 134; III, 249; see Cranganor
Çynocephali, II, 169; IV, 94
Čynstn, I, 215
Cyollos Kagon, I, 117; III, 213

Cypress Tree, II, 103
Cyprus, I, 168, 169; III, 139, 140, 144, 145, 166, 168, 199, 226, 246
Cyrenaica, I, 221
Cyrênê, I, 221
Cyrillic Alphabets, I, 245
CYRUS, I, 9; II, 108
Cytiaca, III, 212
Cytra, III, 247
Czernikov, I, 305

Dabag, I, 127
Daban Shan Pass, IV, 141
Dabihat, III, 192
Dabil, I, 255
DABRY, *Pisciculture en Chine*, II, 191
Dabul, III, 194
Dacca, I, 243; IV, 152
Dacca muslins, I, 197
Dagoba, I, 248
Dah-din, IV, 238
DAHLMANN, Father J., III, 253
Daibal, I, 255
Daibul, I, 86, 227, 309
Daich (Iaik), I, 212
Daïdu (Peking), III, 114, 115, 116, 125, 128
Daifû, III, 120
Dailam, III, 22, 23; IV, 184
Dailui (Talifu), III, 127, 131
DAIMING Khan, I, 291
DAIMIR Can, I, 291
Dairim, IV, 182
Daitu (Peking), I, 93; II, 227
Dájis (Ta Jen), I, 273
Dak-choki, II, 234
Dakli, III, 131
Dala, I, 243
Dalaï Lama, II, 250; III, 269
Daldili, II, 115
DALGLEISH, IV, 230, 234, 235, 238
Dalmatians, I, 221
DALRYMPLE, IV, 159
DALTON, II, 157, 162, 168
Damascus, I, 43, 307; III, 22, 23, 199, 226, 241, 244, 245; IV, 3, 36, 37, 109, 126
Damashk (Damascus), III, 23
Dambadenia, II, 170
Damghan, I, 189, 190, 293
Damietta, I, 306
Damiyat, I, 306
Damna, I, 195
Damnae, I, 195
Damonela, I, 309
DAMPIER, W., II, 151
DAN, II, 130, 179
Dangchi, Dangdji, I, 273
DANIBEG, I, 71; IV, 183, 228
DANIEL, Patriarch, II, 17
DANIEL, Prophet, I, 27; II, 110
Daniele in Friuli, S., II, 15, 16
DANISHMANJA, III, 34; IV, 162
Dankshi, IV, 242
DANTE, III, 198
Danube, I, 245
DAPPER, II, 147
Dara-i-Aingharan, IV, 259
Darail, I, 313
Darásun, darassun, I, 209, 276; II, 199
Darband, III, 90
Darband Niás, III, 131
Dard, I, 314
Dardas, III, 156
Daric, I, 229
DARIUS, I, 10; II, 102, 115
Darjiling, I, 184
Darkness, Land of, IV, 7
Darkot, I, 61; IV, 259
Dark Sea, I, 247
Darmut, I, 306
Daron, I, 94
Darwáz, I, 313; IV, 216
DARWIN, II, 242
Dasfetidae, Lake of, II, 115
DÁSHIMAN, III, 121, 126
Dast, IV, 135
Dates, I, 251; IV, 39
DĀṬHOPATISSA II, I, 70
Daulatabad, I, 310; IV, 14, 21, 23, 85
Daumghan, III, 76
DAVÁ KHAN, IV, 161
DAVÁ TIMUR, IV, 161
DAVID, Armand, II, 181, 182
DAVID, Metropolitan of China, I, 103
DAVID, King, II, 152; III, 213, 243; IV, 224
DAVID, King of the Tartars, III, 17
DAVIS, Sir J. F., I, 132, 135; II, 177, 179, 184, 187, 188, 192, 194, 199, 213, 215, 220
Daxata, I, 195
DAY, Dr., II, 134; III, 218, 219
Daya, II, 146
Dayaks, II, 168
Daybul (Dabil), I, 255
Daylam, IV, 184; see Dailam
Dead, disposal of, in Cathay, III, 99; in Tibet, II, 252–4; in India, III, 63
Dead Sea, I, 307; II, 105, 160
DEANE, Major H. A., I, 74
Death of Odoric, II, 275
DE' BIANCHI, II, 100
Deccan, II, 144; see Dekkan

Decency of Hindus, III, 249
DEFRÉMERY, I, 245, 246; IV, I, 142, 151, 162, 165, 166
Degenerations in Geographical knowledge, I, 21
DE GOEJE, I, 135, 136, 137; II, 147
DE GROOT, J. J. M., I, 112
DE GUBERNATIS, II, 61, 81; III, 11
DE GUIGNES, I, 3, 20, 21, 30, 32, 42, 52, 53, 56, 57, 65, 72, 86, 88, 89, 91, 92, 94–6, 104, 125, 140, 194, 205, 206, 208, 210, 247; II, 104, 180, 183, 213, 226, 227, 257; III, 33, 34, 39; IV, 5, 142, 163, 165, 166, 201, 212, 228, 229
Dehfattan, IV, 76
Dehi-Kherján, Dehi-Kherkán, Dekergán, III, 76
Deh-i-Parian, IV, 259
Dekkan, I, 242, 243; II, 144; IV, 177
DELFIN, II, 17
Delhi, I, 78, 131; II, 115, 127, 142, 143, 226; III, 69, 131, 218, 231; IV, 12, 13, 14, 16, 18, 20, 21, 23, 46–8, 80, 81, 128, 138–140, 149, 225
Deli, II, 115
Deli-Baba, III, 162
Delights, River of, II, 262–4
DELISLE, Léopold, I, 300, 305; II, 52, 73, 83
Della Decima, III, 137 *seq.*
Dellai, IV, 230, 231
Delly, I, 310
Delly, Cape, IV, 72
Deluge did not reach Adam's Peak, III, 234, 245
Demawend, I, 189; II, 102
DEMETRIUS, III, 15
DEMETRIUS, Companion of Goës, IV, 202, 208, 221, 222, 224, 226, 227
DEMETRIUS, Friar and Martyr, II, 117, 119, 122, 124; III, 76
DEMIRLAN, I, 297; see Tamerlane
Demons, II, 260–1
Dengadda, II, 115
DENHA, I, 119, 120, 127
DENNYS, N. B., II, 157, 158, 160
Deogiri (Daulatabad), I, 310; IV, 14, 21
Derbend, I, 304; IV, 123
Derbend, Pass of, I, 163
Desert of Lop, II, 264
Deserts, Haunted, II, 264–5; IV, 39
DESGODINS, II, 250
DESIDERI, I, 71; II, 249
DES MICHELS, A., II, 165
Despina Khatun, IV, 7
Devagiri, II, 115; III, 70
DEVÉRIA, G., I, 99; III, 186
Devil's Advocate, II, 17
Devil crying in the night (Devil Bird), III, 42
Devils cast out by Franciscans, II, 260
Devi-patam, IV, 35
Devoutness of Saracens, III, 260
Dewagiri, II, 115; III, 70
Dewal, I, 86
Dewar, III, 68
Dhafar, III, 68; IV, 36, 149, 150
Dhār, IV, 23
DHARMÂKARA, I, 73
DHARMÂPALA, I, 73
Dharmapatam, IV, 76
Dhibat-ul-Mahal, IV, 31
Dhungzil, IV, 235, 238
Dhungzil Langar, IV, 234
Diabolic Art, II, 222
Diacoregan, III, 76
Diadin, III, 162, 163
Diagorgan, III, 75, 76
Diamonds, II, 172
Diarbakr, Diarbekir, I, 216; II, 223; IV, 3
DIAZ, Em., I, 106
Dibajat, I, 127; III, 192
DICKENS, I, 192
DIEDO, Nicolas, I, 270
DIEULAFOY, II, 110
Digun, I, 243
Dilem, II, 258
Dili, II, 115, 127; see Delhi
Dilivar, II, 115
Dim Islands, II, 160
Dinár, II, 150; IV, 56 *seq.*, 112, 113
Dinarpore, IV, 153
Dinawar, IV, 33
DIOCLETIAN, I, 94
DIODORUS of Tarsus, I, 26
DIODORUS, I, 189
Diogil, I, 310
DIONYSIUS, III, 219
DIONYSIUS PERIEGETES, I, 183, 201; III, 186; IV, 266
DIOSCORIDES, I, 184, 185
Dioscoris (Sumatra), I, 220
Dirhem, I, 229; IV, 56 *seq.*; IV, 113
Dirpe, II, 103
Dishes of plaited cane, III, 99; IV, 135
DISMAS, I, 151
Diu, I, 86

Diul, I, 86, 227; see Daibul
Division of tongues, III, 263
Divrighi, III, 161
Divrik, III, 161
DIZABUL, DIZABULUS, I, 59, 205, 206, 207, 209, 210, 211
Dizfúl, II, 110; III, 23
Djagorgan, III, 76
Djankou, I, 130
Djāwaga, I, 127
Djegdelèh, IV, 206
Djeguid-Ali, IV, 206
Djehaz, II, 113
Djéteh, IV, 163
Djihan River, III, 160
Djordjanieh, III, 82
Dnieper, I, 245, 305
Dniester, I, 245, 305
Doab, IV, 20
Doana (Dogana), III, 144
Dobaha, I, 306
DOBNER, Gelasius, editor of Marignolli, III, 199–201, 204, 207, 209, 210, 212, 213, 216, 217, 219, 224, 225, 229, 230, 241, 247–9, 256, 259
Dofar, III, 68; see Dhafar
Dog-faced people, II, 168, 187; IV, 94
DOKUZ-Khatun, II, 246
DOLBEZER, IV, 141
Dolphin, I, 225
Doltalay, II, 115
Domasch, I, 307
DOMINICHELLI, T., II, 36, 38, 49, 50, 55, 61, 64, 65, 73, 74, 82, 262
DOMINICUS, III, 14
Don, I, 158, 305; II, 105; III, 81, 184
Doncola, I, 306
Dondardane, III, 170
Dondin, II, 25, 30, 31, 32, 34, 173, 174
Donfermellino, III, 170
Dong-hoi, II, 163
Dongola, IV, 40
Donkola, I, 306
Dora, IV, 259
DOREZ, Léon, III, 180
Dorpat, II, 102
DORVILLE, II, 249; IV, 176, 268
DOST MAHOMED KHAN, IV, 209
DOZY, G. J., IV, 160
DOZY, R., II, 110; III, 199
Dragoian, II, 174
Dragomen, Hints on, III, 151
Dragon Lake, II, 174; III, 221, 222
Dragons, Fiery, III, 231
Drangiane, I, 99
Dravida, I, 242
Dream, Coleridge's verses made in a, curious coincidence, II, 227
Dress of people of Cathay, II, 29
Drinking habits of the ancient Turks, I, 209
Dristra, I, 245
Drosache, I, 195
Dru gu, I, 62
Drum at Emperor's Gate, I, 131
Drums, Hill of (Sounding Sand), IV, 3
DRUZES, I, 101; II, 188
DUA Khan, III, 132; IV, 162, 163
DUA TIMUR, III, 30, 35
DUBOIS, Abbé, II, 138, 145
DUCANGE, I, 46, 47, 229; II, 110, 111, 153, 204, 219; III, 47, 51
Dúdkárán, IV, 136
Dudriaga, III, 161
Duecalydonian, I, 187
DU HALDE, I, 159, 298; II, 165, 187, 188, 192, 205, 210, 227, 256
DU JARRIC, I, 134, 220; IV, 170, 172, 174, 177, 179, 180, 183, 201–3, 207, 217, 218, 221, 223, 225, 254
DULAURIER, I, 50, 82, 244, 253; IV, 148, 155, 157
Dumb trade, I, 193, 200, 202, 218–9; III, 258
Dumi, I, 243
Dun chuan, I, 140
Dundalk, III, 206
Dundrennan, III, 170
Dunfermline, III, 170
DUNKUL, IV, 23
DUNS SCOTUS, II, 23
Dúr, III, 23
DURAND, E. M., II, 167
Durga, III, 65
Durian, II, 150
Durmapatnam, III, 40
Durúdgarán, IV, 136
Duson, I, 276
DUTREUIL de RHINS, I, 4, 311
Duvriaga, III, 161
Duwán, I, 317, 318
Dvárasamudra, Dwarasamudra, I, 82; II, 115, 143; III, 66
Dwarfs, II, 229–230
Dyaks, II, 158, 162
Dzungaria, I, 154, 163; IV, 160, 192, 228, 235

Earth, Length and Breadth of Inhabited, I, pp. 215 *seq.*
Earth as fuel, IV, 113, 114
Eastern Atlantic, I, 255

Eastern Bengal, I, 243
Eastern Turkestan, I, 248, 304
Eastern Turks, I, 247
Eastern Volga, I, 304
East India Gazetteer, II, 135; see HAMILTON, W.
Eating the aged, II, 173–5
Ebib, I, 219
EBLIS, III, 228
Ebony, I, 253
EBRÁHIM Sultan, Mirza, I, 286
Ebron, III, 245; see Hebron
Ecbatana, I, 189; II, 102, 153; III, 16
ECCARD, II, 9; III, 14, 17
Echmiazin, I, 308; III, 163
Ectag (Altaï), I, 209
Eden, III, 199, 209, 221
Edessa, II, 141; III, 199, 253
Edict, Chinese, regarding Christian Churches, I, 104 *seq.*
Edil (Volga) River, I, 307; II, 105
EDKINS, J., I, 55
EDRISI, I, 22, 31, 71, 86, 87, 99, 114, 127, 129, 130, 131, 135, 141, 143, 144, 152, 214, 230, 242, 243, 247–9, 253, 254, 256, 306, 309, 313, 314, 316, 318; II, 98, 112, 133, 139, 141, 146, 147; III, 23, 24, 27, 180, 192, 247, 263; IV, 184, 209, 235, 258
EDWARD I, King of England, I, 167
EDWARD II, III, 10, 166
EDWARD III, III, 140, 206
Eghar Bulak, IV, 238
Egriár, IV, 227, 229
Egypt, I, 102, 202, 216, 217, 220, 224, 306; III, 197, 218, 222–4, 229, 241, 245, 263, 269; IV, 37
Egyptians, I, 219, 221
Eier Tau, Lake, III, 194
Eigg Island, II, 262
EITEL, E. J., I, 9
Ektag, I, 209
Elaeagnus, IV, 228
Elam, III, 248
Elamites, I, 220; III, 22
El Arish, I, 306
El Berki, I, 130
Elborz-Kuh, II, 103
Elburz, I, 189
Elburz Mountains, II, 103, 258
El Cheki, I, 130
ELCHIGADAY, III, 30, 39; see ILCHIGADAÏ
ELEAZAR, III, 267
Elephants, I, 230, 231, 243; II, 34, 164, 171, 236; III, 194; IV, 33, 48, 97, 156, 159
Elephants, Cave of, II, 114
Elettaria Cardamomum, II, 154
Eleuths, IV, 192
ELIAS, Patriarch, I, 127
ELIAS, Metrop. of Damascus, III, 24
ELIAS, the Hungarian, III, 211
ELIAS, Ney, I, 60; III, 20; IV, 160, 164, 193, 271; see *Tarikh-i-Rashidi*
ELIAS, Legends, III, 192, 194, 266, 267
ELIAS, son of TUGHLAK TIMUR, IV, 189
Eliim, I, 306
Elim, I, 221
El I'nba, I, 130
Elis, I, 202
Elisabetpol, III, 23
ELLIOT, H. M., I, 309; II, 134, 180; III, 112
Elly, I, 309
ELPHINSTONE, II, 139, 140, 264; IV, 187, 205, 217, 258
EL WARDI, I, 87, 247
Ely, Kingdom, IV, 74
EMANUEL, King, III, 224
Emba, I, 212
Embassies, from Roman Empire to China, I, 51 *seq.*; from Byzantium to Turkish khagans, I, 205; from Shah Rukh to Peking, I, 179, 271 *seq.*; from Great Khan to the Pope, in 1338, III, 179; and in return, 188; from Emperor of China to Delhi in 1342, IV, 17; and return embassy, IV, 18; to China, commercial expeditions in guise of, IV, 218–9, 242–5
Emeralds, I, 230
Emese, I, 258
Emodon, I, 203
Emodus, I, 200
EMPOLI, GIOVANNI d', I, 124; see GIOVANNI da Empoli
Encyclopædia Britannica, I, 158, 197; II, 90
Encyclopédie de l'Islam, I, 83
Engaddi, II, 115
English Cyclopædia, II, 17, 154, 166, 242
ENMELINE, I, 262
ENOCH, the founder of Monkery, III, 245
EPHTHALANUS, I, 205
Ephthalites or White Huns, I, 58, 59, 205, 207, 229; see Hepthalites

EPIPHANIUS, I, 212
Epiphi, I, 219
Epirus, I, 102
Equius of Rubruquis, I, 272, 287, 288
ERATOSTHENES, I, 11
Erdil, II, 211; see Volga
Ergol, IV, 188
Eri, I, 293, 300; see Herat
Erkeun, III, 121; see **Arkaun**
Erman, II, 242
Ermenie, I, 262
Erminia, III, 159
Ermon, Mt., I, 307
ERNEST of Saxony, Duke, III, 223–4
ERSKINE, II, 139, 234, 264
Erythraean Sea, I, 11, 13, 183, 202, 212, 216, 254
Erzingan, Erzinghian, Erzinjan, III, 161, 162, 168
Erzinghian, III, 161
Erzrum, Erzerum, II, 10, 30, 34, 99, 100, 101; III, 161, 162, 163, 164
ESCANDEL, Matthew, I, 122
Eski Baghdad, III, 23
Esneh, I, 306
ESPINHA, J. d', I, 313
Essfahán, I, 286
Essiongeber, I, 306
ESTHER, II, 102
Estierenda, III, 171
Etāwa, IV, 22
Ethaguri, I, 195
Ethil, II, 242; see Volga
Ethiopia, I, 187, 212, 217, 218, 220, 223, 224, 227, 230, 231; III, 6, 7, 222, 223, 247, 252; see Abyssinia
Ethiopians, I, 101, 195, 222, 230
Etna, III, 267
EUGENE III, III, 16
EUGENE IV, I, 121, 178, 268
Eupatoria, I, 305
Euphirattes, Lake below Paradise, III, 220
Euphrates, I, 84, 86, 87, 188, 189, 304, 307; II, 101, 111, 171; III, 161, 162, 197, 198, 222, 226, 261, 262; IV, 45, 137
EUPHROSYNE, IV, 7
Europe, III, 242, 247
Europe, invaded by Tartars, I, 152
EUSEBIUS, I, 221
Euxine, II, 98
EVA, III, 197
EVE, II, 171; III, 227, 228, 232, 236, 244
Evi, I, 300
Evil Spirits in Deserts, II, 265
Evilach, III, 224
Excursions et Recon., II, 164
Expenses of Mercantile venture to Cathay, III, 153
Exterior China, I, 143
EZECHIEL, I, 20, 304; II, 103, 208; III, 239
EZPELATA, Jerome, IV, 173

FABRI, Padre Stefano, I, 238
FABRIS, Luigi, II, 88
Facfur, Faghfúr, I, 33, 94, 141, 256; II, 210; see **Baghbugh**
Fachatim, I, 307, 308
FADL ALLAH RASHID ED-DIN, see RASHID ED-DIN
FA HIAN, I, 42, 67, 74, 75; II, 132, 184, 263; III, 231, 233, 259; IV, 204, 222, 235
Fahri, I, 253
Faizabad, I, 315, 317, 318; IV, 185, 211, 216
Fakanúr, IV, 35
FAKHAR-UL-DIN, I, 273
Fakhrah, IV, 84
FAKHRUDDIN, IV, 84, 85, 86
Fakirs, IV, 223
Faknur, I, 309
FALCON of Toul, N., I, 168
FALCONER, II, 166
FALMERAYER, II, 99
Fals, II, 196
Fan, III, 217
Fana, II, 151; see Java
Fanchan, III, 121, 127
Fan ch'eng, I, 168
FAN Ch'eng-ta, I, 75
Fandaraina, II, 133, 134; IV, 27, 77
Fanduk, IV, 116; see **Fondacum**
FAN SHAN, I, 66
FAN SIUN, I, 66
Fansur, II, 159; IV, 157
Fansuri Camphor, IV, 98
Fap ši, I, 108
Faráb, III, 147; IV, 164
Farang, IV, 38
Farghan, I, 315
Farghânah, I, 18–20, 36–8, 90, 98, 191, 192, 249; IV, 160, 166, 191, 211, 212
FARID-ul-Hakkwa-ud-Din, IV, 12
Faringal, IV, 259
FARIS ABU IMÁN, IV, 37
Farrah, I, 99
Farrukhabad, IV, 271
Fars, I, 99; II, 129; III, 23, 68, 85
Farsetti, II, 57, 266

Farwan, IV, 209
Fa-shi, I, 108
Fatan Malifatan, III, 68
Fatsu, I, 314
Fattan, I, 81; IV, 35
FATTEH ALI SHAH's large family, II, 164
Faughán, I, 315
FAULCON of Toul, Nicholas, I, 168
FAULDS, Henry, III, 123
Feasts at Court of Great Khan, II, 237
FEDERICI, CAESAR, III, 262; IV, 99
Fedo, III, 145
Feet, Little, II, 236
Fei lai fong, II, 204
Fei lai Hill, II, 203, 204
Felt, I, 248; IV, 268
Felt Idols, II, 261
Female, dress in Baghdad, II, 110; schools, IV, 24
Female rule, III, 194
Femenat, I, 309
Fenchui-matheu, II, 214
Fenchui-Nanwang, II, 214
Fenghua, II, 189
Feng-hwang Hill, II, 193
FERDUSI, I, 9, 151
FERGUSON, Donald, I, 199
FERIDUN, I, 9
FERINGEES, I, 9
FERRAND, Gab., I, 2, 11, 88, 127, 128, 129, 139, 141, 244, 245–255, 257; II, 139, 147
Ferrara, II, 195, 214
FERRIER, *Caravan Journeys*, I, 190
FÉRUSSAC, Bon de, III, 202
Fez, IV, 37, 39, 40, 150
Fezzan, I, 220
Fiera, III, 146
Figs (misqali), II, 107
Fiji, II, 162
Fijians, II, 224
FILIPPO the Carmelite, III, 197
Fin, I, 210
Finger prints, III, 123
FINLAY, *Greece*, II, 99
Finno-Ugrians, I, 245
Finns, I, 245
FIRDUSI, I, 9, 151
Fire, Tartar Ceremony of passing persons and goods through, I, 208
Fire Ship, IV, 133
FIRISHTA, I, 78, 79; II, 135; IV, 10
FIRISHTAJÁN, III, 26
FIRÓZ, FIRÚZ, son of YEZDEJIRD III, I, 96, 97, 99, 100, 205
FIRÚZ, Rebellious Nephew of Great Khan (fictitious), IV, 140, 145
Firuz-Koh, I, 293
FISCHER, *Tartars*, II, 207
Fish in Champa, II, 164, 165
FISHER, Capt., IV, 151, 152
Fisheries Exhibition, *Cat. Chinese Collection*, II, 189
Fishing, II, 190, 191; by cormorants, II, 188–9
FISQUET, H., II, 87
Fista, I, 300
Fistuchi, III, 167
FITZ-GEOFFRY, Raymund, II, 118
FITZ-RALPH, Richard, III, 206
Fiume di Piaceri, II, 263
Fiume Rosso, II, 31
Five Dynasties, I, 114
Fizzat, IV, 59
FLAMEL, N., II, 69
Flandrina, II, 133, 134; see Fandaraina
Flaviopolis, III, 139
Flemings, IV, 210
FLEURIAIS, II, 216
Florence, I, 123; III, 178, 200, 227, 237, 241, 255, 256
Florin, Florentine, III, 140; IV, 58
FLORUS, I, 18
Flying Leeches, II, 172
FO, I, 278; IV, 201
Foda, III, 145
FODIM, III, 182
Foe Koue Ki, II, 264; III, 231
Foglia Nuova, III, 43
Fo lin, I, 97; see Fulin
Fo ling (Radix China), I, 292
Follero, III, 159
Follis, IV, 112, 113
Fondaco, III, 144, 145, 229, 230; IV, 116; see Fondacum
Fondacum, III, 229; see Fanduk and Fondaco
Fontana, III, 171
FONTANINI, Archbishop, II, 15
Fonte Dennisinni, I, 241
Fonteghi, I, 270
Foot-posts in Cathay, II, 232
Footprint on Adam's Peak, III, 227, 232
Formosa, II, 168
Fornace, III, 171
FORSTER, G., IV, 206
FORSTER, J. R., II, 86
Fortunate Islands, I, 188, 191
Fortunatus, III, 243
FORTUNE, R., II, 180, 181, 185, 188, 189, 191
Forum Julii, II, 4

Foschia, II, 90
Foucher, A., I, 74
Fountain of Paradise, III, 220, 234; of Jonah, III, 225
Four Garrisons, I, 61, 62; IV, 222, 231, 235, 237
Fournier, James, III, 188, 209
Four Rivers, III, 220–2
Fou ting, III, 182
Foveo, III, 145
Fowl-rabbit, II, 186
Fox, III, 206
Fozo, I, 301
Fræhn, I, 34
Francis, St., II, 13; III, 231
Francis, Franciscan, I, 180
Francis of Alessandria, Friar, III, 32, 212
Francis I, of France, I, 304
Francis of Perugia, II, 104
Francis of Pisa, II, 119, 123
Francis Xavier, St., I, 220
Franciscan Monks, martyred at Tana in India, II, 117 *seq.*; at Almaliq, III, 32, 212; at the Court of Cambalec, II, 225, 239; III, 215; in Cathay, I, 169; III, 100; expel devils, II, 260; most acceptable missionaries to Cathayans, III, 215
—— Houses at Tabriz, II, 102; at Soltania, II, 105; at Zaitún, I, 169; II, 131, 183; III, 229; at Yang chau, I, 169; II, 210; at Cambalec, I, 169; III, 215; in Kipchak, III, 82, 83; in Cathay, I, 169
Francus of Perugia, III, 37
Frankland, III, 180, 210
Franks, I, 221, 293
Franzi, C., II, 82
Frederick II, Emperor, I, 152; II, 257; III, 210
Fremant, B., II, 88
French spoken at Aleppo, III, 226; and in Cyprus, III, 226
Frescobaldi, II, 122; III, 138, 224, 236
Freytag, I, 20; II, 197, 221
Friccia, the word, III, 250
Friedmann, Dr. E., *Pegolotti*, I, 172
Friedrich, I, 128
Friuli, II, 3–6, 8, 14
Fruit, forbidden, discussed, III, 238
—— trees, bearing men and women, II, 138
Frumentius, I, 217
Fu chau, I, 175, 257, 301; II, 10, 183, 185, 186; III, 126, 128, 150; IV, 121, 126
Fujita, I, 81
Fuju, II, 186
Fu Kien, I, 39, 122, 136; II, 10, 177, 183, 186, 187; III, 12, 128; IV, 109
Fu lang (Europe), III, 214
Fūlāt, I, 129
Fu-li-la River, I, 85
Fu-lin, I, 42, 44–6, 48, 49, 54–7, 97, 235; III, 12
Fu Nan, I, 8, 66, 193
Fundacum, III, 230; see **Fondacum**
Funeral Ceremonies, IV, 143
Fung chau, I, 3
Fu Ping Hien, I, 106
Furness, III, 171
Fús, I, 98
Fusco, III, 158
Fushi Taifu, III, 21
Futim Joens, III, 181
Fu ting, III, 182; IV, 271
Fu Tso-lin, I, 313
Futteh Ali Shah, II, 164
Futtehpur Sikri, IV, 172
Fu-tu Hiung, IV, 222
Fuzo, II, 185

Gabak, IV, 163
Gabala, III, 15, 22
Gaban, III, 160
Gabar Castle, II, 106
Gabella, III, 144
Gabelli, II, 6, 8, 16, 20, 21, 84
Gabet, I, 200; II, 239, 245, 248, 250; IV, 143
Gabriel, Angel, III, 228
Gabriel, Priest, I, 108
Gadeira, I, 212
Gades, I, 212, 216, 221
Gadue, III, 160
Gaeta, III, 169
Gag, III, 213
Gaillard, *Nankin*, II, 205, 206
Gaïtros, River, I, 14
Gai-ya-szu-ting, I, 79, 80
Galafron, King of Cathay, I, 173
Galanga, Galangal, I, 137; III, 168
Galata, III, 81
Galatians, I, 102
Galbanum, III, 167
Galdan Khan, IV, 192
Galilee, III, 199, 226
Galisci, John, IV, 203
Galiúr, IV, 22
Galle, I, 77, 226, 253; IV, 33
Gallus ferrugineus, II, 186
Gallus lanatus, II, 186

GALTON, III, 124
Gálu, III, 193
GAMA, da, I, 179; II, 134; III, 230; IV, 169, 201
Gamalec for Cambalec, III, 149
Gamora, Sea of, I, 307
Gampola, IV, 33
GAMS, *Series Episcop.*, III, 13, 14, 28
Gaṇḍakī, I, 69
Gandamak, IV, 206
GANDAR, D., *Canal impérial*, II, 213; III, 115; IV, 63
Gaṇḍavatī, I, 69
Gandhara, I, 69, 74, 242; IV, 204
Gandon, III, 160
Ganfu, I, 89
Ganges, I, 69, 142, 176, 177, 183, 194, 195, 203, 303; II, 163; III, 198, 221, 222, 225; IV, 22, 151, 152
Ganpu, IV, 137
Gantur District, III, 70
Gao, IV, 40
Gaoloshan, IV, 210
Gaou, I, 226
Garaghat, IV, 176
Garamaeans, I, 189
Garamaei, III, 23
Garamantes, I, 188, 220
GARCIA da Horta, I, 184, 185, 225
GARDĒZI, Abu Said 'Abd al-Haiy Ibn Duḥak, I, 140
Garenaei, I, 195
Garine, II, 100
Garo, I, 184
Garuda, IV, 146
Gascony, I, 120
Gasō, IV, 231
Gates of China, I, 256
Gatzaria, I, 305
GAUBIL, I, 82, 111, 112; II, 153, 217, 226, 228; III, 186, 214
Gaudia (gaou), I, 226
Gauls, I, 216
Gaur, I, 124, 177; IV, 83, 84, 154
Gauta, I, 293
GAUTAMA, IV, 242
GAUTHIOT, R., I, 215
Gauze, I, 143, 197
Gaza, I, 43, 143
GAZAN Khan, II, 103, 105; see GHAZAN KHAN
Gazaria (Crimea), I, 305; III, 48, 52, 58, 81, 84, 169, 183
Geben, III, 160
Geech, I, 245
Geese, II, 181, 186; IV, 110
Gem Fishery in Ceylon, II, 171
GEMBOGA EVENZI, III, 181, 182; IV, 271
GEMELLI-CARRERI, II, 205
Genoa, I, 120, 171; II, 105; III, 154–6, 210
Genoese Merchants; in Cathay, III, 73; in Indian Sea, III, 257
Geographical Notions of Marignolli, III, 247, 261; of Ibn Batuta, IV, 44
GEORGE, I, 211
GEORGE, King (of Prester John's Family), III, 15, 47, 48, 50
GEORGE, Mar, I, 119
GEORGE, Saint, Church of, in Malabar, III, 218
Georgia, I, 94; III, 177
Georgians, I, 246
Geraldon Abbey, III, 171
GERARD, III, 10, 28, 72
GERARD of Prato, III, 5
GERARDE, *Herball*, II, 153, 154
GERBILLON, II, 227, 245
Gerfalcon, II, 229
GERINI, G. E., II, 156, 157, 169; IV, 157
German Engineer in Cathay, I, 167; Traveller in Central Asia, anonymous, I, 311, 318; IV, 182
Germany, III, 247, 252, 255
Gerondon, III, 171
Gete, IV, 163
Geu-gen, I, 208; see Juan Juan
Geukoun, III, 160
Ghaggar, IV, 12
GHAIASSUDDIN NAKKASH, I, 179, 271
GHAIASSUDDIN of Damghan, IV, 34
GHAIASUDDIN, III, 109
Ghalchas, IV, 210
Ghalwa, I, 306
Ghanah, I, 243
Ghand, I, 313
Ghandara, IV, 204; see Gandhara
Gharu wood, IV, 101
Ghazan Khan, I, 103, 105; III, 52, 108, 114, 156, 161, 162; IV, 7
Ghazár, I, 129, 143
Ghazni, I, 74; IV, 160
Gheez, I, 222
Ghelzo, III, 170
Gherofani, III, 168
Ghes, I, 145
GHIAS-UD-DIN BAHADUR BURAH, IV, 84, 86
Ghideli, IV, 180, 206
Ghilan, I, 290; see Gilan

Ghirinsula, III, 125
GHIYAS-UDDIN of Bengal, I, 80
GHIYAS-UD-DIN-TUGHLAK, II, 115, 127
GHODLEE BEABAN, II, 263
Gholáláy, IV, 259
Ghorāghāt, IV, 176
Ghorband, IV, 208, 255, 256, 257, 259
Ghorbund Valley, IV, 183
Ghori, IV, 257
Ghorraib, I, 137
Ghotaians, I, 163
Ghūbāliq, I, 60
Ghuz, I, 149, 152, 245, 247
Giacha Barca, III, 237
Gialalabath, IV, 211
Giants, II, 230; III, 259
Giava maggiore, IV, 146
GIBB, E. J. W., III, 112
GIBBON, I, 29, 32, 46, 47, 49, 84
Gibraltar, IV, 38, 39
Gierondona, III, 171
Giervalse, III, 171
GIGLIOLI, E. H., II, 181
Gihon, III, 197, 222
Gilan, I, 290, 315; III, 23
GILDEMEISTER, I, 86, 242, 243, 253; II, 133, 141; IV, 152
Gilead, I, 307
GILES, H. A., I, 5
Gilgit, I, 61, 314; IV, 216, 267
GILISH, III, 69
GILISHDIUR, Raja, III, 69
GILOTT, GILLOTT, III, 33, 212
Gilt-Teeth, III, 127, 131
Ginger, I, 264; II, 137, 181; III, 62
Gintarchan, III, 146; see Gittarchan
GIORGI, II, 249, 250–3
GIOVANNI da Empoli, I, 124, 267; II, 130
GIOVANNI Ferdinand, IV, 250
GIOVANNINO of Pisa, II, 131
Gipte, Desert of, I, 306
Giraffe, I, 223
GIRARDENGO, Nicolas, III, 179
Girdi, IV, 206
Girgenti, I, 241
GIROLAMO, Pope (NICOLAS IV), III, 215, 216
Gittarchan, III, 82, 146, 147, 152; see Astrakhan
Giu Gimmoncota, III, 65
Giudea, I, 240, 241
GIUNTI, T., I, 290, 295; II, 28
Glenluce, III, 170
GNAUCK, Max, II, 91
Goa, I, 309; II, 130, 134, 142, 212; III, 222, 253; IV, 24, 64–6, 72, 173, 177, 179, 198, 199, 202, 226, 250, 253, 254
Gober, IV, 144
Gobi, II, 263; III, 213
Gobidar, III, 160
GOD upon earth, James Fournier claims to be, III, 188
GODFREY of Viterbo, III, 226, 239–240
GODINHO de EREDIA, II, 162
GOËS, Benedict, I, 49, 181, 182, 242, 250, 251, 272, 273, 275, 276, 289, 291, 293, 310, 311, 318; II, 221; III, 11; Map to illustrate, I, 310–318; Introductory Notices regarding, IV, 169–194; Bibliography, IV, 194–7; Journey from Agra to Cathay, IV, 198–254; IV, 258; see Table of Contents
GOG, I, 151, 255, 304; IV, 123
Goga, I, 309
Gogha, III, 78
Gogo, I, 309; III, 78; IV, 40, 63, 64, 66
Gojenang, I, 74
Gold, I, 316; II, 146, 148, 150; IV, 9, 111
Golden Gate of Byzantium, I, 47; Chersonese, I, 193
Golden Land, I, 183
Golden Mountain, I, 209
Golden-Teeth, III, 127, 131; see Zardandan
GOLDSMID, Sir F. J., I, 99
GOLIAH, I, 151
GOLIUS, I, 114
GOLLÂS, I, 229
GOLOBEV, I, 311
Gomiti, II, 229, 230
Gomul, III, 265
Gondar, I, 218
GONDOPHARES, III, 252
Goose with two heads, II, 173
Gorahkpúr, I, 68
Gordico, Monte, II, 102
Gordyene, I, 93
Goritz, II, 14
GÖRRES, III, 5
Gosjú, III, 131
Gosse, II, 161
GOSSELIN, I, 24
Gota, II, 249, 250
Goths, I, 221; III, 184; of Gazaria, III, 48; Land of the, III, 48; IV, 269
GOTTWALDT, I, 83
GOVEA, Ant., IV, 170
Gozan, IV, 257

Gozart, I, 119
GRÄBERG de HEMSO, II, 105; III, 220
Graduale, III, 50
GRAHAM, Cyril, I, 101; II, 188
Grains of Paradise, II, 153, 154
Granada, III, 230; IV, 39
Grand Canal; see Great Canal
Grand Cham, II, 14, 19
Granum Paradisi, II, 153
Grapes, II, 107; IV, 109
GRAY, J. H., *China*, II, 178, 182
Great Caan, Estate, III, 89 *seq.*
Great Canal, II, 10, 213, 215; IV, 44
Great Desert, I, 303
Greater Sea, II, 98
Great India, III, 249
Great Kaan, I, 267; II, 152, 155, 164, 178, 186, 193, 195, 196, 217, 218, 236, 238, 242, 246, 247, 248; III, 209
Great Kauli, I, 303
GREAT MOGUL, III, 252
Great S'lamat, III, 194, 267
Great Wall, I, 38, 58, 165, 175, 252, 274; IV, 123, 239
Greboco, III, 161
Greece, III, 81
Greeks, I, 221; II, 177
Greenland, II, 208
Green Mount at Peking, II, 218–220
Green Sea, III, 180
GREGORY of Armenia, St., I, 94
GREGORY IX, Pope, I, 154
GREGORY X, Pope, III, 4
GREGORY of Hungary, III, 188
GRENARD, I, 60, 106; IV, 231
Grenelusso, III, 170
Grideghorda, III, 170
GRIGORIEV, V., IV, 164
GRIMANUS, Leo, IV, 202, 208
GROENEVELDT, W. P., II, 146, 148, 149, 150, 152
GRUEBER, II, 249; IV, 176, 268
GRUM GRŽIMAILO, IV, 141
GRÜNWEDEL, I, 63
GUALTERIUS OFAMILIUS, II, 115
Guardafui, I, 212
Guase, I, 144
Guaycurûs, II, 147
GUBERNATIS, Angelo de, III, 11; see DE GUBERNATIS
GUCCELLI, GUECELLI, II, 15
GUCCIO, George, IV, 2
Gu chen, III, 55; IV, 141, 237
GUCHLUK, III, 87
GUDENUS, V. F. de, II, 46
Gūdnaphar, III, 253
GUEBEK, I, 301
Guebers, I, 112
Guendoumek, IV, 206
GUERIN, Mgr. Paul, II, 89
Guidè, I, 306
GUIDOTTO, Friar, II, 98, 266
GUILIELMUS de Prato, III, 14
GUILLAUME de Nangis, I, 162
GUILLIELMUS de Nassio, III, 180
GUIWARGUIS, Mar, I, 119
Gujarat, I, 127, 228, 241, 242, 254, 309; II, 115; III, 76, 78, 229
Gulbahar, IV, 257
Guldingamo, III, 170
GULLIVER, IV, 158
Gumik, III, 84
GUMMÁ, A., II, 91, 174
GUNDAPHAR, III, 253
GŪNDOPHARUS, III, 252
GUPTA, I, 68
Gūrdezī, I, 140
Guriev, III, 85
Gurkhan, I, 149; III, 21, 22, 25; IV, 141
Gushtasp, I, 10
GUYARD, Stan., I, 33, 255, 256; II, 210
Guzerat, I, 309; III, 229; see Gujarat
GWAGNINI, I, 305
Gwalian, IV, 257, 259
Gwalior, IV, 20, 21, 22
Gwazyar, IV, 257, 259
Gyantsè, II, 251, 253
Gybeit, III, 192, 194, 267
GYLLIUS, Peter, I, 46
Gyon, I, 262, 304; III, 222

Habagateth, IV, 227, 229
Habang, Habank, III, 132; IV, 90, 151–4
Habanga, IV, 152
Habangiah Tilah, IV, 151
HABIL, I, 151
Habsh, III, 223
HACKLUYT, R., II, 78; see HAKLUYT
Hadhramaut, IV, 149
Hadith, I, 308
HADJI KHALFA, IV, 164
HAENEL, MSS., II, 23, 41, 48, 58
Haft Bacha, IV, 257
Haft Iklim, IV, 165, 193
Hagabateth, IV, 227, 229
Hagarenes, III, 85
HAGECIUS, III, 200, 201
HAGEN, H., II, 58
Haidarabad, I, 255
HAIDAR MAHOMET, IV, 166

HAIDAR RAZI, IV, 234
Hainan, Hainam, I, 100, 130, 301; II, 174; III, 129, 130
Hair, I, 251; IV, 269
Hair plaited, II, 251
Hair, yellow, IV, 210
Hairy Folk, III, 255
Hai si, I, 42
Haitam, III, 131
HAITHON, HAI TON, HAYTHON, HETHUM I, King of Little Armenia, I, 161, 163, 164, 195, 289; III, 139
HAITON II, I, 164; II, 118
HAITON, Friar, the Historian, I, 118, 162, 164, 168, 169, 178, 258; II, 34, 98, 102, 107, 168; III, 53, 85; IV, 174
HAITUN NOYÁN, III, 121
HAJAJ, I, 90
Hajigak, IV, 255
Hajiyak, IV, 255, 257, 259
HAJJI AZIZ, IV, 225
HAJJI KHANUM, IV, 207
HAJJI MAHOMED, I, 30, 131, 181, 275, 277, 290, 294, 295; IV, 234, 241
Hajr, IV, 5
Haj Tarkhan (Astrakhan), III, 147; IV, 7
HAKIM MIRZA, IV, 203
Hakkar, IV, 40
HAKLUYT, II, 27, 78, 180
Halabidu, III, 66
Halacha, III, 23
Halah, III, 23
Halaha, III, 24
Halala, III, 22
Halawan, III, 22
HALL, Dr. F., IV, 256
HALL, Prof. I. H., I, 108
HALL, Robert, I, 27
HALMA, Abbé, I, 190
Haloes round Buddhist Saints, II, 153
Halwan, III, 23, 24
Halys, III, 161
Hamadan, III, 22, 108
Hamade, II, 262
Hamath, I, 257; IV, 37, 45
Hami, I, 40, 58; III, 55, 148, 265; IV, 237, 238, 239
Hamid, IV, 5
HAMILTON, Alex., I, 129; III, 252
HAMILTON, Walter, II, 135
HAMMER, V., I, 246; II, 133; III, 107; IV, 142
HAMY, E. T., II, 256
HAMZA-al-Iṣfahānī, I, 83, 84
HAN, I, 4, 5, 7, 41, 42, 51, 57, 58, 60, 95, 114, 234; III, 12; IV, 228, 231
HANANJESUS, I, 108
Hanaul, IV, 22
Hanceu, I, 240; see Hang chau
Hancialix, IV, 227, 229
Hang chau, I, 89, 136, 142, 150, 171, 173, 175, 236, 240, 256, 258; II, 10, 177, 180, 187–9, 192–4, 198–200, 203, 205, 213; III, 128, 148, 229; IV, 129, 137; see Khansa, Cansay, Quinsai, etc.
Han Haï, I, 62
Hāniḳu, IV, 138
Han mi mo mo ni (Emir), I, 89
HANNIBAL, IV, 45
Hanoi, I, 4, 51, 193
Hansi, IV, 12
HAN YÜ, II, 182
Hanzawadi, I, 243
Hapaniya Tillah, IV, 153
Hara, III, 22
Harach, Mount, II, 102
Harah, I, 190; III, 23; see Herat
HARAPÂLA, II, 115
Harba, I, 308
Hardalah, IV, 98
Hardwār, IV, 18
Hariana, IV, 258
Harira, I, 145
Harkah, I, 244
Harkand, Sea of, I, 127; II, 149
Harkat, I, 244
HARLEZ, C. de, I, 8
Harmakut, IV, 18
Harráqah, IV, 133
HARRIS, I, 125
HARSA ÇĪLADĪTYA, I, 69
HARTMANN, I, 31, 83, 137, 141, 257, 258
HARÚN AL RASHÍD, I, 92
Haryr, I, 137
Hasam, III, 130
Hashísh, II, 257
HASSAN, II, 258
Hassan-ghar, III, 22
HASSAN JUJÁK, III, 125
Hassan Kala'a, Hassan Kaleh, II, 101; III, 162
HASSAN SABAH, II, 257
Hat island, II, 146
HATTHADĀṬHA, I, 70
HAUGHTON, IV, 208
Hau Han Shu, I, 8, 23, 41, 50, 52, 53; II, 243; IV, 266
Haulak, IV, 235
Haunted Deserts, II, 264
HAU SHU, I, 140
HAU T'ANG, I, 140

Havilah, II, 111
HAVRET, H., I, 105–9
Hawak, IV, 255
Hawaráwún, III, 131
Hawâz, II, 109
Hawking, the Great Khan, II, 229
HAYAM WURUK, II, 156
HAYM, N. F., II, 92
HAYTHON, see HAITHON
Hazah, II, 109; III, 23
Hazaras, I, 250; IV, 183
Hazlakh, I, 249
HAZRAT AFAK, IV, 166, 185, 192
Hazrat Imám, I, 317; IV, 210, 211
Head Dress, II, 222, 223, 251
Heat, great, at Hormuz, II, 112
Heaven, City of, see Hang chau
HEBER, II, 172, 252
Hebron, III, 240, 244, 245
HEDIN, Sven, IV, 223
Hedyphon, III, 23
Hedypnus, III, 23
Hei yi Ta shi, I, 92
Hekatompylos, I, 23, 43, 189, 190
Hellespont, I, 188, 190
Hemodus, I, 194, 195
Henna, III, 166
Hennins, II, 223
HENRICUS, II, 16
HENRION, Baron, II, 87
HENRY II, Duke, I, 152
HENRY of Glatz, II, 24, 27, 28, 52, 80, 93, 267, 271, 277
Hens, II, 186; IV, 110
Hephthalites, I, 58, 59, 205, 207, 229; see Ephthalites
HERACLEONAS, I, 54
HERACLIUS, I, 54; IV, 8
Herat, I, 34, 103, 104, 123, 189, 190, 205, 271, 286, 287, 293, 300; II, 115; III, 22, 23, 155; IV, 160
HERBELOT, d', I, 34, 54, 55, 247, 251, 296; II, 112, 133, 198; III, 223; IV, 223
HERBERT, Sir T., II, 34, 106, 107
Hercules' Gates, III, 219
Herdil, II, 242; see Volga
Here, II, 115; see Herat
Herenj, I, 244
Heri, I, 190, 300
Heriunitis, III, 22; see Herat
Herkend, Sea of, I, 127; II, 149
HERMANN, A., IV, 266
Hermaphrodite, III, 261
Hermon, I, 307
HERODOTUS, I, 22, 151, 213; II, 33, 157, 173, 252; III, 158, 242, 249, 259; IV, 143, 204
Heroöpolitan, I, 221
Herpestes ichneumon, II, 114
HERSCHEL, Sir W. J., III, 124
Heruli, I, 221
Hesdin, III, 199
HESE, John of, III, 197, 198, 251, 253
HETHUM, see HAITON
HEWETT, II, 147
HEYD, W., II, 90, 107, 133, 134
HEZEKIAH, I, 27
HHÁLÁ, III, 126
Hhamál, III, 241
Hharash, I, 222
Hharshan, I, 222
HHURNASAB, IV, 34
Hiacán, IV, 229
Hiang Shan, III, 182; IV, 271
HIAO WU TI, I, 67
Hiarcan, Hiarchan, IV, 215, 217, 218, 221; see Yarkand
Hia T'ien-chu-sze, IV, 267
HIBELIN, Jehan de, I, 262
HIDAYAT-ALLAH, IV, 166, 185, 192
Hiddekel, III, 197
HIE-LI Qagan, I, 62
H'IEN, Ye-liu, I, 147
HIEN CHW'EN, I, 81
HIEN-PHU, I, 148
HIEN TSING, I, 148
HIEN TSUNG, I, 70; III, 149
Hien Yang, III, 122; IV, 89
Hierapolis, I, 188, 189
HI LEANG (YE LIU), IV, 228
Hili, I, 309; II, 115; IV, 26, 74, 75
Hílú, IV, 21
Himalaya, I, 184, 185, 224; II, 208, 248; IV, 176
Himatala, II, 188, 223
Himyarites, I, 251
Hind, I, 87, 142, 151, 230; II, 111; III, 23, 28
Hindeki, II, 111
Hindu Kush, I, 98, 230, 250, 311, 314; II, 263; IV, 9, 181, 183, 205, 206, 209, 255 *seq.*
Hindus, I, 101, 150, 151; II, 25
Hindustan, IV, 207
HING TSUNG, I, 147
Hiong nu, Hiung nu, I, 7, 35–40, 62, 64, 65; see Huns
Hiontius, III, 240
Hippopotamus, I, 224
Hippuri, I, 199
Hira, I, 43, 83, 84
HIRTH, Fried., I, 18, 19, 23, 41, 42–6, 48, 52, 54, 55, 57, 109, 197, 199, 233; II, 169, 183, 192, 194, 242; III, 13; IV, 4, 266
Hisar-shaduman, I, 287
Hispaniola, I, 272

Hissar, I, 286
Hissar-shaduman, I, 286
HI TSUNG, I, 133
HIUAN TSANG, HIUEN TSANG, I, 63, 69, 70, 74, 75, 110, 191, 192, 210, 227, 228, 242, 254, 274, 277, 303, 313–6; II, 188; III, 221; IV, 186, 215, 222, 231, 235, 258
HIUAN TSUNG, Emperor, I, 63, 105, 110
Hoa, I, 205
HOASENG, I, 237
Ho chau, III, 113
Hocibelch, I, 310
HODGSON, B. H., I, 73
Hog stag, I, 224
HOJAH APPAK, IV, 192
Hojahs, IV, 192, 193
Ho K'iu-ping, I, 38
HO-LI-DAN, II, 248
Holin, III, 128; see Karakorum
Holm Cultram, III, 171
HOLM, Frits V., I, 106
Holong, I, 72
HOLUBEIM, I, 300
Holy Land, II, 34; III, 226, 247
HOMER, II, 240
Homerite, I, 213, 218, 220, 227, 231
Ho Nan, I, 108; II, 152, 209, 231; III, 126, 128
HONDIUS, I, 308; IV, 159
Honey, II, 157
Honey, Trees producing, II, 156; III, 61
Hongkong, I, 135
Hong Merchants, II, 213
HONG WU, I, 57; see HUNG WU
Honor, IV, 73
Honore, I, 309
HONORIUS IV, Pope, I, 120, 166
HOPKINSON, J., III, 197
HORACE, I, 186
Horma, IV, 227–9, 231
Hormes, III, 68
HORMISDAS, II, 112
Hormisiom, I, 309
Hormuz, I, 85–7, 144, 171, 309; II, 10, 106, 112, 113, 242; III, 49, 68, 69, 75, 199; IV, 4, 5, 36
Horn, worn by women of some aboriginal Tribes in China, II, 188
Hornbill, II, 173
Horses, with six legs, II, 229; Trade in, to South India, III, 69; to Ceylon, I, 230; Great, carried to Great Khan by Marignolli, III, 213; commemorated in Chinese Annals, III, 214
HOSEÍN, III, 122
Ho shang, II, 251
Hosol, IV, 230
Hostelries in Cathay, II, 232; IV, 116, 117
HO TI, I, 50, 66
HO TU, I, 23
Houang chang yu, II, 191
HOUDAS, II, 236
Hou-jen, I, 116
HOUTUM-SCHINDLER, II, 103
HOVEDEN, Roger, III, 17
HOWARD, Rev. G. B., II, 135, 136
HOWARD, Broadley, III, 219
HOWORTH, Sir H. H., I, 246
HOYSALAS, II, 115
HR'IPSIMÊ, St., III, 163
Hsing-ch'a Shêng-lan, II, 150
Hsing-hsing, I, 161
Hu, II, 237, 238
Huai yu, III, 12
HUART, Cl., II, 258; IV, 133
Hua yang, I, 161
Hua yang kuo chih, I, 161
Hubbigunge, IV, 153
HUBER, Ed., I, 75
HUC, E., I, 200; II, 87, 184, 239, 245, 248, 250, 251; IV, 143
HUDSON, I, 290; II, 160
Huen-ba-sheng, IV, 228
HUET, III, 198
Hu-eul-man, IV, 228
HUGO of Cyprus, IV, 3
Hujan, II, 105
Hujetabad, II, 107
Hu Kwang, I, 167; II, 231; III, 128, 129
HÚLAKÚ, I, 153, 272, 288, 289; II, 102, 197, 244, 258; III, 4, 40, 111; IV, 7, 87, 144, 160
Hu-la-ma, IV, 228
Hu lu, IV, 231
Human Sacrifices, II, 139; IV, 98; at Tartar Funerals, IV, 142–3; in Súdán, IV, 144
HUMĀYŪM, I, 9; IV, 18, 204, 207
HUMBOLDT, A., I, 178, 190; II, 154; IV, 187
Humi, I, 191
Hu Nan, III, 129
Hunawar, Hunawúr, IV, 24, 30, 31, 35, 63, 64, 65, 73, 124
Hund, I, 74
Hungarian, White, I, 245
Hungary, I, 122; III, 188, 246, 247
H'UNG KI, YE-LIU, I, 147

HUNG WU, I, 57, 73; II, 216; III, 12, 127, 157
Hun ho, III, 117
Huns, I, 104, 215, 220, 244; III, 184; see Hiong nu
Huns, White, I, 36; see Hephthalites
HUNTER, W. W., *Gaz. of India*, II, 129, 134
Hunting Matches of Great Khan, II, 234
Hunza Nagar, I, 314
Huo Chou, III, 133
HUO-TSI-CHAN, IV, 185, 228
Hu pao tze, IV, 141
Hu Pe, III, 129
Hurma, I, 306
Hus, II, 109; III, 85; see Huz
HUSAIN, IV, 165, 211
HUSAMUDDÍN, III, 125
Husnabad, I, 278, 285
Husn Amárat, I, 309
Huz, II, 106, 109; see Hus
Huzia, II, 109
Huzitis, II, 109
Hwang, I, 141
HWANG CHAO, I, 133
Hwang Ho (Yellow River), I, 278, 285; II, 165, 213, 244, 245; III, 24, 47, 115, 126, 128, 148, 221, 225; IV, 108, 188
HWANG TI, I, 7, 8, 149; II, 216
Hwan-na, IV, 222
HWAN TI, I, 51, 52, 66
Hwa ting, I, 136
Hwei Ho, I, 62, 88; III, 55
Hwei Hu, I, 62, 88
Hwei Hwei, I, 88; II, 198
Hwei Sheng sze, I, 88
HWEI SING, I, 75
HWEI TI, I, 76
HWEI T'UNG, I, 147
Hwei Yuan, IV, 193
HWEN TSUNG, I, 90
HYACINTHE, Father, II, 252; see BITCHOURIN
Hyacinth, stone, I, 226, 228
Hyperperae, IV, 9
Hyphasis, III, 219
Hyrcania, I, 34, 190
Hyrcanian Sea, I, 187, 213
Hyrcanians, I, 221

Iaic, Iaik, I, 212, 245, 308; see Jaic
Iakonich, IV, 215
Iam, I, 275
Iamceu, Iamzai (Yang chau), II, 209, 210, 212
Iana, I, 303; II, 151
Iangio, II, 209
Iangsé, II, 210
Iascot, I, 159
Iberia, I, 216
Ibex, I, 224
Ibir, I, 152
IBI SHABOLO SHEKU KHAN, IV, 164
IBN AL-FAKIH, I, 128
IBN AL-KALBI, I, 2
IBN BATUTA, I, 44, 75, 80, 82, 131, 135, 143, 151, 173, 177, 226–8, 242, 253, 254, 257, 258, 272, 277, 282, 289, 296, 299, 302, 304, 306–310; II, 24, 122, 127, 132, 133, 141, 146, 164, 168, 171, 172, 179, 180, 183, 187, 192, 196, 197, 201, 223, 233; III, 34, 146, 185, 192, 194, 217, 218, 230–3, 237, 256, 259; IV, 1–166, 169, 208, 225, 258, 271
IBN EL WARDI, I, 87, 247
IBN HAUKAL, I, 20, 86, 245
IBN JUBAIR, III, 145; IV, 43, 156
IBN JUZAI, IV, 40, 41, 42
IBN KHALLIKAN, I, 308
IBN KHURD'ADHBAH, I, 18, 127, 135, 137, 225, 243, 247, 256; II, 147
IBN MUHALHIL, I, 101, 138, 242, 244, 250, 253, 254, 255; IV, 190
IBN ROSTEH, I, 137
IBN SA'ID, I, 256
IBN WAHAB of Basra, I, 133
IBRAHIM, III, 109
IBRAHIM SULTÁN, Mirza, I, 273
Icarus, I, 315
Ich River, I, 212
I chau, I, 73
Ichneumon, II, 114
Ichthyophagi, I, 195
Iconium, I, 57; III, 125; IV, 5
IDBUZID, I, 108, 110; IV, 266
IDES, Ysbrand, I, 276; II, 199
Idiqut, IV, 141
Idiqut Shahri, I, 64; III, 55, 133
Idolatry, in India, III, 63; ascribed to Catholics by Orientals, III, 264
Idols, Feeding of the, II, 185
Ierken, IV, 215
Iescilbas, I, 293, 295
Iest (Yezd), II, 107, 108
Ieuch, I, 306
Ighúrs, III, 120; see Uighúrs
IKÉ FANCHÁN, III, 122
IKE-MESE, II, 152
I-Khanam, IV, 211
IKHTYYAR UD-DIN, IV, 86

Ilak khans, I, 60, 148; IV, 164
Ilchi (Khotan), I, 311, 312; IV, 223
ILCHIGADAÏ, I, 65; III, 30, 35, 39; IV, 161
Ili, I, 33, 35, 37, 38, 40, 164, 171, 248, 272, 288, 289; III, 21, 87; IV, 164, 187, 193, 222, 228, 230, 239
Ili baliq, I, 163, 164
I-LIE YE-LIU, I, 148; III, 21
Iliskoye, I, 164
ILIYAS, IV, 85
Ilkhan, I, 149
Illustration, II, 166
Illyrians, I, 221
Il Milione, II, 228; see MARCO POLO
Imád-ud-daulah Abu'l Khair, III, 108
Imaus, I, 16, 190, 192, 194, 286
Imil, IV, 163, 164, 235
IMIL KHWAJA, IV, 163
Imil River, IV, 271
Imperium Medium, III, 85
Incense, IV, 97
Inchi, III, 230
Incineration, II, 167; see **Cremation**
India, I, 6, 37, 151, 215, 227, 263, 309, 310; II, 110–2; III, 22, 23
—— Inland (Lower Euphrates), II, 111
—— Upper (for S. China), II, 176
—— Upper (for S. India), III, 59, 67
—— Great, and Maxima (S. China), III, 228, 373
—— Little (Malabar), III, 373
—— Lower (Malabar), III, 230
—— Tertia of Jordanus is in Africa, I, 213; III, 27
—— the term, how used by Portuguese, IV, 198
—— Nestorian Archbishopric of, III, 22
—— Climate of, etc., III, 59, 60
Indian and China Trade in Pliny's time, cost of, I, 200
Indian Antiquary, I, 271; II, 130, 135, 142
Indian Caucasus, II, 262
Indian Ocean, III, 234
Indians, I, 15; III, 241, 246
Indian Words used by Ibn Batuta, IV, 15; coins mentioned by Ibn Batuta, IV, 54 *seq.*; weights in time of, IV, 62, 81
Indies, I, 15; III, 247
Indies, the Three, III, 28
Indigo, III, 165
Indigo, Red, I, 251
Indo-China, I, 143
Indo-Scythians, I, 36
Indostan, III, 217
Indulgences, III, 83
Indus, I, 61, 86, 87, 101, 104, 150, 177, 227, 243, 303; II, 207; III, 198, 209, 221, 222, 225, 229, 253; IV, 9, 154, 180, 203, 216, 238
Industry of Chinese, II, 179
Ingachar, IV, 217
Ingtien, I, 175
I-ning Fang, I, 110
INNOCENT IV, Pope, I, 154, 156; III, 199, 210
INNOCENT VI, III, 203
Inshan, III, 24
Invulnerability, how procured, II, 161, 162
Io, III, 242
Iolci, IV, 227
Iouvia, I, 215
Ipoh, II, 158
Irak Ajami, II, 257
Irak, Iraq, I, 84, 90; IV, 136, 139
Irak, Pass, IV, 259
Iran, I, 152
IRAVI CORTTAN, II, 135; III, 254
Irawadi, I, 176, 177; III, 222
Ireland, II, 241; III, 204, 206
Irkhan, I, 248
Iron of Seres and Chinese, I, 17, 254; presented by Turks to an ambassador, I, 208; ships without iron, II, 114; weapons without iron, II, 162; láth at Delhi, IV, 47; at Charikar, IV, 208
Iron Gates, I, 247
Iron Mines, IV, 209
Irtish River, I, 247, 289; IV, 162
ISAAC, III, 245
ISAAC, servant of GOËS, IV, 178, 180, 202, 215, 221, 224, 240, 244, 248, 250–2, 254
ISABEL of Bavaria, II, 223
ISA BEN THÂTHA, IV, 150
ISAI, IV, 201, 225
ISAIAH, I, 3, 10, 11, 20; II, 122
ISAN BUGHA, IV, 161, 163, 166
Isauites, IV, 175
Isfidjab, IV, 164
ISHAK BIN AMRAM, I, 244
Ishkamán, IV, 259
Ishkashm, IV, 211
Ishma, IV, 238
ISHWAR, III, 68
ISIDORE, St., I, 22

Islands of India and Cathay, their great number, I, 258; II, 176; III, 64; subject to Great Khan, II, 231
ISMAEL, II, 257; IV, 166
ISMAEL Shah, I, 216
Ismaelians, I, 153
ISMAIL KHAN, IV, 192
Isnicmid, IV, 8
Ispahan, I, 182; II, 104, 106, 257; III, 228; IV, 3, 36, 139
ISRAEL, I, 224
Israelites, I, 221, 222
Issa, III, 65
ISSÉ or YI SE, I, 110
Issedon Serica, I, 195
Issedones, I, 195
Issedonians, II, 252
Issik Kul, I, 36, 60, 272, 311; IV, 160
Issus, II, 190
IṢTAKRÎ, I, 84, 85
Istambul, I, 44; IV, 8
ISTÄMI, I, 58
Istan-polin, I, 44
Istria, II, 4
ISU MANGU, IV, 161
ISUN TIMUR, III, 34; IV, 162
ITI, II, 200
Itu, Mountains, I, 288
Iūchi, III, 230
Iurmen, I, 308
Iusce, IV, 219
Iuvernia, I, 189
Ivory, I, 253
I-wu, IV, 239; see Ha mi
I-wu-lu, IV, 239; see Ha mi
IZDBUZID, I, 108, 110; IV, 266
IZZET ULLAH, I, 317; IV, 183, 190, 234, 238, 239

Jaba (Zabadj), I, 127
Jabah, I, 243
JABALAHA, Mar, I, 109, 116, 120, 121, 127, 166; II, 135; III, 253
Jabkan River, I, 289
Jaca, III, 237
Jaci, III, 127; see Yachi
Jack fruit, II, 139; III, 40, 237
JACKSON, A. W. W., *Persia*, II, 106
JACOB, III, 245
JACOB, Syrian Bishop, I, 127
JACOBI, Hermann, I, 6
JACOBUS, Bishop of Khanbaliq, III, 14
JACOBUS de Paduâ, II, 117; see JAMES of Padua
Jacorich, IV, 215
JACQUES de Novelles, III, 209
JACQUES de Vitry, II, 34
JACQUET, E., II, 72; III, 36, 37
Jadah, I, 246
Jade, II, 221, 246; IV, 219, 244
Jádú, I, 246
Jaghjagha, I, 216
Jah Jirm, I, 189
Jaház, II, 113
Jaic, I, 212, 245, 308; II, 242; III, 85
Jaidi-urtang, IV, 229
Jaiguouden, IV, 239
Jaimur, I, 227, 254
Jainas, III, 251
Jaintia, IV, 152
Jajali, I, 254
Jajullā, I, 254
Jakonig, IV, 215
Jalalabad, I, 74; IV, 180, 183, 206, 210
Jalālī, IV, 20, 21
JALALUDDIN, I, 33, 80; II, 115
JALAL UDDIN AHSAN, IV, 13
JALALUDDIN, Sherif, IV, 34
JALALUDDIN TABRIZI, IV, 87–90, 131, 151, 152–4, 209
JALANSI, Raja, IV, 22, 65
JÁLASTI, III, 231
Jaleym, I, 310
Jalgáh, I, 272
Jalish, IV, 234; see Chalish
Jálna, I, 310
JALUT, I, 151
Jam, IV, 230
Jamâkûd, I, 258
JAMALUDDIN, III, 69
JAMAL UDDIN, IV, 30, 31, 36
JAMBRES, I, 151
Jambu, IV, 95
Jambu Air, IV, 96
JAMES, Friar, Irish comrade of Odoric, II, 11, 15, 241
JAMES of Florence, Archbishop, III, 28
JAMES of Padua, Friar and Martyr, II, 117, 119, 121, 122, 124; III, 76
Jami'ut Tawárikh, the History of Rashid, III, 107, 110, 112, 131
Jamjál, III, 115
Jamkût, I, 257, 258
Jamrūd, IV, 204
JAMSHID, I, 9
Jamún, IV, 95
Jana, I, 303; II, 151; III, 194; see Java
Janatabad, IV, 83
Janci, III, 248; see Yang chau
Jandishapur, Jandisabur, III, 22 23
Janfu, I, 136

Jangali Admi, II, 230
JANIBECH, JANIBEG, I, 301
JANIKAH, IV, 166
Jan Kila'h, I, 317
Janku, I, 136, 143; II, 210
Jankūt, I, 255
JANNES, I, 151
Japan, I, 88, 131, 136, 301; II, 163; IV, 159
JAPHET, I, 151; III, 247
Jar in Peking Palace, II, 220
Jarga, I, 151
JARRA, IV, 12
Jase, II, 113
Jasper, IV, 219
Jatah, IV, 163
Jats, IV, 233
Jaua, I, 302; see Java
JAUBERT, I, 86, 142, 143, 243, 256, 314, 315; II, 133, 147; IV, 184, 209; see EDRISI
Java, I, 77, 124, 128, 275, 302, 303; II, 10, 31, 34, 151, 152, 154, 156, 161, 183, 219; III, 192–5, 267; IV, 67, 68, 71, 92, 94, 145, 147, 148, 155–8, 198
Java the Less, I, 176; II, 150, 174; see Sumatra
Java Major, I, 176; II, 162; see Java
Javan, I, 101
Jāwa, Jāwi, II, 151
Jáwalamukhi, IV, 18
Jaxartes, I, 23, 34, 37, 61, 191, 211; III, 147, 221; IV, 164, 166, 216, 235
JAYANBOGHA, III, 182
Jayawardanapúra, III, 244
JAZEDBOUZID, I, 108
Jazia, or Poll-tax, IV, 18
Jazírah, an island, II, 146
Jazirah, on the Tigris, I, 199; on the Volga, I, 308
Jazirat ul-Andalus (Andalusia), IV, 156
JEBE NOYON, I, 60
JEHAN de Saint Denys, II, 249, 266
JEHAN LE LONG, II, 266; III, 36, 89
JEHOIADA, III, 266
Jehol, III, 116
Jelu, valley, I, 114
Jelum, IV, 154
Jenasdan (China), I, 93
JENKINSON, Anthony, I, 181; III, 82, 84, 85, 126; IV, 201, 241
Jenpagur, I, 93
Jen-pa-kur, I, 94
Jenpakuriani, I, 94
Jenuyeh, I, 149
JEREMIAH, III, 222
Jerm, IV, 185
JEROME, III, 266
JEROME, Friar, III, 11
JEROME of Ascoli, Cardinal, I, 120
JEROME-XAVIER of Navarre, IV, 173–7
Jerusalem, I, 119, 252, 263; II, 106, 135, 141, 178; III, 16, 24, 199, 226, 240, 245; IV, 37
JESMAS, I, 151
Jessam, III, 130
Jesuit Missions in China, I, 121; IV, 169 *seq.*; their surveys, I, 311 *seq.*
Jesuit Tables, I, 312
JESUJABUS of Adiabene, Patriarch, I, 103; II, 129
Jews, I, 112, 222; II, 133, 134, 135; III, 199; IV, 175; in China, III, 215; Statesmen in Mongol Service, III, 108
Jezia, IV, 18
Jháláwár, IV, 64
Jibal, I, 135; III, 16
Jibal Nákus (Hill of the Bell), sounding-sand in Sinai Desert, II, 262
Jibal-Sindi, I, 241
Jibal-ul-Thabúl (Mount of the Drums), IV, 3
Jibul Judi, II, 102
Jidda, Jiddah, I, 306; III, 228; IV, 5
Jidiáh, I, 79
Jigdah, IV, 234, 238
JIHANGHIR, IV, 135
Jihán Numá, IV, 164
Jih nan, Ji nan, I, 3–6, 51, 193, 234
Jih-pên-kwé, III, 129
Jihun R., I, 247, 313–5; III, 221; IV, 160; see Oxus
Jikil, I, 245, 246
Jil, I, 315
Jilahd, I, 307
Jilan, III, 198
JINKISHAI, III, 34; IV, 161
JINKSHI, III, 33, 35
Jinseng, I, 292, 298
JIN TSUNG, I, 148; II, 223
Jîrun, I, 85
JIV, I, 9
JIWANI, III, 20
JO, II, 249
JOANNES, St., III, 84
JOANNES IUCHOY, III, 181
JOB, II, 34; III, 226; land of Job, II, 109
Jogis, IV, 21, 23, 135, 223

JOHANNES SCOTUS, III, 220
Johannina, III, 230
JOHN, St., not dead, belief, III, 44
JOHN'S, St., Convent at Sarai, III, 83
JOHN XXII, Pope, II, 12, 16, 22, 104, 126, 130; III, 5, 33, 36, 37, 89, 179, 205, 211
JOHN IV Comnene, IV, 7
JOHN III, King of Portugal, III, 253
JOHN, Metropolitan of Masin, I, 121
JOHN BAPTIST, St., III, 211
JOHN of Cora, I, 169; III, 36, 37, 89
JOHN the Cordelier, III, 6
JOHN FERDINAND, a Chinese Christian sent to aid Goës, IV, 180, 181, 245, 247–252
JOHN of Florence, see JOHN de' MARIGNOLLI
John of Hese, III, 197, 198, 251, 253
JOHN of India, Master, a black man, III, 32
JOHN, Patriarch of the Indies, III, 252
JOHN LE LONG of Ypres, II, 68, 73, 244, 266; III, 36, 89
JOHN of Luxemburg, III, 99
JOHN de' MARIGNOLLI, III, 9, 13, 177–269
JOHN of MONTE CORVINO, I, 52, 118, 122, 169, 170, 299; II, 10, 11, 22, 114, 118, 141, 200, 245, 270; III, 3–7, 10, 11, 12, 14, 15, 26, 36, 37; First letter, 45–51; Second letter, 51–8; 59, 100, 179, 210, 211, 216
JOHN PALAEOLOGUS, III, 211
JOHN de PLANO CARPINI, see CARPINI
JOHN of ST. AGATHA, III, 5
JOHN of Udine, II, 22
JOHN of Winterthur, II, 8; III, 14, 31
JOHNSON, F., *Persian Dict.*, I, 20, 141, 185, 253, 292; II, 221
JOHNSON, Richard, I, 181; III, 85
JOHNSTON, Keith, I, 117, 299, 310; II, 213; IV, 227
Johore, II, 157
Jolah, II, 147
JONAS, III, 225
JONES, Winter, I, 175, 176, 177; III, 243
JOPPI, Dr. V., of Udine, II, 19, 36, 38, 82, 89
JOR, an Indian King, I, 242
JORDANUS, Friar, I, 82, 170, 171, 213, 227, 303; II, 10, 11, 22, 24, 98, 102, 103, 114, 116, 118, 125, 128–131, 141, 163, 164, 168; III, 27–31, 38, 68, 75, 76, 78, 80, 203, 217, 218, 223; Addit. Notes to his *Mirabilia*, III, 39–44; First Letter, III, 75–8; Second Letter, III, 78–80
Jorján, I, 190
Jorjaniah, III, 82
Jorman, I, 307, 308
Jorvaulx, III, 171
JOSEFUS, Bishop, III, 14
JOSEPH, III, 245
JOSEPHUS, III, 184
Jo-shui, I, 235
Jöujen, I, 149; see Juan Juan
JOVIAN, Emperor, I, 216; III, 23
JOVIUS, Paulus, II, 208
Juan Juan, I, 58, 59, 149, 205, 208
Judaea, III, 12
Jugdulluk, IV, 206
Jugglers' tricks at Kanchau, I, 296; at the Khan's Court, II, 239; at Khansa, IV, 134
Juggurnath, II, 145
Júјú, III, 117
JULIAN, Emperor, III, 23
JULIEN, Stanislas, I, 10, 18, 23, 65, 68, 69, 71, 72–5, 107, 295, 298, 317; III, 223
Julman, I, 307
Jumna R., III, 221; IV, 16, 82, 83
Jún R., IV, 82
JÚNA KHAN, IV, 10
Junks, II, 131; III, 230; IV, 25, 103
Jurfattan, IV, 76, 77
Jurga, I, 281
Juri, I, 242
JURZ or JUZR, an Indian King, I, 241, 242, 243
Justice with a vengeance, IV, 30
JUSTIN II, Emperor, I, 59, 205, 207, 208; II, 252; III, 122, 147
JUSTIN Martyr, III, 243
JUSTINIAN, Emperor, I, 24, 49, 55, 203, 204
Ju-tê-a, III, 12
Juvia, I, 215
Juz, IV, 19

Káan, Kan, Khan, Khakan, Khagan, I, 149; III, 213; see Great Kaan and Khan
Kabadián, I, 191

KABAK KHAN, IV, 161
Kaber, I, 228
KABIL (Cain), I, 151
Kabul, I, 98, 230, 242, 254, 281, 310, 314; II, 10, 262; IV, 9, 180, 181, 185, 203, 204, 206–9, 215, 221, 255
Kabulistan, I, 152
Kadáh (Queddah), I, 127, 253
Kadhil, II, 139; III, 237
KADIJA, III, 192; IV, 31
KADIR KHAN, IV, 85–6
Kadranj, Kairanj, Herenj, I, 128, 244
Kafche-kué, Kafchekuo, III, 130
Káfilas, IV, 257, 259
Kafiristan, I, 74, 314; II, 263; IV, 204, 205, 256, 259
Kafirnihan, I, 315
Kafirs, I, 242; IV, 204–6, 221, 256, 258
KAFUR, I, 253; III, 69; IV, 19, 20
Kahārs, IV, 14
KAÏANÊ, St., III, 163
Kaibars, I, 283
KAIDU, III, 4, 15, 49, 132; IV, 162, 163, 234
K'aidu Gol, IV, 234, 235
K'ai fung, Khai fung, I, 114, 156; II, 192; III, 126, 128
K'AI HWANG, I, 88
KAIKHÁTU, III, 150
KAI KHUSRU (Cyrus), I, 9, 10
KAIKOBAD, I, 9
Kail, III, 63, 68, 70, 131; IV, 35
Kailas, III, 221, 222; IV, 18
Kaili, IV, 159
Kailúka, IV, 159
Kailúkari, IV, 104, 159
Kaimāk, I, 246
Kaiminfu, II, 227; III, 116, 117, 118
Kainak, IV, 235
Kai p'ing, II, 227; III, 113, 116, 117
Kais, I, 84, 85, 144; IV, 5, 45; see Kish
Kajarrá, Kajraha, Kajrai, IV, 22
Kakali, IV, 96
Kakam, IV, 25
Kakula, IV, 96, 97, 100, 103, 157
Kalacha, IV, 210
Kalah, I, 252, 253
Kalāh-Bār, I, 127, 253
Kal'ah-i Atashparasṭān, II, 106
Kalakah, IV, 159
Kala-Kambing, II, 157
Kalamita Bay, I, 305
Kalank, I, 246
KALATIN-BIN-UL-SHAKHIR, I, 138, 140
Kalcha, IV, 180
KALESA, III, 69
KALESA-DEWAR, IV, 58
Kalib, I, 251
Kali Nadi, IV, 22
KALIN BIN-SHAKHBAR, I, 138
Kaliq, IV, 235
Kalka Mazar, IV, 235, 238
Kalkan, I, 245
Kallats, Turkish Tribe, I, 210
Kalliana, Kalliani, Kaḷliena, Kalyani, I, 210, 220, 227, 230, 243, 253, 254
Kalmaks, Kalmuks, I, 246, 281; IV, 165, 166, 188, 192, 234, 235
Kalsha, IV, 210
Kaluganga, III, 231
Kalyanapuri, I, 220
Kama, I, 307, 308
KAMAL-UDDÍN ABDALLAH, IV, 16, 119
Káman, I, 243
Kamara, IV, 96, 100
Kamári Aloes, IV, 100
Kāmarūb, I, 253
KAMARUDDIN DUGHLAK, IV, 165, 189
Kamarún, I, 253
Kamārupa, I, 253; IV, 252
Kambaia, III, 76
Kambálik, II, 233
Kambalu, IV, 174
Kamboja, I, 193
Kamchau, Kamchu, I, 276, 277; III, 128, 148; IV, 241; see Kan Chau
Kamkhu, III, 127
Kampot, I, 193
Kampsay, III, 269
Kāmrān, IV, 207
Kamrú, IV, 86, 87, 90, 96, 151, 152
Kamrub, IV, 152
Kamrun, I, 243, 253; IV, 101, 152
Kamrup, I, 79, 254; IV, 152
Kams, III, 18
Kamul, Kamil, I, 73, 140, 273, 281, 304; III, 148, 190, 213, 216, 265; IV, 189, 191, 233, 234, 238, 239, 241
Kan, IV, 138; see Káan
Kanauj, I, 69, 74, 90, 241, 315; IV, 13, 20, 21, 22, 271
Kanbalu, IV, 174
KANCHANA WUNGU, III, 193
Kan Chau, I, 38, 64, 73, 118, 139, 276, 277, 278, 286, 291, 293, 302; III, 128, 148; IV, 241

Kanchekue, III, 130
Kançou, I, 136
Kand, III, 23
Kandábil, I, 139
Kandahar, I, 74, 98, 242; III, 127, 131; IV, 22, 63
Kandar, III, 127, 131
Kandesh, IV, 177
Kanfu, II, 179, 180
Kangar, I, 272
K'ang chü, I, 23; III, 186; see K'ang Kiu
K'ANG HI, I, 50; II, 236, 239
Kang Kao, I, 193
K'ang Kiu, I, 23, 37, 30; III, 186
Kangli, I, 210, 287
K'ANG TAI, I, 66
KAN HSING, II, 152
Kanjanfu, I, 292; III, 127; IV, 126, 127, 129, 145, 149
Kanjút, I, 314
Kankar, I, 272
Kan Kiang, ginger, II, 181
Kan Kiang, IV, 121
Kanklis, I, 210
Kanphu, I, 89; IV, 137
K'an pu, I, 136
Kansan, II, 246; III, 127
Kán-sang-i-Kásh, IV, 219
KAN SHIN, I, 100
Kan Su, Kan Suh, I, 35, 61, 64, 106, 278; II, 231, 246, 247; III, 126, 128, 129, 148; IV, 241
KAN T'IEN HAU, I, 148
Kantu, I, 136, 137
Kanya Kubja, I, 74
KAN YING, I, 18, 41, 50, 51
Kao ch'ang, I, 64, 247, 248; III, 55, 153; IV, 237
Kao li (Corea), I, 257, 258, 303; III, 113, 125, 128, 129
Káoshán, IV, 259
KAO SIEN-CHI, I, 61, 71, 91
Kao t'ai, I, 293
Kao t'ang, II, 208
KAO TSU, I, 147
KAO TSUNG, I, 97, 110; II, 192, 194, 205
KAPAK, I, 301; IV, 163
Kapchak, III, 147
Kapila, I, 68
Kapiša, I, 112
Kaptar Köl, IV, 228
Kara Balgasún, I, 64; III, 55
Karachi, I, 86
Karachil, IV, 17, 18
Káragáty, IV, 164
KARA HÚLAKÚ, IV, 161
Karáјáng (Yun nan), III, 126, 127, 130, 131, 187; IV, 270
Karakand, III, 163
Kara Kash, IV, 219
Kara Khanids, I, 148
Kara Khodja, I, 140, 272, 281; III, 132, 133; IV, 141, 162, 189, 238
Kara Kilisse, III, 162, 163
Kara K'itai, Kara Khitaï, I, 148, 149; III, 21, 22, 87; IV, 141, 163, 164, 230
Kara Kizil, IV, 238
Kara Korum, I, 116, 156, 158, 159, 163, 288, 289, 311; II, 231, 237; III, 19, 25, 128, 186, 187; IV, 140, 141, 145, 161, 163, 164, 205, 217
Karakorum Pass, I, 71, 317; IV, 190
Karakul, I, 318
Karambar, IV, 259
Kárami, IV, 111
Karamoran, Karamuran, I, 278, 286; II, 244; III, 125
Karamuren, II, 213; III, 148, 225; see Hwang Ho and Caramoran
Karana Kiuje, I, 74
Karangui Tagh, IV, 219
Kárani, IV, 104
Karaoul, I, 287; see Karaul
Karashahr, I, 7, 40, 58, 62, 64, 73; III, 225; IV, 188, 191, 222, 227, 231, 233–5, 238
Karasi, IV, 5
Kara Su, III, 161
KARATAI, IV, 133
Kara tau, I, 288; IV, 182
Karategin, I, 190–2, 315, 316
Karaul, I, 175, 274, 287; IV, 230, 239
Karawal, IV, 230
Kara-yulgun, IV, 230
Karazan, III, 127; see Karáјáng
Karchu, I, 317; IV, 217
Karens, III, 80, 127
Kargalagga, IV, 215
Kargú, I, 275; II, 233
Karikal, I, 309
Kari-Sairam, I, 272
Karkadan, rhinoceros, I, 243
Karkha, III, 23
Karliq, IV, 235
Karluk, I, 59, 91
KARMÁNAH, III, 122
Karmisin, I, 308
Karnabul, I, 143
Karnali, III, 198, 222
Karoramawár, III, 131
Kars, I, 163; II, 100, 101
Karsi, III, 114, 117
Karsput R., II, 99

Kartag, I, 152
KARTI, Emir, IV, 132
Karua, I, 185
Karun R., IV, 154
Karwan, IV, 209
Karwar, IV, 72
Kasan, II, 223
Kasbin, II, 243
Kaschan, II, 106; see Kashan
Kasghara, I, 143
Kashan, II, 10, 31, 106
Kashgar, I, 36, 40, 60–2, 71–2, 90, 99, 119, 123, 143, 191, 192, 194, 286, 287, 311, 314; III, 24, 55, 221, 225; IV, 160, 162–6, 175, 177, 182, 183, 185–193, 203, 207, 215–7, 222, 223, 228, 231, 235
Kashgaria, I, 61, 148
Kashibín, I, 243
Kashimghar, III, 22, 24
KASHIN, IV, 162
Kashish, IV, 223
Kashíshá, I, 108; II, 223
Kashish Daghi, IV, 223
Kashmir, I, 24, 36, 69–71, 73, 242, 254, 292, 310, 314; IV, 174, 177, 183, 191, 216, 227
Kashmiri, II, 249
Kash Tash, II, 221
Kasia, I, 185, 194; IV, 152, 206
Kasia Hills, I, 184, 185
Kasian Mountains, I, 194, 195
Kastamuni, IV, 5
Kasturi, I, 224
KASYAPA, II, 132
Kataghan, IV, 184, 211
Kataia, I, 146
Kataka, IV, 46
Katak-Banāras, IV, 203
Kataur, Mountains, IV, 205
Katay, III, 247
Katban, III, 131, 132
KATHAN KHAN, III, 52, 53
Kāthiāwār, III, 78
Katif, III, 68
Katighora, I, 143
Katmandu, IV, 176
Kattigara, I, 4, 5, 143, 188, 191, 193–5; IV, 266
KATULPHUS, I, 206
Kaukau, IV, 40
Kaulam, I, 80, 253, 309; II, 137; IV, 2, 26, 29, 30, 35, 148, 149; see Quilon, Columbum
Kaulam-Malé, I, 220
Kauli, I, 257; see Korea and Kao li
Kaungmüdhau Pagoda, I, 243
Kautiliya, I, 6
Kâvêra, I, 228
Kâvêrîpattam, I, 228
Kávil, III, 68
Kawadián, I, 191, 315
Kāwār, IV, 72
Kawe, IV, 22, 63
KAY, Dr., III, 243
Káyal, IV, 35
Káyal, Old, IV, 35
Kayaliq, Kayalik, I, 288–9; IV, 271; see Cailac
Kayam Koulam, Kayan Kulam, II, 134, 135; IV, 79
Kayans, II, 157, 168
Kaymäk, I, 246
Kays, I, 84, 85; see Kais and Kish
KAZAN, III, 33–5; IV, 164, 165
Kazan, IV, 6
Kazbin, IV, 184
Kazerún, IV, 120
Kazi, I, 130
Keibung, II, 227
Keimak-Baigur, I, 247
KEITH, Marshal, IV, 128
Kelantan, I, 82; IV, 157
Kelso, III, 170
Kena, I, 144
Kenchac, Kenchak, I, 287, 288, 289
KEN CHAM, III, 19
Kenchan, II, 246; see Kenjan
Keneh, IV, 4
Kenia, III, 197
Kenjan, Kenjang, I, 175; II, 246; III, 127, 128
Kenn, I, 145
Kerait, I, 116, 178; II, 246; III, 17, 19, 24, 25, 48; IV, 140, 186
Kerbela, II, 132
Keriahs, II, 147
Kerit, Kerith, III, 19, 24
Kermanshah, I, 308; III, 23
Kermian, IV, 5
KERN, H., II, 151; IV, 155
KER PORTER, II, 110
Kerulan, Kerulen, R., II, 221; III, 26
Keshikten, II, 228
Kesho, I, 193
Kesimur, II, 253
Kessair, I, 152
KETCHPOLE, Allan, I, 129
Keumitho, I, 191
Khabur, I, 308
Khaighun, I, 143
KHÂJAH GHAYÂTH-UL-DIN, I, 271
Khâju, I, 255, 258
KHALLACH, IV, 210

Khamdan, I, 31, 140, 141, 256, 258
Khamil, IV, 239; see Kamul
Khan, I, 149; see Kaan
Khanabad, IV, 210
Khanam, IV, 211
Khanbaliq, I, 119, 149, 153, 169, 170, 258, 275, 278, 280, 285; II, 179, 216; III, 13, 22, 24, 113, 114, 115, 125, 128, 148; IV, 90, 108, 118, 123, 137, 138, 140, 149, 161, 164; IV, 138; see Pe King
Khan Chalish, IV, 227
Khan Chau, Khamčau, I, 141; see Kan Chau
Khancou, I, 129, 130
Khâncu, I, 135
Khândjou, I, 136
Khandy, Island, I, 144
Khanfu, I, 104, 112, 129, 132, 133–6, 142, 143, 256, 257, 258; II, 179; IV, 120, 137
KHANIKOV, I, 311
Khánikú, IV, 137, 138
Khânjû, I, 256
KHĀNKAJŪ, IV, 204
Khanku, I, 142, 256, 258; IV, 137
Khansa, I, 89, 256–8; II, 179, 193, 194, 195; IV, 89, 90, 118, 129, 130, 137, 142, 145, 149, 223
Khansáwiyah, IV, 135
Khan t'ang, I, 31; see Khumdan
Khanzai, II, 178, 193
Khanzi, I, 152
Kháqán, I, 149
Khara-Kitat, IV, 230
Khara-Yurgun, IV, 231
Kharezmchâh, II, 197
Khari, I, 315
Khari-ab, I, 315
Kharkah, I, 244
Kharliks, Kharlikhs, I, 210, 247, 249, 250
Kharlok, I, 249, 250
Kharpont, III, 161
Kharteza, IV, 259
Khartum, I, 306
Khasgar, IV, 164; see Kashgar
Khata, I, 258, 271, 273, 281
Khat Angusht, III, 123
Khatay-Muqranus, I, 275
Khathlakh, I, 250
Khatiyan, I, 250; IV, 190
Khatun, I, 149
Khaulak, IV, 235
Khavanda, I, 191
Khawak, IV, 183, 255, 256, 258, 259
Kháwand-i-Tahur, IV, 166
Khayzoran, II, 148
Khazars, I, 20, 99, 245; III, 169
Kherkhis, I, 210
Khia pwan to, I, 191
KHIDR, III, 194, 267
KHIENTOLO, I, 74
Khientowei, I, 69
KHILIJÉ, II, 115
Khilkhis, I, 247
Khingan Mountains, I, 146
Khingsaï, III, 115, 126, 128; see Khansa
KHINIE, I, 75
Khinjan, IV, 257
Khinsá, III, 131
Khirkhiz, I, 248
Khitai, I, 7, 146, 148, 151, 157; II, 177; IV, 164, 170; see K'itai
Khitan, I, 148, 288; III, 21, 24; see K'i tan
Khitat, I, 148
Khithá, IV, 137
Khiva, III, 82; IV, 160
Khizilji Turks, I, 143, 247, 249, 316
KHIZR KHWAJA, IV, 165
KHMER, I, 8; IV, 157
Kho cho, III, 55
KHODABANDAH, I, 166; see OLJAITU
Khodjo tulas, IV, 230
Khoi, III, 164
Khojand, I, 23; IV, 166
Khokand, IV, 160; see Kokand
KHONDEMIR, IV, 162, 163
Khorasan, I, 98, 99, 102, 119, 134, 163, 244, 246–8, 251, 252, 286; II, 10; III, 22, 24, 85, 156; IV, 9, 11, 136, 160, 184
KHOSRU I, of Armenia, I, 94; IV, 14
KHOSRU NAOSHIRWAN, I, 59, 95, 206
Khotan, I, 24, 40, 58, 62, 73, 119, 141, 146, 191, 205, 246, 250, 251, 286, 287, 311; II, 207, 221; IV, 162, 188–192, 207, 217, 219, 221–3, 231, 235, 249, 253
Khotcho, I, 64
Khotl, I, 192; see Khutl
Khozars, III, 169; see Khazars
Khubdan, I, 31; see Khumdan
KHUDAIDÁD, Amir, I, 272; IV, 165, 189, 190
Khulum, I, 72, 73; IV, 210, 259
Khumdan, I, 31, 108, 133, 142, 143
Khutl, I, 192, 315, 316
Khutlán, I, 315; see Khutl
Khutlukh, I, 250

Khuttan, I, 246; see Khotan
Khuzistan, I, 308; II, 109; III, 22, 23; IV, 3, 154
Khuzluj, I, 249
KHWAJA RASHID, III, 108
Khwaja Regruwán, II, 262
KHWAJA, Amir, III, 128
KHWAJA, ELIAS, IV, 165
KHWAJA JAHÁN, III, 231; IV, 11, 34
KHWAJA, KHIZR, IV, 165
Khwajas, IV, 185, 192
Khwalis, I, 210
Khwaresmians, II, 198
Khwarizm, I, 90, 99, 154, 256, 315; III, 21, 82; IV, 9, 160, 209, 225
Khyber Pass, IV, 204
Ki, II, 216
Kiā, I, 279
Kia cheng, II, 210
KIA K'ING, II, 213
Kian Chau, I, 136
Kiang, I, 30, 65, 150, 177; II, 209, 231
K'iang (Tibétain), I, 36, 40, 60
Kiang Chau, II, 194
Kiang Che, II, 231; III, 128
Kiang Nan, I, 142; II, 165, 205, 207, 209; III, 128
Kiang Ning, II, 205
Kiang Pe, II, 231
Kiang Si, II, 187, 209, 231; III, 128, 129; IV, 110, 121, 126
Kiang Su, I, 121; III, 120
Kiao chi, I, 4–6, 8, 18, 51, 52, 193; III, 130, 255
Kiao ho, IV, 237
KIA TAN, I, 85
Kiao Ti, I, 4, 5
Kiau chi, I, 193; see Kiao chi
Kia yu kwan, I, 117, 274; IV, 239, 271
Kibla, I, 246
Kidifu, I, 275, 276; II, 233, 234
Kie ku, I, 248
Kien ch'ang, IV, 126, 127
KIEN CHEN, I, 100
KIEN-FUH-TING, I, 79, 80
KIEN-HUT-DING, I, 80
Kien Kang (Nan King), I, 139–140; II, 205
K'IEN LUNG, III, 117; IV, 178
Kien ning (Nan King), II, 205
K'ien-to-wei, I, 69
Kien wei, I, 65
KIEN WEN, I, 76, 248
Kien Yeh, II, 205
KIEPERT, I, 184, 191, 310, 311, 317
Kie sie, II, 228
Kiev, I, 157, 305
Kiho, I, 56, 110
Kij, I, 309
Kilagai, IV, 257
Kila'h Chap, I, 317
Kilasiya, IV, 210
Kilif, I, 315
Kilimanjaro, III, 197
Killah, I, 85
Killa-Karai, Killi-Karai, IV, 35, 158
KILLICH, IV, 210
Killoss, III, 170
Kimak, I, 246, 247
Kimkhwa, III, 155; IV, 118
KIN, I, 147, 148, 150, 254; II, 115, 177, 192, 205, 216, 220; III, 21, 126, 149
Kinara, II, 108
Kinbaiat, IV, 21, 23; see Cambay
Kincha, III, 186
Kinchang, III, 127
Kin chi, III, 131; see **Golden Teeth**
Kin ching, I, 237
Kin cob, III, 155
King chao (Si ngan), III, 127, 128
King d'Or, II, 115
King-hing-ki, I, 235
King-kiao-pei, I, 105
King R., I, 113
Kings of the Earth, Great, I, 241; IV, 37
King-Shan, II, 220
King sze, King se, I, 150; II, 180, 187, 192; III, 115, 128, 148, 260; IV, 17, 44, 129; see Hang chau, Khansa, Cansay, etc.
King te chen, IV, 110
KING-TSING (Adam), I, 112, 113
KING TSUNG, I, 147
KING Ye-liu, I, 147
Kin hwa fu, II, 188
Kin ling fu, II, 205
Kin Ling koo kin t'oo k'aou, II, 205
Kin Ling t'oo yung, II, 206
Kin-man, IV, 141
Kinsay, II, 193, 200
Kin shan, I, 205; II, 255
Kin Sheng Sze, I, 106
K'in yuen, I, 136
Kiong shan, I, 65
Kioto, I, 68
K'io wei, II, 200
Kipchak, I, 149, 154, 167, 210, 245, 301; II, 223; III, 82, 89, 188, 190; IV, 6, 160, 255, 256, 270
KIRAKOS GANDSAKETSI, I, 164

KIRCHER, Athan., I, 106, 182; II, 182, 186, 242, 249; IV, 193
Kirghiz, I, 64, 210, 248, 249; II, 223; III, 130; IV, 183, 210
Kiria, I, 246, 251
Kirkaldy, IV, 129
Kirkstall, III, 171
Kirkstead, III, 171
Kirman, I, 85, 309
Kirmanshah, I, 308; III, 23
Kirmesin, I, 308
Kis, III, 68; IV, 4
Kish, I, 85, 144, 146, 309; III, 69; IV, 5, 45; see Kais
Ki-shi (Kish), I, 85
Kishm, II, 107; IV, 211
Kishmis, II, 107
Kishna, II, 139
Kishnabad, IV, 257
Kishtabad, IV, 257
Kishtiwánán, IV, 136
Kisiwa, IV, 155
Kisliar, III, 84
Kissen, III, 148
K'i tai, I, 7, 146, 157; II, 177; see Khitai
K'i tan, I, 17, 147, 148, 247, 288; II, 177, 216; III, 21, 24; IV, 163; see Khitan
Kiuchen, I, 5, 51
KIUHOTÓ (Kobád), I, 95
K'iu lan, IV, 222, 271; see K'iu tan
Kiu mi, Kiu-mi-tho, I, 40, 191, 192
K'iu-p'i-lo, IV, 230, 231
Kiu she, I, 40, 41
Kiu shi, IV, 141
K'iu tan, IV, 222, 271
Kiu T'ang Shu, I, 48, 55; IV, 141
K'iu tze, I, 40; IV, 222, 231
KIWAMUDDIN the Ceutan, IV, 128
Kiyān, I, 141
KI YE, I, 75
Kizil, IV, 230, 231
Kizil bash, I, 295
Kizil Chai, III, 164
Kizil Dagh, III, 161
Kizil Irmak, III, 161
Klysma, I, 221
KNIGHT, II, 189, 190
KNOX, Robert, II, 172; III, 233, 237
KOBÁD, I, 95
Kochkiri, III, 161
Kodangulor, Kodungalùr, II, 134; IV, 78
K'ODZISHAN, IV, 185, 228
Koh-Daman, Valley, II, 263; IV, 208, 255
Koh-i-Baba, IV, 256
Koh-i-Khanam, IV, 211
Kohistan, IV, 209, 255
Koh Tralàch, I, 129
Koïk, IV, 45
Koil, IV, 35
Koilam, II, 129
KOKAN BEG, IV, 186
Kokand, I, 191; IV, 160, 183, 235
Kokan-Tana, I, 309
Kokcha, I, 317; IV, 211, 216, 256
Kokkonagara, IV, 157
Kokshal, IV, 228
Ko ku rye, I, 257; see Corea
Kól (Aligarh), IV, 20, 21
Kôla, II, 130
Kolāba, I, 254
Kolam, II, 130
Kolamba, II, 130
Kolechi, IV, 172
Koli, III, 113, 125; IV, 157
Koli Akoli, I, 152
K'O-LI-KI-SZE, III, 15
Kolis, III, 219
Kollam, II, 129
Ko-lo, IV, 57
Kolo lu, I, 59; see Karluk
Kolzum, I, 221
Komar, IV, 96
Komedi, I, 191, 192
Komul, III, 265; IV, 239; see Kamul
Konges, I, 36, 272; see Kungis
Kong tien, I, 31
Konieh, IV, 5; see Iconium
Konjeveram, I, 242
Konkan, I, 241, 254, 309; II, 114; IV, 254
Konkana, I, 74
Kookoo, II, 224
Koosiara R., IV, 153
Kopal, I, 288; IV, 235, 271
Kopantho, I, 191
Kophen, I, 212
Korea, I, 257; II, 237; see Corea
Korgeun, III, 162
Korgha Utra, IV, 239
Kornegalle, III, 233; IV, 33
Koshang, I, 116, 119; IV, 268
Kosseir, I, 306; IV, 4
Kota, III, 244
K'o teis, I, 221
Kothian, I, 243
Kotow, I, 90, 91; II, 238
Kotroba, III, 23
Kotta, III, 244
Kotulo, I, 315
Kotwâl, II, 122; IV, 139
Kouchan, I, 248
Koumdan, I, 108; see Khumdan
K'outché, I, 99

Kouyunjik, III, 225
Kowelaki, III, 130
Kow-r-ki, III, 15
Kozan, III, 160
Krim (Solghat), IV, 6
Krishna, I, 254; III, 70
Ksatriya Mahānāman, I, 67
Kshatriyas, I, 2
Ktesiphon, I, 43, 120, 216
Kuang chow, I, 89
Kuan yin, III, 269
Kuban, I, 212; III, 83
Kubeis, III, 267
Küber, IV, 144
Kublai Khan, I, 65, 82, 110, 134, 141, 149, 153, 167, 301; II, 134, 152, 197, 216, 219, 227, 230, 231, 236, 237, 246, 248, 270; III, 4, 5, 10, 15, 45, 113, 114–7, 119, 121, 122, 125, 127, 130, 132, 133, 149, 150, 155, 186, 301; IV, 129, 137, 140, 156, 162
Kucha, I, 35, 40, 58, 61, 64, 73, 141, 248, 251; IV, 189, 190, 222, 228, 230–1, 234, 235, 237, 238
Kuchar, IV, 231; see Kucha
Kúch Bihár, IV, 176
Kuchluk, I, 148; III, 21
Kudra-mali, I, 199
Kuei-shui, I, 23
Kuen-lun, I, 129; IV, 219; see Kwen lun
Kuesie, II, 228
Kûfah, I, 83, 84; IV, 3
Kúkah, III, 78; IV, 23, 64, 66
Ku kung i lu, II, 220
Ku ku nor, I, 61
Kulam, I, 254; II, 10, 129, 130, 137; III, 68
Kulaybu, I, 251
Kuldja, Kulja, I, 164, 289; III, 87; IV, 183, 193, 228
Kulesa-Dewar, III, 69
Kuma, III, 84; IV, 6
Kumagusu Minakata, III, 124
Kumar, I, 253, 254; III, 245
Kumára, IV, 96, 157
Kumara Dás, I, 67
Kumari Aloes, IV, 96
Kumbashi, IV, 227
Kumblah, IV, 74
Kumdan, I, 108; see Khumdan
Kumēdh, I, 192
Kumid, I, 191
Kumidha, I, 191
Kúmín Nikúlún, I, 57
Kumis, I, 209
Kumish, IV, 238
Ku mo, I, 40; IV, 231; see Aqsu
Kumo-chou, IV, 231
Kumuk, III, 84
Kumuki, I, 247
Kumul I, 140; see Kamul
Kunakar, IV, 33
Kúnar, IV, 33
Kundalika, I, 254
Kundrandj, I, 128
Kundrang, I, 128
Kunduz, IV, 160, 184, 186, 210, 211, 257, 258
K'ung hua tao, II, 220
Kungis, I, 36, 272; see Konges
Kuningan, III, 193
Kunjuk Khan, IV, 161
Kunki, III, 126
Kun lun, I, 129; IV, 219; see Kwen lun
Kunstmann, Prof. F., I, 176; II, 9, 57, 88, 129, 141, 204; III, 5, 192, 229, 231
Kur, II, 105; III, 23
Kurd de Schloezer, I, 139
Kurdish Armenia, I, 93
Kurdistan, I, 114, 308; II, 10, 102, 109; III, 85
Kurgan-i-Ujadbai, IV, 211
Kurgos, III, 87
Kuria Muria, I, 152
Kurkarausu, IV, 239
Kurla, I, 58; IV, 234, 235, 238
Kurtai, Amir, IV, 131–3, 136
Kurumbas, II, 147
K'u run, IV, 239
Kurunaigalla, IV, 33
Kús, I, 306; IV, 4
K'u sa ho, I, 97
Kush, IV, 189
Kushan, I, 247, 248; IV, 257
Kush-tam, IV, 230
Kustána, IV, 222
Kutaiba, I, 20, 90, 100
Kutás, I, 273
Kutb Minar, IV, 46
Kutb-uddin Mubārak, IV, 214
Kutchin Indians, II, 147
Kutchluk Khān, IV, 222
Kutlugh Khwaja, III, 132
Kuverachal, IV, 18
Kuyuk Khan, I, 149, 157, 161, 209, 289; II, 246; III, 19, 186; IV, 163, 164
Kuz-i-Búznah, IV, 108
Kwang binh, I, 51; II, 163
Kwang chau (Canton), I, 86, 89, 256
Kwang fu, I, 89
Kwang han tien, II, 220
Kwang Si, III, 129, 130
Kwang Tung, I, 136; II, 182; III, 12, 129

KWAN YIN, III, 269
Kwawa, II, 156
Kwei, II, 237
Kwei Chau, III, 128
Kwei Hwa Ch'eng, II, 245
Kwe lin fu, III, 130, 131
Kwen lun, I, 7, 129; II, 183; IV, 187, 219
Kylantin, I, 83
Kymkhãw, I, 137
Kynloss, III, 170
Ky yu, II, 191

Laccadives, I, 226
Lackered Ware, IV, 136
Ladakh, I, 71; II, 249; IV, 177, 217
Ladanum, III, 157, 167
Ladies at Mongol Court, Head-dress of, II, 222
Ladoga, Lake, III, 246
Laghman, I, 74
Lagoon Maeotis, I, 183
Lahari, IV, 9, 10
Lahore, II, 115; III, 217; IV, 173, 174, 177, 180, 183, 202, 203, 208, 227, 249, 254
L'Ahsa, III, 68
Laias, II, 115; see Aias
LAICHAI, I, 237
Lai lai, I, 82
LÁJAN FANCHÁN, III, 122
Lajazzo, III, 160; see Aias
Lake into which offerings were cast, II, 144
Lakhnaoti, I, 124; IV, 83–5
LALADĪTYA, I, 70
LA LOUBÈRE, I, 124
Lama, Grand, II, 250; III, 93
La Magna (Germany), II, 115
Lamb, Tartar, II, 31, 116; IV, 267
Lambri, Lamori, Lamúri, Lāmeri, II, 34, 146, 148, 149, 150, 168; III, 131
LAMECH, III, 244
Lamghan, I, 74
LAMI, *Cat.*, II, 6[illegible]
Lamreh, II, 146
Lan Chau, I, 278, 285
Land of Darkness, IV, 7
LANE, II, 163
LANE-POOLE, Stanley, IV, 161
Langabālūs, Lankhabālūs, Lanjabalus, I, 127
Langar, I, 272; IV, 238
Langkawi, Pulo, I, 127
LANGLÈS, I, 125
Langtin, III, 117
Lanha, I, 225
Lanka, I, 226
Lankin (Nan king), II, 205
Lanpo, I, 74
Lan She, I, 36, 37
Lanterns, Feast of, I, 282; III, 269
Lan-wou-li, II, 146; see Lambri
Laodicea, III, 16
LAONICUS CHALCONDYLAS, see CHALCONDYLAS
Laos, III, 221
Lapais, I, 168
LAPIED, II, 216
Lar, I, 127
Lara, I, 74
Lárán, I, 254
Laranja, II, 115
LARDNER'S *Cyclop.*, I, 197, 202; II, 86
LA RENAUDIÈRE, II, 87
LARGAIOLLI, D., II, 89
Larissa, I, 306
Larkhana, IV, 9
Laroccia, III, 171
LA RONCIÈRE, C. de, III, 180
Lārwī, I, 127
LASSEN, I, 3, 13, 16, 18, 25, 41, 69, 70, 73, 74, 128, 184, 185, 195, 205, 220, 224, 226, 227, 229, 241–3; II, 134, 141, 153; IV, 66–71, 156, 157
Latin Conquest of Asia, Prophecy of, III, 80
Latin Church of Malabar, III, 218
Latin of Marignolli and Jordanus, III, 203
Latitudinarian notions of Chinese, III, 74
Latoo, IV, 153
LATOUS, I, 198
Lau ch'eng, II, 216
LAUFER, B., I, 6; III, 124; IV, 267, 268, 269, 270
Laulan, I, 39
LAURENT, J. C. M., *Peregrinatores*, II, 22, 47, 104, 111, 250; IV, 1
Lavaldio, III, 171
LAWRENCE of Alessandria, Friar, III, 32
LAWRENCE of Ancona, Friar, III, 33, 212
Lawsonia inermis, III, 166
LAYARD, I, 114, 115; III, 22, 225, 262
Layazo, I, 307; see Aias
Laybach, II, 5
LAZARI, V., II, 74, 80, 81, 103
LAZARUS, II, 115
Lazice, I, 221
Lead, Mines of, I, 253
LEANG, LIANG, Dynasty, I, 114; II, 208
Leang Chau, I, 38, 63

Leang Shu, I, 66
LEAO, LIAO, Dynasty, I, 7, 60, 147, 148; II, 177, 216; III, 21; see K'i tan
Leao Tung, I, 147; III, 128
Leao Yang, I, 147; II, 231; III, 128
Leather-money, III, 149
Lebanon, Mount, III, 226, 240
LEBEAU, *Bas Empire*, I, 49, 54, 210; II, 221
LE BLANC, Vincent, *Travels*, II, 98, 166, 174
LE COMTE, II, 205
LE COQ, von, I, 36, 63; III, 55, 126
LE CORBEILLER, Ed., II, 154
Ledáki, II, 249
LEE, Henry, *Vegetable Lamb*, II, 242, 243; IV, 268
LEE's *Ibn Batuta*, IV, 155, 159
LEECH, Major, I, 311; IV, 183, 206, 208, 209, 256, 258
Leeches, Plague of, in Ceylon, II, 171
Leeches (i.e. Doctors) at the Khan's Court, II, 226
LEGGE, J., I, 8
Leicestershire, III, 171
Lelda, Leuda, III, 144; IV, 271
LE LONG, Jehan, II, 68, 73, 244, 266; III, 36, 89
LEMON of Genoa, Master, III, 191, 196, 259
Lemons against leech bites, II, 171
Lemyin, IV, 239
Lengten, III, 117
Length of Ibn Batuta's Travels, IV, 41
Lenzin, II, 212, 213
LEO, Chinese Mandarin, I, 236
LEO the Isaurian, I, 55, 56
LEON II, III, 139, 160
LEON III, III, 165
LÉON, T. R. P., II, 91
LEONARDUS, Bishop, III, 14
LE QUIEN, I, 306; II, 103, 104, 242; III, 13, 14, 33, 37
LERCH, IV, 164
LE STRANGE, Guy, I, 83–5, 102
LE THANH-TONG, II, 163
LETRONNE, I, 220
Letters of Prester John, III, 17; for other Letters, see Table of Contents
Lettres édifiantes, I, 104; II, 140, 249
Leuchieu, IV, 243
LÉVI, Sylvain, I, 67, 69, 72, 73, 76; II, 142
LEVY, E., IV, 270, 271
LEWIS, St., I, 158
LEWIS of Bavaria, II, 12; III, 199, 205
LEYDEN, Dr., II, 139
Lhadan, I, 61
Lhásá, I, 61, 71; II, 10, 248–250, 252, 253; IV, 176, 268
LI, eunuch, I, 87
Lialeyse, I, 306
Liampo, II, 205
LIANG, Dynasty, see LEANG
LIAO, see LEAO
Liber de Ætatibus, II, 22
Library, Laurentian, I, 123; at San Daniele, II, 15
Libya, I, 187, 220
Li Chau, II, 152
Lichfield, III, 206
Lidebo, I, 306
Liegnitz, I, 152
Life in the Forests of the Far East, II, 162
Lighthouse in the Persian Gulf, I, 86
Lign-aloes, II, 148, 150
Ligno, Dominus regnabit a, III, 243
Ligor, IV, 157
Ligurti, III, 162
LI HUNG-CHANG, III, 120
LI I-PIAO, I, 69
Li Kam, I, 23, 41
Li Kiang, III, 127
Li Kien, I, 41, 233
LI KWANG-LI, I, 38, 39
LI LING, I, 39, 64
LI MA-TEU, IV, 178; see RICCI, M.
Limyrice, I, 183
Lincegam, II, 213
Lin ching, II, 213
Lincolnshire, III, 171
LINDSAY, Robert, IV, 151
Ling Pe, II, 231; III, 187
LING ROTH, II, 158
Ling-yin sze, IV, 267
Linju, II, 213
Lin-ngan (Hang Chau), II, 177, 192, 205
LINSCHOTEN, I, 184, 185; II, 113, 146, 180, 181; III, 252; IV, 98, 99
Lin-tsin-chu, II, 214
Lin Ts'ing, I, 122; II, 213, 214
Lin Yi, I, 8; II, 163; see Champa
Lin Yin, II, 203, 204
LIONE, Dottor, I, 240
Lions, Black, II, 115; trained, at Khan's Court, II, 239
LIRUTI, G. G., II, 9, 23, 57, 79, 86

Lisbon, I, 268, 313
Lisciadro, III, 167
Literary Information regarding China previous to Mongol Era, I, 24; see Table of Contents
LI TSUNG, II, 205
Little Pamir, IV, 211
Little Sea, I, 100
LITTRÉ, *Dict.*, II, 98, 162
Liu-kia-kiang, I, 77
Liu sha, I, 235
Livenza, II, 5
Livre des Merveilles de l'Inde, II, 166
Lo Abassi, II, 250, 251
Loahc, II, 117
Loan King, II, 227
Loan, river, II, 227
Lobaes, for Lamas, II, 250
Lob Nor, I, 40, 58; III, 225; IV, 188
Locche, III, 163
Loch'a, II, 168
LOCKHART, Col., IV, 211
Log, Legend of St. Thomas and a huge, III, 250
Lohac, IV, 159
Lo-hing-man, II, 168
Lohoc, II, 117
LOHRASP, I, 10
Lolo, I, 74
LOMBARD, Surgeon, I, 170
Lombards, II, 4
Lomelic, the word, II, 122
London (in Pegolotti), III, 170
Longa, II, 237
Longa Solanga, I, 152
Longevity, case of, II, 215; IV, 123
Longitudes, of places adjoining the Bolor Mountains, and their discrepancies, I, 311
Lop, IV, 188
Lop, Lake, IV, 188; see Lob Nor
Lophaburī, I, 124
LORD, IV, 258
LORENZO DE' MEDICIS, I, 180
Loretto, II, 178
Loukin, Loukyn, I, 129, 135; see Lukin
Loundrás, I, 250
Louth Park, III, 171
Lo Yang, I, 91, 93, 108, 110, 114, 133, 139
Luban, IV, 97
Lubus, II, 147
LUCALONGO, Peter of, I, 170; III, 55
LUCAN, I, 14
LUCARDIE, Capt. M. J. C., II, 146
LUCCHINO TARIGO, II, 105
Luchac, III, 130
LUCULLUS, I, 216
LUDOLF, I, 222; II, 157, 217, 218; III, 7, 27, 222–4; IV, 146
LUD. II di Teck, II, 4
LUDDUR DEO, III, 70
Lúfú, I, 276
LU-HO (LUKE), III, 15
Lui Chau, III, 130
LUIZ GONÇALVEZ, IV, 170
Lujak, III, 130
LUKE, II, 263
Lukin, I, 129, 135, 143; III, 126, 128, 130
Lu kou, III, 117
LU KWANG, IV, 231
Lumghán, I, 314
Lumkali, I, 135; III, 126, 128, 130
Lung hing, III, 128
Lung men, II, 165
LUNG-SIU, Ye-liu, I, 147
Lung Wan, I, 78
LUN TSANG, I, 60; IV, 266
Lun yü, II, 224
Luqsor, Luxor, I, 306; IV, 4, 45
Lúristan, II, 109; IV, 3, 138, 139
LUSIGNAN, I, 262; III, 226
Lussom, R., I, 305
Lutzŭ, II, 189
L'Uzi, R., I, 305
Lybian Desert, I, 306
Lydians, III, 249
Lyons, I, 156
Lyons, Council of, I, 154; III, 211

Maabar, Ma'bar, Maebar, Mobar, I, 82; II, 31, 34, 130, 134, 141, 143, 168; III, 5, 30, 61–3, 65–70, 231, 249; IV, 13, 27, 34, 66, 67
Mabad, I, 244
Macao, II, 212; IV, 242, 253
MACARTNEY, Lord, II, 197; III, 116; IV, 121, 187, 216, 217
MACARTNEY'S Map in ELPHINSTONE'S *Caubul*, I, 310, 313, 316
Maccao, IV, 242; see Macao
McCRINDLE, J. W., I, 25, 27, 212–219, 221–3, 226, 228–232
Mace, I, 264
Macedonia, I, 102, 247
Macerata, IV, 178, 181
MACFARLANE, Ch., II, 87, 264
MACGOWAN, D. J., II, 188
Machin, Mahachin, I, 9, 34, 68, 73, 78, 121, 150, 151, 177, 179, 281; II, 177, 180; III, 68, 115, 116, 131
Machindránáth, II, 249
Machini, I, 269

Machli-bander, III, 70
Machli-patam, III, 70
MACHOMET, II, 23, 119, 123, 125; III, 269; see MAHOMED
Machú, III, 127
Macini, I, 151
MACINI, EL, III, 223
Macinus, I, 266
MACLEOD, Capt., IV, 201
MACRAY, G. D., II, 43
Madagascar, I, 138, 167; II, 154
Madai, island, I, 242
MADDEN, II, 70
Madhyadesa, I, 75
Madínata Wasit, I, 309
MÂDJÛDJ (MAGOG), I, 255
Madonna delle Grazie, II, 89
Madras, I, 81, 309; II, 10, 134; III, 6, 49, 65, 250, 253; IV, 135
Madras Journal, I, 81; II, 135
MADRI, I, 164
Madura, II, 140; III, 69, 70, 218; IV, 35
Maeandrus, I, 184
Maebar, III, 61; see Maabar
MAËS TITIANUS, I, 188, 191, 192
MAFFAMET CAN, IV, 207
MAFFEI, III, 251, 252
Ma fú, I, 276
Magadha, I, 67–9, 74; II, 132
Magadoxo, I, 87; IV, 4
MAGAILLANS, II, 177, 178, 234
MAGALHÃES, II, 147
Magar, III, 84
MAGELLAN, II, 162; IV, 159
Magellanic Cloud, III, 195
Mager, III, 84
Maghuz, I, 152
Magi, I, 112, 246
Magi, the three, II, 106; III, 192, 267
Magians, I, 112
MAGINI, I, 182, 302, 304, 305; II, 109
Magnus Canis, II, 217
MAGOG, I, 151, 255, 304
Mahabalipuram, I, 81
Mahaban, I, 243
Mahabharat, I, 2
Mahachin, Mahachina, Maha Čina, see Machin
Mahachinasthana, I, 68; see Machin
MAHADEVA, III, 252
MAHAMET HÀN, MAHAMETHAN, MAHAMETHIN, IV, 220
MA HA MU, III, 121
MAHANAAMA, Raja, I, 67
MÁHANG, I, 9
MAHÂPADMA, I, 73
Mahapadma, Lake, I, 70
MAHARA, III, 131
Mahāvamsa, I, 67
Mahe, IV, 76
MAHENK, I, 9
MAHMUD KHAN, IV, 166
MAHMUD SABAKTAGIN, I, 242
MAHOMED, MAHOMET, the Prophet, I, 83, 88; II, 23, 119, 123, 125; III, 110, 269; IV, 192, 202, 224, 250
MAHOMED, Sultan of Khwarizm, I, 33
MAHOMED KHAN, son of KHIZR KHWAJA, IV, 165
MAHOMED, Khan of Kashgar, IV, 191, 207, 220
MAHOMED KHAN SHAIBANI, IV, 166
MAHOMED BAKHTIYAR KHILJI, I, 78, 79; IV, 152
MAHOMED IBN KASSIM IN SIND, I, 90
MAHOMED AL MASMÚDI, IV, 80
MAHOMED SHAH, son of KHUDAIDAD, IV, 190
MAHOMED TUGHLAK, of Delhi, I, 75, 79; II, 144; III, 150; IV, 10, 11, 14, 18, 19, 34, 51, 62, 69, 84, 135, 138, 225
MAHOMED UZBEK, I, 301; IV, 6, 158
Mahomedanism professed by no Mongol Emperor of China, II, 237
Mahomedans in China, I, 89; IV, 130, 175; their devoutness, III, 260; and brotherly feeling, III, 1
Mahrattas, I, 242; II, 140
MA HUAN, I, 76, 77, 79, 87; II, 172; IV, 4, 24, 91, 92
Mai, IV, 189
Maiceram, IV, 74
Maidán, II, 121
MAIDARI, I, 164
Mailamanagara, III, 251
Mailapur, I, 309; II, 141, 142; III, 250–2
Mailapurâm, III, 250
MAILLA, de, I, 65; II, 205, 228, 237; IV, 142
Mainpúri, IV, 21
MAITREYA, I, 164
Majapahit, II, 152, 156; III, 193, 194
Majar, IV, 66
Majars, Majgars, I, 246
MAJOR, R. H., I, 124, 125, 127, 144, 176, 266; II, 160, 166, 181; III, 40; IV, 146

Majorca, III, 166
Makam ul Báb, I, 251
Makhna, a tuskless male elephant, I, 231
Malabar (Minibar, Mulebar, etc.), I, 80, 86–8, 127, 171, 185, 220, 225, 226, 228, 253; II, 10, 31, 34, 115, 130, 132–6, 140–2, 154; III, 49, 65, 68, 167, 191, 196, 216, 217, 237, 249, 252, 254; IV, 3, 27, 36, 63, 72–9, 223
Malabathrum, I, 184
Malacca, I, 127, 180, 215, 253; II, 147, 149; IV, 98, 253, 259
Malaga, IV, 39
Malaiur, II, 157
MALALA, or MALELA, John, I, 213
Malantan, I, 82
Malascorti, I, 308; II, 258
Malasia, I, 307
Malasjerda, I, 308
Malasjird, II, 258
Malatia, I, 307
Malatolto, Malatolta, III, 144
Malaur, I, 314
Malaya, I, 214
Malay Islands, I, 128
Malay Peninsula, I, 78, 128, 253; IV, 156, 157
Malays, II, 147
MALCOLM (*Persia*), I, 10, 96, 100
MALCOLM, Lieut., III, 233
Maldah, IV, 83
Maldive Islands, I, 127, 214, 226; II, 174; III, 192, 193; IV, 31, 32, 34, 36, 50, 67, 74, 80, 149, 225
Malé (Malabar), I, 86, 220, 227, 228, 230
Malifatan, Malifattan (Molephatam, Manifattan), III, 30, 68; IV, 35
MALIK, BAKHSHI, I, 282, 283
Malik, II, 122
MALIK-AL-JIZR, I, 242
MALIK-AL-SÁLAH, II, 149
MALIK KAFUR, III, 66
MALIK SUNBUL, IV, 29
MALIK TAKI-ULLAH, III, 68
MALIK-UL-ZÁHIR, IV, 145, 147
MALIK YUHANA, III, 26
MALIK YUZBEK, I, 79
MALIK ZÁDA, IV, 11
Malipattan, III, 63
Malḳat, III, 68
MALKÍKARIB, I, 251
Malli, IV, 39
Malmistra, I, 307; see Mamistra
MA-LO-FU, I, 234
Malta, III, 189
MALTE-BRUN, I, 288
MALVOISIN, II, 89
Malwa, I, 74; IV, 21, 22, 23
Mama Khatum, III, 162
MAMBRE, I, 290, 293
Mambroni Cini, I, 292
MAMIGONIANS, I, 94
Mamira, Mamiron, I, 292
Mámírán-i-Chini, I, 292
Mamistra, I, 307; III, 229
MAMKON, I, 94
Mamre, II, 103
Mamuvi, III, 84
Mán, II, 177
Manaar, I, 199; III, 65
Manar Mandali, IV, 32
MANASSEH, II, 133, 135
MANCASOLA, Thomas of, Catholic Bishop of Samarcand, III, 39
Manchuria, I, 118
Mandal al-Kamarūbī, I, 253
Mandal Kamruni, I, 253
MANDEVILLE, I, 171, 221; II, 33–5, 91, 98, 103, 113, 115, 123, 145, 166, 217, 244, 255; III, 44, 99, 155, 211, 219, 236, 263; IV, 2
Mandurafin, I, 254
Mandura-patan, I, 254
Manekir, I, 241
MANES, I, 248; see MANI
MANGALA, II, 246; III, 127
Mangalapura, I, 74
Mangalore, I, 220, 228, 309; IV, 21, 73
Manganor, I, 309
Mangaruth, I, 228
Mangi, Manzi, Manci, I, 146, 150–2, 172, 302; II, 34, 134, 176, 177, 178, 180, 186, 192, 200, 206, 231, 254–6; III, 71, 113, 130, 207, 216, 228, 248, 249; IV, 137
Mango, fruit, II, 150; III, 236, 237; IV, 271
Mangona, III, 145
Mangouste, II, 116
MANGU KHAN, I, 149, 153, 160, 161, 163, 210, 240, 248, 288; III, 19, 54, 113, 156, 187
MANI, I, 62, 248
MANIACH, I, 206–8, 210, 211
MANIAGO, II, 21
MANICHAEANS, I, 64, 248
Manichaeism, I, 62, 63
Manjaim, IV, 76
Manjarur, IV, 73
Manjeshwaram, IV, 74
Manjin, II, 177
MAÑJUÇRI, I, 73, 112

MAÑJUGHOSA-BISSŌCHTMA, I, 73
Mank, I, 315, 316
Mann, IV, 81; see **Maund**
MANNING, Thomas, II, 249, 253
Mansūra, I, 255
MANSUR KHAN, IV, 234
MANTEGNA, II, 142
Mantra, II, 147
Man tsu, Man tze, I, 146; II, 177
Mantua, I, 304
MANU, I, 2
Manuscripts of Odoric, II, 28 *seq.*, 39 *seq.*; of Marignolli, III, 207; of Ibn Batuta, IV, 41
Manviti, III, 84
Manzi, see Mangi
Manzil-Sindi, I, 241
Maps in this work, Notes on the, I, 299 *seq.*
Maori, IV, 22
Maoris, III, 221
Mao-Shan, II, 168
Mapaeul, I, 82, 83
Maparh, I, 82
MAR-ABA, I, 26
Maragha, I, 119, 121, 308; III, 75, 76
Maralbashi, IV, 228, 229
Marallo, I, 228
Maramati, III, 156, 169
Marand, III, 164
Maranel, Marabia, IV, 74
Marasch, I, 163
Marawa, Marawar, I, 228; II, 140, 141; III, 67, 69; see Maabar
MARCEL, Gabriel, II, 83
March, the, III, 169
MARCHESINO of Bassano, II, 12, 27, 80, 266, 270
Marching in India in 1340, IV, 14
MARCIANUS OF HERACLEA, I, 12, 13, 195; III, 27
MARCO DA LISBONA, II, 12, 84
MARCOS, Rabban, I, 119, 120
MARCUS AURELIUS, I, 6, 21, 51, 52, 66, 193
Mar di Bachu, II, 211; see Bacu
Mardin, I, 119, 216
Mare Majus, II, 98
Mare Maurum, II, 98
Mare Ponticum, III, 81
Marga, I, 304, 308
Margarita, II, 141
Margiana Antiochia, I, 190
MAR HANAM ISHU'A, I, 108
MA-RH YE-LI-YA, I, 118
MARIGNOLLI, John de', I, 80–2, 117, 119, 123, 170, 171, 213; II, 23, 24, 27, 107, 110, 129, 130, 132, 133, 136, 142, 171, 179, 180, 183, 192, 203, 225; III, 6, 11, 28, 31, 33, 35, 177–269; IV, 34, 161
MARINO SANUDO, III, 53, 180
Marinus of Tyre, I, 11, 19, 187, 188, 190, 192, 194
MAR JABALAHA; see JABALAHA
MARKAUNT, Thomas, II, 39
MARKHAM, C. R., I, 33, 174, 266, 293; II, 99, 249, 251, 262
Mark Sterling, Value of, III, 140
Marmalong Bridge, III, 252
Marmora, Sea of, III, 246
Marmorea, I, 308
Maroga, III, 75; see Maragha
MARQUART, J., I, 138–140, 206, 244–7, 251, 252, 255; II, 142
Marrah, I, 283
Marriage Customs in Chaldaea, II, 111; at Tana, II, 116
Marriage Customs of Tartar Chiefs with Greek Princesses, IV, 7
MARS, I, 248
MAR SARGIS, SARGHIS, I, 108, 118, 199
MARSDEN, I, 165; II, 98, 103, 115, 149, 214, 218
MARSHALL, Henry, III, 233
Martaban, I, 124, 177, 243
Martaban, IV, 107
Martamam, I, 124
Martignac, II, 5
MARTIN, II, 234
MARTIN, P., II, 140
MARTIN, St., II, 221
Martin, Church of St., Padua, II, 165
MARTINEZ, Fernando, I, 178, 266, 267
MARTINI, Mart., I, 6, 122, 123, 159, 175, 182, 291; II, 177, 182, 183, 186, 188, 192, 201, 205, 209, 210, 214, 216, 217, 233, 242, 246; IV, 243
MARTINS, F., see MARTINEZ, F.
Martyrdom of Four Franciscans at Tana in Salsette, II, 117–132; III, 14, 76, 77, 79; of six Franciscans and another at Almaliq in 1339, III, 31–3, 212; of Stephen, a young Friar at Sarai, III, 83; of two Franciscans in Tartary, III, 28; of ten thousand Christians in Armenia, III, 40
Marulló, II, 141
Marv, I, 97, 102–4, 123, 190; III, 22–4; IV, 184
Marv-ar-Rûd, I, 102
Marv-ash Shâhijân, I, 102

Mary, St., Island, II, 147
Masalak-al-absár, I, 307; II, 144, 194, 195; IV, 138
Masin (Mahachin), I, 121, 127, 151
Maskat, II, 112; III, 68; IV, 36
MAS LATRIE, Count of, III, 138
Masnad, IV, 139
MASPERO, Georges, II, 163
MASPERO, H., I, 66; IV, 267
Massagetae, I, 34; III, 184
Massawah, I, 219
Massis, III, 163
Massissa, III, 160
Massius, Mount, I, 216
MASSON, Map, I, 310
Mastauj, I, 315
Mastra, I, 152
Masudabad, IV, 12
MAS'UDI, I, 31, 33, 43, 44, 47, 83, 84–6, 90, 96, 97, 126, 127, 136–8, 230, 241–3, 245, 247–9, 251, 306, 307; II, 111, 139, 144, 248; III, 192, 225, 245, 265
Masufah, IV, 144
Masulipatam, III, 70
Matan, II, 162
Matheu, the word, II, 214; III, 119
Mattancheri, II, 134, 135
MATTHEW, St., III, 7, 222
MATTHEW of Arezzo, III, 5
MATTIOLI, II, 153, 154
MATTIUSSÍ, II, 6, 7
Matto Grosso, II, 147
MA TWAN-LIN, I, 57, 161, 199, 200; III, 150; IV, 157
MAUI, I, 50
Maund, IV, 81
MAURICE, Emperor, I, 29, 30, 34, 115
MAURICE, Gabriel, I, 106
Mauritania, I, 221
MAURO, Fra, I, 142, 151, 176, 177, 303, 304; II, 23, 103, 115, 130, 133, 160, 211, 267; III, 27, 53, 147, 219, 233, 244, 246, 247
MAURY, Alfred, I, 127, 128, 253
Mauttama, I, 243
Mā-warā-n-Nahr, I, 20, 98, 244; III, 33; IV, 137, 145, 160, 161, 164, 165, 190, 212
Mayad, I, 244
Mayandur, IV, 73
MAYERS, W. F., I, 78
MAYILÂ DEVÎ, II, 142
Mayn, II, 109
Māzandarān, I, 100, 163, 275
MAZDAI, III, 253
Meau tze, II, 187
Meaux Abbey, III, 171
Mecca, Mecha, I, 131, 246; II, 123, 137; III, 228, 267; IV, 3, 5, 37, 192, 207, 208
Mecchino, II, 137
Mecrit, I, 152
Meda, I, 306
Medan, II, 121
Medeia, I, 301; III, 85
Medes, I, 102, 206; II, 98; III, 16, 28
MEDHURST, Jr., W. H., I, 10
Media, I, 135, 189; III, 22
Medina, IV, 3, 190, 207
Mediterranean, I, 300; III, 180, 246
MEDLYCOTT, II, 126, 142
Megna, IV, 152
Mehar, III, 161
Mehrán, I, 86
Meiling Pass, IV, 121
MEINERT, J. G., Commentator on Marignolli, II, 207; III, 180, 192, 193, 202, 207, 210, 213, 216, 217, 219, 229–231
Meï Shan, II, 220
Mekke, I, 246; see Mecca
Mekong, I, 128
Mekran, I, 309; IV, 160
Melaguette, Meleguette, Melegetae, etc., II, 153, 154
Melanchlaeni, IV, 204
MELA, POMPONIUS, I, I, 15, 16, 196, 197; II, 252; III, 222
MELCHIZEDEK, III, 209
Melek-i-Rûm Kaisar, I, 57
Meliancota, IV, 78
Meliapur, Meliapor, III, 250, 251; see Mailapur
Melibar, II, 134; see Malabar
MELIORANZI, Canon, II, 14
Meliori Foro, II, 181
Melistorte, II, 258
Melle, IV, 40
Melli, I, 219; IV, 40
Melon producing a lamb, II, 240
Melons, I, 267; II, 107, 240
Melrose, III, 170
Memak, III, 84
Membaj, I, 307
Mena, III, 156
Menabar, III, 65
Menam, I, 124
MENANDER, I, 23, 46, 96, 149, 205, 206, 274
MENAS, III, 223
MENDOZA, G. de, II, 181, 188
MENENTILLUS of Spoleto, Friar, III, 5–6, 58–9

MENEZES, Alessio di Gesù de, IV, 226, 253
MENEZES, Duarte, II, 142
MÊNG K'I, II, 152
Meng-ku-yu-mu-ki, IV, 141
MENG-LIANG-LU, II, 194
MENINSKI, II, 255; III, 54; IV, 142
Menteshé, IV, 5
Mentz, II, 34
Menzu, II, 209, 211, 212
MEODEUS, III, 252
Mercato, III, 145
MERCATOR, I, 308; IV, 159
Merdacas, II, 221
Merdachascia, applied to silk, II, 221
Merga, III, 76
Mergeo, IV, 73
Merkit, III, 19, 20
Meroe, I, 306
Merososso, III, 170
MERTA WIJAYA, III, 193
Meru, III, 198, 222
Merv, see Marv
Merveilles de l'Inde, II, 146
Meselelec, IV, 229
Mesene, I, 42
Mesetelech, IV, 227
Meshed, I, 189; III, 39; IV, 3
Meshid Ali, IV, 36
Mesmeric Influence, IV, 124
Mesopotamia, I, 83, 84, 102, 189, 220, 225, 226, 252
MESSIAH, I, 113
Metaxa, the word, II, 221
Metropolitan Sees of the Nestorians, III, 22, 23
Metroxylon laeve,—Rumphii, II, 160
Mexicans, III, 80
Mexico, I, 180
MEYENDORFF, I, 34, 71; IV, 183, 210, 228
MEYER, Paul, II, 67
MEZZABARBA, III, 215
Miako, I, 131; IV, 169
MICAEL of Tar'el, St. Mar, I, 119
MICHAEL, Friar, II, 15
MICHAEL, Patriarch, III, 223
MICHAEL, a Convert, III, 258
MICHAEL DUCAS, I, 56
MICHAEL PALAEOLOGUS, treats about the Union of the Churches, III, 4; see PALAEOLOGUS, M.
MICHAEL the Syrian, I, 50
MICHEL, Francisque, II, 40
MICHELE MAMBRE, I, 290, 293
MICHELL, IV, 182
Michem, I, 301, 302
Middle Empire, III, 85; see Medeia
MIÉ-LI-I-LING-KAI-SA, I, 44, 56
Mien, I, 301, 302; II, 236
Miesa, III, 171
MIGNE, *Patrologia*, II, 100
Mijnere, I, 306
MIKIA-I-LING, I, 56
MIKIALING, I, 56
MIKLUCHO-MACLAY, II, 147
Milan, I, 86
Milazzo, III, 169
Miliaresion, I, 44, 229
MILI-I-LING KAISA, I, 56, 57
MILIS, I, 108
Milk, Trees that give, III, 96
MILLAIS, III, 214
MILLER, Hugh, II, 262
Millestorte, Millescorte, II, 257, 258
Millet, III, 41
MILTON, III, 227
Min, R., I, 77, 175; III, 12; IV, 121
Minâb, I, 85
Minabar, III, 65
Minao, I, 85
Mines de l'Orient, II, 257
MING, I, 73, 76, 79, 87, 131, 175, 179, 237, 268, 271, 274; II, 146, 205, 206, 216, 232; III, 150; IV, 189
Mingaur, Minglaur, Mingora, I, 74
Mingchu, II, 212; see Ning Po
Mingieda, IV, 227–9
Mingio, I, 301; II, 212; see Ning Po
Ming-oï, IV, 231
Ming shi, II, 152; III, 13
MING TI, I, 66
Minibar, II, 65, 74, 132; III, 230; see Malabar
Minieh, I, 306
MINISSIMI, Luigi, II, 90
Minister of the left; — of the right, I, 134
Minnagara, I, 241
Minocchi, II, 230
MINOR HAN, I, 139
Mints or Treasuries in Cathay, III, 98
Min Yue, I, 39
MIQUEL, II, 157
Miracles, alleged of Odoric, II, 11, 13–16, 275–6; by bones of friars, II, 128 *seq.*; by St. Nicholas's finger, III, 200; at tomb of St. Thomas, III, 376
Mirapolis, III, 250; see Mailapur
Mirapor, I, 309; III, 250

Miraporam, R., iv, 74
Mir Izzet Ullah, iv, 219, 230, 239
Mirjai, ii, 221; iv, 219
Mir Jumla, iv, 176
Mirkhond, i, 271; ii, 236
Mir Shah, i, 315
Mirza Abu Saïd, iv, 166
Mirza Baisangar, i, 271
Mirza Hakim, iv, 207
Mirza Ibrahim, i, 313
Mirza Mahomed Haidar Kurkan, iv, 193
Mirza Ulugh Beg, i, 271; iv, 166
Misermans, iv, 233
Misqali, ii, 107
Mi-shi-ho (Messiah), i, 113
Misr, iii, 263
Missionary Friars, i, 213; see Table of Contents
Missioni Francescane, ii, 214
Missions to pacify the Tartars, i, 154; First to Cathay, iii, 4; see Franciscans, Jesuits, John of Monte Corvino, etc.
Missions Catholiques, i, 122; ii, 250
Missis, iii, 160
Mississa, i, 307
Mithras, i, 27
Mitridanes, i, 173
Miyako, i, 131; iv, 169
Moal, i, 117; iii, 20
Moawiyah, i, 44, 48, 50; iv, 130
Mobar, see Ma'bar
Moccoli, Moccols, iii, 147, 146, 164
Mo Chu, i, 148
Modilial, iii, 257
Mogal, iii, 20
Mogaung, Mogoung, Moquan, i, 10, 177
Moghan, ii, 105
Moghulistan, iv, 163, 164, 165, 166
Mogòr, i, 238; iv, 198
Mohabar, see Ma'bar
Mohamedans, i, 88, etc.
Mohammed II, ii, 99
Mohammed Khudabendeh, ii, 104
Mohammed Khwarizm Shah, i, 60
Mohammed Tughlak, iv, 14; see Mahomed Tughlak
Mohl, Jules, i, 9
Moho, ii, 200
Mohochintan, i, 68
Mohonoan, Chacha, i, 67
Mo-i, i, 44, 48
Mokan, Khan, i, 205, 206
Molai (Malé), i, 86
Molephatam, iii, 30, 68; iv, 35; see Malifatan
Molini, G., ii, 61
Mollah Suleïman, iii, 162
Mo-lo, i, 85
Molopama, i, 70
Moltan, i, 310; see Multān
Molucas, ii, 156, 161, 168, 208; iv, 158
Mombasa, iv, 4
Monasteries and Monks, Buddhist, ii, 184; iii, 57, 94, 229, 233, 234, 242, 243
Monde illustré, ii, 166
Monet, Henry, ii, 83
Money Paper, iii, 97
Mong Ch'ang, i, 140
Mong Chi-siang, i, 140
Mongol, Cathay under the, from Rashíduddín, iii, 113 *seq.*
Mongol Conquests, i, 148 *seq.*; Dynasty in China, i, 146 *seq.*; its Fall, i, 172
Mongol Empire divided, i, 153
Mongol Expeditions to Java, ii, 151
Mongol Khans, their diplomatic communications with Europe, i, 166
Mongolia, i, 200, 286; iv, 163, 205
Mongols, i, 136, 288; ii, 144, 177, 245, 248; iii, 20, 248
Mo-ni, i, 62, 63
Monkey Mountains, iv, 108
Monod, Gabriel, ii, 83
Monreale, i, 241
Mons Beatus, iii, 267
Monsol, iii, 225
Monsters and Strange Beasts, ii, 230; iii, 255, 258, 259; in the cloister at Cansay, ii, 202; iii, 260
Montanus, ii, 210
Montaperti, iii, 178
Monte Corvino; see John of Monte Corvino
Montecroce, Ricold of, i, 155, 170; ii, i, 22, 98, 104, 111, 223, 250; iii, 225, 234, 260; iv, 135, 143
Monteniani, Girolamo, ii, 20
Montereale, Count Pietro, ii, 17
Montfaucon, i, 25, 27, 212–6, 218, 219, 227, 228, 230, 231; ii, 56
Montgomerie, Capt. J. G., i, 311, 312; ii, 248, 254
Montignac, ii, 20
Monument of Odoric, ii, 17 *seq.*

MOOR, *Notices Indian Arch.*, II, 149, 157, 168, 174
MOORCROFT, I, 317, 318; IV, 230
Moors in China, singular meeting of, IV, 128
Mootapilly, III, 70
Mophi, I, 151
Mopsuestia, I, 307
Moquanne, III, 8
Moradabād, IV, 18
MORANVILLÉ, H., III, 37
Moray, III, 170
Morda sangue, III, 167
Morea, III, 153
MOREL-FATIO, I, 299
MORELLI, J., II, 64
Morilloum, I, 228
Morocco, III, 145; IV, 39
Morpeth, III, 171
MORRISON, Dr. R., II, 232
Mortiliano, II, 22
Moscov, I, 305
MOSES, I, 221; III, 209; IV, 175, 224
MOSES of Chorene, I, 93, 94, 159
MOSHEIM, I, 114, 162; III, 5
MOSINANG, I, 73
Mosque, Forcible driving to, IV, 32, 225
MO SSU PAN, I, 97
MOSTANSIR, III, 223
MOSTAS'IM BILLAH, I, 153; IV, 87
Mosul, I, 119, 189; II, 109; III, 22, 23, 199, 225; IV, 3
MO TSUNG, I, 147
MOUHOT, H., I, 128
MOUKHINE, I, 311
MOULE, A. C., II, 215; III, 15; IV, 269, 270
MOULE, G. E., II, 192, 193, 195, 203, 204
Mountain of the Moon, III, 198
MOUNTAIN, OLD MAN of the, II, 257 *seq.*
Mountain of Ceylon, III, 220, 227, 228, 232; IV, 32; see ADAM, Peak
Mount Deli, II, 115; IV, 75
MUAWIA, see MOAWIYAH
MUBÁRAK SHAH, IV, 161
MUBÁRIK, II, 115
Mubids, I, 112
Muchal, III, 147
Mudiliar, III, 257
Mughisar, III, 161
Mughuls, I, 272
MUHAMMAD, III, 34; IV, 162
MUHAMMAD ABDUL KERIM MOONSHY, IV, 206
MUHAMMAD BAKHSHY, I, 271
MUHAMMAD BEG, I, 272
MUHAMMAD BIN KĀSIM, I, 254
MUHAMMAD KHĀVEND SHAH, I, 271
MU HAN, I, 206
Muh hu, I, 112
Muhupa, I, 112
Mujah, I, 244
Mujelibè, III, 262
Mukim, II, 146
MUKTOPIDA, I, 70
Mu ku tu su, I, 87; see Magadoxo
Mulahi, Mulahidah, II, 258
Mulehet, Mulhet, II, 258
Mul Jawa, IV, 48, 67, 68, 96, 97, 149, 155–8
MÜLLER, And., I, 182
MÜLLER, C., I, 11, 13, 14, 17, 183–5, 201, 205, 212, 217, 219, 304
MÜLLER, F. W. K., I, 36, 63
MÜLLER, Max, II, 241
MULLIK YUZBEK, IV, 153
Multān, I, 254, 310; IV, 10, 12, 17, 238
Münchener Gelehrte Anzeigen, III, 5
Múnchú, III, 125
Munda, III, 145
MUNEDJIM BASHI, IV, 64
Mungali, I, 74
Mung-kie-li, I, 74
Mungkien, I, 316
Munich, III, 205
Munkan, I, 316
MUNSHÍ MAHOMED HAMID, I, 311
MÜNTZ, E., II, 83
MURAD, Sultan, IV, 173
MURAD Beg, IV, 186
Murad Su, III, 163
Murano, I, 290
MURATORI, II, 153
Muria, I, 152
MURRAY, Hugh, I, 302; II, 86, 146; IV, 189
Murz, IV, 256
Musa Sapientium, II, 150
MUSCI, Jerome, III, 216
Mushar, III, 161
Musical maidens, service by, II, 254
Musk, I, 224, 227, 248, 251, 264, 316
Mussauites, IV, 175
Mussi, II, 150
Mus-Tagh, IV, 215, 228
Mustakhraj, IV, 140
Musulmans in China; see **Mahomedans**
Mutafilly, Mutfili, I, 309; III, 70

Mutammid, I, 135
Mutapali, III, 70
Mu T'ien tze chuen, I, 9
Mutlam, II, 135
MUTOPI, I, 70
Muttra, IV, 35
MU WANG, I, 9
Muyiri Kodu, III, 249
Muzart, IV, 228
Muzart Daria, IV, 231
Muziris, III, 249
Mygdonia, I, 216
Mynibar, II, 130; III, 207, 249
Mysore, I, 243; III, 66

Nâband, I, 84
Nabannae, I, 195
Nabi Yunus, III, 225
Nacchetti, Nacchi, III, 155, 169
Nadhabár, Naderbar, Nandarbar, IV, 23
NADIR SHAH, IV, 205, 207
Nadjaf, I, 83
NA-FU-TI O-LO-NA-SHOEN, I, 69
NAGAIA KHAN, IV, 7
Nagarahara, I, 74
Nāgara kretāgama, II, 156
Nails, long, in Manzi, II, 256
Naïmans, I, 148, 195, 287; III, 19–21, 25, 53; IV, 222
Naïn, II, 106
Naja, I, 244
Najah, I, 143
Naked Folk, I, 303; III, 42
Nakh, III, 155, 156; see **Nacchetti**
Nakhodah, IV, 104
Nakhschiwan, III, 37
Nakkaras, II, 262, 264
NAKKÁSH, I, 179
Nakkut, III, 156
Nakur, II, 149
Nala, I, 10
Nalopatana, I, 228
Nam King (K'aï fung), III, 125, 126
Nam tai, I, 175
NANA, I, 70
Nanaor, I, 309
Nan ch'ang, II, 212; III, 128
Nan chao, I, 61; III, 127
Nan che, II, 182
Nandor, I, 309
Nanggolokialo, I, 74
Nanghin, III, 126
Nangiás, Nangkiass (Southern China), I, 34, 150
Nan King, I, 18, 30, 67, 76, 78, 93, 122, 123, 175, 278; II, 10, 184, 193, 204–6, 209, 216; III, 126, 128
Nan Shan, II, 187, 188
NAN SUNG, II, 205, 206
NANTÉ, I, 67
Nan Ts'i Shu, IV, 267
Nanwuli, I, 82
Nan Yue, I, 39
NAOSHIRWAN, I, 95; see KHOSRU NAOSHIRWAN
NAPIER, Sir Robert, IV, 22
Naples, I, 120; III, 97, 190, 200, 210
NAPOLEON I, II, 19
NAPOLEON III, II, 230
NARAM SIN, I, 8
Naranja, II, 115
Nard, I, 184
Nardostachys, I, 227
Nargah, I, 151
Nárgil, I, 225; III, 236, 241
NARSES, I, 97
NARSES, General, I, 115
NASAWI, I, 33, 256
Nasçarini, II, 130
Nasi, island, II, 146
Nasicci, the word, see **Nacchetti**
NASIRUDDIN, *Tables of*, I, 290, 314; IV, 184
NASIR UDDIN, son of BALBAN, III, 132; IV, 85
NASIR UDDIN, Sultan of Ma'bar, III, 231; IV, 34
NASRI BIN AHMED BIN ISMAIL, I, 138
NASR-UD-DÍN, Seyid, III, 122
NA SU LA TING, III, 122
NATHAN, I, 173
NATIGAY, II, 261
NA-TU-LU, I, 206
Natuma, Natuna, I, 128
Nature, La, II, 256
NAU, F., I, 109
Nauakath, III, 24
Nava pura, I, 124
Náwús, IV, 142
Naysâbûr, I, 102
Nazareth, III, 200, 226
Nazavicium, I, 203
Nazzareni, II, 130
Nebo, I, 307
NEBUCHADNEZZAR, II, 135; III, 262
Necuveram, Necuveran, II, 169, 173
Negapatam, I, 81; II, 140; IV, 35
Negrais, IV, 93
NEGRO, G. del, II, 79, 87, 90
Negropont, III, 29
Nehāwend, I, 96
NEIGEBAUER, I, 176
Nelcynda, IV, 74, 75

Nêlê, I, 10
Nelliseer, IV, 74
Nellore, II, 141; III, 68
Nemnai, Nemtai, Nemptai, I, 175, 266
Neng kai chai man lu, I, 116
Nepal, I, 60, 69, 73
Nepalese, II, 249
Nephrit, I, 246
Nerbudda, III, 221
Nêrê, I, 10
Neruala, I, 310
NESSAWI, I, 33
NESTOR, *Chronique*, I, 245
Nestorians, I, 44, 101, 116, 119, 121, 122; II, 111, 117, 132, 142, 166, 210; III, 16, 18, 19, 22, 101, 102
Nestorian Envoy to the Pope in 15th Century, I, 177
Nestorian Metropolitan Sees, III, 22, 23
NESTORIOS, Mar, I, 119
NESTORIUS, I, 102; III, 48
NEUMANN, I, 31, 107, 141
Newars, I, 73
Newbattle, III, 170
NEWBOLD, Capt., II, 262
New Guinea, II, 159
New York, I, 106
New Zealand, III, 221
NGAI TI, I, 66
Ngan hwei, II, 207
Ngan kwo, I, 131
Ngan si, I, 61, 63, 140; III, 127; IV, 231, 237
NGAN TI, I, 57
NGAO-LA-HAN, II, 210
Nghe-an, I, 4, 135
Ngo Hu, II, 182
Nhut-nam, I, 4
Nia, I, 251; IV, 190
Niandor, I, 309
NICEPHORUS, I, 49, 55
NICEPHORUS GREGORIAS, I, 46; III, 49
NICEPHORUS MELISSENUS, I, 44
NICHOLAS's finger, Saint, III, 200
NICHOLAS, Friar, Archbishop of Khanbaliq, III, 12–14, 34, 35; IV, 161
NICHOLAS, Son of ARSLAN, III, 187
NICHOLAS III, Pope, I, 301; III, 5
NICHOLAS IV, Pope, I, 120, 166; III, 4, 216
NICHOLAS of Bantra, III, 13, 75
NICHOLAS COMANUS, I, 57
NICHOLAS of Molano, III, 188
NICHOLAS of Pistoia, II, 141; III, 5, 6, 45, 58, 59, 65
Nicobar Islands, I, 127; II, 168–170; IV, 93
NICOLAS, *Chron. of Hist.*, I, 219
Nicosia, III, 246
Nicoveran, II, 167, 168
Nicoverra, II, 25, 30–2, 34
NIEH-KU-LUN, III, 12, 13
Nieito, I, 71
Nien yu, II, 191
NIEUHOF, I, 80; II, 210, 213, 214; III, 80
Niger R., III, 221; IV, 39, 40
Nigri K'itai, IV, 230
NIKITIN, Athan., I, 151, 179, 254; III, 194
NIKPAI, IV, 161
Nikpha, I, 144
Niláwar (Nellore), III, 68, 70
Nile, I, 10, 202, 219; II, 207; III, 221–4; IV, 3–5, 40, 45
Nileshwar, Nileshweram, Nilexoram, IV, 74
Nili, I, 10
Nimbar, III, 217, 230; see Nymbar
NIMROD, II, 122; III, 209, 261, 263
NIN, III, 265; see NINUS
Ninarkovil, Nínarqáwal, IV, 35
Nine Oguz, I, 248
Nine Provinces, a name for China, I, 177
Nineveh, I, 34; III, 23, 225
Ning Chu, I, 111
Ning Hia, I, 116; II, 244
Ning po, I, 301; II, 189, 205, 212
NI NIE SHI, NI-NÍ-SSE (NARSÈS), I, 97
NINUS, III, 264; see NIN
Ninus, I, 34; see Nineveh
Niobottoli, III, 170
Niomostriere, III, 171
Nirwana, IV, 242
Nisabur, Nishapur, III, 155, 156
Nisibis, Nissibin, Nisibin, I, 119, 216; III, 22, 23
Nit-nam, I, 4, 6
NIU CHE, NIU CHEN, I, 147, 148; II, 177, 192, 200; III, 123
Niu kwo, I, 303
Niya, I, 251; IV, 190
Nizahdars, IV, 139
NIZAMUDDÍN, III, 69
NOAH, I, 26, 234, 240, 246; II, 102; III, 163
NOAH, son of NASRI, I, 138, 252
NOBREGA, Em. de, III, 252
Nocran, I, 309
Nocueran, II, 168
NOE, III, 163; see NOAH
NOGODAR, IV, 9

Noisettes de Saint Gratien, III, 97
Nomisma, I, 44, 229
Noncello, II, 5
NONNOSUS, III, 9
Norai, I, 10
Norbonucche, III, 170
North-China Herald, II, 182; IV, 269
NORTHERN CHAU, I, 63
NORTHERN SUNG, I, 92
NORTHERN WEI, I, 95
Northumberland, III, 171
Notes and Queries on China and Japan, I, 98; II, 177
Nottingham, II, 182
Nottinghamshire, III, 171
Nottola, the word, II, 116
Nouveau Dict. d'Hist. naturelle, II, 181, 186
Nouvelle Biographie générale, II, 87
Nouvelles Annales des Voyages, I, 114, 191
Novgorod, I, 305
Novus Orbis, II, 134
NOYÁN TAKIN, III, 127
Nuábah, I, 306
Nuachet, III, 22
Nubia, I, 220, 306; III, 7, 127
Nubians, I, 220
Nuksán, IV, 259
NU'MÂN, I, 83
NÚMÚGHÁN, III, 127
Nuovo Archivio Veneto, II, 5, 91
Nutmegs, I, 264; II, 153
Nuts of St. Gratian, III, 96, 97
Nyakot, III, 22
Nyas, II, 149, 168
Nymbar, III, 207, 249; see Nimbar

Obillah, Obolla, I, 84, 85, 86; II, 111
OCCAM, II, 16, 23; see OCKHAM
OCCIONI-BONAFFONS, G., II, 93
Ocean, II, 112; III, 180
OCKHAM, William, II, 16, 23; III, 205
OCTAÏ, IV, 162; see OKKODAÏ
Octorar, III, 147
Ocymum Sanctum, II, 116
ODO, Gerard, III, 33
ODORIC, I, 45, 76, 80, 119, 122, 127, 153, 169, 171, 257, 276, 279, 301; II, see Table of Contents; III, 3, 11; IV, 258, 266, 268
ODORICUS, Ludovicus, II, 7
Oech, R., I, 211
Oechardae, I, 194, 195
Oechordas, Oechardus R., I, 194, 195, 203
Oedisius, I, 217
Ögan, IV, 231
OGUZ KHAN, I, 210
Ohind, I, 74
d'OHSSON, I, 33, 34, 167, 177, 223, 289, 299; II, 105, 144, 178, 180, 193, 197, 234, 238, 257, 263; III, 107; IV, 142, 156, 162, 163, 184, 235
Oikhardai, I, 194, 195
Oitograc, Oï-togrhaq, IV, 231
Oitograch Gazo, IV, 230
OKKODAI, I, 149–151, 153, 162; II, 201, 234; III, 33, 34, 113, 132, 156, 186, 248; IV, 162, 163
O-KO-TA, I, 148
OKTAI, III, 34; see OKKODAI
Olachi, III, 246
OLAUS MAGNUS, II, 208
Olcholtam, III, 171
Oldaraese, III, 171
Old Cairo, III, 263
OLDENBURG, Wilibrand of, I, 307
OLD GERARDE, III, 236
OLD MAN OF THE MOUNTAIN, II, 257, 259
Olibanum, IV, 97
Olives, IV, 118
OLJAI TARKHAN, III, 121
OLJAÏTU, I, 121, 166; II, 104; III, 10, 108–110; IV, 7
OLOBET EBADASCAN, IV, 213
Olo Ot, II, 147
OLOPUN, OLOPAN, I, 105, 109, 110
O-LO-SSŬ, I, 109
Oltrarra, III, 147, 148, 156
OLUGH BEGH, I, 273, 284, 300
Oman, I, 85, 126, 132, 138, 244, 253; II, 112; III, 222; IV, 4, 5
OMAR, I, 84; III, 121
OMAR BEN KHATAB, II, 102
OMAR FANCHÁN, III, 122
OMAR KHWAJA, III, 126
O-mei Shan, I, 75
OMONT, H., II, 71
Omyl, IV, 163, 164
ONESICRITUS, I, 14
Onon, I, 148
Onore, IV, 73
Onyx, III, 224
Ophir, III, 76
OPPERT, III, 262
Opurocarra, I, 203
Orange, Oranges, II, 115; IV, 239
Orang Sakai, II, 147
Orang Tanjong, II, 147
ORANUS, IV, 177
Orbo, I, 308
Orchoë, I, 43
Orderly Administration of China

always strongly impressed Eastern nations, I, 134
Ordos, II, 10, 244
Ordu, III, 161
Organae, Orgune, III, 82, 84
ORGANAH Khatún, IV, 161
Organci, I, 304; III, 147, 148, 154, 156; see Urghanj
Organisation, in Chinese manner, of states in Central Asia, I, 98
Organum, Orgonum, I, 287, 289; IV, 161
Orinoco, III, 196
ORION, I, 144
Orissa, I, 69, 73, 177; II, 145
Orkhon, I, 64, 248; III, 19, 55
Orlando Innamorato, I, 173
Ormes, II, 110, 112, 117; III, 65, 256; see Hormuz
Ormi, I, 308
Ormis, I, 309
Ormuz, I, 78
Orontes, I, 304; III, 198; IV, 95
Orosana, I, 195
OROSIUS, I, 221
ORPELIANS, I, 94
Orpiment, III, 166
Orrhatha, Orrhotha, I, 227, 230
Orte Bellanda, III, 171
Ortus, II, 244
Oryx, I, 224
Ossetes, Ossethi, II, 223; III, 185
Ostriches with two heads, II, 229
OTHMAN, IV, 5
OTHMAN BIN AFFÁN, IV, 130, 131
Othmani plums, IV, 209
Otrar, I, 163, 174, 288; III, 147, 148
OTTOKAR, King of Bohemia, II, 5
Ottorocorrhas, Ottorocorrhae, I, 194, 195, 203
Ouch, I, 99
Oudh, III, 85
Oukaka, III, 84
OUSELEY, IV, 184
Outchah, IV, 238
OVIDIUS NASO, Publius, I, 186, 305
Oviedo, II, 166
Owair, I, 152
Oweke, III, 84
Ox idol, II, 138, 169
OXENHAM, *Atlas*, II, 231
Oxford, III, 205, 206
Oxus, I, 23, 36, 37, 41, 59, 61, 72, 98, 104, 191, 192, 230, 248, 278, 304, 310, 312–8; III, 82, 221, 225; IV, 160, 182, 184, 186, 210, 211, 215–7, 255, 258
OZAR, III, 87
Pacamuria, IV, 73
Pacchino, IV, 244, 252; see Peking
Pachan, IV, 238
Pacific Sea, IV, 103
Padaville, III, 231
Paddaei, II, 173
Pâdsháh, IV, 139
Padua, II, 12, 30, 98, 142, 165, 195
Pa-eul-ch'u-k'o, IV, 228
Pagan, I, 177; II, 153
PAGANO DELLA TORRE, II, 14, 17
Pagdatine, I, 34
Pagi Islanders, II, 148, 149
Pagine Friulane, II, 83
PAGIUS, III, 18
PAGNINI DEL VENTURA, G. F., III, 137, 138, 141, 142, 148, 229
Pa hang, I, 82
PAIGHAMÍSH FANCHÁN, III, 122
Paigu, I, 177; see Pegu
Paijamas, II, 110
Paik- tjyei, I, 257
Pai-t'a shan, II, 220
Pai-ti-yen, I, 205
Pajajaran, II, 152
Pakhpos, IV, 210
PAKOR, PAKUR, I, 94
Pāk Pattan, IV, 12
Pala and Ariena of Pliny, not the plantain, III, 41
Palabadulla, III, 233
Palace of Great Khan at Cambalec, II, 218 *seq.*; IV, 139 *seq.*
PALAEOLOGUS, Michael, III, 4, 211, 230; IV, 7
Palam, IV, 12
Palambang, Palembang, II, 157, 161
Palanka, III, 162
Palankin, III, 241
Palatine Library, Florence, *Cosmographia* of, and its real date, I, 176; MS. of Odoric, I, 60, 94; Appendix II, II, 337 *seq.*
Palawán, IV, 158
Palermo, I, 115, 144, 145, 241
Palestine, I, 119, 120, 143, 220; II, 23; III, 224; IV, 3
Palestrina, I, 120; III, 216
Paliana, I, 195
Palibothra, Palimbothra, I, 183, 190, 194
PALISHANU, IV, 205
Paliuria, IV, 78
PALLADIO, G. F., II, 85
PALLADIUS, I, 33, 117, 118; II, 227, 229, 247, 248; III, 15, 53, 55
PALLAS, *Voyages*, II, 223

PALLEGOIX, I, 132
Palm leaves used to write on, III, 242; IV, 71
PALUDANUS, I, 184; III, 236
Pa-lu-ka, IV, 231
Palur, IV, 78
Palus Mæotides, I, 305; III, 81
Pamech, IV, 217
Pamir, I, 40, 61, 192, 248, 313, 314; III, 221, 222; IV, 181, 182, 184, 186, 211, 216, 217, 219
Pamir-i-Wakhán, IV, 211
PAMPHILA, I, 197, 198, 199
Panamé, IV, 78
PAN CH'AO, I, 40, 42, 43, 50, 57; IV, 188, 231
Panche, II, 117
Panchshir, Panjshir, II, 263; IV, 9, 209, 255–9
Panconia, Pancovia (Pegu), I, 177, 267
Pandarani, II, 10, 133; IV, 77
Panduah, Pandua, IV, 83, 85, 154
PAN HIONG, I, 41; IV, 231
Pan hwei tien, IV, 141
Panichiero, III, 146
Panja, I, 313, 314; IV, 211
Panjalin, II, 161
Pansala, III, 234
Pan She Ta Tchen, IV, 239
Panteh, II, 156
Panten, II, 155, 156
Pantheon of GODFREY of Viterbo, III, 240
P'an tou, I, 23
P'an-tsu, I, 23
PAN YONG, I, 41; IV, 231
PAOLINO, I, 220; II, 132, 135, 173; III, 218; IV, 172
PAOLO, Dr., I, 240
Paoting fu, II, 152
Pao yew cheng, II, 210
Papas, I, 108
Paper Currency, II, 196–8, 240; III, 149–151; IV, 112
Papši, I, 108
Paracels, II, 183
Paradise, III, 196–198, 220
Parasol, III, 256
PARASTER KHAN, III, 26
Paravanor, IV, 78
Parco di Livia, III, 171
Pardadáriyah, IV, 139
PARDESSUS, I, 20
PAREBANDI, III, 69
Paremporam, IV, 78
Paris, I, 120
PARIS, Matthew, III, 18
PARKER, E. H., I, 142; II, 193, 232; IV, 269
PARKES, Harry S., I, 10
Parliament of Friuli, II, 4, 21
Parocco (Baroch), III, 76–8
Paroche, II, 117
Parrakad, IV, 79
Parrocia, the word, III, 165
PARROT, Prof., II, 102
Pars, I, 99
Parshiam, I, 307
Parsis in China, I, 58, 112; IV, 130
PARTA of Edessa, I, 95
Parthia, I, 23, 41, 189
Parthians, I, 23, 52, 102, 216
Parthura, I, 23
Parti, I, 228
Partridges, II, 99
Parvata, I, 242
Parwan, IV, 9, 21, 22, 180, 183, 209, 211, 255, 256–9
Paryan, IV, 256, 258
Pasalain, I, 308
Pasargadae, III, 232
PASCHAL or PASCAL of Vittoria, II, 98; III, 31, 32, 35, 55, 81, 83, 85, 212
Pascherti, I, 307, 308
Pasei, II, 149
Pashai, IV, 9, 139, 258
Passaur, IV, 203
Passes of Hindu Kush, note on, II, 255
Pass of Siking, III, 117
PA-TA-LIK, I, 55
Paṭaliputra, I, 69
Pa-tan, I, 81
Patani, II, 155
Patefula, IV, 172
PATKANOV, K. P., I, 164
Patlam, IV, 32, 33, 34
Patna, IV, 76
Patria del Friuli, II, 82, 89
PATRICIUS, I, 26
Pattan, III, 63; IV, 173
Pattan Fattan, III, 70
PATTERSON, B. C., I, 121
Patti, III, 169
Patuk, II, 252
PAUSANIAS, I, 16, 21, 52, 202
PAUTHIER, G., I, 2, 7–10, 28, 30, 31, 41–5, 47–57, 70–2, 79, 80, 82, 91, 95, 96, 99, 103, 105, 107–110, 112, 114, 117, 131, 132, 134, 141, 165, 177, 237, 273, 278, 280, 285, 291, 295, 299, 302, 303, 309, 314; II, 165, 177, 178, 184, 192, 198, 205, 210, 211, 213, 215, 216, 219, 220, 234, 238, 244, 245; IV, 4, 159, 162, 189, 238

PAVET DE COURTEILLE, I, 84, 137; II, 236
Paychinor, I, 309
PEACOCK, II, 255
Peacocks, II, 222; III, 250
Pearls, II, 146, 169; II, 225; III, 168
Pe Che-li, I, 278; II, 213; III, 128
PE CHEN, IV, 231
Pechin (Peking), I, 239
PECHINEGS, I, 244, 245, 247
Pedaggio, III, 144
Pedir, I, 124; II, 149
PEDRO JUAN, III, 26
Peepul tree, III, 242
PEGOLOTTI, F. Balducci, I, 159, 172, 229; II, 101, 102, 130, 137, 146, 154, 157, 192, 196, 197, 221; III, 48, 82, 85, 97, 99, 137–171, 263; IV, 241
Pegu, I, 124, 128, 151, 177, 183, 228, 243; II, 161, 166; III, 194; IV, 201
Pegua, the word, III, 41
PEHLVÁN SSULLÁH, I, 278
Pei ho, III, 115
Pei lin, I, 105, 106
Pein, I, 251; IV, 189, 190
Pei p'ing fu, II, 216
Pei shi, III, 186
Pei t'ing, I, 59, 62; III, 55; IV, 141, 237
Pe Kiang, IV, 121
Pe King, I, 93, 114, 122, 147, 148, 150, 153, 169, 173, 181, 258, 278, 285, 313; II, 10, 177, 192, 205, 213, 216, 220, 227, 234, 236, 249; III, 3, 13, 22, 115, 117, 128, 190, 216; IV, 44, 140, 150, 169, 180, 181, 235, 236, 239, 243, 252
Peling, II, 147
PELLETZ, Joann. de, III, 14
Pelliceas and **Filiceas**, Scripture criticism by Marignolli, III, 227, 241
PELLIOT, Paul, I, 5–8, 32, 45, 53, 63, 64, 81, 88, 89, 105, 108–110, 113, 114, 116, 129, 136, 215, 278, 318; II, 168, 173, 210; III, 15, 126, 127, 182, 214; IV, 170, 228, 230, 231, 267, 268, 270, 271
Penances of Hindus, II, 143
Penta, Pentam, I, 301; II, 157
Pentapolis, I, 221; IV, 141
Penthexoire, II, 244
Pen-ts'au Kang-mu, I, 109; IV, 98, 101
Pepper, I, 225, 227, 253; II, 34, 129, 130, 132, 133, 136, 153, 154; III, 62, 217
Pera, III, 164, 165, 211
Perak, IV, 99
Perath Mesenae, III, 22
Peregrinatores Medii Ævi Quatuor, see LAURENT, J. C.
PEREGRINE of Castello, III, 10, 28, 71, 73
Perepen Angarry, IV, 78
Perescote, I, 293
Pergunnah, IV, 153
Perhé, I, 177
Periapatan, IV, 35
Periaville, III, 231
PERIEGETES, see DIONYSIUS
Perim, IV, 64
Perimula, IV, 157
Periplus, I, 43, 227, 254
PERITCHEHREH, I, 9
Periyár, II, 134
Perjan, IV, 256
PEROZES, I, 96, 205
Persarmenians, I, 220
Persepolis, II, 10, 108; III, 232
Persia, I, 74, 84, 85, 92, 94, 95, 96, 98–104, 112, 178, 215, 218, 220, 227, 231, 238, 248, 272, 293, 309; II, 164; III, 22, 69
Persian Gulf, I, 83, 85, 88, 146, 215, 227, 304; II, 10, 111, 112, 180
Persian Song, IV, 133
Persians, I, 89, 102, 204, 205, 245; II, 98; III, 16, 186
PERTZ, *Archiv*, II, 44, 45, 48, 49
Peru, II, 262
Perugia, I, 156; III, 75
Perum, I, 305
PERUMAL, II, 130; III, 69
PERUZZI, III, 140
Pervilis, III, 231
Pesadone, Pasidum, Pasidonum, III, 144
Pescamor, I, 309
Peshāwar, I, 73, 242; IV, 180, 181, 203–6, 249
Pesth, I, 152
Pe tai, I, 146; II, 177
PETER of Abano, III, 6, 195, 196
PETER of Florence, III, 11, 100
PETER of Lucalongo, I, 170; III, 55
PETER of Provence, III, 32
PETER of Sienna, II, 117, 119, 125; III, 76
PETER, Indian, Friar, III, 212
PETER the Tartar, I, 167
PETER DELLA VALLE, II, 113

PETERMANN, *Mitt.*, I, 218, 288, 289, 310; II, 262
PÉTIS DE LA CROIX, I, 212, 283, 293, 305; II, 105, 197; IV, 142, 163, 233, 238, 256
PETLIN, Evesko, II, 250
Petra, I, 43
Petri, I, 184
PETRUS RODULPHIUS, II, 12, 21
Pe tsi, I, 257
PETZIGAUDIAS, Ioannes, I, 48
Peudefitania, III, 40; IV, 76
PFEIFFER, Ida, III, 194
Phalacrocorax sinensis, II, 189
Pharan, I, 221
PHARAOH, I, 151
Phari, II, 224, 252
Phasianus lanatus, II, 186
Phasis, I, 212
Phazania (Fezzan), I, 220
PHEITOLI, I, 54
PHILEMON, I, 189
PHILIP, Christian Mandarin, I, 236
PHILIP the Physician, III, 17, 18
PHILIP, Prior of Dominicans at Jerusalem, III, 18
PHILIP III, IV, 199
PHILIP the Fair, I, 120, 166, 167
PHILIP of Valois, III, 37
Philippine Islands, II, 174; IV, 160
PHILIPPS and GÖRRES, III, 5
PHILIPPS, W. R., II, 142; III, 253
PHILLIPS, Geo., I, 48, 77, 79, 86, 87; II, 168, 172, 183, 186
PHILO, I, 221
PHILOSTORGIUS, I, 221
PHILOSTRATUS, II, 240
PHINEAS, III, 267
PHIRADAM SCHYECH, IV, 124
Phison R., I, 227; III, 197, 224, 225
Phoca, I, 225
Phocæa Nova, III, 43
Phoenicia, I, 220; III, 236
Phoenix Fructifera, IV, 70, 71
Phokpochengrá, II, 249
Photius, I, 14, 221
Phrygians, I, 102
Phryni, I, 17
Piaceri, Fiume di, II, 263
Piada, Piaddae, I, 195
Pian fu, I, 285
Pian la Magione, I, 156
Piazza, III, 144, 145
Piazza Ballarò, I, 241
Picco, III, 157
Pi chan, IV, 238, 239
Pijan, IV, 191, 234, 238
Pi sha, IV, 222
Pi Shan, IV, 223
P'ien liang, III, 128
Pien Yi tien, I, 72
Pietra Santa, III, 255
PIEVTSOV, I, 311
PIGAFETTA, II, 162, 163; II, 208; IV, 146
Pigeon Island, IV, 35
PILACORTE, II, 21
P'I-LO-KO, I, 61
PI LOU SSÉ, PI LU SSU, I, 96, 97
Pima, I, 251
PIMENTA, N., IV, 199
P'ing ling, I, 40
Ping yang fu, I, 285
PINHEIRO, Em., IV, 173, 183, 203, 254
PINKERTON, I, 125
Pinna squamosa, II, 243; IV, 267
PINTO, F. M., I, 122, 124; II, 33, 205; III, 221, 223
P'i pi, III, 149
Pirabar, II, 132
PIREBANDI, III, 69
PIREZ, I, 180
Pirs, traditions of, in Silhet, IV, 153
Pisa, II, 12, 122; III, 244
PISANUS, Barth., II, 16
Pisga, I, 307
PISHING, I, 295
Pishpek, I, 288
Pistachios, III, 167
Piyádahs, IV, 136
PIZARRO, I, 170
PIZZIGANI, III, 161
PLANO CARPINI, John of, see CARPINI
Plantain, II, 150; III, 236
PLATO, I, 134
PLAYFAIR, II, 205, 208
PLINY, I, 15–7, 21, 22, 184, 185, 192, 196–9, 224, 228, 254, 315; II, 33, 208, 217, 263; III, 259
Plum, IV, 109
Po, II, 195, 213; III, 12
Pochang, I, 177
Pó chăng tze, IV, 141
Poggi Islanders, II, 147, 148
POGGIO BRACCIOLINI, I, 174–8
Pohwan, IV, 231
Poison, II, 157, 158
Poland, III, 247
Pole Star, III, 195
POLI, the three, I, 169
Poliars, III, 259
Polin, I, 45
Poliu, Great and Little, I, 71; IV, 267
POLLARD, A. W., II, 78

POLO, Maffeo, I, 277
POLO, Marco, I, 2, 76, 81, 82, 87, 89, 93, 105, 111, 114, 117–9, 121, 128, 131, 139, 141, 144, 150, 152, 153, 161, 165, 167, 168, 173, 175, 180, 181, 214, 249, 251, 257, 267, 273, 277, 283, 285, 290, 291, 294, 296, 301–4, 309, 313; II, 24, 26, 33, 35, 98, 103, 106, 107, 112–6, 129, 130, 132–4, 139, 140, 146, 149–153, 156, 157, 159, 162–4, 168–170, 172, 174, 177, 182, 183, 186, 192, 193, 198–201, 209, 210, 212–4, 216, 217, 219, 220, 224, 227–9, 232, 234, 236, 239, 240, 242, 244–8, 250, 253, 255–8, 261, 263, 264; III, 18, 187, 194, 195, 253; IV, 3, 4, 137, 149, 159, 186, 188, 189, 198, 211, 238, 241
POLO, Nicolo, I, 168
Pololo, I, 313
Polorbech, III, 162
Poltava, I, 305
Polumbum, II, 117, 125, 129, 131, 137
POLYBIUS, II, 153
Polypodium barometz, II, 242
Pomegranates, II, 107
POMPONIUS MELA, I, 1, 15, 16, 196, 197; II, 252; III, 222
Ponani, IV, 78
Pondicherry, IV, 69
PONTANO, Iacobo, I, 232
Ponteamas, II, 156
PONTICO VIRUNIO, II, 76
Pontus, I, 183, 221; II, 98; III, 81
Pootoo, II, 184; III, 269
Pope, of the idolaters, II, 250; III, 93; of the Mahomedans, III, 250; considered immortal, III, 216
POPE, the Poet, II, 240
Pope, I, 108
Poperti, I, 307
POPOV, IV, 141
POPPO, Wolfgang, II, 4
Population, of China, vast, II, 178; III, 95, 213, 228; of Cansay, II, 194; of Shensi, II, 247
Porca, IV, 79
Porcelain, IV, 109, 121
Porcelain phials from Egyptian tombs, I, 10
Pordenone, II, 3, 5, 7, 19, 21
Port Customs in China, IV, 115
Portenau, II, 5
Porto Pisano, I, 305
Portrait of Strangers, IV, 115
Portraits of Odoric, II, 21
Portraiture, Chinese skill in, IV, 114
Ports of Malabar, decay of, IV, 26; list of medieval, IV, 72
Portuguese, first arrival of, in China, I, 180
Portulano Mediceo, I, 301, 309; III, 147, 148
Portus Naonis, II, 5
PORUS, King, II, 114
PO-SI-LI, I, 44
P'o sse, Po ssu, I, 89, 95, 97, 99
POSTERIOR WEI, I, 62
Posts, system of, in China, II, 233; III, 92
PO-TO-LI, I, 44, 54, 55
Potsu, I, 314
POTTINGER, Eldred, IV, 208
Pou lu, I, 71; IV, 267
POUTIMSTEFF, I, 288
Poyang, II, 212; IV, 129
Po yeh, II, 152
PRABU KANYA KANCHANA WUNGU, III, 193
Prague, III, 199, 200, 201, 203, 204, 207, 227, 259, 264
PRAJÑA, I, 112, 113
PRAPAÑCA, II, 156
PRASRINMO, II, 251
PRATAPA VIRA RUDRA DEVA, III, 70
PRESBYTER COHEN, III, 26; see PRESTER JOHN
PRESTER JOHN, I, 116, 155; II, 244, 245, 257; III, 15–21, 25–7, 47, 222–4; IV, 177
PRETIOSUS JOANNES, III, 26; see PRESTER JOHN
PRIDHAM, II, 171; III, 231, 233, 235
PRIMAUDAIE, Elie de la, I, 305
PRINSEP, *Tibet*, II, 249
Printing in China, I, 295, 298
PRISCIANUS, I, 183, 201
Probatica, III, 240
PROCOPIUS, I, 24, 46, 203, 204, 221
Prome, I, 177
PROPERTIUS, Sextus Aurelius, I, 186; II, 140
Prophecies of Latin Conquest of India, III, 80
Propontis, II, 98; III, 81
PROU, M., IV, 270
Provence, III, 144
Provinces of the Great Khan's Empire, I, 231; twelve, 246; list of them, III, 125 *seqq.*
PRYSE, W., Rev., IV, 152, 154
PSEUDO-CALLISTHENES, I, 304; III, 219

PSEUDO-ODORIC, II, 22
Ptolemais, I, 221
PTOLEMIES, I, 220
PTOLEMY, Cl., I, 4, 6, 11–16, 22, 93, 110, 143, 146, 159, 176, 183, 184, 187–192, 194, 195, 203, 213, 217, 227, 228, 241, 254, 286; II, 112; III, 23, 27, 184, 197, 247, 263; IV, 228
Pu-cheng, II, 163
Pucian, Puccian, IV, 237, 238
Pudopatana, I, 228; IV, 65, 69, 76
Pudripatam, IV, 76
Pugman Range, IV, 255
Pu hwan, IV, 231
Pu ku chen, I, 59
PU-LA, III, 12
PÚLAD CHINGSANG, III, 111
PULAKOMA BAZAE LACHA, I, 77
Pu-lam, Pu-lan, I, 45
Pulisanghin, III, 17
PULLÉ, G., I, 157
Pulo Condor, Pulo Condore, I, 78, 128, 129; II, 183; IV, 159
Pulovois, II, 174
Pulowei, II, 174
Pulse, Chinese skill in the, I, 159
Pulu, I, 71
Pu-lu-sha-pu-lo, I, 74
Pumpkin Island, I, 129
Punjab, I, 146, 292; IV, 203
Punkahs, II, 113
PURÁNVÁR SHAIKH, IV, 166
PURCHAS, I, 33, 182; II, 35; IV, 193
Purchase of children to bring up as Christians, III, 46, 55
Purgatory, III, 198
Purshavar, Purushavar, Puruṣapura, I, 74; see Peshāwar
Purslain, I, 246
Purut, I, 71
Puryan, IV, 256
P'U SA, I, 62
Pussé (Persia), I, 98, 99
Putlam, I, 226
Pygmies, II, 207, 208
Pyramids, IV, 45
Pyramus, III, 160, 221

Qa'an, I, 149; see Kaan
Qala'h, I, 253; see Kalah
Qala'i, I, 253
QĀLIN B. AŠ SACHĪR, I, 138
Qalmáq, I, 281; see Kalmak
Qamjû, I, 258
Qamul, I, 249; see Kamul
Qanun, I, 33, 256
Qaqola, IV, 96, 157; see Kakula
Qaráwul, I, 274; see Karaul
Qaschi, II, 106
Qashān, II, 106, 107; see Kashan
Qáyl, I, 273, 286
Qazwin, II, 258
QAZWINI, I, 138, 139
QIR THAY, IV, 133
Qomul, IV, 239; see Kamul
Quang-binh, II, 163; see Kwang binh
Quantone, IV, 245, 251; see Canton
QUATREMÈRE, Et., I, 34, 149, 152, 165, 167, 179, 246, 271, 275, 276, 278, 280–2, 286–8, 313; II, 105, 193, 195, 197, 201; III, 108–133; IV, 138, 166, 193, 201, 216
Quedda, Queddah, I, 127, 253
Quelinfu, II, 205
Quengianfu, II, 246; III, 127
Quesitan, II, 228; see Kie sie
QUÉTIF, III, 5, 37, 177
Quiloa, IV, 4
Quilon, II, 129, 130, 133, 191, 218, 220; IV, 79
Quinsai, I, 89, 180, 267, 268; II, 192, 193, 198; III, 126, 148; see Hang chau
Quisci, I, 144; see Kish
Qum Aryq, IV, 228
Qum bashi, IV, 228
Qum turâ, IV, 231
QUOLIBEY, I, 301; III, 5; see KUBLAI
Quotan, IV, 222, 253; see Khotan
Qyzyl, IV, 231; see Kizil

Raba, III, 145
Rabat Lodansa, IV, 230
Rabban, I, 109; II, 118
RACHIAS, I, 200
Radix China, I, 292
RADLOFF, I, 64; IV, 269
RAFFLES, II, 151, 173, 174
Rahma, Rahman, I, 243
Rahmaniya, Ramaniya, I, 243
Rai, I, 309; II, 257; III, 22, 23
RAINALLUCI, Petrus, de Vico Corbario, II, 12
Rainstones, I, 246
Raisins, I, 165, 166
Raithu, I, 221
Ramanancor, IV, 35
Ramāyana, II, 151
Rāmgulis, IV, 204
Ramgunga, IV, 18
Ramin, II, 146
Ramisseram, III, 67
Ramnad, II, 140; III, 65, 67; IV, 35

Ramni, Ramny, II, 146–8
RAMUSIO, I, 131, 175, 179–181, 184, 218, 270, 290, 296; II, 25, 28, 31, 32, 77, 78, 94, 96, 134; III, 259; IV, 234
RAN, III, 126
Rangoon, I, 243
Raphidin, I, 221
Rasalain, I, 308
RASHIDUDDIN, I, 135, 152, 153, 167, 246, 272, 307–9; II, 133, 146, 177, 179, 180, 228, 231, 232, 246; III, 21, 24, 30, 54, 107–133, 186; IV, 133, 176, 241, 242
Ratnapura, III, 233; IV, 33
Rats, II, 116
Ratu Dewa, III, 193
Ravend Cini (Rhubarb), I, 293
Ravenna, III, 247
RAVERTY, I, 140
Rāwalpindi, IV, 203
Rawánd-i-Chini (China Rhubarb), I 293
RAWLINSON, G., I, 8; II, 153, 164; III, 158, 259
RAWLINSON, Sir H., I, 84, 99, 149, 192, 308, 311; II, 102, 111, 232; III, 23
RAYMOND of Provence, Friar, III, 32, 33
RAYMOND DELLA TORRE, II, 8
Razichitis, III, 22
Rebat, IV, 177
Recueil des Historiens des Croisades, I, 260, 262
Recueil des Historiens des Gaules, I, 162, 263
Recueil de Voyages Soc. Géog., I, 156; II, 28; see AVEZAC, d'
Red River (Araxes), II, 102
Red River (So'ng koy), I, 6
Red Sea, I, 88, 199, 200, 221, 306; III, 27, 180; IV, 3, 4
REES, *Cyclopaedia*, II, 153, 154
Regio Feminarum, I, 303; III, 194
Reg Rawán, II, 263
Regruwan, II, 262, 263
REHATSEK, Edward, I, 271–4, 277–9, 281–7
Rei, Land of, I, 293
REINAUD, I, 11, 16, 21, 31, 52, 70, 74, 83, 84, 86, 90, 98, 114, 125–8, 131, 133, 138, 228, 241, 243, 248, 253, 254–6, 285; II, 133, 196, 208; IV, 5, 137, 152
REISKE, I, 255
REJAM, I, 151
Rejang, II, 25, 150, 151
Rekem, I, 43, 52
Relations des Voyages par les Arabes, I, 257; II, 149
Religious Houses in Scotland and England supplying wool, III, 170
RÉMUSAT, Abel, I, 1, 20, 23, 41, 51, 70, 71, 83, 90, 92, 96, 98, 100, 107, 165, 166, 191, 195, 209, 223, 272; II, 156, 163, 164, 201, 208
RENAN, I, 107
RENAUDOT, Eusèbe, I, 31, 125, 127
RENNELL, I, 310; III, 262
RESED, I, 129
Resengo, II, 150, 151
REUILLY, *Tibet*, II, 250
Revatikshetra, I, 254
Revesbi, Revesby Abbey, III, 171
Revolving Pagoda, I, 277
Revue Critique, II, 73, 83, 142
Revue de Géographie, II, 83
Revue des Questions scientifiques, II, 83
Revue du Monde musulman, II, 135, 199
Revue historique, II, 5, 82, 83, 89
Revue des Traditions populaires, I, 74
Rewa, I, 74
Rey, I, 246, 309
Rhabana, I, 195
Rhaptum, I, 213
RHEEDE, I, 185, 225; III, 236
Rhinoceros, I, 222, 243; III, 42
Rhio Strait, II, 157
Rhodes, I, 190; III, 166
Rhoncosura (palm wine), I, 225
Rhubarb, I, 269, 290, 292; II, 247
Rhyming double names, I, 150 *seq.*
Riāu, II, 156
RICCI, Matteo, I, 121, 182, 239; II, 216; III, 255; IV, 171, 178–181, 198–200, 209, 227, 236, 244–6, 248, 250, 253, 254
Rice, III, 166
Rice-Wine, I, 276; II, 199; see Darasun
RICH, II, 108; III, 262
RICHARD, S. J., II, 213
RICHARD, Archbishop of Nazareth, III, 200
RICHARD, Bishop of Armelec, III, 32, 33, 212
RICHARDSON, II, 197, 200
RICHARDSON, Dr., Traveller in Burmah, IV, 201
RICHTHOFEN, Baron F. von, I, 3, 5, 83, 192, 193; IV, 266
RICOLD of Montecroce, I, 170; II, 22; III, 260; see MONTECROCE

RIEU, *Cat. Pers.*, I, 140
Right, left, and centre, Masters of Chinese titles, I, 135
RIPA, Father, II, 131, 181, 188, 199, 236
Risam, I, 151
RITTER, I, 81, 191, 286, 293, 307; II, 135, 141, 245; III, 216, 221, 222; IV, 182, 186, 190, 194, 216, 217, 219, 229, 233, 255
Rivalse, III, 171
Rivaulx, III, 171
River of China, IV, 108
Rivers of Paradise, III, 198, 220
Rivers from a common source, frequent allegations of, III, 221
Rivista friulana, II, 88
Roasting of pepper denied, III, 217
Robaihat, III, 192
ROBERT, King of Naples, III, 140, 214
Robinson Crusoe, II, 244, 255
ROCHA, Felix da, I, 313
Roche Abbey, III, 171
ROCKHILL, W. W., I, 85, 116, 117, 149, 156, 157, 159–161, 233, 288; II, 144, 169, 200, 223, 224, 234, 237, 245, 247, 253, 258, 261, 265; III, 18, 20, 186; IV, 4, 164, 235, 271
Rock-salt, I, 68; II, 104; IV, 5, 39
ROCN UDDIN KHURSHAH, I, 153
RODULPHIUS, Petrus, II, 12, 21
ROGER II, of Sicily, I, 141
Roha creek, I, 254
ROHRBACHER, II, 88
ROLANDUS PATAVINUS, II, 153
Roman Empire, Chinese knowledge of, II, 35 *seq.*
ROMANET DU CAILLAUD, I, 122; II, 166, 174, 214
Romania, I, 101, 212; II, 98; III, 153, 167, 169
Romans, I, 197, 199, 204, 221
Rom. of Nat. Hist., II, 161
Rome, I, 44, 120, 216; III, 247, 255, 266
Ronda, IV, 38
Rosa sinensis, I, 198
ROSE, Sir Hugh, IV, 22
ROSS, E. D., I, 314; IV, 160, 193
Rossia, I, 305
Rosso, Fiume (Araxes), II, 102; III, 164
Rostaor, I, 305
Rostov, I, 305
Rotin, II, 161
Roukn Eddin, II, 197
Roussie, I, 263
ROUSTOUM, I, 99; see RUSTUM
Rozāt ul Janāt, II, 197
RUBEN, RUPEN, I, 109
Rubeo, I, 307
RUBEUS PINZANUS, III, 181
RUBRUQUIS, William, I, 116, 149, 152, 156, 158, 160, 161, 163, 164, 209, 210, 272, 287–9; II, 40, 98, 102, 144, 199, 200, 222, 224, 234, 237, 240, 252, 258, 261, 263, 264; III, 18, 20, 22, 25, 81, 83, 125, 146, 185, 212, 216; IV, 70, 161, 230, 233, 235, 271
Ruby, II, 169, 172
Ruby Mines, I, 317
Rūdbār Mountains, II, 258
RUDOLF of Hapsburgh, II, 5
RUDRAMA DEVI, III, 70
Rufford, Rufforte, III, 171
Ruhmi, I, 243
Rukh, II, 117; IV, 146, 147
RUKH-UD-DÍN KAI-HAUS, IV, 85
Ruknaddin Abishari Fanchán, III, 126
Rúm, I, 45, 57; III, 125; IV, 38
Rúm and Farang, distinctive use of, IV, 38
Rumford, III, 171
Rumis, IV, 175
RUMPHIUS, II, 161
Ruotolo, III, 157
RUPEN of Armenia, III, 139
Rūpya dvīpa, II, 151
Russia, I, 264; III, 186
Russians, I, 245, 283; II, 177
Russians in Central Asia, I, 288, 289, 310, 311, 317; see VALIKHANOFF
Rustam Khail, IV, 255
RUSTUM, I, 10, 99
RUSTUM, Mirzá, I, 286
RUYSBROEK, see RUBRUQUIS
RYMER, *Foedera*, I, 166

SAAD-UD-DÍN, III, 108
Saba, or Sava, in Persia, II, 106, 107
Saba, or Sheba, Queen of, I, 218; II, 31, 107; III, 220, 240, 241, 258, 259, 264, 265, 267
Saba, Island, I, 123, 191–4, 196
SABAR ISHU'A, I, 108
Sabba, II, 31
Sabjú, III, 131
Sacae, I, 196, 208
SACCHIENSE (PORDENONE), II, 21
SACHR, IV, 130
Sacred Tooth, I, 67
Sacrithma, IV, 214, 216
SACY, de, I, 90, 220; II, 104, 141

Sadaj, I, 185
Sadchu, I, 143
SADIK ISFAHANI, I, 33; IV, 8, 235
Sadinfu, I, 278, 285
Sadkáwan, IV, 82, 84–6
SADOZAI Dynasty, IV, 207
SADR-UD-DÍN, III, 108
Sadr-ul-Jihán, IV, 138, 141
Safed Chir, IV, 256
Saffi, Sea of, II, 108
Safflower, III, 166
Saffron, I, 228
Sagae, I, 196
Sagatin, I, 308
Saggio, III, 157
Sághanián, I, 315, 316
Sāghar, IV, 23
Sagharj, IV, 138, 141
Sagina, III, 41
Sago, II, 26, 34, 158–160
Sagus Rumphiana, II, 160
Sagwire, II, 157
Sáhadji Hindi, I, 185
Sahra, II, 154
Saianfu, I, 167
Sai-Arik, IV, 229
SAID ALI, IV, 190
SAIDUDDAULAT, III, 108
SAIFUDDIN, III, 126
Saimur, I, 227, 253, 254
SAINSON, C., II, 163
St. James, II, 142
St. John, II, 162; III, 44
St. Mark's Library, II, 27, 130
SAINT-MARTIN, *Arménie*, and ed. of LEBEAU, I, 3, 20, 49, 54, 93–6, 210; III, 24
Saint Petersburg, IV, 182, 183
St. Susan, III, 170
Sairam, I, 271, 272; IV, 164, 230, 231
SAI TIEN CH'E, III, 121
Sak, Sakas, I, 36
Sakai, II, 147
Sakaia, I, 202
Sakatu, IV, 144
Saknia, I, 316
Saksak, IV, 227
SAKYA MUNI, I, 74, 112, 113, 164, 272, 277; IV, 238
SALAHUDDIN, I, 278
Salatuyah, IV, 19
Salawat, IV, 33
SALDANHA, Arias, IV, 199, 226
SALE, III, 248
SALGHUR Atabeg, III, 69
SALIBAZACHA, I, 103
SALIVAHANA, III, 70
Salleo, III, 171
Salmasa, III, 22
SALOMON, III, 241
Salopatana, I, 228
Salsette, II, 114, 123; IV, 172, 173
Salt, II, 104, 112
SALT, *Travels*, I, 218, 220, 222
Salt Range, I, 146
Salulang, IV, 257, 258
Salutation, Chinese, IV, 176
Saluyú, I, 272
Salvastro (Sivas), III, 161
Salwen, III, 221
Samander, III, 84
SAMANIDS, I, 101, 138; IV, 266
Samara, II, 149
Samarcha, II, 149
Samari (Zamorin), IV, 24
Samaria, III, 226
Samarkand, I, 23, 90, 99, 103, 104, 117, 118, 123, 134, 162, 163, 174, 211, 251, 264, 265, 269, 271, 272, 286, 287, 293, 295–7; II, 198; III, 22–4, 39, 117; IV, 138, 162, 164, 165, 166, 182, 211
Samarlanga, II, 149
Samarykand, I, 287
Sambhal, Samhal, IV, 17, 18
Samiard, III, 16
Samkuk, I, 257
Samlaî, II, 165
Sammour, I, 137
Samrequant, I, 162; see Samarkand
Samshu, II, 200
Samudra, II, 149
Samulcotta, III, 65
Samundra, I, 82
SANBUL, IV, 20
Sand, Sea of, II, 106, 107; Hills, III, 213
Sandābīl, I, 252
Sandábur, I, 139, 309; IV, 23, 24, 31, 64–6, 72; see Sindábur
Sandai, I, 176
Sandal-wood, I, 227, 253, 267; III, 194
Sandar-Fulat, I, 128–9
Sandoddi, III, 164
Sands, Sounding, II, 262 *seq.*; IV, 3
Sandu (Shang tu), II, 227, 270
Sandy Sea, II, 30, 34
Sanf (Champa), I, 128, 129, 135, 143, 253, 254; II, 163; IV, 96; see Champa
Sanfi, I, 143
Sanghârâma, I, 113
Sanghin, III, 117
Sang Kan, III, 117
Sang Kan ho, III, 117

Sanir, I, 307
SANJAR, III, 33; IV, 161
Sankjû, I, 255
SANK WO CHI, I, 58, 257
Sanmarcant, I, 269
SAN MICHELE of Verona, I, 290
SAN PAO T'AI KIEN, I, 76
Sanpo, III, 198, 222
Sansasano, III, 170
SANSEVERINO, III, 200
SANSON, N., I, 308
Santa Croce, Florence, III, 178
SANTAREM, I, 300; IV, 199
San Thome, San Tome, II, 141, 142; III, 250–2
SANTI, Philip de', II, 17
SANTO CONCORDIO, Bartholomew di, III, 58
SANTO STEPHANO, Hieron., I, 124
SANUTO, SANUDO Marino, I, 171, 304; III, 80; IV, 3, 23
Sanyr, I, 307
SAPOR, I, 102, 141, 216; II, 112; III, 23
Sapphire, I, 226
Saqifah, IV, 139
Saqnán, I, 313
Sara, Sarra, Sarai, Sarray, on the Volga, I, 154, 288, 301, 307, 308; III, 10, 13, 14, 48, 53, 55, 82–5, 146, 147, 154, 156, 190, 212, 216, 225; IV, 7, 9, 49
Sarabula, III, 110, 111
Saracanco, III, 147
Sarachik, Saraichik, III, 85, 147
Saraga, I, 109, 196
Saragh, I, 93, 108, 159
SARAH, III, 265
Sarakinú, IV, 8
Saraláng, IV, 259
Sarandip (Ceylon), III, 131
SARAT CHANDRA DAS, II, 252, 253
Sarawasti, III, 221
Sarbisacalo, II, 101; III, 163
Sarc Guebedal, IV, 227
Sarchil, Sarcil, IV, 180, 210, 214, 216, 217
Sarcobolus Spanoghei, II, 157
Sardha, III, 221
Sardinia, IV, 37
Saregabedal, IV, 227, 228–231
SAREL, Col., I, 65
SARGHIS, MAR, I, 108, 118, 199
Sarha, IV, 95, 96
Sari, I, 100
Sarikbaee, IV, 216
Sarikul, Sarikol, I, 191, 311–4, 317, 318; III, 221; IV, 126, 210, 215–7, 249; see Sirikul
Sarik Kumish, IV, 239
Sarkel, I, 245
Sarmatia, I, 187
Sarnau, I, 124, 178
Sarsati, IV, 12
SARTACH, I, 158, 163; III, 19
Sárú R., IV, 108
Sarug, I, 307
Sarus, III, 160, 221
Sarwál, II, 110
Sarygh-Abdal, IV, 228, 231
Sas, Sasu, I, 217, 218
Sasam, I, 227
SASSANIANS, I, 83, 94
SASSANIDS, I, 42, 59, 60, 96; IV, 266
Sasus, I, 219
Satganw, Satgauam, I, 177; IV, 82
Sati, IV, 111
Satin, IV, 118
SATOK BOGHRA KHAN, I, 60
Satpâramitâ-Sutra, I, 113
SATURNE, I, 245, 248
Satyr's Cape, I, 195
Saukjû, I, 258
SAUL, I, 151
SAULCY, F. de, II, 53, 59
Saumah, see **Sommi**
Saunghar, IV, 23
Saurequant, I, 162
Sautequant, I, 262
Sava, II, 106
Savast, I, 307
SAVI, V., II, 5, 6, 83, 91
SAWERS, S., III, 233
Sawley, III, 171
Sayad, I, 317
SAYFUSTORDT, Ulrich, III, 10, 75
Saymúr, I, 253; see Saimur
SBARALEA, II, 8, 22; III, 177, 179, 200
Scala, II, 98
SCALIGER, J. C., II, 241, 242
Scanderún, Scanderoon, I, 307; III, 139, 198
Scaracanti, III, 163
SCHEFER, Ch., I, 83; II, 83, 197; IV, 133, 136, 206
Schelaheth, Sea of, II, 149
Scherpi, II, 116
SCHILTBERGER, I, 174; IV, 124
SCHLAGINTWEIT, I, 246, 310, 311, 312, 317; II, 253; IV, 22
SCHLEGEL, G., I, 75, 303; II, 83, 168, 173, 177, 200, 223, 234, 242
SCHLOETZER, I, 245
SCHMIDT, I, 30, 93, 283, 291; II, 221, 227, 263
SCHMIDT, F. M., I, 158
SCHOLASTICUS of Thebes, I, 184

SCHUYLER, Eugene, IV, 164
Scialik, IV, 234
Sciapodae, Marignolli accounts for story of, III, 254, 256
Scibetto, III, 154
Scierno, I, 177
Scintilla, La, II, 83
Scio, II, 99, 100; III, 153
Scisia, I, 307
Sclaves, I, 245
Sclavonia, III, 81
Scorpions, II, 106
SCOTT, Sir Walter, I, 163
SCOTUS, Johannes, III, 220
Scripture criticisms by Marignolli, III, 239
Scythia, I, 16, 93, 187, 194, 203
Scythians, I, 15, 196, 202, 206, 221, 252
Sea of Andaman, I, 127
—— of Azov, III, 180
—— of Bacuc (Caspian), see Bacu
—— of Damascus, III, 180
—— of Harkand, I, 127
—— of India, III, 64
—— of Jorjan (Caspian), III, 180
—— of Lar, I, 127
—— of Marmora, III, 180, 181
—— of Persia, I, 127
—— of Pontus, III, 180
—— of Venice, III, 180
Sea Trade between China and India, I, 80, and Persian Gulf, 83 *seq.*
Seal, II, 190
Seam, I, 309
Sebaste, I, 307; III, 161
Sebur, I, 307, 308
Sedasheogarh, IV, 65, 72
Seetlagunga, III, 234, 235
Segelmessa, IV, 2, 39, 119
Segin, I, 116
Se hoen R., IV, 231
Sehwán, IV, 9
Sejistan, Seistan, I, 85, 98, 99, 123, 251, 300; III, 22, 24
Se kin, I, 206
Sekjin, I, 280, 283
SELA, III, 248
Selangor, II, 147
Selediba, I, 214
Selekur, I, 191
Selenga, I, 62; III, 20
Seleucia, I, 52, 120, 216
Seleucia Elymaidis, III, 23
SELEUCIDS, I, 41, 216
SELEUCUS NICATOR, I, 216
Selgie, II, 168
SELIM I, I, 216
Selitrennoi Gorodok, III, 82
SELJUKID TURKS, II, 100; IV, 5
SELMAN FARSY, I, 83
SEM, III, 239
Semali, III, 117
SE-MA TS'IEN, I, 4, 8, 9, 37
SEMEDO, Alvarez, I, 107, 122, 235, 237; II, 187, 201; IV, 243
SEMENOV, I, 288, 289
Semin, I, 306
Semipalatinsk, IV, 183, 227
SEMIRAMIS, III, 264, 265
Semiriechie, I, 60
Semiscat (Samarkand), III, 39
Semnan, I, 293
SEMPAD, Constable of Armenia, I, 161, 262, 266; IV, 266
Semulla, I, 254
Semur, city of, III, 40
Senaar, III, 261
SENART, Emile, II, 142
Sendi Foulat, I, 129; see Pulo Condor
SENECA, I, 14, 197, 199
Senfy, I, 129
Sengkili, Senghili, I, 82; II, 134
Seng king, Seng ling, III, 117
Seni Keuï, III, 162
Senus R., I, 195
Septuagint, III, 222
Sequin, Venetian, IV, 58
Sēr, I, 202
Sera, I, 15, 19, 188, 189, 191, 194, 195
Serabula, II, 111
Serachuk, III, 85
Sera-Hassan-Kala'a, II, 101
Serans, I, 309
Serendib, I, 127; III, 228, 234; IV, 2, 32
Seres, I, I, 14–18, 20, 21, 24, 25, 32, 90, 102, 104, 110, 134, 158, 159, 183, 188, 192, 193, 196–200, 202–5; III, 219, 259
SERGIUS, I, 108, 118; III, 15
Seria, I, 202
Serice, Serica, I, 13–16, 159, 187, 192, 194, 195; III, 219
Sericum, possible origin of, I, 20; etymology according to Rubruquis, I, 158–9
Sericus, I, 194, 195
Seriginez, II, 228
Serinda, I, 24, 204
Seringapatam, III, 66
Sermessacalo, II, 101; III, 163
Serpanil, IV, 180, 214, 216
Serpents, II, 170, 182
Seruj, Serug, I, 307
Serwal, II, 111

Sesadae, I, 183, 185
Sestoria, the word, II, 163
Setemelti, I, 81, 309
SETH, III, 234, 240, 245
Sethu, III, 67
Sethu Pati, III, 67
Setines, IV, 8
SETTA, Count A. A. della, II, 62
Setu, III, 67
Setupatis, III, 69
Seuth, I, 306
Sevan, III, 40
Seven Pagodas, I, 81, 309; III, 251
Seven Seas, III, 180
Seven greatest Sovereigns, IV, 31
Seychelles, II, 166
Seyllan, III, 220, 221, 227, 231, 235, 239, 241, 242, 244, 245, 250, 268; see Ceylon
SEYYID EDJELL SHAMS UD-DÍN, III, 121, 122; IV, 89
SEYYID NASR UD-DÍN, III, 122
SEYYID TADJ EDDIN HASSAN BEN EL KHALLAL, III, 120
Shabait, Shabat, III, 194
SHABAR, IV, 162
Sha Chau, I, 73, 117, 140
SHÁDY KHÁJAH, I, 271, 285
SHA GELAAL, IV, 151
Shágnan, I, 313, 316; IV, 216
Shah, IV, 154
Sháhábád, III, 23
SHAH ABBAS, II, 104
SHAHAB-UD-DÍN BUGHRAH SHAH, IV, 86
SHAH JAHÁN, I, 80; IV, 13
SHAH JALÁL, IV, 151
SHAH JELALL, IV, 153
SHÁHI BEG KHÁN, IV, 166
Shah Kataur, IV, 205
SHAH MADAR, IV, 123
Sha-ho, III, 115
SHAH PUR, I, 41; see SAPOR
Shahr-i-nao, Shahr-i-naw, I, 124, 177; IV, 91; see Gaur
Shahrmandi, III, 69
Shah-rood, Shah-rud, I, 190
SHAH RUKH, I, 139, 175, 179, 209, 252, 271–289; II, 196, 233, 234; III, 92, 126, 182, 265; IV, 165, 188, 190, 191, 233, 238, 239, 241
SHAHÚ, IV, 17
Shahyar, IV, 230
SHAIBEK, IV, 166, 212
Shaikh mysterious, at Sinkalan, IV, 123 *seq.*
Shaikh of Islam, IV, 41
SHAIKH JAMALUDDÍN, III, 68
SHAIKH-UL-JIBAL, II, 257; see OLD MAN OF THE MOUNTAIN
Shajrat ul Atrák, I, 33
SHAKAMUNI-FU, I, 277
SHAKEMONIA, I, 163
SHAKHBAR, I, 140
SHAKHIR, I, 140
Shaki, IV, 95; Shaki Barki, III, 237
Shakyar, IV, 227
Shali, IV, 77
Shâliyat, II, 133; IV, 77
Shalwár, II, 110
Shamál, IV, 229
SHAMS-UDDIN (IBN BATUTA), IV, 1
SHAMS-UDDIN (Iliyas), IV, 85, 86
SHAMS-UDDIN ALTAMSH, I, 131
SHAMS-UDDIN FIRUZ, IV, 86
Shan, I, 153, 161
Shan baf, IV, 19
Shang Hai, I, 77, 136
Shang kho, IV, 238
Shang Tu, II, 227, 244; III, 116, 133
Shang yuen tsié, III, 269
Shanjû, I, 256, 257
Shans, III, 131
Shan Shan, I, 40; III, 127
Shan si, I, 32, 35, 73, 114, 278, 285; II, 245; III, 128
Shan tan, II, 247
Shan Tung, II, 213, 214; III, 128
Shan yü, I, 149
Shao Hing, II, 189, 200
SHARIFUDDÍN, I, 33, 175, 212, 305; IV, 233, 234, 256
SHARÍF-UDDÍN of Tabriz, IV, 119
Sharkhu, I, 143
Sharshuk, IV, 234, 238
Sha Shan, III, 213
Shatpal, IV, 257, 259
SHAW JULOLL, IV, 151
Shayok, I, 71
Sheba, I, 217; III, 191, 265; see Saba
Sh'e ch'eng, I, 40
Sheertoo, IV, 256
SHEFFIELD, D. Z., II, 213
Sheher-al-nawi, I, 124
SHEHU, I, 210
SHEIL, Sir J., II, 100
SHEIL, Lady, *Glimpses*, II, 100
SHEM, III, 246, 248
Sheng, II, 231; III, 128
SHENG TSUNG, I, 147
Shenir, I, 307
Shen si, I, 30, 31, 175, 235, 237, 238, 278; II, 10, 231, 246; III, 127, 128; IV, 241, 247
Shen tu (India), I, 37, 65
SHER SHAH, IV, 83, 93
SHE-TIE-MI, I, 58, 59, 206
Shetik, II, 157, 158

SHI, YE-LIU, I, 148; III, 21
Shiang tsû, I, 108, 109
Shibrtu, IV, 255, 256–8
Shighnán, I, 191, 192, 316
SHIHAB-AB-DIN BAYAZID SHAH, I, 80
SHIH-PI, II, 152
SHIHU, I, 74
SHI HWANG TI, I, 11, 38
Shikhini, Shikini, I, 316
Shi ki, I, 41, 42
Shilder Dawan Pass, IV, 230
Shilder Kumish, IV, 239
SHI-LI, I, 97
SHI LO SHUKIA, I, 71
SHILOYTO, I, 68, 70
Shinas, I, 11
Shindi Valley, IV, 215
Shinjû, Shindjû, I, 256, 257
Shinkali, Shinkala, I, 82; II, 133, 134; see Cranganor
Shi-po, I, 136
Shipping, vast and splendid in China, II, 180, 211
Ships stitched with twine, II, 113; III, 67; Indian, their insecurity, III, 67; Chinese, described, IV, 25
Shiraz, I, 84, 99, 286, 309; II, 10, 109, 178; III, 125; IV, 3, 36, 120, 131
SHIR BEHRAM, I, 272
Shirinbaf, IV, 19
SHIR MUHAMMAD OGHLLAN, I, 272; IV, 165
Shisham, I, 227
SHI-TAO-AN, I, 75
SHI TSUNG, I, 147
SHÍYAS, II, 257
Shonghár, I, 283
Shor Kuduk, IV, 229
Shorshuk, IV, 234, 238
Shuh, Shu, kingdom of, I, 4, 65, 139, 140; III, 12
Shui king, IV, 223
Shui Yang, II, 242
Shu King, I, 8
Shu kiun ku shi, I, 116
SHUN TI, I, 79; III, 187, 214; IV, 139, 142
Shushan, II, 102, 106
Shustar, I, 309
Shuster, II, 110; III, 23
Shwa, IV, 256
Shy-king-shan, III, 117
Shyok R., I, 71
Shyraz, I, 286; see Shiraz
Si, capital of Yu t'ien, IV, 223
Siam, I, 77, 124, 128, 151, 178, 214, 277; II, 174; III, 221, 252; IV, 98, 155–8, 242, 243
Siang Yang Fu, I, 167, 168
Siao Jen, II, 208
Sia She, IV, 231
Sia wush, I, 9
Siberia, I, 245, 246, 302, 304
Sibir, I, 152, 307
Sibor, I, 227, 230; III, 76
Sicilies, Two, IV, 156
Sicily, II, 4; III, 169, 188, 229
Siculi, I, 246
SIDI ALI, IV, 211
SIE, I, 40
Siele, I, 214
Sielediba (Ceylon), I, 214, 225, 227, 228, 230
Sielediva, I, 214
Sie-mi-se-kan (Samarkand), III, 39
Sie-mi-sze-hien (Samarkand), I, 118
Sien pi, I, 61
Si fan, I, 238; II, 248
Sigàn, I, 238, 239; see Si ngan
SIGOLI, S., III, 223, 224, 236
SIGURD, I, 46, 47
SI HABAHU, I, 226
SIHAB UDDÍN, IV, 16
Si Hai, III, 225
Si Hai tsu, III, 115
Si hala, I, 225, 226
Sihaladipa, I, 225
SI HALO, I, 226
Si ho, I, 226
Si Hu, Western Lake of Hang chau, I, 256; II, 201, 204
Si Hu Che, II, 203
Sihun, I, 272; III, 147, 221; IV, 164
Sijistan, I, 85; see Sejistan
Sikhs, IV, 204
Sikhû, I, 256; see Si Hu
SI-KI-LI-SZE, III, 15
Si King, I, 114, 116; III, 117
Sikkah, IV, 59
Sila, Silah, I, 131, 136, 137, 255, 257
Silam, I, 103
Silat Tebrau, II, 157
Siláwar, III, 68, 70
SI LEAO, I, 148; III, 21
Silhet, I, 184, 310; III, 132; IV, 151–5
SILIUS ITALICUS, I, 186
Silk, I, 197–9, 202–4, 227; II, 215; III, 155; IV, 111
Sillan (Ceylon), II, 170
Silsilah, I, 306
Silver, IV, 111
Silver Mines, I, 316
SILVEȘTRE, *Paléographie*, II, 70
SILZIBUL, I, 59, 206

Simbirsk, IV, 6
Sim Kargha, IV, 238
SIMOCATTA, Theophylactus, I, 7, 209, 232; see THEOPHYLACTUS
SIMON, Metropolitan of Fars, II, 129
Simylla, I, 254; see Symulla
Sin, I, I, 5, II, 20, 127, 144, 151, 230, 248; III, 23; IV, 137
Sinae, I, I, 3–6, 11–3, 15, 32, 90, 110, 183, 187, 188, 191–3, 195; III, 22
Sinai, I, 27, 122, 221; II, 262; III, 224
Sinaitic Inscriptions, I, 222
Sincapura (Singapore), IV, 253
Sind, I, 65, 87, 138, 142, 151, 205, 230, 255; III, 28, 67, 68; IV, 17
Sindabil, I, 139, 252
Sindábur, IV, 23, 24, 31, 64–6, 72; see Sandábur
SINDAR BANDI, III, 69, 70
SINDAR LEDI, III, 68, 70
Sindh (Indus), IV, 160
Sindhu (Indus), I, 86
Sindifu, I, 139
Sindu, I, 227, 230
Sinestan (China), I, 108
Sing, I, 258
Sing, provincial administrations of Cathay so-called, II, 231; III, 122, 123, 125, 128
Si-ngan, I, 30, 31, 43, 56, 88, 91, 93, 105, 106, 112, 114, 116, 159, 175, 215, 235, 237, 292; II, 246; III, 23, 54, 127, 128; IV, 223, 247; see Ch'ang ngan, Kenjan, Khumdan
Si-ngan, Monument, I, 105–112, 159, 235–7
Singapore, I, 253; II, 156, 157, 159, 181; IV, 156, 159, 253
Singing men and women in Great Khan's Court, II, 239
Singo, II, 231
Singugli, II, 133
Singui, II, 215
Singuimatu, II, 214
Singulir, II, 133, 134
Singuyli, I, 82; see Cynkali
Sinhala (Ceylon), I, 71, 225
Sínia-ul-Sín, I, 143
SINIBALD, I, 161
Sinim, I, 3, 10, 11
Sinistan (China), I, 108
Sin jabgu, I, 206
Sinjumatu, II, 213–5
Sín Kalán (Canton), II, 179; III, 130; IV, 25, 67–9, 109, 120, 121, 123; see Chin kalan and Sin Kilan
Sin Kiang, IV, 193
Sin Kilan (Canton), II, 180; IV, 68; see Sín Kalan
Sin la, I, 257
Sin ling, I, 276
Sinope, III, 161
Sin Pao-cheng, II, 210
Sinra, I, 257
Sin T'ang Shu, I, 46
Sin teu (Indus), I, 86
Sinthao (Indus), I, 68
Sinthus (Indus), I, 227
Sin-ul-Sín, I, 135; IV, 25, 108, 120, 121, 123
Sipahis, IV, 136, 139
Sipahsalár, IV, 104
Si pei ti, III, 248
Sir Daria (Jaxartes), I, 211; III, 147; IV, 160
Sira R., I, 146
Sirab, IV, 256, 258
Siraf, I, 84–6, 125, 132, 308; II, 133; IV, 5, 45
Siras, I, 309
Sirhind, I, 24
Sirian, I, 124
Sirikul, I, 191, 311–4, 317; III, 221; IV, 216; see Sarikul
Sir-i-lung, IV, 257
Sir-i-Pamir, IV, 216
SIRIUS, I, 245
Sirkek, I, 158
Siro-Khaghan, I, 93
Sirsa, IV, 12
Sis, I, 161, 162, 307; III, 139, 160
Sisam logs, I, 227
Sissu, I, 227
Sista, I, 300
Sita, III, 221
Sitia, III, 67
Sittarkent, III, 146
Sitting in the air, IV, 134
Siu chau fu, I, 65
SIUEN TEH, I, 78
Siumenna, I, 82
Siurhia, I, 93, 159
Siu Simmoncota, III, 65
Siút, I, 306
SIVA, II, 138; III, 65
Sivas, I, 307; III, 161
Siva-Samundra, III, 66
SI WANG MU, I, 9, 235
Siwastán, IV, 9; see Sehwán
Six-fingered folk, III, 255
Siyalik, IV, 234
Siyalis, IV, 234
Siyaposh, IV, 204, 205
Si-yü shui tao ki, IV, 141

Si yü t'u che, IV, 228
Sizyges, I, 195
Sjahar-nouw (Siam), I, 124
SKEAT, *Pagan Races*, II, 147
Skikhini, I, 191
Skins, coats of, Marignolli's remarks on, III, 227, 241
Skulls, goblets of paternal, in Tibet, II, 252 *seq.*
Slamat, mountain in Java, III, 267
Slavs, I, 245
SMITH, Rev. J. J., II, 41
SMITH's *Dict.*, I, 10, 14, 29, 94, 189, 192, 197
Smuggling, punishment of, IV, 115
Smyrna, I, 190
Soap, III, 166
SOARES DE ALBERGARIA, Lopo, I, 267
Sobah, Sobaha, I, 306
Sobissacalo, II, 34
Soccabula, II, 111
Socceo, IV, 239; see Su Chau
Soceda, the word, II, 164
Socieu, IV, 241, 244, 245, 247, 250; see Su Chau
Socotra, I, 27, 123, 220; III, 7, 8, 23, 38, 252
Sodania, I, 308
Soer, I, 87; III, 68
Soffi, I, 293
Sofi, I, 295
Sogdia, I, 205, 207
Sogdiana, I, 40, 96, 134; III, 186
Sogdians. I, 23, 59, 205, 208
Sohan, I, 306
SO-HO-TO, II, 248
Soï, Soyi R., I, 71
Sokcheu, II, 233; see Su Chau
So Kiu, I, 40; IV, 218, 231
Solagna, II, 267; see WILLIAM of.
Solana, I, 195
Solanga, I, 152
Solangka, I, 177; III, 125
Solánka, III, 128
Solankis, II, 115
Soldaia, I, 305; III, 169; IV, 2, 7
Soldania, II, 102, 104, 105; see Sultania
Solghat, IV, 6
Soli, Solli, I, 76
Solidus, I, 229
SOLIMAN, I, 57
SOLINUS, C. J., I, 22
SOLOMON, I, 218; III, 76, 232, 240, 264, 265
Soltania, I, 118, 293; II, 10; III, 36, 89, 110; IV, 136; see Sultania
Somali, I, 28, 217
Somdoma, II, 105
SOMMERVOGEL, IV, 171, 173
Sommi, I, 159; III, 148
Somnath, Sumnath, I, 82, 309; II, 134
So mo chung, II, 199
Sonaparanta, I, 183
Sonargauam, Sonargaon, Sonarganw, I, 177; IV, 83, 85, 91, 92, 93, 149
SONDER BANDI DAVAR, III, 68
Sondor, Sondur, I, 128, 152; IV, 159
Sone, III, 221
Song Koi, I, 5
Soolo, IV, 158, 159
Soorma R., IV, 153
SOPATRUS, I, 25, 228, 229
Soratha, I, 228
Sorici di Faraone, II, 114
Sornau, I, 124
Sornaquam, see Sonargauam
Sorrabula, II, 111
SOTER MEGAS, I, 36
Soucat, IV, 159
Sounding Sands, see **Sands, Sounding**
Sournau, I, 124
Sowchick, III, 126; IV, 241
Spain, I, 264; III, 31, 227
Spaniards, I, 216, 221
Spartel, Cape, I, 221
SPECHT, Ed., I, 205
Spectator, III, 27
Spedicamento, III, 144
SPEKE, Capt., III, 221
Spigo, III, 168
Spike, III, 168
Spikenard, I, 185, 227; II, 150
Spilimbergo, II, 21
Spinning and knitting by men, II, 129
Splitting silk stuffs to weave again, unfounded stories about, I, 196
Spodium, IV, 99
Spoleto, Friar MENENTILLUS of, III, 58
Spolia Zeylanica, I, 77
SPRENGEL, M. C., II, 86; III, 146
SPRENGER, I, 33; II, 180
SPRÜNER, *Atlas*, I, 299
Sramanas, III, 242
SRI KUMARA KAKATIYA PRATAPA GANAPATI RUDRA DEVA, III, 70
Srinagar, I, 24
SRI PERUMAL, II, 130; III, 69
SRI ROMA, IV, 156

SRONG BTSAN SGAM PO, I, 60, 69
Ssadyn-Qúr, I, 278
SSANANG SSETZEN, I, 30, 93, 276, 283; II, 227; III, 54
Sse-jin, I, 280
Ssŭ ch'uan, I, 161; see Sze ch'uan
Standard, II, 166
STANFORD, I, 310; II, 245
Stater, I, 229
Statera, III, 218
Stationery, II, 204
STAUNTON, II, 188
STECKEL, Corrado, II, 74
Steelyard, right of the privilege of St. Thomas' Christians, III, 218, 229
STEIN, Sir Aurel, I, 38, 63, 190, 192, 215, 251, 274, 318; IV, 231, 249
STEPHEN, Friar, a Bohemian, I, 156
STEPHEN of Peterwaradin, Friar, III, 83
STEWART, *Bengal*, I, 79
STIELER, *Hand-Atlas*, II, 156
Stod Bod, II, 248
Stone, green, for the eyes, I, 251
Stone, Red, for the spleen, I, 251
Stones, Precious, II, 171, 172
Stone Tower, I, 19, 183, 188–192, 194, 286
STRABO, I, 11, 14, 17, 22, 146, 189, 221; II, 252; III, 14
STRAHLENBERG, Phil. Joh. v., IV, 215
Straits, the, I, 77, 213
Straits of Bali, II, 160
—— of Macassar, IV, 158
Strigenes, II, 228
Suabia, III, 189
Suákin, I, 306; IV, 4
Suali, III, 77
Subahlika, III, 76, 77
Subára, III, 76; see Supera
Su Bashi, IV, 238
SUBUTAI, III, 133
Su chau (in Kiang Nan), I, 142; II, 192, 205
Su Chau (in Kan Su), Su Chow, Sukhchau, Sukchur, Succuir, I, 38, 58, 117, 140, 275, 276, 286, 290–3, 296; II, 233, 247; III, 126, 128, 129; IV, 178, 180, 181, 239, 241, 242, 244, 245, 247, 249, 250
Su Chau Chi, II, 247
Sudak, I, 305; IV, 2
Sudan, IV, 39, 144
Sudkāwan, IV, 82
Sueves, III, 184
Suez, I, 221
Sufala, Sufálah, III, 76, 77
SU FANCHÁN, III, 122
SÚFÍS, IV, 131
Sug, IV, 159
Sugar, abundance of, in China, II, 184; III, 96; IV, 108; from trees, II, 157; III, 61, 236
Sugo, III, 145
Suhár in Oman, I, 87
SUHAYL, I, 245
SUI, I, 30, 32, 44, 54, 63, 68, 88, 95, 97, 98, 191
Suicides of devotees in India, II, 145
Suigim, IV, 239
Suisis, II, 102
Sui ye, IV, 164
Sukadana, IV, 159
Súk-Balhara, I, 241
Sukchu, see Su Chau
Su-le, Su-lei, I, 40; IV, 222, 231; see Kashgar
SULEIMAN, merchant, I, 126; III, 120
SULEIMAN UL SAFADI-UL SHÁMI, IV, 27
SULEYMAN-KHEYL, IV, 206
Suli, IV, 29
SU LI P'U, I, 90
Sulphur, III, 167
Sultania, I, 169, 308; II, 102, 104, 105, 106, 131; III, 36, 37; see Soldania and Soltania
SULTÁN SHAH, I, 271, 282; IV, 185, 186
Súlúk, IV, 158, 159
Sumatra, I, 77, 78, 82, 124, 127, 128, 152, 302, 303; II, 10, 25, 31, 34, 146–151, 157, 164, 168, 174; III, 131, 194–6; IV, 68, 94, 95, 97, 100, 145, 147, 149, 155–7, 159, 198
Sumenna, I, 82, 83
Summerkeur, Summerkent, III, 146
Sumpit, II, 31
Sumpitan, II, 156, 158
Sumuntala, I, 82
Sunarganw, IV, 83, 85, 91, 92; see Sonargauam
SUN CH'ÜAN, I, 19
Sunda, II, 174; IV, 65
Sundara, I, 129
SUNDARA-PANDI, III, 69
Sundar Fūlāt, I, 128, 129
Sundiva, IV, 81
SUNG, I, 10, 60, 72, 81, 88, 92, 114, 136, 150; II, 177, 193, 194, 203, 206, 210, 212, 223; III, 130, 149, 186; IV, 137, 243

Sungari, III, 125
Sungei Malāyu, II, 156
Sungei Selitar, II, 156
Sungora, I, 82
SUNG YUN, I, 66, 75
Sun Trees, II, 103
Sunur Káwán, IV, 91
Sunzu-matu, II, 214
Suors, II, 102
Supera, Suppara, I, 227; II, 128; III, 76–8
Sura, I, 225
SURAJJUDÍN, III, 69
Surashtra, I, 74
Surat, I, 87, 228; II, 10; III, 77; IV, 64
SUREN, I, 94
Surkhāb, I, 316, 317
Surma, IV, 151, 152, 154
Súrpáraka, III, 77
Susa, II, 110
Susah, in China, I, 142
Susis, II, 102
Suspha, I, 213, 214
Sustar, I, 309
SU-SUNG, II, 207
Su-tan, I, 234
Sutlej, II, 207; III, 198, 221, 222
SU-TSUNG, I, 63, 91, 110
Suttee, II, 31, 32; II, 139, 140
Suvar-i-Akalím, IV, 164
Suvarna Bhumi, I, 183
Suvarṇa dvīpa, II, 151
Svind Bheel, IV, 153
Svinsivede, III, 171
Swāt, I, 74, 204
Swineshead, III, 171
SWINHOE, II, 189, 220
Swords, I, 253
Sycee, IV, 112
Sydrapetta R., III, 252
Syênê, I, 216; IV, 3, 5
SYKES, P. M., II, 107
Sylhet, IV, 151; see Silhet
Symbolon Limen, III, 14
Symulla, I, 227, 254
Syo, II, 236
Syr Daria, I, 211; III, 147; IV, 160; see Jaxartes
Syria, I, 101, 102, 104, 110, 113, 120, 153, 220, 307; III, 16, 22, 166, 186, 226; IV, 3, 5
Syrian Lamb, IV, 267
Syr Jabgu, I, 206
Syro-Chinese **Monument**; see Singan
Syrtis, I, 221
Sze ch'uan, I, 4, 37, 61, 65, 75, 116, 139, 140, 153, 161; II, 186, 231, 246; III, 12, 113, 126, 128
SZE-MA TS'IEN, see SE-MA TS'IEN
Szesna R., III, 247

Tabari, I, 91, 96
Tabaristan, Taberistan, I, 100; II, 107; III, 22, 23
TABAS KILI, I, 290
Tabashír, II, 161; IV, 99
Tabγač, Ταυγάστ, I, 7, 32; IV, 266; see Taugas
Tabis, I, 197
Tablets, I, 279; II, 237
Tabor, I, 304
Tabriz, Tauris, I, 154, 163, 167, 170, 174, 265, 293, 308; II, 10, 31, 101–5; III, 4, 5, 45, 53, 55, 67, 75, 76, 109, 111, 143, 155, 158–161, 162–4; IV, 87
TACCHI-VENTURI, IV, 181
Taccolino, III, 160
Ta cheng, II, 210
Ta chin, I, 281
Tachṭach, Takhṭakh, I, 244
Tacin (Ta Ts'in), I, 240, 241
Tadmor, IV, 36
Táfan, I, 243
Tafilet, IV, 39
Taganrog, I, 305
Tagazgaz, Taghazghaz, I, 131, 132, 143, 247, 248
TAGHABUN, I, 91
Taghájar Noyan Batu Kerkháhi, III, 126
Taghár, II, 255
Tagh-dum bash Pamir, IV, 211, 215
Tagliamento, II, 82, 90
TAGMA, I, 211
TA-GÖEI (WEI), I, 32
Ta Hia, I, 36, 37, 39, 65
Tahouristan, I, 108
Taianfu, I, 114
Taican, IV, 211
Taichau, I, 256
Tai du, II, 216, 217; see Taï tu
Tai hsü Pass, II, 183
Tailasán, III, 86
T'AI MOU, I, 7
T'AI P'ING, II, 192, 213; III, 120
Taissan, I, 29, 30
TAI TING, II, 222, 270
T'AI TSU, I, 53, 111, 147, 148; III, 12
T'AI TSUNG, I, 29–31, 54, 55, 59, 61, 62, 68–70, 96, 98, 110, 147; IV, 266
Taï tu (Daïdu), III, 114–6; see Tai du

Taiuna, I, 114, 143
T'AI WU, I, 7
Taiwust, I, 309
T'ai yuen fu, I, 114
Tájah, I, 114, 143, 256
Ta Jen, I, 273
Tajiks, I, 42, 88; III, 120; IV, 210, 211, 227
Tájuddin of Ardebil, IV, 119
Takadda, IV, 40
TAKAKUSU, I, 100, 112
Takazzé, I, 218
Ta Kiang, II, 207; see Yang tze
TAKIUDDIN ABDARRAHMAN, III, 68, 69
Taknas, I, 33
Takōla, IV, 157
Tala, a tank, III, 69
Talaga Masin, II, 155
Ta'lah, I, 241
Talai, Talay, II, 115, 204, 206, 209, 211; see Yang tze
Talaings, III, 127
Talaji, III, 69
Talakan, IV, 256; see Talikhan
Talaoch, III, 145
Talas, I, 91, 99, 119, 209, 210, 272, 288, 289; III, 24; IV, 162, 164
Talay, see Talai
Talhan, IV, 209, 211
Ta li, I, 61; III, 127, 131
Talikhan, I, 205; IV, 180, 183–5, 210, 211, 217, 256
TALIKU, IV, 161
Talilo, I, 313
Talisman, III, 86
Tallec, IV, 229
TA LO PIEN, I, 206
Ta-lo-sz', IV, 164
TALUT, I, 151
Talysian, II, 156; IV, 159
TAM (T'ang) family, I, 239, 240
Tamalapatra, I, 184
Tamasak Island, II, 156
Tambapanni, Tambapanniyo (Taprobane), I, 225, 226
Tame, I, 33
TAMERLANE, I, 297
Tamgama Jában, I, 33
Tamgeran, IV, 215
Tamgha, III, 143
Tamghaj, I, 33
TAMGHÂJ KHAN, I, 33, 256; II, 210
Ta-ming, I, 114
TA MING, Dynasty, I, 291
Tamlifatan, III, 131, 132
Tamositieti, I, 314, 316
Tamotas, III, 99
Tamul Annals of South India, III, 67, 69
Tamraparni (Taprobane), I, 226
Tamraparni River, IV, 35
Tamunga, III, 143
Tana (Azov), I, 179, 269, 270, 305; III, 48, 81, 143, 146, 151–4, 156, 158, 159, 169, 224, 225; IV, 201
Tana (Salsette, India), I, 171, 241, 254, 309; II, 8–10, 30, 31, 34, 113–5, 117, 123, 125, 126; III, 14, 29, 30, 76, 78, 80, 84, 207; IV, 3, 64
Tana Martyrs, II, 117–132, 184
Tana-Malayu, I, 72; II, 156
Tanais, I, 305
Tanay R., I, 305
Tanazzar, I, 124
Tancaullaggio, III, 161
Tancharan, Tancharas gold, I, 218
Tanchat, I, 162
Tanchet, III, 22; see Tangut
T'ANG, I, 10, 19, 34, 41, 42, 44, 54, 59–62, 66, 69, 71, 86, 88, 89, 91, 97, 98, 105, 108, 110, 111, 114, 116, 133, 191, 257; II, 184, 205, 216; III, 124, 126; IV, 141, 149, 164, 188, 228, 235, 267
T'ang Shu, IV, 164, 230
Tangat, I, 263; III, 24; see Tangut
Tangath, I, 291; see Tangut
Tangauls, III, 161
Tang chi, I, 273
Tanghetar, Tangitar, etc., IV, 180, 215–7
T'anghsichên, II, 189
Tangier, IV, 1, 38, 128
Tangi-i-Badakhshan, IV, 184, 214, 216
Tangis, I, 33
TANG KIANG, I, 4–5
T'ang king kiao p'ai sung cheng ts'iuen, I, 106
Tangkut, III, 126, 127
Tangmash, I, 33
Tangtash, I, 33
TANGUS, I, 33, 174
Tangut, I, 116, 118, 119, 123, 143, 150, 162, 277; II, 244; III, 22, 128, 132, 133, 148
TANIBEK, III, 211
Tanjore, I, 242; II, 140; III, 218
Tankah, Tankhah, Tanga, IV, 54, 59, 63, 138
TANKIZ Khan (for CHINGHIZ), IV, 110, 142
TAN KO FANG, I, 97
Tanmaling, II, 156
Tanmoeilieu, I, 72

Tanore, IV, 78
Tan tan, II, 173
Tanúmah, I, 128
T'ao-hua-shi, I, 33
Tao t'ai, I, 273
TAO TSUNG, I, 147
Tao yi chi lio, I, 81; III, 194; IV, 27, 271
Taprobane, I, 104, 198, 199, 214, 215, 220, 222, 224–8, 303
Tapti, III, 77; IV, 21, 23
TA PU-YEN, I, 148; III, 21
Târanâtha, I, 73
Taranchi, IV, 238
Tarapaca, II, 262
Taras, IV, 164
Tarasu, I, 276
Taraz, I, 60, 91, 97; IV, 164
Tarbagatai, I, 289; IV, 163
Tarchan, I, 211; III, 147; see Tarkhan
Tarchis, III, 84
TARDU, I, 206
Tarighurghan, I, 143
Tarik Baba, III, 232
Tarikhi Ahmed, IV, 206
Tarikh-i-Rashidi, I, 314; II, 198; IV, 160, 161, 166, 193, 271
Tarikh Jahan Kushai, II, 197; IV, 164
Tarik-i-Wassaf, IV, 156
Tarik Mama, III, 232
Tarim, I, 35, 58, 192, 194; IV, 188, 190, 217
Tark, III, 24
Tarkhan, I, 211; III, 147; IV, 49
Tarkhu, III, 84
Tarmapatam, IV, 76
TARMASHIRIN Khan, III, 30, 33–5; IV, 161
Tarmedh, I, 191, 315, 316
Tarsa (Naiman), III, 20
Tarse, I, 259, 260, 262; III, 53
Tarsia (Uighúr Country), III, 53
Tarsic Letters (Uighur), III, 53
Tartar City of Peking, II, 217
Tartar Lamb, II, 31, 116; IV, 267
Tartari schenari, III, 147
Tartars, I, 179; III, 215, 248
Tartary, I, 15, 195, 264; III, 198
Tartary Cloth, III, 99
Taschan, I, 297; see Tashkand
Tashbaliq, I, 191, 192, 286; IV, 186
Ta Shi (Arabs), I, 48, 62, 85, 88–92, 97, 103, 233–5; IV, 231
TA SHI (YE LIU), I, 148; III, 21
Tashkand, I, 98, 164, 271, 272, 297; IV, 166, 233
Tash Kurghan, I, 191; IV, 211, 215–7
TASTU, I, 299, 300
TATE, G. P., I, 99
TA T'EU KHAN, I, 206
Tathung, II, 244, 245; III, 24, 47, 48
TA TI, I, 19
Ta Ts'in, I, 18, 41–6, 49–54, 56, 57, 63, 105, 110, 112, 113, 116, 193, 233–5, 240, 241; III, 12
Tattooed Faces, II, 149
Ta tu, II, 216; III, 128
Tau, I, 223
Taugas, Taugast, I, 7, 29–34, 143, 233; IV, 69, 266
TAUGAS, I, 264
Taun-murun Pass, I, 192
Taurelaphus, I, 223
Tauris, see Tabriz
Taurus, I, 196; III, 160, 221
TAVANTI, Angelo, III, 137
Tavern Customs in China, II, 211
TAVERNIER, I, 71; II, 108, 112, 251; III, 262
Tavilgo, IV, 238
Tawal, IV, 157, 159
Tawálisi, IV, 68, 103, 108, 145, 149, 157–160
Ta Wan, I, 18, 36–9
Tawat, IV, 40
Tawi-tawi, IV, 159
Taydo, II, 216, 217
Ta Yi, I, 103
TAYLOR, I, 199; III, 251
Tayu, II, 208
Ta Yue Chi, I, 36, 205
Ta yun Kwang ming, I, 63
Tazi, I, 88
Tchao-Naiman-Soumé-hoton, II, 227
Tch'a-pouo-ho-lo, I, 69
TCH'ENG YUEN, I, 62
Tchen la, I, 8
TCHERKASOV, III, 147–8
Tchetchetlagh, IV, 217
Tchöl, Tchöle, III, 213
TCHÖ-YEN-P'OU-HOUA, III, 182
Tea, I, 131, 161, 292
Teak, I, 244, 254
Tears of Adam and Eve, II, 171; III, 235
Tebet, II, 248, 253; see Tibet
Teghdáriyah, IV, 139
Tegia, I, 306
Tehran, I, 293; II, 106, 243; III, 22, 23
Teichungyu, I, 131
TEIGE, Jos., *Zizi*, I, 232
TEIXEIRA, II, 140

Tejpat, I, 185
Tekes, I, 36, 272
Tekkeh, IV, 5
TEKLA HAIMANOT, Saint, II, 132
TE KWANG (YE LIU), I, 147
Telai, III, 69
Telinga, I, 242
TELLEZ, F. B., I, 217
Tellicherri, III, 40; IV, 76
TEMPLARS, I, 169
TEMUCHIN, TEMUJIN, I, 148, 149; III, 25, 26; see CHINGHIZ
Tenasserim, I, 12, 124
Tendek-Shahr, II, 244
Tenduc, I, 118; II, 10, 244, 245; III, 15, 24, 25
Tenes, IV, 37
Tenghi Badascian, IV, 214; see Tang-i-Badakhshan
TENNENT, Sir J. E., *Ceylon*, I, 25, 67, 68, 70–2, 75, 78, 84, 184, 199, 200, 226, 227, 253, 277; II, 130, 166, 170, 172; III, 219, 231, 233, 234, 245, 259
Tents in felt, II, 248; IV, 268
Tephrice, III, 161
Terek Dawan, I, 191, 192, 286
Terek-lak-Payin, IV, 190
Terek River, III, 84
Terivagante, IV, 76
Terki, III, 84
Termedh, I, 191; see Tarmedh
Terracina, II, 199
Terra del Fuego, III, 198
Terra Incognita, I, 194, 195
Terre Sainte, II, 105
Terrible Valley, II, 25
TERRIEN DE LACOUPERIE, I, 4–11, 149
Terter R., III, 23
TERTULLIAN, III, 243
Teskan, Teshkan, IV, 211
Tetcaul, I, 175
TE TSUNG, I, 72, 110, 113, 148
Teu-Beu, II, 248
Tewan-tâgh, IV, 228
Texel, III, 193
Thāban, I, 242, 254
Thabashir, see Tabashir
Thabis, Mountain, I, 196
Tháfak, Tháfan, I, 242, 243
Thágiah, IV, 38
Thagurus, Mount, I, 194
Thaifand, I, 242
Thaifu, III, 120
Thai-i-chi, II, 220; III, 115
Tháïkán, IV, 211
Thai Nguyên, II, 165
Thai Noi, I, 124
Thai Yai, I, 124
Thajuye, I, 114, 143
Thakbat, I, 32
Thal, IV, 259
Thalamasin, II, 31, 155, 160
Tha'lán, I, 315
Thalec, IV, 227
Thalictrum foliosum, I, 292
Thämerlin, I, 174
Than, I, 315
Thana, II, 34; see Tana
Thangáj, I, 34
Thanh hoa, I, 51
Tharrhana, I, 195
Thatháh, I, 244
Thebaid, IV, 4
Thebe, II, 202, 204
Thebes, I, 190; III, 29; IV, 45
Themistetan, I, 180
THEODORUS, I, 54
THEODORUS of Mopsuestia, I, 26
Theodosiopolis, II, 100
THEODOSIUS, I, 47, 54; II, 100
THEOPHANES BYZANTINUS, I, 24, 49, 115, 204
THEOPHYLACTUS SIMOCATTA, I, 7, 25, 29, 30, 32–4, 50, 115, 134, 143, 209, 232; IV, 266
Theriodes, gulf, I, 195
THÉVENOT, I, 25, 227, 232; II, 183, 205, 210, 242
Thiante, Thiante-Kiun, II, 244, 245
Thiantsé, I, 29, 30
Thin, I, 11, 13, 183, 184
Thinae, I, 3, 5, 11, 13, 19, 43, 159, 183, 196
Thoantac, IV, 227; see Toan Tac
Thogara, I, 195
THOGAY, III, 179, 180
Thoi, IV, 133
Thokarestan, I, 108
THOMAS, George, IV, 12
THOMAS, St., I, 81, 101, 162, 235, 263, 309; II, 34, 130, 132, 134, 141; III, 6, 10, 11, 17, 45, 61, 191, 219, 249–253; IV, 4
THOMAS, St., Christians of, I, 112; III, 217
THOMAS-À-KEMPIS, II, 11
THOMAS of Mancasola, III, 39
THOMAS of Tolentino, II, 117, 118, 121, 122, 124, 126, 131; III, 8, 29, 76
THOMAS, sent Bishop to Cathay, III, 11
THOMSEN, Vilh., I, 248; III, 126; IV, 266
Thoth, I, 219
Three Children in the Furnace, III, 263
Three Churches, Tre Chiese, III, 163

Three Kingdoms, I, 66, 139
Three Kings, I, 162; II, 34; III, 16
Threshold of the Khan's Palace not to be touched, II, 224
Throani, I, 195
THSIN, I, 2; see TS'IN
Thsining chau, II, 215; see Ts'i ning
Thsinju, II, 215; see Ts'inju
Thsungling, I, 191; see Ts'ongling
THUILLIER, Col., IV, 154
Thule, island, I, 194
THUNMANN, I, 245
Thurn and Taxis, I, 151
Thuwai, IV, 133
Thyni, I, 151
T'ian chuh (India), II, 203; see T'ien Chu
T'iao chih, I, 18, 23, 42, 50, 51
Tiazkarai Hojaghian, IV, 193
TIBERIUS II, I, 206; IV, 143
Tibet, I, 37, 60, 62, 68–71, 131, 132, 136, 139, 142, 143, 238, 251, 281, 313, 315, 316; II, 10, 23, 224, 247, 248, 251, 252, 263; III, 131, 221, 269; IV, 86, 170, 176, 177, 183, 187, 191, 205, 268
Tibetans, I, 36, 40, 60–2, 92; II, 207, 248; III, 222
Tic, I, 212
T'ie le, I, 62; III, 55
Tien (Yun Nan), I, 4, 6, 39; III, 122
Tien R., II, 213
T'ien Chu (India), I, 52, 65, 66; II, 203
T'ien fang, I, 131
T'ien Shan, I, 58, 117, 191, 272, 308, 311, 312; III, 265; IV, 160, 162, 163, 166, 187–9, 191–3, 228, 230, 231, 233–5, 237, 239, 271
T'IEN SHUN, I, 30
T'ien Tsin, II, 215
T'IEN TSO, I, 147
T'ientze, I, 141
Tie sie, III, 53
Tifer, I, 305
Tiflis, III, 177
Tigers, II, 116
TIGRANES I, the Great, I, 48
TIGRANES II, I, 216
TIGRANES VI, I, 93
Tigré, I, 217
Tigris River, I, 167, 189, 199, 216, 304, 308, 309; II, 171; III, 16, 23, 84, 125; IV, 133; the Volga called so, III, 84
Tikodi, IV, 77
Tiladae, I, 184
Tilanchoug, island, II, 169
Tiling, III, 70
Tillah, IV, 153
TILLE, II, 6
Tilputa, IV, 21
Timbuktu, I, 219; IV, 39
TIMGHAJ KHAN, I, 33
TI-MI-TI-R (DEMETRIUS), III, 15
TIMKOWSKI, II, 217, 220, 221, 236, 255; IV, 190, 228–230
TIMOSINA, I, 70
TIMOTHY, Patriarch, I, 103, 115
Timulla, I, 227, 254
TIMUR the Great, I, 33, 34, 174, 175, 178, 179, 211, 264, 265, 271, 272, 283, 305; II, 100, 104, 105, 229, 233; III, 23, 34, 37, 82, 146, 147, 182, 185; IV, 12, 162, 163, 165, 166, 186, 190, 205, 207, 233, 234, 238, 256, 258
TIMUR, grandson of Kúblái, III, 45, 116, 121
TIMUR FANCHÁN, III, 122
TIMUR KURKÁN, Amir, I, 285
Tin, I, 253; Tin money, II, 150
Tindail, IV, 104
Tingdsapuho, I, 317
Ting hoeul, I, 82, 83
Tingis, I, 221
Tingkorh, I, 82
TINTI, Luigi, IV, 266
Tioman, I, 128
Tipura Hills, IV, 152
Tira, I, 307
TIRABOSCHI, II, 14, 25, 86
Tirawari, IV, 30
Tirhut, IV, 176
TIRIDATES, I, 94
TITANS, III, 222
TITEUPULI, I, 205, 206; IV, 266
Tithe, III, 265
TITIANUS, see MAËS TITIANUS
Tiulo R., I, 305
Tiuman, I, 128
Tiyu, I, 86
Tiyūma, I, 128
Tiznaf R., IV, 210
Tjerimai, Mountain in Java, III, 267
Toan Tac, IV, 227, 228, 229, 271
TOBA (WEI), III, 55
TOBBA AL AKRÁN, I, 251
Tobbat, I, 246, 248
Tobolsk, I, 307
TOCATIMUR, III, 187
Tocchetto, III, 157
TOCTAI, IV, 270
TOCTAMISH Khan of Saraî, III, 185

Toddy, I, 225; II, 117
Todorag, III, 161
Todurga, III, 161
TOGAN TEMUR, I, 79; see TOGHON TEMUR
TOGHON, TOGON TEMUR, I, 79; II, 227; IV, 139. 142
Toghrak Dung, IV, 230
TOGHRAL BEG MALIK YUZBEK, IV, 152
Toghuzghuz, I, 140, 247, 248
Tograchi, IV, 238
TOGRUL, III, 25
Togto, II, 245; IV, 270
Toguz Oguz, I, 248
Tohfat-ul-Mujahideen, II, 135
Tokharestan, I, 36, 37, 96, 97, 100, 191, 215; IV, 184
Tokharians, I, 36
Tokhlasun, IV, 234
Tokhtasun, IV, 238
Tokmak, I, 60, 288; IV, 164, 235
Tokto, II, 245; IV, 268
Tōkyō-gakuhō, I, 81
Tolentino, II, 118
Toloneo, III, 145
Tölös, I, 58, 62
Tongan, III, 76
Tong Hai, I, 39
Tong King, I, 3–5, 51, 52, 114, 167, 193; II, 163, 165; IV, 157, 158
Tong shu, II, 212
T'O PA, I, 32
Torachi, I, 305
TORBITA, III, 193
Torissi, III, 159
Toroff, IV, 153
TORRE, Raymond della, II, 8
TORRES, José de, IV, 170, 171
Torrid Zone, III, 213
Torshok, I, 305
Tortoises, II, 32, 165, 166
TOSCANELLI, Paolo del Pozzo, I, 177, 178, 267, 268
TOSTATUS, Joannes, III, 197
Toto Ch'eng, Tou Ch'eng, II, 245
TOÛGHÂDJ, TOOGHAJ, I, 33
Toukiue, see Tu Kiue
T'oung Pao, I, 7, 8, 32, 41, 44, 45, 50, 53, 55, 88, 105, 109, 110, 113, 180, 215, 298, 303; II, 83, 139, 163, 168, 173, 194, 200, 215, 223, 234, 243; IV, 267, 268, 271
TOURNEFORT, II, 99–101
Tower of Babel, II, 34; III, 261, 262
Toyuk, III, 133
Tozan, II, 245; IV, 268
Traces of former Christianity found by Ricci in China, I, 122; in Indo-Chinese Countries, I, 123
TRAJAN, I, 216
Tranquebar, I, 228
Transit of Venus, II, 216
Transmigration, as exhibited to Odoric and Marignolli, II, 203; III, 260
Transoxiania, I, 19, 140, 154; III, 33, 85; IV, 136, 160, 163, 166
TRANSTORNA, Friar Gonsalvo, III, 81
Travancore, II, 129, 130, 135; IV, 172
Treasuries or Mints in Cathay, III, 98
Trebizond, I, 212; II, 9, 10, 30, 31, 34, 97–100, 102; III, 133, 162–4
Trees producing flour, II, 156; wine, II, 157; honey (i.e. sugar), II, 156
Trees of Paradise, III, 226
—— worshipped, III, 242
TREO, Lucrezio, II, 6
Treviso, II, 178
Tribute paid by Egypt to Ethiopia on account of the Nile, III, 223
Trichinopoly, II, 140
Trieste, II, 3
TRIGAULT, N., I, 122, 295; II, 210, 214; III, 53, 255; IV, 179–181, 198, 213, 219
Triglia, III, 158
Tropea, III, 169
Troy, I, 266
Trübner's Record, II, 243
Trucins, III, 93, 94
TRU'O'NG-VINH-KY, II, 167
Trutius, III, 93
TRYPHO, III, 243
Ts'ai chau, II, 152
TS'A LI MO-HO-NAN, I, 67
Tsen, I, 4, 5
Tseu thung, II, 183; see Zaitún
TSEU TSING-CHANG, I, 237
Ts'I, II, 205
TSIANG FU, I, 63
Tsiang Kiun, IV, 193
Tsiang shi, I, 273
Ts'ian ts'iuan, I, 38
Ts'i chau, II, 183
Ts'ien Han Shu, I, 8, 23, 35, 41, 42, 149
Ts'IEN SHU, Dynasty, I, 140
Ts'ien tang R., II, 188, 195
Ts'ien Wen ki, I, 78
Ts'i lan, IV, 228
Tsi ling, I, 97, 99

Tsi mu sa, IV, 141
TS'IN, Dynasty, I, 2, 3, 5–7, 11, 41, 215; II, 205, 243; IV, 266
TSIN, Dynasty, I, 41, 50, 66, 67, 93, 114, 147, 235; IV, 266
Tsin, I, 144
Tsi-nan fu, II, 214
Ts'in ju, II, 215
Tsin ling, I, 237
TS'IN LUN, I, 18
Ts'i ning chau, II, 213, 215
TS'IN SI HWANG TI, I, 11, 38
Tsiompa, II, 163
Ts'iuan chau, I, 88, 136, 142; II, 152, 183, 184, 186; IV, 117, 118, 120, 121
Tsomoling, II, 252
TSONG KHABÁ, II, 250
Ts'ong ling, I, 35, 40, 191, 192
Tsuan feng, II, 194
Ts'ui lan, II, 168, 169
TSUNG-CHIN (YE-LIU), I, 147
Ts'ung jin, I, 237
Ts'ung ling, I, 35, 40, 191, 192
Ts'wan chau, II, 152, 183, 184, 186; IV, 117, 118, 120, 121; see Ts'iuan chau and Zaitún
Ttsitsikling, I, 318
Tuam, III, 204
Tübät, I, 246
Tubbat, I, 246
Tubot, II, 248; see Tibet
T'u fan, I, 60, 62, 71; II, 248
TUGAN, son of Kúblai, III, 130, 131
Túgh, I, 223
Tûghâj, I, 256
TUGHLAK, of Delhi, Mahomed; see MAHOMED TUGHLAK
TUGHLAK TIMUR KHAN, IV, 161, 163, 165, 189, 191
Tugrakdan, IV, 230
TU HUAN, I, 235
Tuin, I, 117, 160; II, 144; III, 93
Tukai Nám, III, 126
TU K'ANG, II, 200
TUKA TIMUR, IV, 161
Tukhára, I, 316
Tu Kiue, I, 58–62, 97; IV, 164, 235, 266
TUKTUKA, IV, 7
Túl, Tool, Pass of, IV, 255, 256, 258
Tula, III, 19
TULABUKA, IV, 7
Tulasi, II, 116
TULI, III, 25, 26
TULIK, Amir, IV, 189
Tulsi Trees, II, 25
TULUN, I, 149
Tumapel, II, 152
Tuman, II, 198, 199
TUMÁN, Amir, IV, 141
Tumchuk, IV, 229
T'U MEN, I, 58, 206
T'U MI TU, I, 62
Tungani, IV, 238
T'ung Che, I, 273
Tungeetar, IV, 217; see Tanghetar
Tung King, Tun kin; see Tong King
Tung kup, II, 146
Tung kwo, I, 131
Tung sheng chau, IV, 268
Tun hwang, I, 38, 40, 41, 58, 63, 113, 140
Tunis, III, 247; IV, 37
Tupalak, I, 315
Tupha, I, 223
T'u po, T'u bod, T'u po t'è, I, 60; see Tibet
TUR, I, 9
Turan, I, 152; II, 263; IV, 164
Turbit, III, 168
Turfan, I, 40, 41, 58, 64, 140, 247, 272; III, 55, 133; IV, 141, 189, 191, 231, 233, 234, 237–9, 293
Turkestan, I, 99, 138, 288, 302, 312; II, 197, 199; IV, 145, 160, 163, 164, 186, 228, 237
Turkey, II, 263; III, 81
Turkish Khans, intercourse between the Byzantine Court and the, I, 54 *seq.*; 205 *seq.*
Turkmen, Turcomans, I, 149, 163, 247
Turk and Mongol Tribes, Christianity among the, I, 115 *seq.*
Turks, I, 44, 58, 59, 96, 204–8, 245, 315; II, 177, 216; IV, 238
Turlú, I, 305
TURNER, T. Hudson, I, 167
TURNOUR, *Epitome*, I, 226, 243
Turpia, III, 169
Tursi, Turshi, IV, 20
Turtle, I, 225
Turusium, III, 247
Tús, I, 102
Tuscany, I, 120; III, 255
Tusce, IV, 217, 219
T'u se wei, I, 106
Tusks, II, 251; IV, 269
Tuster, IV, 36
Tút, I, 219
Tutan Dara, IV, 257
Tuticorin, IV, 35
TU TSUNG, I, 81
T'U WU, I, 58, 206
T'u yu huen, I, 61
Twer, I, 305

Tygris, III, 84, 225; see Tigris R.
Tyras, I, 305
Tyre, I, 169
Tyuinus, III, 93
Tzana Lake, I, 218
Tze tung, I, 257
Tzinia, I, 108
Tzinista, I, 12, 28, 214, 215, 227, 228
Tzinisthan, I, 28, 107, 108

Ubashi, a Class of Lama, II, 250
Uboh, IV, 12
Uchaar, III, 121
Uchh, IV, 10, 238
Uchkilisi, Uchkilisse, I, 308; III, 163
Uch Turfan, I, 40
UDALRIC, ULRIC, 7
UDALRIC, Duke of Carinthia, II, 5
UDALRIC, St., II, 21
Udhyana, Udyana, I, 71, 74
Udine, II, 3, 8, 9, 13, 14, 16, 36, 38
Uduyut, III, 20
Ufa, I, 308
Ugan, IV, 230, 231
UGHELLI, *Italia Sacra*, III, 10, 178
Uguech, Ugueth, III, 84
Uighúr Characters, I, 166, 167
Uighúrs, I, 58–60, 62–4, 72, 88, 91, 116, 119, 178, 194, 195, 212, 247, 248; II, 232; III, 20, 21, 53, 54, 132, 186; IV, 160, 163, 164, 239
Ujah, IV, 10
Ujan, I, 314
Ujjain, I, 230; IV, 23
Ujjayani, I, 74
Ukak, IV, 7
Ukek, III, 84; IV, 7
UKHAGATU, IV, 139
Ukoli, III, 125
UKUNAÏ, I, 148
Ulús, IV, 164
Uman, III, 131, 132
Umbeyla Campaign, I, 310
Umbrella, III, 256
UMEIRA, III, 264
Umraz, Pass of, IV, 256
Umri, IV, 22
UNC, UNC CHAM (PRESTER JOHN OF POLO), III, 19, 20, 25
Ungaria, III, 247
Unicorn, I, 222, 224, 243
Unnia, I, 215
Unona Ethiopica, II, 153
Upper India, II, 176, 177, 180
Ural, I, 85, 212, 246
Urat, III, 48
URBAN VIII, II, 16
Urda lik, IV, 238
URDUJA, IV, 104–8, 158
Urdukand, I, 60
Urfa, Urfah, I, 307; II, 223
Urga, IV, 239
Urganj, Urganth, Urghandj, I, 304; III, 82, 83, 85, 87, 147, 190
Urgence, III, 82
Urh-sze, I, 38
URRETA, III, 223
Urumia, Urmia, I, 304, 308; II, 197; III, 22, 163
Urumtsi, I, 117; IV, 141, 234, 238, 239
Urza, IV, 256
Ush, I, 191, 286
Ushak Tal, IV, 238
Ush Kara Langar, IV, 238
Ushnej, I, 119
Ussn, I, 309
Utak, III, 84
Utakhanda, I, 74
Utara Kuru, I, 195
Utiennang, I, 74
UTTUNGADEWA, II, 152
Uz, I, 245
UZBEK, I, 295; III, 84, 89, 90, 190, 211, 212, 216, 246, 247; IV, 9, 160, 166, 186
Uzes, I, 247
Uzi, I, 305
UZIELLI, G., I, 268, 290
Uzma Dung, IV, 238
UZUN HASSAN, I, 178
Uzun Tati, I, 40, 251
UZZANO, Gio. da, II, 98, 137, 153, 219; III, 142, 148, 153, 155; IV, 99, 118

VÂGÎÇVARA, I, 73
VALENTIJN, I, 124
VALENTINE, I, 206; IV, 49, 143
VALENTINE CAESAR, I, 54
VALENTINELLI, II, 84–7, 92
Valenza, III, 166
VALIGNANI, IV, 178
VALIKHANOFF, *Russians in Central Asia*, I, 288, 289, 310, 311, 317; III, 55, 88; IV, 82, 193, 210, 235
Valley of Terrible Things, II, 262
VALONTE, Giov., III, 4
VALVASONE, Jac., II, 6
VAMBERY, III, 213; IV, 269
Van, Lake, I, 304, 308; II, 107; III, 22, 40
VAN BERCHEM, I, 88
Vancouver island, II, 174
Vandals, III, 184
VAN DEN GHEYN, II, 83
VAN DE PUTTE, Samuel, II, 249

VAN DER LITH, IV, 155, 157, 160
Varami, I, 293
Vardoj R., IV, 211
VARIN, P., II, 220
VARRO, I, 315
VARTHEMA, I, 124, 178; III, 243
Vatami, I, 293
Vatuk, III, 84
Vaudey, III, 171
Veddahs, I, 184; III, 245, 259
Vegetable Lamb, II, 242
Veil in further India, IV, 147
Velez, IV, 39
Velletri, III, 37
Velogesia, I, 43
VELUDO, II, 56
Velvets, II, 106
Venia, II, 143
Venice, I, 171, 290, 295; II, 3, 4, 10, 15, 23, 30, 100; III, 154, 159, 166, 169, 179, 188, 197, 207, 229
VENIUKOV, I, 310, 311, 317; IV, 182
VENNI, II, 5, 11, 17, 18, 20, 21, 27, 28, 36, 57, 77, 78, 80, 96, 119, 140, 267
VENUS, I, 248
Veramin, I, 293
Vercelli, II, 16
Verde, Cape, III, 230
Veremi, I, 293
Verona, II, 218
Vertical Writing, III, 54
Verzino, II, 137
VESPUCCI, Amerigo, III, 230
VETULUS DE MONTANIS, II, 257
Viatka, I, 307
Vicenza, II, 178, 246
Vienna, II, 3
VIEYRA, IV, 223
VIGNAUD, Henry, I, 268
VIGNAY, Jean de, II, 67, 266, 271
Vijayanagar, II, 140; III, 69
VILA, Jose Maria, II, 214
Villa Franca do Campo, IV, 171
VILLANI, G., III, 178
VILLANI, Matteo, III, 255
Villa Nova, II, 6, 19–21
VINCENT de Beauvais, II, 34, 223
VINCENZO MARIA, P., II, 116, 135, 136, 140, 173; III, 217, 236, 237, 252
VINCENZO the Carmelite, IV, 223
Vinegar, IV, 45
VIRA-PANDI, III, 69
VIRGIL, I, 20, 21, 185
VIRGIN worshipped in China, III, 269
VISDELOU, I, 42
VISHNU, III, 198, 222; IV, 146
Visiapur, I, 243
VISSCHER, III, 218
VISSIÈRE, A., II, 192, 199, 204
VITRY, Jacques de, I, 21
Vittoria, III, 31
VIVIEN DE SAINT-MARTIN, I, 74, 212, 217, 229
Vociam, Vocian, I, 301, 302; III, 131
Vodaric, II, 7
Vokhan, I, 313, 318; see Wakhán
Volga, I, 45, 140, 154, 156, 163, 179, 212, 245, 246, 287–9, 307, 308; II, 105, 211, 242; III, 82, 84, 185, 198, 225, 247; IV, 6, 158
VOLTAIRE, I, 107
Vost, IV, 259
Votíak, II, 223
Voyages au Nord, I, 181
Vritranes, for Buddhist Monasteries, III, 102
Vulgate, II, 103, 110, 208; III, 243
Vypín harbour, II, 134

Waddakare, IV, 77
WADDELL, L. A., I, 62; II, 224, 249, 252, 253
WADDING, I, 301; II, 9, 11–14, 22, 24, 84, 85, 118, 119, 123, 125, 126, 131, 258, 262; III, 3, 4, 6, 28, 29, 31, 33, 199, 200, 206
Wadi Araba, II, 262
Wadi-ul-Makám, I, 251
Waghand, I, 313
Wagish River, I, 317
Wahabi, IV, 5
WAHĪ ARDŪJĀ, IV, 104
Wahlstatt, I, 152
Wahman, I, 243
Wai ch'eng, II, 216
Waihand, I, 74
WAIS, IV, 165
Waján, I, 314
Wakf, I, 153
Wakhán, I, 248, 313, 316, 318; IV, 211, 216, 259
Wakhijrui, IV, 211
Wakhjir, IV, 216
Wakhs-ab, I, 192, 315, 316
Wakhsh, I, 286, 313–7
Wakhshjird, I, 313, 315, 316
Wak-Wak, II, 139
WALCKENAER, Baron, I, 12, 127, 128, 228; II, 153; III, 194; IV, 157, 159
WALID, Khalif, I, 254
Wali-Kambing, II, 157, 158

WALKER, Col., I, 310–312; IV, 206
WALKER, John, I, 317; IV, 183, 256, 259, 310, 311
Wall of China, Great, I, 165, 175; see Great Wall
WALLACE, A. R., II, 159
Wallachia, the Greater, III, 246
Wallachians, III, 246
WALLIN, Dr., II, 262
WALTER (o' the) Mill, II, 115
WANG CHING-HUNG, I, 76
WANG Hiuen-ts'e, I, 67, 69
WANG KANG, I, 65, 161; III, 15, 25, 26
WANG KIEN, I, 140
WANG KU, III, 15
WANG MENG, I, 7
Wang Mu, I, 7
WANG NIEH, I, 75
WANG PHEITOLI, I, 54
WANG YEN-TE, I, 248; III, 133
WAN-LI, III, 12
Wanshi, III, 120
Wan sui chan, II, 220
WANZLEBIUS, III, 223
Waracha, III, 237
Warangal (Tilinga), III, 70; IV, 14, 45
WARD, *Hindoos*, II, 116
WARD, II, 149
WARNER, II, 34, 113, 166
Wasit, I, 309
Wasjird, I, 316
WASSAF, II, 178, 179, 193, 197; IV, 223
WASSAIF SHAH, III, 223
Water, Population on the, in Cathay, III, 95, 224
Water-leeches, II, 172
Water Melon, IV, 109
WATHEK BILLAH, Khalif, IV, 123
WATTERS, IV, 231
Wazipur, IV, 22
Wealth of Idol Temples in Ma'abar, II, 142–3
WEI, I, 32, 66, 93, 95, 139, 208, 247; III, 55
Wei choui, I, 30
Wei Ho, I, 113; II, 213, 214
Wei jung, IV, 231
Wei kan, IV, 231
WEIL, *Biblical Legends*, II, 122, 171
Wei lio, I, 41, 52, 199
Wei ngan, III, 122
Wei Shu, II, 223
Wei wu eul, Wei wu rh, I, 62; III, 55
Well, IV, 229
WELLBY, Capt., III, 121
Wen Chau, I, 136; II, 188
WEN CH'ENG, I, 61
Wen Ho, II, 213, 214
Wen Su, I, 40
Wen Su Chau, IV, 231
WESSELS, Rev. C., IV, 171
WESTERMARCK, E., II, 147
Whales, IV, 5
WHALID, Khalif, I, 90
WHEELER, J. T., I, 81
WHITE, Lieut. Charles, II, 173
White Horses, II, 239
White Huns, I, 205, 229; see Hephthalites
White Lake, III, 247
White Mountain, IV, 192
White Sea, III, 246
Widow-burning, see Suttee
Wihara, III, 242
Wijaya, I, 226
WILBRAND of Oldenburg, II, 22
Wild beasts in Ceylon do not hurt foreigners, II, 172; IV, 33
Wild Men, III, 259
Wild Ox (Yak), I, 223
WILFORD on Goës, IV, 216
WILKEN, Prof., II, 147
WILKINSON, IV, 154
WILLIAM, Dr., I, 298
WILLIAM the Campanian, Friar, III, 28
WILLIAM de Cigiis, II, 103
WILLIAM of Modena, I, 171; III, 33
WILLIAM of Nassio, III, 179
WILLIAM of Prato, III, 13
WILLIAM of Solagna, II, 12, 27, 32, 266, 267, 271
WILLIAM of Villa nova, III, 9, 10
WILSON, H. H., IV, 182
Wine, I, 160, 248, 267; II, 117, 199, 200; IV, 205, 267, 268
Wodok, I, 23
Woga, I, 77
Wogouls, I, 245
Women, kingdom of, III, 192–4
WOOD, I, 17, 248, 250, 310–18; II, 263, 264; IV, 183–6, 205, 206, 209, 211, 216, 255–9
Wou k'i, IV, 235
Wou yi, IV, 235
WREDE, Baron, II, 108
WRIGHT, Thos., II, 40; III, 219
WU, I, 66, 139; II, 205; III, 12
Wu ch'ang, I, 71; III, 128, 129
Wu ch'eng che ti, IV, 141
Wu ch'wan lu, I, 75
WU HAU, I, 61
Wu-i-shan-li, I, 23
Wu-ki, I, 276

WU KIAI, I, 64
Wu Sun, I, 35, 36, 38, 40
Wu Sung, I, 77
Wu T'ai Shan, I, 73
WU TI, I, 4, 18, 23, 35–9, 54, 58, 68, 96
WU TSUNG, I, 111
WU TZU-MU, II, 194
Wu wei, I, 38
WYLIE, A., I, 35, 39, 41; II, 205

Xanadu, see Sandu
Xan baliq, IV, 138; see Khan baliq
XAQUEM DARXA, IV, 71
XAVIER, Jerome, IV, 201, 202, 220, 253
Xetaia (Khitai), IV, 174
Xeythona, I, 267

Yabtuar, IV, 182
Yachi, III, 126, 127
Yaconic, IV, 180, 215, 217
Yadah, I, 246
Yadava, I, 254; II, 115
YÂDJÛDJ, I, 255
YAFATH (JAPHET), I, 2
Yak, I, 223, 273, 295
Yaka-arik, IV, 215, 230, 231, 238
Yaka-kuduk, IV, 229
YAKUB BEG, III, 127
Yākūt, I, 2, 138
Yaldúz, I, 272
Yam or Post House, I, 275, 276; II, 232–4
Yampa, II, 150
Yamsé (Yang Chau), II, 210
Yamzai (Yang Chau), II, 209
Yandjoû, Jangju, I, 33
Yaneku, II, 210
Yang Chau, I, 100, 136, 169, 256, 257; II, 10, 177, 205, 209, 210; III, 248; IV, 120
Yanghikand, III, 24
Yangi hissar, Yanghi hissar, I, 191, 318; III, 24; IV, 187, 217, 223, 238
Yangi Yuli, IV, 255
YANG MA-NO (DIAZ), I, 106
YANG TI, I, 54, 56, 68, 95, 98
Yang tze, I, 77, 136; II, 115, 207, 213, 255
Yangui, II, 209
Yanjû, I, 256, 257
YAO, I, 7, 8
Yao Chau, IV, 129
Yarkand, I, 40, 117, 246, 311, 312, 314, 317; II, 221, 234; III, 213; IV, 162, 163, 180–3, 187–8, 190, 191, 193, 207, 210, 215–221, 223, 225, 228, 231, 249
Yar Khoto, IV, 237
Yarmuk, I, 59
Yasa, IV, 142, 238
Yasak, IV, 142
YASAM, III, 128
Yasdi, II, 107
Yashm, IV, 219
Yasin, I, 314
Yatimak, IV, 256
Yat-nam, I, 4
Yau-ch'eng, I, 39
Yava-Koli, II, 151
Yaxartes (Syr Daria), IV, 164; see Jaxartes
YAZDBŌZĒD, I, 110; see IZDBUZID
Ydyqut Shahri, III, 133; see Idiqut Shahri
YEFREMOFF'S Travels, IV, 183
YEH, I, 51
Ye li k'o wen, Ye li ke un, I, 118; II, 210; III, 121
YE-LIU A-PAO-KI, etc., I, 147
Yellow River, I, 116, 136, 147, 150; II, 244, 245; see Hwang Ho
Yemen, I, 83, 251; IV, 3, 35, 153
Yen, Kingdom, II, 216; III, 12
YEN FU, III, 15
Yenghi abad, IV, 238
YEN HI, YELIU, I, 147
Yenisei, IV, 162
Yen k'i, I, 40; IV, 222, 231, 234, 235; see Karashahr
Yen King, I, 47, 177; II, 216; see Pe King
Yen ngan, III, 122
Yen ta, II, 223
YENTHUHOLO, I, 55
Yen t'o man, II, 168
YENYO, I, 48
Yer-ka-lo, II, 250
YESONTIMUR, YESUNTIMUR, II, 222, 226, 270; III, 33, 35
YESSUGAI, III, 25
YE SU, III, 12
Ye ta, I, 205, 229
YE-TAI-I-LI-T'O, I, 205
Ye-tha, II, 224
Ye-tu, I, 114
Yezd, I, 31, 290; II, 10, 106–8
YEZDEGERD, YEZDIJIRD III, last Sassanian King, I, 55, 59, 96, 97
YEZID BEN MUAWIA, I, 44
Y-ho, II, 213
Ying tien, II, 216
YING TSUNG, I, 30; II, 222
Ying-yai-shêng-lan, I, 77; II, 146, 148–150

Yi-se, i, 110
Yissessé (Yezdegerd), i, 96
Yisun Timur, see Yeson Timur
Yi Tsing, i, 51; iv, 100
Yi ts'u ssu, i, 97
Yi-Yun, i, 288
Ynde, i, 262
Yogurs, iii, 53
Yong Lo, i, 73, 76, 77, 80, 87; ii, 134, 205, 216
Yong Yu, ii, 191
Yotkán, iv, 222
Young, John, ii, 43
Youngmyo, i, 243
Yoyada, iii, 266
Ypotamuses, iii, 254
Yrcanum, M., i, 304
Ysenbras, Sir, iii, 214
Ytanor, iv, 78
Yu, iii, 12
Yu, Emperor, i, 177; ii, 237, 200
Yu (Jade), ii, 221; iv, 219
Yuan Dynasty, i, 136, 173, 267; ii, 152, 198, 199, 206, 219, 227, 231; iii, 15, 128, 185, 187, 214
Yuan ch'ao pi shi, ii, 248; iii, 82, 156
Yuan-chuang, ii, 223; see Hiouen Tsang
Yuan Shi, ii, 152, 198, 217, 248; iii, 82, 182, 186, 239, 248
Yuan tien chang, ii, 210
Yu chau, ii, 216
Yu ché, iii, 125
Yu chu, iv, 231
Yue chi, i, 35–8, 40, 66, 229
Yuëh, iii, 12
Yuei-ai, i, 68
Yuen, Dynasty, see Yuan
Yuen, Ye liu, i, 147
Yuen chao, i, 112
Yuen Pao, iv, 112
Yué-shang shi, i, 7, 8
Yu-hwang-ho, ii, 213
Yulduz, i, 272; iv, 233, 234
Yü-lung-ghie-ch'i, iii, 82
Yung chan, i, 161
Yung ch'ang, iii, 131
Yung Cheng, ii, 249
Yung Lo, see Yong Lo
Yung ting, iii, 117
Yung-yau-tiao, i, 53
Yun Ho, ii, 213
Yun Nan, i, 39, 61, 72, 76, 118, 122, 177, 244; ii, 231, 248; iii, 122, 127, 128, 187
Yunus Khan, iv, 166, 191
Yunus, an Alan Chief, iii, 182
Yur, iv, 259
Yurgun, iv, 231
Yurung Kash, iv, 219
Yusce, iv, 217
Yu she, iv, 219
Yusuf, i, 280, 284
Yuthia, i, 124
Yu t'ien, i, 40, 205; iv, 222, 223, 231; see Khotan
Yü Ya, Yü Ying, ii, 189

Zab, i, 304, 308
Zaba, Zabai, i, 193
Zabaj, Zabadj, Zabag, i, 127, 138
Zabid, i, 306
Zabulistan, i, 152
Zacharia, Martin, iii, 38
Zachary, Archbishop of St. Thaddeus, iii, 40
Zafernameh, iii, 82, 88
Zagan, i, 167
Zagatai, i, 174, 264, 269, 270; iii, 147
Zahir-uddín, the Zinjani, iv, 19, 29
Zahir-uddin ul Kurláni, iv, 127
Zahn, J. von, ii, 5, 6; ii, 82, 89
Zaila, iv, 4
Zaitún, Zaytún, i, 51, 169–172, 256, 257, 267, 301; ii, 131, 177, 179, 180, 183, 184, 186, 212; iii, 10, 11, 28, 71–5, 100, 115, 126, 130, 131, 180, 191, 216, 229, 230, 241, 248; iv, 2, 17, 25, 40, 67, 109, 117–121, 126, 127, 145, 149, 270
Zaituníah, iv, 118
Zam, i, 315
Zambesi, iii, 221
Zambrini, ii, 62, 89, 92
Zamorin, iv, 24
Zampa, ii, 163; see Champa
Zanguebar, i, 213
Zanj, i, 85, 138
Zanzibar, i, 85, 138; iii, 259; iv, 155
Zao, iv, 25
Zarafshán, i, 38; iv, 216
Zaraguelles, ii, 110
Zarangiane, i, 99
Zaranj, i, 99
Zardandan, i, 302; iii, 127, 131
Zarefpod, iii, 82
Zaritzin, i, 308
Zarûn, i, 85
Zarya, Pass of, iv, 256
Zar-Zamin, i, 316
Zavolha, ii, 241, 242
Zayd, i, 246
Zedler, *Lexicon*, ii, 154
Zedoary, iii, 167

Zegana, Ziganah, II, 99
ZEMARCHUS, ambassador from Byzantium, I, 149, 208–212
ZENKSHI, III, 33
ZENO, II, 6
ZENOB, I, 94
Zerzumen, I, 316
Zhafár, IV, 149
Zhi-nan, I, 193
Ziamba, II, 163
Zibillo, III, 165
Zihar, IV, 23
Zi-ka-wei, I, 107
Zilan, IV, 228
ZIMMERMAN, IV, 182
Zindan, III, 232
Zindan Baba, III, 232
Zindan-i-Suleiman, III, 232
Zinghi, III, 195
Zingion, I, 218
Zingium, III, 259
ZINGUO, III, 85
Zinj, I, 212, 213, 218, 230; III, 28
Zin Zin, I, 161
Zion, Mount, III, 265
Zipangu, II, 163; III, 129
Zizera, I, 308
Zohab, III, 22, 23
ZOHAK, I, 9
Zohak, ruins, IV, 257
ZONARAS, I, 204
ZOROASTER, II, 103; III, 53
ZOSKALÈS, I, 216
Zuanapur, I, 177
Zurich, III, 14
ZURLA, I, 176; II, 257; III, 195, 246

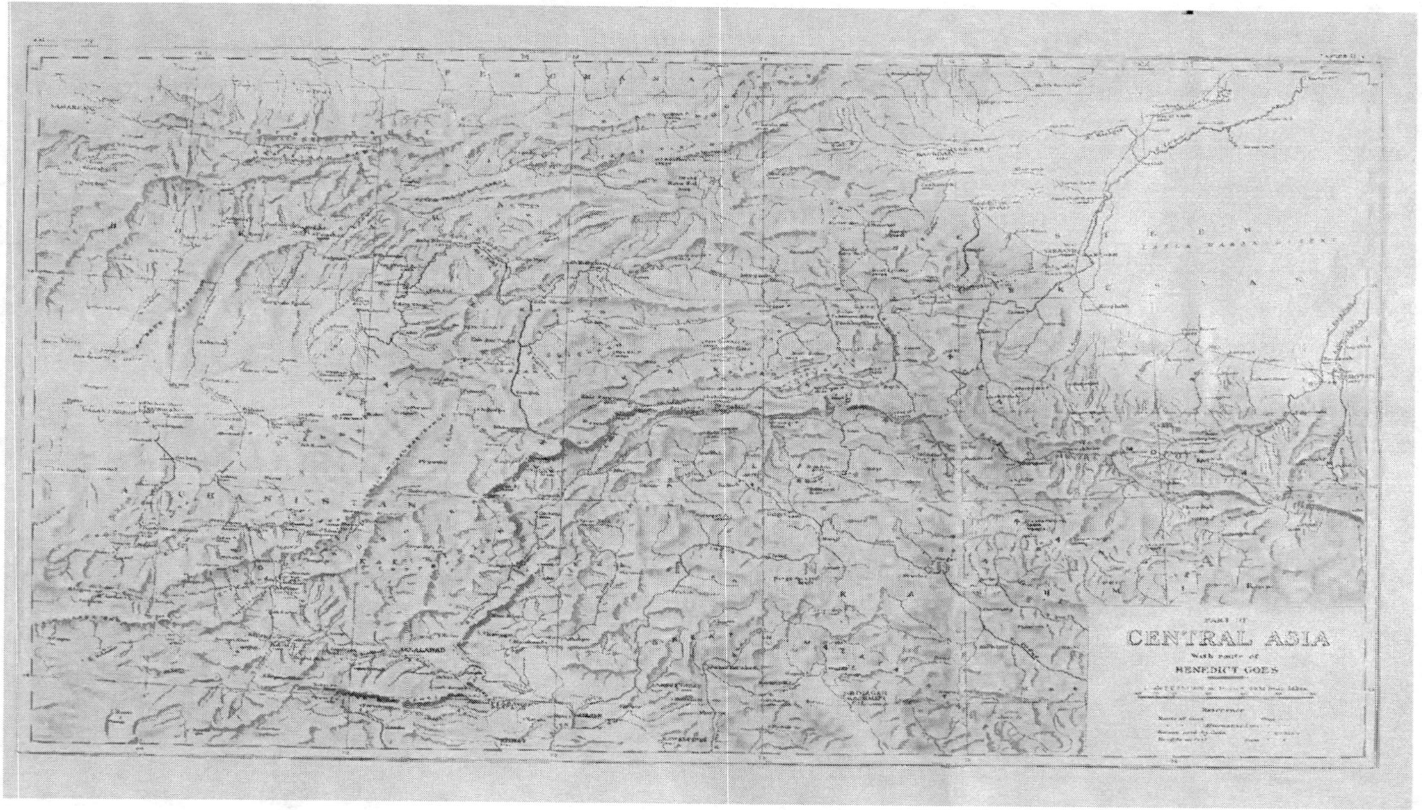
PART OF
CENTRAL ASIA
With route of
BENEDICT GOES